EXO-VATICANA

EXO-VATICANA

Petrus Romanus, Project L.U.C.I.F.E.R. and the Vatican's Astonishing Plan for the Arrival of an Alien Savior

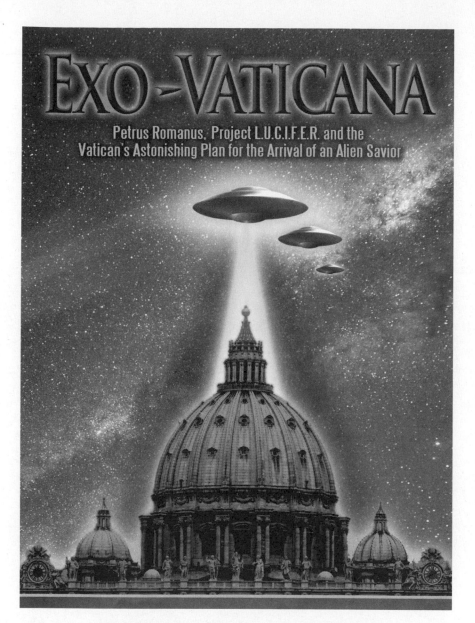

CRIS PUTNAM
& THOMAS HORN

DEFENDER

CRANE, MO

Defender

Crane, MO 65633

©2013 by Thomas Horn

A collaborative work by Thomas Horn and Cris Putnam.

All rights reserved. Published 2013.

Printed in the United States of America.

ISBN 13: 978-0984825639

A CIP catalog record of this book is available from the Library of Congress.

Cover illustration and design by Daniel Wright.

All Scripture quotations from the King James Version; in cases of academic comparison, those instances are noted.

Acknowledgements

We wish to acknowledge the following people, without whose friendship, inspiration, assistance, and research this book would have been difficult to finish on time: our lovely wives Shelley Putnam and Nita Horn, Gary Stearman, J. R. Church, Chuck Missler, Michaeal Hesier, Merlyn and Majel Hyers, T. Horton, and to Daniel Wright for a superior cover design. Of course editor Donna Howell and proofreader Angie Peters must be shown gratitude for making us sound better than we are, and typesetter Pamela McGrew, whose world-class interior designs are consistently unparalleled. Finally, to the many thousands of friends who visit our websites and constantly express their love and support, please know how much your affection lifts us up in these critical times.

Contents

SECTION THREE
WHEN CHARIOTS OF THE GODS APPEAR

SECTION FOUR
THE COMING GREAT DECEPTION

Prologue

The Year of Three Popes and the UFO Invasion

A book with a cover as sensational as this one has a lot of explaining to do. We fully expect a barrage of criticism from all sides. On one hand, many who believe space aliens are visiting Earth from other galaxies are going to take offense, and, on the other hand, many skeptical Christians will charge us with sensationalism. However, we believe we have good grounds for the ideas behind this book, and, if one is willing to engage in the arguments, they will stand up to scrutiny. Even so, a few caveats are in order:

First: The UFO/ET subject is murky water, to say the least. But once the hoaxes, hallucinations, and nonsense are extracted, there is a genuine unexplained phenomenon.

Second: We are not taking a hard line on the existence of extraterrestrial life, but we do make a case for why we are skeptical.

Third: We are not generalizing that all paranormal (another vague category) phenomena are necessarily demonic, but we are basing our epistemology on the proven guide to the supernatural, the sixty-six books of the Bible.

Given that our presuppositions are now clear, let's explain that sensational book cover.

For Roman Catholics, the year 1978 will long be remembered as the year of the three popes. Pope Paul VI, the pope who forebodingly declared, "The smoke of Satan…has entered the Sanctuary,"[1] died on August 6, 1978. In extraordinary agreement with the centuries-old prediction "from the midst of the moon" by Saint Malachy, on August 26, 1978, the precise day of a half moon, Cardinal Albino Luciani was elected on the second day of the conclave and became Pope John Paul I. Whereas we explained the preternatural circumstances connecting these events to the nine-hundred-year-old apocalyptic oracles of Saint Malachy O'Morgair in our previous work *Petrus Romanus: The Final Pope Is Here*, we did not realize that these events coincided with a major UFO flap over Rome that spanned the ill-fated rule of John Paul I through the early reign of John Paul II and with a reoccurrence upon his demise in 2005.

Within the midst of the doomed Pope John Paul I's brief pontificate, numerous cigar-, disc-, and triangular-shaped craft were seen haunting the skies across Italy by people from all walks of life, including Vatican officials. According to the Mutual Unidentified Flying Object Network (MUFON):

> At 5:50 a.m. on September 14, people in Rome saw a triangular object for five minutes. At about the same time, people near Florence reported seeing a cigar-shaped object. Early on the morning of the 16th, highway police near Rome received calls about a "luminous triangle" and "a beam of greenish light."[2]

The early-morning, triangular craft sighting on September 14 in Rome was reported by police, Vatican guards, and airline workers.[3] The purpose and effect of the green radiation beam remains

UFOs Light Up Italy's Skies

(c) New York Times Service

Rome, Italy — The skies of Italy, it seems, are full of OVNIS, the Italian version of UFOs.

Unidentified flying objects that give off green, red or white light and have a doughnut-like hole, have been reported recently, and sometimes photographed, at dozens of places between Palermo in Sicily and Milan.

Last week, the phenomenon of the OVNI — "oggetto volante non identificato" in Italian — hit Rome for the first time. Dozens of persons called police, all with essentially the same message: "We see an enormous beam of green light just overhead." A lieutenant and a noncommissioned officer, "driven by curiosity," as they said later, then ran out on the terrace at police headquarters and confirmed the sighting.

Camera Was Ready

Last week in Palermo a bank clerk, Nino Raffagnino, spotted an object just before midnight, made a dash for his telephoto lens and came up with a series of pictures that appeared in the press. One, taken when the object was stationary, according to Raffagnino, showed a disc of light with a hole in the middle.

Officers of the Palermo police, alerted by calls, also took pictures and sent them to newspapers. They showed a long, wide streak of light in a dark sky. Reports of sightings also came from a night patrol of the elite national police corps, at Lecce, in the south, and from two soldiers

standing guard at Brindisi near the Adriatic.

Newspapers all over the country have been getting calls for weeks — so many that Paese Sera, a Communist newspaper in Rome, said it might have to consider a daily column.

The most alarming item so far has been one from San Benedetto del Tronto, a fishing village near Pescara, where two fishermen were reported to have disappeared without a trace on a clear night when the sea was as smooth as a mirror and the moon full. Fishermen in the area refused to go out at night after that, and there has been talk of an "Adriatic Triangle."

Italy's national UFO center has not made a public appraisal of the reported sightings, nor has the corresponding service of the Defense Ministry. In Corriere della Sera, the influential Turin newspaper, Francesco Alberoni, a sociologist, expressed surprise that so many sightings were being reported.

Normally, he said in an interview, such reports come at times of great national anxiety, but Italians are rather less worried just now than usual.

Pot Issue Sent Back to 1st Panel

A proposal to decriminalize first time possession of small amounts of marijuana was sent back Monday to the same committee that endorsed the proposal last week.

Even though the Common

unknown. John Paul I mysteriously died two weeks later, on September 28, 1978. It was time to elect the third pope within a few months.

On October 16, 1978, a few weeks after the UFO incident, the College of Cardinals elected the prophesied "labor of the sun," John Paul II, to the pontificate. Born and buried on solar eclipses, his life also eerily synchronized with the medieval mottos of Saint Malachy. As the third pope within the calendar year and prophesied penultimate to Armageddon, the spiritual warfare in Rome was at a fever pitch. The UFOs grew more invasive—so much so that the story made the *New York Times* news service and appeared in newspapers across the US in December 1978.

Dozens of persons witnessed and photographed a strange, doughnut-shaped craft emitting a beam of green light above Rome on December 14, 1978. According to the article, Rome's police department corroborated the UFO sighting. More disturbing, two fisherman in a nearby village disappeared, and their fate is unknown. This unprecedented level of UFO activity above Rome coincided with the infamous year of three popes. At minimum, the correlation is suggestive, but that is not the end of the story.

The sole survivor of the 1978 tri-pontificate, John Paul II, died on April 2, 2005, after a long and well-received reign. He probably did more to popularize the papacy than any pope in recent memory. His body was dressed in his vestments and moved to Clementine Hall on the third level of the Apostolic Palace on April 3. The next day, three red pillows were secured endearingly beneath his head, and the coffin was moved onto a red velvet platform to facilitate the various ceremonies and sacraments that were to continue for days. As the pope must be buried between the fourth and sixth day after his death, Friday, April 8 was chosen as the last possible burial date. The Mass of Requiem led by Cardinal Joseph Ratzinger was scheduled for 10:00 a.m., but early that morning they received an unannounced visitation of the Close Encounter II variety, and this time it was caught on video.

COURTESY WISH-TV

April 9, 2005, at 6:00 a.m.

Raiders News Update featured a story that weekend that explained the above video still:

> Indianapolis News Channel 8 released a video taken Thursday evening of St. Peter's Basilica in Vatican City showing what appears to be an unidentified flying object moving across the upper left portion of the screen. The video, taken from a network feed camera at around 6:00 a.m. Roman time, was filmed as Pope John Paul II lay in state.[4]

We contacted the Indianapolis station WISH-TV about the video footage, but unfortunately, they do not have archives reaching back to 2005. Another Internet story preserves the incident:

Unusual Light Appears Over Vatican

Saturday, April 9, 2005:

> The light pictured here appeared over St. Peter's Basilica. It was
> 6:03 a.m. Italian time on the morning of April 8, 2005, 6 hours
> before Pope John Paul II's funeral. AnUnknowncountry.com
> reader writes, "I watched this as it happened live on TV. It was
> awesome and just a little chilling. I feel that this event (sign) is of
> great significance.…"
>
> Night video is notoriously deceptive and difficult to analyze,
> and there is no way to be certain that this is an anomalous object,
> but numerous viewers who called our attention to it claim that it
> appeared much larger than a bird, and to have an internal light
> source. It moved very quickly, with a swift gliding motion. No
> other similar objects appear on the tape.[5]

This photograph alone would justify our cover, but 1978 and
2005 are not the only incidents. In our former work, *Petrus Romanus*,
we suggested a nine-hundred-year-old prophecy may have predicted
the rise of the biblical False Prophet. Though it is hard to draw any
definite connection, there was another UFO incident that may bolster these suspicions.

Cardinal Trarcisio Bertone, the official Secretary of State of the
Vatican who presides as second in command, has attracted the atten-
tion of many with his ambition to become Petrus Romanus. On
June 22, 2006, Benedict XVI appointed Cardinal Bertone to replace
Angelo Sodano as the Cardinal Secretary of State, and four days later
(June 26, 2006), Cardinal Bertone was awarded the Knight Grand
Cross of the Order of Merit of the Italian Republic. During the
forty-eight hours between his appointment and Grand Cross award,
it appears *they* came back.

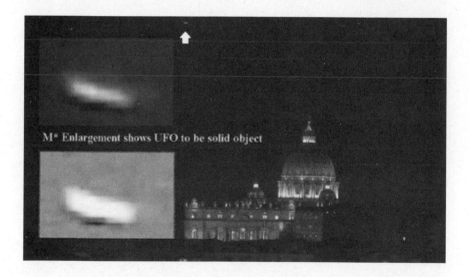

The photo above was taken in Rome by a Polish tourist on June 24, 2006, and submitted to a Polish ufologist. According to photographic analysis performed by *UFO Digest*, in the top left corner, the enlargements indicate a solid object above Rome.[6] This sequence of events fortuitously positioned Bertone—according to the *National Catholic Reporter*—as "the most powerful figure in the Vatican after Benedict XVI, himself. Since the era of Paul VI, the Secretariat of State has played the role of a 'super-dicastery,' to some extent coordinating the work of all the other departments of the Vatican. It is also responsible for the Vatican's relations with states, hence its 'foreign policy.'"[7] Could the UFO visitation also indicate Bertone's status as a chosen one?

Naturally, this brings to mind the book *Apollyon Rising*'s epic revealing of the eschatological beliefs of the Occult Elite pertaining to the return of Apollo, whom they believe will rule a final earthly empire. In both *Apollyon Rising* and *Petrus Romanus*, a synchronicity between Vatican City and Washington DC was suggested. The capitols in both cities feature an occult architecture between a dome (feminine) and an obelisk (phallic Egyptian symbol of fertility), which seems to suggest a sorcerous birth.

Vatican Dome Facing Obelisk

Washington Dome Facing Obelisk

Our present investigation has yielded another link between Vatican City and Washington DC—a ufological one. Some readers might be familiar with this old photo seen on various UFO websites:

This photo clearly shows Saint Peter's obelisk with a formation of UFOs in the sky above. However, what most websites do not say is that the photo is not genuine, but rather was created as an illustration by the Italian weekly, *L'Europeo*, for a story that ran on February 3, 1957, describing an actual sighting that occurred on November 6, 1954, by an Italian government official, Console Alberto Perego.[8] This illustration was created based on Perego's eyewitness testimony, and it was never represented as an actual photo of the event. However, this was a real event with lots of supporting evidence.

On November 6, 1954, Italian diplomat Dr. Alberto Perego reported seeing a fleet of UFOs over Vatican City to numerous agencies including the Vatican and its astronomical observatory. The National Investigations Committee on Aerial Phenomena (or NICAP) was a civilian UFO research group active in the United States from the 1950s to the 1980s. They preserved the following record:

> According to Italian diplomat Alberto Perego, at that time working in Rome (he was later attached to the Italian Consulate in Belo Horizonte, Brazil) hundreds of people watched a display of numerous small lights like "white spots, sometimes with a short white trail" which formed and reformed in rough geometrical patterns resembling successively the letters "V" and "X", then separated into two "serpentine curves" which moved off in different directions.[9]

Perego published his testimony along with diagrams of the formations in books published only in Italian, but, fortunately, also in English for a 1985 issue of *Flying Saucer Review* (the article is included on the free data DVD provided with the first release of *Exo-Vaticana: Petrus Romanus, Project L.U.C.I.F.E.R., and the Vatican's Astonishing Plan for the Arrival of an Alien Savior* when purchased from SurvivorMall.com). He indicated they flew in formation directly over the Vatican:

At noon, a large formation of twenty machines, the largest formation I had yet seen, appeared from the East, flying towards Ostia, and almost immediately after that I saw a similar night of twenty more coming from the opposite direction, i.e. from Ostia. The two "V"-shaped squadrons converged rapidly until the vertices of the two "V"s met, thus forming a perfect "St. Andrew's Cross" of forty machines, with ten to each bar. The convergence occurred at an estimated altitude of 7,000 or 8,000 metres over the Trastevere Monte Mario district of Rome, and consequently right over the Vatican City itself.[10]

A few days later, Perego went to the Vatican Observatory, where his sighting was corroborated. "Then I visited the Vatican Observatory at Castel Gandolfo, near Rome. There the Director of the Specola Vaticana, Father Zilwes, informed me that at about 11:00 a.m. on November 12 a Brazilian priest who was on duty in the Observatory had seen some strange objects pass twice over the Observatory, very low at terrific speed, and with no sound."[11]

Thus, it seems the Vatican astronomers have been aware of the UFO reality for much longer and to a greater extent than formerly admitted. But this is where the story gets even more bizarre, because the article we extracted this testimony from was titled, "'Great Crosses' Over Rome and Washington, D.C., in November 1954."

A US Navy commander based in Washington, DC, Alvin E. Moore, was working for the Scientific Intelligence Department of the CIA at the time. Not a man prone to fanciful imaginings, he reported a remarkably similar phenomenon involving flying saucers on November 9, 1954, over the US Capitol:

When I left the office at 5 p.m. I saw in the western half of the sky—and mainly in the southwestern quadrant—above the long, narrow, horizontal skyribbon—two huge X's or crosses of pearly white vapor. I thought that in medieval days an observer of such huge crosses in the sky probably would have considered them an omen. They looked, however, more like X's than crosses having right-angle parts; and I concluded that each of four flying saucer emissions of propulsion materials had crossed another to form the X's above the horizontal ribbon-like line of gas or vapor.[12]

While we are not exactly sure what to make of all this, the parallel formations are suggestive, given the occult architecture of the two cities. Additionally, Gordon Creighton, the editor of *Flying Saucer Review* and the reporter who broke the story, has written elsewhere concerning UFOs, "I do believe that the great bulk of these phenomena are what is called satanic."[13] Might these corresponding cities be the chosen locations where an Alien Savior stages *The Revealing*?

The Revealing is the name of our friend and colleague L. A. Marzulli's third novel in the Nephilim series. The cover of that book features a fleet of flying saucers over Jerusalem. What most people don't know is that the back story to the cover comes from a purportedly ancient text that surfaced in the late 1990s and made a brief splash in the media before disappearing into obscurity, the *Angel Scroll.* Scholars derived the scroll's name from one of its verses, which describes a mystical tour of the heavens undertaken by the scroll author in the company of an angel with the obscure Hebrew name Pnimea. The text features accounts of a number of mystical, celestial journeys, in which the author is shown the secrets of the universe. According to the press at the time:

Rumors have circulated for years among scholars in the Holy Land that one of the scrolls—the religious writings of the Essenes found in caves near the Dead Sea between 1947 and 1954—made its way to an antiquities dealer in one of the nearby Arab capitols.

On Monday, the Jerusalem Report magazine reported

that in 1974, Benedictine monks bought the parchment filled with 1,000 lines of Hebrew text, spirited it to a monastery on the German-Austrian border and secretly studied it. The monks were sworn to secrecy, but one—identified only by the pseudonym Mateus—broke the vow, bequeathing a transcript and his commentary to a German friend after his death in 1996.[14]

According to all available accounts, the Benedictine monks of the Roman Catholic Church have intentionally kept this scroll from public view. Believing it too important to remain hidden, German Benedictine, Matheus Gunther, reportedly said, "I promised that I would not carry the secret of this missing scroll with me to my grave."[15] Accordingly, he had arranged for it to be publicized upon his death, which occurred in 1996. Stephen Pfann, a leading Dead Sea Scrolls scholar, examined the copies of the text and determined that it could be authentic. However, the promised scroll was never delivered for a true investigation. At this point, a hoax seems unlikely, because there was never a profit motive involved. Could it be that the Benedictines were able to stifle the revelation? According to Phann, the text is full of "divine chariot-throne themes with elaborate details of angels ascending heaven's multiple gates."[16] Dr. Michael Heiser, a colleague of Phann, was shown a copy of the text and used it as the "Apocalypse Scroll" in his novel *The Façade*. The line that inspired the cover of Marzulli's book involved Jerusalem under attack by "thousands of sun disks."[17] The Angel Scroll remains an enigma, but could its prediction of a UFO invasion over Jerusalem be the reason for its suppression by the Benedictine order?

Whatever the case may be, readers will come to understand the book cover for *Exo-Vaticana* is not simply the product of someone's fanciful imagination. According to reliable witnesses and photographic evidence, something like what we have pictured has occurred more than once. The 1978 tri-papacy tangential to an extraordinary

UFO display over the Vatican, along with its return upon John Paul II's death, more than justifies the artist's rendering. However, it is not as simple as a few random sightings. The year of three popes marked one of the greatest UFO flaps across Europe in modern history. The correlation suggests spiritual warfare is involved and the events of February 11, 2013 indicate that it is about reach unprecedented levels.

Lightning strikes Vatican as Pope Benedict XVI announces his retirement

Just as we were about to turn the final draft of the manuscript over to the printer, something incredible occurred. Pope Benedict announced that he will step down at the end of the month. This is almost unprecedented as the last pope to resign was Pope Gregory XII, in 1415. In his case, he stepped down to end the "Western Schism," a decades-long disagreement that resulted in two, and later three, men claiming to be headof the Catholic Church. Back in April of 2012, Tom Horn and I revealed the obscure work of a Belgian Jesuit, Rene Thibaut, who predicted the papacy would change hands in April of 2012 based on a nine-hundred-year-old prophecy by Saint Malachy. In our previous book, *Petrus Romanus*, his work was verified using a software spreadsheet and calculated down to the days. Interestingly, we wrote specifically on pages 58–59 and 470 that Pope Benedict would likely step down for health reasons. The year 2012 came and went and we assumed Thibaut was mistaken. As it turns out, he was *far more correct than anyone ever knew*! According to the NY Times:

> That the resignation was long in the planning was confirmed by Giovanni Maria Vian, the editor of the Vatican newspaper, *L'Osservatore Romano*, who wrote on Monday that the pope's decision "was taken many months ago," after his trip to Mexico and Cuba in March 2012, "and kept with a reserve that no one could violate."[18]

This is astounding! The French book entitled, *La Mystérieuse Prophétie des Papes* ("The Mysterious Prophecy of the Popes"), by Thibaut, published in 1951, predicted Benedict's decision with pinpoint accuracy. This suggests that the ending of the Malachy prophecy looms near and Petrus Romanus will assume the papacy by the time this book is in print.

With the long-dreaded *final* conclave set for March, it appears there could be another portent in the sky heralding the arrival of a Pope—this time, Petrus Romanus. In early March, the comet Pan-STARRS will pass by the Earth as it dips inside the orbit of Mercury. Experts expect it to become a naked-eye object about as bright as the stars of the Big Dipper, but it has the potential to put on a more dramatic display than expected. Karl Battams of the Naval Research Lab says, "Prepare to be surprised. A new comet from the Oort Cloud is always an unknown quantity equally capable of spectacular displays or dismal failures."[19] If that's not enough, Comet ISON coming in November 2013 promises to be the "comet of the century."[20] Interestingly, Saint Hildegard, also known as "Sibyl of the Rhine," was a German mystic, Benedictine abbess, visionary, and polymath, who predicted a great comet would appear as an end-time portent. She prophesied:

> Before the Comet comes, many nations, the good excepted, will be scoured with want and famine. The great nation in the ocean that is inhabited by people of different tribes and descent by an earthquake, storm and tidal waves will be devastated. It will be divided, and in great part submerged. That nation will also have many misfortunes at sea, and lose its colonies in the east through a Tiger and a Lion.[21]

Many interpreters believe that great nation of many tribes to be the great melting pot of the United States of America. If so, expect rough weather ahead.

Finally, most of our readers are probably aware that the Vatican has made quite a few of its own sensational statements concerning aliens. For example, try a simple Google search using the terms "baptize" and "extraterrestrial" and discover how it returns thousands of results pointing to recent claims made by Jesuit astronomers of the Vatican Observatory Research Group (VORG). Add to that recent editorials in popular media like "The Salvation of Extraterrestrials" by Thomas F. O'Mera, and it becomes clear that a book like this is needed.[22] Even more, the Internet is humming with rumors that the Jesuits named their telescope "Lucifer" after Satan, himself. Now if that is the case, then someone *does* have a lot of explaining to do. As you are probably aware from the promotional video, this prompted us to visit the Vatican Advanced Technology Telescope (VATT) within the Mt. Graham Observatory Complex in Arizona to get to the bottom of this matter. You are now invited to follow us on that journey.

2 Introduction
Prolegomena

W**arning:** This book may shatter the comfort of closely held presuppositions and may result in the wholesale alteration of crucial priorities.

A Vortex of Convergent Scenarios

Even the marginally informed are beginning to recognize that the entire world's horizons are drastically changing. Numerous ostensibly independent scenarios are converging. In fact, one can easily map an entire vortex of convergencies that are altering virtually every rule book of conduct in every field of endeavor:

In the field of physics, scientists are alarmed that even the constants of physics appear to be changing. If the constants are changing, that implies that our physical reality "is but a shadow of a larger reality."[23]

The foundational discovery of twentieth-century science is that the universe is not infinite: it may be expanding, but it is *finite*. And it clearly had a beginning. (That's what led to the family of speculations known as "the Big Bang.") What is even more disturbing is that there is also a definite limit to "smallness"! Whether one is dealing with length, mass, energy, or even time, we run into the Planck Limit. Between the finite limit to the macrocosm (the region of astronomy and astrophysics) and the indivisible units in the microcosm (the region of subatomic particles and quantum physics), we discover that our physical reality is actually a virtual *digital* simulation! (This is one of the underlying insights of movies such as *The Thirteenth Floor*, or the popular *Matrix*.) This entire universe now appears to be a subset within (for lack of an alternative, inclusive term) the *metacosm*. Much of this book will explore the nature and implications of the metacosm.

The convergence of several cutting-edge technologies—genetics, robotics, nanotechnologies, and artificial intelligence—is collectively ushering in astonishing ambitions for the "transhuman"—even with the potential of immortality. (Will God draw His line in the sand as He did in Genesis 11?)

The continuing global economic crisis has now affected the entire West—even America, as the world's largest debtor, now has its financial future in doubt. The centroid of power—initiated in Mesopotamia, migrated from Babylon, to Persia, to Greece, then Rome—continued westward, which then resulted in an era of dominance throughout Northern Europe, in the fifteenth through the eighteenth centuries. This migration of power ultimately arrived to make the twentieth century the "American Century."[24] However, the centroid of power has migrated toward the "Asian Century." As this book will detail, it appears that it will ultimately return westward to where it all began—but with some astonishing surprises en route.

The emergence of Unidentified Flying Objects (and their associated myths) continues to lurk behind the hoaxes and (often deliberate) misinformation, harboring many surprises to the uninformed. (Why do they enjoy a higher military classification than our most sensitive weapons systems? And, what is their *biblical* significance? The prophet Daniel speaks of those who will "mingle themselves with the seed of men" [Daniel 2:43]. If they are not "of the seed of men," who are they?)

Meanwhile, a shocking moral decay continues in virtually all sectors of society—political, financial, educational, and ecclesiastical. This decline seems to continue unparalleled in modern history. Man's predicament used to be regarded as a quest for truth; yet we now live in a society that denies the existence of truth.[25] In America, the republic that was based on the rule of law, now effectively ignores the foundational documents upon which it was founded.[26] We have abandoned the sanctity of commitment in business as well as in our families; we change partners like a fashion statement. Furthermore, the cancer of "entitlement mentality" has infected the traditional work ethic, and the path toward tyranny seems unlikely to be stemmed. Some observers even suggest that God's "Abandonment Wrath" has begun. With the outlawing of God in the schools and public places, and the murder of 50 million innocents since *Roe v. Wade*, it shouldn't come as a surprise.

Many of us have traditionally regarded the Roman Catholic Church as the most exclusive club on the Earth. Now we find it reaching out to be among the most inclusive: even Islam is embraced! (Yet the anathemas against Protestants still stand.) And now, as the first occasion in six hundred years, a pope (Pope Benedict XVI) is resigning! His deteriorating mental and physical strength is presented as the motivating reason, but is the decision really based on internal politics? How will this impact the succession? How will this mesh with the fabled papal prophecies?[27]

Many politicians continue espousing "change." There are, indeed, changes afoot—more than most people have any awareness of. Yet, global problems lead to proposing global solutions. There are growing suspicions that many of these converging scenarios are the result of a deliberate design—a preparation for a cosmic deceit.

The Age of Deceit

The Bible clearly warns of a coming era of unprecedented deceit and delusion:

> Let no man deceive you by any means: for that day shall not come, except there come a falling away first, and that man of sin be revealed, the son of perdition; Who opposeth and exalteth himself above all that is called God, or that is worshipped; so that he as God sitteth in the temple of God, shewing himself that he is God.… And for this cause God shall send them strong delusion, that they should believe a lie. (2 Thessalonians 2:3–4, 11)

Note the definite article, the "lie": a specific deception that will deceive the entire world.

> For then shall be great tribulation, such as was not since the beginning of the world to this time, no, nor ever shall be. And except those days should be shortened, there should no flesh be saved: but for the elect's sake those days shall be shortened. (Matthew 24:21–22)

And, "Take heed that no man deceive you" (Matthew 24:4; see also Luke 21:8; Mark 13:5). This is a command—not just a suggestion. But how can we accomplish this?

There is an ultimate deception in the making—the preparation for the white horse of Revelation 6. These emerging preparations will be clear to those who know what to be looking for…*and they will alter your personal priorities.*

This book is intended to be an introductory part of your field manual. Much of this may come as a surprise—even to those with substantial biblical literacy at their disposal.

(Don't attempt to appraise the following discourses until you have completed a careful review of this entire book. And be prepared for some well-defended discoveries.)

Introduction Author Bio

Dr. Charles "Chuck" Missler has spent four decades in the boardrooms of high-technology corporations, serving as chief executive officer of six of them. He is a founder of the Koinonia Institute, a Christian "think-tank" with members in more than eighty countries. He has contributed to over one hundred publications on biblical exposition and international conferences on strategic perspectives, many of which can be viewed on www.KItrust.org.

SECTION ONE

THE INVESTIGATION BEGINS

1 | Mount Graham and the L.U.C.I.F.E.R. Project

The Investigation Begins

"A new instrument with an evil-sounding name is helping scientists see how stars are born. L.U.C.I.F.E.R., which stands for 'Large Binocular Telescope Near-infrared Utility with Camera and Integral Field Unit for Extragalactic Research,' is a chilled instrument attached to a telescope in Arizona. And yes, it's named for the Devil, whose name itself means 'morning star' [and which] happens to be right next to the Vatican Observatory on Mt. Graham in Tucson."
—Rebecca Boyle, *Popular Science* magazine

Following the release of our 2012 best seller, *Petrus Romanus: The Final Pope is Here*, we were inundated with invitations from around the world to be interviewed on radio, television, and in print media. These included segments in The History Channel's *Countdown to Apocalypse*, which premiered November 9, 2012; a special feature on VisionTV, Canada's largest Christian channel, titled, *I Prophesy: The Apocalypse Series* (complete with reenactments) that aired nationwide on Tuesday, November 20, 2012; invitations to Rome to discuss with Italian media our findings on René Thibaut, a Belgian Jesuit whose meticulous analysis of the Prophecy of the Popes predicted the arrival of Petrus Romanus in

2012; a "best of" interview with George Noory on *Coast to Coast AM*, and dozens more.

But it was two shows in particular (which we did on *The Omega Man Radio Program* with popular author and radio man Steve Quayle) that prompted our interest in writing this book and, more importantly, our visit to Mt. Graham in southeastern Arizona to start our investigation. The first show we did with Steve rocketed *Omega Man* to the number-one *Blog Talk Radio Show* in the world for over a week. It focused on the ancient Prophecy of the Popes and the fact that the pontiff following Benedict XVI will be the final one on this mysterious list of popes, a prophecy that was concealed inside the secret vaults of the Vatican for hundreds of years and that many believe points to the arrival of the False Prophet of end-times infamy. (Note that at the writing of this book, Benedict XVI had just stepped down, and whoever was scheduled to follow him in the role of Petrus Romanus was still an open question. Whoever it turns out to be is the final pope, according to the medieval Catholic prophecy.)

In the second *Omega Man* show, which aired Wednesday, April 4, 2012, we broached the subject of a "Vatican ET" connection. That program sent *Omega Man* into the stratosphere for an unprecedented one-month position as the top *Blog Talk Radio Show* on the planet, illustrating to these authors that the world is more than casually interested not only in the final pope, but in the connection between Rome and its work on extraterrestrial intelligence, astrobiology, and the intriguing connection between those issues and Petrus Romanus.

Thus, on a mild morning in September 2012, we (together with our cameraman Joe Ardis, a.k.a., the "Wild Man of the Ozarks") departed the small desert town of Safford, Arizona (which normally has a warm, high-desert climate, that is much hotter than most places in eastern Arizona due to its relatively low elevation of 2,953 feet),[28] en route to the Mt. Graham Observatory Base Camp, eighty miles from Tucson and a few miles south of Safford on State Route 366. Located near the northern limit of the Chiricahua Apache and Western Apache territories, *Dził*

Nchaa Si An, as it is known in the Western Apache language, is one of the four holiest mountains in America for the Apache and is considered sacred to all of the region's native peoples. (The San Carlos Apache Tribe had originally joined environmentalists who sought, among other things, to protect the Sacred Grounds and American Red Squirrel, in filing dozens of lawsuits before a federal appeals court to stop the construction of the observatories on Mt. Graham, but the project ultimately prevailed after an act by the United States Congress allowed it.)

We had been warned by our guide that the trek up the steep mountainside from 2,953 feet to over 10,700 feet was precarious, coupled with more hairpin turns, switchbacks, and narrow segments of roadway overlooking deep canyon walls than we might have imagined. To top it off, there would be no guardrails along the harrowing, winding path. We were scheduled to arrive at the Mt. Graham International Observatory a couple hours after departure. We would meet with astronomers and engineers at the Large Binocular Telescope (LBT)—currently one of the world's most advanced optical telescopes—where, among other things, the new LUCIFER device is attached between its gigantic twin mirrors (either of which would be the largest optical telescope in continental North America). We were later told by the LBT systems engineer who spent significant time with us that day that another instrument—LUCIFER II—is scheduled to arrive at the observatory anytime and will complete the two multi-object and long-slit infrared spectrograph imagers needed for studying the heavens in search of, among other things, exoplanets that may host intelligent life. We would also visit the Heinrich Hertz Submillimeter Telescope that day, which sits between the LBT and the real target of our quest—the Vatican Advanced Technology Telescope and the Jesuits who work there.

Before leaving base camp, Dramamine for motion sickness was suggested ahead of departure, and the two men in our research team who declined that offer would soon wish they hadn't. Once we were underway, it was nonstop reeling back and forth, bouncing up and down, as the driver—who seemed a little too much to enjoy being in one gear faster than he should have been given the circumstances—occasionally looked at us in the rearview mirror and smiled. As we went from Sonoran Desert scrub at the mountain's floor to alpine spruce-fir forest closer to the summit, our guide, who sat in the opposite front seat from the driver, occasionally pointed to something off to one side, describing how more life zones and vegetative varieties existed here than on any other North American mountain, including almost two dozen plants, animals, and insects that are not found anywhere else. Of course, this included the celebrity of Mt. Graham—the endangered red squirrel—which Arizona has already spent at least 1.25 million dollars protecting. But it was hard to appreciate these facts while some of us were growing queasy and wondering how far down the canyon wall we would roll if at any moment the driver were to lose control and barrel off the side. Thankfully, just when we were starting to think this excursion had been a bad idea, we stopped approximately two-thirds of the way up the mountain at the Columbine Ranger Station, a United States Department of Agriculture (USDA) Forest Service administrative complex that had been built circa 1935 by the Civilian Conservation Corps, a public work-relief program that was part of President Franklin D. Roosevelt's New Deal that had provided unskilled manual labor jobs to relieve unemployment during the Great Depression.

We had packed a sack lunch and used the ranger station as a place to rest a while, eat, and let our bellies recover a bit from the roller coaster ride. While munching on a sandwich and looking at the aging black-and-white pictures that hung on the walls here and there of the Depression-era men who had built the modest encampment, we met a volunteer, an interesting old chap who told us how he had been coming there for many years to keep a fire in the fireplace and to greet hikers who wandered into the park. When we told him where we were going, he got quiet. When we added that our plan was to speak with the Jesuits at the Vatican Advanced Technology Telescope (VATT) in the restricted area further up the mountain, he lost interest in the conversation and started stirring his fire again.

Minutes later, lunches consumed and stomachs still uneasy, we were back in our vehicle. From that point forward, the road (if we can call it that) became little more than a glorified goat trail until finally, about a mile from our destination, we arrived at a security gate with "No Trespassing" warnings posted in several languages. The guide had a key to the gate. She unlocked it, then relocked it behind us after we drove through the opening. At that point, the driver pulled out a radio we had not noticed before, and radioed somebody that we were heading up the incline. Evidently this was necessary, because from this point forward, the steep, gravel lane was barely wide enough for one vehicle at a time, and we didn't want to risk running up against another vehicle that might be coming down from the observatories. No one answered the driver's call, so he radioed again, then a third time, with still no response. The silence must have meant the road was clear, as just like that, he slipped the vehicle into low gear and we began our final thirty-minute crawl up the mountainside.

"And one more thing," the guide warned as we jerked over the rocky track, tires spinning against the loose gravel and dirt. "When we get to the restricted area you'll see brightly colored cables roping off most of the land around the buildings. Do not—I repeat—*do not* step over those lines, or you will be arrested immediately and hauled off to jail." She wasn't smiling, and when we got to the observatories, we saw the security lines and enforcement vehicles, just as she had described them.

Searching for Lucifer from Atop the Holy Mountain

It was approximately eleven in the morning (Pacific Standard Time) when we rounded the final bend and saw just ahead the towering edifices housing the LBT, an optical telescope for astronomy and currently one of the world's most advanced systems. Near it was the Submillimeter Telescope (SMT) or, as it is also known, the Heinrich Hertz Submillimeter Telescope, a "state-of-the-art single-dish radio telescope for observations in the sub-millimeter wavelength range…the most accurate radio telescope ever built."[29] And last but not least, about a block away from them, we observed our primary reason for trudging to the top of this peak—the Vatican Advanced Technology Telescope (VATT).

Of course, before making the trip, we had read the official story from the Vatican Observatory website describing how VATT truly lives up to its name:

> Its heart is a 1.8-m f/1.0 honeycombed construction, borosilicate primary mirror. This was manufactured at the University of Arizona Mirror Laboratory, and it pioneered both the spin-casting techniques and the stressed-lap polishing techniques of that Laboratory which are being used for telescope mirrors up to 8.4-m in diameter. The primary mirror is so deeply-dished that the focus of the telescope is only as far above the mirror as the mirror is wide, thus allowing a structure that is about three times as compact as the previous generation of telescope designs.[30]

Such technical language aside, the "observers" who are approved to operate VATT and what they are using it for these days are who would take us through the looking glass. This was confirmed minutes later by the Jesuit father on duty that day (whom we got on film), who told us that among the most important research occurring with the site's Vatican astronomers is the search for extrasolar planets and advanced alien intelligence. He then proceeded (as did our guide) to show us all around the observatory, from the personal quarters of the Church's astronomers—where they ate, slept, relaxed, studied—to the control rooms, computer screens and systems, and even the telescope itself. While we were given complete and unrestricted opportunity to question how the devices are used and what distinctively sets each of the telescopes on Mt. Graham apart, we had not expected the ease with which the astronomers and technicians would also speak of UFOs! This was especially true when we walked up the gravel road from VATT to the LBT, where we spent most of the day with a systems engineer who not only took us to all seven levels of that mighty machine—pointing out the LUCIFER device (which he lovingly referred to as "Lucy" several times and elsewhere as "Lucifer") and what it is used for, as well as every other aspect of the telescope we tried to wrap our minds around. He also stunned us as we sat in the control room listening to him and the astronomers speak so casually of the redundancy with which UFOs are captured on screens darting through the heavens. Our friendly engineer didn't blink an eye, neither did any of the other scientists in the room, and we were shocked at this, how ordinary it seemed to be.

Authors Tom Horn and Cris Putnam in front of VATT

Standing on the platform beneath VATT

Walking from VATT to the Large Binocular Telescope

LBT systems engineer in control room with Tom, Cris, and an astronomer (out of frame on right) describing how often UFOs are captured during observations

But as much as the commonality of UFO sightings on Mt. Graham's telescopes intrigued, this was not the primary reason for our being there. We had come with deeper questions concerning high-level Vatican astronomers and what they had been leaking to, and discussing with, the media in recent years—including captivating comments from Jesuit priests like Guy Consolmagno, a leading astronomer who often turns up as a spokesman for the Vatican. He has worked at NASA and taught at Harvard and MIT, and currently splits his time between the Vatican observatory and laboratory (Specola Vaticana) headquartered at the summer residence of the Pope in Castel Gandolfo, Italy, and Mt. Graham in Arizona. Over the last few years, Consolmagno has focused so much time and effort in an attempt to reconcile science and religion in public forums, specifically as it relates to the subject of extraterrestrial life and its potential impact on *the future of faith*, that we decided to contact him. He agreed to be interviewed via the Internet from Rome. However, it seemed once he knew who we were and what we wanted to examine, he kept his answers short, if not altogether evasive. On the upside, he was gracious enough to send us a copy of his private PDF file for a booklet that he authored entitled *Intelligent Life in the Universe: Catholic Belief and the Search for Extraterrestrial Intelligent Life*, which had been pulled by the publisher shortly after it was authorized by Rome in 2005 and is no longer available anywhere. It is a gold mine of what he and the Vatican are considering regarding the ramifications of astrobiology and specifically the discovery of advanced extraterrestrials (this is perhaps the reason it was pulled). In it, he admits how contemporary societies will "look to The Aliens to be the Saviours of humankind."[31] To illustrate the theological soundness of this possibility, Consolmagno argues that humans are not the only intelligent beings God created in the universe, and these non-human life forms are described in the Bible. He starts by pointing to angels, then surprises us by actually referencing the Nephilim:

> Other heavenly beings come up several times in the Psalms. For example, look at the beautiful passage in Psalm 89 that calls out, "Let the heavens praise your wonders, O Lord, your faithfulness in the assembly of the holy ones. For who in the skies can be compared to the Lord? Who among the heavenly beings is like the Lord?... The heavens are yours, the earth also is yours; the world and all that is in it—you have founded them." Likewise,

God asks Job (38:7) if any human can claim to have been around at the creation, "when the morning stars sang together and all the heavenly beings shouted for joy."

Are these "heavens," "holy ones," those "in the sky," the "morning stars…and heavenly beings" more references to angels? Or do they refer to some other kind of life beyond our knowledge?

…And these are not the only non-human intelligent creatures mentioned in the Bible. There's that odd, and mysterious, passage at the beginning of Genesis, Chapter 6, that describes the "sons of God" taking human wives. With it is a frustratingly oblique reference to "The Nephilim…the heroes that were of old, warriors of renown."

Most Biblical scholars suggest that the Nephelim [*sic*] and the Sons of God in Genesis can be explained away as a left-over reference to the creation stories of the pagans who surrounded ancient Israel, that they were written by the kind of people whose culture saw anyone Not Of My Tribe as being unspeakably alien. Likewise, the references to heavens and stars singing and praising the Lord can be seen simply for the beautiful poetry that it is.

But whether you interpret these creatures as angels or aliens doesn't really matter for the sake of our argument here. The point is that the ancient writers of the Bible, like all ancient peoples, were perfectly happy with the possibility that other intelligent beings could exist.[32]

Read that again, then ask yourself: Did the Vatican's top astronomer actually mean to use the story of the Nephilim from the Bible as an example of the kind of "space saviors" man could soon look to for salvation? This incredible assertion is only topped by what he says next. In quoting John 10:16, which says, "And other sheep I have, which are not of this fold: them also I must bring, and they shall hear my voice;

and there shall be one fold, and one shepherd," Consolmagno writes: "Perhaps it's not so far-fetched to see the Second Person of the Trinity, the Word, Who was present 'In the beginning' (John 1:1), coming to lay down His life and take it up again (John 10:18) not only as the Son of Man but also as **a Child of other races?**[33] (emphasis added).

Do Vatican scholars actually believe Jesus might have been the Star-Child of an alien race? Do Consolmagno and/or other Jesuits secretly hold that the virgin birth was in reality an abduction scenario in which Mary was impregnated by ET, giving birth to the hybrid Jesus?

All this would seem impossible theology if not for the fact that other high-ranking Vatican spokespersons—those who routinely study from the "Star Base" (as local Indians call it) on Mt. Graham—have been saying the same in recent years. This includes Dr. Christopher Corbally, vice director for the Vatican Observatory Research Group on Mt. Graham until 2012, who believes our image of God will have to change if evidence of alien life is confirmed by scientists (including the need to evolve from the concept of an "anthropocentric" God into a "broader entity"[34]), and the current Vatican Observatory director, Father Josè Funes, who has gone equally far, suggesting that alien life not only exists in the universe and is "our brother," but will, if discovered, confirm the "true" faith of Christianity and the dominion of Rome. When the *L'Osservatore Romano* newspaper (which only publishes what the Vatican approves) asked him what this meant, he replied: "How can we rule out that life may have developed elsewhere? Just as we consider earthly creatures as 'a brother,' and 'sister,' why should we not talk about an 'extraterrestrial brother'? It would still be part of creation,"[35] and believing in the existence of such is not contradictory to *Catholic doctrine*.[36]

Such statements are but the latest in a string of recent comments by numerous Vatican astronomers confirming a growing belief (or inside knowledge?) that discovery may be made in the near future of alien life, including intelligent life, and that this encounter will not challenge the authority of the Roman Catholic Church.

Brother Guy Consolmagno with Pope Benedict XVI

From the '70s through the '90s, it was Monsignor Corrado Balducci—an exorcist, theologian, member of the Vatican Curia (governing body at Rome), and friend of the Pope—who went perhaps furthest, appearing on Italian national television numerous times to state that ETs were not only possible, *but were already interacting with Earth and that the Vatican's leaders were aware of it.* Furthermore, speaking as an official demonologist, he said that extraterrestrial encounters "are not demonic, they are not due to psychological impairment, and they are not a case of entity attachment, but these encounters deserve to be studied carefully."[37] He even disclosed how the Vatican itself has been closely following the phenomenon and quietly compiling material evidence from Vatican embassies (nunciatures) around the world on the extraterrestrials and their mission. For example, at a forum concerning the enormous UFO flap in Mexico, he stated, "I always wish to be the spokesman for these star peoples who also are part of God's glory, and I will continue to bring it to the attention of the Holy Mother Church."[38]

Whatever you make of his claims, Balducci was a member of a special group of consultants to the Vatican, a public spokesperson for

Rome on the matter of extraterrestrial life as well as UFO and abduction phenomenon, and his assertions have never been contradicted by the Catholic Church.

Perhaps most intriguing was Catholic theologian Father Malachi Martin who, before his death in 1999, hinted at something like imminent extraterrestrial contact more than once. While on *Coast to Coast AM* radio in 1997, Art Bell asked Malachi why the Vatican was heavily invested in the study of deep space at the Mt. Graham Observatory we visited. As a retired professor of the Pontifical Biblical Institute, Malachi was uniquely qualified to hold secret information pertaining to VATT. His answer ignited a firestorm of interest among Christian and secular ufologists when he replied, "Because the mentality…amongst those who [are] at the…highest levels of Vatican administration and geopolitics, know…what's going on in space, *and what's approaching us*, could be of great import in the next five years, ten years" (emphasis added).[39]

Those cryptic words, "what's approaching us, could be of great import," were followed in subsequent interviews with discussion of a mysterious "sign in the sky" that Malachi believed was approaching from the north. While this could have been an oblique reference to an end-time portent, the Catholic prophecy of the Great Comet, people familiar with Malachi believe he may have been referring to a near-future arrival of alien intelligence. (Interesting note from the authors: When we asked Father Guy Consolmagno what he thought of Malachi's claims, he actually seemed miffed by the man, saying, "I have heard stories about the late Malachi Martin which make me rather suspicious of statements that come from him. I was at the observatory in the 1990s, and he never visited us nor had anything to do with us."[40] This reaction seems consistent with how many other Catholic priests despised Malachi's willingness to disclose what Rome otherwise wanted buried, especially the satanic cabal within the Jesuit order Malachi wrote about in his best-selling books.)

Yet, if ET life is something Vatican officials have privately considered for some time, why speak of it so openly now, in what some perceive as a careful, doctrinal unveiling over the last few years? Is this a deliberate effort by church officials to "warm up" the laity to ET disclosure? Are official church publications on the subject an attempt to soften the blow before disclosure arrives, in order to help the faithful retain their ortho-doxy in light of unprecedented forthcoming knowledge?

Writing for *Newsweek* in the May 15, 2008, article, "The Vatican and Little Green Men," journalist Sharon Begley noted that "[this] might be part of a push to demonstrate the Vatican's embrace of science... Interestingly, the Vatican has plans to host a conference in Rome next spring to mark the 150th anniversary of the Origin of Species, Charles Darwin's seminal work on the theory of evolution. Conference organiz-ers say it will look beyond entrenched ideological positions—including misconstrued Creationism. The Vatican says it wants to reconsider the problem of evolution 'with a broader perspective' and says an 'appropri-ate consideration is needed more than ever before.'"[41]

The "appropriate consideration" Begley mentioned may have been something alluded to by Guy Consolmagno three years earlier in an interview with the *Sunday Herald*. That article pointed out how Consolmagno's job included reconciling "the wildest reaches of science fiction with the flint-eyed dogma of the Holy See" and that his latest mental meander was about "the Jesus Seed," described as "a brain-warp-ing theory which speculates that, perhaps, every planet that harbours intelligent, self-aware life may also have had a Christ walk across its methane seas, just as Jesus did here on Earth in Galilee. The salvation of the Betelguesians may have happened simultaneously with the salva-tion of the Earthlings."[42] This sounds like a sanctified version of panspermia—the idea that life on Earth was "seeded" by something a long time ago, such as an asteroid impact—but in this case, "the seed" was divinely appointed and reconciled to Christ.

The curious connection between the Vatican's spokespersons and the question of extraterrestrials and salvation was further hinted at in the May 2008 *L'Osservatore Romano* interview with Father Funes in an article titled "The Extraterrestrial Is My Brother." In the English translation of the Italian feature, Funes responds to the question of whether extraterrestrials would need to be redeemed, which he believes should not be assumed. "God was made man in Jesus to save us," he says. "If other intelligent beings exist, it is not said that they would have need of redemption. They could remain in full friendship with their Creator."[43]

By "full friendship," Funes reflected how some Vatican theologians accept the possibility that an extraterrestrial species may exist that is morally superior to men—closer to God than we fallen humans are—and that, as a consequence, *they may come here to evangelize us*. Father Guy Consolmagno took up this same line of thinking when he wrote in his book, *Brother Astronomer: Adventures of a Vatican Scientist*:

> So the question of whether or not one should evangelize is really a moot point. Any alien we find will learn and change from contact with us, just as we will learn and change from contact with them. It's inevitable. And they'll be evangelizing us, too.[44]

But hold on, as this disturbing rabbit hole goes much deeper: In a paper for the Interdisciplinary Encyclopedia of Religion and Science website, Father Giuseppe Tanzella-Nitti—an Opus Dei theologian of the Pontifical University of the Holy Cross in Rome—explains just how we could actually be evangelized during contact with "spiritual aliens," as every believer in God would, he argues, greet an extraterrestrial civilization as an extraordinary experience and would be inclined to respect the alien and recognize the common origin of our different species as being from the same Creator. According to Giuseppe, this contact by nonterrestrial intelligence would then offer new possibilities "of better understanding the relationship between God and the whole of creation."[45] Giuseppe states this would not immediately oblige the Christian "to renounce his own faith in God simply on the basis of the reception of new, unexpected information of a religious character from extraterrestrial civilizations,"[46] but that such a renunciation could come soon after as the new "religious content" originating from outside the Earth is confirmed as reasonable and credible. "Once the trust-worthiness of the information has been verified," the believer would have to "reconcile such new information with the truth that he or she already knows and believes on the basis of the revelation of the One and Triune God, conducting a re-reading [of the Gospel] inclusive of the new data."[47] How this "more complete" ET gospel might deemphasize or significantly modify our understanding of salvation through Jesus Christ is discussed in the Exotheology section of this book, but former Vatican observatory vice director, Christopher Corbally, in his article, "What if There Were Other Inhabited Worlds?" may have summarized the most important aspect when he concluded that Jesus simply might not remain the *only Word* of salvation: "I would try to explore the alien by letting 'it' be what it is, without rushing for a classification category, not even presuming two genders," Corbally said, before dropping this bombshell:

> While Christ is the First and the Last Word (the Alpha and the Omega) spoken to humanity, he is not necessarily the *only* word spoke to the universe… For, the Word spoken to us does not seem to exclude an equivalent "Word" spoken to aliens. They, too, could have had their "Logos-event". Whatever that event might have been, it does not have to be a repeated death-and-resurrection, if we allow God more imagination than some religious thinkers seem to have had. For God, as omnipotent, is not restricted to one form of language, the human.[48]

That high-ranking spokespersons for the Vatican have in recent years increasingly offered such language acknowledging the likelihood of extraterrestrial intelligence and the dramatic role ET's introduction to human civilization could play in regard to altering established creeds about anthropology, philosophy, religion, and redemption may become more future-consequential than most are prepared for.

And then there is that LUCIFER device at Mt. Graham, which

LBT engineer showing authors the LUCIFER device and explaining how it uses infrared

is curiously described on the Vatican Observatory website as "NASA AND THE VATICAN'S INFRARED TELESCOPE CALLED [LUCIFER]—A German built, NASA and The Vatican owned and funded Infrared Telescope…for looking at NIBIRU/NEMESIS."[49] Why has the Vatican Observatory website allowed this caption to remain? Nibiru and Nemesis are hypothetical planets that supposedly return in orbit close to the Earth after very long periods of time. They have been connected in modern myth with "Planet X" and most darkly with the destruction of planets that some believe occurred during a great war between God and Lucifer when the powerful angel was cast out of heaven. Are Rome and other world powers using the LUCIFER device to observe something the rest of us cannot see—something they believe represents this ancient war (or worse, keeping an eye on approaching end-times angelic transportation devices/UFOs—something Father Malachi Martin hinted at)? The latter theory is interesting in light of the demonic name of the infrared device. Infrared telescopes can detect objects too cool or far away and faint to be observed in visible light, such as distant planets, some nebulae, and brown dwarf stars. Additionally, infrared radiation has longer wavelengths than visible light, which means it can pass through astronomical gas and dust without being scattered.

Objects and areas obscured from view in the visible spectrum, including the center of the Milky Way, can thus be observed by LUCIFER's infrared technology.[50] But what UFO researchers have fascinated about for some time now is how infrared technology can also be used to spot and track unidentified flying objects *that cannot be seen with other telescopes or the naked eye*. In fact, some of the most astonishing UFOs ever caught on film have been recorded with infrared.

Years before this type of technology was brought to Mt. Graham in the form of the LUCIFER device, we speculated in our book *The Ahriman Gate* how the governments of the world might secretly be using infrared and modified high-sensitivity telescopes to monitor a hidden UFO armada parked just beyond the planet Mars. On page 205, we fictionalized:

> One hundred and twenty miles away, a senior technician on duty at the U.S. Air Force's top-secret Satellite Control Facility was glancing over his *Outdoorsman* magazine when he unexpectedly caught sight of something unusual on his SCF monitor. Whatever it was, it looked ablaze. He dropped from his reclined position and rolled his chair toward the screen. "Somebody find the colonel," he said a second later. "Tell him to get in here… quick."
>
> The sergeant tossed the magazine aside and readjusted the cameras to optimize mapping sensitivity. An early-warning satellite was reporting anomalous changes both inside and outside Earth's atmosphere, unlike anything the senior tech had seen before.
>
> He changed the RTC settings and raced outside to look at the sky.
>
> Nothing unusual could be verified visually.
>
> He returned to his station and stared at the monitor again. The huge flare was growing, indicating incredible temperature increases.
>
> Why the instruments were reporting what his eyes could

not substantiate was a mystery. As far as the computer was concerned, the sky was on fire, burning through and coming apart like a rip in the fabric of space.

"Dadgummit!" he said impatiently, "Where's the watch commander!?"

Just then the colonel raced into the room. "What is it, Sergeant!?"

"We've got unknown acquisitions, sir…take a look at this."

Quick-stepping to the remote tracking computer, the colonel leaned over the sergeant's shoulder. The screen was detailing a rapidly expanding redness.

"Are you mapping this?" he questioned.

"Yes, sir."

"Is it monochromatic? Oriental bird flashing?" he asked, insinuating that the Chinese might be pointing a laser at the satellite to confuse the Americans.

"It's no laser, sir."

The colonel stepped backwards, still watching the screen as he picked up the hot line to NORAD.

The commander-in-chief at the North American Aerospace Defense Command Center answered. "CINC-NORAD."

"This is Cricket Control," the Colonel said. "KH-20 is picking up massive energy readings. Do you have unscheduled thermals?"

"We have activity from terrestrial to celestial."

"To celestial?"

"Yes."

"How wide?"

"From the blue to the red planet."

"Are you certain?"

"Yes."

"What is it? Heat?"

"Negative."

"Solar flare?"

"No."

"What, then?"

"We cannot substantiate the cause at this time, Colonel, but whatever it is…it's growing exponentially. Cricket is to continue coordination of SGLS auto-tracking and range/range data to Mission Control."

"Roger that," the Colonel said, and hung up.

At the computer, the senior tech was mumbling under his breath, "M-maybe Hell opened its mouth to let us peek inside."

"What?"

He looked at the Colonel apprehensively. "Something Grandma told me…something from the Bible."

"What's your grandma's Bible got to do with this, Sergeant?"

"She said in the last days Hell would open and a great furnace with bug-headed demons would crawl out of it…or something like that…"

"Hell! Bugs! Stop acting stupid, Sergeant, and readjust those satellite settings!"

"Y-yes, sir."[51]

Then, on page 218, we gave the first hint of what was coming:

Outside and above the Earth, the rip in the fabric of space continued to widen. It had grown during the night and now spanned an area sixty-six thousand miles wide and millions of miles long, the current distance from Earth to Mars.

Peering into the rift at 6:00 AM Pacific Daylight Time, NASA's most powerful telescope had turned up nothing unusual. To make matters worse, NORAD's infrared and ultraviolet detections were still undeciphered. Top-level specialists from NASA's Chandra X-ray Observatory had been called in, and had rushed to the military center to study the phenomenon.

Then at 7:35 AM, astronomers working at the Marshall

Space Flight Center came up with something unusual. Using a modified high-sensitivity "hard" x-ray telescope, mysterious objects deep inside the rift had been located—hundreds of thousands of them—some bigger than football fields and others smaller than houses, moving toward Earth. The researchers couldn't explain the curiosity, only that the armada of objects would breach the rift's opening and enter Earth's atmosphere in less than an hour.[52]

VATT, Giants, Hybrids, and LUCIFER's Light Spectrum

A fascinating and potentially prophetic connection exists between the LUCIFER device's infrared capacity for seeing farther into the light spectrum, the technology used by "Watchers" to create the legendary giants, UFOs, and the prophecy by Jesus Christ in response to His disciples when they asked, "Tell us, when shall these things be? And what shall be the sign of thy coming, and of the end of the world?" to which Jesus answered, "As the Days of Noe [Noah] were, so shall also the coming of the Son of man be" (Matthew 24:3; 37).

As the director of the Future of Humanity Institute and a professor of philosophy at Oxford University, Nick Bostrom (www.NickBostrom.com) is a leading advocate of what has come to be known as transhumanism—the idea that we will use emerging fields of science including genetics to alter Homo sapiens and to create a new form of man. Like the Watchers in the Days of Noah, Bostrom envisions remanufacturing humans with animals, plants, and other synthetic life forms through the use of modern sciences. When describing the benefits of man-with-beast combinations in his online thesis, *Transhumanist Values*, Bostrom acknowledges that animals have "sonar, magnetic orientation, or sensors for electricity and vibration," among other extrahuman abilities. He goes on to explain that the range of sensory modalities for transhumans would not be limited to those among animals, and that there is "no fundamental block to adding say a capacity *to see infrared radiation* or to perceive radio signals and perhaps to add some kind of telepathic sense by augmenting our brains" (emphasis added).[53]

Bostrom is correct in that the animal kingdom has levels of perception beyond human. Some animals can "sense" earthquakes and "smell" tumors. Others, like dogs, can hear sounds as high as 40,000 Hz—and dolphins can hear even higher. It has also been shown that at least some animals see wavelengths beyond normal human capacity that, according to the biblical story of Balaam's donkey, may allow certain animals to *see into the spirit world.*

At Arizona State University, where the Templeton Foundation is currently funding a series of lectures titled, Facing the Challenges of Transhumanism: Religion, Science, Technology,[54] transhumanism is specifically viewed as possibly effecting *supernatural,* not just physical, transformation. Called "the next epoch in human evolution," some of the lecturers at ASU believe radical alteration of Homo sapiens could open a door to unseen intelligence. Consequently, ASU launched another study in 2009 to explore communication with "entities." Called the SOPHIA project (after the Greek goddess), the express purpose of the study is to verify communication "with Deceased People, Spirit Guides, Angels, Other-Worldly Entities/Extraterrestrials, and/or a Universal Intelligence/God."[55]

Imagine what this could mean if government laboratories with unlimited budgets working beyond congressional review (and perhaps with entities they have been led to believe represent advanced alien intelligence) were decoding the gene functions that lead animals to have preternatural capabilities of sense, smell, and sight, and were blending those genetic instructions with Homo sapiens. Among other things, genetically engineered modern "Nephilim" could be walking among us now—alien/human hybrids that appear to be Homo sapien but that hypothetically can see and even interact with invisible forces, including those "Other-Worldly Entities/Extraterrestrials" that VATT astronomers and transhumanists are looking for. Sound far-fetched? Consider what Ludovico Maria Sinistrari (1622–1701; an Italian Franciscan theologian and advisor to the Supreme Sacred Congregation of the Roman and

Universal Inquisition in Rome) believed. He was considered an expert on exorcism and sins relating to sexuality, including investigations of those individuals accused of sexual relations with demons. He wrote:

> Now, it is undoubted by Theologians and philosophers that carnal intercourse between mankind and the Demon some-times gives birth to human beings; that is how is to be born the Antichrist, according to some Doctors, such as Bellarmin, Suarez, Maluenda, etc. They further observe that, from a natural cause, the children thus begotten by Incubi are tall, very hardy and bold, very proud and wicked.[56]

We will examine what other experts believe about "alien-human hybrids" in a different section of this book, but the pattern for hybridity and the result of a part-man that can see into nonhuman realms may have been documented in the Bible! The story of Nimrod (Gilgamesh/Apollo/Osiris) in the book of Genesis illustrates how, through genetic influences such as a retrovirus or germ-line genetic engineering, a living specimen's DNA could be coded to make it a "fit extension" for infection by an other-dimensional entity. Genesis 10:8 says about Nimrod: "And Cush begat Nimrod: he began to be a mighty one in the earth." Three sections in this unprecedented verse indicate something very peculiar happened to Nimrod. First, the text says that "he *began* to be." In Hebrew, this is *chalal*, which in its Qal (simple active) stem means "to become profaned, defiled, polluted, or desecrated ritually, sexually or genetically" but in the Hiphil stem (causative) means "begin." It is certainly conceivable that the inspired author's word choice might imply word play for a "profaned beginning." Second, this verse tells us exactly *what* Nimrod began to be—"a *mighty* one" *(gibborim)*, possibly one of the offspring of the Nephilim. As Annette Yoshiko Reed says in the Cambridge University book, *Fallen Angels and the History of Judaism and Christianity*, "The Nephilim of [Genesis] 6:4 are always…grouped together with the gibborim as the progeny of the Watchers and human women."[57] And the third part of this text says the change to Nimrod started while he was on "earth." Therefore, in modern language, this text could accurately be translated to say:

> And Nimrod began to change genetically, becoming a gibborim, the offspring of watchers on earth.

To understand how as a mature, living specimen, Nimrod could have begun to be a gibborim, it is helpful to imagine this in terms of biology as we know it. For instance, not long ago, one of the authors of this book "began to be" a diabetic. Because of poor choices of food, diet, and exercise, the doctor assumed a genetic inherent was triggered that began changing the author in powerful, metabolic ways. Yet just because the heritable, disease-related genotype that can lead to diabetes was present, this did not necessarily mean that it would develop into the medical condition. It is entirely possible to be a carrier of a genetic mutation that increases the risk of developing a particular disease without ever actually becoming afflicted with the disorder in the course of a lifetime. Due to an earlier lifestyle, or maybe even certain environmental conditions, the gene mutation involved in the action of insulin "turned on" and the author "began to be" a diabetic.

We've often wondered if the record of Nimrod that says he "began to be" a "gibborim" indicated something similar about his genetics, DNA, or bloodline that "turned on" as a result of his decisions, triggering a change in him from one type of being to another. It is also possible that Nimrod became afflicted with a retrovirus that integrated with his genome and, in essence, "rewrote" his genetic makeup, fashioning him into a "fit extension" for an underworldly spirit. When we asked Sharon Gilbert, author of *The Armageddon Strain* whose formal education includes molecular biology and genetics, if she thought this was possible, she responded in a personal email:

> Absolutely! Retroviruses essentially inject single-stranded RNA strands into somatic (body) cells during "infection." These

ssRNA strands access nucleotide pools in the host cell and form a double-stranded DNA copy. This dsDNA can then incorporate itself into the host chromosome using a viral enzyme called "integrase." The new "fake gene" then orders the cell to make more mRNA copies of the original virus RNA. These then travel out of the cell and infect the next cell, and so on.

Perhaps this type genetic rewriting is implied in Genesis 10:8, which says, "And Cush begat Nimrod: he began to be a mighty one [gibborim] in the earth."

In addition to such scientific deduction, another reason we believe this story is suspicious has to do with Nimrod's sudden ability to "see" what others apparently could not. Note what he did immediately following Genesis chapter 10. As soon as he "began to be a mighty one" in the earth, one chapter later, Nimrod set out to build a tower whose top would "reach unto heaven" (Genesis 11:4). This was the infamous Tower of Babel, and Nimrod was designing it so that the top of it would extend into *Shamayim* ("heaven"), the abode of God. The *Jewish Encyclopedia* confirms several historical records that Nimrod, whom it establishes was also identified by various ancient cultures alternatively as Osiris, Orion, Apollo, and Gilgamesh, built the Tower of Babel in an attempt to ascend into the presence of God. Jehovah, Himself, came down and said of the Tower's design: "Nothing will be restrained from them, which they have imagined to do" (Genesis 11:6). In other words, according to the Lord, Nimrod would have accomplished what he "imagined" to do—to build a tower whose top would reach into the abode of God.

That this section of Scripture could be viewed as a secondary support for the concept of Nimrod having become "revived Watcher offspring" is supported by Nimrod seeming to abruptly be aware of *where* and *how tall* to build a tower so that the top of it would penetrate the dwelling place of God. Were his eyes suddenly opened to realities that are outside man's normal mode of perception? Did he develop LUCIFER-like abilities of sight, perhaps including infrared? As he became *gibborim*, he would have taken on Watchers' propensities, which, as angels, could see into the supernatural realm including where heaven is located and possibly where to enter it. Even the name "Babylon" implies this, echoing the North and South American Indian beliefs about towering gateways and the meaning "gate of God" or "gateway *to* God." That there could be sacred locations where those beings that can see into the supernatural realm could literally walk up onto a high place—such as Mt. Graham—and enter heaven is not as farfetched as it sounds. Numerous records, including from the Bible, appear to substantiate the idea that heaven could be attained on high towers or mountainous locations. Consider Moses meeting with God on Sinai, Jesus returning atop the Mount of Olives, the two hundred Watchers that "descended in the days of Jared on the summit of Mount Hermon" (Enoch 6:6) and other examples, including Jacob's ladder. This could also explain why, in the deep recesses of our psyche, people tend to believe they can draw closer to God when going up onto mountains.

In addition to the possibility of suddenly seeing into the supernatural realm as a result of integration with fallen angels, if Nimrod was genetically modified according to the original Watcher formula, he would have inherited animal characteristics within his new material makeup, and animals, like angels, can perceive "domains" that humans cannot. This includes obvious things, such as wavelengths of the electromagnetic spectrum, but possibly something even more substantial, like the spirit realm. This is important to keep in mind as we consider in another chapter of this book how the move by modern scientists and transhumanists to revive Watcher technology and to blend humans with animals could be a subset of a larger alien-human breeding program already in motion…

…and a deeper, more disturbing proposition involving what all this has to do with the Vatican, astrobiology, Petrus Romanus, great deception and the coming of the Antichrist.

2 | The Sky Island's Assimilation for Extraterrestrial Evangelism

"The highest levels of Vatican administration and geo-politics, know that, now, knowledge of what's going on in space, and what's approaching us, could be of great import in the next five years, ten years."[58] —Father Malachi Martin, adviser to three popes

"You want to know about UFO[s] and little green men? Contact the Vatican. They have an observatory out in Arizona, and that's what they are looking for."[59] —Gordon Cooper, NASA astronaut

(Cris Putnam) am sitting in the Tucson International airport drinking an overpriced coffee while collecting my thoughts. There's much to ponder; yesterday was a milestone. Gazing out the window, palm trees offset the arid, cacti-flecked terrain framed by jagged mountains in the distance. Since I have a few hours to wait, I am reviewing our tour of the Mt. Graham International Observatory, home of the Vatican Advanced Technology Telescope (VATT), the Submillimeter Telescope (SMT), and the most powerful telescope in the world, the Large Binocular Telescope (LBT). From where I sit, Mt. Graham is about a hundred miles northeast through an unremarkable desert bramble of scrub brush and uninviting cacti near the little town of Safford. Just yesterday, Tom Horn and I began our journey from the Discovery Park base camp traversing an hour and half of stomach-churning switchbacks and hairpin turns until we reached the top. Our expedition was instructive on a number of levels, some quite unexpected.

Upon ascent, we were cautioned to only sojourn the designated areas because our mere presence posed a mortal threat to an exceedingly rare breed of red squirrel, a rubicund rodent allegedly residing exclusively on this peak. While the locals voiced skepticism concerning its peerless status, they were, nevertheless, adamant that we would be arrested if we so much as landed a foot fall in its safe zone. Being a North Carolina native, I couldn't help but make a few wisecracks about squirrel hunting, but this was serious business. In fact, Arizona spent $1.25 million on rodent rope bridges to avert road kill.[60] It's safe to say the squirrels have been, well, assimilated into the observatory complex. Even so, a deep dissonance drones between the stark reality of a billion human beings in famine and the extravagant squirrel spans adjoining a multimillion-dollar facility searching for dark matter, black holes, and aliens. Nevertheless, the case of the Mt. Graham red squirrel is instructive concerning life in the universe, a point we will develop in the chapter on astrobiology.

Elite rodents aside, if astronomers do discover a planet suitable for extraterrestrial life, Mt. Graham is probably the facility that will make the announcement. Of course, a lot of people are wondering what the Vatican is doing up there—astronaut Gordon Cooper sure expressed an interesting opinion—and we hope to shine some light on that question.

While touring VATT, we met a Jesuit engineer eager to pontificate on the compatibility of science and faith. Of course, we agree that the war alleged by secularists is more about poor philosophy than a concrete conflict, but some Jesuits are part of the problem (more on that later). The VATT is a cherry assignment for a Jesuit interested in science. While the living quarters are tight, wealthy benefactors furnished a plush leather sofa and chairs for the otherwise rustic retreat. Amenities aside, this facility is for serious astronomy, and it houses an impressive instrument on an ideal location. The mission of VATT is displayed prominently outside the entrance in Latin and in English indoors.

Translation of Latin in image above: "THIS NEW TOWER FOR STUDYING THE STARS HAS BEEN ERECTED ON THIS PEACEFUL SITE SO FIT FOR SUCH STUDIES AND IT HAS BEEN EQUIPPED WITH A LARGE NEW MIRROR FOR DETECTING THE FAINTEST GLIMMERS OF LIGHT FROM DISTANT OBJECTS DURING THE FIFTEENTH YEAR OF THE REIGN OF JOHN PAUL II MAY WHOEVER SEARCHES HERE NIGHT AND DAY THE FAR REACHES OF SPACE USE IT JOYFULLY WITH THE HELP OF GOD" (photo by author)

By way of surveying the role of astronomy in astrobiology and the search for extraterrestrial intelligence, this chapter will follow our tour. First, we'll look at how the Mt. Graham complex came to be and examine some of the Vatican's contributions. Then, we will stroll up the gravel road to the LBT and discuss the search for exoplanets. Finally, we will look at the Submillimeter and radio telescopes, especially their use in the Search for Extraterrestrial Intelligence (SETI) program. Along the way, we will try to unpack why the Jesuit in charge of the Vatican Observatory Research Group told the media in 1992 that the purpose of VATT and the Mt. Graham International Observatory was to *contact extraterrestrials and baptize them into the Roman Catholic Church.*

Resistance is Futile

The VATT facility is really the brainchild of Jesuit George V. Coyne, who became director of the Vatican Observatory in 1978. In addition to his duties as a Jesuit, he was an adjunct professor in the University of Arizona's astronomy department, as well as associate director of the Steward Observatory. As a darling of the atheist community, he appeared with Richard Dawkins advocating a deistic form of Darwinism and stunned the high priest of atheism by also promoting a radical form of pluralism, the idea that all religions lead to the same God.[61] Of course, to those familiar with the radical revisionism of Vatican II (Second Vatican Council), it was no big surprise, but Coyne stretches the bounds of orthodoxy even given Rome's embrace of postmodernism. He profaned the film *Religulous* hosted by atheist Bill Maher, claiming that the Scriptures are scientifically inaccurate obscurantisms to the cheers of secularists and pagans universal. As we will address in a later chapter, it seems that just as Malachi Martin lamented in *The Jesuits: The Society of Jesus and the Betrayal of the Roman Catholic Church* (1987), this sort of reductionist postmodernism has become the stock and trade of third-millennium Jesuitism.

Back in 1980, Coyne brokered an agreement between the University of Arizona and the Vatican wherein it was stipulated that Rome would pay a fee so that members of the Vatican Observatory Research Group (VORG) could use the Steward Observatory facilities and office space. The choice of location is no accident. Sometimes called the "Old Pueblo," Tucson is a virtual "Holy See" for astronomers, because the climate and atmosphere of the surrounding mountains make it one of the best viewing locations in the world. As the second-largest populated city in Arizona behind Phoenix, it is home to the Smithsonian Astrophysical Observatory and National Optical Astronomy Observatories, as well as the University's Steward Observatory. The University of Arizona, boasting the largest undergraduate and second-largest graduate astronomy program in the US, also hosts a cutting-edge Center for Astrobiology, and offers an undergraduate and graduate minor in astrobiology.[62] The area is fast becoming a magnet for extraterrestrial ambitions.

Accordingly, Arizona is home to some of the more vocal exponents for astrobiology, like cosmologist Chris Impey, the best-selling author of *The Living Cosmos: Our Search for Life in the Universe* (2011) and many other popular titles and textbooks, who serves as the center's astrobiology education and outreach point man. Impey has also collaborated extensively with the VORG, contributing to volumes on the intersection between science and theology, as well as presenting at the 2009 Astrobiology Conference hosted by the Vatican in Rome.[63] Another outspoken figure who attended that 2009 conference, Paul Davies, is conveniently nearby at Arizona State in Tempe, which is part of the Phoenix metropolitan area, a city famous for its 1997 visitation by a mile-wide, delta-shaped craft witnessed by then-acting Arizona Governor Fife Symington, numerous citizens, and law enforcement personnel. We will return to the high strangeness within, but now we must explain the assimilation of Mt. Graham.

Through a highly contentious process, the Mt. Graham International Observatory has come to be the premiere astronomical site on the planet. It all came about because the University of Arizona began to campaign for a new international observatory using the latest technology back in the early 1980s. At that time, all of the Tucson sites were occupied, so, at an altitude of two miles above sea level, Emerald Peak on Mt. Graham seemed a promising choice.

The VORG, already in a symbiotic relationship with the university, was a seminal ally in forming an international consortium including not only Catholic institutions like Notre Dame University and a large group of Italian observatories, but also the Max Planck Institute of West Germany. The influential conglomerate is known to consist of these partners:[64]

Vatican Observatory Research Group	U.S. Universities	Italy	Germany
Specola Vaticana (Castel Gandolfo)	University of Arizona (Tucson)	Osservatorio Astronomico di Roma (Rome)	Max-Planck-Institut für Astronomie (Heidelberg)
V.O.R.G. Steward Observatory (Tucson)	University of Notre Dame (Notre Dame)	Osservatorio Astrofisico di Arcetri (Florence)	Max-Planck-Institut für Extraterrestrische Physik (Munich)
	Northern Arizona University (Flagstaff)	Osservatorio Astronomico di Bologna (Bologna)	Max-Planck-Institut für Radioastronomie (Bonn)
	Arizona State University (Tempe)	Osservatorio Astronomico di Padova (Padua)	Leibniz-Institut für Astrophysik Potsdam (Potsdam)
	Ohio State University (Columbus)		Landessternwarte (Heidelberg)
	University of Minnesota (Minneapolis; St. Paul)		
	University of Virginia (Charlottesville)		

Consisting of four nation states (Vatican, United States, Italy, and Germany), the international juggernaut still had a small problem... those pesky American environmental laws and the local Indians who hold the mountain sacred.

Dzil Nchaa Si An (Apache for "Big Seated Mountain") is one of the Western Apaches' four holiest mountains. The mountain was named in 1846 when, during the war with Mexico, Lieutenant William Emory, a topographer for the Army, labeled the mountain on his map as Mt. Graham after his friend and fellow officer James Duncan Graham. Following a series of presidential executive orders, it was assimilated into the United States as public land in 1873. Accordingly, it came under the purview of the US Forest Service, under whose administration it still remains. The mountain has a majestic presence in the landscape as seen from the San Carlos Apache Reservation, where a remnant of the indigenous population now resides. The local Apache harbor a deep sense of violation from past events like the Camp Grant Massacre, during which American troops wiped out an entire village without provocation. It was so heinous that President Ulysses S. Grant threatened placing Arizona under martial law unless the perpetrators were brought to trial. In response, a Tucson grand jury indicted one hundred of the assailants with one hundred and eight counts of murder. Even so, it took the Tucson jury a mere nineteen minutes to find them not guilty.

With such horrific historical precedent, it comes as little surprise that many of the surviving Apache deeply resent the appropriation and desecration of their sacred lands. Calling it "cultural genocide," they initiated a campaign to terminate construction. Environmentalists joined them, arguing that the astronomical mecca would contaminate the endangered ecosystem. Elizabeth A. Brandt, an activist for *Cultural Survival*, writes:

> The astronomers have the resources of the scientific establishments of four nation-states on their side, and the best lobbyists and lawyers that money can buy. They have the support of many politicians in each country, and receive millions of dollars in research grants. The Apache opposition survives by donation and a spiritual conviction of the rightness of their cause. Environmentalists have also opposed the project because of their concerns with the damage it will cause to the unique ecosystems and endangered species on the mountain.[65]

As a part of the Pinal Mountain range surrounded by the Sonoran-Chihuahuan Desert, the Nature Conservancy reports that the area contains "the highest diversity of habitats of any mountain range in North America."[66] Often referred to as a "Sky Island" ecosystem, the old growth forests on Mt. Graham's peak are Arizona's equivalent to tropical rain forests. It is home of at least eighteen species and subspecies of plants and animals found nowhere else on the planet, including the aforementioned endangered red squirrel.

The beginning of the struggle traces back to the mid 1980s, and, for some, it is a holy war. Over the years, the resistance has staged road blockades and engaged in acts of small-scale domestic terrorism—making headlines when some twenty thousand dollars worth of equipment was stolen from the construction site in 1986.[67] Interestingly, at the same time this controversy raged, Pope John Paul II paid a questionably serendipitous visit to Tucson in September of 1987, receiving Coyne along with a delegation from the university. The pope gave the project his blessing. Not surprisingly, wealthy Catholic benefactors for VATT were soon to fall in line. However, the timing also begs the question concerning possible papal persuasion of Roman Catholic congressmen and wildlife officials. According to the *Syllabus of Errors* promulgated by Pope Pius IX, Roman Catholics necessarily swear allegiance to the pope over any national interest.[68] Many believe Rome has consistently worked behind the scenes to subvert US interests as documented by Justin Dewey in the nineteenth-century exposé, *Washington in the Lap of Rome* (a free resource with this book when purchased at SurvivorMall.com).

In 1984, the conglomerate proposed the construction of *thirteen* telescopes on the two highest peaks of Mt. Graham: Emerald Peak and High Peak. Anticipating opposition, members of the international consortium threatened to build the complex in another country if it could not be built on Mt. Graham's two highest peaks. In 1985, The US Fish and Wildlife Service recommended only allowing the consortium to build five telescopes on one of the peaks. Then-acting director of the US Fish and Wildlife Service, Frank Dunkle, was widely criticized by environmentalists for paying more attention to politics than natural resources, later prompting his resignation.[69] During this time, the red squirrel was put on the endangered species list and the revised "Biological Opinion," an official document/assessment by US Fish and Wildlife released in 1988, clearly indicated that the university proposal would jeopardize the red squirrel. The official opinion consisted of three options, two of which allowed for limited construction and one that prohibited the project. That could have been the end, but it was never allowed to be decided due to an unprecedented intervention by Congress suggesting high-level skullduggery.

One might expect the Roman Catholic delegation to be somewhat sympathetic and sensitive to the ecological concerns. However, it was decidedly the most caustic and aggressive proponent of the project. Responding to the environmentalists' concerns, acting VORG director Coyne ranted:

> Nature and the Earth are just there, blah! And there will be a time when they are not there.… It is precisely the failure to make the distinctions I mention above [between Nature, Earth, cultures, human beings] that has created a kind of environmentalism and religiosity to which I cannot subscribe and which must be suppressed with all the force that we can muster.[70]

While this sort of violent language harks back to the Crusades and Inquisition, it also sounds eerily similar to Jean-Luc Picard's *post* assimilation, "I am Locutus of Borg. Resistance is futile. Your life, as it has been, is over. From this time forward you will service us."[71] Even worse were statements by his Jesuit brother and history professor at the university, Father Charles W. Polzer, who claimed, "The opposition to the telescopes and the use of Native American people to oppose the project are part of a Jewish conspiracy that comes out of the Jewish lawyers of the ACLU to undermine and destroy…the Catholic church."[72] One marvels at the anti-Semitic vitriol coming from the so-called Society of *Jesus* (Himself, a Jew), but it also begs the question of how preventing the VATT project could destroy the Catholic Church. This suggests that something more than Jesuitical stargazing is at stake. Shortly subsequent to the pope's visit, a congressional power play rendered the legal controversy academic.

The consortium and its supporters lobbied and convinced Congress to grant exemptions from the National Environmental Policy Act (NEPA) in order to begin construction of the first three telescopes, with

VATT taking the lead. But these weren't just exemptions; rather, this was a whole-scale reworking of federal law. By decree of Arizona Senator John McCain's deceptively titled "Idaho and Arizona Conservation Act of 1988," along with a half-million dollars paid for the services of the Washington, DC, lobbying powerhouse Patton, Boggs, and Blow, the project was given the green light. According to Dr. Randy Maddalena, a scientist in the Exposure and Risk Analysis Group at Lawrence Berkeley National Laboratory,[73] this move amounted to an extraordinary subversion of the legal process:

> Congress responded by adding Title 6 to the Arizona-Idaho Conservation Act which was quickly enacted into law. In essence, Congress took over the job of the Forest Service by choosing "Reasonable and Prudent Alternative" Three from the Biological Opinion. In Title 6, Congress divided the construction of the astrophysical complex into two phases. Congress then ordered the issuance of a special use permit and instructed the Secretary of Agriculture to "immediately approve" the first phase of the astrophysical project. In legislating their decision, Congress circumvented the decision making process crafted by law and refined through judicial interpretation.[74]

In response, two Arizona physicians, Robin Silver and Bob Witzeman, met with McCain in 1992 in order to voice their concerns. They describe the senator throwing a violent fit at the mere mention of Mt. Graham: "He jumped up and down, screaming obscenities at us for about 10 minutes. He shook his fists as if he was going to slug us. It was as violent as almost any domestic abuse altercation."[75] By hook or crook, the environmental exemptions were granted and the project realized. Exclaiming, "Resistance is futile," the VORG officially inaugurated the VATT facility in September of 1993…Mt. Graham was assimilated.

Refusing to accept said futility, the resistance movement rages. As it stands today, the initial three telescopes are in operation, but the

University of Arizona has requested a new evaluation from the Wildlife Service proposing at least *seven* telescopes. As recently as December 2010, a new lawsuit was filed:

> On Dec. 22, 2010, the Mount Graham Coalition, the Maricopa Audubon Society and the Center for Biological Diversity (CBD), filed a Notice of Intent to Sue the U.S. Department of Agriculture (USDA) and the U.S. Forest Service (USFS) for failing to reinitiate Endangered Species Act (ESA) consultation with the U.S. Fish and Wildlife Service (USFWS) regarding the Mount Graham Telescope Project which is situated atop Mount Graham, a mountain considered sacred since time immemorial to the San Carlos Apaches.[76]

Even though the real battle was decided when VATT went operational, the bitter dispute remains a constant news item in Arizona. Of course, all of this is fueled by big science and the search for extraterrestrial intelligence, but the technological innovation that drove this hard-fought quest came from the Steward Observatory mirror lab. Now we turn to what in the world—or out of *this* world—the Jesuits are looking into!

The Vatican Advanced Technology Telescope

You have probably been wondering about the "advanced technology" in the acronym VATT; in that regard, when it comes to high-end telescopes, power comes down to the primary mirror. The Steward Observatory Mirror Lab also had its impetus around 1980 with the backyard experimentation by Professor Roger Angel. Melting his own ovenware in a homemade kiln, he pioneered the use of Pyrex glass, employing a honeycomb structure for crafting superior quality telescope mirrors. The honeycomb design allows the lab to produce lightweight, yet extremely rigid, mirrors of unprecedented size. Using spin-casting techniques and a special polishing process, the Steward lab produces superior mirrors. Some have suggested this innovation was fueled by more than astronomical ambitions.

While science and technology afford us great luxury and convenience, they also bring us nuclear weapons and mustard gas. Jeffrey St. Clair, writing for *Counter Punch*, reports a little-known connection to the infamous Star Wars Defense Initiative: "The giant mirrors that power the Mt. Graham scopes have also been touted for their dual use nature: both as stargazers and as a potential component in the Star Wars scheme, wherein the mirrors would reflect laser-beam weapons on satellites and incoming missiles."[77] While it is unknown (and likely classified) whether the military industrial complex is secretly using the Steward Lab for space weapons, it has had prodigious success.

The first production test of the Steward lab in 1985 was a 1.83-meter mirror that was subsequently offered to the VORG in exchange for an agreement to share a quarter of its viewing time with the school. In astronomy, viewing time on a state-of-the-art instrument is a precious commodity, and you won't find anyone sleeping at night on top of Mt. Graham. The VORG represents another novel nocturnal species inhabiting the "Sky Island."

The VATT is a Gregorian telescope, a type of reflecting telescope designed by Scottish mathematician and astronomer, James Gregory, in the seventeenth century. Nearly all major telescopes in use (including the Hubble Space Telescope) are reflecting telescopes. A reflecting telescope uses a concave mirror to capture and focus the rays of light, reflecting it to another mirror and then to a magnifying lens or electronic instrument (like LUCIFER). They are the first choice for professional astronomers, amateur astronomers, and hobbyists. They will all tell you, "size matters" —mirror size, that is. In order to see deeper into space and farther back in time, it is necessary to collect as much light as possible; of course, the fainter the light, the farther the object and the older the light. "Back in time?" you might balk. Indeed, for example, it takes light eight minutes to travel from our sun to the Earth, so we don't see the sun as it really is; rather, we see it how it *was* eight minutes ago. This applies even more to the night sky. The next closest star, Proxima Centauri, is 4.22 light years away. That means if it were to burn out, we would not even know about it until more than four years later. In this way, telescopes literally facilitate looking back in time, and the bigger the mirror, the more light can be gathered and the farther back into the cosmic past we can see. So, what are they looking for up there?

Given its superior optics and location, VATT has been used primarily for imaging and photometric work where it regularly outclasses much larger telescopes. The facility is celebrated for its discovery of Massive Astrophysical Compact Halo Objects (MACHOs) in the Andromeda Galaxy. A MACHO is a body that emits little or no radiation and drifts through interstellar space on its own. Since these bodies do not emit any light of their own, they are very hard to detect, and VATT's optics are ideal. They include black holes, neutron stars, brown dwarfs, and planets not associated with a system. MACHOs are one possible way to explain the mysterious presence of dark matter in the universe. As discussed in chapter 13, "The Extradimensional Hypothesis," braneworld theory, as proposed by Paul Steinhardt of the Princeton University Astrophysics Department, suggests that dark matter may indeed evidence a parallel universe, and black holes could be portals connecting our universe to the unknown. Do these heralded discoveries of dark matter in the Andromeda Galaxy suggest that the Jesuits really are looking for ET? Many journalists think so.

Just days before VATT went into operation, Coyne granted interviews and the subsequent press from that time is rather astonishing. For example, Bruce Johnston of the *London Daily Telegraph*, a conservative newspaper with a good reputation, reported on October 28, 1992, that the "Vatican Sets Evangelical Sights on Outer Space":

THE Roman Catholic Church is to team up with America's space agency to look for life in outer space and so spread the Gospel to extraterrestrials.

Jesuit priests who run the Vatican Observatory near Rome say they are joining forces with the US NASA agency to hunt for UFOs and signs of life on planets in solar systems similar to Earth's.

NASA's job will be to monitor for "alien" communication signals; the Vatican, which has helped to build a new reflector telescope in Tucson, Arizona, would search for planets displaying conditions for life....

Should intelligent alien life be found, Fr. Coyne said, "the Church would be obliged to address the question of whether extraterrestrials might be brought within the fold and baptized."[78]

It goes without saying that these salacious claims sparked a storm of speculation. Why did he make these statements just days before VATT's official launch? Coyne appears to have been quite serious. The assertion concerning VATT's partnership with NASA was intentional and unqualified. A few months later, on January 8, 1993, Dr. Robin Silver of the Mt. Graham Coalition contacted NASA demanding an explanation. Freedom of Information Officer Patricia Riep-Dice responded, "NASA has no contact with either the Vatican Observatory or the Vatican Observatory Research Group."[79]

Accordingly, someone is not being truthful. There are two possibilities: Either Coyne lied or he let the cat out of the bag. While NASA is notorious for obfuscation, why would Coyne lie about VATT working with NASA to find aliens? The VORG quickly went into damage-control mode. Speaking as vice director of the VORG, Chris Corbally explicitly denied teaming up with NASA to spread the Gospel to extraterrestrials. Even so, Coyne's precedent frames more recent comments by Balducci, Consolmagno, and Funes in an eerie new light. Perhaps their so-called speculations are meant to prepare mankind for disclosure? If so, we believe it will be the strong delusion predicted in biblical prophecy.

VATT and LUCIFER?

Speaking of delusions of grandeur, the grandest of all is attributed to Satan: "How art thou fallen from heaven, O Lucifer, son of the morning! how art thou cut down to the ground, which didst weaken the nations!" (Isaiah 14:12). The taunt song found in Isaiah 14:12–15 is where the popular name for the devil, Lucifer, is derived from the Hebrew phrase "הֵילֵל בֶּן־שָׁחַר" (*Helel Ben-Shachar*) in verse 12, meaning "morning star, son of dawn." This name has been interpreted to be varying entities but there is a good case for the traditional understanding as the devil. In its original context, scholars agree that this is related to Ugaritic mythology concerning Baal and Athtar.[80] While Isaiah could be simply borrowing from local mythology for an illustration, it seems as if the prophet sees through the King of Babylon to the wicked spiritual power behind him. Psalm 82 and the book of Daniel suggest that earthly kingdoms have cosmic overlords (Daniel 10:13; 20), a paradigm which fits nicely with the Beast of Revelation who is similarly empowered by the great red dragon identified as Satan (Revelation 12:9; 13:2).

In Ugaritic lore this usurper is argued to be Athtar, who was referred to as Venus (morning star), who seeks to displace Baal.[81] Other scholars relate this passage to an ancient Babylonian or Hebrew star-myth, similar to the Greek legend of Phaethon.[82] Even so, one can imagine that, in a cosmic sense, all of these myths stem from a common netherworld event. The New Testament is clear that angels rebelled (Matthew 25:41; Revelation 12:9) and the Earth is currently under the power of a usurper (2 Corinthians 4:4; 1 John 5:19). While the King of Babylon could hardly hope to "ascend to heaven above the stars of God" it certainly speaks to his extreme hubris. Author C. S. Lewis famously said, "It was through pride that the devil became the devil: Pride leads to every other vice: it is the complete anti-God state of mind."[83] *Helel Ben-Shachar's* frustrated divine ambition harkens the account of a war in heaven in Revelation 12:7–17 where Satan is thrown to Earth suggesting commonality with "the man who made the Earth tremble" (Isaiah 14:16).

During the intertestamental period, this account of the angels' fall associated with the morning star was subsequently associated explicitly with the name Satan, as seen the second Book of Enoch (29:4; 31:4). Accordingly, the association of Lucifer to Satan continued with the church fathers because he is represented as being "cast down from heaven" (Revelations 12:7–10; cf. Luke 10:18). For example, Origen wrote, "Again, we are taught as follows by the prophet Isaiah regarding another opposing power. The prophet says, 'How is Lucifer, who used to arise in the morning, fallen from heaven!'"[84] Thus, prior to the Vulgate it was already being applied to the devil. It seems there is a good historical case for applying the name Lucifer to the devil.

Did the Vatican really name its telescope *Lucifer*? Actually, there is an astronomical instrument with that name, but the VORG's association with the LUCIFER instrument is alleged to be only by proximity. The Jesuits deny any part in the naming of the infernal instrument adjacent to VATT. It appears that their consortium partners, the Germans from the odious Max Planck Institute (a group that gave assistance to the murderous experiments of Nazi scientist Dr. Mengele in the 1940s[85]), are responsible for the satanic allusion.

Chelsea Schilling, a reporter for *World Net Daily*, called the Center for Astronomy of Heidelberg University and spoke to a Roman Catholic astronomer, Andreas Quirrenbach, who denied that the name Lucifer from Isaiah 14 had any real association to the devil, arguing, "This is due mostly to a misreading of the relevant biblical verses. However, these misreadings have propagated into folklore."[86] While centuries of Catholic scholars would disagree, he then contradicts himself by admitting the device was named after a German politician who is literally named after the devil. According to the *WND* article:

"Now, as it happens, the name of this governor is Teufel, which is the German word for 'devil,'" Quirrenbach explained. "Again, absolutely no offense to anyone; this is a fairly common name in Germany. So to those familiar with the local state politics in

Southwest Germany, it is plainly obvious that the two Lucifer instruments are named in honor of Teufel, who helped the state observatory become a member of the LBT."[87]

What makes Quirrenbach's explanation odd is that, on one hand, he argues that Lucifer in Isaiah 14 is not really about the devil, but on the other hand, he says it was named after a German politician whose name literally means "devil" or "demon" according to a German dictionary.[88] Apparently, *they named it after the devil regardless of Isaiah 14.*

At a minimum, they went to extravagant lengths to force the diabolic name into an acronym. Although the Jesuit we encountered denied it, it seems likely they were taking a shot at their Jesuit neighbors. Rather than its satanic sibling, VATT employs another sophisticated instrument called the Cornell Massachusetts Slit Spectrograph (CorMASS), which serves a similar function to LUCIFER on the LBT. This near-infrared spectrograph is ideal for confirming brown dwarf stars and has likely contributed to VATT's discovery of new MACHOs. While VATT is impressive, it sits in the shadow of the most powerful telescope on the planet, which does employ LUCIFER.

The Large Binocular Telescope

As Horn and I, a little winded by the elevation, strolled up the gravel road toward the monstrosity housing the Large Binocular Telescope, we saw the scorched black landscape through the few remaining trees, evidence of the wildfires that nearly reached the observatory on more than one occasion. Consequently, the Forest Service has taken measures to keep the telescopes out of harm's way. The Indian lawsuit mentions several acres of trees that were clear-cut around the telescopes. According to our guide, during the last lightning-prompted fire, they performed a controlled burn near the LBT in order to prevent the wildfire from reaching the $87 million facility, the largest, most sophisticated optical telescope on Earth.

In the 1940s, the Hale telescope at Mt. Palomar Observatory in California was considered state of the art, with its 5.1-meter mirror. That world-class facility owned and operated by the California Institute of Technology has been used to discover distant objects at the edges of the known universe (called quasars) and thousands of asteroids. It is still an awesome telescope. In fact, using the old glass, only one other mirror was ever made topping its size: a six-meter monster for the BTA-6 Special Astrophysical Observatory of the Russian Academy of Science. In contrast, the LBT on Mt. Graham boasts *two* 8.4-meter diameter mirrors for a total collecting area corresponding to a single circular mirror with a diameter of 11.8 meters! It's over twice the size of the Hale. This explains why Mt. Graham International Observatory can see deeper into space and farther back in time than any other facility on Earth, and also why we suggest that if astrobiologists do discover an Earth-like exoplanet, Mt. Graham is probably where it will happen.

A main goal of the LBT program is to search for Earthlike planets and extraterrestrial life. The LBT is equipped especially for this purpose. For instance, most terrestrial observatories are limited because the Earth's atmosphere acts like a lens that distorts ground telescope images. The LBT's adaptive optics and interferometry help overcome such distortions. No one is looking through a peephole lens on a system like this; rather, the light is sent to high-tech, computer-controlled observing instruments. Because distant exoplanets are also obscured by dust and space debris, interferometry, a technique of superimposing wavelengths in order to filter the image, helps for detecting Earthlike planets orbiting other stars and then searching them for signs of life. The official LBT website states the project goal: "The key science objective is to survey nearby stars for debris disks down to levels which may obscure detection of Earth-like planets."[89] Using its two mirrors in an adaptive manner, the LBT has even surpassed the Hubble Space Telescope's sharpness. Each of the two mirrors is equipped with three single-beam instruments: a prime focus camera, an optical spectrograph (MODS), and a near-infrared instrument (LUCIFER).

The instrument infamously named LUCIFER (which the staff affectionately abbreviates to "Lucy") is really nothing more than a fancy camera of sorts. As discussed above, it was named by the secular German scientists at the Max Planck Institute, not the Vatican group. While the device baptized after Old Scratch has inspired great speculation, it is a rather forced acronym for "LBT Near Infrared Spectroscopic Utility with Camera and Integral Field Unit for Extragalactic Research." They went to exorbitant lengths to make it work:

L	U	C	I	F	E	R
LBT	Utility	Camera	Integral	Field	Extragalactic	Research
Near	with	and		unit		
Infrared				for		

Spectroscopy pertains to the dispersion of an object's light into its component colors (i.e., energies or wavelength). By performing spectrographic analysis of an object's light, astronomers can infer the physical properties of that object (such as temperature, mass, luminosity, and chemical composition). This is how they look for conditions favorable for life like the presence of liquid water, carbon, and oxygen. Infrared spectroscopy deals with the infrared region of the electromagnetic spectrum—that is, light with a longer wavelength and lower frequency than normal visible light. Because some organic compounds vibrate in such a way as to be detectable by infrared spectroscopy, LUCIFER is a valuable tool used in the quest for extraterrestrial life. When we toured the LBT, only one LUCIFER device was installed; the second is due in 2015 or so. So far, they have only been calibrating and testing the system; the actual search for ET life is expected to launch in earnest in early 2013.

From there, we moved next door to the Heinrich Hertz Submillimeter Telescope, a huge, ten-meter dish owned by the Arizona Radio Observatory.

Will the Sub Ever Wow Us?

The Submillimeter Radio Telescope was the second of the three allowed by congressional fiat to be constructed, and it was inaugurated shortly after VATT in 1993. While radio waves lead us to immediately think of SETI, the sub's range lies between infrared and radio, albeit overlapping a little into both. It is also employed in astrobiological research, since radio astronomy is the most powerful method for detecting individual chemical species. Radio telescopes have detected more than a hundred interstellar atoms, molecules, or fragments, including life-indicative compounds like acids, alcohols, aldehydes, and ketones. The Arizona Radio Observatory operates two radio telescopes in Southern Arizona (another outside of Tucson). Combined, the two telescopes routinely cover extremely short wavelength radio and far-infrared frequencies. Physicists classify light waves by their energies (wavelengths). Labeled in increasing energy, we might chart the entire electromagnetic spectrum as shown below:

Radio waves	Sub-mm	Infrared far---- near	Visible light Red---purple	Ultraviolet	X – rays	Gamma rays

Whereas Lucifer handles near-infrared energy, far-infrared is a lower energy with a longer wavelength, and may be used for rotational spectroscopy. Because it is a region of the spectrum where the electromagnetic waves are strongly diminished by water vapor or clouds in the air, the dryness of the air around and above Emerald Peak is optimal for far-infrared observations. This makes it ideal for rotational spectroscopy, which can detect interstellar glycine, the simplest amino acid, a building block for life. This telescope is used nine–ten months of the year, and it is nonoperational only when there is too much water vapor in the atmosphere, primarily during the summertime, as was the case during our July visit.

The Submillimeter is currently being used in array of radio telescopes worldwide in an ambitious effort to take the first picture of the ever-elusive black hole.[90] If brane-world cosmology turns out to be accurate, a picture of a black hole could, in fact, "wow" us with evidence for a parallel universe!

The Submillimeter Radio Telescope in operation (note the LBT building to the right)

As Horn and I toured the Submillimeter Radio Telescope facility, he asked me if this was the same sort of dish that received the famous "Wow!" signal. That signal actually fell in a longer wavelength of the spectrum (radio), and those dishes naturally use a much larger collecting area. The "Wow!" signal was a strong, narrow-band radio signal detected by Jerry R. Ehman on August 15, 1977, while he was working on a SETI project at the Big Ear radio telescope at Ohio Wesleyan University's Perkins Observatory. The signal bore the expected profile for a transmission of intelligent extraterrestrial origin. Astounded at how closely the signal matched the expected ET signature, Ehman circled the signal on the computer printout and wrote the comment "Wow!" in the margin. Of course, this comment inspired the name.

The "Wow!" signal's frequency of 1420 MHz is noteworthy to SETI researchers, because hydrogen, the most common element in the universe, resonates at about 1420 MHz. Consequently, it seems logical that extraterrestrials would use that frequency to transmit a strong signal across light years of space. Even more, 1420 MHz is a protected spectrum, meaning its bandwidth is forbidden for terrestrial transmissions due to its astronomical purposes. This makes it extremely unlikely that it was an Earth signal reflected back, as some skeptics have suggested. However, it has never been heard again… (That is, if the "powers that be" are telling us everything.)

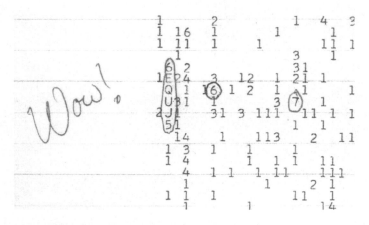

The famous "Wow!" signal data

Having a basic knowledge of how radio astronomy works makes then-acting VORG director George Coyne's public statements in 1993 concerning the collaborative VORG/NASA ambitions to baptize ETs all the more inexplicable. Robert S. Michaelsen's essay in the scholarly book *American Sacred Space* preserved some astounding assertions by the chief Jesuit astronomer. Drawing from interviews at the time of VATT's inauguration, Michaelsen wrote:

> Coyne envisions asking extraterrestrials contacted through the sub-millimeter radio frequency technology (built in phase one) if they had "ever experienced something similar to Adam and Eve, in other words, 'original sin,'" and "Do you people also know Jesus who has redeemed you?".… Apparently the sacred calling of the Mount Graham International Observatory extends beyond the quest for epiphanies to a willingness to spread the Gospel's universal message.[91]

As peculiar as it seems, Coyne apparently really said these things, and multiple news outlets represented him as being forthright. Accordingly, many researchers believe the Vatican is hiding knowledge about ET. If the VORG really wanted to disabuse us of the nefarious image they seem to inspire, they couldn't do any worse than Coyne. Perhaps he was only having some fun, but his intent is still a matter that inspires intense speculation.

Is the Sky Island a Dimensional Portal?

Mountains are universally associated with deities and spirits. History suggests part of the reason native peoples considered Mt. Graham "holy" involved unusual heavenly activity there in ancient times, when UFOs called "spirit lights" moved through the sky, something that seems to have contributed to their attribution of "powers" to the solar system and natural phenomena. Interestingly, the base of the mountain hosts the Saint Paisius Orthodox Monastery, a women's cenobitic community dedicated to intercession by the alleged Marian phenomenon. As biblical Christians, we do not accept Marian dogmas. Our position is that the so-called Marian apparition is likely one and the same as the deceptive UFO phenomenon. For example, note this description of the October 13, 1917 Fátima sighting witnessed by an estimated seventy thousand people who had stood in the rain all day to see it, as recorded by Vallée:

> The sun appeared as a disk of brilliant silver, "a weird disk that turns rapidly on its own axis and casts off beams of colored lights in all directions. Shafts of red light shot out from the rim of the sun and colored the clouds, the earth, the trees, the people; then shafts of violet, of blue, of yellow and of other colors followed in succession." These colors have been described by an objective skeptic as "monochromatic sectors," and they were definitely revolving. The reports speak of a flat disk rather than a globe. After a while it stopped spinning and "plunged downward in zig-zag fashion toward the earth and the horrified spectators."...

Finally the disk reversed its motion and disappeared into the sun, the real sun, once again fixed and dazzling in the sky. The astounded crowd suddenly realized that their clothes were dry.[92]

While the Orthodox presence at Mt. Graham is not officially under the Roman Pontiff, it does share many heterodox Marian doctrines, including the belief that apparitions like Fátima are visitations by Jesus' deceased mother.[93] It also affirms problematic doctrines like Mary's perpetual virginity[94] despite the Scriptures' many explicit attestations to Jesus' siblings (Mark 6:3; Matthew 13:55–56; Galatians 1:19). The Saint Paisius Monastery home school for teenage girls is dedicated to the "Protection of the Theotokos," meaning the protection afforded them through the intercessions of the Theotokos ("Virgin Mary"). Yet, as addressed in our former work, *Petrus Romanus: The Final Pope Is Here*, Scripture states there is only one mediator between God and man, the Lord Jesus Christ (1 Timothy 2:5). Perhaps Mt. Graham's association with Marian idolatry is more than coincidence?

Saint Paisius Orthodox Monastery at the foot of Mt. Graham

Arizona is quite famous for UFO activity. Witnessed by thousands of people across Nevada and Arizona, as well as the Mexican state of Sonora, the Phoenix lights UFO was the United States' largest mass sighting—not just because of the sheer number of witnesses, but because of the quality of their testimony. Then-acting Governor Fife Symington has testified in writing:

> Between 8:00 and 8:30 on the evening of March 13, 1997, during my second term as governor of Arizona, I witnessed something that defied logic and challenged my reality: a massive, delta-shaped craft silently navigating over the Squaw Peak in the Phoenix Mountain preserve. A solid structure rather than an apparition, it was dramatically large, with a distinctive leading edge embedded with lights as it traveled the Arizona skies. I still don't know what it was. As a pilot and a former Air Force officer, I can say with certainty that this craft did not resemble any man-made object I had ever seen.[95]

Documented activity like this suggests something inherently strange about the area, begging the question, "Does Arizona host a dimensional portal or wormhole?" While extradimensionality is addressed generally in chapter 13, needless to say, the area provides a uniquely hospitable climate for the well-yoked marriage between Jesuits and extraterrestrials. According to Apache lore, this geographic proclivity toward the peculiar has ancient roots.

The San Carlos Apache have preserved an ancient tale concerning a race of giants known as the Jian-du-pids, who were judged and destroyed by the Great Father, the sun.[96] In fact, the enormous Phoenix metropolitan area, covering Maricopa and Pinal counties, is often referred to as the "Valley of the Sun." According to the legend, a miniature race of three-foot-tall Indians called the Tuar-tums lived in the valley as peaceful farmers. They prospered until one day they were invaded by the Jian-du-pids, described as goliaths who used tree limbs for toothpicks.

These Nephilim, led by a massive man named Evilkin, allegedly came from the Northeast and were headed south to their home beyond the Gulf of Baja. The giants nearly wiped out the Tuar-tums before they hid themselves underground in the mountains and Father Sun threw a huge fireball that seared the monstrous Nephilim into the scorched mountain rock. While elements of the tale are obviously mythological, it has a remarkable thematic coherence with Genesis 6.

The Apache Creation Myth is also interesting in this regard, as a particular version involves the "One Who Lives Above," who descended in a flying disc at the start of Creation. "In the beginning nothing existed—no earth, no sky, no sun, no moon, only darkness was everywhere," the legend starts before noting that "suddenly from the darkness emerged a disc, one side yellow and the other side white, appearing suspended in midair. Within the disc sat a bearded man, Creator, the One Who Lives Above."[97]

While no single Apache Creation Myth dominates all tribal beliefs, most groups share key precepts as well as symbolism within their oral histories. Besides the creator who rides in a heavenly disc, a Dragon with the power of speech turns up, bargaining with men, as well as supernatural gateways associated with mountains (ch'iná'itíh) through which spirit beings can come. Sometimes these spirits are represented by the Owl (to an Apache Indian, dreaming of an Owl signified approaching death, while the Hopis see the Burrowing Owl [Ko'ko, "Watcher of the dark"] as the god of the dead and the underground), which is fascinating, given the connection with "alien abduction" accounts in which the Owl is a disguise wherein the abductee is led to believe the bug-eyed alien in their memory was actually an Owl they had seen somewhere and had lodged in their memory. Throughout Christian history, owls have been associated with sorcery and flying witches, and the source of these legends seems to mirror many abduction tales, which we shall consider later. Suffice it to say that these ancient native ideas involving flying discs, flying creators, spirit lights, owls, a talking dragon or great serpent, and even supernatural gateways tied to mountain ranges began long before the Vatican cast its eyes on Mt. Graham.

3 | Days of Noah

"But as the days of Noe were, so shall also the coming of
the Son of man be."—Matthew 24:37

In Luke 17:26 and Matthew 24:37, Jesus draws a provocative parallel between the days of Noah and the days of the
Son of Man. While it is clear He is characterizing the disposition of civilization as His return approaches, what exactly does this
antediluvian allusion imply? Beginning with George Hawkens Pember
(1837–1910), the phrase "days of Noah" has perhaps fueled more
speculation concerning end-time, otherworldly phenomenon than any
other passage of Scripture. Pember was an English theologian affiliated
with the Plymouth Brethren, a group that emphasized biblical prophecy and believed that current events could be signs or signals that heralded Christ's Second Coming. In Pember's classic work, *Earth's Earliest
Ages and Their Connection with Modern Spiritualism and Theosophy*, the
original preface states that he "endeavored to show the characteristic
features of the Days of Noah were reappearing in Christendom, and
therefore, that the Days of the Son of Man could not be far distant."[98]

His prescient work of evangelical counter-cult apologetics addresses the spiritual deception in the Spiritualist movement, Theosophical Society, and Buddhism. He believed these occultic movements were characteristic of the end-time, black awakening. Working from the allusion to the days of Noah, he listed seven parallels between the antediluvian age and the days of the Son of Man: 1) an overemphasis on God's mercy at the expense of His holiness; 2) a disregard for gender roles and contempt for marriage; 3) how technology and entertainment entice man away from worshipping God; 4) the alliance between the nominal Church and the world; 5) a vast population increase; 6) the rejection of prophetic warnings and preaching; and the most pertinent to our discussion, 7) "the appearance upon earth of beings from the Principality of the Air, and their unlawful intercourse with the human race."[99]

Turning back to the Luke passage, Jesus connects the time of His return to the judgment of the antediluvian world and that of Sodom and Gomorrah (Luke 17:28). While Pember lamented these emergent trends in the late nineteenth century, we suggest that the violence of Noah's day and perversion of Lot's are close to their ultimate fruition. We are eager to address the extraterrestrial question, but first, in deference to his faithful service, let us briefly examine Pember's seven points in a twenty-first century context.

1: Pember's first point finds ready correspondence in a humanistic denial of human sinfulness and the theological liberal's denial of hell. Postmodern theologians blur the concept of truth and trendy books denying the reality of hell, like Rob Bell's *Love Wins*, are "Christian" best sellers. For Roman Catholics, Christ's exclusivity (John 14:7) has been replaced by politically correct Vatican II pluralism. The fear of the Lord has been relegated to an anachronism, and Jesus is seen as simply a wise teacher. Pember railed, "They neither confess Him to be the Only Begotten Son of the Father, nor feel the need of His atonement. Consequently, they reject His revelation, as an absolute authority at least, trusting rather to the darkness within them which they call light."[100] Has this trend improved?

Of course, this situation has only festered. A recent Pew Forum on Religion and Public Life study determined that 52 percent of self-identifying Christians say eternal life is not exclusively for those who accept Christ as their Savior. President of Southern Seminary, Al Mohler, commented, "We are in an age when we want to tell everyone they are doing just fine. It's extremely uncomfortable to turn to someone and say, 'You will go to hell unless you come to a saving knowledge of Jesus.'"[101] We wonder how many Christians have the courage to say that in public in 2013.

2: Normative gender roles are increasingly anachronistic, and the institution of marriage is being attacked in ways Pember would not have conceived in his most hellish nightmare. With pastoral concern, he was direly troubled by the nineteenth-century divorce rate. According to scholars, "In 1870, it was calculated that 81 divorces took place per 0.1 million of the married population of the US."[102] That calculates to a mere 8 percent, whereas today, up to *50 percent* of marriages end in divorce.[103] Accordingly, many Generation X, Y, and Zs forgo marriage altogether. Others, believing it to be a hedge against divorce, opt for a trial period or, in popular parlance, "shack up." Today, between 50 and 60 percent of all marriages begin with cohabitation.[104] Unfortunately, secular wisdom fails, as it turns out that living together before marriage actually *increases* the chances of divorce with a remarkable 67 percent of cohabitating couples eventually divorcing.[105]

3: Pember believed science, art, and luxury were leading to depravity. Keep in mind this was during an age with no electricity, Internet porn, or Hollywood films. Since then, man's achievements in science and technology have grown exponentially and collaterally fostered the rise of radical secularism. Aiden Wilson Tozer characterized this secular trend as zombification: "Secularism, materialism, and the intrusive presence of things have put out the light in our souls and turned us into a generation of zombies."[106] If mindless forms of entertainment occupy too much of our time, it takes a toll. Many young people watch so much television that they can no longer follow a written linear argument. This is devastating to Christianity, as biblical faith is dependent on the written word. Similarly, pornography is one of the highest earners in any given entertainment medium and has infected conservative evangelicalism.[107] Others are zombified by arrogance.

Leading the ghoulish charge, physicist Stephen Hawking brazenly denied the Creator in his 2012 best seller, *The Grand Design*, writing, "Because there is a law such as gravity, the universe can and will create itself from nothing. Spontaneous creation is the reason there is something rather than nothing, why the universe exists, why we exist."[108] In other words, to create itself, the universe had to exist, *before* it existed. Now that is futile thinking! I guess Hawking's "Grand Design" is actually no design…but how grand is that? Unfortunately, man's accomplishments have fostered scientism—the assumption that science is the only path to true knowledge. Yet, clearly, this assumption is not arrived at by the scientific method. Thus, scientism cannot meet its own standard. In truth, we must assume a great deal of discovered truths, like the laws of logic and mathematics, to make science possible. Scientism is woefully incoherent, but prideful men live as if it were true.

The so-called four horseman of the "new atheism" dominated the first decade of the third millennium with best-selling tripe like *The God Delusion* by Richard Dawkins, *The End of Faith* by Sam Harris, *Breaking the Spell: Religion as a Natural Phenomenon* by Daniel Dennet, and *God is Not Great* by Christopher Hitchens. Of the notorious four, it is a safe bet that one is no longer an atheist. Christopher Hitchens became a believer December 15, 2011, albeit it was an unsalvific postmortem conversion. Still more, the astonishing hubris exhibited by transhumanists like Ray Kurzweil has led to the supreme arrogance that man will create God in his own image.

4: The alliance between the nominal Church and the world, which began in the fourth century Constantinian synthesis and the formation of Catholicism, has reached new levels of decadence as the Protestant mainline denominations Episcopal,[109] Evangelical Lutheran Church of America (ELCA),[110] and Presbyterian Church in the United States of

America (PCUSA)[111] not only condone homosexuality, they promote homosexual clergy. Ignoring the clear warnings in Scripture, they thumb their noses at God while inverting His created order. "Likewise also as it was in the days of Lot; they did eat, they drank, they bought, they sold, they planted, they builded" (Luke 17:28). Accordingly, Jesus' allusion to Lot living in Sodom is analogous to the widespread acceptance of sexual immorality. Some commentators believe it was the societal approval of perversion more than individual acts that beckoned God's wrath in Lot's day. Even worse, predatory pedophiles are abusing children under the protection of the Roman priesthood while others proudly march in parades.[112] We cannot be far from what God saw during the days of Noah and Lot.

<u>5</u>: World population has more than tripled from around 2 billion, when Pember wrote, to 7.4 billion today. This even has secularists screaming the "end is nigh" as the Inter-Academy Panel Statement on Population Growth called the current growth "unprecedented" and prognosticated that rising levels of atmospheric carbon dioxide and pollution will lead to an environmental Armageddon.[113] While the science is dubious, the angst is appropriate, though for other reasons. Burying its head in the sand, the secular world has attempted to push God out of everything. From public schools to politics, secularization works to relegate God's truth to the upper story realm as explained in another chapter. Religious beliefs are considered mere private opinions. As a result, the violence of Noah's day is paralleled by new levels of depravity in our own. The FBI records around 1.4 million violent crimes per year in America, and entertainment media glorifies the behavior.[114] The year 2012 has provoked multiple instances of assailants biting, even eating, their victims, prompting the media to sensationalize the catchphrase "Zombie Apocalypse."[115] Even so, there is nothing as subtly violent as the unmitigated slaughter of innocent babies. Indeed, over 40 million infants are legally murdered each year with global government approval. In China, many abortions are forced by the state but in the United States they willingly sacrifice to the idol of easy sex on the altar of convenience.

6: Jesus makes an allusion to past divine judgment with an emphasis on the credulity of the general population. By credulity we mean they were oblivious. Not only did the people in Noah's day not heed the warnings given, they carried on their day-to-day activities as if God were inconsequential. They were caught off-guard because they were so wrapped up in everyday life that they had no concern for the warnings Enoch and Noah had given about spiritual realities. In contrast, Noah and his family prepared for the future Flood even though they saw no material evidence of its coming and did not know the exact time of its arrival until it came. The author of Hebrews confirms, "By faith Noah, being warned of God of things not seen as yet, moved with fear, prepared an ark to the saving of his house; by the which he condemned the world, and became heir of the righteousness which is by faith" (Hebrews 11:7). Vigilance is appropriate; Jesus is saying that we face a similar situation today.

The notorious generations of Noah and Lot are frequently employed in Jewish texts as symbols of great wickedness and God's corresponding judgment. For example, the apocryphal book Sirach 16:7–8 reads: "He did not forgive the ancient giants who revolted in their might. He did not spare the neighbors of Lot, whom he loathed on account of their arrogance." In like fashion, Jesus is telling us these things will increase and divine judgment will fall. This belief entails an apocalyptic worldview. The term "apocalyptic" from the Greek *apokalypto,* meaning "reveal," occurs in v. 30 with: "the Son of Man is revealed" (*apokalyptetai*). God's dramatic disruption of everyday life is part of the divine ordering of history. The revealing of Christ is the consummation of salvation history, the fulfillment of the *Original Revelation*, the *protoevangelium* in Genesis 3:15. Accordingly, Christians expectantly welcome the apocalypse as the long-awaited solution to the so-called problem of evil.

In the New Testament, 1 Thessalonians 5:1–3 parallels the preparedness of Noah's family: "But of the times and the seasons, brethren, ye have no need that I write unto you. For yourselves know perfectly that the day of the Lord so cometh as a thief in the night. For when they shall say, Peace and safety; then sudden destruction cometh upon them, as travail upon a woman with child; and they shall not escape" (1 Thessalonians 5:1–3). Then verses 4–6 respectively speak to the timing: "But ye, brethren, are not in darkness, that that day should overtake you as a thief. Ye are all the children of light, and the children of the day: we are not of the night, nor of darkness. Therefore let us not sleep, as do others; but let us watch and be sober" (1 Thessalonians 5:4–6). Paul is implying that believers will sense the arrival of the "days of Noah." While no one knows the day or hour of the apocalypse, there is widespread consensus in the Christian community that the hour is late. While the above is certainly the main thrust of Jesus' "days of Noah" warning, we agree with Pember on his final point as well.

UFOs and the Days of Noah

SEVENTH POINT: Back in 1884, long before the coining of terms like "flying saucer" and "extraterrestrial," Pember asserted, "The seventh and most fearful characteristic of the days of Noah was the unlawful appearance among men of *beings from another sphere*" (emphasis added).[116] He predicted the return of the "Principality of the Air" and argued that the rise of spiritualism was its fruition. Of course, Pember has taken a lot of ribbing for his assertions since the nineteenth century because we still await the apocalypse. In like fashion, imagine the ridicule Noah endured as an apocalyptic prophet building a huge ark far removed from the sea. It is not difficult to imagine Noah was accused of something akin to "hate speech" as a pre-Flood preacher of righteousness. Also easy to conceive is that, by an assortment of antediluvian affronts, he was called a crackpot for his strange beliefs.

Similarly, a twenty-first-century evangelical can expect ridicule merely for believing the Bible, but a Christian ufologist attracts double disdain. One attracts scorn from both sides, secular and Christian. Just as it was business as usual in Noah's day, it seems many people, especially Christians, are oblivious to the incredible aerial phenomena regularly reported by reliable witnesses worldwide. Once the hoaxes and mistaken natural phenomena are weeded out, we believe an element of those phenomena is supernatural. We will argue for the psycho-spiritual nature later, but in this chapter we want to focus on public incredulousness. Jesus' admonition was that people would ignore the signs. Facilitating that is a very real taboo on the subject. In spite of overwhelming evidence, UFOs are not taken seriously.

That UFOs are real and deserve serious scrutiny is beyond question. Recalling that the "U" in UFO denotes "unidentified," estimates of the number of unexplained cases in official files by qualified scientists like astronomer J. Allen Hynek, computer scientist Jacques Vallée, and nuclear physicist Stanton Friedman range between 15 and 25 percent of cases. We prefer to call these unexplained cases *residual* UFOs or RUFOs, whereas the explained cases become IFOs or identified flying objects. Even a more conservative estimate like that from astrophysicist Hugh Ross (an evangelical Christian) still merits the 5-percent mark. Still, Ross elaborates, "If only 1 percent of UFO reports remain unexplained, the number of RUFOs sighted over the last five decades could range into the tens of thousands, if not many more."[117] Although we believe the number is much higher, the salient point is that even by the most minimal estimate, tens of thousands of inexplicable aerial craft have been baffling trained observers. Even more perplexing are the millions of reported personal encounters with their occupants.

Otherworldly encounters and alien abductions seem to suggest the eccentric and delusional, but then you read works like *Abduction* (1994) and *Passport to the Cosmos* (1999) by respected Harvard psychiatrist and Pulitzer Prize winner John Mack. Now deceased, Mack was a serious academic who risked his reputation and career to publicize the strange similarities he found in a broad spectrum of non-pathological experiencers. Were these mere delusions, the detailed correspondences should not have occurred. To his surprise, after counseling scores of abductees, he detected a remarkable coherence that inferred veracity. Intriguingly, he still determined that abduction was more spiritual than physical, albeit very real. While Mack is the academic superstar of ufology, he is by no means alone.

Another respected academic, David Jacobs, a historian specializing in popular culture at Temple University whose doctoral dissertation was published as *The UFO Controversy in America* by Indiana University Press in 1975, came to similar but more alarming conclusions. His subsequent works, *Secret Life: Firsthand Accounts of UFO Abductions* (1992); *The Threat: Revealing the Secret Alien Agenda* (1998); and *UFOs and Abductions: Challenging the Borders of Knowledge* (2000), came to the conclusion that extraterrestrial biological entities (ETBEs) are not only visiting Earth but are actually abducting millions of human beings worldwide to extract genetic material for the purpose of creating a race of hybrids. Another academic, Karla Turner, who authored *Into the Fringe* (1992); *Taken: Inside the Alien-Human Abduction Agenda* (1994); and *Masquerade of Angels* (1994), not only concurred with Jacobs, she testified in great detail that it was happening to her!

Kenneth Arnold Points to a Drawing of the UFO

Since qualified scientists and otherwise credible academics draw these conclusions, why is the UFO subject still routinely ridiculed? One simple explanation is that the ambiguous nature of the term UFO invites equivocation. The acronym "UFO," meaning "Unidentified Flying Object," was the brainchild of Capt. Edward J. Ruppelt, chief of the official Air Force investigating agency, Project Blue Book, to replace the then-dominant terms "flying saucer" or "flying disk."[118] In truth, even "flying saucer" was a misnomer, because Kenneth Arnold actually said he saw a boomerang-shaped craft that skipped along like a saucer skims the water when tossed over a lake. Nevertheless, the term "flying saucer" captured the imagination of the public and popular press and became an infectious idea.

Speaking of that famous sighting by Arnold, Ruppelt wrote, "It is well known that ever since the first flying saucer was reported in June 1947 the Air Force has officially said that there is no proof that such a thing as an interplanetary spaceship exists. But what is not well known is that this conclusion is far from being unanimous among the military and their scientific advisers because of the one word, proof; so the UFO investigations continue."[119] Even so, it is important to note that the same year, Air Force General Nathan Twining admitted in a classified document that, "The phenomenon is something real and not visionary or fictitious."[120] Ruppelt goes on about military fighter planes pursuing and firing upon unknown craft, craft that were simultaneously locked on ground radar and seen by pilots, and craft that evaded and sped away with ease. He then asks rhetorically, "Doesn't this constitute proof?"[121] As incredible as it seems, the dogfight situation has occurred many times, as documented by recent authors Richard Dolan and Leslie Kean mentioned below.

It is apparent that Ruppelt usually meant something like "flying saucer" when he employed the term "UFO" in his own writings. While it usually implies something more than "unidentified," the operative term, "UFO," stuck. The problem is that most people mean something more like flying saucer but the imprecise terminology leaves enough ambiguity for skeptics like Neil deGrasse Tyson to equivocate and ridicule. In his keynote address at a skeptic convention, Tyson ridiculed UFOs:

> [When] someone says they saw a UFO, remind them what the U stands for! Okay? *Un*-identified! Because then they say, "I saw a UFO"; I say, "Oh! What did it look like?" [They said,] "Oh! It was like, a spaceship and it came from another planet" and then, then I said, "But you just said, you didn't know what it was 'cuz... you said it was unidentified!"[122]

Tyson then accuses the witness of making an argument from ignorance. This is a disingenuous equivocation based on the imprecise nature of terminology, because, in truth, the person had a description of what he saw. Part of the problem is that the term "UFO" is inclusive of what can later turn out to be IFOs. Accordingly, RUFO (residual unidentified flying object) offers some much-needed precision. It still begs the question of why, in the face of so many RUFO cases, the intelligentsia remains so skeptical.

Jacques Vallée has addressed this sort of behavior as part of an intentional disinformation effort to subvert honest research: "To prevent genuine scientific study from being organized, all that is needed is to maintain a certain threshold of ridicule around the phenomenon. This can be done easily enough by a few influential science writers, under the guise of humanism or rationalism."[123] While we do not know that Tyson is intentionally filling this role, we find his demeanor to be exactly what one would expect given Vallée's analysis. Even so, it is probably that Tyson has the best of intentions.

Another reason otherwise smart people, like Tyson, snicker at the subject is ignorance. A 1979 poll of scientists and engineers reported that 18 percent had seen a UFO.[124] The UFO Skeptic website reports that:

> When Prof. Peter Sturrock, a prominent Stanford University plasma physicist, conducted a survey of the membership of the

American Astronomical Society in the 1970s, he made an interesting finding: astronomers who spent time reading up on the UFO phenomenon developed more interest in it. If there were nothing to it, you would expect the opposite: lack of credible evidence would cause interest to wane. But the fact of the matter is, there does exist a vast amount of high quality, albeit enigmatic, data.[125]

The people who snicker have not done their homework. The fact of the matter is that the more informed one is about the subject of RUFOs, the more likely one is to believe something extraordinary is occurring. The problem, even among brilliant scientists, is lack of appropriate education.

Friedman, who has been lecturing on the subject at colleges and universities in eighteen countries for a few decades, reports, "In my lectures I review 5 large scale scientific studies and ask after each one how many have read it. Typically fewer than 2% have read any."[126] In view of that, we believe *the evidence is there* if people are willing to study. There exists a wealth of high-quality scholarship stretching back fifty years from the early works of Hynek and Vallée to the recent works by historian Richard Dolan and investigative journalist Leslie Kean. Data wise, there is such an embarrassment of riches that contemporary researchers do not think collecting new case studies is the most profitable way to proceed. We will discuss methodology in a later chapter, but for now, let's review some of the latest literature. These are recent books that we feel will convince nearly anyone except the most determined, close-minded skeptic.

Richard Dolan's first volume, *UFOs and the National Security State: Chronology of a Coverup, 1941–1973*, and second volume, *The Cover-Up Exposed, 1973–1991*, from a meticulously documented, two-part, chronological narrative of the US national security dimensions of the UFO phenomenon from 1941 until modern history. Working from a wealth of recently declassified documents, there are many startling cases demonstrating government culpability. Solid cases reported by military witness with corroborating radar and visual confirmations, alleged crash retrievals, and even some involving the death of military personnel have been recorded in official documents. This book demonstrates conclusively that, contrary to the party line, secrets *are* being kept. The evidence is weighty, and Dolan boils it all down to two possible conclusions: It is either secret, man-made antigravity technology or "UFOs are the product of an alien technology."[127] He argues the likelihood of the former is slim to none, as that craft appeared long before the technology seems remotely feasible. He supports this argument by referring to the fact that the early intelligence efforts to assess the German and Soviet abilities evidenced in the declassified1947 Schulgen memo came up empty-handed and consequently suggested the extraterrestrial hypothesis (ETH).[128] In 1948, Project Sign came to a similar conclusion. Dolan concedes that the only evidence for the ETH is eyewitness testimony, photographs, and radar tracking. He makes a good case for alien technology, but the elephant in the room is the complete lack of evidence that these craft originate from distant galaxies. While terrestrial radar sightings are abundant, we know of no documented occasion when a craft was tracked coming from another solar system.

While Dolan certainly acknowledges that "it is quite possible that UFOs have existed for millennia,"[129] a limitation of his focus is that one could walk away with the mistaken impression that RUFOs are a modern phenomenon. Nonetheless, he argues cogently that the exponential advances in aircraft and radar technology during World War II contributed to more reporting of the phenomenon and a consequentially more diverse phenomenology. In other words, one reason more RUFOs are reported today is because we are technologically more capable of seeing them, but it may also imply a transformation in our consciousness.

Carl Jung believed the latter to be the case, and we will discuss some of his observations within this book. Yet, strange craft in the sky are nothing new. In the forward of Dolan's first volume, Vallée asserts, "UFOs have been with us since the beginning of recorded history."[130] Indeed, Vallée's *Passport to Magonia* (1969) and recent work coauthored with scholar Chris Aulbeck, *Wonders in the Sky: Unexplained Aerial Objects from Antiquity to Modern Times* (2010), are seminal works preserving that history. Be that as it may, an intellectually honest reader will not come away from Dolan's volumes unimpressed. In addition, Leslie Kean's effort on contemporary cases is of similarly high quality.

Kean's work, *UFOs: Generals, Pilots and Government Officials Go on the Record*, offers only unimpeachable cases with multiple reliable witnesses and corroborating data. Chapters are authored by military personnel like Major General Wilfried De Brouwer from Belgium, airline pilots like Captain Ray Bowyer, and government officials like Fife Symington, the former governor of Arizona. Preference is given to officially documented cases, often involving skeptical, trained observers, and the international scope of this book confirms a global phenomenon. Astonishingly, Kean reports mass sightings of huge craft like the Belgian wave, the Hudson Valley wave, and the mile-wide, delta-shaped craft that silently glided over Phoenix, Arizona, that brings to mind scenes from the film *Independence Day*, including gape-mouthed bystanders standing roadside. Yes, events like that have really happened and the 1917 sighting at Fátima arguably belongs in the same category.

Overall, Kean's book offers cogent analysis and further suggests a rationale for why the government seemingly has "a powerful desire to do nothing"[131] or a UFO taboo. Departing from Dolan's perspective, Kean takes the position that the government is likely concealing its *ignorance* rather than its knowledge. Either way, there is a conspiracy of silence. As with Dolan's work, an open-minded reader who digests Kean's book will be convinced that RUFOs are very real, extremely strange, and by no means resolved by conventional explanations. In addition, there is a documentary film, *I Know What I Saw*, based on Kean's book.[132]

Commenting on the lack of outcry concerning the Westchester Boomerang, a massive V-shaped craft seen close up by thousands of awestruck New Yorkers between 1982 and 1985, Hynek mused, "As a homely analogy, one might say that such a totally novel idea 'overheats the mental human circuits' and the fuse blows (or the circuit-breaker cuts out) as a protective device for the mind. The time is not yet right for the age and the new idea might just as well not [have] been there in the first place. Mankind was not yet able to handle it."[133] In other words, perhaps it is a psychological denial mechanism, and most people, consciously or unconsciously, simply prefer not to know. Neil Tyson's argument from ignorance comes full circle.

Nevertheless, a recent poll by *National Geographic* indicated that only 36 percent of Americans (80 million people) believe RUFOs exist.[134] The results align with more scientific studies like the 2008 survey conducted by Scripps Howard News Service and Ohio University, which also found that one-third of adults believe it's either "very likely" or "somewhat likely" that intelligent extraterrestrials have visited Earth. Even more, 56 percent say it is either "very likely" or "somewhat likely" that intelligent life exists on other planets. One in twelve said he or she had personally seen a UFO that might have been an alien spaceship. The study also reported that people who had recently attended church, and who personally identify as born again, are less likely to believe in UFOs or the existence of ETs. We hope to convert you, our readers, from the former—to believe RUFOs exist—while encouraging you to remain skeptical as to the latter. Of those 36 percent of Americans polled who believe, it is safe to assume the majority, we think unfortunately, agree with Friedman that RUFOs are alien spacecraft.

Friedman, an articulate and persuasive speaker, is a leading advocate for the ETH or the idea that RUFOs are spacecraft from other planets. Like Dolan, he is convinced the government is covering something up. He argues, "I have spent time at 20 archives, had a security clearance for 14 years, and find it perfectly obvious that crucial data has been withheld and many government people have lied with regard to UFOs."[135] It appears that 79 percent of Americans in the *National Geographic* survey agree with Friedman and Dolan that the United States government is involved in a cover-up. Even so, it is important to note that one does not necessitate the other. For example, the government could be hiding the fact that UFOs are *not* alien spacecraft. This also explains the 43-percent gap between 36 percent with ET belief and 79 percent with conspiracy belief. While most likely assume it is top-secret military aircraft, there is another, less terrestrial, possibility. In fact, of the four scientists listed above, Friedman is in the minority.

While differing in particulars, Hynek, Vallée, and Ross lean toward the interdimensional hypothesis (IDH), which posits what is, for all intents and purposes, a *supernatural* explanation. Ross defines the IDH as the idea that "such phenomena belong not to extraterrestrial spacecraft but to another realm of reality beyond the time-space continuum."[136] As a result, Hynek coined the term "meta-terrestrial," and Vallée wrote, "I do not think they are extraterrestrial in the ordinary sense of the term. In my view, they present an exciting challenge to our concept of reality itself."[137] We will discuss the arguments against the ETH in chapter 7, "Astrobiology and the Extraterrestrial Worldview." It is intriguing that Vallée's ideas find more coherence with a biblical worldview than most. It is quite clear from his writings that he maintains a supernatural worldview if not a Christian one.

From Vallée, we learn that another reason RUFOs are routinely dismissed is that they behave in absurd and arguably diversionary ways. In other words, they avoid detection by betraying coherent patterns. For instance, researchers have cataloged thousands of ships of varying colors, shapes, and sizes. It seems unimaginable that thousands of races of ETs are visiting Earth and even more absurd that one race would use such a diversity of ships. John Keel wrote, "Because the witnesses seem to be telling the truth, we must assume that UFOs come in myriad sizes and shapes. Or no real shapes at all. This leads us to the old psychological warfare gambit once more. If the phenomenon has built-in discrepancies, then no one will take it seriously."[138] In other words, if sightings worldwide were consistent, it would cause alarm, but the lack of consistency serves as camouflage. Either the so-called ETs employ their ships once and discard them, or the ships are not really machines in a conventional sense. We affirm the latter. Even more perplexing are the entities themselves.

Although the diminutive grey alien seems to dominate the public consciousness, there are a wide variety of entities attested to in the literature. Because the likelihood of one truly extraterrestrial race on Earth seems low to scientists, the odds of so many races *visiting* Earth simultaneously seems ludicrous. Even so, this is what the evidence from witnesses seems to imply. Sergeant Clifford Stone of the US Army testified to the National Press Club in Washington, DC about having catalogued fifty-seven different species of aliens as a part of his official military duty.[139] Thus, for a critical thinker, the sheer variety begs incredulity and casts doubt on such testimony. Furthermore, if the ETs are biological entities, why do they so closely resemble occult phenomena, as in the case of Aleister Crowley's drawing of the demonic entity Lam summoned through ritual magick, decades before the grey alien entered the public consciousness?

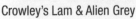
Crowley's Lam & Alien Grey

Next, one does not have to survey much of the literature to notice that the messages coming from these entities are often contradictory and absurd. Contactees and channelers—like George Adamski in the 1950s,

Ruth Norman in the 1980s, and recently Blossom Goodchild—are routinely betrayed and played for fools by the so-called space brothers. The diversity of beings and deceptive, occult connotations leads many critics to assume the phenomenon is wholly delusional.

While some of this diversity is indicative of hoaxes, the sheer volume of credible cases infers an underlying reality. Perhaps the RUFO phenomenon and the associated beings are intentionally promoting an absurd veneer. This is where Vallée makes a keen observation:

> If you wanted to bypass the intelligentsia and the church, remain undetectable to the military system, leave undisturbed the political and administrative levels of a society, and at the same time implant deep within that society far-reaching doubts concerning its basic philosophical tenets, this is exactly how you would have to act. At the same time of course, such a process *would have to provide its own explanation* to make ultimate detection impossible. In other words, it would have to project an image just beyond the belief structure of the target society. *It would have to disturb and reassure at the same time, exploiting both the gullibility of the zealots and the narrow-mindedness of the debunkers.* This is exactly what the UFO phenomenon does.[140]

In all likelihood, RUFOs and their associated entities have a method to their madness. Like shape-shifting tricksters, they confound, subvert, and divide, leaving believers confused and skeptics assured. A survey of technical professionals determined that only one in twelve bothered to report a UFO encounter.[141] This is not surprising, given the taboo with the ridicule and career risk from naturalist orthodoxy. Consequently, the likelihood of widespread underreporting causes a vicious circle of ignorance. Why is this the case?

It seems the elite have a vested interest in keeping the topic out of bounds. Taking a cue from Kean, we obtained an astonishing analysis of this UFO taboo from a scholarly political science journal, *Political*

Theory, called "Sovereignty and the UFO" by Drs. Alexander Wendt and Raymond Duvall, an article of unprecedented significance. The analysis determined that governments, specifically the United States, intentionally avoid the subject because it threatens their authority. They describe the situation that, "Considerable work goes into ignoring UFOs, constituting them as objects only of ridicule and scorn. To that extent one may speak of a 'UFO taboo,' a prohibition in the authoritative public sphere on taking UFOs seriously, or 'thou shalt not try very hard to find out what UFOs are.'"[142] On a rational basis, the taboo does not make sense.

The writers list several arguments as to why the subject merits study. At the top of the list is the fact that if genuine ETs are verified, it would be one of the most important discoveries in history. After all, millions of dollars are being funneled into astrobiology with absolutely no evidence behind it, yet we have mountains of UFO data that is dogmatically ignored. In contrast to official pronouncements, the authors write, "UFOs have never been systematically investigated by science or the state, because it is assumed to be known that none are extraterrestrial. Yet in fact this is not known, which makes the UFO taboo puzzling given the ET possibility."[143] The real reason for the taboo lies in the elite's lust for power.

The two political scientists determined that political sovereignty is man-centered or anthropocentric. It follows that the elites base their status on the assumption of naturalism and *man being the pinnacle of nature* places themselves as universal sovereigns. In this way, the existence of entities other than man threatens the elite's claim to power. Politically, the nation-state would be forced to concede as ET's "confirmed presence would create tremendous pressure for a unified human response, or world government."[144] A provocative analogy is made between Christ's Second Coming and ET disclosure, "Imagine a counterfactual world in which God visibly materialized (as in the Christians' "Second Coming," for example): to whom would people give their loyalty, and could states in their present form survive were such a question politically salient?"[145] In other words, the powers that be have a vested interest in squelching any belief system that threatens their power, be it God or ET. It is not so much that they are hiding the truth about RUFOs as it is that they do not want it investigated. Even so, the poignant analogy above also begs the question, given the alternatives of Christ or self-proclaimed ET saviors: To whom would the people give their loyalty?

Summary

By way of summary, we believe the following points contribute to a vicious cycle leaving the public uninformed and ill-prepared to deal with a disclosure-type event involving extraterrestrials.

- We argued that because only a small percentage of UFOs are extraordinary, the large number of intentional hoaxes and mistaken identification of natural phenomenon discredits legitimate research.
- All of these are lumped together under the same classification and, consequently, imprecise terminology leads to confusion and equivocation.
- The phenomenon itself promotes absurdities as a form of camouflage.
- Consequently, ridicule of the subject discourages investigation and most cases go unreported.
- Despite the evidence for extraordinary craft, the elite promote a taboo because it threatens their sovereignty.
- The taboo ensures that rigorous scientific study does not occur.
- Widespread ignorance of the data creates a vicious cycle which circles back around.

It seems that the prophetic trends enumerated by Pember and the sanctified ignorance of the elite strongly support that we live in days like those of Noah—days when, despite the extraordinary signs and things coming upon the Earth, people turn a blind eye, maintaining the status quo just as it was "until the flood came, and destroyed them all" (Luke 17:27).

4 | They Live

"An experiment that has led to the deliberate creation of a human chimera—named after the Greek monster that was part lion, part serpent and part goat—was presented to the European Society for Human Embryology in Madrid on Wednesday…"—*The Telegraph*

In 1988, an American science fiction-horror film, titled *They Live* (directed by John Carpenter), depicted a nameless drifter—played by professional wrestler "Rowdy" Roddy Piper—who discovers the ruling elite are in fact aliens that have hypnotized the human race and are managing human social affairs through subliminal messages concealed in memes and mass media. In an important early scene, Nada, as the Piper character is called, notices strange behavior coming from a nearby church and, upon further inspection, discovers that the church is a front, holding little more than cardboard boxes and playing a fabricated choir from strange, scientific machinery in a back room. Within the walls of the counterfeit church, Nada locates a hidden compartment containing another box. When the police tear down the building, driving its inhabitants to escape, he returns to find that the box is still in the secret compartment, retrieves the box, enters an alleyway, and opens it to learn that it contains multiple pairs of black sunglasses. He puts on a pair, discarding the rest, and soon discovers they include a very special filter. Looking through the lenses, he can see "the reality of the bleak world": that global media and advertising actually contain totalitarian commands of obedience and conformity in consumerism to control an unwitting human population by humanoid aliens with grotesque, skull-like faces.[146] Though a commercial failure at the time, the film eventually made its way to the top twenty-five cult classics ("The Cult 25"), where it remains presently, according to *Entertainment Weekly* magazine.[147] The film and theatrical posters can often be found today in mocking editorials depicting the goals of totalitarians and elitists, but another suggestion of the work that usually goes without discussion is how the world really might be infested with nonhuman agents of an unknown reality, about which the bulk of mankind is unaware.

First, from a purely incorporeal reality, we know that demons and their militaristic interest in people and geography are ontological facts, according to the Bible. In the Old Testament, demons are seen as the living dynamic behind idolatry (i.e., Deuteronomy 32:17), and in the New Testament, every writer refers to their influence. Extrabiblical texts including ancient pseudepigraphical works like the first Book of Enoch and post-New Testament writings such as the *Didache*, Ignatius' *Epistle to the Ephesians*, and the *Shepherd of Hermas* agree with this concern. Early church fathers also reinforced the belief that evil spirits seek to thwart the will of God on Earth through attacks on the Body of Christ in particular and against society in general, as unseen intermediaries—both good and evil—interlope between spiritual and human personalities at home, in church, in government, and in society. Understanding how and why this is true is defined in demonological studies such as the Divine Council (a term used by Hebrew and Semitic scholars to describe the pantheon of divine beings or angels who administer the affairs of heaven and Earth). Experts typically agree that, beginning at the Tower of Babel, the world and its inhabitants were disinherited by the sovereign God of Israel and placed under the authority of lesser divine beings that became corrupt and disloyal to God in their administration of those nations (Psalm 82). Following Babel, these beings quickly became idolized on earth as gods, giving birth to the worship of "demons" (see Acts 7:41–42; Psalms 96:5; and 1 Corinthians 10:20) and the quest by fallen angels to draw mankind away from God. While the dominion of these entities and their goals are frequently overlooked, close collaboration between evil ones and unregenerate social architects operates on a regular basis outside the purview of the countless multitudes who are blinded to their reality. In other words, as suggested in the film *They Live*, behind governors, legislators, presidents, dictators, and even religious leaders, wicked spiritual powers move throughout the machine of ecclesiastical and civil governments and media as freely as they are allowed. Whenever such principalities recognize a religious or political body that has become a force for moral good, they set about—through a sophisticated labyrinth of visible and invisible representatives—to bring that organization down, one righteous soul at a time.

It is within this concealed arena of evil supernaturalism that unregenerate men are organized. Under demonic influence, they are orchestrated within a great evil system (or empire) described in various scriptural passages as a satanic order. In more than thirty important biblical texts, the Greek New Testament employs the term *kosmos*, describing this "government behind government." It is here that human ego, separated from God, becomes hostile to the service of mankind while viewing people as commodities to be manipulated in the ministration of fiendish ambition. Some expositors believe the origins of this phenomenon began in the distant past, when a fire in the mind of Lucifer caused the powerful cherub to exalt himself above the good of God's creation. The once-glorified spirit, driven mad by an unequivocal thirst to rule, conquer, and dominate, spawned similar lust between his followers, which continues today among agents of dark power who guard a privileged, "cause-and-effect" symmetry between visible and invisible personalities.

At Satan's desire, archons command this supernatural, geopolitical sphere, dominating kosmokrators (rulers of darkness who work in and through human counterparts) who, in turn, command spirits of lesser rank until every level of earthly government, secular and religious, can be touched by this influence. If we could see through the veil into this domain, we would find a world alive with good against evil, a place where the ultimate prize is the souls of men and where legions war for control of its cities and people. With vivid testimony to this, Satan offered Jesus all the power and the glory of the governments of this world. Satan said, "All this power [control] will I give thee, and the glory of them [earthly cities]: for that is delivered unto me: and to whomsoever I will I give it. If thou therefore wilt worship me, all shall be thine" (Luke 4:6–7).

According to the epistle of the Ephesians, it is this dominion, not flesh and blood, where opposition to God's will on Earth is initiated. Whereas people and institutions often provide the "faces" on our problems, the conflict originates beyond them, in this place where unseen forces scheme. These forces may indeed be more influential than anyone ever imagined. In fact, there is a strong likelihood that the first murder recorded in Genesis was demonically inspired (in a manner that parallels the so-called alien abduction phenomenon in interesting ways). Have you ever wondered why "sin" is personified when God issues the following warning to Cain in Genesis 4:7? "If thou doest well, shalt thou not be accepted? and if thou doest not well, sin lieth at the door. And unto thee shall be <u>his desire</u>, and thou shalt rule over <u>him</u>" (underline added). Doesn't it seem odd that sin is a "him," and if Cain does not do well, he will be sin's desire? How can "sin" have desire? Apparently, there is something more going on here, and scholars have uncovered surprising answers.

The wonderful thing about archeology is that we have a greater understanding of the Bible's context now than at any other time in history. Scholars have translated a wealth of tablets from Mesopotamia that not only add contextual clues to scriptural references, but provide insight into borrowed Semitic vocabulary. In this case, a careful examination of the Hebrew text leads many evangelical inerrancy-upholding scholars to see the participle rendered "lieth" (Hebrew *rōbēs*) in the KJV (or "is crouching" in other versions) as an Akkadian loan word, *rābiṣu* for a demon (ancient Hebrew has no vowels, so *rbs* offers this flexibility).[148] Of course, there are other scholars who balk, preferring a less supernatural exegesis, but the context of the passage supports the demonic interpretation. Sin does not lie in wait, but demons do. Biblical scholar John Walton agrees: "The fact that the text mentions the desire to master Cain favors *rābiṣu* as a demon."[149] Thus, just prior to the first murder in history, "sin" is depicted as a doorway demon waiting for an opportune time, an invitation that comes all too soon.

The ancient Akkadian literature reveals more astonishing data. In medical texts, inflicted individuals are depicted in the following ways: 1) "[as having] walked in the path of a *rābiṣu*," and 2) "a *rābiṣu* has seized him." The root meaning of *rābiṣu* is "one who lies in wait."[150] Uncanny parallels to modern abductions are seen in the descriptions of demons who ambush their victims in various locations: *rābiṣ ūri*, "the *rābiṣu* of the roof"; *rābiṣ nāri*, "the *rābiṣu* of the river"; *rābiṣ ḫarbati*, "the *rābiṣu* of the wasteland." It seems there was a *rābiṣu* for just about anywhere, even a *rābiṣ musâti*, "the *rābiṣu* of the toilet." Now that's disturbing! Ill manners aside, consider the *rābiṣ urḫi*, "the *rābiṣu* of the road."[151] Might Barney and Betty Hill (of the famous alien abduction case), while driving late at night on that lonely road, have encountered something like the latter manifest physically in modern garb?

But What if There Is Something More—Something Embodied?

What if the incorporeal or uncarnate reality described above is only part of the story? What if, in at least some instances, there is something more physical than the whispered influence demons can have on the human mind? What if, walking among us, there are tangible human hybrids, fit extensions for incarnation or embodiment of powerful alien-demonic entities, such as the creatures in the movie *They Live* or the Nephilim of ancient days? Is such a concept too incredible to be substantive? Would you be surprised to learn that some very intelligent people—including academics and scholars—believe (to borrow a line that the character Carol Anne so ominously expressed in the 1982 film *Poltergeist*), "They're here"?

Among secular and religious researchers today, there is a contentious behind-the-scenes debate going on in this regard, which has been growing in intensity over the last few years among those who recognize first of all that genetically modified plants, animals, and yes, humans are now reality (documented within the following pages). Unnatural forms of life first sprang up in ancient days and, according to the Bible, *this is a repeatable phenomenon*—that is, human hybridization not only happened in the earliest of times, but was followed by at least a second wave during the days of Abraham, Moses, and the Davidic kingdom, and, more importantly, was prophesied to erupt once more in the latter days. Therefore, we shall show unequivocally that the question is not whether humans were, can be, or are being hybridized, but whether alien/demon agencies are involved in the process. If so, does this imply something very uncomfortable, which most of us do not want to think about— that a form of "human" exists that quite possibly cannot be redeemed?

First Record of Human Hybrids

Stories and legends extending as far back as the beginning of time in every major culture tell the astonishingly consistent story of "gods" that descended from heaven and materialized in bodies of flesh. The renowned Christian apologist, Francis Schaeffer wrote, "More and more we are finding that mythology in general, though greatly contorted, very often has some historic base. And the interesting thing is that one myth that one finds over and over again in many parts of the world is that somewhere a long time ago supernatural beings had sexual inter-course with natural women and produced a special breed of people."[152] This extends to the UFO alien mythos as well. Our working hypothesis is that the so-called extraterrestrials are nothing new. Indeed, they have been with us all along. They appear in our literature as far back as records extend. In some of the earliest texts, we see a diverse population of strange entities being created by the gods. For instance, in the *Akkadian Epic of Creation,* we read of the female chaos monster, Tiamat, employing a host of oddities:

> She deployed serpents, dragons, and hairy hero-men,
> Lion monsters, lion men, scorpion men,
> Mighty demons, fish men, bull men,
> Bearing unsparing arms, fearing no battle.[153]

As the cuneiform tablets recount, the deity Enki believed correctly that Apsu, upset with the chaos they created, was planning to murder the younger deities, and so Enki captured him, holding him prisoner beneath his temple called E-Abzu. This angered Kingu, their son, who reported the event to Tiamat, whereupon she fashioned eleven monsters to battle the deities in order to avenge Apsu's death. These were her own offspring: Bašmu, "Venomous Snake"; Ušumgallu, "Great Dragon"; Mušmaḫḫū, "Exalted Serpent"; Mušḫuššu, "Furious Snake"; Laḫmu, the "Hairy One"; Ugallu, the "Big Weather-Beast"; Uridimmu, "Mad Lion"; Girtablullû, "Scorpion-Man"; Umū dabrūtu, "Violent Storms"; Kulullû, "Fish-Man"; and Kusarikku, "Bull-Man." These entities are recorded in the most primitive records, and we can find astonishing parallels in later literature. From the Sumerians through the Akkadians to the ancient Hebrews, these legends have remained consistent. Later, "ancient Greek and Roman myths were populated not only by gods, heroes, and demons," Brother Guy Consolmagno from VATT at Mt. Graham reminded us, "but by any number of strange and monstrous beings."[154]

Thus, from Rome to Greece—and before that, from Egypt to Persia, Assyria, Babylonia, and Sumer—the earliest records of civilization reveal an era when powerful beings known to the Hebrews as *Watchers* and in the book of Genesis as the *benei ha-elohim* ("sons of God") descended to Earth, mingled with humans, and gave birth to part-celestial, part-terrestrial hybrids known as *Nephilim*. The Bible says this happened when civilization expanded and daughters were born unto men. When the "sons of God" saw the women's beauty, they took wives from among them to sire their unusual offspring. In Genesis 6:4, we read the following account: "There were giants in the earth in those days; and also after that, when the sons of God came in unto the daughters of men, and they bare children to them, the same became mighty men which were of old, men of renown."

When this Scripture is compared with other ancient texts (including those by early church fathers such as Justin, Irenaeus, Athenagoras, Commodianus, Julius Africanus, Clement, Tertulluan, Methodius, and Ambrose, not to mention works like the books of Enoch, Jubilees, Baruch, Genesis Apocryphon, Philo, Josephus, Jasher, The Testament of the 12 Patriarchs, and many more), the firmly held ancient belief becomes clear that the giants of the Old Testament, such as Goliath, were part-human, part-animal, part-angelic offspring of a supernatural interruption into the divine order and natural propagation of the species.

The first-century Romano-Jewish historian, Flavius Josephus, described part of the story this way:

> For many angels of God accompanied with women, and begat sons that proved unjust, and despisers of all that was good, on account of the confidence they had in their own strength; for the tradition is, that these men did what resembled the acts of those whom the Grecians call giants. But Noah was very uneasy at what they did; and being displeased at their conduct, persuaded them to change their dispositions and their acts for the better: but seeing they did not yield to him, but were slaves to their wicked pleasures, he was afraid they would kill him, together with his wife and children, and those they had married; so he departed out of that land.[155]

The early church father Irenaeus added that the angels used women not only to produce "giants," but taught them enchantments specifically for the purpose of casting lust-potions to lure both men and angels to their beds:

> And for a very long while wickedness extended and spread, and reached and laid hold upon the whole race of mankind, until a very small seed of righteousness remained among them and illicit unions took place upon the earth, since angels were united with the daughters of the race of mankind; and they bore to them sons who for their exceeding greatness were called giants. And the angels brought as presents to their wives teachings of wickedness, in that they brought them the virtues of roots and herbs, dyeing in colors and cosmetics, the discovery of rare substances, love-potions, aversions, amours, concupiscence, constraints of love, spells of bewitchment, and all sorcery

and idolatry hateful to God; by the entry of which things into the world evil extended and spread, while righteousness was diminished and enfeebled.[156]

While the prophet Daniel called certain powerful angels "Watchers" in canonical Scripture (Daniel 4:13, 17, 23), it was the apocryphal Book of Enoch that first described their cosmic conspiracy. We read:

> And I Enoch was blessing the Lord of majesty and the King of the ages, and lo! the Watchers called me—Enoch the scribe— and said to me: "Enoch, thou scribe of righteousness, go, declare to the Watchers of the heaven who have left the high heaven, the holy eternal place, and have defiled themselves with women, and have done as the children of earth do, and have taken unto themselves wives: Ye have wrought great destruction on the earth: And ye shall have no peace nor forgiveness of sin: and inasmuch as they delight themselves in their children [the Nephilim], The murder of their beloved ones shall they see, and over the destruction of their children shall they lament, and shall make supplication unto eternity, but mercy and peace shall ye not attain." (1 Enoch 10:3–8)

According to Enoch, two hundred of these powerful angels departed "high heaven" and used women (among other things) to extend their progeny into mankind's plane of existence. David Flynn referenced an interlinear Hebrew Bible that offers an interesting interpretation of Genesis 6:2 in this regard. Where the King James Bible says, "The sons of God saw the daughters of men that they were fair," Flynn interprets as, "The B'nai Elohim saw the daughters of Adam, that they were *fit extensions*" (emphasis added).[157] In other words, they wanted to incarnate themselves into the material world. The New Testament also suggests this idea when Jude, the brother of our Lord, wrote, "And the angels which kept not their first estate, but left their own habitation [*oikētērion*]" (Jude 6). This Greek term, *oikētērion*, is used by Paul in 2 Corinthians 5:2 to denote the transfigured body given to believers in heaven. This implies that these fallen angels indeed sought to extend part of themselves into earthly bodies. The rendering "fit extensions" seems applicable when the whole of the ancient record is understood to mean that the Watchers wanted to leave their proper sphere of existence in order to enter Earth's three-dimensional reality. They viewed women—or at least the women's genetic material—as part of the formula for accomplishing this task. Ancient records suggest the Watchers modified animals as well. For instance, *Jubilees* implies that interspecies mingling eventually resulted in mutations among normal humans and animals whose "flesh" (genetic makeup) was "corrupted" by the activity, presumably through cross-genetic integration:

> And injustice increased upon the earth, and all flesh corrupted its way; man and cattle and beasts and birds and everything which walks on the earth. And they all corrupted their way and their ordinances, and they began to eat one another. And injustice grew upon the earth and every imagination of the thoughts of all mankind was thus continually evil. (Jubilees 5:2 underline added, cf. 7:21–25)[158]

Even the Old Testament contains reference to the mutations that developed among humans following this time frame, including "men" of unusual size and physical strength, who had six fingers, six toes, an animalistic appetite for blood, and even lion-like features (2 Samuel 21:20; 23:20). Early church father Eusebius adds other important details:

> And they begat human beings, with two wings; and then others with four wings and two faces and one body and two heads... still others with horses' hooves, and others in the shape of a horse at the rear and a human shape at the front...they also made bulls with human heads and horses with dogs' heads as well as other

monsters with horses heads and human bodies…*then all kinds of dragon-like monstrous beings.* (emphasis added)[159]

Of the "winged humans" and "dragon-like monsters," prophecy expert, J. R. Church, once made an interesting point that since this activity was satanic in nature, it refers to the "seed of the serpent" that was at enmity with Christ. "The concept of a reptilian race continues throughout the Bible as a metaphoric symbol of the devil," Church wrote in *Prophecy in the News* magazine, February 2009. "Later Scriptures add the term 'dragon,' with the implication that these otherworldly creatures were designed with the DNA code of a reptilian race." Church went on to state that some of these satanic creatures were depicted as "bat-like gargoyles, or winged dragons" in ancient art, and that we should not be surprised that "a humanoid-type reptilian race could cohabit with human women and produce a race of giants."[160] In what could be historical support of Dr. Church's premise, a document fragment found in Cave 4 among the Dead Sea Scrolls contains an admonition by Amram, the father of Moses, to his children. In a badly damaged segment of the text, Amram sees the chief angel of darkness, a Watcher named Melkiresha in the form of a *reptilian* (bracketed suspension points represent scroll damage/irretrievable text):

I saw Watchers in my vision, a dream vision, and behold two (of them) argued about me and said […] and they were engaged in a great quarrel concerning me. I asked them: "You, what are you […] thus […] about me?" They answered and said to me: "We have been made masters and rule over all the sons of men." And they said to me: "Which of us do you choose […]

I raised my eyes and saw one of them. His looks were frightening like those of a viper, and his garments were multi-coloured and he was extremely dark […]

And afterwards I looked and behold […] by his appearance and his face was like that of an adder [a venomous snake], and he was covered with […] together, and his eyes […]"[161]

The fact that the Watchers are described in explicitly *reptilian* terms by the ancient Hebrews grounds the ufological discussion of such beings and their interactions with man firmly in ancient history. As a case in point, Dr. John Mack's seminal work on the abduction phenomenon cites many cases involving entities meeting the same description as that found in the Dead Sea Scrolls. For example, this description by an abductee named Sara: "The head was the most prominent part of the body and was 'shimmery,' looking 'reptilian,' almost 'snake like, serpent like' and quite elongated."[162] Furthermore, contrary to the revisionist accounts given by ancient astronaut theorists, this implies the so-called reptilians are, in fact, Watchers pursuing a more sinister agenda than scientific exploration. Yet, abductee testimonies also suggest that their interest in genetic material is very real.

Perhaps the most scientific description concerning the Watcher experiments and their genetic modification of humans and animals comes to us from the Book of Jasher, a Hebrew text that appeared in the medieval period claiming to contain material from the ancient book mentioned in the Hebrew Bible. While its origin is debatable, this text preserves the familiar story of the fall of the Watchers, and then adds an exceptional detail that none of the other texts is as unequivocal about, something that can only be understood in modern language to mean advanced biotechnology, genetic engineering, or transgenic modification of species. After the Watchers had instructed humans in the secrets of heaven, note what the text says occurred:

[Then] the sons of men [began teaching] the mixture of animals of one species with the other, in order therewith to provoke the Lord. (Jasher 4:18)

It does seem likely that the phrase "the mixture of animals of one species with the other" means Watchers had taught men something more than natural animal crossbreeding, as this would not have "provoked the Lord." God made "like" animals of different breeds capable of reproducing. For example, horses can propagate with other mammals of the Equidae classification (the taxonomic "horse family"), including donkeys and zebras. It would not have "provoked the Lord" for this type of animal breeding to have taken place, as God, Himself, made the animals able to do this.

If, on the other hand, the Watchers were crossing species boundaries by mixing incompatible animals *of one species with the other*, such as a horse with a human (creating, then, a centaur), this would have been a different matter altogether and may cast light on the numerous ancient stories of mythical beings of variant species manufacturing that fit perfectly within the records of what the Watchers were accomplishing. Understandably, this kind of chimera-making would have "provoked the Lord," and currently raises the serious question of why the Watchers would have risked eternal damnation by tinkering with God's creation in this way. Several theories exist as to *why* Watchers would have corrupted natural genotypes, including the ideas that: 1) Because Yahweh had placed boundaries between the species and strictly ordered that "each kind" reproduce only after its "own kind," the Watchers as rebels sought to break these rules in order to assault God's creative genius by biologically altering what He had made; and 2) The corruption of antediluvian DNA by Watchers was an effort to cut off the birth line of the Messiah. This theory posits that Satan understood the protoevangelium—the promise in Genesis 3:15 that a Savior would be born, the seed of the woman, and that He would destroy the fallen angel's power. Satan's followers therefore intermingled with the human race in a conspiracy to stop the birth of Christ. If human DNA could be universally corrupted or "demonized," they reasoned, no Savior would be born and mankind would be lost forever. Those who support this theory believe this is why God ordered His people to maintain a pure bloodline and not to intermarry with people from the other nations. When the Hebrews breached this command and the mutated DNA began rapidly spreading among men and animals, God instructed Noah to build an ark and prepare for a flood that would destroy every living thing, the purpose of which would be to purge the Earth of the contaminated genotypes and phenotypes.

Finally, a third theory as to why Watchers merged the genetics of various life forms incorporates the voluminous ancient "Watcher" texts into a consistent account regarding the overriding motive for what the Watchers had apparently used DNA for. When this is done, it becomes clear that genetic substances were for them an Earth-centric and organic construction material (or, as Dr. Jacques Vallée called it, "living energy"[163]) for building a composite body that would allow them to leave their plane of existence and to enter man's (see Jude 1:6; 2 Peter 2:4). The challenge of this theory becomes how intermingling various species would satisfy this goal or provide the Watchers with a method of departure from "high heaven" and incarnation into man's "habitation." While we will not take time here to explain every detail, the hypothesis involves the Watchers combining species in order to create a *soulless or spiritless body*—a living but empty "large organism" or "shell" into which they could extend themselves. The rationale here is that every creature as it existed originally had its beginning in God, who wove a barrier between the species and ordered each creature to reproduce "after its own kind." The phrase "after its own kind" verifies what type of spirit can enter into an intelligent being at conception. When the sperm of a dog meets ovum of a dog and the life of a dog is formed, at the first spark of life, the spirit (or "nature" when speaking of an animal) of a dog enters that embryo and it grows to become a dog in spirit and form. The spirit of a man does not enter it, in the same way that a man is not born with the spirit of a horse or cow. This creature/spirit integrity is part of the divine order and would have kept the Watchers, who wanted to incarnate within the human realm (not just "possess" creatures), from displacing the spirits of humans or animals and replacing them with their own. How did the Watchers overcome this problem? It appears, based on the ancient records (and like modern scientists are doing today), that they blended existing DNA of several living creatures and made something that neither the spirit of man nor beast would enter at conception, for it was neither man nor beast. As *Mysterious World*, in its 2003 feature, "Giants in the Earth," noted:

The Nephilim were genetically manufactured beings created from the genetic material of various pre-existing animal species.… The fallen angels did not personally interbreed with the daughters of men, but used their godlike intellect to delve into the secrets of YHWH's Creation and manipulate it to their own purposes. And the key to creating or recreating man, as we have (re)discovered in the twentieth century, is the human genome—DNA.[164]

According to this extrapolation from the ancient accounts, the manipulation of living tissue by the fallen angels led to an unusual body made up of human, animal, and plant genetics known as Nephilim, an "Earth-born" facsimile or "fit extension" into which they could incarnate. While this theory significantly adds to the ancient record, it seeks to modernize the ancients' description of what they, perhaps, did not fully grasp through the lens of a prescientific worldview and vocabulary. Interestingly, science has uncovered unexpected evidence for this in the human genome.

The Washington Post recently published a story on findings that a "mystery" species with partial human DNA once walked the Earth. The story, titled "Sex with Early Mystery Species of Humans Seen in DNA, UW Researcher Says," is just the latest in a series of similar recent finds, and while no fossilized giant bones were found in this case, a calling card was left in present-day Africans: *snippets of "foreign" DNA*. "These genetic leftovers do not resemble DNA from any modern humans," the writer of the article reports before adding this bombshell: "The foreign DNA also does not resemble Neanderthal DNA, which shows up in the DNA of some modern Europeans.… That means the newly identified DNA came from *an unknown group*"[165] (emphasis added).

Given the above theories, the biblical story of Nephilim offspring offers the most satisfying answer to this enigma.

One objection occasionally raised against the idea of part-men hybrids born as a result of union between angelic and human "genetics" is the belief that angels are supposedly sexless, since Jesus said at the resurrection that people will neither marry nor be given in marriage but shall be "like the angels in heaven." However, as James Montgomery Boice points out, the words recorded in Matthew 22:30 are "not the equivalent of saying that the angels are sexless or that they could not have had sexual relations with women if they had chosen to do so. In heaven human beings will not marry but will nevertheless retain their identity, which includes their being either male or female. In the same way, the angels could also have sexual identities. It is significant perhaps that when the angels are referred to in Scripture it is always with the masculine pronoun 'he,' and they are always described as men."[166] Thus, when Jesus said the angels in heaven do not marry, this is a separate matter from what those angels that departed (or were cast out of) heaven were capable of doing and apparently did. Jude 1:6–7 adds a deep and important point about this when it says:

And the angels which kept not their first estate, but left their own habitation, he hath reserved in everlasting chains under darkness unto the judgment of the great day. Even as Sodom and Gomorrha, and the cities about them in like manner, giving themselves over to fornication, *and going after strange flesh*, are set forth for an example, suffering the vengeance of eternal fire. (emphasis added)

It is remarkable here that Jude connects the sin of the fallen angels with the sexual sins of Sodom and Gomorrha using the telling commentary that they had gone after "*strange flesh*." This is the Greek *sarkos heteros* and contains a very important meaning connected to how the men of Sodom and Gomorrha wanted to have *sex with angels* (see Genesis 19). Thus, their sin is compared by Jude to those angels of one verse earlier, who departed their proper habitation in heaven to comingle with women. The Apostle Paul also resonates these demarcations in 1 Corinthians 15:40 when he says, "There are also celestial bodies, and bodies terrestrial: but the glory of the celestial is one, and the glory of the terrestrial is another." When explaining that the *heavenly* body is made up of something entirely different than the *earthly* body, is Paul speaking metaphysically, or can a difference in the *raw material* of these bodies be assumed? Certainly it can, because in the previous verse he speaks of the differences between the flesh of men, beasts, fishes, and birds, yet points out how these are all of earthly composition, as opposed to the following verse, in which he clearly divides the celestial body as "another" type of body not of the same "terrestrial" (terra firma, of the Earth) kind.

According to the second-century Apostolic Father, Athenagoras, Lucifer had been the angel originally placed in charge of the earthly "matter" (see the ancient text, *Plea for the Christians*). After his fall, Satan used his knowledge of creation and genetics to corrupt what God had made. This is interesting in light of modern science and the recent suggestion that genetic abnormalities "may predispose a man to antiso-cial behavior, including crimes of violence."[167] One of the hottest topics in biology today is the science of "epigenetics," which involves heritable changes in gene expression or cellular phenotypes that can be caused by "mechanisms" other than normal changes that occur in underlying DNA sequences—thus the title "epi-(Greek: ἐπί, over, above, outer)-genetics." Whether supernaturalism can play a role as one of these "outer mechanisms" is suggestive, and many scholars believe demonic posses-sion (for instance) can negatively affect chromosomal health. The New Testament is replete with connections between sickness and genetic disorders as directly connected to demonism. According to theologian and spiritual warfare expert Dr. Neil Andersen, "Approximately one-fourth of all the healings recorded in the Gospel of Mark were actually deliverances."[168] For example, "They brought unto him many that were possessed with devils: and he cast out the spirits with his word, and healed all that were sick"; and, "when he had called unto him his twelve disciples, he gave them power against unclean spirits, to cast them out, and to heal all manner of sickness and all manner of disease" (Matthew 8:16; 10:1).

The Difference between Demonized Humans and Soulless Hybrids

Whereas physical and spiritual sickness was and can be healed (including when it is the result of demonism), a question of significantly greater distress arises over genetically altered humans known as "Nephilim" and whether such creations had a redeemable soul in the Judeo-Christian sense (i.e., the soul of a human as different than the nature of any animal in that man alone was made in God's image and the essence of the human person is capable of union with God now and transcendence from mortal to redeemed immortality after death). The debate over this question extends as far back as the early church fathers, throughout the Middle Ages, and especially during the Inquisition by the Roman Catholic Church. One of the foremost figures of the twentieth century and a pillar of both the Irish and British literary establishments, William Butler Yeats, examined this subject in his Sea Stories Notes concerning Abbot Anthony and his confrontation with human chimeras:

> Throughout the Middle Ages, there must have been many discussions upon those questions that divided Kirk's Highlanders. Were these beings but the shades of men? Were they a separate race? Were they spirits of evil? Above all, perhaps, were they capable of salvation? Father Sinistrari…tells a story which must have been familiar through the Irish Middle Ages, and the seed of many discussions. The Abbot Anthony went once upon a journey to visit St. Paul, the first hermit. After travelling for some days into the desert, he met a centaur of whom he asked his road and the centaur, muttering barbarous and unintelligible words, pointed to the road with his outstretched hand and galloped away and hid himself in a wood. St. Anthony went some way further and presently went into a valley and met there a little man with goat's feet and horns upon his forehead. St. Anthony stood still and made the sign of the cross being afraid of some devil's trick. But the sign of the cross did not alarm the little man

who went nearer and offered some dates [food] very respectfully as it seemed to make peace. When the old Saint asked him who he was, he said: "I am a mortal, one of those inhabitants of the desert called fauns, satyrs, and incubi, by the Gentiles. I have come as an ambassador from my people. I ask you to pray for us to our common God who came as we know for the salvation of the world and who is praised throughout the world." We are not told whether St. Anthony prayed but merely that he thought of the glory of Christ and thereafter of Christ's enemies and turning towards Alexandria said: "Woe upon you harlots worshipping animals as God." This tale so artfully arranged as it seems to set the pious by the ears may have been the original of a tale one hears in Ireland today. I heard or read that tale somewhere before I was twenty, for it is the subject of one of my first poems. But the priest in the Irish tale, as I remember it, tells the little man that there is no salvation for such as he and it ends with the wailing of the faery host. Sometimes too, one reads in Irish stories of hoof-footed creatures, and it may well be that the Irish theologians who read of St. Anthony in Sinistrari's authority, St. Hieronymus, thought centaur and homunculus were of like sort with the shades haunting their own raths and barrows. Father Sinistrari draws the moral that those inhabitants of the desert called "fauns and satyrs and incubi by the Gentiles" had souls that could be shrived, but Irish theologians in a country full of poems very upsetting to youth about the women of the Sidhe [Irish Gaelic term for a supernatural race in Irish and Scottish mythology comparable to fairies or elves] who could pass, it may be even monastic walls, may have turned the doubtful tale the other way. Sometimes we are told following the traditions of the eleventh-century poems that the Sidhe are "the ancient inhabitants of the country" but more often still they are fallen angels who, because they were too bad for heaven and not bad enough for hell, have been sent into the sea and into the waste places.

More probably still the question was never settled, sometimes Christ was represented as throwing them into hell till some- one said he would empty the whole paradise, and thereupon his hand slackened and some fell in this place and some in that other, as though providence itself were undecided.[169]

Perhaps this explains the more recent Roman Catholic position on extraterrestrials? Sinistrari, the seventeenth-century demonologist, clearly believed in "rational creatures besides man, endowed like him with a body and a soul, that are born and die like him, redeemed by Our Lord Jesus-Christ, and capable of receiving salvation or damnation."[170] According to the original text, *Demoniality*, from which Yates was quot- ing, "It is clear that it was no devil or pure spirit ejected from heaven and damned, but some kind of animal."[171] The subject of whether hybrid humans (call them satyrs, centaurs, or Nephilim) can be redeemed sur- faced again a few years ago when one of the writers of this book (Horn) was having lunch with State Superintendent Capp Marks of the Oregon District Assemblies of God and several other state representatives. Marks leaned forward and said, "Tom, this week I read the novel *The Ahriman Gate* that you and Nita wrote. It was very good, but one thing troubled me greatly. That part where human genetics were combined with what the scientists in the book thought was alien DNA, which led to the revival of Nephilim. I never liked talking about that subject when I was a pastor because I hate the implications—that there could be mutant humans that cannot be saved." Capp's abhorrence of the issue is shared by all people of goodwill, but, whether we like it or not, it doesn't change the fact that Nephilim, as described in the Old Testament and in the ancient Book of Enoch, seemed to be devoid of natural-redeemable souls/spirits. Recall in Genesis 6:9 that only Noah, and by extension his children, was found "perfect" in his generation. The Hebrew word for "perfect" in this case is *tamiym*, which means "without blemish" or "healthy," the same word used in Leviticus to describe an unblemished, sacrificial lamb. The meaning was not that Noah was morally perfect—

after all, he got drunk shortly after the Flood subsided—but perhaps this suggests that his physical makeup (his DNA) had not been contaminated with Nephilim descent, as apparently the rest of the world had become. In order to preserve mankind as He had made it, God destroyed all but Noah's family in the Flood. The ancient records, including those of the Bible, consistently describe the cause of this Flood as a response to "all flesh" having become "corrupted, both man and beast." Additionally, on the question of whether the corrupted or altered humans had redeemable souls, note what happened when the Watchers asked the prophet to beseech God for the salvation of their children (the Nephilim):

> Then I went and spoke to them all together, and they were all afraid, and fear and trembling seized them. And they besought me to draw up a petition for them that they might find forgiveness, and to read their petition in the presence of the Lord of heaven. For from thenceforward they could not speak [with Him] nor lift up their eyes to heaven for shame of their sins for which they had been condemned. (Enoch 13:3–5)

Enoch takes this petition to God, and then informs the Watchers of their—and their hybrid children's—situation, regarding whether they can be redeemed:

> I wrote out your petition, and in my vision it appeared thus, that your petition will not be granted unto you throughout all the days of eternity, and that judgment has been finally passed upon you: yea [your petition] will not be granted unto you. And from henceforth you shall not ascend into heaven unto all eternity, and in bonds of the earth the decree has gone forth to bind you for all the days of the world. And [that] previously you shall have seen the destruction of your beloved sons and ye shall have no pleasure in them, but they shall fall before you by the sword. And your petition on their behalf shall not be granted, nor yet

on your own: even though you weep and pray and speak all the words contained in the writing which I have written. (Enoch 14:4–7)

Thus based on the Book of Enoch and reflected in the Bible in such places as Genesis, Jude, and 2 Peter, redemption was not possible for any of the fallen Watchers or their hybrid offspring, though the Nephilim *were part human*. In this sense, Nephilim could be compared to an extraordinary primate—intelligent like men and angels, even possessing human DNA, but not Homo sapien as fashioned by God in His image. In further confirmation of their status as unredeemable, we also learn from this strange narrative of a primeval belief concerning two types of resurrection from the dead—one that is strictly terrestrial (i.e., a dead Nephilim can return from the grave to inhabit another corruptible body of flesh) and a second future resurrection in which eternal glorified bodies are promised only for those who sleep in Christ. Isaiah makes it clear that the Watcher's offspring (called *Rephaim* in this text) cannot participate in the latter. In chapter 26:14 of his book, he says: "They [Rephaim] are dead, they shall not live; they are deceased, they shall not rise: therefore hast thou visited and destroyed them, and made all their memory to perish." The word rendered "deceased" from the Hebrew implies "shades" or "ghosts of the dead."[172] From this we see echoed how the term Rephaim was used in two senses: one for human (and Nephilim) spirits in the underworld and another for terrestrial giants.

In the *Ras Shamra* texts (ancient writings found in Ugarit in northern Syria), the Rephaim were described as demigods who worshipped the Amorite god Ba'al, the ruler of the underworld. For example, this ancient Ugaritic text preserves a Canaanite ritual for summoning the Rephaim:

You have summoned the Rephaim of the netherworld;
You have commanded the Council of the Didanites!
Summon ULKN, Rapha!

Summon TRMN, Rapha!
Summon SDN-w-RDN, [Rapha!]
Summon TR-'LLMN, [Rapha!]
[All] summon the most ancient Rephaim!
You have summoned the Rephaim of the netherworld!
You have commanded the Council of the Didanites![173]

Scholars think the Ugaritians, probably the Amorites of Northeastern Syria, traced their origins to the enigmatic Didanum people, and thus summoned the Council of the Didanites from the underworld of the Rephaim. While these Canaanites beckoned them, the prophet Isaiah describes these shades greeting defeated Babylon within the infernal region:

Hell [Sheol] from beneath is moved for thee to meet thee at thy coming: it stirreth up the dead [Rephaim] for thee, even all the chief ones of the earth; it hath raised up from their thrones all the kings of the nations. And they shall speak and say unto thee, Art thou also become weak as we? Art thou become like unto us? (Isaiah 14:9–10)

This passage mocks the king of Babylon as spirits of dead royalty welcome him to the underworld. It also prefigures the final fall of Babylon the Great (Revelation 17:15–19:3) and the defeat of Satan (Luke 10:15; Revelation 12:7–9; 20:10), as well as looks back on the fall of Babel's Nimrod (Genesis 11:1–9), who also was believed to be a giant.

However, it is also clear that the term "Rephaim" designated earthly giants, because in Numbers 13:33, the "sons of Anak" are said to be descended from (literally "children of") the Nephilim. These Anakim are described as Rephaim in Deuteronomy 2:11. The ancient Hebrews who translated the Septuagint into Greek understood the prophet Isaiah (chapters 13 and 14) as using Rephaim in this second sense to predict a return of these "giants" with "monsters" at the advent of the destruction of Babylon in the final age. From the Septuagint, we read:

The vision which Esaias son of Amos saw against Babylon. Lift up a standard on the mountain of the plain, exalt the voice to them, beckon with the hand, open the gates, ye ruler. I give command and I bring them: giants are coming to fulfill my wrath.... For behold! The day of the Lord is coming which cannot be escaped, a day of wrath and anger, to make the world desolate.... And Babylon...shall be as when God overthrew Sodom and Gomorrah.... It shall never be inhabited...and monsters shall rest there, and devils shall dance there and satyrs shall dwell there. (Isaiah 13:1–3, 9, 19–22)[174]

The sixteenth chapter of the Book of Enoch also tells of the deceased offspring of Watchers, the spirits of the giants, or Nephilim, as being released at the end of time to bring slaughter and destruction upon man:

From the days of the slaughter and destruction and death of the giants, from the souls of whose flesh the spirits, having gone forth, shall destroy without incurring judgement—thus shall they destroy until the day of the consummation, the great judgement in which the age shall be consummated, over the Watchers and the godless, yea, shall be wholly consummated. (1 Enoch 16:1)[175]

Of course, this all comes to pass as part of God's Day of the Lord or Great Tribulation, when Satan and his angels punish the unbelieving world before they are resigned to the pit. According to scholars, "This defines the temporal extent of the evil spirits' activity. They will continue their brutality, unabated and unpunished from the death of the giants until the day of judgment."[176] This particular prophecy mirrors those of Isaiah and the apocryphal works, which indicate a future date in which Watchers will rise for judgment while the spirits of their giant offspring manifest to wreak havoc upon Earth.

The Book of Jubilees—an ancient Jewish religious work that is considered inspired Scripture by the Ethiopian Orthodox Church as well as Jews in Ethiopia—parallels the frightening scenario, prophesying spirits of the Nephilim on Earth in the last days. In this passage, God is ready to destroy all these demons after the Flood, and Noah prays that his descendants be released from their attacks. Mastema (an alternate name for Satan) intervenes, imploring God to allow him to retain and control one-tenth of these demons in order to exercise his authority, because they are needed "to corrupt and lead astray before my judgment." In other words, this corruption will peak just before Satan is judged (Revelation 20:2, 10):

> And the Lord our God spoke to us so that we might bind all of them [Nephilim spirits]. And the chief of the spirits, Mastema, came and he said, "O Lord, Creator, leave some of them before me, and let them obey my voice. And let them do everything which I tell them, because if some of them are not left for me, I will not be able to exercise the authority of my will among the children of men because they are (intended) to corrupt and lead astray before my judgment because the evil of the sons of men is great." And he said, "Let a tenth of them remain before him, but let nine parts go down into the place of judgment." (Jubilees 10:7–9)[177]

According to this text, God has allowed Satan to exercise dominion over the Earth with an army of demons, including the spirits of the Nephilim spawned in the ancient world. Their job description is the corruption of humanity. One escapes their purview through believing the Gospel. While Christ defeated them on the cross, His kingdom is inaugurated but not manifest. One impending day, this necessarily comes to an apocalyptic culmination. Given the Septuagint's rendering of Isaiah 13, this could include an end-time incarnation as giants.

Finally, a prophecy in the second chapter of the book of Joel with a parallel in Revelation 9 seems to include an end-times volcano of hybrids. While some expositors claim Joel was describing an army of locusts with phrases like "[They are] a great people and a strong" and "they shall run like *mighty men* [*gibborim*, a term associated with the Nephilim]," it is hard to accept these verses as talking about grasshoppers. We think this describes a demonic invasion that could possibly include Nephilim.

[They are] a great people and a strong; there hath not been ever the like, neither shall be any more after it...and nothing shall escape them. The appearance of them is as the appearance of horses; and as horsemen, so shall they run.... They shall run like mighty men [*gibbowr, gibborim*]; they shall climb the wall like men of war.... They shall run to and fro in the city; they shall run upon the wall, they shall climb up upon the houses; they shall enter in at the windows like a thief. The earth shall quake before them.... And the LORD shall utter his voice before his army: for his camp is very great: for he is strong that executeth his word: for the day of the LORD is great and very terrible; and who can abide it?" (Joel 2:2–11)

Of course, this passage finds a striking parallel in the fifth-trumpet judgment, with its freak-show locust horde (Revelation 9). These monstrosities are described to be shaped like horses, having human faces and hair, lions' teeth, scorpion tails, and wings that sound like chariots rushing to battle. John MacArthur describes these freakish creatures:

But these were not ordinary locusts, but demons, who, like locusts, bring swarming destruction. Describing them in the form of locusts symbolizes their uncountable numbers and massive destructive capabilities. The fact that three times in the passage (vv. 3, 5, 10) their power to inflict pain is compared to that of scorpions indicates they are not actual locusts, since locusts have no stinging tail as scorpions do. Scorpions are a species of arachnid, inhabiting warm, dry regions, and having an erect tail tipped with a venomous stinger. The stings of many species of scorpions are excruciatingly painful, and about two dozen species are capable of killing humans. The symptoms of a sting from one of the deadly species, including severe convulsions and paralysis, resemble those of demon-possessed individuals (cf. Mark 1:23–27; 9:20, 26). Combining in the description of the demons both locusts and scorpions emphasizes the deadliness of the demon invasion.[178]

Taken at face value, these demons cannot be immaterial spirits. Scholars, those who take end-time prophecy seriously, invariably conclude that these end-time hordes manifest in mongrelized bodies. Arnold Fruchtenbaum also notes their hybrid nature:

The description of these "locust-scorpions" given in verses 7–10 clearly shows that they are something other than literal scorpions or locusts. Their origin being the Abyss further shows that they are demons. It is not unusual for demons and other angelic beings to have animal-like features.[179]

When the numerous ancient texts are added up, there is persuasive evidence that Joel's army is much more than simple grasshoppers, and that the massive army of demonic *gibborim* that run upon the wall and from which nobody can escape are the corporeal crossbred creations of demonic Watcher biotech and the spirits of the ancient Nephilim.

Some may be shocked to learn that, in addition to the citations above, the Bible actually describes an end-times confrontation between the "mythological gods" and Christ. "The Lord will be terrible unto them: for he will famish all the gods of the earth," says Zephaniah 2:11. "The Lord of hosts, the God of Israel, saith; Behold, I will punish the… gods" (Jeremiah 46:25). Human followers of the pagan deities will also join the conflict, calling upon their "idols of gold, and silver, and brass, and stone, and of wood" (Revelation 9:20) to convene their powers against the Christian God, uniting with "unclean spirits like frogs…the spirits of devils working miracles, which go forth unto the kings of the earth…to gather them to the battle of that great day…[to] a place called in the Hebrew tongue Armageddon" (Revelation 16:13–14, 16).

Other places in the Bible, such as Job 26:5, may also reflect the idea of a demonic mechanism that can, under some circumstances, return Rephaim from the underworld to temporal, physical bodies. "Dead things are formed from under the waters," Job 26:5 says. The dead in this text are *rapha* (Rephaim), and the phrase "are formed" is from *chuwl*, meaning to twist or whirl as in a double helix coil or genetic manufacturing. The startling implication of these various texts is that beneath the surface of Earth or even another dimension, agents of darkness await the recurrent moments of their fleshly reconstitution. What's more, the long history of demonological phenomena related to manipulation of biological matter suggests that versions of this curious activity have been repeated ever since that first incursion described in the books of Genesis and Enoch. The reanimation of Nephilim certainly occurred after the first advent in the Days of Noah, for Genesis 6:4 includes the telling phrase, "and also after that," verifying the strange undertaking was not confined to the antediluvian age. Indeed, almost immediately following the Great Flood, Scripture confirms the return of hybrid humans, including Og, the King of Bashan, whose bed was approximately fourteen feet long by six feet wide; Anak and his Anakim; and other beings among the tribes of Emim, Horim, and Zamsummim. An interesting note is that, by the time Og arrived, though he was very large, he was dwarfed by the size of the first giants, who were recorded in excess of twenty feet tall. Does this suggest that the Nephilim offspring were intentionally being bred down in size with each generation, thus allowing for eventual seamless, secret integration among human societies of pseudo-humans with "corrupted" genetic code?

Most significant for us today are the ancient texts that forecasted this final repeat of hybridized humans and animals for the latter days, and the question of whether man in his arrogance has now set in motion a prophetic repeat of that activity associated with "the days of Noah."

5 | The Return of Hybrid Humans

"Up in the tree branches, they could make out a huge set
of yellowish, reptilian eyes. The head of this animal had to
be three feet wide, they guessed. At the bottom of the tree
was something else. Gorman described it as huge and hairy,
with massively muscled front legs and a doglike head."
—*The Las Vegas Mercury*

On November 28, 2012, during the third season of
Conspiracy Theory with Jesse Ventura, the TruTV program looked into "human-animal hybrid experi-
ments that supposedly have gone beyond the Petri dish with rumors
that a real-life 'Planet of the Apes' is being created."[180] The producers
had contacted one of the authors of this book (Horn) late in 2011 with
a request for help. They wanted to know whether scientists had secretly
crossed the Rubicon with regard to human-animal genetic experiments, as they were preparing for the filming of season 3, episode 4,
titled "Manimal," described on Ventura's website this way: "Science has
made major breakthroughs in drug research and transplant technology
by experimenting on 'chimeras'—human/animal embryo hybrids. But
these seemingly noble goals may be covering up a much more nefarious purpose—to create half human, half ape super soldiers, paving the
way for a real life Planet of the Apes showdown."[181] (The producers

actually offered, on three separate occasions, to fly Horn to set locations in the United States to meet with Ventura and the film crew, but he turned them down for reasons that will be revealed later. Conversely, though Horn declined their repeated invitation to be on the show, he did spend numerous hours with them as a consultant, providing documentation and expert witnesses. Horn saw to setting them up with Professor William B. Hurlbut, consulting professor for the Department of Neurology and Neurological Sciences at Stanford University Medical Center and a member of the US President's Council on Bioethics, who will be featured with both of the authors of this book and over a dozen experts in an upcoming documentary exposé on transhumanism, tentatively scheduled for release in 2013.)

Scene from the movie *Splice*

Among the scores of research papers, Defense Advanced Research Projects Agency (DARPA) budget line items, suspect locations where human-animal experimentation ethics may have passed the curtain of acceptability, and media reports that Horn forwarded to the producers was a Reuters news article dated November 9, 2009, titled "Scientists Want Debate on Animals with Human Genes," which hinted at just how far scientists have come and how far they intend to go with human and animal hybridization. The news piece started out, "A mouse that can speak? A monkey with Down's Syndrome? Dogs with human hands or feet? British scientists want to know if such experiments are acceptable,"[182] and then continued with revelations that scientists inside Britain were comfortable now with up to 50/50 animal-human integration. The article implied that not all the research currently under design is kept at the embryonic level, and that fully matured monstrosities (like the creature in the 2010 movie *Splice*) are quietly under study.

It didn't take long to surmise whether the Reuters article was simply speculating or if indeed there were scientists already experimenting with human-animal creations beyond the embryonic stage. In July 2011, Britain's Academy of Medical Sciences (AMS) admitted in a 148-page report that such science is advancing so quickly and being conducted in so many laboratories around the world without appropriate oversight that an international regulatory commission is urgently needed to oversee the creation of these part-human, part-animal, part-synthetic chimeras. Interestingly, the AMS did not call for a prohibition of the science, but rather for an international supervisory body under which the science can fully and officially proceed. In the précis of its analysis, the AMS considered "research that involves the introduction of human DNA sequence into animals, or the mixing of human and animal cells or tissues, to create *entities* we refer to as 'animals containing human material'" (ACHM).[183] The academy then confessed: "Such approaches are long-established, and thousands of different ACHM have been used in biomedical research, yet they have received relatively little public discussion."[184] What type of beings did Britain's leading scientists know of or suspect as now being secretly under study? From the summary of the AMS paper, we find:

- Extensive modification of the brain of an animal, by implantation of human derived cells, which might result in altered cognitive capacity approaching human "consciousness" or "sentience" or "humanlike" behavioural capabilities.
- Situations where functional human gametes (eggs, sperm) might develop from precursor cell-types in an animal; and

where fertilisation between human and animal gametes might then occur [yes, folks, we are talking here about animals that can conceive from human sperm and give birth to human-animals].

- Cellular or genetic modifications which could result in animals with aspects of humanlike appearance (skin type, limb or facial structure) or characteristics, such as speech [in other words, Nephilim].[185]

Only one day after the AMS circulated this report, the popular *UK Mail Online* published a story detailing that, in just one instance alone (of potentially tens of thousands):

Scientists have created more than 150 human-animal hybrid embryos in British laboratories. The hybrids have been produced secretively over the past three years by researchers looking into possible cures for a wide range of diseases. The revelation comes just a day after a committee of scientists warned of a nightmare "Planet of the Apes" scenario in which work on human-animal creations goes too far.[186]

While such chimeras are supposedly destroyed at the embryonic level, experts involved in the field who were interviewed by *Reuters* admitted, "Some scientists in some places want to push boundaries."[187] In other words, there are most likely *Splice*-like creatures in laboratory settings now, locations that these scientists have left unmentioned. Martin Bobrow, professor of medical genetics at Cambridge University, hinted why this is the case: "There is a whole raft of new scientific techniques that will make it not only easier *but also more important to be able to do these cross-species experiments*" (emphasis added).[188] One place where researchers may have already considered this research to be so "important" that it justifies pushing those "boundaries" the British scientists alluded to is the Yerkes National Primate Research Center at Emory University in Georgia (originally located in Orange Park, Florida). It is one of eight national primate research centers funded by the National Institutes of Health (NIH); both Yerkes and the NIH have shown interest in combining animal and human genetics to create a new species. The Discovery Channel (in an episode of "Unsolved History" on March 27, 1998) discussed a report by Dr. Gordon Gallup, a psychologist from the University at Albany, on the Yerkes National Primate Research Center in which he confessed "a human-chimp hybrid was successfully engendered and born [at the center] but was destroyed by the scientists soon after."[189] This should come as no surprise, as Emory's professors, including Rabbi Michael Broyde, have argued very recently that Jewish law would support animalized humans so long as the technology produces superior people. In an October 7, 2011, article on the University's website, Broyde says:

> Genetic engineering (GE), in which the traits of different individuals, or animals, are combined, already has resulted in amazing combinations.... Jewish law would support similar intentional human-human chimerism, in which the embryonic material of two fetuses is mixed, or human-animal chimerism, in which the cells of a human are mixed with cells of another mammal...processes and technologies that result in healthy, or healthier, children are intrinsically good and should be embraced, not feared.[190]

Professor Broyde is correct in stating that genetically altering "the traits of different individuals... has resulted in amazing combinations." In fact, the first *known* genetically altered humans were born over a decade ago as a result of an experimental program at the Institute for Reproductive Medicine and Science of Saint Barnabas in New Jersey. An article at that time explained part of the research, saying, "The babies were born to women who had problems conceiving. Extra genes from a female donor were inserted into their eggs before they were fertilized in an attempt to enable them to conceive. Genetic fingerprint tests on two one-year-old children confirm that they have inherited DNA from three adults—two women and one man."[191] Concerning these experiments, Dr. Joseph Mercola points out something very important:

> Today, these children are in their early teens, and while the original study claims that this was "the first case of human germline genetic modification resulting in normal healthy children," later reports put such claims of absolute success in dispute [meaning not all the genetically engineered children were necessarily healthy]. Still, back in 2001, the authors seemed to think they had it all under control, stating:
>
>> These are the first reported cases of germline mtDNA genetic modification which have led to the inheritance of two mtDNA populations in the children resulting from ooplasmic transplantation. These mtDNA fingerprints demonstrate that the transferred mitochondria can be replicated and maintained in the offspring, therefore being a genetic modification without potentially altering mitochondrial function.
>
> It's relevant to understand that these children have inherited extra genes—that of two women and one man—and will be able to pass this extra set of genetic traits to their own offspring. One of the most shocking considerations here is that this was done—repeatedly—even though no one knows what the ramifications of having the genetic traits of three parents might be for the individual, or for their subsequent offspring. Based on what I've learned about the genetic engineering of plants, I'm inclined to say the ramifications could potentially be vast, dire, and completely unexpected.[192]

For those inclined to believe the astonishing report above was an isolated incident, British scientists repeated the same experiments in 2008, and the Oregon Health & Sciences University (OHSU) conducted similar research aimed at producing genetically engineered "super babies" in 2012.[193] Yet, regardless of how many times this and other forms of human genetic tinkering have been secretly conducted outside public or congressional review (historical precedence suggests many, many times), it is important to understand how germline genetic engineering was used in this one example in which thirty genetically modified children were created, as it reflects the very modus operandi that fallen angels used with Nephilim—to introduce heritable modifications to the human genotype that give birth literally worldwide to changes in the gene pool through natural propagation. Dr. Mercola's concerns are thus highly appropriate in that current genetic engineering (GE) models on humans carry the same potential as when "all flesh" was corrupted in the Old Testament and had to be destroyed by God. As a result, germline engineering is considered by some conservative bioethicists to be the most dangerous of human-enhancement technology, as it has the power to truly reassemble the very nature of humanity into posthuman, altering an embryo's every cell and leading to transferable modifications extending to all succeeding generations.

Debate over germline engineering is therefore most critical, because as changes to "downline" genetic offspring are set in motion, the genotype and phenotype (nature, physical makeup, and behavior) of mankind will be altered with no hope of reversal, thereby permanently reshaping humanity's future. In spite of that, according to "ethicists" like Oxford University Professor Julian Savulescu, not only do we have "a moral obligation" to engineer such people, but embryos that do not meet certain genetic improvements in the future should not be allowed to live.[194] Dr. Richard Seed, a physicist in Chicago, goes further, warning anybody who has plans of standing in the way of this dream that they had better rethink their opposition: "We are going to become gods, period. If you don't like it, get off. You don't have to contribute, you don't have to participate, but if you are going to interfere with me becoming a god, you're going to have trouble. There'll be warfare."[195] Professors Seed and Savulescu are not alone in their strong beliefs. Dr. Gregory Stock, a respected proponent of germline technology, argues that man not only has a moral responsibility to "improve" the human genotype, but also that powerful new technology now at our disposal for transcending existing biological limitations is making the schemes of transhumanists inevitable, if not imminent. "We have spent billions to unravel our biology, not out of idle curiosity, but in the hope of bettering our lives," he says. "We are not about to turn away from this."[196] Elsewhere, Stock does admit, however, that this could lead to "clusters of genetically enhanced superhumans who will dominate if not enslave us."[197]

Thus, from the "Human-Ape Army" plans of Ilya Ivanov under Soviet dictator Joseph Stalin,[198] to the early part of the twentieth century when Adolf Hitler instructed Josef Mengele to perform horrific experiments on live human beings in concentration camps to test their genetic theories, and to the US, where up until the 1970s, more than sixty thousand Americans were sterilized after being deemed of inferior genetic stock, the dream of one day advancing the next step in human evolution through engineering homo-superior has always had its champions. The difference until lately has been that the Frankensteinian visionaries lacked biotechnological skills and the public's will to enable "large-scale genetic and neurological engineering of ourselves."[199] Today, that has changed: The technology has arrived, and the will to birth a new form of man has at least entered its fledgling state, if not secretly advanced altogether. Even the recent Olympics underscored this science, pointing out the specter of clandestinely modified humans. Chinese swimmer Ye Shiwen's superhuman-like performance led John Leonard, the director of the World Swimming Coaches Association, to describe the sixteen-year-old's world-record-setting feat as "suspicious," "disturbing," and "unbelievable." Authorities who tested Ye Shiwen for drug abuse also should have checked to see "if there is something unusual going on in terms of genetic manipulation," he said.[200] Dr. Ted Friedmann, chair of the genetics panel of the World Anti-Doping Agency, agreed, saying he "would not be surprised at all" if genetic enhancements were now being secretly used on humans.[201]

In other words, Aldous Huxley's dystopian *Brave New World* is already slipping in under most of the public's radar. Human prenatal diagnosis, screening fetal genomes, and designer children were just the first cracks in the dam holding back incremental changes due the human genetic reservoir this century, and experts are now admitting it. This includes the Academy of Medical Sciences mentioned earlier, the same astute science body that more recently joined the British Academy, the Royal Academy of Engineering, and the Royal Society to produce a narrower joint study in 2012 titled, "Human Enhancement and the Future of Work," wherein they documented the alarming trend aimed at augmenting humans both cognitively and physically. In this new study, the collaborative team characterized serious concerns over the burgeoning "hybrid age" as having already started and in which the arrival of a new form of man is upon the horizon. What new breeds of hominid do they foresee? An example from page 26 of their work highlights how people could be engineered to have *serpentine qualities*:

> Participants discussed how these kinds of techniques may in the future aid research into the extension of the range of human vision to include additional wavelengths. Examples exist in animals, such as snakes that can detect infrared wavelengths, which might provide a source of research for developing approaches that can be used in humans. Potential applications could be envisaged in the military, but also in other employment, from night watchmen, safety inspectors, gamekeepers, etc, including the possibility of enhanced vision at night.[202]

To assure tomorrow's "snake people" not only see in the dark but are appropriately plugged into the end-times grid they will serve, the looming reptilian-humans will also have Borg-like "physical and digital enhancements such as cybernetic implants and advanced machine-interfacing technologies," according to another study by the Academy of Medical Sciences.[203]

Whenever these authors speak on the subject of transhumanism and the looming "human enhancement" era, people are surprised to learn the many ways in which the United States government has committed taxpayer money to institutions such as the Case Law School (Cleveland, Ohio) for developing the actual guidelines that will be used for setting government and public policy around the next step in human evolution through genetic alteration. Maxwell Mehlman, professor of bioethics at the Case School of Medicine, received nearly a million dollars not long ago to lead a team of law professors, physicians, and bioethicists over a two-year project "to develop standards for tests on human subjects in research that involves the use of genetic technologies to enhance 'normal' individuals."[204] Following the initial study, Mehlman began traveling the United States offering two university lectures: "Directed Evolution: Public Policy and Human Enhancement" and "Transhumanism and the Future of Democracy." These talks are designed to inform and persuade college students about the need for society to comprehend how emerging fields of science have already set in motion what some are calling "the Hybrid Age," a time when what it means to be human will be forever changed.

It's revealing that many of these technocrats admit being influenced by the works of men like Friedrich Nietzsche (from whom the phrase "God is dead" derives) and Goethe, the author of *Faust*. Nietzsche was the originator of the *Übermensch* or "Overman" that Adolf Hitler dreamed of engineering, and the "entity" that man, according to Nietzsche, will eventually evolve into. Like the ancient Watchers before them, transhumanists dream of giving life to Nietzsche's Übermensch by remanufacturing men with animals, plants, and other synthetic life forms through, among other things, the use of recombinant DNA technology, germline engineering, and transgenics, in which the genetic structure of one species is altered by the transfer of genes from another. While president of the United States, George W. Bush once called for legislation to "prohibit…creating human-animal hybrids, and buying, selling, or patenting human embryos,"[205] the prospect of animalized humans "is a subject of serious discussion in certain scientific circles," writes senior counsel for the Alliance Defense Fund, Joseph Infranco. "We are well beyond the science fiction of H. G. Wells' tormented hybrids in the *Island of*

Doctor Moreau; we are in a time where scientists are seriously contemplating the creation of human-animal hybrids."[206] The former chairman of the President's Council on Bioethics, Leon Kass, may have said it best in the introduction to his book, *Life, Liberty and the Defense of Dignity: The Challenges of Bioethics*:

> Human nature itself lies on the operating table, ready for alteration, for eugenic and psychic "enhancement," for wholesale redesign. In leading laboratories, academic and industrial, new creators are confidently amassing their powers and quietly honing their skills, while on the street their evangelists [transhumanists] are zealously prophesying a posthuman future. For anyone who cares about preserving our humanity, the time has come for paying attention.[207]

But Are "They" Involved with "Them"?

Based on facts detailed above, we started this chapter saying the question is not whether humans were, can be, or are being hybridized, but whether alien/demon agencies are involved in the process. Today, what some call "alien abduction," in which a breeding program allegedly exists resulting in alien/human hybrids, seems but a contemporary retelling of similar DNA harvesting and genetic manipulation by those mysterious beings called "Watchers" whose genetic modification activities we have discussed.

In his book, *Confrontations—A Scientist's Search for Alien Contact*, highly regarded UFO researcher, Dr. Jacques F. Vallée, once argued: "Contact with [aliens is] only a modern extension of the age-old tradition of contact with nonhuman consciousness in the form of angels, demons, elves, and sylphs."[208] Later, Vallée more closely identified the operative power behind these "aliens" as equivalent to the fallen Watcher angels of the Days of Noah:

> Are these races only semi-human, so that in order to maintain contact with us, they need crossbreeding with men and women

of our planet? Is this the origin of the many tales and legends where genetics plays a great role: the symbolism of the Virgin in occultism and religion, the fairy tales involving human midwives and changelings, the sexual overtones of the flying saucer reports, the biblical stories of intermarriage between the Lord's angels, and terrestrial women, whose offspring were giants?[209]

Another highly respected and often-quoted UFO researcher, John Keel, echoed the same when he stated in *Operation Trojan Horse*:

Demonology is not just another crackpot-ology. It is the ancient and scholarly study of the monsters and demons who have seemingly coexisted with man throughout history.... The manifestations and occurrences described in this imposing literature are similar, if not entirely identical, to the UFO phenomenon itself. Victims of demonomania [possession] suffer the very same medical and emotional symptoms as the UFO contactees.... The Devil and his demons can, according to the literature, manifest themselves in almost any form and can physically imitate anything from angels to horrifying monsters with glowing eyes. Strange objects and entities materialize and dematerialize in these stories, just as the UFOs and their splendid occupants appear and disappear, walk through walls, and perform other supernatural feats.[210]

Associate professor of psychology Elizabeth L. Hillstrom was even more inflexible on comparisons between "alien" experiences and historical demonic activity, quoting in her book *Testing the Spirits* an impressive list of scholars from various disciplines who concluded that similarities between ETs and demons is unlikely coincidental. Hillstrom cites authorities of the first rank including Pierre Guerin, a scientist associated with the French National Council for Scientific Research, who believes, "The modern UFOnauts and the demons of past days are probably identical,"[211] and veteran researcher John Keel, who reckons, "The UFO manifestations seem to be, by and large, merely minor variations of the age-old demonological phenomenon."[212] Harvard psychiatrist and Pulitzer Prize-winner John Mack risked his career when he announced that the abduction phenomenon is very much real albeit an assault of a quasi-spiritual nature. The following is a chilling excerpt from Mack's *Passport to the Cosmos*:

> Some abductees feel that certain beings seem to want to take their souls from them. Greg told me that the terror of his encounters with certain reptilian beings was so intense that he feared being separated from his soul. "If I were to be separated from my soul," he said, "I would not have any sense of being. I think all my consciousness would go. I would cease to exist. That would be the worst thing anyone could do to me."[213]

He records page after page of transparently demonic phenomenon. Another victim described her horror: "I knew instinctively that whatever that thing was next to me wanted to enter me. It was just waiting to enter me."[214] Of course, this screams demon possession, but, against the evidence, Mack's naturalistic worldview steered him toward the extraterrestrial hypothesis. In contrast, Vallée connects the dots: "The 'medical examination' to which abductees are said to be subjected, often accompanied by sadistic sexual manipulation, is reminiscent of the medieval tales of encounters with demons."[215] With these sorts of characterizations coming from the secular scholars, it should be no surprise that we also connect UFO/ET phenomenon with demonic activity.

Incubi, Succubi, Daemons, and Elementals

In contrast to the "demons" of later Judeo-Christian belief, French UFO researcher, Aimé Michel (1919–1992), preferred the *daemons* of earlier Greek antiquity as the culprits of UFO and ET activity. The difference between what most people today think of as a demon (an incorporeal, malicious spirit that can seduce, vex, or possess a human) and the dae-mons of ancient Greek Hellenistic religion and philosophy is that dae-mons were corporeal (though often invisible and constituted of material unlike human or animal genetics) and could be good (*eudoaemons*) or evil (*cacodaemons*). *Eudoaemons* (also called *agathodaemons*) were some-times associated with benevolent angels, the ghosts of dead heroes, or supernatural beings who existed between mortals and gods (as in the teachings of the priestess Diotima to Socrates in Plato's *Symposium*), while *cacodaemons* were spirits of evil or malevolence who could afflict humans with mental, physical, and spiritual ailments. (In psychology, cacodemonia or *cacodemomania* is the pathological belief in which the patient is convinced he/she is inhabited, or possessed, by a wicked entity or evil spirit.) This delineation, and its potential spiritual and physical ramifications on humans, was reflected in the works of Italian Franciscan theologian, exorcist and advisor to the Supreme Sacred Congregation of the Roman and Universal Inquisition in Rome, Ludovico Maria Sinistrari (1622–1701). Sinistrari, who was regarded as an expert on sexual sins, wrote extensively of individuals accused of amorous relations with demons. His work, *De daemonialitate, et incubis et succubis*, refer-enced by Yeats, may be considered today among the earliest accounts of what could otherwise be called "alien abduction" resulting in hybrid offspring because the *incubi* and *succubi* of Sinistrari's opinion were nei-ther evil spirits nor fallen angels, but corporeal beings "created midway between humans and angels."[216] Sinistrari found that monks and nuns were of particular interest to the incubi/succubi, presumably due to pent-up sexual frustrations resulting from celibacy oaths that made them easier targets (which makes one wonder what the venerated Saint Cecilia really meant when she said to Valerian, "There is a secret, Valerian, I wish to tell you. I have as a lover an angel of God who jealously guards my body"[217]). Physical evidence, including semen, left on site following intercourse with the phantoms was often copious, negating the possi-bility in at least some cases that the event was psychological. One such incident between a sleeping nun and an incubus in the form of a spectral "young man" had multiple eyewitnesses and was recorded by Sinistrari in his work, *Demoniality*. The Catholic Father writes:

In a Monastery (I mention neither its name nor that of the town where it lies, so as not to recall to memory a past scandal), there was a Nun, who, about trifles usual with women and especially with nuns, had quarrelled with one of her mates who occupied a cell adjoining to hers. Quick at observing all the doings of her enemy, this neighbour noticed, several days in succession, that instead of walking with her companions in the garden after dinner she retired to her cell, where she locked herself in. Anxious to know what she could be doing there all that time, the inquisitive Nun betook herself also to her cell. Soon she heard a sound, as of two voices conversing in subdued tones, which she could easily do, since the two cells were divided but by a slight partition. [There she heard] a peculiar friction, the cracking of a bed, groans and sighs, her curiosity was raised to the highest pitch, and she redoubled her attention in order to ascertain who was in the cell. But having, three times running, seen no other nun come out but her rival, she suspected that a man had been secretly introduced and was kept hidden there. She went and reported the thing to the Abbess, who, after holding counsel with discreet persons, resolved upon hearing the sounds and observing the indications that had been denounced her, so as to avoid any precipitate or inconsiderate act. In consequence, the Abbess and her confidents repaired to the cell of the spy, and heard the voices and other noises that had been described. An inquiry was set on foot to make sure whether any of the Nuns could be shut in with the other one; and the result being in the negative, the Abbess and her attendants went to the door of the closed cell, and knocked repeatedly, but to no purpose: the Nun neither answered, nor opened. The Abbess threatened to have the door broken in, and even ordered a convert to force it with a crow-bar. The Nun then opened her door: a search was made and no one found. Being asked with whom she had been talking, and the why and wherefore of the bed cracking, of the sighs, etc., she denied everything.

But, matters going on just the same as before, the rival Nun, become more attentive and more inquisitive than ever, contrived to bore a hole through the partition, so as to be able to see what was going on inside the cell; and what should she see but an elegant youth lying with the Nun, and the sight of whom she took care to let the others enjoy by the same means. The charge was soon brought before the bishop: the guilty Nun endeavoured still to deny all; but, threatened with torture, she confessed having had an intimacy with an Incubus.[218]

These entities were associated with the forest sylvans and fauns by Augustine in his classic, *De Civiatate Dei* ("City of God"):

There is, too, a very general rumor, which many have verified by their own experience, or which trustworthy persons who have heard the experience of others corroborate, that sylvans and fauns, who are commonly called "incubi," had often made wicked assaults upon women, and satisfied their lust upon them; and that certain devils, called Duses by the Gauls, are constantly attempting and effecting this impurity is so generally affirmed, that it were impudent to deny it.[219]

These devils usually appeared at night as either a seductive demon in a male human form (*incubi*, from the Latin *incubo*, "to lie upon") having phantasmagoric intercourse with women, or elsewhere as a sensual female presence (*succubi*) who collected semen from men through dream-state copulation. Some believe these entities are one and the same. That is, the same spirit may appear as a female in one instance to collect male seed, then reappear elsewhere as a male to transfer the semen into a womb. The etymology (the study of the history of words, their origin, form, and meaning) of the word "nightmare" actually derives from the Old English *maere* for a "goblin" or "incubus" and variously referred to an evil female spirit that afflicted sleepers with a feeling of suffocation and bad dreams and/or elsewhere as a seductress. While religious credo involving incubi and succubi was widespread in mythological and legendary traditions, Sinistrari defied established church theology on the topic when he wrote: "Subject to correction by our Holy Mother Church, and as a mere expression of private opinion, I say that the Incubus, when having intercourse with women, begets the human foetus *from his own seed*" (emphasis added).[220] Ironically, Sinistrari considered the worst part of this sinful intercourse to be that the incubus—a morally superior being in his mind (as currently suggested by modern Catholic theologians regarding ET, discussed elsewhere in this book)—had lowered itself by taking up with a human! "The incubus, (or succuba) however, does, he holds, commit a very great sin considering that we belong to an inferior species," notes twentieth-century writer William Butler Yeats from Sinistrari's own writings.[221] In this sense, Sinistrari's interpretation of the incubi and succubi is similar to the alien abductors of modern tradition and the daemons of Hellenistic Greek religion. They also reflect the beliefs of the alchemists who preceded Sinistrari, especially German-Swiss occultist Paracelsus, who believed in the Aristotelian concept of four elements (earth, fire, water, and air),[222] as well as the three metaphysical substances—mercury, sulfur, and salt—the finest of which were used by the entities to constitute the more majestic "bodies" of those elemental beings. Elementals are referred to by various names. In the English-speaking tradition, these include fairies, elves, devas, brownies, leprechauns, gnomes, sprites, pixies, banshees, goblins, dryads, mermaids, trolls, dragons, griffins, and numerous others. An early modern reference of elementals appears in the sixteenth-century alchemical works of Paracelsus. His works grouped

the elementals into four Aristotelian elements: 1) gnome, earth elemental; 2) undines (also known as nymph), water elemental; 3) sylph,
air elemental (also known as wind elemental); and 4) salamander, fire
elemental. The earliest known reference of the term "sylph" is from
the works of Paracelsus. He cautioned that it is harmful to attempt to
contact these beings, but offered a rationale in his work, *Why These
Beings Appear to Us*:

> Everything God creates manifests itself to Man sooner or later.
> Sometimes God confronts him with the devil and the spirits
> in order to convince him of their existence. From the top of
> Heaven, He also sends the angels, His servants. Thus these
> beings appear to us, not in order to stay among us or become
> allied to us, but in order for us to become able to understand
> them. These apparitions are scarce, to tell the truth. But why
> should it be otherwise? Is it not enough for one of us to see an
> Angel, in order for all of us to believe in the other Angels?[223]

A book that popularized this concept in the late sixteenth century
was the work *Le Comte de Gabalis, ou entretiens sur les sciences secrete*
("Count Gabalis, or Secret Talks on Science"), which helped the revival
of the third-century mystical philosophy based on the teachings of Plato
and earlier Platonists known as Neoplatonism. It explained:

> The immense space which lies between Earth and Heaven has
> inhabitants far nobler than the birds and insects. These vast seas
> have far other hosts than those of the dolphins and whales; the
> depths of the earth are not for moles alone; and the Element of
> Fire, nobler than the other three, was not created to remain use-
> less and empty. The air is full of an innumerable multitude of
> Peoples, whose faces are human, seemingly rather haughty, yet
> in reality tractable, great lovers of the sciences, cunning, obliging
> to the Sages, and enemies of fools and the ignorant.[224]

The incubus in Henry Fuseli's famous 1781 oil painting *The Nightmare*

"According to Count Gabalis," Robert Pearson Flaherty explains, "these elementals were—like Sinistrari's incubi and the ETs of current lore—corporeal and capable of begetting children with humans."[225] This occult concept holds potential for deep deception and future malevolence, as, according to the doctrine, it was "the original intent of the Supreme God that humans should join in marriage with the elemental races rather than with each other, and the 'fall of man' occurred when Adam and Eve conceived children with each other rather than with elemental beings. Unlike humans, elemental beings had mortal souls; hence, they had but one hope of immortality—intermarriage with humans."[226] Flaherty compares this to modern ET abduction stories and the messages received by those who are part of the "alien" breeding program:

Through hybridization with humans, ETs of current lore do not seek immortality but rather to avoid extinction. Historian of religions Christopher Partridge describes how the concept of malevolent ETs is rooted in Christian demonology (belief in evil spirits). Here, "ET religion" is used to refer to the positive valorization of ETs, *who are portrayed not as fallen angels and scheming demons, but as our saviors, creators, and (in the hybridization myth) partners in continued evolution and survival.*[227] (emphasis added)

Close Encounters of the Skinwalking, Shapeshifting, Demonic Werewolf Kind

The history of elemental beings including incubi and succubi or "alien-demons" by any other name is often closely associated with a variety of shapeshifting monsters and "cryptids" (from the Greek "κρύπτω" [*krypto*] meaning "hide"), whose existence is difficult to prove by means of their ability to apparently move in and out of Earth's dimension or man's visible spectrum—the human range of sight. Examples of these would include the Yeti in the Himalayas, the famous Bigfoot or Sasquatch of mainly the Pacific Northwest region of North America and Canada, and the Loch Ness Monster of Scotland. Hoaxes aside, literally tens of thousands of people throughout history and around the world (including reputable individuals such as clergy, professionals, military, law enforcement personnel, and even anthropologists) have seen, found biological samples of such in hair and footprint evidence, and even filmed and recorded the creatures' unidentifiable language vocalizations, but have up until now failed to capture a single physical specimen. Witness testimonies often include reports of fantastic sizes—from enormous dragons in the sea to giant bipeds ranging in height from eight to twelve feet, with footprints up to twenty-four inches. And then there are the phenomena frequently connected with the appearance of cryptids that are typical of occult activity—a retching or sulfuric odor, mysterious rapping on walls and windows, shadows and ghostly lights inside or outside homes, disembodied voices, the levitation or disappearance of furniture and other household items, etc.

Possibly the earliest account of a Bigfoot sighting in the US was published over 125 years ago in a historical pamphlet that told of frontiersmen coming across a "wild man" in the Siskiyou Mountains of Northern California. "The thing was of gigantic size—about seven feet tall—with a bulldog head, short ears, and long hair; it was also furnished with a beard, and was free from hair on such parts of its body as is common among men."[228] Another barely known confrontation with a large, hairy biped was actually reported by President Theodore Roosevelt, an avid outdoorsman. Noah Hutchings writes of this event: "The story appeared in *The Wilderness Hunter* published in 1893. The account given by Roosevelt related that some kind of a wild beast had killed a man and had eaten half his body in a mountain range between the Salmon and Windom rivers. The following year, two hunters were camping in the same area when they became aware that they were being watched by a strange creature walking on two legs. The next day, the hunters separated. One of the hunters arrived at camp to find the other hunter dead with his neck broken and severe wounds to the throat area. In the article, Mr. Roosevelt reported his belief that the hunter was killed by 'something either half-human or half-devil, some great goblin-beast.'"[229] There are even reports of apelike creatures shot and killed followed by similar creatures coming to retrieve the corpse. One such story tells of a Bigfoot being put down and afterwards, similar large, hairy beings coming out of the woods to recover the body. The same creatures returned again later to attack the cabin of those miners who had killed the beast. An account of this event states:

> At night the apes counterattacked, opening the assault by knocking a heavy strip of wood out from between two logs of the miners' cabin. After that there were assorted poundings on the walls, door, and roof, but the building was built to withstand heavy

mountain snows and the apes failed to break in…. There was… the sound of rocks hitting the roof and rolling off, and [the miners] did brace the heavy door from the inside.

They heard creatures thumping around on top of the cabin as well as battering the walls, and they fired shots through the walls and roof without driving them away. The noise went on from shortly after dark till near dawn…. The cabin had no windows and of course no one opened the door, so in fact the men inside did not see what was causing the commotion outside.

Nor could Mr. Beck say for sure…that there were more than two creatures outside. There were [at least] that many because there had been one on the roof and one pounding the wall simultaneously. However many there were, it was enough for the miners, who packed up and abandoned their mine the next day.[230]

One of the more disturbing and better documented cases concerning large nonhuman primates occurred on October 25, 1973, near Greensburg, Pennsylvania, when a young farmer named Stephen Pulaski and more than a dozen others observed a bright red ball of light accompanied by large humanoids. The twenty-two-year-old farmer with two younger boys watched from a hilltop as a bright, "dome shaped" object, making a "sound like a lawn mower," settled over a field. He guessed it measured about one hundred fifty feet in diameter. Suddenly, Pulaski caught sight of two large creatures, which at first he thought were bears—one about seven feet tall and the other taller than eight feet—walking by a fence line. He was able to approximate their size fairly accurately, because they were silhouetted against the railing boards. They were covered with long, dark hair and had arms that hung down like a gorilla's. The beings were making a sound like babies whimpering, and a terrible odor like burning rubber was wafting up the hill from them. The entities saw Pulaski and the two young men and started toward them. As the younger boys ran toward the farmhouse, the twenty-two-year-old fired a warning shot over the creatures' heads with his hunting rifle. When they continued forward, he shot three more times, this time directly at the larger of the two. The big, hairy biped acted like it was hit, raised its right hand, and the dome-shaped object went silent, disappearing instantaneously, but being replaced by a glowing area on the ground. At that, the beings turned and headed into the woods. A few minutes later, a state trooper arrived to investigate the shooting. He went with the farmer down onto the field to within two hundred yards of the incident area. The officer later reported that the ground was still glowing when they got there. Trees began breaking in the forest, and the men thought something large was moving towards them from the woods. It abruptly stopped, then, thirty minutes later, it started moving again. A large, brown figure could be seen coming their direction, so they jumped into the patrol car and sped to safety.

Early the next morning, members of the Westmoreland County UFO Study Group arrived at the farm to begin an investigation. They noted that Pulaski's dog seemed to be tracking something they couldn't make out in the woods. As they were talking with the young farmer and his father, Pulaski inexplicably began behaving as if he were demon possessed—convulsing, growling, and flailing about. His own dog ran at him, and he attacked it. At the same moment, two of the investigators started feeling lightheaded and were having difficulty breathing. Pulaski suddenly knocked his father down as he fainted onto the ground, face first into manure. When he snapped out of it a few moments later, he started growling like an animal and warned, "Get away from me. It's here. Get back." A sulfuric aroma filled the air as Pulaski reported seeing a figure cloaked in all black garbs saying something to him about a man "who is coming to save the world." Pulaski was subsequently evaluated physically and psychologically and found to be of sound mind and truthful. Numerous witnesses at various phases of the incident also testified that the event actually happened as reported.

The Pulaski farm is one example of thousands of comparable events wherein cryptids have appeared accompanied by spiritualistic and demonological characteristics. In another account, both a giant and small creature teamed up to torture a young woman. This was not only captured by multiple eyewitnesses, but also was played out repeatedly in a prison cell before dumbfounded police officers, prison guards, medical staff, and dozens of reporters in the heart of Manila, capital city of the Philippines. In this case, physical evidence was even captured in the form of long, black hair from a beast that was never identified. At the center of the episode was one of America's most well-known ordained ministers, Dr. Lester Sumrall, who formed the LeSEA broadcast network.

In the early 1950s, Dr. Sumrall was in Manila building a church, which today is known as the Cathedral of Praise. On May 12, 1953, the *Daily Mirror* in Manila published a startling story under the headline, "Police Medic Explodes Biting Demons Yarn," in which a most unusual story unfolded of law enforcers and medical examiners being mystified by an inmate whose body continuously bore deep teeth marks. The frightened girl claimed that two beings were appearing and biting her. One of the devils was big and dark with long hair all over his head, chest, and arms. He had fangs like a dog and large, sharp eyes, and his feet were at least three times larger than normal. He was dressed in a black robe with what appeared to be a hood on the back. His voice was deep, with a tunnel-like echo. The second being was squatty, maybe thirty inches tall, and it was also dark, hairy, and deformed. As the witnesses watched, the girl's facial expressions would suddenly change, and she would begin glancing about, as if she was seeing something the others could not. (What she was seeing was dubbed "The Thing" by the press.) Then the girl would start screaming and struggling against an invisible force, before collapsing, half-conscious, into the arms of the prison staff member holding her. At that moment, there would be teeth marks wet with saliva marking her body. Dr. Mariano B. Lara, then chief medical examiner of the Manila Police Department and a university professor of pathology and legal medicine, was convinced of the genuineness of the possession and exorcism and provided his own description, recounted in this excerpt from the official medical report filed at the prison:

I find it difficult and near impossible to accept anything of a supernatural character.... Equipped with a magnifying lens and an unbelieving mind about this biting phenomena, I scrutinized carefully the exposed parts of her [Clarita Villanueva's] body, the arms, hands, and neck, to find out whether they had the biting impressions. I saw the reddish human-like bite marks on the arms.... At that very instant, this girl in a semi-trance loudly screamed repeatedly.... I saw, with my unbelieving eyes, the clear marks or impressions of human-like teeth from both the upper and lower jaws. It was a little moist in the area bitten on the dorsal aspect of the left hand, and the teeth impressions were mostly from the form of the front or incisor teeth. Seeing these with my unbelieving eyes, yet I could not understand nor explain how they were produced as her hand had all the time been held away from the reach of her mouth....

In full possession of her normal mind, I asked her (Clarita Villanueva) who was causing her to suffer from the bites. She answered that there are two who are alternately biting her; one big, black, hairy human-like fellow, very tall, with two sharp eyes, two sharp canine teeth, long beard like a Hindu, hairy extremities and chest, wearing a black garment, with a little whitish piece on the back resembling a hood. His feet are about three times the size of normal feet. The other fellow is a very small one about two or three feet tall allegedly also black, hairy and ugly.[231]

After first hearing the report on the radio then reading the newspaper story the next day, Dr. Sumrall, who believed the girl was demon possessed, grew convicted that the Lord wanted him to procure permission from prison authorities to pray for the prostitute's deliverance. Through his church architect, who was a friend of the mayor of Manila, he received the okay to visit with the chief medical advisor of the police department, Dr. Mariano Lara. While talking with the doctor inside the prison morgue, Lara acknowledged to Sumrall that something beyond his professional knowledge was happening and that he was actually afraid of "The Thing" after witnessing the bite marks appear before his own eyes. With Lara's approval, Sumrall was allowed to pray for the girl while observers watched. She was very resistant, cursing him in English (which she could not speak), screaming, and fighting every moment to get away. The first day of prayer failed to provide healing, and Sumrall believed he needed to fast and pray for another day. That evening, the newspaper published his picture on the front page, three columns wide, with the headline, "The Thing Defies Pastor."[232] The next day would be different. Following a spiritual battle reminiscent of an Old Testament prophet challenging the followers of Baal, and with repentance of her sins and acceptance of Jesus as Savior, the girl was delivered, yet, that was not the end of the story. Sumrall explains what happened next:

> As I was leaving I told Clarita that I was sure these devils would return. "After I am gone," I said, "they will come. Then you must demand them to leave without my being present. You must say, 'Go, in Jesus' name,' and they will obey." With this I left the compound.
>
> We asked the newsmen not to write about the morning's events, but they said they were obliged to. The story had run for two weeks and it must be concluded. Since the Methodist Church is the oldest Protestant denomination in the islands, they presumed I was a Methodist, and it was in the papers that way. They did not know how to write of such an experience; therefore, some of what they said was not correct. But I feel mostly responsible for this, as I gave them no interview and left the city to get away from publicity.
>
> The devils did return to attack Clarita, and a strange thing happened when she called on them to leave. *She was engaged in a mortal struggle and went into a coma, her fists clenched. The doctor pried her hands open and to his astonishment, there lay some long, black, coarse hair. Dr. Lara placed this hair in an envelope and put*

it in a guarded place. Under the microscope he found that the hair was not from any part of the human body. The doctor has no answer to this mystery—how an invisible being, presumably a devil, could have lost hair by a visible being pulling it out.[233] (emphasis added)

The notion of physical material like hair having been pulled from a wraithlike demon opens the fascinating proposal that ultraterrestrial beings (call them angels, demons, or aliens) can migrate back and forth between different realities and take forms that are both material and immaterial. This sounds crazy to the natural mind, yet the concept is biblical. The writer of Hebrews reminds us to "be not forgetful to entertain strangers: for thereby some have entertained angels unawares" (Hebrews 13:2), and when the disciples of Jesus saw His return from the grave, they "were terrified and affrighted, and supposed that they had seen a spirit." Jesus told them to touch Him and see that "a spirit hath not flesh and bones, as ye see me have" (Luke 24:37–39). Similarly, Abraham was visited by three angels in the plains of Mamre (Genesis 18:1–8). They appeared as men and walked, talked, sat, and ate. But the truth was they were not human at all, but spirit-beings from heaven, illustrating one of the most dynamic facts of Scripture: that otherdimensional life forms have power to assume tangible matter whenever it fits their cause. Does this explain how cryptids can be there one moment and gone the next, leaving man perplexed by their appearance and disappearance? Does this not remind of the Rephaim, which exist in the spirit world but could also have the ability to manifest on Earth as giant, hairy bipeds known in the Bible as Nephilim and perhaps today as Bigfoot?

Incidentally, hair from the Manila "Thing" is not the only example found.

In October 2012, a headline in the *UK's Mail Online* read: "Sasquatch in Siberia? Hair Found in Russian Cave 'Belonged to Unknown Mammal Closely Related to Man.'" The story claimed that DNA tests on suspected "Yeti hair" found in a Siberian cave during an international expedition in 2011 was of an unknown mammal closely related to man, but not a human. Nor did the hair belong to any known animal from the region such as a bear, wolf, or goat, the article said. Analysis was conducted in Russia and the US, which "agreed the hair came from a human-like creature which is not a Homo sapien yet is more closely related to man than a monkey."[234]

Then, on November 24, 2012, another press release was issued involving a team of experts in genetics, forensics, imaging, and pathology led by Dr. Melba S. Ketchum of Nacogdoches, Texas, and their five-year long DNA study (submitted for peer review), which claimed "the existence of a novel hominin hybrid species, commonly called 'Bigfoot' or 'Sasquatch,' living in North America." The DNA sequencing suggested that the legendary Sasquatch is actually "a hybrid cross of modern Homo sapiens with an unknown primate species." Dr. Ketchum reported that her team sequenced three complete Sasquatch nuclear genomes and determined the species is a human hybrid. "Our study…utilized next generation sequencing to obtain 3 whole nuclear genomes from purported Sasquatch samples," Ketchum said. "The genome sequencing shows that Sasquatch mtDNA is identical to modern Homo sapiens, but Sasquatch nuDNA is a novel, unknown hominin related to Homo sapiens and other primate species. Our data indicate that the North American Sasquatch is a hybrid species, the result of males of an unknown hominin species crossing with female Homo sapiens."[235]

Ketchum, a veterinarian whose professional experience includes twenty-seven years of research in genetics, including forensics, continued:

> The male progenitor that contributed the unknown sequence to this hybrid is unique as its DNA is more distantly removed from humans than other recently discovered hominins like the Denisovan individual. Sasquatch nuclear DNA is incredibly novel and not at all what we had expected. While it has human nuclear DNA within its genome, there are also distinctly non-human, non-archaic hominin, and non-ape sequences.

We describe it as a mosaic of human and novel non-human sequence. Further study is needed and is ongoing to better characterize and understand Sasquatch nuclear DNA.[236]

That Ketchum and her team's findings were reported before being peer reviewed is suspect and may turn out to be erroneous. On the other hand, if validated, it could be another baffling evidence fragment connected to that mysterious creature we call "Bigfoot" and "Sasquatch."

Another cryptid sometimes associated with Bigfoot, which was first reported in the 1980s on a quiet country road outside of Elkhorn, Wisconsin, is called "The Beast of Bray Road." A rash of sightings between the '80s and '90s prompted a local newspaper (*Walworth County Week*) to assign one of its reporters named Linda Godfrey to cover the story. Godfrey started out skeptical, but because of the sincerity of the eyewitnesses, became convinced of the creature's existence. In fact, she was so impressed with the consistency of the reports from disparate observers (whom the History Channel's TV series *MonsterQuest* subjected to lie detector tests in which the polygraph administrator could find no indication of falsehoods) that she wrote not only a series of articles for the newspaper but later a book, titled *Real Wolfmen: True Encounters in Modern America*. In her book, she claims that "the U.S. has been invaded by upright, canine creatures that look like traditional werewolves and act as if they own our woods, fields, and highways. Sightings from coast to coast dating back to the 1930s compel us to ask exactly what these beasts are, and what they want."[237] Her book presents a catalogue of investigative reports and first-person accounts of modern sightings of anomalous, upright canids. From Godfrey's witnesses, we learn of fleeting, as well as face-to-face, encounters with literal werewolves—canine beings that walk upright, eat food with their front paws, interact fearlessly with humans, and suddenly and mysteriously disappear. While Godfrey tries to separate her research from Hollywood depictions of shapeshifting humans played by actors like Michael Landon or Lon Chaney Jr., she is convinced there really are extremely large, fur-covered, anthropomorphic, wolf-like creatures that chase victims on their hind legs.

Eighteenth-century engraving of a werewolf

Werewolves, like other cryptids, are deeply connected in history not only with occultic lore but with the alien-similar fauns and incubi that sought and obtained coitus from women. In the ancient Bohemian Lexicon of Vacerad (AD 1202), the werewolf is *vilkodlak*, on whom the debauched woman sat and was impregnated with beastly seed.[238] Saint Patrick was said to have battled with werewolf soldiers and even to have transformed the Welsh king Vereticus into a wolf. (The strange belief that saints could turn people into such creatures was also held by Saint Thomas Aquinas, who wrote that angels could metamorphose the human form, saying, "All angels, good and bad have the power of transmutating our bodies."[239]) Long before the Catholic saints believed in such things, the god Apollo was worshiped in Lycia as Lykeios or

Lykos, the "wolf" god. The trance-induced utterances of his priest-esses known as Pythoness or Pythia prophesied in an unfamiliar voice thought to be that of Apollo himself. During the Pythian trance, the medium's personality often changed, becoming melancholic, defiant, or even animal-like, exhibiting a psychosis that may have been the original source of the werewolf myth, or *lycanthropy*, as the Pythia reacted to an encounter with Apollo/Lykeios—the wolf god. Pausanias, the sec-ond-century Greek traveler and geographer, agreed with the concept of Apollo as the original wolf man who, he said, derived his name from the pre-Dynastic Apu-At, an Egyptian god of war. But Virgil, one of Rome's greatest poets, held that "the first werewolf was Moeris, wife of the fate-goddess Moera, who taught him how to bring the dead back to life."[240] Romans of that era referred to the werewolf as *versipellis*, or the "turn-skin," reminiscent of later indigenous peoples of America who still believe in "skinwalkers," or humans with the supernatural ability to turn into a wolf or other animal.

According to local legend, a ranch located on approximately four hundred eighty acres southeast of Ballard, Utah, in the United States is (or at least once was) allegedly the site of substantial skinwalker activity. The farm is actually called "Skinwalker Ranch" by local Indians who believe it lies in "the path of the skinwalker," taking its name from the Native American legend. It was made famous during the '90s and early 2000s when claims about the ranch first appeared in the *Utah Deseret News* and later in the *Las Vegas Mercury* during a series of riveting articles by journalist George Knapp. Subsequently, a book titled *Hunt for the Skinwalker: Science Confronts the Unexplained at a Remote Ranch in Utah* described how the ranch was acquired by the now defunct National Institute for Discovery Science (NIDS), which had purchased the property to study "anecdotal sightings of UFOs, bigfoot-like creatures, crop circles, glowing orbs and poltergeist activity reported by its former owners."[241] A two-part article by Knapp for the *Las Vegas Mercury* was published November 21 and 29, 2002, titled, "Is a Utah Ranch the Strangest Place on Earth?" It told of frightening events that had left the owners of the ranch befuddled and broke—from bizarre, bullet-proof wolf-things to mutilated prize cattle and other instances in which animals and property simply disappeared or were obliterated over-night. As elsewhere, these events were accompanied by strong odors, ghostly rapping, strange lights, violent nightmares, and other paranor-mal phenomena. Besides the owners of the Skinwalker Ranch, other residents throughout the county made similar reports over the years. Junior Hicks, a retired local school teacher, catalogued more than four hundred anomalies in nearby communities before the year 2000. He and others said that, for as long as anyone could remember, this part of Utah had been the site of unexplained activity—from UFO sight-ings to Sasquatch manifestations. It was as if a gateway to the world of the beyond existed within this basin. Some of the Skinwalker Ranch descriptions seemed to indicate as much. For example, in one event repeated by Knapp, an investigator named Chad Deetken and the ranch owner saw a mysterious light:

> Both men watched intently as the light grew brighter. It was as if someone had opened a window or doorway. [The ranch owner] grabbed his night vision binoculars to get a better look but could hardly believe what he was seeing. The dull light began to resemble a bright portal, and at one end of the portal, a large, black humanoid figure seemed to be struggling to crawl through the tunnel of light. After a few minutes, the humanoid figure wriggled out of the light and took off into the darkness. As it did, the window of light snapped shut, as if someone had flicked the "off" switch.[242]

In 1996, Skinwalker Ranch was purchased by real-estate developer and aerospace entrepreneur Robert T. Bigelow, a wealthy Las Vegas busi-nessman who founded NIDS in 1995 to research and serve as a central clearinghouse for scientific investigations into various fringe science, paranormal topics, and ufology. Bigelow planned an intense but very private scientific study of events at the farm. He was joined by high-ranking military officials, including retired US Army Colonel John B. Alexander, who had worked to develop "Jedi" remote viewing and psychic experiments for the military as described in Jon Ronson's book, *The Men Who Stare At Goats*, former police detectives, and scientists including Eric W. Davis, who has worked for NASA. In the years before, Bigelow had donated 3.7 million dollars to the University of Nevada at Las Vegas "for the creation and continuation of a program that would attract to the university renowned experts on aspects of human consciousness."[243] Bigelow's Chair for the university program was parapsychologist Charles Tart, a man "famous for extended research on altered states of consciousness, near-death experiences and extrasensory perception."[244] But what Bigelow's team found at the Skinwalker Ranch was more than they could have hoped for, at least for a while, including "an invisible force moving through the ranch and through the animals."[245] On this, the *Las Vegas Mercury* reported in November of 2002: "One witness reported a path of displaced water in the canal, as if a large unseen animal was briskly moving through the water. There were distinct splashing noises, and there was a foul pungent odor that filled the air but nothing could be seen. A neighboring rancher reported the same phenomena two months later. The [ranch owners] say there were several instances where something invisible moved through their cattle, splitting the herd. Their neighbor reported the same thing."[246]

Yet of all the anomalous incidents at the ranch, there was one that took the prize. On the evening of March 12, 1997, barking dogs alerted the NIDS team that something strange was in a tree near the ranch house. The ranch owner grabbed a hunting rifle and jumped in his pickup, racing toward the tree. Two of the NIDS staffers followed in a second truck. Knapp tells what happened next:

Up in the tree branches, they could make out a huge set of yellowish, reptilian eyes. The head of this animal had to be three feet wide, they guessed. At the bottom of the tree was something else. Gorman described it as huge and hairy, with massively muscled front legs and a doglike head.

Gorman, who is a crack shot, fired at both figures from a distance of 40 yards. The creature on the ground seemed to vanish. The thing in the tree apparently fell to the ground because Gorman heard it as it landed heavily in the patches of snow below. All three men ran through the pasture and scrub brush, chasing what they thought was a wounded animal, but they never found the animal and saw no blood either. A professional tracker was brought in the next day to scour the area. Nothing.

But there was a physical clue left behind. At the bottom of the tree, they found and photographed a weird footprint, or rather, claw print. The print left in the snow was from something large. It had three digits with what they guessed were sharp claws on the end. Later analysis and comparison of the print led them to find a chilling similarity—the print from the ranch closely resembled that of a velociraptor, an extinct dinosaur made famous in the Jurassic Park films.[247]

Stories of anomalous cryptids moving in and out of man's reality, the opening of portals or spirit gateways such as reported at Skinwalker Ranch, and the idea that through these openings could come the sudden appearance of unknown intelligence was believed as fact in ancient times, a phenomenon we will continue to investigate in the next chapter.

6 | Fairies, Changelings, and the False Messiah from Magonia

"I believe there is a machinery of mass manipulation behind the UFO phenomenon; it aims at social and political goals by diverting attention from some human problems and providing a potential release for tensions caused by others. The (UFO) contactees are part of that machinery. They are helping to create a new form of belief: an expectation of actual contact among large parts of the public. In turn, this expectation makes millions of people hope for the imminent realization of that age-old dream: salvation from above, surrender to the greater power of some wise navigators of the cosmos. They may be from outer space [but] their methods are those of deception."—Dr. Jacques Vallée

Stories of anomalous cryptids moving in and out of man's reality such as described in the previous chapter were once considered fact in ancient times. Early people around the world viewed "them" as coexisting with man and having the capability of being seen whenever the netherworld beings willed it. This included the opening of portals or spirit gateways, such as reported at Skinwalker Ranch, and the idea that through these openings could come the sudden appearance of werewolves, ghosts, goblins, trolls, and those mythical beings of legend that have an even more interesting connection to modern UFO lore known as *fairies*. Fairy variety is considerable, and listing each type here is beyond the scope of our interest. However, some of them are virtually identical with ancient descriptions of demons, including a particular one called the *bogie* or "bogeyman" who haunts the dark and enjoys harming and frightening humans. These fairies appear very similar to traditional descriptions of "Bigfoot," with the same furry bodies, together with fiery red eyes. Other fairy classifications are practically indistinguishable from the flying witches of classical antiquity and the ancient Near East. Olaus Magnus, who was sent by Pope Paul III in 1546 as an authority to the Council of Trent and who later became canon of Saint Lambert in Liége, Belgium, is best remembered as the author of the classic 1555 *Historia de Gentibus Septentrionalibus* ("History of the Northern Peoples"), which chronicled the folklore and history of Europe. In it, he provided engravings of fairy-demons carrying women away for intercourse. Before him, in 1489, the legal scholar Ulrich Molitor did the same, providing etched plates in his Latin tract on sorcerous women (*De laniis et phitonicis mulieribus*) depicting demons abducting women for coitus. Besides such similarities to current UFO and alien-abduction activity, these fairies often left "the devil's mark"—a permanent spot or scar believed to have been made by the demon (or the devil himself) raking his claw across the flesh or by the red-hot kiss of the devil licking the individual. This happened at night, at the conclusion of the nocturnal abduction episode. This mark was also known as "fairy bruising" and as the "witche's teat" and appeared overnight as a raised bump or scoop mark in the flesh, often on the most secret parts of the body. In modern times, alien abductees often bear the same marks as those described in olden days as the devil's mark—cuts or scoops on the backs of the legs, arms, and neck; purplish, circular spots around the abdomen and genitals; and in patterns consistent with those from medieval times ascribed to witches, incubi, and fairies. Thus, the actual mythology of these creatures and the "little people" who traveled with them between our reality and fairyland or "Elfland" portrays an image quite different than that of cutesy Tinker Bell fluttering overhead at Disneyland! Fairy legend includes the identical alien-sounding roles of abduction, inducing some type of paralysis in which the victim can see what is happening but is powerless to intervene (the *Oxford Dictionary of Celtic Mythology* says the colloquial English usage of "stroke" for cerebral hemorrhage derives from its relationship with "paralysis" and originated with the "fairy-stroke" or "elf-stroke" of legend[248]); levitating people and flying them away to "fairyland" (or what some today call "Magonia"); and traveling in UFO-like discs or circular globes of light.

In the 1960s, legendary French UFO researcher Dr. Jacques Vallée began to explore these commonalities between UFOs, alien abduction, and fabled figures like fairies in his book, *Passport to Magonia: From Folklore to Flying Saucers*. (This work by Vallée is no longer available, but is provided free in searchable pdf format with the purchase of this book from Defender Publishing). Out of this research, he developed a "multidimensional visitation hypothesis" beyond spacetime that would allow for undetected coexistence between humans and nonhuman beings, which have been seen and detected for thousands of years and seem to present themselves in a way that suggests either: 1) they are mutating their persona to match our current belief systems (i.e., they once were called the little people of elfin lore who stole and replaced children with "changelings," while today they are the little greys of ET abduction who steal and replace embryos with hybrid babies); or 2) they are doing what they have always done and *we* are the ones interpreting their presence in ways that accommodate our current understanding of science and religion. For Vallée, the comparisons between the ancient fairy stories and modern alien-abduction phenomena were too similar to be coincidence. He cites the work of Walter Yeeling Evans-Wentz (1878–1965), an anthropologist and expert on "fairy-faith" in Celtic countries (whose 1911 book/dissertation on the subject is also free with the data packet that comes with this book from the publisher), as powerful evidence for consistency of the phenomena throughout history.

Evans-Wentz, also a theosophist, is famous for compiling and editing the sacred texts on Tibetan Buddhism that were published by Oxford University Press in the early twentieth century. Consequently, he is widely credited with pioneering western Buddhism associated with astrobiologist Chris Impey. However, before his travels to Sri Lanka and India, Evans-Wentz wrote his doctoral thesis at Oxford University on the Celtic belief in fairies. He approached the subject as a scholar examining the history and folklore of the British Isles through the lens of anthropology and psychology. It is perhaps one of the most thorough and scholarly endeavors ever conducted on the subject.

As the nineteenth century rolled over into the twentieth, the industrial revolution was driving the populations toward the cities, and the population was booming. Evans-Wentz did extensive ethnographic fieldwork interviewing folks in Ireland, Wales, Scotland, Brittany, and the Isle of Man. Encounters with fairies were plentiful enough to be commonplace in the early nineteenth century, but as modernity approached, they waned. Today, fairies are largely forgotten, relegated to old wives' tales and legend, albeit the phenomenon still exists.

Jacques Vallée is convinced that the fairies were not only real, but that they currently endure under the modern guise of extraterrestrials. What Evans-Wentz was able to capture was the time of transition when the entities plagued by the encroachment of modernity transformed themselves. Through his field work, Evans-Wentz noted that nearly all of the older folks had witnessed fairies or believed in them. It transcended legend as a commonly accepted fact. However, the next generation, influenced by the industrial zeitgeist, lacked fairy belief. John Bruno Hare, founder of the Sacred-Text.com Internet archive, surmised, "We come away from this study with a multi-dimensional view of the fairies, who, much like the grey aliens of UFO belief, inhabit a narrative which seems too consistent to be the product of insanity, yet too bizarre for conventional explanation."[249] This suggests a line of congruence between the accounts of fairies and that of today's so-called extraterrestrials. Vallée writes:

> We have now examined several stories of abductions and attempts at kidnappings by the occupants of flying saucers.

These episodes are an integral part of the total UFO problem and cannot be solved separately. Historical evidence, gathered by Wentz, moreover, once more points in the same direction.

> This sort of belief in fairies being able to *take* people was very common and exists yet in a good many parts of West Ireland.... The Good People are often seen there (pointing to Knoch Magh) in great crowds playing hurley and ball. And one often sees among them the young men and women and children who have been *taken* (emphasis in original).

Not only are people taken, but—as in flying saucer stories—they are sometimes carried to faraway spots by aerial means. Such a story is told by the Prophet Ezekiel, of course, and by other religious writers. But an ordinary Irishman, John Campbell, also told Wentz:

> A man whom I have seen, Roderick Mac Neil, was lifted by the hosts and left three miles from where he was taken up. The hosts went at about midnight.

Rev. Kirk gives a few stories of similar extraordinary kidnappings, but the most fantastic legend of all is that attached to Kirk himself: the good reverend is commonly believed to have been taken by the fairies.

> Mrs. J. MacGregor who keeps the key to the old churchyard where there is a tomb to Kirk, though many say there is nothing in it but a coffin filled with stones, told me Kirk was taken into the Fairy Knoll, which she pointed to just across a little valley in front of us, and is there yet, for the hill is full of caverns and in them the

"good people" have their homes. And she added that Kirk appeared to a relative of his after he was taken.

Wentz, who reports this interesting story, made further inquiries regarding the circumstances of Kirk's death. He went to see the successor to Kirk in Abcrfoyle, Rev. Taylor, who clarified the story:

> At the time of his disappearance people said he was taken because the fairies were displeased with him for disclosing their secrets in so public a manner as he did.[250]

Some UFO researchers go so far as to call the Reverend Robert Kirk "the first genuine martyr of the exo-politics movement."[251] His seminal *The Secret Commonwealth of Elves, Fauns and Fairies* provides a wealth of parallels to modern ufological research (and is also included in the free data packet). Was Kirk spirited away to the ever-enigmatic place called Magonia?

Vallée documented that:

> The physical nature of Magonia, as it appears in such tales, is quite enigmatic. Sometimes, it is a remote country, an invisible island, some faraway place one can reach only by a long journey. Indeed, in some tales, it is a celestial country.... This parallels the belief in the extraterrestrial origin of UFO's so popular today. A second—and equally widespread—theory, is that Elfland constitutes a sort of parallel universe, which coexists with our own. It is made visible and tangible only to selected people, and the "doors" that lead through it are tangential points, known only to the elves. This is somewhat analogous to the theory, sometimes found in the UFO literature, concerning what some authors like to call the "fourth dimension"—although, of course, this expression makes much less physical sense than does the theory of a parallel Elfland. (It does sound more scientific, however!)[252]

Vallée's argument is persuasive, given the history of demonic entities and their deceitful record of assuming any appearance that gains them acceptance into society. Recall the creatures in the film *They Live* and their ability to appear quite human. According to 2 Corinthians 11:14, even Satan, himself, can manifest as "an angel of light"! Vallée also notes that this deception on the part of the modern alien-fairies seems to be for the purpose of taking and replacing babies or smaller children with "changelings."

In alien abduction, many women report the removal of their fetus, followed later by introduction to (supposedly) the post-gestational baby. In fairy lore, the child is removed and replaced with a "changeling," a human-looking copy—especially of Western European folklore and folk religion. Numerous theories were developed between the thirteenth and fifteenth centuries to explain the reason for this abduction and replacement of children, including that the earthly child was a "tithe to hell" or tribute paid by the fairies to the devil every seven years. But Vallée updates this point, noting how the modern alien abduction phenomenon and the numerous accounts of abductions by the fairies focused "especially on pregnant women or young mothers, and they also are very active in stealing young children."

He says:

Sometimes, they substitute a false child for the real one, leaving in place of the real child…one of their children, a changeling: By the belief in changelings I mean a belief that fairies and other… beings are on the watch for young children…that they may, if they can find them unguarded, seize and carry them off, leaving in their place one of them.[253]

Vallée then points to a television series that capitalized on the aspect of UFO lore and the connection between modern and ancient abductions:

In the show, the human race has been infiltrated by extraterrestrials who differ from humans in small details only. This is not a new idea, as the belief in changelings shows. And there is a well-known passage in Martin Luther's Table Talk, in which he tells the Prince of Anhalt that he should throw into the Moldau a certain man who is, in his opinion, such a changeling—or killcrop, as they were called in Germany.

What was the purpose of such fairy abductions? The idea advanced by students of folk tales is again very close to a current theory about UFO's: that the purpose of such contact is a genetic one. According to Hartland:

> The motive assigned to fairies in northern stories is that of preserving and improving their race, on the one hand by carrying off human children to be brought up among the elves and to become united with them, and on the other hand by obtaining the milk and fostering care of human mothers for their own offspring.[254]

Baby switched with a changeling in *The Legend of St. Stephen* by Martino di Bartolomeo

Thus the idea of deceptive, nighttime creatures probing humans to gather genetic material for use in generating hybrid offspring agrees with Vallée and his contemporaries who, following extraordinary research, determined that whatever the modern alien abduction encounters represent, their goal is a repeat of ancient activity involving the collection of DNA for: 1) a *Breeding Program*, followed by; 2) a *Hybridization Program*, and finally; 3) an *Integration Program*, exactly what Watchers accomplished with Nephilim in ancient times.

But why would "aliens" be involved in such a program? Over the last few decades, secular alien abduction researchers like Budd Hopkins and Dr. David Jacobs have posited that the aliens are a dying race and must pass on their genetic material through hybrids to maintain their species. The Barney and Betty Hill case of September 19–20, 1961, marked the first widely publicized claim of such alien abduction and the beginning of the public's knowledge of the phenomenon. Yet the part of their story that is often overlooked is how ova was reportedly retrieved from Betty Hill's body and sperm from her husband, Barney, presumably for use in the hybridization scheme. In the years since, tens of thousands of people have slowly emerged from around the world to claim they, too, have been subject to a mysterious alien procedure in which human genetic material is harvested, including sperm and eggs for a reproductive agenda involving human hosts as surrogates and incubatoriums for fetuses wherein alien-human hybrids are produced. Entire communities have grown up around the idea that children now exist on Earth who are part human and part alien. Some claiming to be parents of hybrid children have their own websites, host conferences, and are building social networks across the web. These people include academics, physicists, psychologists, attorneys, actresses, and school teachers. Furthermore, according to researchers, it isn't just child hybrids that are now among us. Adult versions have spread throughout society, too. Budd Hopkins— who, before he died of cancer at the age of eighty in 2011, was considered the father of the alien-abduction movement—claimed that he and Dr. Jacobs especially were building new case files containing disturbing evidence related to specific entities and their integration within human society. He was planning to illustrate that the science-fiction/horror film *They Live* was not that far off after all, and that, from local bread factories to halls of Congress, alien-human hybrids are now firmly entrenched within Earth's cultures. Not long before he passed away, he wrote on the Journal of Abduction-Encounter Research (JAR) website:

> I investigated the reports of two women who described seeing an adult male hybrid wearing glasses. Each made a drawing of the hybrid, and the two drawings are amazingly similar. Both portray a strange-looking man, with sharp cheeks, wearing oddly-shaped glasses. The two women independently drew the same person. Some of these hybrid beings have been seen by more than three people at once and they are described by the witnesses the same way. As far as hybrids operating in the human world, we have many reports of them driving automobiles, shopping in stores, and behaving more or less naturally in other mundane places, but manifesting the kinds of powers aliens seem to have, i.e., the ability to control minds, and to communicate telepathically. The powers the gray aliens possess in the world can entail a complex series of repeated similar events, as if these adult hybrids do not really understand our world and our behavior but are trying to learn exactly how we act and what we say, all of which gives us an uneasy feeling of what their agenda might be leading to. There definitely is strong evidence that an infiltration into human society is taking place.[255]

Portals, Occult Magic, and the Collins Elite

Approximately six years ago, following the release of the book *Nephilim Stargates: The Year 2012 and the Return of the Watchers*, I (Horn) did a series of televised shows with J. R. Church and Gary Stearman for their *Prophecy in the News* broadcast, in which we discussed the idea of supernatural "portals, doorways, and openings." The concept is actually an ancient one—that gateways between our world and other dimensions exist or can be created through which those entities described above can pass. At one point, the programs with Church and Stearman (available online at YouTube.com[256]) focused on a theory I had briefly raised in *Nephilim Stargates* involving infamous occultist Aleister Crowley, Jet Propulsion Laboratory founder Jack Parsons, and Church of Scientology founder L. Ron Hubbard. A portion of that original material reads:

> As is referenced in chapter 2, in 1918 famed occultist Aleister Crowley attempted to create a dimensional vortex that would bridge the gap between the world of the seen and the unseen. The ritual was called the Amalantrah Working and according to Crowley became successful when a presence manifested itself through the rift. He called the being "Lam" and drew a portrait of it. The startling image, detailed almost ninety years ago, bears powerful similarity with "Alien Greys" of later pop culture.
>
> L. Ron Hubbard and Jack Parsons attempted to do this very thing by inviting the spirit of Babylon [their magical working was called *Babalon*] through a portal during a sex ritual. Their hope was to incarnate the whore of Babylon—a demon child or Gibborim. Parsons wrote that the ritual was successful and that at one point a brownish/yellow light came through the doorway. At the same moment he said he was struck by something invisible, and a candle was knocked out of his hand.
>
> It is interesting that following Crowley's magic portal (which produced the alien-looking LAM) and Hubbard and Parson's Babalon Working ritual, Crowley died in 1947—the same year as the Roswell crash and the same year Kenneth Arnold [a friend of Parsons] saw his flying saucers and sightings of "aliens" increased around the world. Was a portal indeed opened by these men's invitations?[257]

J. R. Church was very interested in the idea that men heavily involved in the occult with a strange UFO-alien twist and covertly connected with segments of this government's aerospace endeavors might actually have opened a portal allowing the increase into our world of powerful demonic influences.

Interview with Nick Redfern[258]

Several years after *Nephilim Stargates* was published and the *Prophecy in the News* shows aired, a book by Nick Redfern titled *Final Events* was released that repeated the basic outline of my work, but this time around reportedly had the backing of a secret government group commissioned to get to the bottom of the UFO phenomenon. The group ultimately concluded that the mysterious manifestations are demonic and directly connected to Parsons and company and their Babalon Workings. According to Redfern, they are called the "Collins Elite."

Initially skeptical of the *Final Events* outline and sensing somebody somewhere had simply repeated to Redfern what I had said and extrapolated it into a full-blown fabrication, I decided to talk to him on the phone and then conduct a follow-up Q & A over email. Below is a portion of the email exchange in which Redfern describes how he became aware of and eventually met with the Collins Elite:

HORN: Nick, tell me how you became aware of the Collins Elite.

REDFERN: In 2007, I had a lengthy conversation with an Anglican priest named Ray Boeche, who is also a former state-director for the Mutual UFO Network. Back in 1991, Ray met—in a Lincoln, Nebraska hotel—with two Department of Defense scientists who were working for a classified Pentagon project to try and contact what were termed Non-Human Entities, or, NHEs. The NHEs being the intelligences behind the UFO phenomenon. The idea was to try and understand, and duplicate, their technology: to make weapons out of it, in other words. However, the more the group looked into it all, the more they came to believe the NHEs were not extraterrestrial in origin, but were using that image as a cover. Their real origin, the group finally believed, was literally demonic. Ray related this and much more to me, which collectively demonstrated that there was a group—or probably groups—within the US Government that believed the UFO phenomenon is real, but is of a negative, spiritual nature. One of those groups called itself the Collins Elite, and that's the one I had contact with.

HORN: Under what circumstances did you first meet with them?

REDFERN: This chiefly came by following all the data that Ray Boeche gave me, including some that Ray preferred I left out of my book on the subject, titled *Final Events*. And I did indeed leave out of the book that data Ray asked me not to include. The collective data—names, dates, places etc.—let me chase things down further. And I openly phoned a number of places linked to the story—government and military facilities—and laid my cards on the table and told them what I was looking for: a group in the government that concluded UFOs have demonic origins. I often find that taking a very forthright and very alternative approach like this can open doors. Sometimes, letting people know you're looking is actually a good thing and makes them wonder why, and it can lead to positive developments. Not always, but sometimes it works. And in this case it did. That led me to a handful of people from the Collins Elite. They initiated all—literally all—of the contact I had with them, by phone and in person, but which is not ongoing now. Meetings occurred chiefly at diners, restaurants, and in hotels of their choosing.

HORN: What was the conclusion of the CE in relation to the UFO phenomenon?

REDFERN: Their belief is that the UFO phenomenon is 100 percent real, but that its origin is satanic. As they see it, the "aliens are visiting us" angle is a camouflage to allow Satan—if he really exists, of course—to get his grips into us. They believe that the presence of the UFO phenomenon, right now, and since 1947, is the commencement of an "end times" scenario, where the "E.T. landing" angle may be played out to con the world into believing the "Grays" are friendly extraterrestrials. The CE believes that belief and prayer, rather than weapons, can hold off this infiltration and invasion.

HORN: How do Jack Parsons, Aliester Crowley, and gang tie in?

REDFERN: In its very earliest years—the late 1940s to the early 1950s—the CE focused a great deal of its attention on Crowley and Parsons, their connections, Parsons' interest in UFOs and rocketry, and Crowley's manifestation of the grey-alien-like "Lam" during the Amalantrah Working of 1918. It was, chiefly, these two men—and their actions—that laid the foundation for the "how and why" of the CE's beliefs concerning the theory that the UFO phenomenon is demonic, deceptive, manipulative and deadly. From there, the CE began looking at the early Contactees and George Adamksi's Crowley connection, and George Hunt Williamson's use of Ouija boards to contact alleged alien entities. This is how their beliefs began to be constructed, by putting all these threads together and trying to make some collective sense of it all.

HORN: Did the CE provide you with any documentation?

REDFERN: I was given access to some documents. Some of them are in the book, others I have never revealed, for various reasons, mostly based on requests not to from the CE. One lengthy document came to me via the group, and was one of their own reports, which further bolstered their beliefs that the UFO phenomenon is a satanic deception. They also provided me with other documents…that have surfaced via the Freedom of Information Act [and] which they had on file as it was all relative to their research, such as the FBI's and Air Force' files on Jack Parsons, and official documentation on remote-viewing. The CE-created documentation is not covered by FOIA provisions because the CE is technically not an agency or group of government. Its members are government employees, but their work for the CE is done in a private capacity. So, while they have definitely received government funding and support, their research is technically not "government work," and therefore, their self-created documents are not subject to government secrecy laws. However, the CE has deeply influenced powerful figures in government for decades, which makes the group's work—and its position—extremely important in terms of what people in government, the military, and the intelligence community thinks about the demonic theory.

HORN: As far as you know, were members of the Collins Elite Roman Catholic or did they ever convey a Roman Catholic theological worldview?

REDFERN: Not as far as I know. But, I could be totally wrong, for the following reason: It's important to note that the overwhelming majority of the data given to me was provided to me in the form of statements and disclosures. That's to say, they shared what parts of the story, and their work, that they wanted to share. I was rarely given the opportunity to ask questions.

HORN: You mention Lieutenant Colonel Nelson Pacheco's work *Unmasking the Enemy* in your book. Are you aware it promotes Mary as deity?

REDFERN: Yes, I am aware of that. I've read the book a couple of times. A lot of the conclusions are similar to those reached by the CE.

HORN: Is CE member "Richard Duke" willing to talk to me?

REDFERN: I have no idea. The meetings I had, which covered 2007 to 2010, were always at the control of the people I spoke with. I was never, ever, able to initiate a contact, aside from when I put out those initial feelers. After that, it was always a case of them pulling the strings and advising me "when" and "where" information. So, all I can say is this: given that [you are] covering very similar territory and research to that contained in my *Final Events* book it would not surprise me if an approach is one day made or an exchange of data occurs. But, I'm not able to influence that.

HORN: Can we see the photocopies of "The Collins Report"?

REDFERN: Maybe one day, and the other documents too. This is a bit of a grey area, as the report was prepared by the CE and for CE members and for interested parties in the government, military, and intelligence community. But, because the CE is not technically an agency or arm of government, the report itself falls—copyright-wise—under the ownership of the man who wrote it. I was allowed to reproduce a couple of pages of its text in my *Final Events* book—chiefly as it relates to the demonic theory for Roswell. But, because the document is the private work of an individual and intended for the membership of the CE and other interested people in government, it's still his private work. In that sense, it's as protected as any author's book is. So, it's not a document that can be obtained via the Freedom of Information Act, as it's not a government document. Permission would have to come from the author. Just like in any normal situation where an author's permission is sought to quote from their books, etc.

Following the phone and email exchanges with Redfern, I continued making fairly significant efforts to verify his story concerning the Collins Elite. I also repeated my willingness to meet with a member of the Collins group anywhere, anytime, and have been told a meeting between them and I could occur, though as of this date I am still waiting. Meanwhile, my sources in the United States—which extend from US military intelligence to national defense employees with both Department of Defense and intel top-secret security clearances—came back empty-handed. This included our friend Colonel Steve Bauer, who served longer as a US government military aide than anyone in the history of the White House under five US presidents—Nixon, Ford, Carter, Reagan, and Bush. Bauer had never heard of the "Collins Elite" and couldn't locate a single intelligence resource that otherwise would substantiate Redfern's claims. But I knew, having said that, that this didn't mean the story as detailed in *Final Events* was untrue. Counterintelligence, Majestic 12-level compartmentalization, and official denial is a well-established part of the government's past and present protocols when handling questions concerning UFOs and so-called alien abduction activity—a fact that every significant investigator into this phenomenon has run into when trying to separate fact from fiction. So I moved on and checked with one of my international contacts—former director of Britain's Military of Defense's department for UFO research, Nick Pope—and was surprised when he cautioned against disbelief and even confirmed the existence of a Collins Elite-like group among Britain's aristocracy. Following this, I reached out to Gregory Richford, a Ball Aerospace contact who works with advanced systems and technologies for Space Control & Special Missions. He, too, cautioned against doubting the Collins reality and sent me a four-page document outlining the following main points, ending with an ominous warning. Below are just some of the talking points from his meticulous outline.

Security levels and Compartments

- Start with the understanding that a Top Secret DOD (Department of Defense) or SCI (Sensitive Compartmented Information; intelligence world) clearance is the first level of clearance required before one gets to SAP programs.
- There are at least four levels of Top Secret (TS) special access programs (SAPs) that currently exist in the US DOD/Intel world:
  - o Acknowledged top secret SAPs
    - ▪ (Security cleared) Congress (or staff) has access to full knowledge of program name, mission, budget, etc.

- o Unacknowledged top secret SAPs
  - Cleared Congress (or staff) has access to full knowledge
- o Unacknowledged/Waived top secret SAPs
  - Program, Budget, customer, and mission are all highly classified
  - Only two Senators and two Congressmen are made aware of the program, typically at a very high level only
  - Typically referred to as a "Black" program
- o Completely Unacknowledged top secret SAPs
  - No acknowledgement or overview to the Congress
  - Accountable only to the agency that authorizes mission and money ostensibly related to a Presidential Order
  - Really known as "Deep Black" in the vernacular.
  - *This level is itself not acknowledged; can't be acknowledged for obvious reasons*
  - Two agencies in particular make great use of this: CIA and NSA
- o With more than 25 years in this world, I personally have experience with levels 1 through 3 only. Level 4 is outside my scope.
- o Most of the high level UFO work is done at level 4. It is not acknowledged and specifically not even known except to those briefed into the compartment/program. Only leaks aid in the process of discovery.
- o This is likely a strong reason why Nick Pope is reluctant to spell out unambiguously what by definition is meant to be concealed at an unacknowledged level.

Formation of the Collins Elite

- A number of intelligence agencies looking at the UFO situation are drawn into the orbit of a larger picture held by the CIA.

- o Army Intel; Naval Intel; Air Force Intel; Defense Intel Agency (DIA), etc.
- o This seems consistent with how high level exchange takes place; they contribute to larger efforts out of their own agencies and budgets.
- A subgroup of this CIA-dominated and controlled compartment, informally sees things differently and begins to form a counterpoint voice to the research. They call themselves after a time the "Collins Elite."
  - o This seems plausible based on the discussions and factions I have seen over the years. Independent thinking is valued. Like-minded experts gather around themselves.
- Over time, the Collins Elite position becomes more refined, more emphatic, more concerned.
  - o One notes that most of these guys are industry old timers, with an old Christian worldview, having been in this covert intel circle for 30–40 years.
- The Collins Elite seems to be an internal but underlined informal collection of guys who maintain their independence of thought about matters in this highly classified and clearly controversial realm.

Review

- U.S. Intelligence agencies are trying to understand UFOs in early 1950s
- Same intel agencies also trying to understand the occult sorcery of two key figures: Aleister Crowley and Jack Parsons—and how it could be applied as a National Defense asset.
- Deeply covert CIA-controlled intel group wants to pursue research on psychotronic weapons and remote viewing "technologies" and embarks on a deluding journey, a perverted scheme and Faustian bargaining.
- After years and decades of incremental research in this arena, several deaths more recently occur to test subjects in these realms; things are going badly awry.

- A sub-group watching all this, loosely confederated, calling itself the "Collins Elite" begins to recognize this as completely occult, demonic/Satanic, and begins to organize itself as a counterpoint to the general research direction.
- The Collins Elite begins to see a much larger and terrifying picture of what this whole unleashed enterprise is leading to; the connection to fallen angels, the Nephilim, and a plan for taking over the world.

Conclusion

- This unsettling story has every indication of being true; it follows directly from everything you and I know about UFOs and their ultimately nefarious mission tied to an end-time prophetic scenario
- Unraveling this further is loaded with known and unknown complexities—*and that includes dangers.*[259] (emphasis added)

DNA Harvesting, Genetic Manipulation, and the Seed of the Serpent

When former Christian college professor and BBC correspondent, Dr. I. D. E. Thomas, in his highly recommended book, *The Omega Conspiracy*, chronicled the burgeoning of so-called alien abduction activity in the 1980s, he made similar enlightening connections between the alien-abduction phenomenon and end-time prophecy concerning a return of Nephilim, something other writers have since built upon. Documentation by "abductees" worldwide and the stories of DNA harvesting by "aliens" reminded him of the history of biological misuse by the Watchers. Dr. Thomas told us personally that the special desire by the "aliens" for human and animal molecular matter could explain "why animals have been killed, mutilated, and stolen by the aliens," a point Vallée repeated in his book, *The Invisible College: What a Group of Scientists Has Discovered About UFO Influences on the Human Race*, when he wrote:

In order to materialize and take definite form, these entities seem to require a source of energy…a living thing…a human medium…. Our sciences have not reached a point where they can offer us any kind of working hypothesis for this process. But we can speculate that these beings need living energy which they can reconstruct into physical form. Perhaps that is why dogs and animals tend to vanish in [UFO] flap areas. Perhaps the living cells of those animals are somehow used by the ultraterrestrials to create forms which we can see and sense with our limited perceptions.[260]

Evidence concerning the collection of "living cells" from animal (and human) mutilations indicates something very unusual and unworldly. The precision by which the material is collected has often been compared to "laser-like" precision, but Lieutenant Colonel Philip J. Corso (1915–1998), who is best known today for his book, *The Day After Roswell* (which disclosed his involvement in allegedly back-engineering extraterrestrial technology recovered from the UFO crash site at Roswell, New Mexico, in 1947), was working on a manuscript before he died, titled *Dawn of a New Age* that described an unknown technology beyond laser accuracy used by unsympathetic Extraterrestrial Biological Entities (EBEs) for tissue removal:

A study and laboratory reports show that the tissue taken from animals and humans by the alien EBEs also centers around cell structure. So delicate and perfected is their advanced approach that when they cut out the private reproductive parts (vagina, penis, testicles) and the rectum, eyes ears, udders, etc., they do not cut through cells. The cells are separated not cut through. Even the brain is taken in a manner where there is no cerebral trauma.

In their animal and human mutilations, the aliens have shown a callous indifference concerning their victims. Their behavior has been insidious and it appears they might be using our earth and manipulating earth life. Skeptics will excuse them that possibly they are benevolent and want to help, however, there is no evidence they have healed anyone or alleviated human ailments. On the other band, they have caused pain, suffering and even death.[261]

As the battalion commander of European air defense in World War II, the chief of the Special Projects branch of the Intelligence Division under General Douglas MacArthur, and a staff member of President Eisenhower's National Security Council for four years, Corso's unpublished work illustrates that the science and purpose behind the alleged modern ET-human-hybridization agenda is so clouded in mystery that not even leaders from the world's most prestigious intelligence bureaus seem to fathom it (except, of course, if at above-top-secret levels there are black government agencies participating with the alien entities in some sort of cosmic Watergate wherein the breeding program transpires). Plenty of so-called whistle-blowers, books, and leaked files have suggested the same, but Vallée's suspicion is that many, if not most, of these "sources" are actually concoctions by complicit government proxies, which are disseminated in order to so completely muddle the factual objectives of the *program* with duplicity, half-truths, and subterfuge that the public can never really know what is happening. "There is a genuine UFO phenomenon and it is not explained by the revelations of alleged government agents bearing fancy code names like Condor or Falcon,"[262] he concluded in *Revelations: Alien Contact and Human Deception*.

Dr. David Jacobs, a historian specializing in popular culture at Temple University, has concluded from over twenty years of research that the overriding purpose of the UFO phenomenon is abduction with nefarious intent. He explains:

For example, the evidence strongly suggests that the majority, if not all, of "close encounter" UFO sightings are the beginnings or endings of abduction events. Even high-level sightings may be indicative of abductions. Statistics from Gallup Polls on UFO sightings have varied from 9 percent to 14 percent since the 1950s. If a percentage of these sightings mask abductions, then the number of abduction events is high.[263]

This proposes a more sinister agenda behind UFOs than scientific exploration. At the same time, that a modern "alien" program of breeding and hybridizing humans is covertly occurring similar to what the ancient Watchers did is something, no matter how absurd it may seem, a growing body of scholars, based on accumulative physical and eyewitness evidence, are coming around to.

In his book, *Secret Life: Firsthand, Documented Accounts of UFO Abductions*, Professor Jacobs combined scientific and investigatory methods to analyze the accounts of dozens of "abductees" including more than three hundred independently corroborated stories of such experiences, describing in unsettling detail the reproductive procedures that abductees claim were administered by "small alien beings." Jacobs' profoundly unsettling conclusion paralleled that of Vallée and others— that alien abductors are conducting complex reproductive experiments involving the conception, gestation, hybridization, and integration on Earth of alien hybrid beings.

Jacobs wrote:

[The aliens] want to use the ability humans have to recreate themselves. They want human sperm and eggs. They want human physical involvement with the offspring. They want complete knowledge of the reproductive physiological processes. [And this] abduction program appears to be vast. Abductees routinely report rooms with as many as two hundred tables holding humans in various stages of examination. The aliens hustle them out as soon as possible after the procedures are completed, presumably so that more humans can be brought in. The evidence suggests that this goes on twenty-four hours per day, month after month, year after year. The amount of time and energy invested in the breeding program is enormous.[264]

Besides Jacobs and Vallée, other noteworthy scientists who believed something unearthly was happening in connection to alien activity included: Dr. Josef Allen Hynek, the United States astronomer and professor in charge of Project Blue Book; Dr. Hermann Julius Oberth, one of the founding fathers of rocketry and astronautics; Lynn E. Catoe, senior bibliographer for government publication research by the Library of Congress for the US Air Force Office of Scientific Research; Dr. Karla Turner, an academic who gave up her career to speak out after discovering her own abductee status; and the late Harvard Medical School professor and Pulitzer Prize winner, Dr. John Edward Mack. After working with abduction "experiencers," including interviews with over one hundred people of various ages and backgrounds, Mack showcased the narratives of thirteen subjects in astonishing detail in his book, *Abduction: Human Encounters with Aliens*, where he reached very much the same conclusion as his peers:

> What is amply corroborated [is] that the abduction phenomenon is in some central way involved in a breeding program that results in the creation of alien/human hybrid offspring.... My own impression is that we may be witnessing...an awkward joining of two species, engineered by an intelligence we are unable to fathom.[265]

Yet, if demons pretending to be aliens are actually behind a fantastic breeding and hybridization scheme, what would be their purpose? Biblical scholar and prophecy expert Gary Stearman believes they are dark overlords, come forth to repeat what happened in the Days of Noah, to create a generation of genetically altered pseudo-humans for the service of Satan and Antichrist in preparation of Armageddon. He points to Matthew 24:37, which says, "But as the days of Noe [Noah] were, so shall also the coming of the Son of man be." Stearman then goes on to elaborate:

Here, Jesus is clearly speaking of future judgment, the Tribulation, Second Coming and certain events that will surround it.

He says that His coming will happen at a time when social conditions will resemble those that plagued the world in the days of Noah. From Genesis 6, we now discern that these will include an invasion of dark forces from the heavens.… The UFO abduction phenomenon is only a mask for fallen angels who have departed from their natural domain to engage in the filthy work of creating an alternate race that will act as their proxies.… Now, as [in the Days of Noah], they pry into the forbidden areas of human procreation. Lascivious and power hungry, they seek to set up their own race, and their own province of control.

But only in the last fifty years have their activities acquired a speed and purpose that tells us what time it is, prophetically speaking. Jesus told us, in effect, that when we begin to see such things come to pass, His appearance would not be far behind.[266]

On the Watcher website, our dearly departed friend and late Christian genius, David Flynn—whose early online research first broke many of today's most popular theories regarding the alien-hybrid scheme as an end-times deception aimed at misleading mankind—reaffirmed the warnings made by Gary Stearman:

The Book of Enoch explains that the Sons of God descended first onto the mountain called Hermon.… The rebel angels intended to thwart God's plan for the earth by destroying the descendants of Adam. Satan's goal in organizing the Nephilim/human hybridization program was to pollute the bloodline that would produce Jesus Christ, the Messiah, the Kinsman Redeemer.

Now that it is so close to the end times, Satan has orchestrated human/rebel angel interaction on a grand scale. The plan is now to prevent any flesh from being saved. By manipulating human genetics, whether through the guise of "alien abduction" or by supplying willing mortal accomplices with the proper technology…there is currently being created humanoid hybrids who are not-quite-human…. The second wave of hybrid "Nephilim creation" is Satan's last effort to destroy all Sons of Adam, so that none can be redeemed when Jesus Christ returns at the End of the Age.[267]

One cannot read the conclusions by Gary Stearman and David Flynn without calling to mind Genesis 3:15, which says, "And I will put enmity between thee and the woman, and between *thy seed* [zera, meaning "offspring," "descendants," or "children"] and *her seed*" (emphasis added). From the Middle Ages forward, church leaders believed this genotype or "seed" would provide for the mystical arrival of Antichrist and ultimately represent the return of Nephilim—the reunion of demons with humans. Back in 1976, academician N. P. Dubinin, the first director of the Institute of Cytology and Genetics of the Siberian Branch of the USSR Academy of Sciences (1957–1959) may have understood a key element related to how Satan's "seed" would animate Antichrist on Earth in the last days. He described by what means in his opinion the genetics revolution would lead to *"an exchange of living forms"* taking place *"between the earth and other worlds."*[268] After reading his material, Russian Orthodox Archpriest Vladislav Sveshnikov expressed apocalyptic fears, saying: "We have to admit that contemporary science is preparing the ground for the coming of the Antichrist." Why did Sveshnikov imagine the "exchange" of genetic material "between the earth and other worlds" leading to Antichrist? He saw something reminiscent of the Watchers advent being repeated in "the manipulation of genes in order to produce the 'superman' or 'man-god' of Nietzsche's imagination, who will be at the same time the 'devil-man' or 'Antichrist' of Christian patristic teaching."[269]

English theologian George Hawkins Pember agreed with this premise, and in his 1876 masterpiece, *Earth's Earliest Ages*, he analyzed the prophecy of Christ that says the end-times would be a repeat of "the Days of Noah." Pember outlined the seven great causes of the antediluvian destruction and documented their developmental beginnings in his lifetime. Like Stearman, Flynn, and Sveshnikov, he concluded that the seventh and most fearful sign would be the return of the Nephilim and the arrival of Antichrist—"The appearance upon earth of beings from the Principality of the Air, and their unlawful intercourse with the human race."[270]

Thus, it appears those social, spiritual, and academic intellectuals who now believe we are close to integration with intelligent alien life (and who also believe that this discovery could ultimately reconfigure established doctrines of science, religion, and salvation) may be closer to the truth than some of them have imagined. Events unfolding over the past decade portend a near future in which "alien influences" led by a man of unusual intelligence will arrive on Earth as champions of a "new" gospel. Numerous Scriptures foretold the otherworldly leader's coming for what he actually is—paganism's ultimate incarnation; the "beast" of Revelation 13:1. As Jesus Christ was the "seed of the woman" (Genesis 3:15), the Antichrist will be the "seed of the serpent." But the prophet Daniel may have provided an even greater clue as to the identity of this coming false savior. He says in chapter 11, verse 39 of his book that the Antichrist will be a worshipper of the *god of forces—a god whom his fathers knew not*, a text that can literally be interpreted to mean, *an alien god*.

SECTION TWO

ESSENTIAL HISTORY AND ASTROBIOLOGY

7 | Astrobiology and the Extraterrestrial Worldview

"Sometimes I think we're alone in the universe, and sometimes I think we're not. In either case the idea is quite staggering."—Arthur C. Clarke[271]

"We shall not cease from exploration, and the end of all our exploring will be to arrive where we started and know the place for the first time."—T. S. Eliot[272]

Who hasn't gazed at the sky in wonder and considered the possibility of extraterrestrial life? It seems only natural, given our modern understanding of the vastness of space. To the secular person, the idea that outer space could be uninhabited seems like a terrible waste of space, but to the biblical theist, the heavens declare the glory of God. Consider that the concept of "waste" only applies where resources are limited and, of course, God has no such constraints. Even so, throughout history, many Catholic theologians and today Jesuit scientists assert that claims like "God did not create space aliens" limit God. For these thinkers, the astrobiological project offers a route to discovery. According to José G. Funes, the director of the Vatican Observatory Research Group (VORG), "The study of astrobiology is quite appropriate for the Pontifical Academy of Sciences, which is based on a multi-disciplinary collaboration."[273]

While one wonders what business a Church has doing science in the first place, the VORG is involved with the top secular astrobiologists in the field.

In 2009, the Pontifical Academy of Sciences hosted an astrobiology study week at the Casina Pio IV on the Vatican grounds from November 6–11. The pope's academy gathered over thirty astronomers, biologists, and geologists, as well as Catholic theologians, to discuss the existence of extraterrestrials and the theological implications of disclosure. Welcoming perspectives from atheists, New Agers, Buddhists, and Catholics alike, the conference primarily focused on the scientific disciplines investigating the existence of extraterrestrial life and making contact. The program was organized progressively into eight segments: 1) Origin of Life; 2) Habitability Through Time; 3) Environment and Genomes; 4) Detecting Life Elsewhere; 5) Search Strategies for Extra Solar Planets; 6) Formation of Extra Solar Planets; 7) Properties of Extra Solar Planets; and 8) Intelligence Elsewhere and Shadow Life. As one can see, the program was designed to progress sequentially, culminating in the last segment, intelligence elsewhere and "shadow life"—a cryptic label for alien life with unknown biochemistry—and in their own words, "the question of whether sentient life forms exist on other worlds, and whether <u>forms of life alien to our own in fact coexist with us— today—on our own home world</u>"[274] (underline added).

Paul Davies' discussion of "shadow life" opened the door to discussion regarding weird terrestrial life as well as on distant planets, a fascinating suggestion that we will develop in this book. The crux of his presentation was, "If life arises readily in earthlike conditions, as many astrobiologists contend, then it may well have started many times on Earth itself, raising the question of whether one or more shadow terrestrial biospheres of alternative life forms have existed in the past, or still exist today."[275] Whether or not prevailing science recognizes it, we believe evidence for unconventional life, known as cryptids, exists in our ancient records as well in as the case files of modern cryptozoologists. We suggest that what many folks call "extraterrestrial" might be better explained as an indigenous phenomenon.

Astrobiologists are convinced they will discover genuine ET life very soon. To say that they are hopeful would be an understatement. Really, the tone of the pontifical conference gave the impression that the existence of extraterrestrials is a foregone conclusion and that the world should be prepared for such an announcement within a few short years. Cosmologist and astrobiology education and outreach designate Chris Impey from the University of Arizona, also associated with "Science for Monks," a peculiar coalition engaging Tibetan Buddhism,[276] delivered the final presentation of the week, entitled "Reflections on the Future of Astrobiology," in which he expressed confidence of a forthcoming discovery and disclosure:

> It is plausibly estimated that there are hundreds of millions of habitable locations in the Milky Way, which is just one of billions of galaxies in the universe. As scientists gather to discuss progress in astrobiology, we still only know of one planet with life: our own. But there is a palpable expectation that the universe harbors life and there is hope that *the first discovery is only a few years away.*[277] (emphasis added)

While Dr. Impey's "few years" are now upon us, recent exoplanet discoveries seem to offer promise. We will look at a few of the more interesting ones within. First, we endeavor to define the astrobiological project.

While astrobiology is a multidisciplinary collaboration between astronomy, biology, paleontology, oceanography, geology, and genetics, the term "astrobiology" represents the matrimony of the first two scientific disciplines. Astronomy is the study of the universe and biology is the study of life. By their union, the study of extraterrestrial life is suggested. However, since there is not a shred of scientific evidence for life anywhere except on Earth, it lacks an actual subject to study. This raises a serious question about its status as a legitimate science. In the prestigious journal *Science*, a famous evolutionary biologist, George Gaylord Simpson, wrote that it is "a curious development in view of the fact that this 'science' has yet to demonstrate that its subject matter exists!"[278] He wrote that in 1964, and the situation remains the same half a century later, despite a great deal of posturing and confident speculation. Accordingly, astrobiology truly is a faith-based initiative necessarily extrapolated from the highly questionable assumptions of naturalistic science. It really is a worldview issue, a topic we will take up at the close of this chapter.

In the interest of objectivity, we present the description of astrobiology found on NASA's website: "Astrobiology is the study of the origin, evolution, distribution, and future of life in the universe."[279] Similarly, a popular astrobiology textbook definition reads: "The study of life on Earth and beyond; it emphasizes research into questions of the origin of life, the conditions under which life can survive, and the search for life beyond Earth."[280] The term "exobiology," sometimes interchanged with astrobiology, is actually much more specific—it covers the search for life beyond Earth and the effects of extraterrestrial environments on living things. Today, it is considered a subdiscipline within astrobiology. While one can readily see they are attempting to answer traditionally religious questions concerning origins, purpose, and the future, they are grounding their faith on some very tenuous assumptions. Naturalism commonly refers to the view that only the laws of nature control the universe, and that nothing exists beyond the natural. In truth, astrobiology is driven more by an ideology than a science.

The creed prompting this research is called the Copernican principle. Named after Nicolaus Copernicus, this tenet states that the Earth is not in a central, preferred position in the cosmos. Although there are arguments that support the idea that our location is special, most astronomers infer much more than our placement within the universe. Naturalists, who exclude God entirely, extrapolate the "principle of mediocrity," the idea that the Earth is a mediocre planet among many and, by combining the assumptions of Darwinism and origins of life research, humanity is merely an evolved primate of no special significance, so that things once thought sacred are really only trifling coincidences of deterministic, natural law. Carl Sagan popularized this idea in his book, *The Pale Blue*

Dot: A Vision of the Human Future in Space, by offering this description based on the picture of Earth from the Voyager spacecraft:

> Because of the reflection of sunlight the Earth seems to be sitting in a beam of light, as if there were some special significance to this small world. But it's just an accident of geometry and optics, look again at that dot, that's here, that's home, that's us.... Our posturings, our imagined self-importance, the delusion that we have some privileged position in the Universe are challenged by this point of pale light. Our planet is a lonely speck in the great enveloping cosmic dark. In our obscurity, in all this vastness, there is no hint that help will come from elsewhere to save us from ourselves.[281]

And so, mankind should not presume we are in any way privileged or that the universe was designed with us in mind. Astrobiologists reason that, because we are nothing special, there must be many similar pale blue dots, and, given the right chemicals and conditions, life should accidentally "poof" into existence on those insignificant planets, too. Therefore, the naturalist fantastically concludes that the universe must be teeming with life. Of course, philosophically, it amounts to a house of cards, and not all naturalists are so inclined; but, believe it or not, this line of irrational thinking inevitably follows from the dominant materialist worldview taught in our major universities. They justify it as a promising scientific field for two underlying reasons: 1) the existence of exoplanets (planets beyond our solar system); and 2) abiogenesis (origin of life from nonlife). First, let's look at exoplanets.

Exoplanets: A Brave New World?

A new study suggests there may be *100 billion* alien planets in our Milky Way galaxy.[282] Note that this is *merely for our galaxy*, not the entire universe. This is a statistical extrapolation based on data from the Kepler satellite and the planets that have been confirmed. Out of those 100 billion, astronomers think about 17 percent of the stars in our galaxy host an approximately Earth-sized planet in a near orbit. Since there are 100 billion stars in the Milky Way, that calculates to around 17 billion Earth-size planets.[283] For many folks, this suggests that the discovery of extraterrestrial life cannot be too far in the future, but these are actually what are called "hot earths" orbiting their stars every eighty-five days and reaching temperatures of 800 degrees Fahrenheit.

The search for planets around other stars is a key component in the search for extraterrestrial life. It is an exciting time in this endeavor. The NASA-owned Jet Propulsion Laboratory hosts a website called "Planet Quest: The Search for Another Earth" (see http://planetquest.jpl.nasa.gov/). In fact, you can even join in on the search at www.planethunters.org by helping sift through the data from the Kepler space probe. To say they are enthused would be an understatement. There are several motivating factors. First, the existence of many extrasolar planets is used to imply that the Earth is not special. This section will introduce the reader to a great deal of scientific evidence that controverts that notion. If you are not familiar with the scientific issues, don't get overwhelmed with the details; let this be an introduction prompting further study. Second, it is assumed that planets positioned similarly to Earth in relation to their star are indeed like Earth. We will argue that position is merely a small part of the requirement. Third, astrobiologists argue that because the universe contains millions of planets, there is a high probability that life has evolved on some of them. We will show why this assumption hangs on faith and not on scientific evidence. The bottom line is that atheistic naturalists believe the existence of extraterrestrial life is a confirmation of their worldview, and this makes the Vatican's involvement all the more peculiar.

In our interview with Vatican astronomer Guy Consolmagno, he indicated the VORG has a new Jesuit point man in the search for exoplanets:

As it happens, one of us, Fr. Paul Gabor, just finished his PhD thesis work at the Paris Observatory on designing an instrument for a proposed European Space Agency spacecraft mission to search for exoplanets, but his work was in optics, not biology. He has just moved to Tucson and is in the process of developing collaborations with people at the University of Arizona, but that is just getting underway right now.[284]

While Vatican Advanced Technology Telescope (VATT) is not well-equipped for exoplanet discovery, the neighboring Large Binocular Telescope (LBT) is considered state of the art. Based on Consolmagno's statement, it seems the VORG will soon have a well-placed insider in the LBT project through its association with the University of Arizona.

Naturally, the astrobiological faith is greatly encouraged by recent discoveries of exoplanets. Prior to 1995, there was no evidence for any planets outside of our own solar system. That has changed dramatically, as scientists now estimate billions of planets exist although only 865 such planets have been identified as of this writing.[285] Although the progress is remarkable, out of those, only nine (a mere 1 percent) are classified as potentially "habitable."

Gliese 581 g: Warm Superterran Exoplanet in the Constellation Libra

Gliese 667C c: Warm Superterran Exoplanet in the Constellation Scorpius

Kepler-22 b: Warm Superterran Exoplanet in the Constellation Cygnus

HD 40307 g: Warm Superterran Exoplanet in the Constellation Pictor

HD 85512 b: Warm Superterran Exoplanet in the Constellation Vela

Tau Ceti e: Warm Superterran Exoplanet in the Constellation Cetus

Gliese 163 c: Warm Superterran Exoplanet in the Constellation Dorado

Gliese 581 d: Warm Superterran Exoplanet in the Constellation Libra

Tau Ceti f: Warm Superterran Exoplanet in the Constellation Cetus[286]

(An exoplanet's name is formed by taking the name of its parent star and adding a lowercase letter. The first planet discovered is given the designation "b" and later planets are given subsequent letters. If several planets in the same system are discovered at the same time, the closest one to the star gets the next letter, followed by the other planets in order of orbital size.)

Even so, the adjective "habitable" is begging the question. As mentioned elsewhere in this book, a "Goldilocks zone" planet refers to a planet that is not too hot and not too cold. "Just right" really means ideal for the existence of liquid water. This is crucial for the existence of life, because if a planet is too hot, then water vaporizes into gas and atoms cannot join together to form the molecules that make up the ingredients for life. On the other extreme, a planet that's too cold will only have ice, not liquid water, for life-sustaining chemical reactions. But, even so, a mere temperature correlation does not make such a world habitable for life, and water has not been confirmed on a single exoplanet.

For example, at the top of list, "Gliese 581 g" is considered one of the most "Earth-like." However, it is about three times the mass of Earth, slightly larger in width and much closer to its parent star—14 million miles away versus 93 million, albeit its star is much smaller. In fact, it's so close to its sun that it orbits every thirty-seven days. Also, it doesn't rotate much on its axis, so one side is almost always sunny, soaring up to a roasting 160 degrees Fahrenheit. On the other side, it is dark, freezing down to 25 degrees below 0. But maybe somewhere in between, scientists speculate, conditions are suitable for life. While these extremes sound pretty brutal to us earthlings, keep in mind this is one of the most hospitable planets to date.

Most exoplanets discovered are far from Earthlike. They are "hot

Jupiters," orbiting perilously close to the surface of their suns in brief "years" of only a few days, a hellish state of affairs not conducive to biological processes. In fact, so far, the majority of exoplanets are like this, but this is a function of the technology used to find them more than the actual situation. The gas giants are obviously easier to find. Because all exoplanets are like tiny little dots orbiting huge, bright stars, looking for one is like searching for a firefly next to a spotlight; only, the firefly would be about six feet from the spotlight, and the light would be in the neighborhood of twenty-six hundred miles away. Obviously, detecting such an object is extremely difficult. Currently, there are really only two basic ways to search for extrasolar planets:

1. Directly: Observation of the planet is direct evidence of its existence.
2. Indirectly: Precise measurements of a star's properties indirectly disclose the effects of orbiting planets.

Of course, direct detection is preferable because it reveals far more about the planet's properties. VORG director José Funes explains, "By examining the spectra of light coming from stars and planets, soon we will be able to identify the elements in their atmospheres, the so-called biomarkers, and see if there are conditions for the emergence and development of life. Moreover, forms of life could exist in theory even without oxygen or hydrogen."[287] Accordingly, one of the big challenges in searching for exoplanets is removing the star light that overwhelms the image and hides the planet. One solution is diffracting light with a special mirror design and high-tech instruments, something the Large Binocular Telescope on Mt. Graham is specifically designed for, a mission scheduled to ensue this year (2013). But, so far, hardly any exoplanets are discovered directly.

In truth, most of the time, astronomers are not *seeing* these planets in their telescopes, but rather are indirectly detecting them with sophisticated computerized instruments that collate massive amounts of data. The techniques involve observing stars carefully for evidence that they are being orbited. Two of the primary methods look for gravitational and luminosity effects:

- The "wobble method" is a simple way to describe the planet tugging on the star gravitationally as it orbits. In reality, the planet and star are orbiting their common center of mass, but a large orbiting planet causes a noticeable wobble on its star.
- The "transit method" is used to detect the planet crossing directly on front of the star. Because stars really only amount to small points of light, this is detected when the brightness dips by a few percent. A small dip in luminosity indicates that something obscured the view. The Kepler space telescope, making many of the current finds, is looking at one wide field of 150,000 stars for four years, trying to detect this small drop in brightness. As of January 7, 2013, Kepler has identified 2,321 exoplanet candidates, and 105 of those have been confirmed.[288]

To make the search a little easier, researchers take advantage of "The M star opportunity," which refers to M-class stars—smaller stars that are consequently better candidates for the transit method, because the planet orbits much closer and is more likely detected. Also, small stars last longer than big stars, so they seem to be better candidates for time-dependent Darwinian evolution. Dr. Sara Seager, professor of Earth, atmospheric, and planetary sciences at MIT, predicted in 2010:

- A big earth transiting a small star would be discovered in three years.
- If we are fortunate, we could find one earth mass planet in an earth like orbit by 2015 by the Doppler (wobble) method.
- Direct imaging to confirm an earth like planet will not be feasible until 2025.[289]

Now that 2013 has arrived, it seems that the first prediction could be satisfied with the recent discovery of an exoplanet circling in the habitable zone of Tau Ceti, a star that is almost identical to our sun.[290] Still more exciting, at twelve light years away, it is relatively close on a cosmic scale, meaning it is feasible to send a spacecraft there in the not-too-distant future or, even more sensational, perhaps "they" might send one to investigate us! More realistically, as mentioned above, we think "habitable" is a misnomer, because in astrobiology it merely means a planet lies in the "Goldilocks zone"—it's hypothetically "just right" in terms of temperatures which allow liquid water. But, thinking soberly, temperature is only a small part of what it means to be habitable.

The Rare Earth

In their book, *Rare Earth: Why Complex Life is Uncommon in the Universe*, Peter Ward, a geologist and paleontologist, and Donald Brownlee, an astronomer and astrobiologist, argue that the emergence of complex life requires a host of fortuitous circumstances not accounted for by most astrobiologists. These include: 1) the right location in the right kind of galaxy; 2) orbiting at the right distance from the right type of star; 3) with the right arrangement of planets; 4) a continuously stable orbit; 5) of the right size; 6) with a large moon; 7) plate tectonics; and 8) evolution from simple cells to complex life. There is a lot of complex science involved, but we will offer a brief summary and make some suggestions for further study.

1: Point one argues that much of the known universe, including large parts of our galaxy called "dead zones," cannot support complex life.[291]

2: The second point describes the aforementioned "Goldilocks zone," which needs no review.

3: Third, a life-supporting system must be structured more or less like our solar system, with small and rocky inner planets and outer gas giants. Without Jupiter, Earth would be bombarded by asteroids.

4: Fourth, the need for stable orbits rules out systems with large planets close to their sun; again, our own solar system reflects an optimal design.

5: Fifth, a large planet's immense gravity is problematic for life, and a small one cannot hold much of an atmosphere. The Earth's size is ideal.

6: The sixth point speaks to how our moon is "somewhat of a freak because of its large size in comparison to its parent planet."[292] The moon's gravity stabilizes the planet's tilt, giving us our seasons; without the moon, the variation would be chaotic, making complex life on land impossible. Also, without the moon, the ocean tides would be only half, effectively excluding tidal pools rich with life. Finally, the moon acts as a protective shield for asteroids and space debris, a fact clearly seen on its crater-pocked surface.

7: Seven, plate tectonics, the movement of the planetary crust across the surface of the Earth, is essential for recycling carbon, providing nutrients, and maintaining our atmosphere. The *Rare Earth* hypothesis argues this could indeed be the decisive factor: "It may be that plate tectonics is the central requirement for life on a planet and that it is necessary for keeping a world supplied with water. How rare is plate tectonics? We know that of all the planets and moons in our solar system, plate tectonics is found only on Earth."[293]

8: Eight, evolution from matter to microbes is assumed as a brute fact. We will take up the origin of life in the next section. Nevertheless, the conjecture that natural selection is an adequate mechanism to explain the incredible complexity found in nature has been deeply challenged by intelligent design theorists, so much so that evolutionist academics prefer censorship over scientific debate.[294] But even granting its adequacy, there are arguments in *Rare Earth* that if life were to emerge on an exoplanet, it would be unlikely to develop beyond simple bacteria. When one considers the sum total of the evidence, the Earth appears designed for complex life.

Clearly, the requirements listed above are far more rigorous than the trivial appeals to the Goldilocks zone (which is merely requirement two) coming from naively optimistic astrobiologists announcing habitable planets. Any legitimate claim to "earthlike" or habitable status should account for all of these points and necessarily faces far greater standards of evidence than the wishful pseudoscience being proffered by many of the more vocal true believers. What makes Ward and Brownlee's work particularly compelling is that they share most of the naturalist presuppositions of their peers. Given their requirements, the Earth is a special place, and the origin of complex life seems miraculous.

The Privileged Planet: How Our Place in the Cosmos is Designed for Discovery is a book by Guillermo Gonzalez and Jay Richards that provides scientific evidence for intelligent design. They not only make a case akin to the *Rare Earth* hypothesis, they contend that those same rare conditions that produce a habitable planet and complex life allow for the best overall place for observing. Our location in the galaxy, the size of the moon, the Earth's rotation, the age of the cosmos, and other factors unite to make scientific discovery possible. For example, complex life, like human beings, requires a certain type of atmosphere. It turns out that this same type of atmosphere provides a remarkably clear view of the near and distant universe. Not only is our atmosphere transparent, but we have dark nights that help us make astronomical discoveries. Other factors contribute as well. For instance, have you ever considered how our moon is exactly the right size to perfectly cover the sun during a full solar eclipse? This makes for ideal study of the sun's chromosphere. No other planet known is blessed with all of these conditions favorable to discovery. The authors conclude "that scientific progress and discovery depend on nature being more than meaningless matter in motion."[295] To sum it up, our ability to even do science suggests that Earth is a very special location rather than a mediocre one. Even so, the majority of scientists demur.

Seth Shostak, a SETI astronomer, exemplifies the normative view: "Unless there is something very very special, miraculous if you will, about our solar system, about our planet earth, unless there's something extraordinarily unusual about it then what happened here must have happened many times in the history of the universe."[296] Naturally, following the SETI orthodox view, he thinks the Earth is mediocre. However, we do feel "miraculous" is an accurate assessment. So does Dr. Hugh Ross, an astrophysicist at Caltech who has argued that the probability of finding just one planet capable of supporting life within the observable universe is less than 1 chance in 10^{174} (the number 1 followed by 174 zeros).[297]

To put that in perspective, the number of atoms in the entire, observable universe is estimated to be within the range of 10^{78} to 10^{82}.

So, taking the larger number giving the smallest probability from this range to be generous, we could say that the odds of randomly picking one particular atom from the universe are about 1 in 10^{82}. The exponents on the tens are multiplying by ten each time, so 10^{174} is 10^{92} times larger than 10^{82}. That means the odds of finding a planet like Earth are 1 in 10^{92} times smaller than the odds of randomly picking one particular atom from the entire known universe. To say it even another way, the odds of finding a planet like Earth are one hundred million trillion trillion trillion trillion trillion trillion trillion times smaller than the odds of randomly picking that one special atom (10^{92} is 1 with 92 zeros after it, and every twelve zeros is multiplying by 1 trillion). If Dr. Ross is correct, astrobiologists are wasting their time.

The Anthropic Principle

As a well-known progressive Creationist, Ross offers this criticism: "Astrobiologists define habitable planets as bodies with the necessary features for surface liquid water to be possible. In truth, even primitive life needs many, many more fine-tuned planetary features."[298] Ross and his team of scientists have derived and presented one hundred forty features of the cosmos as a whole that must fall within certain narrow ranges to allow for the possibility of physical life's existence.[299] In addition, they compiled 402 quantifiable characteristics of a planetary system and its galaxy that must fall within narrow ranges to allow for the possibility of advanced life's existence.[300] These finely tuned essential characteristics, which make life possible on Earth, are known as the "anthropic principle," implying that, contrary to the Copernican principle, the universe appears to be designed with us in mind. We believe this is one of the strongest scientific arguments for the existence of the Creator.

Breaking it down, anthropic means "of or relating to human beings" and principle means "law." Accordingly, the anthropic principle is the law of human existence. As Ross details, our existence in this universe depends on a copious amount of cosmological constants and parameters whose numerical values must fall within a very narrow range of values. If even a single variable were off even slightly, we would not exist. For instance, atoms, the building blocks of matter, are dependent on the strong nuclear force—the force that allows protons and neutrons to stick together in atomic nuclei. If it were too weak, protons and neutrons would not stick together. Ross explains:

> How delicate is the balance for the strong nuclear force? If it were just 2% weaker or 0.3% stronger than it actually is, life would be impossible at any time and any place within the universe. Are we just considering life as we know it? No, we're talking about any conceivable kind of life chemistry throughout the cosmos. This delicate condition must be met universally.[301]

This is but one example from a long list. The extreme improbability that so many variables could align so favorably merely by chance has led many, including the dominant atheist philosopher of the twentieth century, Oxford Professor Anthony Flew, to accept that it was God who providentially engineered the universe to suit mankind's specific needs.[302]

Computer scientist and artificial intelligence researcher Hugo de Garis is also impressed by the anthropic principle, conceding that a valid interpretation is "that our universe is the product, the creation, of a preexisting deity, a hyperintelligence that conceived our universe's laws of physics that are compatible with matter and life, and built our universe according to those laws."[303] In addition, he is enthralled by the "mathematical principle," the idea that the universe appears to have been designed by a mathematician. He writes, "The more humanity knows about how deeply mathematical the laws of physics are, the more plausible it seems that the designer of the universe used mathematical principles as a tool."[304] These evidences have moved de Garis to see the plausibility of a Creator. Yet, astrobiology is founded on the notion that life arose by chance.

Follow the Water: The Sea Monkey Hypothesis

Astrobiology simply presumes that a planet in the Goldilocks zone containing liquid water will somehow produce life. This leads to the "follow-the-water" strategy in the search for ETs. It is a good place to start, as it is widely recognized that the properties of liquid water are exquisitely suited for carbon-based life. These properties include the ability to dissolve and transport the chemical nutrients vital to living organisms and its unmatched capacity to absorb heat from the sun—a process critical for regulating a planet's temperature. However, the mere presence of water, while necessary, is not *sufficient,* because there is no known mechanism explaining how life came from nonlife. If it is a still a mystery on Earth, where we are certain that life exists, what warrant is there to assume it occurs by chance elsewhere? The answer is that there is none; it is simply taken on blind faith. Theologian David Allen Lewis contends, "The same mentality that leads one to accept an origin of life apart from the Creator also leads to the unsupported conclusion that other intelligent life forms must have evolved on other worlds."[305] Of course, that mentality is atheistic naturalism: the worldview behind astrobiological logic.

A colorful illustration can be derived from sea monkeys, a popular item advertised in comic books when we were kids. Abiogenesis, the belief that life evolves from nonlife, is a lot like believing the advertising hype for Sea Monkeys, because it entails a form of magical thinking popular among atheists. Magical thinking is a fallacious type of reasoning that assumes causal relationships between grouped phenomena that aren't necessarily so (i.e., "follow the water"). Appealing to the magical-thinking characteristic in children, the clever comic book ad featured a fantastic, subaquatic kingdom populated with humanoid mermen in front of their medieval-style castle. Invented in 1957 by Harold von Braunhut, the cleverly marketed product promised your very own colony of these alien beings by just adding an "instant-life" packet to a fish tank full of water.

I still remember my excitement as I added the "instant-life" packet to the water in my goldfish bowl. I had been dreaming about the characters in the ad and of all the cool adventures we would have. The water got a little cloudy as I eagerly awaited my mermen to appear. And I waited some more…and then I read the instructions that said I might need a magnifier. Maybe I should have read the fine print? Nevertheless, I was only eight years old and sorely disappointed that my Sea Monkeys didn't look anything like those in the comic book. Even worse, they all died after a few weeks (which was probably my fault, too).

Whereas the "instant-life" concept is compatible with astrobiological assumptions, it was really only clever marketing. In truth, sea monkeys are brine shrimp, a kind of crustacean capable of cryptobiosis, a state somewhat like extreme hibernation in response to adverse conditions like dehydration, freezing temperature, or lack of oxygen. Interestingly, John Glenn took sea monkeys into space aboard Space Shuttle Discovery during mission STS-95. After nine days in space, they were returned to Earth, and hatched eight weeks later apparently unaffected by their travels, a point addressed in the following pages.

Sea Monkey advertisement from 1971

The law of biogenesis, attributed to Louis Pasteur, is the observation that living things come only from other living things, by reproduction. That is, life does not arise from nonliving material. The dominant view held by scientists at the time of Pasteur was called *Spontaneous Generation*. For example, biologists believed that maggots magically popped into being when meat rotted. But Pasteur went against the scientific consensus and boiled the rotten meat, showing that, once sterile, it never produced maggots. Of course, we now know that fly eggs were the culprit. This law proposes an insurmountable obstacle for Darwinian evolution that cannot get started, a state of affairs that prompted Darwin to speculate a "just-so" story about lightning striking a pond of proverbial "primordial soup." Later, Thomas Henry Huxley, known as "Darwin's Bulldog," appended an "a"—for negation of the law of biogenesis—and coined the term "abiogenesis," implying life arising from nonlife, even though it is not clear how this differs significantly from the discredited theory of spontaneous generation other than it is held to be an uncommon, even singular, event in the history of the universe. This state of affairs leads Dr. Ross to conclude that astrobiology is a colossal waste of resources:

> Sometimes, fear of a Christian interpretation of science leads not only to wasted time but also to wasted research talent and money. Astrobiology and SETI (search for extraterrestrial intelligence) serve as examples. In astrobiology, the no-Creator assumption combines with the awareness that life arose on Earth in a geological instant without benefit of prebiotics to compel the conclusion that the origin of life must have been—and still must be—an extremely simple naturalistic event. [A note in original material here included the following citation: P. C. W. Davies and Charles H. Lineweaver, "Finding a Second Sample of Life on Earth," *Astrobiology* 5 (2005): 154–163.] Based on this conclusion, a new branch of science was born. Astrobiology springs from the conviction that literally millions of planets in the Milky

Way Galaxy, as well as several solar system bodies, must be teeming with life.[306]

While naturalists offer up a myriad of "just-so" stories, there are insurmountable problems for the accidental abiogenesis hypothesis.

A prominent example is homochirality, which describes a property of life-essential molecules that consist of only "left-handed" amino acids and "right-handed" sugars. The hand analogy describes chiral molecules, which are mirror images (called isomers) of each other, but the differences are very significant. For instance, the drug naproxen sodium is a wonderful pain killer in one isomer and a deadly poison in its mirror image. To produce the drug, a reaction is done that creates both left-handed and right-handed varieties, and then scientists carefully filter out the poison, leaving the useful isomer for human consumption. But how can a random, accidental process select one isomer over another? A primordial soup would naturally contain equal proportions of left-handed and right-handed molecules. Even more, why does life only use one type? Dr. Fazale Rana, a biochemist, argues, "Homochirality places a demand on naturalistic origin-of-life explanations—a demand that goes beyond the production of life's building blocks and their assembly into complex molecules. And this demand goes unmet."[307] While the probabilities involved in the assembly of even simple proteins are considered absurd, the situation for a natural origin hypothesis is dismal in light of homochirality. In this case, intelligent design is a very reasonable scientific inference.

Of course, the hardened materialist cannot allow a divine foot in the door. Consequently, the origin and development of life are both said to arise via natural selection. Of course, natural selection occurs when a trait provides a survival advantage and gets passed on to offspring while others are eliminated by death. It requires existing life struggling to survive. Although the claim that natural selection functions on nonlife is incoherent, this does not seem to sway naturalists. For instance, the outspoken atheist and professor of zoology, Richard Dawkins, famously wrote:

Natural selection, the blind, unconscious, automatic process which Darwin discovered, and which we now know is the <u>explanation for the existence</u> and apparently purposeful form of all life, has no purpose in mind. It has no mind and no mind's eye. It does not plan for the future. It has no vision, no foresight, no sight at all.[308] (underline added)

While Dawkins' bold proclamation (that natural selection is the explanation for the *existence* of life) represents the worst kind of circular reasoning, his description reveals the haphazard nature of the process. This is where we take issue with theistic evolution advocated by Rome and some evangelicals because Darwinism by definition is not guided. Because of its dependency on randomness, natural selection lacks a mechanism for true convergence, a narrowing-down process that leads to viable results. Mutations are more likely to be harmful than beneficial, and even then they only occur in *living* organisms. Furthermore, convergence, which is necessary to surmount the astronomical probabilities involved in the origin of life, implies a goal that indicates teleology or design, an idea repugnant to atheistic naturalists and, apparently, Jesuit astronomers alike.

Guy Consolmagno has said of intelligent design, "The word has been hijacked by a narrow group of Creationist fundamentalists in America to mean something it didn't originally mean at all…. It's another form of the God of the gaps."[309] By "God of the gaps," he refers to the argument that Creationists simply look for areas that science has not explained—the gaps—and then assert that "God did it." We take his comment rather personally because we believe the scientific *evidence*, not the gaps within, is best explained by design, and, even though they will not admit it, most scientists know it deep down. Francis Crick, the Nobel Prize-winning codiscoverer of the double helix structure of DNA, acknowledged, "An honest man, armed with all the knowledge available to us now, could only state that in some sense, the origin of life appears at the moment to be almost a miracle, so many are the conditions which would have had to be satisfied to get it going."[310] Since then, discoveries of tiny molecular machines inside the cell indicate life is even more complex than Crick was aware. Accordingly, the notion that the origin of life occurred by chance is indefensible. Roger White, a professor at MIT, writes in his paper ("Does Origins of Life Research Rest on a Mistake?") that origins research is marked by two contradictory features: 1) the opinion that life could not arise by chance; and 2) that purposeful agency and intelligent design are not serious options.[311] Naturally, these contradictory tenets cannot coherently coexist. This profound state of cognitive dissonance necessarily extends to astrobiological research.

The Drake Equation

Devised in 1961 by astrophysicist Dr. Frank Drake, the Drake equation is a mathematical equation used to estimate the number of detectable extraterrestrial civilizations in the Milky Way galaxy. The Drake equation states:

$$N = R^* \cdot f_p \cdot n_e \cdot f_l \cdot f_i \cdot f_c \cdot L$$

N = the number of civilizations in our galaxy with which communication might be possible

R^* = the average rate of star formation per year in our galaxy

f_p = the fraction of those stars that have planets

n_e = the average number of planets that can potentially support life per star that has planets

f_l = the fraction of the above that actually go on to develop life at some point

f_i = the fraction of the above that actually go on to develop intelligent life

f_c = the fraction of civilizations that develop a technology that releases detectable signs of their existence into space

L = the length of time for which such civilizations release detectable signals into space[312]

While it is used to justify SETI and the extraterrestrial hypothesis for UFOs, this equation gives the appearance of scientific rigor, but falls well short. The only variable known with any degree of certainty is the rate of stellar formation, R. In the Milky Way, a typical spiral galaxy, new stars form at a rate of roughly four per year.[313] The rest of the variables are probabilities based on evolutionary assumptions. According to Dr. Ross:

Evolutionists argue for a high probability of life elsewhere in the Universe by quoting the following statistic: if only one in a million stars has planets, and if only one in a million of these planets has the right conditions for life, and if only one in a million of these planets has evolved life, then there would still be thousands of life-bearing planets in the Universe.[314]

The variable astronomers feel the least certain about is L, the length of time a civilization remains detectable. A wide variety of estimates have been used for L, yielding divergent results.

Back in 1961, the values that were inserted into the equation by Drake yielded an answer of up to 100 million hypothetical civilizations out there waiting to enlighten us. Now that's a lot of aliens! Of course, all of the figures were manufactured out of whole cloth, but this has not stopped the true believers at SETI. Based on the Cold War and mankind's penchant for self-destructive behavior, Carl Sagan speculated that all of the variables except for L (the lifetime of a civilization) are relatively high, and the determining factor is civilization lifetime. Since Drake and Sagan made their estimates, astronomers have become more conservative. Paul Horowitz, who brazenly guaranteed the existence of extraterrestrial life, generated more modest results, closer to one thousand civilizations. *Skeptic* magazine publisher Michael Shermer argued that astronomers weren't being conservative enough about the length of time a civilization transmits detectable signals. Based on Earth history, he estimated a value for L between 304.5 years and 420.6 years. This yields between 2.44 and 3.36 extraterrestrial civilizations.[315] The astonishing inconsistency between answers like 100 million and *three* ought to suggest something to the reader.

The Drake equation is a poor rationale for belief in ET because the so-called data is merely guesswork. As science-fiction author Michael Crichton stated in 2003:

> As a result, the Drake equation can have any value from "billions and billions" to zero. An expression that can mean anything means nothing. Speaking precisely, the Drake equation is literally meaningless, and has nothing to do with science. I take the hard view that science involves the creation of testable hypotheses. The Drake equation cannot be tested and therefore SETI is not science. SETI is unquestionably a religion.[316]

While ET true believers leap at the Drake equation's feigned rationality, the evidence presented in the *Reasons to Believe Testable Creation Model*[317] is far more rigorous, because it is open to testing and falsification. Even the most enthusiastic SETI believers must admit to the eerie silence after more than forty years of listening to the cosmos.

Fermi's Paradox

The Fermi Paradox is the contradiction between the alleged high probability of extant extraterrestrial civilizations and the lack of confirmed contact with such civilizations. For the reasons of exploration, colonization, and survival, there are good reasons to think an existing ET civilization should be detectable. While we do have UFO sightings, we never see them coming from far away in space. This leads us to suspect they are a localized phenomenon. Since a genuine advanced alien civilization would be expected to spread in a relatively short time, scientists reason, how is it possible that that we do not see them out in space and that our radio telescopes have never collected significant signals of suspect origin? This conundrum has an interesting story behind it.

Back in 1950, a group of brilliant scientists working at Los Alamos National Laboratories engaged in a lunchroom conversation about flying saucers. The conversing colleagues included physicists Enrico Fermi, Emil Konopinski, Edward Teller, and Herbert York. The men discussed a recent UFO flap and an Alan Dunn cartoon facetiously blaming the disappearance of New York City trash cans on extraterrestrial kleptomaniacs.

1950 *New Yorker* Cartoon by Alan Dunn

Emil Konopinski recalls the conversation:

When I joined the party, I found being discussed evidence about flying saucers. That immediately brought to my mind a cartoon I had recently seen in the *New Yorker*, explaining why public trash cans were disappearing from the streets of New York City. The New York papers were making a fuss about that. The cartoon showed what was evidently a flying saucer sitting in the background and, streaming toward it, "little green men" (endowed with antennas) carrying the trash cans. More amusing was Fermi's comment, that it was a very reasonable theory since it accounted for two separate phenomena: the reports of flying saucers as well as the disappearance of the trash cans. There ensued a discussion as to whether the saucers could somehow exceed the speed of light.[318]

The discussion of whether light speed can be surpassed is germane to the extraterrestrial hypothesis for flying saucers because of the prohibitively vast distances that would need to be traversed. According to Ross, "To say that the nearest star is 25 trillion miles away simply does not make the point. An analogy, or scale model, may help, at least a little: if the sun (nearly a million miles in diameter) were represented by a grapefruit, and if someone were to place that grapefruit in the middle of downtown Los Angeles, then a second grapefruit representing the nearest star would lie in downtown Managua, Nicaragua."[319] Accordingly, it would take thousands of years for aliens to reach Earth. This is what prompted the lunchtime discussion of "faster than light speed," which would seem to be a requirement if flying saucers are actually extraterrestrial.

Edward Teller, known as the father of the hydrogen bomb, put the odds of observing beyond-light-speed travel at one in a million, but Fermi argued a much more optimistic one in ten. Later in the day, after pondering the implications, Fermi suddenly exclaimed out of the blue, "Where are they?" According to this account, Fermi then made a series of rapid calculations and concluded that Earth should have been visited long ago and many times over. This extends to the Drake equation as well. If the Drake and Sagan estimates were correct, then the aliens should be self-evident. Hence, the paradox: If the universe is teeming with life, then where are they? UFOs do not behave in a manner that leads us to believe they are ETs doing scientific research. We believe they are better explained by more terrestrial terms, though disturbing. That case is developed within.

Panspermia

Because the evidence for abiogenesis on Earth is so severely lacking, scientists have proposed that life was seeded here from outer space. The term for this idea, panspermia, derives from two Greek terms: *pan*, meaning "all," and *sperma*, meaning "seed." It's actually an old idea. As discussed above, Louis Pasteur proved that spontaneous generation did not occur, but instead the air was full of bacteria, spores, and other forms of reproducing life. This suggested to a few biologists that outer space could be similarly endowed. Near the same time, Charles Darwin published *On the Origin of Species*, which promoted the notion that life was constantly evolving over time. These two nineteenth-century paradigm shifts led to conflicting conclusions regarding the origin of life. Pasteur believed that his work supported Divine Creation, but Darwinists thought that life probably evolved from nonlife. However, when early primordial soup ideas fell into disrepute due to recognition of cell complexity in the early twentieth century, evolutionists postulated that life had never originated, but instead was eternal. Scientists like Englishman William Thomson (Lord) Kelvin and German Hermann von Helmholtz promoted the idea. For example, Helmholtz proposed in 1871:

> It seems to me a perfectly just scientific procedure, if we, after the failure of all our attempts to produce organisms from lifeless matter, put the question whether life has had a beginning at all,

or whether it is not as old as matter, and whether seeds have not been carried from one planet to another and have developed everywhere that they have fallen on a fertile soil.[320]

In like fashion, Svante Arrhenius, a Swedish scientist who won the Nobel Prize for chemistry in 1903, argued that life-producing spores "have been transplanted for eternal ages from solar system to solar system and from planet to planet of the same system."[321] Accordingly, the early forms of undirected panspermia were based on an eternal universe born out of the need to avoid the origin of life entirely. This suggests that modern astrobiology is similarly motivated.

Of course, today, the overwhelming majority of scientists now recognize that the universe had a beginning and, consequently, life must have originated somewhere if not on Earth. Ideas like Arrhenius' journeymen spores have been discredited by the discovery that they would never survive the killer ultraviolet radiation in space or the blazing heat of entry into the atmosphere. For this reason, today's most accepted version postulates that life originated on another planet and was carried to Earth by a large meteor or comet that impacted Earth. Even if allowed, panspermia only offers a solution to how life might have started on Earth. It really does not actually address the origin question; rather, it sidesteps it and projects it onto a fantasy world. We will show below that this sort of irrational leap of faith is characteristic of all nontheistic worldviews. The origin of life still needs an explanation, and we think Divine Creation is the most compelling for evidential reasons.

While former VORG director George Coyne has suggested that the "stars are God's sperm,"[322] naturalistic panspermia faces serious challenges. First and foremost, life in space has never been shown to exist. But even if allowed for argument's sake, only if the seeds are encased deeply inside mineralized rock for protection could their survival be deemed remotely possible. How this could occur is the focus of intense research.[323] Even though he denied the VORG's current involvement in astrobiological research during an interview with the authors of this book,[324] Vatican astronomer Guy Consolmagno, who specializes in meteors, indicated in 2004 that he was working with NASA astrobiologist Lynn Rothschild on whether meteorites are adequate for transporting life to earth.[325] Evidence suggests that some microbes can survive the radiation in space, but the intense heat of entry into the atmosphere still poses a serious challenge. While John Glenn's sea monkeys, mentioned above, were preserved in the comfort of the Space Shuttle Discovery, they would have been instantly incinerated if exposed during reentry. This leads other scientists to suggest that life was intentionally seeded on Earth by extraterrestrials (a form of intelligent design).

In 1973, *directed* panspermia was put forth by the aforementioned Nobel Prize-winning Dr. Francis Crick along with Dr. Leslie Orgel of the Salk Institute. This goes far beyond moss-covered meteorites or wayfaring spores on holiday and we believe provides ample fodder for a diabolic ruse. The abstract of their famous paper, "Directed Panspermia," reads:

> It now seems unlikely that extraterrestrial living organisms could have reached the earth either as spores driven by the radiation pressure from another star or as living organisms imbedded in a meteorite. As an alternative to these nineteenth-century mechanisms, we have considered Directed Panspermia, the theory that organisms were deliberately transmitted to the earth by intelligent beings on another planet. We conclude that it is possible that life reached the earth in this way, but that the scientific evidence is inadequate at the present time to say anything about the probability. We draw attention to the kinds of evidence that might throw additional light on the topic.[326]

They go on to suggest that life could have "started on Earth as a result of infection by microorganisms sent here deliberately by a technological society on another planet, by means of a special long-range unmanned spaceship."[327] It is important to note that Crick and Orgel were driven toward this fantastic notion because of their doubt that random evolutionary processes could account for the complexity of the recently discovered DNA molecule, and we believe that the problem has not significantly changed since. Consequently, directed panspermia is gaining traction, especially in popular parlance.

Science fiction authors and the entertainment industry have been promoting this notion for decades. Recent films like *Prometheus* (2012), *Knowing* (2009), and *Mission to Mars* (2000) have sown this seed into the public psyche. Interestingly, Richard Dawkins made an appeal to directed panspermia in the movie *Expelled* when he was asked about the origin of life by Ben Stein:

Stein: How did it get created?

Dawkins: By a very slow process.

Stein: Well, how did it start?

Dawkins: Nobody knows how it got started. We know the kind of event that it must have been. We know the sort of event that must have happened for the origin of life.

Stein: And what was that?

Dawkins: It was the origin of the first self-replicating molecule.

Stein: Right, and how did that happen?

Dawkins: I told you, we *don't know*.

Stein: What do you think is the possibility that Intelligent Design might turn out to be the answer to some issues in genetics or in Darwinian evolution.

Dawkins: Well, it could come about in the following way. It could be that at some earlier time, somewhere in the universe, a civilization evolved, probably by some kind of Darwinian means, probably to a very high level of technology, and designed a form of life that they seeded onto perhaps this planet. Um, now that is a possibility, and an intriguing possibility. And I suppose it's possible that you might find evidence for that if you look at the details of biochemistry, molecular biology, you might find a signature of some sort of designer.

Stein (as narrator): So Professor Dawkins was not against Intelligent Design, just certain types of designers *such as God.*[328]

As the bestselling author of *The God Delusion*, Dawkins is probably the most famous atheist in the world, so this exchange made for great sport, inspiring quips like "the Dawkins delusion" and the "the aliens of the gaps." However, it is important to note that there are theistic variants of directed panspermia that posit that God providentially guided microbial seeds of life to Earth from space. In the same way that theistic evolutionists believe God used a Darwinian process, a few intelligent design theorists like NASA physicist Dr. Robert Sheldon postulate panspermia as God's means of getting things started on Earth.[329] Thus, if it turns out that there is evidence for panspermia, then belief in God is not necessarily threatened, although Creationism would face a serious challenge. For an excellent treatment of panspermia and the related issues, we recommend Dr. Michael Heiser's chapter in the 2009 Defender publication: *How to Overcome the Most Frightening Issues You Will Face This Century.*

As a theologian, biblical scholar, and ufologist, Dr. Heiser has been carefully thinking through these issues for longer than most. We will draw on his work in exotheology in chapter 11, "Exotheology: Nature and Grace," but he has suggested some possibilities connecting panspermia to the thesis of this book. We suggest that Rome is paving the way, intentionally or not, for widespread acceptance of an alleged alien savior.

We also think an effective end-time deception must be subtle enough to possibly deceive the elect (Matthew 24:24). Heiser sees a strong possibility that evidence for panspermia and extraterrestrials will lead the masses to think God used the extraterrestrials, represented as angels, as His agents in Creation. Accordingly, this could be presented in such a way that does not require one to explicitly renounce his or her faith, but instead, to radically reinterpret it.

Speaking to panspermia, Heiser explains, "It paves the way for a true merging of science and religion. It will be the paradigm that allows the atheist to tolerate religion, and allows literalist Bible-readers, the eastern Buddhist, and the pagan to simultaneously parse the new science the same way. This might in turn be useful fodder for a global religion."[330] Interestingly, an impetus toward globalism is one of the reasons political scientists cite for the US government's ostensibly preferred ignorance concerning the UFO evidence (as discussed in chapter 3, "Days of Noah"). Heiser suspects that, in the near future, scientists will announce a discovery supporting panspermia that will quickly be extrapolated by the public into belief in extraterrestrials. When considered in light of the present public acceptance of ancient astronauts, this ripple effect could eliminate "any discernible obstacle to articulating a global religion that honors the cosmologies of all faiths, united as they are under the reality of panspermia and extraterrestrial influence."[331] We think Dr. Heiser's suggestion has merit, but it begs the question of why people of faith might be so easily swayed. We hope to prepare biblical Christians for what lies ahead. In this case, knowledge is power, so let us examine the basis for astrobiological assumptions.

The Incoherence of the Mediocrity Principle

We come full circle by returning to the foundational tenet of astrobiology: the principle of mediocrity. Recall that this is the idea that the Earth is a mediocre planet among many and, consequently, we should expect to find advanced life throughout the cosmos. But this principle simply assumes that the Earth is a representative example of the habitable zone planets. The logic is deceptive, because it employs a bait-and-switch tactic that may or may not be intentional. The main point is that the Earth is not necessarily representative of all planets in the habitable zone. There is a lot of confusion between necessary and sufficient conditions. As we have shown in this chapter, a great deal of evidence suggests the Earth is a very special place.

The mediocrity argument appeals to a tautology. By this, we mean something that is so obviously true it is basically meaningless, like 1 = 1. In this case, we are given two sets of planets: set A and set B. Just to make the math easy, let's say set A has nine planets and set B has only one, for a total of ten. So when drawing a random sample from the ten total planets, one has a 90-percent chance of getting a planet from set A and a 10 percent chance of drawing one from set B. This is a tautology that no one will dispute. Now, the sleight of hand comes into play.

Astrobiologists are doing something akin to defining A and B together as all planets in the habitable zone. Because Earth is the only habitable zone planet we know about, and it has life, they reason it has a 90-percent chance of coming from the more numerous group (notice this is backwards, as it wasn't drawn from the group). Thus, they assert that set A contains habitable zone planets with life and B has habitable zone planets without life. Therefore, 90 percent of planets in the habitable zone must contain life. In logic, this is called a *non sequitur*—it does not follow. We already know the Earth has life, and they simply assumed it represents the larger group based on the tautology that you are more likely to draw from the more numerous group. But the Earth is not a sample drawn at random from all planets in the habitable zone; as far as we know, it is utterly unique. Therefore, the principle of mediocrity as a justification for astrobiology is fallacious reasoning.

While the principle of mediocrity (evidence for truly Earthlike planets) and abiogenesis is anything but compelling, the Copernican principle itself could be on shaky ground as well. What if it turns out that, in a way Copernicus never could have imagined, we *are* in the center of the universe? On June 30, 2001, NASA launched the Wilkinson Microwave Anisotropy Probe (WMAP), a spacecraft that measures differences in the temperature of the Big Bang's remnant radiant heat called the Cosmic Microwave Background Radiation across the sky. To the astonishment of the scientists, results from WMAP run counter to Copernican expectations.[332] The cosmic structure detected by the WMAP and the orientation of the ecliptic—the plane of the sun as observed from the Earth—are mysteriously aligned. Cosmologist Lawrence Krauss, an outspoken atheist, seems taken aback by the data:

> But when you look at [the cosmic microwave background] map, you also see that the structure that is observed, is in fact, in a weird way, correlated with the plane of the earth around the sun. Is this Copernicus coming back to haunt us? That's crazy. We're looking out at the whole universe. There's no way there should be a correlation of structure with our motion of the earth around the sun—the plane of the earth around the sun—the ecliptic. That would say *we are truly the center of the universe.*[333] (emphasis added)

While we are not claiming the Earth is in the center of the universe, it is interesting that a staunch atheist like Krauss admits to such an anti-Copernican result. Perhaps it will turn out to be the case, but for now it remains a curiosity.

Astrobiology: A Secular Faith

The search for life in the universe is fundamentally a religious quest. According to NASA: "NASA's Astrobiology Program addresses three fundamental questions: How does life begin and evolve? Is there life beyond Earth and, if so, how can we detect it? What is the future of life on Earth and in the universe?"[334] Because the secularist desires answers to the fundamental worldview questions like, "Why am I here?"; "Where did I come from?"; and "What does the future hold?" while at the same time denying the Creator, he gazes hopefully out into space. What follows in an excerpt from a report by the Space Science Board of the American National Academy of Sciences:

> The scientific question at stake in exobiology is, in the opinion of many, the most exciting, challenging, and profound issue, not only of this century but of the whole naturalistic movement that has characterized the history of Western thought for three hundred years. What is at stake is the chance to gain a new perspective on man's place in nature, a new level of discussion on the meaning and nature of life.[335]

Notice it goes well beyond science as a search for *the meaning of life*. It's not as if the naturalist thinks he has much choice. After all, due to a naturalistic worldview, he has nowhere else to look as demonstrated by the famous words of Carl Sagan, "The cosmos is all that is, or ever was, or ever will be."[336] A naturalist believes that the physical universe is the sum total of all that is. Accordingly, if there are any ultimate answers to be found, they must be "out there."

But there are answers! Man's chief end is to glorify God and to enjoy Him forever. This is available for all who will respond to the good news: "That if thou shalt confess with thy mouth the Lord Jesus, and shalt believe in thine heart that God hath raised him from the dead, thou shalt be saved" (Romans 10:9). From our reading of Bible prophecy, we suspect the "god of this world" will soon step up to offer deceptive answers in a manner so compelling that it might "deceive the very elect" (2 Corinthians 4:4; Matthew 24: 23).

Summary Points to Remember:

- The Vatican is not only involved in astrobiology. The Pontifical Academy of Sciences hosted a conference for the top scientists in the field.

- At the 2009 study week that the Pontifical Academy of Sciences hosted, it was announced that a major discovery was expected in a few short years.
- The VORG has worked on panspermia by meteorite and now has a new exoplanet expert in place for accessing the LBT and LUCIFER projects.
- New exoplanet discoveries are being announced every week, but, to date, only nine are called "habitable." We expect this to increase due to the Kepler space probe and LBT telescope.
- "Habitable" is a misnomer, as there is strong evidence that the Earth is unique.
- The anthropic principle or fine-tuning of the universe is so compelling that even famous atheists like Anthony Flew have renounced atheism.
- There is no evidence for abiogenesis (life from nonlife).
- Panspermia is the idea that life came to Earth from space.
- Panspermia may be used to inspire a global religion.
- The Jesuit scientists oppose intelligent design and Creationism.
- The Drake equation is basically meaningless.
- Fermi's Paradox counts against genuine ETs and implies that UFO/UAP are terrestrial.
- The mediocrity principle is based on fallacious leaps in logic.
- Astrobiology is fundamentally driven by a naturalistic worldview.

8 | Astro-Apologetics and the End Times

"I always wish to be the spokesman for these star peoples who also are part of God's glory, and I will continue to bring it to the attention of the Holy Mother Church."[337] —Monsignor Corrado Balducci, Exorcist Archdiocese of Rome

"We are witnessing a masterful satanic subterfuge that appears to involve the appearance of 'angels' and 'aliens.' Many are asking whether the coming of Antichrist can be far removed."[338] —Timothy J. Dailey PhD, Senior Fellow Family Research Council

On July 7th, 2011, Pope Benedict XVI released an encyclical *Caritas in Veritate*, or "Charity in Truth," calling for a New World Order. While we argued in our former work, *Petrus Romanus: The Final Pope Is Here*, that he could be laying the groundwork for his successor, this has surprising connections to the present discussion as well. Section 67 of that document spoke of an "urgent need of a true world political authority" one with "*real teeth.*"

In the face of the unrelenting growth of global interdependence, there is a strongly felt need, even in the midst of a global recession, for a reform of the United Nations Organization, and likewise of economic institutions and international finance, so that the concept of the family of nations can acquire real teeth.[339]

While there are several elite globalist organizations working toward that end, according to their website, "The World Economic Forum is an independent international organization committed to improving the state of the world by engaging business, political, academic and other leaders of society to shape global, regional and industry agendas."[340] In a report entitled *Global Risks 2013*, among the top five "X factors from nature" is the discovery of alien life, which "could have profound psychological implications for human belief systems."[341] The report explains that this might present a challenge to the assumptions of religion:

> Over the long term the psychological and philosophical implications of the discovery could be profound. If lifeforms (even fossilized lifeforms) are found in our own solar system, for example, it will tell us that the origin of life is "easy"—that anyplace in the universe life can emerge, it will emerge. It will suggest that life is as natural and as ubiquitous a part of the universe as stars and galaxies are. The discovery of even simple life would fuel speculation about the existence of other intelligent beings and challenge many assumptions which underpin human philosophy and religion.[342]

In other words, even microbial extraterrestrial life could be perceived as a confirmation of the mediocrity principle explained in our astrobiology chapter. However, it really only entails an expansion of traditional design reasoning, and the existence of simple life does not by any means demand the existence of intelligent life.

Several questions are suggested. Why is it that many evangelical Christians doubt the existence of extraterrestrial life? Why do Christian scholars like Dr. Walter Martin, Dr. Timothy Dailey, Dr. John Weldon, Dr. John Ankerberg, and Dr. Chuck Missler see connections to demons and biblical, end-time prophecy? Would Christians panic or lose their faith given an ET disclosure event? This chapter will answer those questions while addressing the existence of extraterrestrials in light of biblical revelation, examining contemporary Roman Catholic views, and offering a scriptural defense for its connection to eschatology.

Extraterrestrials and the Biblical Philosophy of History

Perhaps one of the most overlooked differences between Christians and unbelievers is the notion that world history is actually heading somewhere. The Bible presents the ultimate account of history with a cosmic scope. It has a very real and decisive goal in the return of Jesus Christ. Theologian Charles Ryrie wrote, "The Scriptures per se are not a philosophy of history, but they contain one."[343] Because God is the creator and sustainer of all things, most theologians agree that the inherent historical trajectory is universal and ultimate. From Genesis to Revelation, a cosmic conflict centering on humankind is the focus. It begins in a perfect garden with an innocent man and woman who are subsequently corrupted by a usurper, and it ends in that garden with the conflict resolved. The bulk of the Scriptures describes the redemptive process, salvation history, as God's relationship to humanity. How comprehensively one views the scope of revealed history is crucial to one's position in this discussion. Even though Scripture is silent on the existence of extraterrestrial life, that silence is suggestive.

The biblical philosophy of history accounts for the range of events from the dawn of Creation to the return of Christ. Genesis 1:1 boldly declares that God created the entire universe "in the beginning," rendered from the Hebrew term בראשית (bereshit), which is also the name of the book in the Hebrew Bible. Dr. John Sailhamer explains that this denotes an unspecified duration of time: "It is a block of time which precedes an extended series of time periods. It is a time before time. The term does not refer to a point in time but to a period or duration of time which falls before a series of events."[344] Modern cosmology affirms that the universe had a beginning. We find the reluctant twentieth-century acceptance of this fact by scientists a verification of what the Bible stated thousands of years prior. Might there have been other worlds prior to our own during this primeval time of the universe? Some have even suggested a civilization on Mars, where the angels rebelled. We will save that for a later chapter, but there is supporting evidence.

There have been dissenting opinions on the use of *bereshit,* but an examination of the biblical data verifies Sailhamer's exegesis.[345] The Bible mentions that the angels were present and singing while God created the Earth (Job 38:7). Angels are created beings and were necessarily created *before* the Earth. It is clear that the Earth is already present before the days of the Creation week have ensued (Genesis1:2). A day is never specified when God created the angels, chemical elements, molecules like water, and the Earth. They are already present as the Spirit hovers over the waters. Thus, there had to be time for all of this to occur prior to day one. This confirms that the rendering of *bereshit* as an unspecified duration is indeed correct. God reveals further details about Creation through the prophet Isaiah, who wrote, "For thus saith the LORD that created the heavens; God himself that formed the earth and made it; he hath established it, he created it not in vain, he formed it to be inhabited: I am the LORD; and there is none else" (Isaiah 45:18). This speaks of God forming the Earth, which is not accounted for in Genesis. Since the Hebrew word תֹהוּ (*tohu*), translated here "in vain," also appears in Genesis 1:2 as "without form," this statement in Isaiah could imply a contrast between the Earth, which was formed to be inhabited, and the other planets, which were not. Indeed, the ones we do know about are not.

For many of us, this begs the question of why God bothered to create the other planets. As we have detailed elsewhere, the concept of wasted space only applies to beings with limited resources and, in this case, the same applies to effort. Again, God used Isaiah to explain: "Hast thou not known? hast thou not heard, that the everlasting God, the LORD, the Creator of the ends of the earth, fainteth not, neither is weary? there is no searching of his understanding" (Isaiah 40:28). He does not get tired, and He does not run out of resources. In fact, we have been given an answer. God reveals in His word that the heavens above serve for: 1) signs; 2) time keeping; and 3) illumination (Genesis 1:14–15). Most importantly, they testify to God's glory and power:

> The heavens declare the glory of God;
> and the firmament sheweth his handywork.
> Day unto day uttereth speech,
> and night unto night sheweth knowledge. (Psalms 19:1–2)

The Bible states that the Earth was originally given to humans, "The heaven, even the heavens, are the LORD's: but the earth hath he given to the children of men" (Psalms 115:16). However, dominion over the Earth was usurped by a rebellious reptilian and is now under his controlling influence (Psalms 82; 2 Corinthians 4:4; Ephesians 6:2; 1 John 5:19). The Apostle Paul alludes to the entire Creation being cursed when Adam sinned (Romans 8:20–22). A strict, literal rendering of the first phrase of the Greek text of Romans 8:20 ("ᾗ γὰρ ματαιότητι ἡ κτίσις ὑπετάγη") reads, "To for futility the creation has been subjected." The one doing the subjecting is necessarily God, because the last phrase, "him who hath subjected the same in hope" (Romans 8:20b) would exclude Satan. The meaning of the term "κτίσις," which the KJV renders "creature," is derivative of the verb "κτίζω," "to create," and can be understood as "creation," or, according to a scholarly lexicon, "the universe as the product of God's activity in creation—'universe, creation, what was made.'"[346] In fact, missionary scholars who translate the New Testament into various foreign languages try to find a term in the receptor language that means "everything that exists."[347] With this in mind, we wonder, is it pressing too hard on this text to understand this curse as applying to the furthest reaches of outer space?

Some may think we stretch it too far, but undeniably, the Fall of man extended into the realm of nature (Genesis 3:17). A better question might be, "Is there warrant to limit it exclusively to Earth?" Based on the universal language in the epistle to the Romans, it does not seem justified. Paul taught, "For we know that the <u>whole creation</u> groaneth and travaileth in pain together until now" (Romans 8:22, underline added). When we consider the toxic conditions in space and on the other planets in our solar system, it seems to apply. If God did create beings similar to man, they would be included in the "whole creation." However, if they were innocent, it would be unjust to subject them to a curse based on Adam's Fall. Because God is just and consistent, this counts against the existence of sinless extraterrestrials as part of God's Creation. Even so, we do know that Satan fell and took a host of angels with him. Taken at face value, the *sin qua non* (absolutely essential element) of history's turmoil is the devil's opposition to God (Genesis 3:1–5; cf. Revelation 20:10).

While sincere Christians have different views concerning eschatology, most agree on humankind's central role in the divine conflict. For example, universal language describes God's covenant with Israel: "For ask now of the days that are past, which were before thee, since the day that God created man upon the earth, and <u>ask from the one side of heaven unto the other</u>, whether there hath been any such thing as this great thing is, or hath been heard like it?" (Deuteronomy 4:32, underline added). This language implies the covenant is unique to Earth, exclusive to humans, and universally unprecedented. It follows that the incarnation of Jesus Christ as our Savior, delivered via Israel, is similarly universal.

The most compelling biblical argument for the uniqueness of terrestrial life is the incarnation. The Second Person of the Trinity, the One who brought the entire universe into existence (John 1:1–3; Colossians 1:16–17; Hebrews 1:1–2), became an everlasting member of the *human* race in the incarnation (John 1:14; 1 Timothy 2:5; Hebrews 7:24–25). He ascended to heaven bodily and sits on His throne as a man. This strongly counts against the existence of extraterrestrials and multiple incarnations on alien worlds, a topic we will address in chapter 11, "Exotheology: Nature and Grace." Furthermore, the doctrine of the

Second Coming is Earth-centered. Jesus taught us to pray: "Our Father which art in heaven, Hallowed be thy name. Thy kingdom come. Thy will be done in earth, as it is in heaven" (Matthew 6:9–10, underline added). This means the Earth, not some alien exoplanet, is God's chosen location for His kingdom. After all, even the angels long to look into these things (1 Peter 1:12).

Apart from divine beings described in Scripture, we cannot say with certainty whether God has created intelligent beings living on other worlds. God is free to do as He pleases. If He did, as C. S. Lewis has argued, perhaps the vast distances involved are "God's quarantine precautions" meant to protect *them* from us![348] We know that *we are fallen*. The twentieth-century death toll of 262 million killed by their governments leaves no room for protest.[349]

Some point out that the Bible is silent about automobiles and myriad other modern developments, but we do not argue that cars or toaster ovens don't exist. For example, Lutheran theologian and professor Ted Peters' critique of the fundamentalist position concludes:

> It seems to me that fundamentalist interpreters perceive with accuracy the salvific structure inherent to the developing UFO myth in our society and, further, that this myth stands at some variance with what Christians want to teach. For this the appropriate response is Christian apologetic theology, to be sure. Yet, the apologetic argument as actually raised here is unnecessarily confused with fallacious appeals to the exclusive authority of the Bible.[350]

While we will address the "UFO myth" in a later chapter, Peters is referring to an argument by Frank Allnut in the book, *Infinite Encounters* (1978), which argues against the existence of ETs somewhat similarly to the above. Peters points out the fallacy of arguing from ignorance (i.e., the Bible does not mention ETs, therefore ETs do not exist.) However, we are not saying that the Bible's silence leads to the definite conclusion that

"ETs don't exist." We concede an argument from silence is tenuous, but we are not arguing from silence as much as from the revelation we *have* been given concerning history's goal. Not to mention, we have scientific doubts, as documented in our chapter on astrobiology. Furthermore, it's somewhat of a category error. Automobiles, Swiss watches, and toaster ovens are not inspiring, theological revisionism. For us, the crux of the matter is the sufficiency of Scripture and, given the implications, we doubt God would leave His church so unprepared. Biblical prophecy lays out a future scenario, and it isn't at all like *Star Trek*. For this reason, we advise militant agnosticism for now and proactive skepticism regarding any future claim to extraterrestrial disclosure.

Does ET Disclosure Threaten Christianity?

A few secular ufologists have suggested that Christians might lose their faith or even panic given an ET reality. Some of this stems from a report commissioned by NASA in 1960 widely known as *The Brookings Report*, which stated:

> The Fundamentalist (and anti-science) sects are growing apace around the world and, as missionary enterprises, may have schools and a good deal of literature attached to them. One of the important things is that, where they are active, they appeal to the illiterate and semiliterate (including, as missions, the preachers as well as the congregation) and can pile up a very influential following in terms of numbers. For them, the discovery of other life—rather than any other space product—would be electrifying.[351]

Since then, several surveys have attempted to determine whether religious folks would panic or lose their faith. The earliest attempt was the *Alexander UFO Religious Crisis Survey* (AUFORCS), conducted in 1994. This survey, directed by Victoria Alexander, wife of retired army colonel, Dr. John Alexander, focused on the responses of a relatively small sample of Protestant ministers, Roman Catholic priests, and Jewish rabbis. The findings were somewhat surprising to secularists because they indicated there would *not* be a crisis of faith. Colonel Alexander wrote of the report:

> Victoria noted in her conclusions, "As the Alexander UFO Religious Crisis Survey illustrates, religion should not be summarily categorized as unresponsive or inflexible to challenging matters. They do not appear to be in danger of disintegration at the news that the UFO community believes would overwhelm them." She goes on to state "that religious leaders did not believe their faith and the faith of their congregation would be challenged by contact with an advanced extraterrestrial civilization—one with or without a religion. According to many respondents, it would confirm God's glory as the creator of the universe."[352]

While this speaks to a greater resilience than expected by many secular ufologists, it has been noted that Roman Catholics were overrepresented in the survey.[353] Since then, Ted Peters has provided a valuable service to the family of faith by performing a more rigorously scientific survey that corroborates the religious *non*crisis. The abstract reads:

> The Peters ETI Religious Crisis Survey was constructed to test the following hypothesis: upon confirmation of contact between earth and an extraterrestrial civilization of intelligent beings, the long established religious traditions of earth would confront a crisis of belief and perhaps even collapse. Responses from individuals self-identifying with seven religious traditions—Roman Catholicism, mainline Protestantism, evangelical Protestantism, Orthodox Christianity, Mormonism, Judaism, and Buddhism—

indicate widespread acceptance of the existence of ETI and incorporation of ETI into their existing belief systems. Religious persons, for the most part, do not fear contact. Forecasts regarding imminent collapse of earth's religious belief systems were found to be more prevalent among non-religious respondents than among religious respondents. This survey provides evidence that tends to disconfirm the hypothesis.[354]

Interestingly, Peters also found the expectation of a religious crisis was largely on the part of the nonreligious. Indeed, it seems that the popular notion concerning collapsing faith in the face of ET disclosure is overstated. Even though the 1960 *Brookings Report* said it would be "electrifying" for fundamentalists, it actually made the case that scientists with a naturalistic worldview might be more threatened:

> It has been speculated that, of all groups, scientists and engineers might be the most devastated by the discovery of relatively superior creatures, since these professions are most clearly associated with the mastery of nature, rather than with the understanding and expression of man. Advanced understanding of nature might vitiate all our theories at the very least, if not also require a culture and perhaps a brain inaccessible to earth scientists.[355]

Indeed, it was Stephen Hawking who warned in 2010 that contact would be "too risky."[356] The Christian faith is based on the resurrection of Jesus Christ and the word of God in Scripture. Our faith is not predicated on something as tenuous as the existence of ETs. We are open to following the evidence where it leads and testing the spirits should such an occasion arise.

At this time we would like to address a few statements within the book, *A. D. After Disclosure: When the Government Finally Reveals the Truth About Alien Contact*, by Richard M. Dolan, Bryce Zabel, and Jim Marrs. Speaking to our position, the authors write:

People do not change overnight. For better as well as for worse, during times of stress, during periods of great uncertainty and even fear, believers will hold more closely than ever to their faith. One key article of faith among Christians is that God will not allow his creation, humankind, to be possessed by dark, Luciferian forces. Instead, it remains within the power of all souls to accept God and reject Satan.[357]

Actually, the Bible teaches that the world has been under the influence of dark forces since the Fall of Adam and remains so until Christ's return (1 John 5:19, 2 Corinthians 4:4). We refer you to the second chapter of the Epistle to the Ephesians. Also, the question of human autonomy in accepting God and rejecting Satan is a matter of intense intermural debate among Christians and is by no means a given. However, both sides of that discussion do agree that only the Holy Spirit can lead one to saving faith (1 Corinthians 12:3).

The authors of *After Disclosure* continue:

If the Christians are right about how they interpret the UFO phenomenon, it is hoped that the rest of humanity will thank them for their stand against a demonic presence masking as extraterrestrials. If they are wrong, or even incomplete, in their analysis, they will be seen as obstructionist or even dangerous, refusing to see the truth that stares them in the face.[358]

This is a fair assessment, but of course we think we are correct. Even so, we advise prayer and skepticism, not fear and violence, for our readers. If these events are connected to prophecy in the way many Christians expect them to be, then it is Jesus Christ, not His followers, who will resolve the situation. If we are incorrect in our view, Michael Heiser and Ted Peters are providing helpful answers as to how evangelical Christians might parse a *genuine* ET reality.

We realize that some of this discussion might seem inconsistent with our argument against ET belief based on a biblical philosophy of history, but an important qualification is in order. In light of the UFO phenomenon and the deceptive behavior of its associated entities, we think the existence of genuine ETs is, for all intents and purposes, a separate issue. David Fetcho made a similar point in the *Spiritual Counterfeits Project Journal*: "The Bible does not demand that we believe one hypothesis or the other regarding the existence of physical beings elsewhere in the universe. The more pressing demand, both biblically and pragmatically, is to discern the activities of the Adversary through the various guises under which he operates."[359] A huge paradigm shift involving benevolent ET advisors guiding us in our spiritual evolution does not fit well with a biblical philosophy of history, but an *alien disclosure deception does*.

Biblical Prophecy

When Jesus' disciples asked Him about His coming at the end of the age, He began with, "Take heed that no man deceive you" (Matthew 24:4). He warned of increasing numbers of false prophets (Matthew 24:5, 11). While those warnings apply generally to false doctrines and religions, He narrows His focus explicitly to a time: "For then shall be great tribulation, such as was not since the beginning of the world to this time, no, nor ever shall be" (Matthew 24:21), which is necessarily connected to the general resurrection of the dead in Daniel 12:1 and cannot be relegated to the destruction of Jerusalem in AD 70, as preterists erroneously assert. Jesus predicted a false messiah would come in "His own name" and would be accepted by the Jews (John 5:43). At this time, the deception will become so convincing that "if it were possible, they shall deceive the very elect" (Matthew 24:24).While it is clear that the time prior to His return will be one of unmatched deception, Jesus' prediction concerning "men's hearts failing them for fear, and for looking after <u>those things which are coming on the earth</u>: for the powers of heaven shall be shaken" (Luke 21:26, underline added) seems to infer something believed to be not of this world, i.e., *extraterrestrial.* Paul's writings confirm the teachings of Jesus.

Paul wrote to Timothy that during the last days, people would depart from Christianity and fall prey to seducing spirits and doctrines of demons (1 Timothy 4:1–3). Although the "latter days" ensued at Pentecost, the temporal language implies a progression culminating in a distinctively universal demonic seduction. Confirming this idea, Paul taught the Thessalonians that prior to Christ's return there will be an apostasy and appearance of "a man of sin" who will proclaim to be God (vv. 3–4). This "man of sin" is widely considered to be the Antichrist or the "the Beast" in the book of Revelation (Revelation 13, 17). In addition, Daniel wrote of a king who would "magnify himself above every god, and shall speak marvellous things against the God of gods" (Daniel 11:36). The title, "God of gods," is revealing, as we believe these events will entail a showdown of divine beings who exercise untold power and influence over this world. According to Paul, this tyrant's appearance will be accompanied by unprecedented signs, and God will allow the unbelieving world to fall under a "strong delusion, that they should believe a lie" (2 Thessalonians 2:11). Of course, Paul is unequivocal that Satan and his rebel angels will carry this out, and, according to biblical theology, the realm they will operate from is *the sky.*

The Prince of the Power of the Air

Paul's description of Satan as the "prince" (*archōn*) "of the air" (*tou aeros*) or "prince of the power of the air" (Ephesians 2:2) is indicative of where this deception will originate. This title speaks to the abode of the fallen angels. According to theologian Fred Dickason's angelology, "This title might be rendered 'the ruler of the empire of this atmosphere.' It pictures Satan's position and activity as a dominating leader operating a kingdom that centers in the atmosphere of the earth."[360] While more liberal interpreters might think we are pressing a metaphor too far, this is certainly the preferred reading. When seeking to understand an ancient text, it is essential to search for the author's intended meaning, and for a first-century Jew, this description was literal. Biblical scholar and recent president of the Evangelical Theological Society, Dr. Clinton Arnold, explains:

> Paul is using spirit here in the sense of a personal being. Likewise, Paul intended air to be understood in a literal sense; both Jews and Gentiles commonly regarded the air as a dwelling place for evil spirits. The following lines from various Greek magical papyri illustrate this perspective:
>
>> For no aerial spirit which is joined with a mighty assistant will go into Hades. Protect me from every demon in the air. I conjure you by the one who is in charge of the air.
>
> A first-century A.D. Jewish document aligns itself with this concept: "For the person who fears God and loves his neighbor cannot be plagued by the aerial spirit of Beliar since he is sheltered by the fear of God" (*Testament of Benjamin* 3:4).
> In Ephesians 2:2, the reference to spirit is simply a reference to a personal evil force, and the reference to air is representative of the common belief that demons inhabit the air.[361]

Another respected biblical scholar, William Hendriksen, argues that the literal meaning is basic to Ephesians 2:2, asking, "Is it not rather natural that the prince of evil is able, as far as God in his overruling providence permits, to carry on his sinister work by sending his legions to our globe and its surrounding atmosphere?"[362] In addition, later in the same letter, Paul similarly positions them, "For we wrestle not against flesh and blood, but against principalities, against powers, against the rulers of the darkness of this world, against spiritual wickedness in high places" (Ephesians 6:12). Also note that in Nehemiah

9:6, the prophet speaks of more than one heaven: He saw the heavens and the "heaven of heavens." These were not peripheral heavens, as taught in Mormonism, but heavenly divisions, as Paul referred to in 2 Corinthians 12:2, saying, "I knew a man in Christ above fourteen years ago, (whether in the body, I cannot tell; or whether out of the body, I cannot tell: God knoweth;) such an one [was] caught up to the third heaven." Some scholars believe that when Paul referred to this "third heaven," he was echoing his formal education as a Pharisee concerning three heavens that included a domain of air or height, controlled by the prince of demons—Beelzeboul, "lord of the flies." In pharisaical thought, the first heaven was simply the place where the birds fly, anything removed from and not attached to the surface of the Earth. On the other end of the spectrum and of a different substance was the third heaven—the dwelling place of God. This was the place from which angelic spheres spread outward. Between this third heaven, "where dwells the throne room of God," and the first heaven, where the birds fly, was a war zone called the "second heaven"—the place where Satan abides as the prince of the power of the "air," a sort of gasket heaven, the domain of Satan encompassing the surface of the Earth. Thus, Satan's kingdom is the atmosphere above Earth, *not* beneath it (or in the center crust of it) in hell. No one will be ruling in hell; it is a place of punishment, and Satan will be in chains (Matthew 25:41, Revelation 20:2). Having a rock-solid biblical basis to locate Satan's kingdom in our atmosphere, we now turn briefly to Unidentified Aerial Phenomenon (UAP), also known as UFOs.

Operation Trojan Horse

While many Christians argue the contactee messages and abductions associated with UFOs and aliens support the demonic nature of the phenomenon, even secular researchers like Jacques Vallée and John Keel have connected the dots. Vallée argues that the phenomenon acts on three levels: 1) physical; 2) biological; and 3) social. First, the physical level constitutes a craft that radiates tremendous energy. Because only 5 percent or so of UAP turn out to be what we term residual (or RUFOs), it is extremely difficult to generalize, but we address the physical more thoroughly in chapter 13, "The Extradimensional Hypothesis." Second, biologically, they cause a variety of psychophysiological effects on witnesses, from hallucinations to lasting personality changes, including paranormal abilities that are associated with demons in the New Testament (Acts 16:16–18).

The third area is the most open to analysis. In the social arena, a broad range of researchers have noted that messages coming from UFO entities betray a deceptive nature. Gary Stearman, host of *Prophecy in the News*, notes:

> From 1947 to the present, UFO aliens have presented themselves as everything from Martians and Venusians to Tau Cetians to Alpha Pegasians. As twentieth-century perceptions have shifted, their identities have shifted to meet current social expectations.
>
> At the dawn of our atomic age they said they were here to save mankind from a hideous extinction by fire and radiation.
>
> With the birth of the environmental movement, they suddenly told their victims that they were here to save mankind from climatic catastrophe.
>
> These days they present no excuse. They simply go about the work that has apparently underlain their comings and goings for many years.[363]

In popular media, movies such as *The Day the Earth Stood Still*, *Close Encounters of the Third Kind*, *Star Trek*, and *ET* have made UFOs and ETs cultural icons. Books by Zecharia Sitchin and Erich von Däniken, along with television shows like *Ancient Aliens*, have inspired an alternative worldview. A Lutheran theologian and ufologist, Ted Peters, has noted that ancient astronaut theory and popular UFO belief offers "an ostensibly respectable way of talking about our deeper religious needs."[364] In other words, these ET beliefs put a scientific gloss on the secularists' inescapable but embarrassing religious sensibilities. However, the contactees and abductees testify to an anti-Christian spiritual agenda, and many folks believe an ET reality falsifies the Bible.

Vallée argues, "Our religions seem obsolete. Our idea of the church as a social entity working within rational structures is obviously challenged by the claim of a direct communication in modern times with visible beings who seem endowed with supernatural powers."[365] Although he is not a Christian, Vallée has a greater grasp of what is going on than most. He has written:

> I believe that UFOs are physically real. They represent a fantastic technology controlled by an unknown form of consciousness. But I also believe that it would be dangerous to jump to premature conclusions about their origin and nature, because the phenomenon serves as the vehicle for images that can be manipulated to promote belief systems tending to the long-term transformation of human society. I have tried to identify some of the manipulators and to highlight their activities, which range from apparently harmless hoaxes such as the false professor George Adamski's meetings with Venusian spacemen to bloody expeditions that have littered the American landscape with the carcasses of mutilated animals. I have found disturbing evidence of dangerous sectarian activities linked to totalitarian philosophies. The ease with which journalists and even scientists can be seduced into indiscriminate promotion of such deceptions is staggering. In the context of an academic attitude that rejects any open investigation of paranormal phenomena, such fanatical conversions must be expected. For me, that is only one more reason for an independent thinker to remain vigilant against false ideas and simplistic political notions planted by those I have called the "Messengers of Deception."[366]

We devote an entire chapter to harmonizing Vallée's "control grid" hypothesis with biblical theology. However, he is not the only secular ufologist supportive of our view.

One of ufology's most influential and widely read authors, John A. Keel, claimed that he did not consider himself a ufologist but a demonologist, even stating, "Ufology is just another name for demonology."[367] While many connections between modern reports of ET activity and the Watchers described in the Old Testament are established within this book, it is essential to note that the Dead Sea Scrolls contain a description of a Watcher that is identical to that of modern, reptilian ETs (see chapter 4, "They Live"). Keel concluded after years of research that the UFO phenomenon was a cosmic bait-and-switch scheme perpetrated by the same entities who opposed Jesus and the disciples:

> The literature indicates that the phenomenon carefully cultivated the religious frame of reference in early times, just as the modem manifestations have carefully supported the extraterrestrial frame of reference. Operation Trojan Horse is merely the same old game in a new, updated guise. The Devil's emissaries of yesteryear have been replaced by the mysterious "men in black." The quasi-angels of Biblical times have become magnificent spacemen. The demons, devils and false angels were recognized as liars and plunderers by early man.[368]

Keel's assessment is astounding given that he was not working from Christian presuppositions. He is credited with coining the term "Men in Black" (MIB) and with charting patterns and cycles in UFO sightings. The fact that researchers like Vallée and Keel come to these sorts of conclusions suggests Christian researchers who connect UFOs to the prophesied demonically inspired "strong delusion" are correct.

In addition, Daniel R. Jennings has documented a dozen similarities between abduction experiences and classical accounts of demonic manifestations.[369] Accordingly, many abductees have found deliverance in Christ. Shortly after the tragic suicide deaths of the Heavens' Gate UFO cult, Guy Malone, a former abductee set free in Christ, moved to Roswell, New Mexico, in response to a missionary call to reach the abductees and ET believers. In addition to his own testimony published as *Come Sail Away*,[370] he started the Alien Resistance movement, which sponsored several conferences and increased public awareness. Many like-minded Christians have joined forces to this end, believing these events forecast the lateness of the hour in God's plan. David Ruffino and Joseph Jordan have written:

> We think that from what we have seen so far that the act of alien abduction isn't just a fad that's occurring, nor it is something imaginary. It is not something that is made up by members of some lunatic fringe; no, it is real and it is a danger to everyone in our society. We think that it is a major part of the "strong delusion" that has come upon the Earth. It fits perfectly into the end time scenario and is a wonderful way to pull people away from the true God and point mankind to the false messiah who will deceive the whole world.[371]

Supporting the notion that so-called alien abductions are demonic attacks, the CE4 Research Group has published testimonies from former victims describing aliens reacting to the name of Jesus (much in the same way that demons responded to His name in the New Testament) and also finding lasting freedom by living a repentant Christian lifestyle.[372]

This makes Rome's heralded demonologist, Monsignor Corrado Balducci, all the much more exasperating. Whereas the majority of evangelical scholars conclude that the contactee phenomenon is connected to the occult, Balducci asserted that so-called extraterrestrial encounters "are not demonic, they are not due to psychological impairment, and they are not a case of entity attachment."[373] Although he was an official Roman Catholic exorcist, it is not clear what he based this dubious evaluation on. Responding incredulously, Michael Heiser wrote:

Anyone who has read more than half a dozen pages of contactee material can see the connections already (and we'll get more specific). One wonders how Msgr. Balducci could have missed this kind of information. No…occult connections to UFOs and alien contact here. Maybe he just doesn't want to see the connections.[374]

(If you would like to read Heiser's scholarly assessment of those occult connections, follow the endnoted link to his blog, *UFO Religions*, for the series "Balducci's Conundrum." The parallels are ubiquitous. We will unpack a few remarkable ones below.)

Referring to UFO aliens, Balducci maintains, "We don't even have to waste a thought on the devil and his demons, who still kept their angelic nature, being fallen angels and therefore also purely spiritual beings, since they are limited in their activity by God and therefore not able to bring all their hatred to us."[375] Balducci was a theologian of the Vatican Curia, a long-time exorcist for the archdiocese of Rome, and a prelate of the Congregation for the Evangelization of Peoples and the Society for the Propagation of the Faith. If one were seeking a Catholic opinion on demonology, it would be hard to solicit a demonologist with more clout. He suggests that originating from the spirit realm precludes any material reality, but Scripture is replete with angels who are mistaken for men (Genesis 19:1; Acts 1:10), and the author of Hebrews warns, "Be not forgetful to entertain strangers: for thereby some have entertained angels unawares" (Hebrews 13:2), which hardly seems possible if they were simply immaterial spirits.

The so-called Nordic aliens are remarkably similar to the messengers in the Bible. The classification "angel" only formally refers to these entities, but it is often used as an umbrella term encompassing a variety of entities. The Bible mentions other strange entities like seraphim and cherubim that have reptilian qualities and, as mentioned already in this book, 4Q544 from the Dead Sea Scrolls describes an evil Watcher named Melkiresha, whose "looks were frightening like those of a viper."[376] Some may argue that angels do not need spaceships. However, we have scant evidence that we are dealing with nuts-and-bolts-type craft, and even if so, it is not a matter of need, rather subterfuge to promote belief in space aliens camouflaging demonic entities. Unfortunately, many modernist theologians have stopped believing in Satan and demons entirely. For example, Roman Catholic theologian Richard McBrien (writing as acting chairman of the theology department at the University of Notre Dame) wrote that he considered the idea of a personal Satan to be "premodern and precritical."[377] We affirm the reality of Satan and demons and believe Keel's analysis was prescient and sound. There is plenty of corroborating evidence in this book supporting this hypothesis. While God does limit their power for now, Balducci ignores the wealth of biblical prophecy that predicts a time when that restraining influence will be lifted (2 Thessalonians 2:7).

The End-Time Deception

Jesus spoke of a time of ὠδίνων "birth pains" prior to His return, and many of us believe we are currently in the throes (Matthew 24:8). Our friend, Dr. Chuck Missler, has written, "What is fascinating about the idiom of childbirth and the Second Coming of Jesus Christ is that they are both preceded by well-known signs given well in advance of the actual event. And yet, an ill prepared mother, like the skeptic, if she chooses to ignore those signs, will be 'caught unaware' when the child is born."[378] Although Jesus already sits on His throne in heaven, He awaits the time His enemies will be completely vanquished (Hebrews 10:13). They will not go down without a fight, and they are going to take a lot folks with them. Among the nominal Church, the demonic realm has been demythologized and brushed aside. As we discuss in another chapter, even most inerrancy-upholding denominations have lost some essential biblical theology concerning the supernatural administration of the Earth. There are "gods" hostile to humanity eager to bring their designs for the Earth to fruition. The popular belief in extraterrestrials, along with the worldwide sightings of UAP and UFOs, seems to indicate that this time draws near.

The Bible predicts an unparalleled demonic deception prior to Christ's return. We believe it has been developing for decades and the stage is now set. Because we live in an increasingly post-Christian society that has elevated scientists as the ultimate arbiters of truth, it seems likely that such an unprecedented deception will be clothed in the credibility of science. A recent Gallup poll asked, "Do you think that UFO's have ever visited Earth in some form, or not?" The ambiguous phrasing of the question assumes the extraterrestrial hypothesis and yielded a whopping 51 percent of men and 40 percent of women who thought it was true.[379] The 2002 Roper Poll on UFOs and Extraterrestrial Life found that 72 percent of Americans believe the government is not telling the public everything it knows about UFO activity, and 68 percent think the government knows more about extraterrestrial life than it is letting on.[380] A 2008 Scripps UFO Poll reported that 56 percent of Americans believe it either "very likely" or "somewhat likely" that intelligent life exists on other planets.[381] Many of these people expect extraterrestrials to have answers for the world's spiritual, economic, and environmental woes. We believe this hope has been intentionally nurtured by deceptive supernatural forces.

Historians write that "the floodgates opened"[382] on the UFO phenomenon only months prior to when Bible prophecy scholars also mark a decisive moment, the restoration of national Israel on May 14, 1948. The correlation is suggestive. Since the time of Israel's reformation, there has been a near-exponential increase in UFO sightings and related phenomena like abduction. This has led an increasing number of theologians to the hypothesis that such entities play a pivotal role in the end-time deception predicted in Scripture. In his classic *Biblical Demonology*, Merrill Unger observed, "Demonism bears a striking relation to the doctrine of last things and all classes of mankind Jew, Gentile, and the church of God will be intimately and vitally affected by the last day upsurge of evil supernaturalism."[383] We believe it's possible that

Operation Trojan Horse will round the knee of its exponential curve as the sixth seal of the seven-sealed scroll is cracked, and the Earth will be led to believe the extraterrestrials have arrived *en masse*.

As we established above, there is an ample exegetical basis to posit the atmosphere around the Earth as the abode of demons. Understanding their penchant for deception, why wouldn't we deduce they are posing as space aliens to bolster a worldview hostile to Christianity? There are other interesting prophetic connections as well. Biblical scholar Robert Utley elaborates:

> In the NT the air is the realm of the demonic. The lower air (*aēr*) was seen by the Greeks to be impure and therefore the domain of evil spirits. Some see this use of "air" as referring to the immaterial nature of the spiritual realm. The concept of "the rapture of the church" comes from the Latin translation of I Thess. 4:17, "caught up." Christians are going to meet the Lord in the midst of Satan's kingdom, "the air," to show its overthrow![384]

Whereas we are well within our rights to suggest anomalous aerial phcnomcna as a probable vehicle by which the end-time deception will be perpetrated, Utley's mention of the rapture is also suggestive.

Inherent in both the pretribulational and pre-wrath rapture positions is a massive worldwide disappearance of Christian believers that necessitates some sort of rationalization from the Antichrist and his authorities (1 Thessalonians 4:15–17). An explanation involving spaceships or something similar seems probable. In their book, *UFO: End Time Delusion*, Lewis and Schreckhise argue, "The rapture will be explained away with a mix of pseudoscience, New Age religion, and both fabricated as well as misinterpreted evidence that will seem to prove that the rapture is an alien invasion."[385] Interestingly, a recent film, *Knowing*, starring Nicolas Cage, has already seeded this idea into popular consciousness.[386] After the rapture, the ET explanation still has force. While much of the apocalyptic imagery in the book of Revelation is symbolic, one marvels concerning the demonic locust hordes associated with the fifth trumpet judgment (Revelation 9). Perhaps these monstrosities are the referents in Jesus' allusions to otherworldly invaders (Luke 21:26)? If the Antichrist attempts to explain these horrific events, an "alien invasion" supplies persuasive explanatory power for the predicted judgments.

Rereading the Gospel?

For these reasons, we are deeply disturbed by the ideas coming from Roman Catholic theologians. As our historical survey in chapters 9 and 10 ("Essential History" chapters) demonstrates, there is a long tradition of Roman Catholic belief in extraterrestrials. Recent statements from Rome indicate this is now accelerating toward the "Omega Point" developed by the French Jesuit Pierre Teilhard de Chardin. Since Chardin's era, Roman Catholic theologians have been working to codify the alien gospel. A leader in this effort is Opus Dei member and professor of theology at the University of the Holy Cross in Rome, Giuseppe Tanzella-Nitti, has written concerning one's response when confronted by an intelligent extraterrestrial reality:

> At the same time, it seems important to note that a believer who is respectful of the requirements of scientific reasoning would not be obliged to renounce his own faith in God simply on the basis of the reception of new, unexpected information of a religious character from extraterrestrial civilizations. In the first place, human reason itself would suggest the need to submit this new "religious content" coming from outside the Earth to an analysis of reasonableness and credibility (analogous to what we are accustomed to do when any religious content is proposed to us, on Earth); once the trustworthiness of the information has been verified, the believer should try to reconcile such new information with the truth that he or she already knows and believes on the basis of the revelation of the One and Triune

God, conducting a re-reading inclusive of the new data, similar to that which would be applied in an ordinary interreligious dialogue.[387]

This is deeply troubling because Rome's track record of rereading revelation in interreligious dialogue is already dismal. Anyone familiar with the theological content channeled by the alleged extraterrestrials is aware of its subversive nature. Naturally, Tanzella-Nitti excludes that material and would argue he is speaking purely hypothetically, but Catholic theology is already wide open enough to accept such content. In the early 1960s, Rome moved from one extreme to another when Vatican II radically reinterpreted the classical position which held "outside of Rome there is no salvation"[388] to one of liberalized inclusivism. In fact, one of the more influential figures at second Vatican council, Karl Rahner, advocated the concept of the "anonymous Christian."[389] In his rebellion against God, Rahner proposes, a sincere Hindu or Buddhist can be saved without knowledge of the Gospel and this view was explicitly endorsed during Vatican II. Not too surprisingly, it is already being applied to extraterrestrials.

Notre Dame theologian Thomas O'Mera implies inclusivism concerning the salvation of extraterrestrials when he rhetorically asks, "Is Jesus so central a figure that only he and his Middle Eastern religious world can reveal God?"[390] What an odd question, given that Jesus *is* God (Romans 9:5). This questioning of Christ's sufficiency is disquieting, considering O'Mera is on the forefront of Catholic exotheology with his 2012 book, *Vast Universe*, and editorials for the *Huffington Post*. This Roman Catholic doctrine called "inclusivism"—that nonbelievers are saved through their own religions or secular philosophies—is considered heretical by Bible-believing Christians (John 14:7; Acts 4:12). Worse yet, the New Testament implies that non-Christian religions are demonically inspired (1 Corinthians 10:20). Consequently, it is without question that these Roman Catholic theologians become enemies of the cross at this point. Inclusivism hinders the spread of the Gospel that true disciples are commanded to communicate (Matthew 28:19). In regard to people of other religions, they presume to respect their beliefs; but, in reality, it amounts to the crassest sort of contempt, because it is guaranteeing their eternal separation from God by withholding from them the *only* message that can save them. In light of this precedent, our sincere concern extends doubly to Tanzella-Nitti's charge that Roman Catholics will be "conducting a re-reading inclusive of the new data"[391] referring to the revealed spiritual "light" of the alleged extraterrestrials. In that regard, Jesuit astronomer Guy Consolmagno has written, "Any aliens we find will learn and change from contact with us, just as we will learn and change from contact with them. It's inevitable. And they'll be evangelizing us, too."[392] Given the profound theological errors inherent in such Catholicism and well documented ET/occult connections, we find this deeply disturbing.

In our astrobiology chapter, we refer to the work of Dr. Michael Heiser, who speculates that scientific evidence seeming to affirm that life on Earth was seeded from space could potentially inspire an inclusivist global religion. In regard to panspermia, he wrote, "It will be the paradigm that allows the atheist to tolerate religion, and allows literalist Bible-readers, the eastern Buddhist, and the pagan to simultaneously parse the new science the same way. This might in turn be useful fodder for a global religion."[393] A Catholic priest and astronomer, Kenneth J. Delano, wrote in an officially sanctioned Catholic book, "Our religious sensitivities ought not be shocked by the idea that the evolutionary history of the human body might be traced back ultimately to a primordial refuse heap left by visiting ETI when Earth was young."[394] In other words, we might have evolved from ancient alien garbage. He adds, "No great theological difficulty should present itself if we discover that ETI played an important part in the formation of the human race."[395] Based on this foundation, Vatican II and the work of theologians like Chardin, O'Mera, Tanzella-Nitti, and Rahner, Roman Catholicism has the theological structure in place to lead that charge. Even more, ever wonder why the Internet is replete with stories concerning the baptism of extraterrestrials by Catholic priests? Are we being conditioned?

Will the Vatican Baptize Aliens?

Several Jesuit members of the Vatican Observatory Research Group (VORG) have made public statements concerning the baptism of extraterrestrials. The first was when then-acting VORG director George Coyne announced at the launch of the VATT facility that "the Church would be obliged to address the question of whether extraterrestrials might be brought within the fold and baptized."[396] In a *New York Times* magazine article—titled "Would You Baptize an Extraterrestrial?"—another VORG astronomer, Chris Corbally, indicated he would baptize extraterrestrials as well.[397] Similarly, when asked whether he'd baptize an alien, Guy Consolmagno replied, "Only if they asked" and then qualified, "Any entity—no matter how many tentacles it has, has a soul."[398] However, Scripture indicates that there are deceiving entities beyond redemption. Satan, who presents himself as an angel of light (2 Corinthians 11:14) and blinds the minds of unbelievers (2 Corinthians 4:4), will be cast into the lake of fire and brimstone forever (Revelation 20:10), and Jesus indicates that this is also the fate of Satan's millions of compatriot angels (Matthew 25:41). This begs the question, "What if such a deceptive entity taking a human form did ask a Catholic priest to baptize him?"

The Catholic belief is that baptism "confers grace *ex opere operato*, that is, the sacrament works of itself."[399] This literally means the ritual itself takes away sin without requiring faith in the Gospel. This is also why unbaptized infants cannot go to heaven, according to Rome.[400] While the dissonance with inclusivism is deafening, theological harmony is not a strong suit for Rome. The Council of Trent declared: "If anyone denies that by the grace of our Lord Jesus Christ, which is conferred in baptism, the guilt of original sin is remitted, or even asserts that the whole of that which has the true and proper nature of sin is not taken away, but says that it is only touched in person or is not imputed, let him be anathema."[401] While that curses just about all evangelicals, biblically based doctrine recognizes baptism as an outward sign of what has already occurred in the heart of the believer (Mark 16:16). When you recognize that you are dead in your sins and believe that Christ died for you and rose from the dead, you are justified in God's eyes (Romans 10:10). It is a heart condition in reference to the propositional content of the Gospel (1 Corinthians 15:3–5). False baptisms and conversions are commonplace. *Baptism does not save anyone or remove sin.* Nevertheless, the Catholic priest erroneously believes the sacrament itself has supernatural power to remove sin and consequently, could be deceived into thinking a baptized alien entity would be in a state of grace as well. Even if these viral media statements about the baptism of aliens seem tongue in cheek, it could be part of a more subtle effort to influence public opinion. It's not lost on ufology researchers either.

Spokesman for the Star Peoples

In the 2012 bestseller, *After Disclosure: When the Government Finally Reveals the Truth About Alien Contact,* Jim Marrs, Richard Dolan, and Bryce Zabel write concerning Roman Catholicism:

> The world's largest church seems to be positioning itself to be at the forefront of Disclosure. The Vatican has long maintained several major astronomical observatories and a collection of radio telescopes. In recent years, its hierarchy has stated, in one form or another, that we have company. Perhaps they know something is afoot, or suspect its inevitability.[402]

After citing a number of provocative statements similar to those we, too, have quoted, the authors conclude, "It is doubtful that all of these Vatican authorities would speak so openly if they felt they were in conflict with official doctrine. Quietly, a policy appears to have been decided upon."[403] It's hard to take issue with this assessment. Given the sheer volume of provocative statements issued by the VORG astronomers and theologians like Chardin, Tanzella-Nitti, O'Mera, and Balducci, it seems academic.

Has the hierarchy of the Roman Catholic Church been deceived by those evil supernatural intelligences? It seems apparent due to Balducci's blanket dismissal of the demonic overtones and occult connections. A close friend of Pope John Paul II, Balducci went on an Italian television show in 1995 and made some startling assertions that prompted a firestorm of speculation in ufology circles. What follows is a transcription of part of that interview given to host Bruno Mobrici, translated into English from the original Italian.

> **Mobrici:** Father Balducci, what would you answer to all of those who claim that the aliens are already among us?
>
> **Balducci:** We can no longer think… is it true, is it not true, are they truth or are they lies, if we believe, or if we don't! **There are already many considerations which MAKES THE EXISTANCE OF THESE BEINGS INTO A CERTAINY. WE CANNOT DOUBT.** Even if we say that among a hundred of these phenomenon there are only… even if we said that 99 were false and that one was true, it's that one that says that **some phenomenon exist**. Therefore this is the first problem…it's not anymore…it doesn't revert anymore to the ambit of human prudence…to doubt…because…the prudence says to be prudent, but not to deny.[404] (suspension points, bold text, caps, and misspelled words in original)

What are we to make of such a highly placed and influential insider announcing on television that the evidence he is aware of "makes the existence of these beings into a certainty?"[405] The title "Monsignor" indicates he has received a special honor from the Pope, so it would be difficult to argue that he was some sort of loose cannon. He went further while speaking at a UFO conference in Mexico: "I always wish to be the spokesman for these star peoples who also are part of God's glory, and I will continue to bring it to the attention of the Holy Mother Church."[406] The context of this public address in Mexico was undeniably speaking to the same "star peoples" widely associated with New Age spirituality and the alien abduction phenomenon.

As mentioned above by Heiser, scholars of comparative religion note the remarkable correspondence between information from contactees like George Adamski and occult groups like the Theosophical Society. Gregory L. Recce, a scholar of cult beliefs, notes the parallels:

> Just as the sources for twentieth-century flying saucer sightings can be traced back to the late nineteenth century so can the sources for twentieth-century contactees, which in this case can be traced back to the life and teachings of Helena Petovna Blavatsky (1831–91), whose Theosophical ideas are clearly paralleled in the claims of many contactees.[407]

Blavatsky maintained that her theosophical teaching came from a long line of enlightened masters, including Jesus and Buddha, as well as masters who dwelt on Venus. Her pantheistic belief system of spiritual evolution finds remarkable parallels to that of Jesuit Pierre Teilhard de Chardin, detailed at the close of this chapter. Fascinatingly, in addition to the satanic connotations ascribed by the Vulgate and King James translations, the Latin name "Lucifer" refers to the morning star otherwise known as Venus. Blavatsky named her magazine *Lucifer*[408] and taught that "Lucifer, as Christ"[409] was the serpent in the Garden of Eden "who spoke only words of sympathy and wisdom to the woman."[410] Also allegedly in contact with the Venusians, George Adamski, a famous 1940s contactee, taught a nearly identical message of evolution and Eastern mysticism to that of Blavatsky and Chardin. Strangely, just like Balducci's ambition to be spokesperson for the "star peoples," Adamski was the self-proclaimed ambassador to the "space brothers." The connections to Roman Catholicism get even stranger.

George Adamski Meets the Pope

In his books *Flying Saucers Have Landed* (1953), *Inside the Space Ships* (1955), and *Flying Saucer Farewell* (1961), Adamski claimed to have,

on numerous occasions, traveled to neighboring planets inhabited by
the benevolent space brothers aboard flying saucers. Like Blavatsky and
Chardin, he incorporated Jesus into his beliefs and used biblical terminology to promote a version of pantheistic monism:

> Jesus continually turned his vision to the Light of his true perfect
> being and he reported that there is no evil in the world, that
> nothing shall by any means harm you. He knew the kingdom
> of heaven; the radiation of his own being transmuted his world
> into a thing of beauty. He did not discriminate between races,
> colors, creeds, or theories. He did not look to a personal deity
> but to an impersonal Creator; his law was not hate but love. And
> if the kingdom of heaven is to be brought upon the earth every
> man must live the life as he lived it. All must behold the oneness
> of life, the unity of being.[411]

Several demonic perversions are immediately apparent:

1: Jesus taught that the world was evil (John 3:19; 7:7; 17:5).

2: Jesus prayed to the Father as a personal God and taught His disciples to do the same (Matthew 6:9).

3: The Kingdom of Heaven will not be brought upon Earth by the
actions of men, but by Christ's return (Revelation 20:6).

While the theology is typical saucer-cult fare, a lesser-known point
is that Adamski claimed to have delivered a message from the Space
Brothers to a receptive Pope John XXIII. A biographer recounts the
incident:

> Adamski nodded and insisted that a meeting with the Pope had
> been arranged. From his pocket he took a package. It contained
> a message, he said, from the Space People, who had asked him
> to deliver it to the Pope. Zinsstag was dubious. But they flew to
> Rome, and were soon making their way to the Vatican. As they
> approached the Apostolic Palace, Adamski looked about for the

papal representative with whom he was supposed to rendezvous.

"There he is, I can see the man. Please, wait for me at this very spot in about an hour's time!"

He descended the steps and, going to the left, entered a doorway—from which Zinsstag thought to discern someone gesturing to him. She was puzzled, though, having expected Adamski to turn right and go in at the main entrance where the Swiss Guards were posted.

After an hour she returned, to find Adamski waiting for her and "grinning like a monkey." On his face was an unforgettable look of sheer joy. The Pope had received him, he said, and accepted the message from the Space People.

Adamski showed her a commemorative coin, and described how the Pope had given it to him—in appreciation of his having delivered the message.[412]

"Golden Medal of Honor" Adamski claimed to have received from Pope John XXIII

While we will probably never know if Adamski was telling the truth about what the Space Brothers allegedly communicated to the pope, this casts Balducci's recent claims in an unsettling light. Also, it is remarkable that Pope John XXIII was the pope who called the Second Vatican Council responsible for the inclusivist framework capable of accommodating the Star Peoples. Finally, recalling how we began this chapter with

Pope Benedict XVI's call for a world political authority with "real teeth," in his 1963 encyclical, *Pacem in Terris*, Pope John XXIII also called for a "universal authority" to deal with global problems:

> Today the universal common good presents us with problems which are world-wide in their dimensions; problems, therefore, which cannot be solved except by a public authority with power, organization and means co-extensive with these problems, and with a world-wide sphere of activity. Consequently the moral order itself demands the establishment of some such general form of public authority.[413]

9 | Essential History I

Atomism and the Occult

"In other parts of space there are other worlds and different races of men and kinds of wild beasts."—Titus Lucretius Carus (50 BC)[414]

I n order to properly assess the philosophical and theological implications of intelligent extraterrestrial biological life, it is essential to review the history of the discussion. Most folks probably assume that it was the dawn of the space age, beginning with the Russian satellite Sputnik in 1957 and culminating with Neil Armstrong taking "one giant leap for mankind" in 1969, that necessitated the ET discussion. Alternately, folks more versed in Western history might think back to the eighteenth-century "age of reason" enlightenment or perhaps even a little farther to the "Copernican revolution," including the infamous sixteenth-century Galileo trial, as the impetus for speculation about ET. While those are certainly remarkable stepping stones, the origin of the otherworldly reaches much deeper into antiquity.

The Ancient World

Some writers (e.g., Erich von Däniken, Zecharia Sitchin) have proposed that intelligent extraterrestrials visited Earth in prehistory and made contact with humans. They cite various artifacts and ancient texts as evidence for ET intervention. A common tenet is that the gods from most, if not all, religions were actually extraterrestrials, and their advanced technologies were wrongly interpreted by primitive peoples as supernatural abilities. Although this demythologizing is quite popular, the so-called ancient astronaut theory has been authoritatively discredited, and it is not taken seriously by most academics.[415] In fact, a program of remythologizing offers more promise.

Scholars are in wide agreement that explicit ET discussion first appeared in the writings of the early Greeks.[416] As early as the sixth century BC, Thales and Orpheus postulated that the moon was much like the Earth. Not much later, Philolaus is reported to have written that the moon was populated. These beliefs are part and parcel of the ancient supernatural worldview.

> Thales (640–548 BC) believed in demoniacal apparitions, Plato in ghosts—deceased people who were compelled to return to the living because they were unable to disassociate themselves from their bodily passions. Democritus (fifth century BC), who could laugh so heartily at human folly, recommended that a man stung by a scorpion should sit upon an ass and whisper in the animal's ear: "A scorpion has stung me." He thought that the pain would thus be transferred to the ass. All the philosophers of old believed in the reality of magic.[417]

While it is clear they believed in the paranormal, the Greek philosophers were in vigorous debate as to the ultimate nature of reality or metaphysics.

At this time, Greek thinkers had reached a conundrum concerning the fundamental laws or underlying principles of nature. In many ways, the ancient debate anticipated the modern evolutionary hullabaloo. On one side was Parmenides, convinced that because reality reflects unity, true change was impossible. On the other side was Heraclitus, who believed that the nature of existence is change. In order to reconcile conflicting schools of thought, Leucippus and his student Democritus asserted that qualitative change (in character or essence) was impossible, but quantitative change (in size or quantity) was real.[418] In other words, they contended that while things appear to change, there is an unseen static reality underneath. This reconciliation was made possible by their theory of atoms.

Originally proposed by Leucippus (fifth century BC), atomism was developed and refined by his protégé, Democritus (460–370 BC). The two intuitively suggested that all matter was composed of very small particles. The thought process went something like this: Imagine slicing a pebble in half, then in half again, and in half again, and again, and so on… This process could continue until, eventually, the pebble is reduced to a grain of sand and becomes too small to see or cut. Based on this, Democritus doubted the process could truly continue infinitely, so he proposed miniscule, indivisible units called atoms. In fact, the Greek word *atomos* means indivisible, and the atomists proposed an infinite number of these basic building blocks.

In this way, they solved the question of unity and change in that the arrangements of atoms were in constant flux while the atoms themselves remained stable. Furthermore, they saw no rhyme or reason governing this mix of atoms. They believed the universe was infinite in size and governed by chance. As a corollary to this, they reasoned that because the Earth and its inhabitants were formed by random combinations of atoms, it naturally followed that the same haphazard amalgamations occurred many times over. In this way, the existence of other worlds and alien life was an inevitable consequence of their worldview.

Known as the laughing philosopher, Democritus speculated that originally the universe was a swarm of atoms churning chaotically, forming larger and larger masses eventually including the Earth, planets, and stars. In antiquity, the term "world" (Greek *kosmos*) meant the observable universe, not a mere planet. Thus, when Democritus asserted a hodgepodge of alien worlds, it is helpful to think in terms of solar systems. According to Hippolytus, "Democritus, son of Damasippus, a native of Abdera, conferring with many gymnosophists among the Indians, and with priests in Egypt, and with astrologers and magi in Babylon…he maintained worlds to be infinite, and varying in bulk; and that in some there is neither sun nor moon, while in others that they are larger than with us, and with others more numerous."[419] Furthermore, he held that some worlds have life while others do not, each has a beginning and an end, and a world could be destroyed by collision with another one. Today, some historians consider Democritus the "father of modern science."[420] Don't tell the donkey.

In the otherworldly discussion, the successor to Democritus was the Greek philosopher Epicurus. He wrote, "A world is a circumscribed portion of the sky, containing heavenly bodies and an earth and all the heavenly phenomenon."[421] From this we can tell that in the late third century BC, when Epicurus invoked the principle of plentitude to defend the existence of innumerable worlds, he meant a vast universe of solar systems. A letter to his student, Herodotus, survives as a prominent example: "There are infinite worlds both like and unlike this world of ours. For the atoms being infinite in number…are borne far out into space."[422] That he believed ETs inhabited these worlds is laid bare by his assertion, "Furthermore, we must believe that in all worlds there are living creatures and plants and other things we see in this world."[423] Although he technically was not an atheist, he was a material reductionist, because he held that even the gods and human souls were made of atoms. Epicurus, like modern deists, argued that the gods were uninvolved in human affairs. He inspired a host of followers.

Atomist thought gave rise to a system of philosophy called Epicureanism, which arguably still survives as modern material reductionism (the idea that everything is reducible to matter and energy as governed by the laws of chemistry and physics). Epicurean philosophy attracted many disciples, one of the most prominent being Titus Lucretius Carus (99–55 BC), known as Lucretius. He popularized atomism in his famous poem, "On the Nature of the Universe." The following is a representative example:

> Granted, then, that empty space extends without limit in every direction and that seeds innumerable in number are rushing on countless courses through an unfathomable universe under the impulse of perpetual motion, it is in the highest degree unlikely that this earth and sky is the only one to have been created and that all those particles of matter outside are accomplishing nothing. This follows from the fact that our world has been made by nature through the spontaneous and casual collision and the multifarious, accidental, random, and purposeless congregation and coalescence of atoms whose suddenly formed combinations could serve on each occasion as the starting point of substantial fabrics—earth and sea and sky and the races of living creatures.[424]

A few decades before Christ was born, the Roman poet Lucretius popularized the materialist worldview, replete with populated alien worlds. Inherent is a denial of Divine Creation and providence, along with the belief that death is simply the disbanding of the atoms, which, consequently, should not be feared. Sounding much like today's transhumanists, he boasted, "Thus religion trod down, by just reverse; victory makes us akin to the gods."[425] In fact, the discovery of Lucretius' writings spawned an atomist renaissance in the sixteenth century AD that has ongoing repercussions. While atomism ran contrary to theism, more renowned philosophers opposed them.

Plato (428–348 BC) and his student Aristotle (384–322 BC) stood in opposition to the atomists and their otherworldly doctrines. Plato solved the metaphysical problem of change by arguing a theory of forms. This system posits a transcendent reality beyond the ever-changing experiential world. It consists of eternal, unchanging forms that are perceived intellectually but not by the senses.[426] For example, there may be many kinds of chairs, but in Plato's thought, there is an ethereal form that defines chairness. While Christian philosophers typically reject Platonism because it undermines the doctrine of *creation ex nihilo* by positing uncreated self-existent forms, much of Plato's thought is consistent with theism.

Plato believed the world was unique because it was a representation of a single creator. He conceived of the *demiurge*, a Greek term for an artisan or craftsman responsible for the creation and maintenance of the material universe. His student, Aristotle, carried this line of thinking forward in his notion of a "prime mover" seen in book 12 of his *Metaphysics*, in which he employed the phrase, "something which moves other things without being moved by anything,"[427] giving rise to the popular term, "unmoved mover." It is from this Aristotelian idea that the cosmological argument for the existence of God derives. He further suggests that because this prime mover set the celestial realm in motion, it follows that there is only one heaven. This necessitates a brief discussion of ancient cosmology.

The ancient Greek word often translated "world" is *kosmos*, which generally meant "order." It carried the idea of bringing order from chaos and—beg your pardon, ladies—this is the idea behind the English term "cosmetics." Over time, it came to represent the Creation order, the observable universe. A Greek lexicon offers discussion:

> The spatial sense of κόσμος and its identification with the universe are found in Plato, though the older idea of world order is still present. For Plato the cosmos is the universe…inasmuch as in it all individual things and creatures, heaven and earth, gods and men, are brought into unity by a universal order.[428]

Thus, a cosmos is orderly because it obeys physical laws. Yet, apart from God, this seems unlikely. It follows that if reality was ultimately chaotic, as the atomists believed, science would not be possible. Accordingly, when Carl Sagan began his classic television show with "*The cosmos is all there is*" he was mistaken. The order observed by science needs an explanation not provided in nature. It must indeed originate from supernature. The universe follows discernible laws, and chaos cannot account for such behavior. Thus, when Plato and Aristotle argued against a plurality of worlds, it entailed an argument against the chaotic randomness of the atomists. They were appropriately arguing for lawful order and design, albeit with an incorrect understanding of physics.

Aristotle believed that the Earth was the geographical center of the cosmos, and, therefore, the Earth was exceptional as a life-supporting planet. Interestingly, he was opposed by Greek astronomer Aristarchus of Samos (310–230 BC), who placed the sun at the center long before Copernicus. Nevertheless, because the stars are so much farther away than anyone then imagined, their expected movement relative to each other as the Earth moves around the sun (parallax) was undetectable. Thus, Aristarchus' speculation, although accurate, was not demonstrable, and Aristotle's geocentrism won the day. In fact, Aristotle's errant cosmology would hold sway for nearly two thousand years, most likely because it accounted for the observed order better than the chaos associated with the competition.

Aristotle also believed that all matter consists of the four elements: earth, air, fire, and water. One of the basic tenets of his cosmology was the doctrine of natural motion and place. This meant that earth (as in soil or matter) moved toward the Earth, water flowed toward the sea, fire moved away from the Earth, and air occupied the space in between. From this he reasoned that, by natural law, all earth is concentrated into our spherical planet; thus, no other worlds could exist. Aristotle wrote:

> Either, therefore, the initial assumptions must be rejected, or there must be only one center and one circumference; and given this latter fact, it follows from the same evidence and by the same compulsion, that the world must be unique. There cannot be several worlds.[429]

He thought unity demanded it. In his classic text, *On the Heavens*, he devotes two entire chapters to the refutation of the existence of other worlds. Of course, we now know that the universe is much bigger than he ever imagined but, even so, his idea of singular "uncaused cause" has gained traction given the standard model of Big Bang cosmology. This "uncreated creator" idea is used in the New Testament in precisely this context.

In Acts 17, the Apostle Paul delivered his famous sermon on the Areopagus in Athens to a group of Epicureans and Stoics who were curious about his strange new teachings. They called Paul a "babbler," which in the Greek text reads *spermologos*, an Athenian slang word meaning "one who picks up seeds." The insult suggested a person who pecks at ideas like a bird pecks at seeds and then spouts them off without fully comprehending what he is saying. Jeering aside, Paul skillfully quoted Greek poets and declared the identity of their "unknown god" as the "God that made the world [*kosmos*] and all things therein, seeing that he is Lord of heaven and earth" (Acts 17:24). In other words, Paul is arguing for the unmoved mover, the one God who created the entire universe and everything within. Of course, this idea and his preaching of the resurrection of the dead surely brought scorn from the atomist Epicureans. Accordingly, some mocked, others wanted another hearing, and a few came to saving faith in Christ. As Christianity grew, Epicureanism, with its many inhabited worlds, waned. However, even today, Epicurean ideas appeal to humanists.

Epicureans and Christians maintain a timeless clash of worldview. It is from the pen of a third-century AD Christian, Lactantius, that the "Riddle of Epicurus," a famous argument against the existence of an all-powerful, benevolent, and providential God (or gods), was preserved:

God either wants to eliminate bad things and cannot, or can but does not want to, or neither wishes to nor can, or both wants to and can. If he wants to and cannot, then he is weak—and this does not apply to god. If he can but does not want to, then he is spiteful—which is equally foreign to god's nature. If he neither wants to nor can, he is both weak and spiteful, and so not a god. If he wants to and can, which is the only thing fitting for a god, where then do bad things come from? Or why does he not eliminate them?[430]

This challenge, broadly known as the problem of evil, inspired two thousand years of apologetics. While an exhaustive answer is beyond the scope of this book, it is enough to say that it is logically possible for God to have morally sufficient reasons for permitting evil. Furthermore, the book of Revelation promises that God will, indeed, one day vanquish evil (Revelation 21:4). It is also important to note that, despite many uninformed skeptics, it is agreed in academia, atheists included, that the logical or deductive problem of evil has been answered decisively by Christian philosopher Alvin Plantinga in his famous book, *God, Freedom, and Evil* (1974).

In retrospect, we must acknowledge the astonishing prescience of the early atomist thinkers in that modern science has confirmed some of their physical reasoning. These ideas inspired modern atomic theory in the hands of scientists with a Christian worldview, like Robert Boyle. Nevertheless, the atomists are the philosophical ancestors of material reductionism, the dominant metaphysic associated with atheism. Even so, we want to avoid the genetic fallacy, the logical error of dismissing a proposition solely on the basis of its source. Yet, Christians who believe in inhabited extraterrestrial worlds should be cognizant that, given its lineage, such a disposition makes for extremely strange bedfellows.

The Early Church

Because Genesis affirms that God created the universe, early Christians were much more attracted to Aristotelian ideas than those of the atomists. Consequently, Aristotle's doctrine of natural place influenced early Christians to believe that all entities existing away from the Earth were necessarily spirits. The doctrine demanded that material beings were earthbound and that beings like angels residing above the Earth, by definition extraterrestrial, were not physical. The church fathers also took exception with atomism's inherent rejection of Intelligent Design. Concerning this fundamental disagreement, little has changed. However, more important is that Scripture casts mankind as the central player in the cosmic drama. Christ incarnated as a man, the last Adam, and the Bible centers on God's plan for humans.

All of the patristic authors who addressed the plurality of worlds, with the exception of one, spoke against it as a heresy. In fact, it is from Hippolytus' *Refutation of All Heresies* that we get some early information about the atomists quoted above. The fourth-century bishop of Brescia, Philastrius, wrote, "There is another heresy that says that there are infinite and innumerable worlds, according to the empty opinion of certain philosophers—since Scripture has said that there is one world and teaches us about one world—taking this view from the apocrypha of the prophets, that is from the secrets, as the pagans themselves called them."[431] Thus, early on, Christian apologists connected it to the occult. In fact, plurality was uniformly condemned except by Origen (185–254 AD), who was troubled by God's seeming inactivity prior to Creation. Origen wrote, "If the world had its beginning in time, what was God doing before the world began? For it is at once impious and absurd to say that the nature of God is inactive and immovable."[432] In other words, because Origen could not imagine that God was idle in eternity past, he thought there must have been previous worlds.

However, it is important to note that Origen did not believe in the simultaneous existence of many earthlike planets with intelligent life, rather a sequence of worlds in a cycle of creation and consummation, as the Scripture posits for our Earth (Isaiah 65:17, 66:22; 2 Peter 3:13; Revelation 21:1). Even so, his view was widely condemned. One of the better-known church fathers, Augustine, who carried the plentitude principle into Christian theology from his Neoplatonist background, addressed the issue indirectly. Apparently, he was responding to folks like Origen who asked why God did not create sooner and, similarly, given infinite size, why He only made our world. Augustine surmises:

For if they imagine infinite spaces of time before the world, during which God could not have been idle, in like manner they may conceive outside the world infinite realms of space, in which, if any one says that the Omnipotent cannot hold His hand from working, will it not follow that they must adopt Epicurus' dream of innumerable worlds? with this difference only, that he asserts that they are formed and destroyed by the fortuitous movements of atoms, while they will hold that they are made by God's hand, if they maintain that, throughout the boundless immensity of space, stretching interminably in every direction round the world, God cannot rest, and that the worlds which they suppose Him to make cannot be destroyed.[433]

As to Origen's temporal objection, he anticipates Einstein's concept of four-dimensional space/time with his contention that "it is vain to conceive of the past times of God's rest, since there is no time before the world."[434] In other words, it is meaningless to ponder "time" prior to Creation because time itself had a beginning. In respect to the spatial objection, his discussion seems to have foreseen Jodie Foster's character Eleanor Arroway's objection in the film *Contact*: "If it's just us, it seems like an awful waste of space."[435] We agree with Augustine that this presumes too much. Wasted space assumes one with limited resources, and God has no such limitations. The vast universe is but a drop in the bucket. Furthermore, our ignorance does not mean space has no purpose. At minimum, it reflects God's glory (Psalms 19), and we will suggest another purpose in chapter 12, "First Incursion of the Chariots of the (Fallen Star) Gods."

The Middle Ages

As documented in our former work, *Petrus Romanus*, the Middle Ages marked a Faustian bargain between the Roman Church and the Carolingian dynasty that served to suppress biblical theology and promote the papal juggernaut. In that work, we discussed the resulting years of darkness (757–1046 AD), ignominiously titled the "Pornocracy" or "Dark Age," by asserting that "demonic weirdness defines the era."[436] In light of that, a bit of arcane lore popularized by Jacques Vallée concerning a Spanish-born priest and archbishop of Lyon, Agobard of Lyon (779–840 AD), seems pertinent. Agobard mentions a folk belief concerning "a certain region, which they call Magonia, whence ships sail in the clouds."[437] Given the historical context, we find the timing of this belief's emergence to be telling. Beginning at this time, there was a developing acceptance that people were visiting the Earth from other worlds in flying ships. The account speaks of four visitors:

> One day, among other instances, it chanced at Lyons that three men and a woman were seen descending from these aerial ships. The entire city gathered about them, crying out that they were magicians and were sent by Grimaldus, Duke of Beneventum, Charlemagne's enemy, to destroy the French harvests.[438]

The extraterrestrials were called "sylphs," and these four contactees were called "ambassadors to the sylphs" (according to Nicolas Pierre-Henri, the abbot of Villars, France). The priest did his best to dispel the belief, and the citizens, while not entirely convinced, let the four ambassadors go free. The esoterica attributed to the abbot of Villars, *The Count of Gabalis: Secret Interviews on Science* (1670), supports the idea that the sylphs were indeed real and the contactees often achieved great success and widespread acclaim.[439] Unfortunately, at this time, many in the priesthood were also involved in the occult arts and were not well trained in biblical theology.

It was the rise of scholasticism, largely inspired by the translation of the ancient Greek philosophers into Latin, that revived scholarly pursuits. Early on, an introduction to the logic of Aristotle by Porphyry was translated into Latin by Boethius, but it was Aristotle's *On the Heavens*, available around 1170 and replete with chapters on otherworlds, that revived astrobiological speculations. An early example is from Saint

Albertus Magnus (1193–1280), who wrote, "Since one of the most wondrous and noble questions in nature is whether there is one world or many, a question that the human mind desires to understand per se, it seems desirable for us to inquire about it."[440] He wrote a complete treatise on astrology and astronomy called *Speculum Astronomiae* ("The Mirror of Astronomy") and a treatise, *De Mineralibus* ("The Book of Minerals"), which dealt with astrological talismans made from minerals. That he was an occult practitioner is laid bare in his assertion that "the [science of talismans] cannot be proved by physical principles, but demands a knowledge of the sciences of astrology and magic and necromancy, which must be considered elsewhere."[441] Magnus discusses various astrological talismans, describes how to make them, and attempts to distinguish between demonic and natural magical powers of the heavens.

Even so, many of his contemporaries accused Magnus of being in league with the devil. Occult tradition holds that he discovered the philosopher's stone and became wealthy from its gold.[442] Nevertheless, he was "beatified" in 1622, meaning that the Catholic Church marked his entrance into heaven and endorsed his alleged postmortem capacity to intercede on behalf of individuals who pray in his name (a practice we have argued amounts to necromancy).[443] On December 16, 1931, Pope Pius XI canonized him as the patron saint of the sciences and honored him as a doctor of the Church, one of only thirty-five persons so privileged. It was his famous student, Thomas Aquinas, who would devote more specific attention to other worlds.

Aquinas was convinced biblical truth could be reconciled with Aristotle's cosmology. Accordingly, he sought to synthesize the Aristotelian science in *On the Heavens* with the Scriptures. Thus, he necessarily denied the existence of other worlds. In his influential work, *Summa Theologica*, he argued in this fashion:

> *Objection* 1. It would seem that there is not only one world, but many. Because, as Augustine says (QQ. LXXXIII., *qu.* 46), it is unfitting to say that God has created things without a

reason. But for the same reason that He created one, He could create many, since His power is not limited to the creation of one world; but rather it is infinite, as was shown above (Q. XXV., A. 2). Therefore God has produced many worlds....

Reply Obj. 1. This reason proves that the world is one because all things must be arranged in one order, and to one end. Therefore from the unity of order in things Aristotle infers (*Metaph.* xii., text. 52) the unity of God governing all; and Plato (*Tim.*), from the unity of the exemplar, proves the unity of the world, as the thing designed.[444]

Aquinas argued God's power is seen in unity and order. One can readily see that he based his argumentation on Aristotle's cosmology. Of course, Aristotle was fundamentally mistaken in his doctrine of natural place. Even so, these arguments stood unchallenged until the heresy hunters of the Inquisition turned their glance his way.

Surprisingly, it was the inquisitors who paved the way for ET belief. In 1277, Etienne Tempier, the bishop of Paris, issued a condemnation of 219 theological propositions that were said to be "true according to philosophy, but not according to the Catholic faith."[445] Church historians believe Tempier was concerned that teachers, like Aquinas, accepted the pagan philosopher Aristotle's views based on their internal logic rather than agreement with church doctrine. Of these 219 heretical propositions, number 34 was "that the first cause [God] could not make several worlds."[446] The disapproval was based on the idea that such a denial encroached upon the doctrine of divine omnipotence. Of course, this objection seemed to overlook the difference between what God *could* do and *would* do, a distinction that was not lost on theologians like William of Ockham (1290–1349) and Nichole Oresme (1320–1382), who argued that although God certainly was capable, He probably did not create other worlds. Even so, the existence of other worlds was now theologically respectable, and the stage was set for more radical divergence from what for centuries had been considered orthodoxy.

In 1440, Nicholas of Cusa (1401–1464), a German philosopher, theologian, and astronomer, had a mystical experience while returning from Constantinople by ship. He described his vision thus, "When by what I believe was a celestial gift from the Father of Lights, from whom comes every perfect gift, I was led to embrace imcomprehensibles incomprehensibly in leaned ignorance, by transcending those incorruptible truths that can be humanly known."[447] What followed was a treatise on mysticism entitled *De Docta Ignorantia* ("Of Learned Ignorance"). Similar to Buddhist practice, Nicholas called this "negative theology," implying a sort of mystical knowing by not knowing. As a result, he conjured up hermetic platitudes like God is "a sphere of which the center is everywhere and the circumference nowhere."[448] He believed that the limits of science could be transcended by means of mystic speculation. Some even contend that this preempted Kepler, famous for his laws of planetary motion, by arguing there were no perfect circles in the universe. His learned ignorance inevitably led him to other worlds inhabited by extraterrestrials.

Nicholas homogenized the heavenly bodies by dismissing the Aristotelian doctrine of unity and natural place. Therefore, he concluded that the Earth, planets, sun, and stars were composed of the same elements, and that there was no center of attraction. He envisioned an infinite universe, whose center was everywhere and circumference nowhere, containing countless rotating stars, the Earth merely being one of equal importance. Consequently, it is not too surprising that it is from Nicholas of Cusa that we encounter the first explicit Roman Catholic argumentation for the existence of extraterrestrials. In *Of Learned Ignorance*, chapter 12, he asserts:

> Rather than think that so many stars and parts of the heaven are uninhabited and that this earth of ours alone is peopled—and that with beings, perhaps, of an inferior type—we will suppose that in every region there are inhabitants, differing in nature by rank and all owing their origin to God, who is the center and circumference of all stellar regions.[449]

Rather than the censure one might expect, Nicholas' work was enthusiastically received. It is important to note that he stated this was revelation from God and it went unchallenged by the Church. Shortly after his shipboard vision, he had become the papal envoy to Pope Eugene IV and assisted in the papal power struggle against the council of Basel, opposing its attempt to reform widespread abuse. He was promoted to the status of cardinal by Pope Nicholas V in 1448. The next person of note was more inclined to science than mystic speculation.

Perhaps one of the greatest contributors to the discussion, Nicholas Copernicus (1473–1543), never actually addressed the topic. Even so, his revolutionary work effectively removed the Earth from the center of the cosmos and seemingly relegated it one among many, perhaps similar, orbs revolving around the sun. He correctly surmised the apparent motion of the stars to be an illusion caused by the rotation of the Earth on its axis and that the Earth orbited the sun once every year. Of course, this meant that the countless stars were potential suns and the observable planets might be other "earths." Of course, if there are other earths, then one might imagine they are populated with people or something else entirely. It really did change everything. Yet, heliocentricism was not widely accepted in his lifetime. A few astronomers, including Germans Michael Maestlin (1550–1631), Johannes Kepler (1571–1630), the Englishman Thomas Digges (1546–1595), and the Italian Galileo Galilei (1564–1642), accepted it, leading historians like N. R. Hanson to quip that the "Copernican revolution" was a minor skirmish that prompted the Keplerian or Galilerian revolution.[450] All the same, at the dawn of the Reformation, Copernicus had planted the seeds for an atomist revival replete with an alien invasion.

The Reformation of ET

Even with heliocentricism creeping toward acceptance, the sixteenth-century revival of philosophical atomism was far more influential than astronomy. In an intellectual climate where Aristotelian cosmology was increasingly challenged, the writings of Lucretius, long lost to the

West, had been discovered by the Italian humanist Poggio Bracciolini. This was also the time of the council of Trent's rabid anathemas and counterreformation Jesuit skullduggery. In 1563, the works of Lucretius were published in Paris, and this printing, known as the Lambinus edition, promoted a resurgence of atomist materialism. In the hands of the French writer Michel de Montaigne, ancient atomism was ample foil for forging a radical new skepticism. He bantered, "Your reason is never more plausible and on more solid ground then when it convinces you of a plurality of worlds."[451] Despairing man's grasp of absolute truth, a chance-driven worldview suited his fancy. It was in this environment that Lucretius' work found its way into the hands of a Roman Catholic friar who became the poster boy of the philosophic alien invasion.

Bronze statue of Giordano Bruno by Ettore
Ferrari (1845–1929), Campo de' Fiori, Rome

Giordano Bruno (1548–1600) is regarded among extraterrestrial apologists, secular and occult, as a free-thought martyr. Born in Naples, Bruno was a Catholic priest, Dominican monk, philosopher, hermetist, Kabbalist, mathematician, and astronomer. Influenced by Lucretius, his cosmology went well beyond the Copernican model by proposing that the sun was merely a garden variety star, and moreover, that the universe contained an *infinite* number of worlds populated by intelligent alien beings. Because space and time were infinite, his cosmogony (theory of Creation) denied divine causation. Still more, he adopted an animistic theory of matter. Animism is the idea that natural things like sticks and stones have immaterial souls. Bruno wrote, "If you speak of the world according to the meaning held among the true philosophers for whom the world is every globe, every star, this our earth, the sun's body, the moon and even others, I reply that the soul of each of these worlds not only ascends and descends but moves in a circle."[452] Delving deeply into occult lore, Bruno preferred magical to mathematical reasoning. Bruno's faith has been described as "an incoherent materialistic pantheism."[453] Moreover, he argued that his beliefs did not contradict Scripture or true religion. Yet, this begs the question: What did he regard as *true religion*?

Bruno defined magic as "the knowledge of the science of nature."[454] Within the renaissance worldview, it was common to merge magic and science because both explore and seek to gain mastery over the structure of the universe. Similarly, religion and magic were conflated because both answered the ultimate questions and offered communion with the divine. Accordingly, for Bruno, magic was the tool for realizing the ends of science and religion. While it seems at odds with the cold, hard, materialist posturing we are accustomed to, naturalist scientists are the heirs apparent to many of the occult traditions. Scholars have traced two streams of occultism in Bruno's work.

Frances Yates, a scholar of Renaissance occultism, traced Bruno's thought to the fifteenth-century rediscovery of the *Hermetic Corpus*, a Gnostic work allegedly authored by Hermes Trismegistus (meaning "thrice-greatest Hermes"), who is a syncretism of the Greek god Hermes and the Egyptian god Thoth. In Hermetic lore, Trismegistus is credited with having delivered all science, medicine, and magic to mankind. Yates makes the case that during the Renaissance, hermeticism spread like wildfire across the intellectual West, inspiring a revival of Egyptian magic practice and alchemy. In the case of Giordano Bruno, she writes:

> Bruno was an intense religious Hermetist, a believer in the magical religion of the Egyptians as described in the *Asclepius*, the imminent return of which he prophesied in England, taking the Copernican sun as a portent in the sky of this imminent return. He patronises Copernicus for having understood his theory only as a mathematician, whereas he (Bruno) has seen its more profound religious and magical meanings.[455]

Bruno cobbled the atomist extraterrestrial doctrine together with Egyptian magic, creating a system all his own. Yates writes,

> Thus that wonderful bound of the imagination by which Bruno extended his Copernicanism to an infinite universe peopled with innumerable worlds, all moving and animated with the divine life, was seen by him—through his misunderstandings of Copernicus and Lucretius—as a vast extension of Hermetic gnosis, of the magician's insight into the divine life of nature.[456]

Just so there is no ambiguity as to Bruno's loyalties, Yates elaborates, "Giordano Bruno's Egyptianism was demonic and revolutionary, demanding full restoration of the Egyptian-Hermetic religion."[457] Popular among the Jesuit order, the hermetic writings combine Greek philosophy with Eastern religion. This is an interesting amalgamation paralleling Bruno's life work in that he contributed both to modern science and to the development of Renaissance occultism.

Hermes Trismegistus

On the other hand, Karen Silvia de León-Jones rejects the popular view of Bruno as hermetic magus and depicts him foremost as a Kabbalist. Kabbalah, meaning "tradition," is the Jewish mysticism that arose in the twelfth century by interpreting the Torah according to secret or hidden knowledge. After the destruction of Jerusalem and subsequent Diaspora, Jews came to conceive of God as utterly transcendent. In other words, God seldom had any interaction with man. Consequently, an emanation doctrine was needed to reconcile the tension of God's distance, and Kabbalah is one such expression. Theurgic Kabbalah, which became popular with Gentiles as well, involves study in three aspects: 1) the emanation (sephiroth) doctrine; 2) methods of interpreting the Scriptures: gematria, notarikon, and temurah; and 3) the redeemer doctrine.

The sephiroth are ten emanations of God's attributes, which for all intents and purposes take the form of divine entities. These ten emanations are structured in a four-level control grid from God to our world. The four levels consist of: 1) the supernatural world: *atziluth*; 2) the world of creation: *briah*; 3) the world of formation: *yetzirah*; and 4) the world of material action: *assiah*. This system seemingly reconciles God's transcendence with His imminence. The upper realms were naturally populated exclusively by spiritual entities, but by Kabbalistic meditation the adept were able to gain access. This was part and parcel of Bruno's extraterrestrial landscape. León-Jones concludes, "Bruno is implementing those 'angelic superstructures' through which demons are controlled, and this is precisely demonic magic."[458] He operated in the transcendent realms, seeking to access the plurality of worlds and alien beings in which Lucretius had only dreamt. He seems knowledgeable of the extraterrestrial channelings in Nicholas of Cusa's *Of Learned Ignorance*, because he outlined a method of obtaining god-like wisdom through "Kabbalistic Ignorance" associated with "certain mystic theologians" within his dialogue *Cabala of Pegasus*.[459] Bruno scholars explain, "To achieve this, individuals must resolve the paradox (by employing a Kabbalistic reading of the *Cabala*) of arriving at that most vile baseness by which they are made capable of more magnificent exaltation."[460] This is a strange paradox indeed.

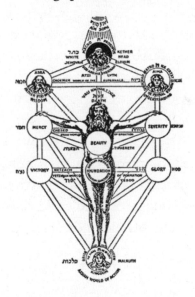

The ten *Sephiroth* form *Adam Kadmon,*
the archetypal man[461]

Bruno wrote in his treatise *Essays on Magic*, "One can prove that demons are material and that they are of several different kinds, by the fact that they have emotions, desires, angers, jealousies and similar feelings found in humans, and in animals composed of observable dense matter. That is why the slaughtering and sacrifice of animals was instituted, for these demons are pleased a very great deal by such ceremonies and fumes."[462] Indeed he seems to have interacted with demonic entities enough to provide details concerning their bodies: "Although they are spiritual substances, nature has given them a body which is very thin and is not endowed with senses. They belong to the genus of animal which, as was said, has more species than do living, composite and sensory animals."[463] The thin body certainly brings to mind modern descriptions of wispy alien greys. Nevertheless, Bruno was no abductee. He sought to control and manipulate them by playing one against the other: "Strong invocations and supplications to make the power of the superior overcome the inferior, for example, to banish evil demons by good ones, and to banish lower evil demons by higher ones. These demons are enticed by sacrifices and holocausts; they are frightened by threats, and they are summoned by the powers of inflowing rays of light."[464] Indeed, the siren song of the occult is the promise of influencing the powers and principalities of this world. Kabbalah was the chosen methodology for reconciling his magic with Scripture.

Gematria

The Kabbalistic methods of interpreting the Scriptures often yield surprising results. Gematria is the well-known practice of creating equivalences from the numerical values of words.[465] Hence, a Kabbalistic proof that God is the first of all beings and, ultimately, good looks like this:

Yahweh   יהוה

Yod (10 or 1+0 = 1)	Hey	Vav	Hey	total
1 +	5 +	6 +	5 =	17

Tov "Good"   טוב

Tav	Waw	Bet	total
9 +	6 +	2 =	17

Rishon "first"   ראשׁון

Resh	Alef	Shin	Waw	Nun	total
2 +	1 +	3 +	6 +	5 =	17

Perhaps gematria offers a solution to the origin of the abduction phenomenon?

חייזר : alien

Het	Yod	Yod	Zayin	Resh	Total
8 +	10 +	10 +	7 +	200 =	235

אינקובוס : incubus

Alef	Yod	Nun	Qof	Bet	Waw	Samek	Total
1 +	10 +	50 +	100 +	5 +	6 +	60 =	235

Notarikon

The second method, notarikon, is an acrostic system in which the letters of a word might be used to form a sentence. One turns a word in Scripture into an acronym, revealing a hidden meaning.

A famous example is אגלא AGLA for *Atah Gibor Le-olam Adonai*, meaning, "The Lord is mighty forever."[466] Esoteric lore holds that the name of AGLA preserved Lot and his family from fire and brimstone that rained down on Sodom and Gomorrah. AGLA was considered a power name of God by magicians of the Middle Ages, and it appeared in magical formulas for everything from protection to flying.

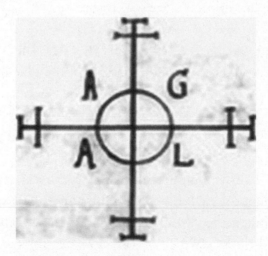

John Dee's AGLA sigil

Themurah

Themurah, תמורה ("exchange") in Kabbalah, denotes "transposition." It consists of transposing the letters of a word by various techniques to coax hidden meanings out of Scripture. For example, each letter can be replaced with the preceding letter in the alphabet, e.g., ET = DS.

Another simple example involves folding the alphabet in half to form a code.

First 13 letters:	A	B	C	D	E	F	G	H	I	J	K	L	M
Last 13 Letters:	Z	Y	X	W	V	U	T	S	R	Q	P	O	N

ZORVM = ALIEN

The third aspect of Kabbalah is the familiar Old-Testament expectation of the coming Messiah. Of course, Christians recognize that He came as the Suffering Servant (Isaiah 53), but Jews await His coming as conquering King (Zechariah 14:9). Interestingly, the single most important Kabbalistic work, *Sefer ha-Zohar* ("Book of Splendor"), predicts the messiah's arrival in the year 5773 (September 16, 2012, to September 4, 2013). A modern edition of the *Zohar* offers:

> In the 73rd year, that is, seven years after Messiah Ben Joseph was revealed, all the kings of the world shall assemble in the great city of Rome. And the Holy One, blessed be He, will shower fire and hail and meteoric stones upon them, until they are wiped out from the world. And only those kings who did not go to Rome will remain in the world. And they shall return and wage other wars. During this time, the King Messiah will declare himself throughout the whole world and many nations will gather around him together with many armies from all comers of the world. And all the children of Yisrael will assemble together in their places.[467]

While we are not aware that the messiah Ben Joseph presented himself to anyone seven years ago, the fruition of this prophecy will likely coincide near the release date of this book. We suspect, if it amounts to anything at all, it heralds the Antichrist.

First and foremost, these methods are used to derive hidden occult meanings from Scripture. It is easy to see that, by such torturous manipulations, one could make the Bible say almost anything. In Bruno's syncretistic faith, Kabbalah provided a biblical support for occult theories such as metempsychosis (the transmigration of the soul associated with reincarnation), an Eastern idea that Bruno sought to prove through atomic theory. In this way, his science was an extension of his magic. While hotly debated among scholars like Yates and León-Jones, it seems fair to accept that Bruno was an adept of multiple occult disciplines. Bruno's occultism was a syncretism of Romanism, hermetism, kabbalah, and atomist philosophy. Fascinatingly, he is among the few sorcerers to be claimed by Catholics, occultists, and secular humanists alike.

In his introduction to a modern edition of Bruno's *Cause, Principle and Unity*, Alfonso Ingegno writes, "This was a philosophy aimed at liberating man from the fear of death and the gods, pointing the way to an escape from the snares which demons use to catch us."[468] Accordingly, modern secularists and ET true believers like to portray Bruno as some sort of scientific messiah. In fact, if you would like to read Bruno's treatise, *On the Infinite Universe and Worlds*, you will find it hosted on the *Positive Atheism* website.[469] Another representative example comes from humanist Edward Howard Griggs who, while doting like a schoolgirl, calls him, "a world wandering scholar, a poet soul among philosophers, intense, passionate, disappearing in the dungeons of the Inquisition, emerging only to meet martyrdom, but in whom the intellectual spirit of our time appears three hundred years in advance."[470] In his book, *Great Leaders in Human Progress*, Griggs titled the chapter on Bruno, "The Martyr of Science." *Au contraire*, he should have been memorialized as a magus. The Inquisition did not doubt.

While visiting Venice, Bruno was betrayed to the Inquisition, jailed, and eventually sent to Rome. Historians are at a loss as to why he was kept in prison for six long years prior to his short tribunal by the Roman Inquisition in 1599. Bruno's most representative work, *The Expulsion of the Triumphant Beast*, a satirical indictment of papal Romanism, published in 1584, was singled out during the inquisitor's summation. According to Gaspar Schopp, Bruno made an ominous overture to the inquisitors, "Perchance, you pronounce this sentence against me with greater fear than I receive it."[471] This quip earned him a wooden vice for his tongue, silencing any protest as Pope Clement VIII declared Bruno a heretic and issued a sentence of death. On February 17, 1600, in a central Roman square called the Campo de' Fiori, he was burned at the stake. As an extension of the unholy union of Church and state, the Roman Church is forever besmirched by its capacity for murderous zeal.

In 1942, Cardinal Giovanni Mercati, after discovering a number of lost documents relating to Bruno's trial, stated that the Church was perfectly justified in condemning him. But is divergence from Roman Catholic Orthodoxy really a justification for a death sentence? *The Catholic Encyclopedia* contends:

> Bruno was not condemned for his defense of the Copernican system of astronomy, nor for his doctrine of the plurality of inhabited worlds, but for his theological errors, among which were the following: that Christ was not God but merely an unusually skillful magician, that the Holy Ghost is the soul of the world, that the Devil will be saved, etc.[472]

On the four-hundredth anniversary of Bruno's death, in the year 2000, Cardinal Angelo Sodano declared Bruno's death to be a "sad episode," but, despite his regret, he defended Bruno's prosecutors, maintaining that the Inquisitors "had the desire to serve freedom and promote the common good and did everything possible to save his life."[473] Suspiciously, the records of Bruno's inquisition are said to be lost. We denounce the Roman Catholic rationale with strong prejudice.

No true Church has any business executing anyone for what he or she believes. While Romanism has begged to disagree, biblical Christianity can compete in the marketplace of ideas without torturing and murdering its critics.

Next, the Copernican Revolution, Galileo, the Jesuits and the Rise of the Scientific Dictatorship.

10 | Essential History II

Galileo to Chardin

"If you direct your mind to the towns on the moon, I shall prove to you that I see them."—Johannes Kepler[474]

Bruno's torturous execution was a terrible injustice, but his involvement in demonic sorcery precludes his celebrated status as a martyr of science. More important to this discussion, it is safe to say that his extraterrestrial beliefs had little to do with his punishment. On the contrary, the principle of plentitude (which basically argued that everything that God could do He would do to maximize His glory) was in place as early as Augustine in the fourth century. But the Middle Ages were the pivot point. Specifically, the inquisitor Etienne Tempier's thirty-fourth proposition and Nicholas of Cusa's *Of Learned Ignorance* rehabilitated faith in the plurality of alien worlds and extraterrestrial life amongst theologians. Ultimately, it was the revival of atomism coupled with Copernican theory that accelerated belief in extraterrestrials to unprecedented levels.

The fifteenth-century rediscovery of the long-buried texts of Democritus, Epicurus, and Lucretius prompted an atomist resurgence. A Roman Catholic priest, Pierre Gassendi (1592–1655), is credited by historians as the one, "who stands at the apex of the revival of a system of atomism faithful to the principles of Epicurus."[475] Given Epicurus' scathing criticism of theism, he made for an unlikely champion. Nevertheless, Gassendi resolved to rehabilitate Epicurean atomism by removing its naturalistic implications. He corrected that there was not an infinite number of atoms, nor were they eternal, but rather finite in number and created by God. During the next two centuries, the writings of the ancient atomists spread all over Europe, helping to inspire the scientific revolution of the seventeenth and eighteenth centuries. In astronomy, the conflict over Copernicus' heliocentric model reached its boiling point in Kepler and Galileo.

When the famous German astronomer Johannes Kepler (1571–1630) received word that Galileo had discovered four moons around Jupiter, he composed an exuberant letter to Galileo, known as the *Dissertatio cum Nuncio Sidereo*. Kepler was convinced that Jupiter's moons were populated with intelligent beings:

> Therefore, if four planets orbit Jupiter at different distances and times: one asks to the benefit of whom, if nobody is on planet Jupiter to admire this variety with his eyes? Then, for what we're are concerned with on this Earth, I wonder; for what convincing reason? Above all, how can they be useful to us who never see them; and we do not expect that everybody can use their eyepieces to observe them.[476]

Thus, Kepler reasoned:

> The new four [planets] are not primarily for us who live on the Earth but without doubt for the creatures who live on Jupiter.[477]

He could not conceive that such bountiful real estate might be desolate. His penchant for eccentrics is prominently displayed in his *Somnium* ("The Dream"), which described a fantastic trip to the moon powered by demonic supernaturalism. The main character, Duracotus, whose mother was a witch, seems to speak for Kepler. Because the grim reaper was calling her, the elderly sorceress decided to preserve her enchanted legacy through her son. She disclosed the surreptitious source of her preternatural powers: *her familiar was a demon who lived on the moon.* Apparently, during a solar eclipse, the lunar demons travel between the Earth and the moon by way of a bridge of blackest darkness. Kepler explained:

> There is no doubt that evil spirits are called powers of darkness and of air. You would therefore regard them as sentenced and, so to say, banished to shadowy regions, to the cone of the earth's shadow. Hence, when this cone of shadow touches the moon, then the daemons invade the moon in a mass, using the cone of shadow as a ladder. On the other hand, when the cone of the moon's shadow touches the earth in a total eclipse of the sun, the daemons return through the cone to the earth.[478]

Duracotus decided to make a journey to the Moon, and, after summoning the demon, he was transported to a place called Levania. From this vantage point he was able to see that the Earth, indeed, orbited around the sun. Some of Kepler's contemporaries took this demonic tale quite seriously and believed that Kepler was divulging his own family history.

According to modern scholars like Carl Sagan, this was the first work of science fiction. Kepler used this tale as a literary vehicle to describe the heliocentric solar system as seen from the moon. However, given that Copernican theory was already viewed as antagonistic to religion, it is perplexing that he set his tale in the occult world of the shadow-land diabolicus. Indeed, many of his contemporaries took it so seriously that his mother was accused of witchcraft and put on trial. They charged that:

> Mrs. Kepler could pass through locked doors without opening them; she'd once ridden a calf to death; she could kill babies by blessing them; she had killed her neighbors' pets and livestock;

she had asked the gravedigger for her father's skull. (That last, it turns out, was true—she intended to have it set in silver as a gift for her son Johannes. She couldn't see what the big deal was, though—she said she'd heard about the ancient custom of making drinking vessels from deceased relatives' skulls in a sermon).[479]

Following her eventual acquittal, a heavy-hearted Kepler added extensive footnotes and explanations to his diabolic fantasy. The bizarre saga of the lunar demons was posthumously published in 1634 by his son, Ludwig Kepler. In some radical, geo-centrist, Creationist circles, the *Somnium* is still taken literally.[480] While that seems extravagant, Kepler's legacy lives on in his namesake space satellite, which is responsible for the recent announcement that billions of planets inhabit the Milky Way galaxy (as discussed in chapter 7, "Astrobiology and the Extraterrestrial Worldview").

At this time, the Vatican Observatory also had its genesis. Roman Catholic historians trace their astronomical heritage back to the Tower of the Winds commissioned by Pope Gregory XIII in 1576. The tower, also known as *Specola Vaticana* and the Gregorian Observatory, is said to be the location where Gregory came to recognize the need for calendar reform based on its highly accurate meridian line that revealed the former calendar's lack of precision. In addition, there was a separate facility at the Roman College that also began research at the time of Galileo in the late sixteenth century. The Gregorian Calendar, which is still in use today, was developed by the Jesuit mathematician Christoph Clavius at the Roman College and promulgated in 1582. During these early centuries, there was no true observatory as the sky was observed from balconies and windows often with less than optimal conditions. While all of this seems terribly progressive, this was also when the Church infamously censured Galileo.

Galileo Galilei (1564–1642) was an Italian astronomer, physicist, mathematician, and philosopher who spearheaded the Scientific

Revolution. His improvements to the telescope facilitated his astronomical observations which supported the controversial Copernican theory. Consequently, Galileo has been called the "father of modern observational astronomy."[481] Most educated people accepted the theories of the Greek astronomer Ptolemy, who held that the Earth was fixed and the sun orbited around it. Copernicus had published his theory in 1543 in a book dedicated to the pope. Copernicus had no physical proof but the heliocentric hypothesis was much better at predicting planetary orbits. Galileo, originally a supporter of Ptolemy's geocentric theory, became persuaded that Copernicus was right that the Earth really did revolve around the sun.

Galileo Galilei

Using a superior telescope of his own design, Galileo made important new observations about the phases of Venus, and sun spots were consistent with Copernican theory while casting doubt on geocentrism. Galileo took these observations to the Jesuits, the leading astronomers of the day, and they agreed with him that his sightings had bolstered the case for heliocentrism. Even so, such a dramatic change threatened volumes of work and scholarship based on Ptolemy. It is important to note that the geocentric universe was a classical pagan (rather than a Christian) concept. Although Christians accepted it, the Bible does not really teach that the sun revolves around the Earth. The writers of the Bible had a prescientific worldview and they described the way things appear to the naked eye. They used the language of the phenomenon.

Phenomenological language is descriptive of the ways things look and does not necessarily affirm scientific facts. For instance, even today, the weather forecaster speaks in terms of sunrise and sunset. However, no one believes that a trained meteorologist is meaning for us to understand that the sun moves around the Earth. Similarly, unless one understands the use of phenomenological language, one might think that the Bible teaches that the Earth is at the center of the universe. But knowing that the biblical authors describe things according to appearance, we understand that, like the weatherman, the Bible is merely saying that the sun rises because, to our naked eye, it appears as if the sun moves around the Earth. The passages in question were not teaching celestial mechanics.

Even so, there are still Creationists, in their misguided zeal to defend Scripture, that argue for a geocentric solar system. This is an unfortunate form of obscurantism that does nothing but discredit legitimate applications of Scripture. However, it does present an interesting challenge for us who would serve to correct them. One way we can rest assured that the heliocentric model is correct is by the remarkable success of NASA's satellite missions, like Galileo to Jupiter, which are based on Kepler's laws of celestial mechanics founded on the heliocentric model. These rockets fly precise trajectories which would inevitably fail if the heliocentric model were not true. Yet, they do succeed, and we have the satellite photographs to prove it, so geocentric Creationism must be false.

Like Galileo's early work, there is another way to prove heliocentrism simply by observations that can be made from Earth with a basic telescope. In geocentric theory, Venus would never be seen in its gibbous phase (where more is lit than not) because Venus is between the sun and the Earth.

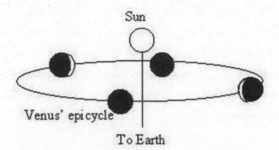

In a geocentric theory, Venus could not
pass through the gibbous phase.

However, in heliocentric theory, Venus can be observed to pass through
all phases, due to the fact that sometimes Venus is closer to the Earth
than the sun and sometimes further away.

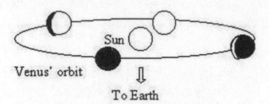

In a heliocentric universe, Venus would
appear to pass through all phases.

Indeed, this can be verified by observation. This photo of Venus in a gibbous phase proves the point. If geocentrism were true, this photograph
would not exist.

Venus in gibbous phase: 12/30/2008

Clearly, Galileo was correct, and those who sought to silence him were misapplying Scripture. Even so, his trial was more the result of poor diplomacy than anything else. When Galileo's lectures supporting the heliocentric theory were reported to the Inquisition, Cardinal Robert Bellarmine met with Galileo. Although the Church believed the Bible supported geocentrism, Bellarmine wrote:

> If there were a real proof that the Sun is in the center of the universe, that the Earth in the third heaven, and that the Sun does not go round the Earth but the Earth round the Sun, then we should have to proceed with great circumspection in explaining passages of Scripture which appear to teach the contrary, and rather admit that we did not understand them than declare an opinion to be false which is proved to be true. But, as for myself, I shall not believe that there are such proofs until they are shown to me.[482]

Thus, it seems the cardinal was open to examining the evidence and modifying the longstanding interpretations accordingly. However, Tyco Brahe, heralded as the greatest astronomer of the period, found Galileo's evidence inadequate. Because the evidence was inconclusive, Galileo agreed he would not teach heliocentrism.

After a few years of quiet work, Galileo was encouraged when Cardinal Maffeo Barberini was elected Pope Urban VIII. Interestingly, Barberini was a native of Florence, which has a red lily on its coat of arms and the Malachy prophecy (see our 2012 book, *Petrus Romanus*) predicting his reign was *Lilium et ro a*, meaning "lily and rose." This was a significant match given that it was after Arnold Wion's publication of the prophecy in *Lignam Vitae* (1595). Before becoming pope, Cardinal Barberini had fought to prevent Copernicus' work from being placed on the list of banned books. Even more, Barberini had written a poem praising Galileo as an intellectual hero. With the scientifically progressive Pope Urban VIII in the Vatican, Galileo was emboldened.

He published *Dialogue Concerning the Two Chief World Systems* in 1632 and claimed that he had proven Copernican theory. While this was obviously a violation of his agreement not to teach heliocentrism, what made it worse was that a major portion of his argument was false. He argued that the motion of the Earth around the sun created the ocean tides. While it was disputed when he wrote it, we now know that the gravity of the moon causes the tides. He made other scientific blunders like arguing against Kepler that the planetary orbits were perfect circles rather than elliptical. Even worse was the way he presented it. Galileo constructed his argument as dialogue between three men, two philosophers and a layman: 1) Salviati: an intellectual who spoke for Galileo; 2) Sagredo: a wealthy nobleman who sought the truth; and 3) Simplicio: an Aristotelian philosopher who put up feeble arguments for Salviati to refute. What made this especially poor form was that *Simplicio*, which in Italian means "simpleton," recited some of the pope's favorite arguments verbatim. Of course, publically humiliating the pope was poor politics and house arrest was a light punishment. Had he handled himself with more diplomacy, he could have avoided censure entirely.

Given his pop-culture status as the champion of science over religion, it may come as a surprise that Galileo did not support belief in extraterrestrials. In 1613, he wrote his *Letter on Sunspots* to the Jesuit astronomer Christopher Scheiner denouncing it in no uncertain terms:

> I agree with Apelles [Scheiner] in regarding as false and damnable the view of those who would put inhabitants on Jupiter, Venus, Saturn, and the moon, meaning by "inhabitants" animals like ours, and men in particular.[483]

Galileo is not known to have ever mentioned Bruno and apparently his opinion concerning ET never wavered, as a letter written three years later to Giacomo Muti reveals:

> I was in a position to prove that neither men nor animals, nor plants as on this earth, nor anything else at all like them can exist

on the moon. I said then, and I say now, that I do not believe that the body of the moon is composed of earth and water, and wanting these two elements we must necessarily conclude that it wants all other things which without these other things cannot exist or subsist.[484]

Thus, contrary to modern opinion, Galileo did not see a necessary connection between Copernican theory and ET life. Stephen Dick concluded, "Exhibiting a mastery of the arguments of Aristotle, Albertus Magnus, and Thomas Aquinas, Galileo concluded that Scripture dictated that there was only one cosmos, because Moses spoke only of the creation of one world."[485] Indicative of the extreme hubris characteristic of Rome, the Catholic Church did not exonerate Galileo until Halloween of 1992 in a public apology by Pope John Paul II. He said:

Thanks to his intuition as a brilliant physicist and by relying on different arguments, Galileo, who practically invented the experimental method, understood why only the sun could function as the centre of the world, as it was then known, that is to say, as a planetary system. The error of the theologians of the time, when they maintained the centrality of the Earth, was to think that our understanding of the physical world's structure was, in some way, imposed by the literal sense of Sacred Scripture.[486]

Of course, we can commend him for *finally* admitting this, but it was a long time coming. While Galileo was an ET skeptic, his contemporaries were not.

For example, the Jesuit Athanasius Kircher (1602–1680) was a German scholar who published around forty works, most notably in the fields of Egyptology, geology, and medicine. He was fascinated by ancient Egypt and, like Bruno, imagined all sorts of fanciful connections between Christianity and Egyptian mythology that were later revealed to be spurious. He was also the champion for a host of alien beings. According to Catholic astronomer, Kenneth Delano:

The Jesuit father Kircher, a contemporary of Huygens, claimed that everyone on Mercury is merry due to that planets lightsome and mischievous influence, the inhabitants of Venus live as in a pagan heaven on account of Venus's influence over men's affections; and on Mars the peoples are rough and warlike, in keeping with Mar's bellicose promptings.[487]

Kircher was on the precipice of an avalanche of such speculation. With the revival of atomic theory, belief in extraterrestrials flourished. Ironically, the Epicurean cosmology, designed to eliminate theism, was now welcomed as an ally.

From 1600 to 1900, there flowed a snowballing torrent of pseudo-scientific theological speculation concerning extraterrestrial life and a plurality of alien worlds. A virtual alien menagerie from every imaginable locale was advanced and promoted by many of the top scientists. For instance, the astronomer who discovered Uranus, Sir William Herschel (1730–1822), asserted that he saw trees, buildings, rivers, streets, and pyramids on the moon. Of course, buildings and roads meant it was populated with lunarians—or lunatics (depending on one's perspective). More perplexing, he thought the sun was inhabited by solarians (ETs who had evolved to survive the extreme temperatures of the sun at a searing 9,940 degrees Fahrenheit). He seemed equally convinced that all of the known planets were occupied by races appropriately endowed for their climates. While it seems ridiculous to us, the existence of solarians was quite a respectable theory in the eighteenth century.

This was also when the *Specola Vaticana* in the Vatican's Tower of the Winds was formally established under the direction of Monsignor Filippo Luigi Gilii (1756–1821). When Gilii died, the *Specola* was closed and its instruments were moved to the college because of its inconvenient location for students, and the dome of Saint Peter's obstructed a large portion of the sky. Astronomical work at the college was initially a Jesuit pursuit. They set about confirming Galileo's work in order to convince the Church authorities, but the Jesuit order was suppressed and disbanded for its pernicious skullduggery by Pope Clement XIV in 1773. By the mid-eighteenth century, the Jesuits had earned a bad reputation in Europe for political maneuvering and economic exploitation bar none. Widely regarded as greedy schemers, prone to meddle in state affairs through manipulation of the royals, they were deported and banished from many European countries. Even so, the astronomical ambitions of Rome endured. Around 1786, Cardinal Zelada had a 125-foot tower constructed and equipped for observation. A few years later, Pope Pius VII went to watch the solar eclipse of 1804, and subsequently took a personal interest in the facility. In fact, when Pius VII went to Paris to crown the ruthless tyrant Napoleon, he also purchased an expensive telescope and pendulum clock for the facility.[488]

Another interesting theologian from this era was Thomas Chalmers, a Scottish minister and a leader of the Free Church of Scotland. He has been called "Scotland's greatest nineteenth-century churchman."[489] A prolific author, he is credited with over thirty volumes; some of the most popular were a series of sermons on the relation between the discoveries of astronomy and the Christian revelation, which was published in January 1817. Chalmers debated skeptics like Thomas Paine who asserted that Christianity would be falsified by the existence of aliens from space. He adamantly believed that biblical faith could accommodate a genuine ET reality, but he also saw that the battle for Earth's dominion was supremely important. Chalmers wrote:

> If, by the sagacity of one infernal mind, a single planet has been seduced from its allegiance, and been brought under the ascendancy of him who is called in Scripture, "the god of this world;" and if the errand on which our Redeemer came, was to destroy the works of the devil—then let this planet have all the littleness which astronomy has assigned to it—call it what it is, one of the smaller islets which float on the ocean of vacancy; it has become the theatre of such a competition, as may have all the desires and all the energies of a divided universe embarked upon it. It

involves in it other objects than the single recovery of our species. It decides higher questions. It stands linked with the supremacy of God, and will at length demonstrate the way in which He inflicts chastisement and overthrow upon all His enemies. We know not if our rebellious world be the only stronghold which Satan is possessed of, or if it be but the single post of an extended warfare, that is now going on between the powers of light and of darkness. But be it the one or the other, the parties are in array, and the spirit of the contest is in full energy, and the honour of mighty combatants is at stake; and let us therefore cease to wonder that our humble residence has been made the theatre of so busy an operation, or that the ambition of loftier natures has here put forth all its desire and all its strenuousness.[490]

While Chalmers believed that a plurality of worlds was possible, he had little doubt that the cosmic conflict between Satan and the powers and principalities over this humble planet Earth were of astronomical, theological significance. The fate of Earth is linked to the ultimate authority of God. As one can readily see, the sorts of ideas put forth in the book you are now holding are not terribly new, albeit the apocalyptic zeitgeist of our age is arguably unmatched.

The nineteenth century picked up where the previous century left off and seemingly cultivated an exponential resurgence in extraterrestrial belief. François Plisson, a French critic of the era's extraterrestrial enthusiasm, wrote, "Almost all the astronomers of our day, and the most eminent among them, freely adopt the opinions that not long ago were viewed as being able to spring only from the mind of a madman."[491] It seems appropriate that this was also the era of a massive rise in occultism and false religions. Spiritualism, Mormonism, Adventism, and the Jehovah's Witnesses all advocated various extraterrestrial doctrines. Panspermia (the theory that life on Earth was seeded from space) originated during this star-struck era. One Catholic theologian from Germany contributed much to Rome's acceptance of alien life.

Joseph Pohle was born in Germany in 1852 and educated in Trier, Rome, and Würzburg. He was ordained to the Roman priesthood in 1878. An accomplished theologian, he also had a great interest in astronomy. His popular book, *Stellar Worlds and Their Inhabitants* (1884), argues that the sheer size of the universe infers that God would maximize His glory by creating countless intelligent alien organisms dispersed throughout the cosmos: material beings, unlike the multiplicity of angels, whose nature is purely spiritual and immaterial. He wrote: "It seems to be the purpose of the Universe that the celestial bodies are inhabited by beings who reflect the glory of God in the beauty of their bodies and worlds as man does, in a limited way, in his world."[492] While God certainly could glorify Himself by creating many populated worlds, given the evidence that deceptive entities have been affecting the modern world in the *guise* of space aliens, we consider the question of genuine ET life a separate issue. Unfortunately, this sort of reasoning, well-intentioned as it may be, only fertilizes the fields of the coming great deception.

The correspondence between Pohle's argumentation—and that coming from modern ET apologists like Thomas O'Meara of Notre Dame—is not too surprising given that Pohle contributed many articles to the *Catholic Encyclopedia* and was a well-respected Roman Catholic theologian whose texts are still in use today. Consequently, his contribution to the extraterrestrial issue was highly influential for the upper echelons of Roman Curia in charge today. In fact, one of the most widely employed European theology textbooks of the twentieth century, *Katolische Dogmatik* (1957) by M. Schmaus, promotes the doctrine of a multiplicity of inhabited worlds derivative of Pohle. Yet, it was the rise of Darwinism and its impact on the Roman Catholic Church that bore the strangest fruit of all.

Pierre Teilhard de Chardin was a Jesuit priest and mystical philosopher who trained as a paleontologist and geologist. He is renowned for his devotion to Darwinism and he famously assisted in the discovery of Peking Man and Piltdown Man, two alleged human ancestors. The

Peking Man was said to be a skull from *Homo Erectus*—an extinct species of hominid that supposedly lived 1.8 million years ago. While casts and written descriptions remain, the original fossils mysteriously disappeared, casting doubt on the discovery. Even worse, the Piltdown Man was an infamous hoax entailing fabricated bone fragments misrepresented as the fossilized remains of a "missing link" allegedly collected in 1912 from a gravel pit at Piltdown, East Sussex, England. In truth, the remains consisted of a dog's tooth, a hippopotamus tooth, an elephant molar, an Orangutan jaw, and a six-hundred-year-old medieval human skull, albeit the hoax was not exposed for some forty years.[493] Chardin's role in this fraud is unclear, but many assert he was also duped.

Pierre Teilhard de Chardin

Chardin conceived of the idea that evolution was progressing to a goal—the maximum level of complexity and consciousness—called the Omega Point (discussed later). Along with the Ukrainian geochemist Vladimir Ivanovich Vernadsky, he also developed the concept of Noosphere, a creative term denoting the numinous sphere of collective human thought. During his prime, he was condemned as a heretic because his mystical Darwinian syncretism severely conflicted with the teaching Magisterium of the Catholic Church, particularly regarding human origins and the doctrine of Original Sin. His primary book, *The*

Phenomenon of Man, presented an evolutionary account of the unfolding of the cosmos that abandoned biblical theology for an occult pantheistic monism. Interestingly, extraterrestrials were an inevitable extension of cosmic evolution. Chardin wrote:

> In other words, considering what we now know about the number of "worlds" and their internal evolution, the idea of *a single* hominized *planet* in the universe has already become in fact (without our generally realizing it) almost as *inconceivable* as that of a man who appeared with no genetic relationship to the rest of the earth's animal population.
>
> At an average of (at least) one human race per galaxy, that makes a total of millions of human races dotted all over the heavens.
>
> Confronted with this fantastic multiplicity of astral centres of "immortal life", how is theology going to react, if it is to satisfy the anxious expectations and hopes of all who wish to continue to worship God "in spirit and in truth"? It obviously cannot go on much longer offering as the only *dogmatically certain* thesis one (that of the uniqueness in the universe of terrestrial mankind) which our experience rejects as *improbable*.[494]

In light of those millions of alien races, Chardin wrote, "We must at least, however, endeavor to make our classical theology open to (I was on the point of saying "blossom into") the possibility (a positive possibility) of their existence and their presence."[495] As we will reveal, Chardin's theological ideas form the epistemological framework for the modernist Jesuit astronomers and even Pope Benedict XVI, himself. With Petrus Romanus assuming the pontificate as the book rolls off the press, ready or not, the False Prophet of the Omega Point is near.

11 | Exotheology: Nature and Grace

"Knowing this first, that there shall come in the last days scoffers, walking after their own lusts, And saying, Where is the promise of his coming? for since the fathers fell asleep, all things continue as they were from the beginning of the creation."—2 Peter 3:3–4

"But in the eternities,
Doubtless we shall compare together, hear
A million alien Gospels, in what guise
He trod the Pleiades, the Lyre, the Bear."
—Alice Meynell, *Christic in the Universe*

Exotheology addresses the theological implications given a genuine, intelligent, extraterrestrial life form. This chapter will address those implications in three areas: 1) the image of God; 2) the incarnation; and 3) Divine Creation. Because the third controverts the assumptions of the astrobiological project and is discounted by the Jesuit scientists, it will be examined through the lens of nature and grace and the divided truth construct taught by Dr. Francis Schaeffer. While you may be wondering why exotheology is important, you should be aware that your tax dollars are funding it.

The Defense Advanced Research Projects Agency (DARPA) doled out around one hundred thousand dollars for a workshop featuring a session asking, "Did Jesus Die for Klingons, Too?" As shocking as it might seem, on October 1, 2011, Christian Weidemann, a philosopher from Ruhr-University Bochum in Germany, lectured on extraterrestrials and theology as part of the 100 Year Starship Study Symposium in Orlando, Florida. The 100 Year Starship organization's mission statement begins, "We exist to make the capability of human travel beyond our solar system to another star a reality within the next 100 years."[496] Intriguing as DARPA's ambition to make *Star Trek* a reality might be, it is downright baffling why it wants to know if the Gospel of salvation is open to aliens. Weidemann, who identified as a Protestant, argued, "If there are extraterrestrial intelligent beings at all, it is safe to assume that most of them are sinners too. If so, did Jesus save them too? My position is no. If so, our position among intelligent beings in the universe would be very exceptional."[497] We think this answer has merit. But why does DARPA care? Historically, skeptics have posited the existence of ETs as a problem for Christianity, but did the first-century apostles anticipate any of this?

When Peter wrote that in the last days, scoffers would come (2 Peter 3:3), he would never have imagined the Church would have entered what historians now call the "space age." He connected skepticism regarding Jesus' return with the disregard of Divine Creation and the Flood of Noah's day. Peter responded to the skeptical objections by suggesting that the present regularity of the world was not indicative of its necessary persistence in the same form. The God who holds the universe together by His word can release it with the same word. Peter also argued that God sees time in a different way than humankind. The seeming delay in Christ's return is an opportunity for sinners to respond in faith to Jesus. Peter understood that the prophecies concerning Christ's return would be fulfilled with destructive power at a time when unbelievers least expect it. In contrast, the scientific enterprise is founded on the uniformity of nature or the belief that today will be much like yesterday and onward in a linear sequence. But the Bible predicts a time when God will intervene. Might that nonlinear event be imminent?

On one hand, the prodigious progress of science has afforded great luxury and benefit, but on the other hand, it promotes arrogance and imagined self-sufficiency. Theologian Merill Unger described the modern Church as, "boastedly wise and scientific but utterly blind to God's truth."[498] During the Holy Roman Empire, the Catholic Church enforced a stranglehold on knowledge and viciously silenced dissent. Soon the evidence mounted against it became overwhelming. The Copernican Revolution's toll on the Renaissance Church's authority has led to what is known as "scientism," the idea that science is the exclusive path to truth. Even though self-refuting, scientism bolsters secular man's denial of Divine Creation and belief in the mediocrity principle. These presuppositions seriously discount biblical revelation.

The doctrine of Creation affords a unique blessing on man. Having been endowed with the image of God, humanity is deemed exceptional (Genesis 1:26–27; 9:6). Systematic theologian Millard Erickson concludes, "The image is something in the very nature of humans, in the way in which they were made. It refers to something a human *is* rather than something a human *has* or *does.*"[499] Implicit in the image is our purpose to know, love, and serve God. In addition, the New Testament grounds the Gospel in Christ's humanity (Hebrews 2:14; 4:15; John 1:14; 1 Timothy 3:16). Humanity's exceptional status and God's incarnation as a man are theological pillars on which the Gospel stands. Thus, it comes as no surprise that John specified the incarnation, "that Jesus Christ has come in the flesh" as a specific test for antichrists (1 John 4:2–3). It naturally follows that the satanic conspiracy will encompass an attack on the image of God, the incarnation, and the doctrine of Divine Creation. We believe that an extraterrestrial ruse staged by evil, supernatural forces uniquely provides the scope to undermine all three while simultaneously offering an attractive spiritual alternative to the world also palatable to inclusivist Roman Catholics and marginal believers in Christ. While the challenges have been around for years, they will gain considerable traction given an alleged ET reality.

Of course, the primary application of this material is to be extremely cautious concerning extraterrestrial claims. As Dr. Michael Heiser has suggested, something as subtle as evidence for panspermia could be just as effective as flying saucers on the White House lawn. If supernatural intelligences perpetrate such a deception, then they will likely immediately attack the veracity of biblical Christianity (Colossians 2:8). However, the teaching will seemingly embrace Christianity in an inclusivist system akin to Eastern religions and Vatican II. Short of directly exposing their demonic origin, which may prove difficult, apologetics are in order.

This discussion also has value given the outside chance of genuine ETs as well. If some sort of disclosure occurs—do not fear—we advise maintaining Christ-like composure and confidence. As fantastic as it seems, the Church should not be caught by surprise if these things come to pass prior to the rapture. We may face what appears to be powerful evidence against our faith. Anticipating this, C. S. Lewis ended his essay "Religion and Rocketry" in a manner supportive of this book's thesis:

> We have been warned that all but conclusive evidence against Christianity, evidence that would deceive (if it were possible) the very elect, will appear with the Antichrist. And after that there will be wholly conclusive evidence on the other side. But not, I fancy, till then on either side.[500]

These sage words from Lewis remind us that no matter how well we anticipate, Satan will likely catch us by surprise. The attack could be much more subtle than we can expect.

Imago De

The image of God, or *imago de*, is generally defined as "that which distinguishes human beings from the rest of God's creatures,"[501] based on the fact that the human is created in God's image (Genesis 1:26). From this definition, it is obvious that extraterrestrial intelligence poses a challenge. Fortunately, Dr. Heiser has been thinking ahead of the curve. In his novel, *The Facade*, he states the problem through his character Brian Scott (loosely based on himself):

> Since theologians of all these traditions have for centuries taught that the image of God is what makes man absolutely unique among created beings, and since—so it's said—the image must refer to things like intelligence, speech capability, moral sense, etc., then the reality of an extraterrestrial intelligence would demonstrate that the Bible has an error.[502]

Interestingly, a Roman Catholic apologetics book by Peter Kreeft, which purports to handle the tough questions, addresses this issue in the form of a dialogue:

> **Sal:** But if we're made in God's image, how can E.T. be made in God's image?
>
> **Chris:** God is spirit. The image of God is in us in the soul, not the body. E.T. would have a soul too, however different his body is.
>
> **Sal:** So E.T. is made in God's image too?
>
> **Chris:** Of course, If E.T.s exist.[503]

Notice how this interpretation of the image does *not* preserve human exceptionalism. In fact, it confirms the principle of mediocrity that undergirds astrobiology. In contrast, the functional view states that humankind is God's unique material image on the Earth, His functional representative (Genesis 1:28; Psalms 8). Heiser explains that the prefixed Hebrew preposition rendered "in" can also be understood to mean "as God's image":

The idea I want to put forth is that humankind was created as God's image. In other words, the preposition tells us that humans work as God's imagers—that they work in the capacity of God's representatives. The image is therefore not a thing put in us; it is something we are. It is not a thing; it is a divinely-ordained or status. Don't think of it as a noun; think of it as a verb. Being created as God's imagers means we are God's representatives on earth.[504]

The beauty of the functional view is that, in contrast to the Catholic view, it *does* give humankind a unique status, even when faced with ETs. It is for this reason that he asserts the functional interpretation of the *imago de* to be more resilient. Theologian Wayne Grudem explains, *"The fact that man is in the image of God means that man is like God and represents God."*[505] Recalling that the text reads, "And God said, Let us make man in our image, after our likeness" (Genesis 1:26a), Grudem argues that to the original readers it meant simply, "Let us make man to be *like* us and to *represent* us."[506] Accordingly, rather than maintain that it is exclusively functional, it seems to us there is room for the likeness aspect to encompass much of what has been classically held true as well. The incarnation issue is somewhat thornier, but can also be answered.

Incarnation

In theology, "incarnation" refers to when Christ, without giving up His deity, became a human being. This invites a challenge given nonhuman intelligent beings. Astrobiologist Paul Davies writes in his book, *God and the New Physics*, "The existence of extra-terrestrial intelligences would have a profound impact on religion, shattering completely the traditional perspective on God's relationship with man.… The difficulties are particularly acute for Christianity, which postulates that Jesus Christ was God incarnate whose mission was to provide salvation for man on Earth. The prospect of a host of 'alien Christs' systematically visiting every inhabited planet in the physical form of the local creatures has a rather absurd aspect."[507] Accordingly, the Church should be prepared to address the alleged contradiction between Jesus' incarnation and the existence of ETs, already a popular canard amongst atheists.

Peter Kreeft's Catholic apologetics treatment approaches it like this:

Sal: And do you think Christ became an E.T. on E.T.'s home planet?

Chris: Why not? Especially if they needed him as we did, if they fell into sin and needed a Savior.

Sal: You mean maybe some planets didn't sin?

Chris: Maybe. We didn't have to sin, you know. That's why we're rightly blamed for it. That much is certain, however you interpret the Garden of Eden story. Sin was out fault, our free choice.

Sal: So maybe E.T. people didn't sin, and then Christ didn't have to come to E.T.'s planct.

Chris: Maybe. But maybe he came anyway, not to die but just to say hello.[508]

Vatican Observatory Research Group (VORG) astronomer Chris Corbally offers a similar response: "While Christ is the First and the Last Word (the Alpha and the Omega) spoken to humanity, he is not necessarily the only word spoke to the universe.... For, the Word spoken to us does not seem to exclude an equivalent 'Word' spoken to aliens. They, too, could have had their 'Logos-event.'"[509] Karl Rahner wrote: "In view of the immutability of God in himself and the identity of the Logos with God, it cannot be proved that a multiple incarnation in different histories of salvation is absolutely unthinkable."[510] As you can see, Roman

Catholic theologians are playing right into the hands of Paul Davies and, more famously, the founding father Thomas Paine, who previously voiced this alleged conundrum:

> Are we to suppose that every world in the boundless creation had an Eve, an apple, a serpent and a redeemer? In this case, the person who is irreverently called the Son of God, and sometimes God himself, would have nothing else to do than to travel from world to world, in an endless succession of death, with scarcely a momentary interval of life.[511]

Of course, Paine merely presupposes the existence of other worlds and ETs, but given an end-time disclosure event, this argument could have real teeth. But certainly all of these skeptics and Catholic theologians alike ignore the repeated instances in Scripture that assert it as a one-time event. Paul couldn't have been any clearer: "Knowing that Christ being raised from the dead <u>dieth no more</u>; death hath no more dominion over him" (Romans 6:9, underlined added). The author of Hebrews makes a major point out of "once" by repeating it five times (Hebrews7:27; 9:12, 9:26, 9:28; 10:10). Also, Peter wrote, "For Christ also hath <u>once suffered for sins</u>, the just for the unjust, that he might bring us to God, being put to death in the flesh, but quickened by the Spirit" (1 Peter 3:18, underline added). It's hard to take the New Testament seriously and imagine multiple incarnations and sacrificial deaths on other planets. The question comes down to sufficiency. It seems much more coherent to believe that if hypothetical ETs do need salvation, then Jesus' unique offering on Earth is enough for all.

C. S. Lewis responded to a similar challenge from astronomer Fred Hoyle by reasoning from Romans 8:19–23 that the longing for redemption is cosmic, and therefore it is possible that Christ's redemption has somehow been extended to other creatures or that perhaps Christians will be the instrument by which it is offered.[512] While it's possible, the Great Commission really only entailed the "ends of the earth" (Acts 1:8).

In addition, the cosmic language in Colossians, "to reconcile to himself all things, whether on earth or in heaven, making peace by the blood of his cross" (Colossians 1:20), seems to imply that any being who can be redeemed is redeemed by the terrestrial cross.

Catholic theologians strangely disagree. For example, Pierre Teilhard de Chardin writes this would be " 'ridiculous', particularly when one considers the enormous number of stars to be 'informed' (miraculously?) and their distance from one another in space and time."[513] Of course, he discounts God's omnipresence and assumes thousands of alien civilizations. In like fashion, O'Meara writes, "Human beings should not project terrestrial religion onto possible peoples elsewhere."[514] Yet, whether or not Rome recognizes it, God is sovereign over the vast universe. Based on dubious alien apologetics like this, Roman Catholics are especially vulnerable to a diabolical ruse. The last area of attack is the doctrine of Divine Creation.

Divine Creation: Nature and Grace

Peter's prophetic warning concerning scoffers was especially prescient in that it connects skepticism of the Second Coming with the denial of Divine Creation (2 Peter 3:4–5). Although skeptics ridicule our confidence in His return, the delay actually reveals God's desire that more will repent and come to faith. Furthermore, Paul specifically connected denial of the Creator to humankind's increasingly futile thinking, idolatrous religion, and immorality (Romans 1:20–32). Those seem self-evident. Nevertheless chapter 3 ("Days of Noah") documents the downward trajectory. Indeed, even the words of the Jesuit scientists seem prophetically significant in that Intelligent Design and Creationism have been castigated to the point that they can no longer be mentioned in a classroom. Divine Creation is foundational to all other doctrines, and skepticism in this area contaminates all others. It really reflects a worldview issue.

While new exoplanet discoveries lead atheists, science fiction fans, and ET true believers to be greatly encouraged, most members of the public are relatively ambivalent because either they are not aware or they do not share the scientists' worldview. The term "worldview" is actually derived from a German term, *weltanschauung*, which means a "look onto the world." An academic definition is "the comprehensive set of basic beliefs in which one views the world and interprets experiences."[515] It is the lens through which one interprets reality. Everyone has a worldview. We all have certain presuppositions and preferences that affect our view of life and reality. Our worldview is formed by our upbringing, education, nationality, and culture. It is fueled by the books we read, music we listen to, art we appreciate, and movies we watch. This is why the Apostle Paul exhorted, "And be not conformed to this world: but be ye transformed by the renewing of your mind, that ye may prove what is that good, and acceptable, and perfect, will of God" (Romans 12:2). The secular world views reality differently than the Christian.

Naturalism commonly refers to the view that only the laws of nature control the universe, and that nothing exists beyond the natural. The public statements coming from the Jesuit scientists are more consistent with the naturalistic worldview than biblical Christianity. For all intents and purposes, the VORG astronomers like George Coyne, Guy Consolmagno, José Gabriel Funes, and Christopher Corbally have adopted a "two-tiered" worldview based on a divided concept of truth as described by the acclaimed evangelical philosopher, Dr. Francis Schaeffer. As it turns out, this is not too surprising, because Schaeffer traced the origin of the divided-truth concept to Roman Catholic Doctor of the Church, Saint Thomas Aquinas (1225–1274). After a brief survey of early Western thought, Schaeffer wrote, "In Aquinas's view the will of man was fallen, but the intellect was not. From this incomplete view of the biblical Fall flowed subsequent difficulties. Out of this as time passed, man's intellect was seen as autonomous."[516] Several passages of Scripture confirm sin's effect on the intellect (e.g., Romans 1:21; 2 Corinthians 3:14–15; 4:4).

According to Schaeffer, Aquinas opened the way for the discussion of what is usually called nature and grace. In his seminal work, *Escape From Reason*, Schaeffer diagrammed grace over nature like this:

GRACE, THE HIGHER
- God the Creator
- heaven and heavenly things
- the unseen and its influence on the earth
- man's soul
- unity

NATURE, THE LOWER
- The created
- earth and earthly things;
- the visible and what nature and man do on earth
- man's body
- diversity[517]

The idea is that truth is divided. There are two kinds of truth: one accessed by reason and evidence and the other by blind faith. If you pay close attention, it becomes easy to spot the truth-divide in the Jesuit scientists' caustic criticisms of Intelligent Design and Creationism. For example, George Coyne, former head of the VORG, disputes the anthropic principle (discussed in our astrobiology chapter) as evidence for Divine Creation:

> To imagine a Creator twiddling with the constants of nature is a bit like thinking of God making a big pot of soup.... It's a return to the old vision of a watchmaker God, only it's even more fundamentalist. Because what happens if it turns out there is a perfectly logical scientific explanation for these values of the gravitational constant and so on? Then there'd be even less room for God.[518]

As you can see, following Aquinas, Coyne has divorced nature the particulars, from grace the universals. Coyne's concept of God need not correspond to objective truths in the material world; rather, it is relegated to the upper story, grace, and need not be detectable. However, his scientific work inhabits the "lower story"—nature—and is accessed by logic and reason. In this realm, Coyne is no different than Richard Dawkins. His view of nature is governed by the laws of physics and chemistry and is therefore mechanistic and determined. Transcendent realities like God's status as Creator and divine providence are in the "upper story" where grace resides. These are known only by faith and have no bearing on his science.

The reason it's so important to thoroughly understand this division is that it is the single most potent weapon used by secularists for delegitimizing the biblical perspective. Obviously, it wasn't always this way. Schaeffer describes how the situation progressed from Aquinas through philosophy, culminating in the twentieth century, when the concept of truth itself was formally divided—a development he illustrated with a two-story building. In the lower story are math, science, and reason, which are considered public truth, binding on all people at all times. Over against it is an upper story of emotional experience, which is deemed purely personal and subjective. This is why you hear people today utter nonsense like, "That may be true for you, but it's not true for me." In this way, ethical claims regarding abortion and marriage are not taken seriously in the marketplace of ideas, because they are simply upper-story beliefs. When Schaeffer was writing, the term "postmodernism" had not yet been coined, but clearly he was ahead of the curve. Today, we call the lower story "modernism," which still claims to have universal, objective truth—while in the upper story, postmodernism, reside spiritual beliefs and morality. Today's fact/value divide is diagrammed like this:

VALUES = POSTMODERNISM
Subjective, Relative, Nonrational

FACTS = MODERNISM
Objective, Universal, Rational

The Jesuit scientists have bought into the divided-truth concept by relegating their faith to the upper story of nonreason while depositing secular, naturalistic science in the lower-story fact realm. This creates serious problems. When religious claims are hoisted into the upper story, they are not only immune from rational criticism, they can hold contradictions with the lower story. Post Vatican II theology thrives on this divide. For example, the division allows Vatican II era Catholics to advocate inclusivism. They celebrated Pope John Paul II leading a prayer vigil alongside witch doctors, shaman, yogis, Buddhists, Muslims and others without offering a single criticism of their beliefs.[519] Unfortunately, all liberal theology is predicated on the divided-truth concept, and the nonbelieving world is completely in its grip.

The secular world is neither wholly rationalist nor postmodern; rather, it is deliberately divided along the fact/values split. Modernism rules the lower-story fact realm, whereas postmodernism has a stranglehold on the upper-story values realm. For example, the secular view of the human person divides human life from personhood. The body in the lower story (the fact realm) is viewed as a biomechanical machine, whereas personhood (the self) is consigned to the subjective upper story. This frames the debate on bioethical issues like transhumanism, euthanasia, sexuality, and abortion. For example, on the lower-story facts side, human life has been opened wide for disturbing experimentation. But in the upper story, scientists are given a wide berth by defining personhood in an unscientific, subjective way so bioethical limits are relaxed. Similarly, this explains why otherwise hard-nosed scientists are prone to believing in extraterrestrials. As Michael Crichton pointed out, SETI is a religious quest. In other words, he means it resides in the upper story and is immune to reason. The divide is why you can get a degree in astrobiology, a field with absolutely nothing to study. The Jesuits who embrace Neo-Darwinism and astrobiology while claiming to represent Christ are trying to have their cake and eat it, too.

The Jesuit scientists and Catholic theologians are far too politically savvy to claim the Bible is false. Exploiting the truth divide, they consign Scripture to the postmodern sphere—as poetry and myth—which takes it out of the realm of true and false altogether. In this way, they can assure us they have faith, while at the same time denying that it has any relevance to science. As Intelligent Design advocate Phillip Johnson puts it, the divided truth concept "allows the metaphysical naturalists to mollify the potentially troublesome religious people by assuring them that science does not rule out 'religious belief' (so long as it does not pretend to be knowledge)."[520] In other words, as long as everyone understands that belief in God is merely a matter of private feelings, then it is acceptable. The two-story grid functions as a gatekeeper that defines what can be taken seriously as genuine knowledge and what can be dismissed as mere wish fulfillment. The secular world celebrates the Roman Catholic embrace of its system.

The Templeton Foundation named Michael Heller, professor at the Pontifical Academy of Theology in Cracow, Poland, the winner of the 2008 Templeton Prize for discoveries about spiritual realities.[521] Whereas the Templeton Foundation purports to honor "exceptional contribution to affirming life's spiritual dimension, whether through insight, discovery, or practical works,"[522] Heller used the press conference as an opportunity to attack intelligent design:

> Adherents of the so-called intelligent design ideology commit a grave theological error. They claim that scientific theories, that ascribe the great role to chance and random events in the evolutionary processes, should be replaced, or supplemented, by theories acknowledging the thread of intelligent design in the universe. Such views are theologically erroneous. They implicitly revive the old manicheistic error postulating the existence of two forces acting against each other: God and an inert matter; in this case, chance and intelligent design. There is no opposition here. Within the all-comprising Mind of God what we call chance and random events is well composed into the symphony of creation.[523]

Manichaeism was a form of Gnostic dualism that gave evil equality with God. Our argument is not that chance has equal status; rather, we believe that *it does not exist* in the way naturalists believe. What does he mean, "There is no opposition" between Creation and randomness? This is hardly intelligible! For communication to have meaning, we must agree on definitions. "Random" and "created" are antithetical. Protestant theologian and philosopher R. C. Sproul explains:

> If chance exists in its frailest possible form, God is finished. Nay, he could not be finished because that would assume he once was. To finish something implies that it at best was once active or existing. If chance exists in any size, shape, or form, God cannot exist. The two are mutually exclusive.
>
> If chance existed, it would destroy God's sovereignty. If God is not sovereign, he is not God. If he is not God, he simply *is* not. If chance is, God is not. If God is, chance is not. The two cannot coexist by reason of the impossibility of the contrary.[524]

Sproul is absolutely correct, but do not misunderstand him. The word "chance" is used in different ways, and secularists often equivocate. In one sense, it simply denotes probability or possibility. Used in this way, it is an abstract concept describing a state of affairs. For example, when you flip a coin, you have a 50-percent chance of getting heads or tails and a 100-percent chance of getting either. However, no one actually believes that some magical force called "chance" causes it to land one way or another. Even so, atheists regularly deify and worship chance in the upper story of nonreason, and apparently Michael Heller has as well.

A coin-toss result is a complex relationship between forces and the environment. If we were to design a machine to precisely flip a coin the same exact way in a vacuum where no outside forces interacted with it, it would land the same way every single time. Chance cannot *do* anything, but atheistic naturalists regularly say that things happen *by* chance, implying causation. This equivocation is a leap into nonreason.

No matter what Heller says, he cannot rationally believe life evolves *by* chance and divine intention; that's nonsense. The Jesuit scientists who advocate evolution by random natural selection are denying God as Creator.

Opus De theologian Giuseppe Tanzella-Nitti characterizes Roman Catholic openness to chance when he argues in respect to ETs, "We do not know if life is a universal and quasi-inevitable phenomena, reproducing itself everywhere that the conditions permit it to do so,"[525] and then, "or if life is equivalent to a mere probabilistic number, the result of chance at the roulette wheel of cosmic evolution and a phenomenon that does not have any significance."[526] It seems the embrace of naturalistic presuppositions follows inevitably once the authority of Scripture has been abandoned.

Appearing with Richard Dawkins, Cardinal George Pell described the biblical story of Adam and Eve as a myth. Much to Dawkins' amusement, he stated, "It's a very sophisticated mythology to try to explain the evil and the suffering in the world.... It's a religious story told for religious purposes."[527] He said it was impossible to know if there was really a first human. The same heterodox view is evident in comments by the Jesuit astronomers. Coyne, who has also appeared with Dawkins, affirms God as the Creator, but qualifies, "I also know that I evolved, that my ancestors came crawling out of the sea, and that they wound up hanging from trees eating bananas."[528] On Genesis, he argues, "Scripture is made up of myth, of poetry, of history. But it is simply not teaching science."[529] The truth divide is obvious, but denial of Adam goes much farther than science, because Adam's sin is a key component of the Gospel (Romans 5:12). If our sin nature is merely a vestigial leftover from our animal past, why would God hold us accountable for it? Worse yet, one wonders why one so inclined would worship Jesus Christ, who was necessarily mistaken in His belief that God created male and female at the beginning (Matthew 19:4). By relegating faith to the upper story of nonreason, these inconsistencies are simply brushed aside. This begs the question, "What is faith?"

Proper faith is neither blind nor wishful thinking, but rather earned trust based on evidence. Richard Dawkins argues that faith is merely "belief without evidence" or even a process of intentional nonthinking.[530] We find this to be disingenuous. We argue that biblical faith is more akin to an earned trust like that between a husband and wife. We have faith based on an earned trust in our spouses' character. In the same way, we trust God and believe His word because of His faithfulness. A theological dictionary supports this by defining it in terms of both an "intellectual belief" and a "relational trust or commitment."[531] Accordingly, biblical faith is based on a unified truth and is supported by evidence detectable in the material world. Ironically, the Jesuit priests have adopted Dawkins' definition.

Guy Consolmagno argues, "The religious fundamentalists, basically, are scared that they don't have faith, which is why they cling so tightly to what little they've got. The science fundamentalists, I think some of them just want to be taken seriously as scientists and they think, well I have to show that I've rejected anything else. So in that sense, science and religion are very separate."[532] While we are not arguing that the Bible is a science book, we do think it should be taken seriously. The Bible not only presents individual truths like God is Creator, the universe had a beginning, and man holds exceptional status over the animals, but it also teaches about the nature of truth. A student of Schaeffer, author, and apologetics professor at Houston Baptist University, Nancy Pearcey, argues, "Because all things were created by a single divine mind, all truth forms a single, coherent, mutually consistent system. Truth is unified and universal."[533] Thus, God either intentionally created, or He did not; it's not possible to coherently believe in random evolution and Creation. There is no excuse for this muddled thinking.

The apostle Paul tells us that God's design is evident in Creation: "For the invisible things of him from the creation of the world are clearly seen, being understood by the things that are made, even his eternal power and Godhead; so that they are without excuse" (Romans 1:20). But even without appeals to Scripture, we think intelligent design is a legitimate program of scientific inquiry. What we are dealing with is two conflicting definitions of science: 1) Science is based on impartial, repeatable observations and follows the evidence where it leads; 2) Science is dedicated exclusively to materialist explanations and philosophical naturalism. It seems that the former is more intellectually virtuous, but we are forced to accept the latter. Intelligent design theory simply states that some things are best explained as the product of a mind, by intelligent causation rather than appeals to chance. For instance, the SETI program is founded on the notion that they can detect design in a radio signal as opposed to random noise. The SETI researcher detects a pattern and makes a design inference and, in this case, no one faults him for it or argues that such an inference is beyond the reach of science. Yet, in other areas of science, such reasoning is not permitted. The Jesuit critics do not understand the design inference.

As a case in point, when Christopher J. Corbally, vice director of the Vatican Observatory, was interviewed at VATT for the German television show, *In Focus,* he displayed this ignorance:

> Intelligent Design means yes there has been development...but there are certain sort of jumps in the development that cannot come through just the physics and the biology working. There has to be something else, an intelligent designer producing that new thing.[534]

It's quite telling that the Jesuit critics do not actually understand intelligent design theory. The design inference is not an appeal from ignorance; rather, it is an appeal to the evidence for intelligent causation. Design is inferred because of positive arguments like irreducible complexity and fine tuning, not gaps. He is also assuming that intelligent design theorists and Creationists make no legitimate use of scientific methods for gathering evidence. As shown above, Dr. Hugh Ross and his team have presented volumes of evidence for design in Creation. This evidence needs to be addressed instead of summarily disqualified.

Contrary to popular opinion, intelligent design is certainly a scientifically investigable cause. In his landmark book, *The Design Inference: Eliminating Chance through Small Probabilities* (1998), mathematician and philosopher William Dembski proposed an "explanatory filter" for processing three modes of competing explanations: regularity, chance, and design. This process demonstrates a rigorous methodology in which regularity and chance can be ruled out, leading to a reasonable inference of design. Yet, intelligent design critics never consider such a process. In this way, intelligent design *critics* are the ones that are closing off legitimate avenues of research and preventing investigation where it is scientifically appropriate. Darwinism is a science stopper.

In addition, the Jesuits commit the "either/or" fallacy by asserting that a view is either scientific or religious. The two areas often overlap. For example, Jesus either rose from the dead or He did not. Paul wrote, "And if Christ be not risen, then is our preaching vain, and your faith is also vain" (1 Corinthians 15:14). Even so, as a scientific endeavor, intelligent design is not a religious position and makes no *a priori* demands. However, naturalism is an antireligious position and does make metaphysical demands. Opposition to intelligent design is not motivated by intellectual integrity; rather, it is motivated by a commitment to philosophical naturalism. The truth divide rules. Thus, it should not be too surprising that Jesuits have embraced belief in New Age mysticism and extraterrestrials.

Malachi Martin's Exposé: The Mystical Darwinism of Pierre Teilhard de Chardin

Malachi Martin, former Jesuit and advisor to three popes, wrote a bestselling expose, *The Jesuits: The Society of Jesus and the Betrayal of the Roman Catholic Church*, accusing the order of systematically undermining Church teachings and replacing them with communist doctrines. Martin claimed there was a diplomatic agreement between the Vatican and the USSR, called the Metz pact. According to Martin, Pope John XXIII promised not to condemn communism in exchange for the participation of two Russian-Orthodox prelates as observers at the Second Vatican Council.[535] This sort of skullduggery and compromise with communism led Martin to leave the Jesuits in order to write books exposing their many heresies. In light of our present discussion, one individual's influence stands above all others.

Pierre Teilhard de Chardin, S. J. (1881–1955), more than any other Roman Catholic, typifies the modernist embrace of Darwinism and extraterrestrials. Martin believed the Jesuits "had been impregnated with his outlook,"[536] undermining the Church in fundamental ways. Concerning Darwinism, Martin wrote that prior to Chardin:

> Roman Catholics had always held that the emergence of *Homo Sapiens* was the direct act of separated creation by God, as outlined in the Garden of Eden account in the book of Genesis. For man, in Catholic doctrine, has a spiritual and immortal soul which could not "evolve" in any acceptable sense from material forms, even from "higher animals." This is still the teaching of the Roman Catholic Church. When Roman Catholic scholars who had accepted Evolution as a fact tried to reconcile official doctrine with Evolution, they assumed that God the Creator intervened at a certain moment in the evolutionary process and infused a spiritual and immortal soul into an already highly developed "higher animal."[537]

Pope Pius IX, the very same pope who declared papal infallibility, referred to Darwinian evolution as "a system which is repugnant at once to history, to the tradition of all peoples, to exact science, to observed facts, and even to Reason herself."[538] Furthermore, the Pontifical Biblical Commission affirmed a literal fundamentalist reading of the first three chapters of Genesis in 1909.[539] The modern revisionism is remarkable.

The absurdity of Catholic claims to an infallible teaching magisterium aside, like the VORG, Chardin dismissed any historicity to the Genesis narrative whatsoever. He wrote, "It is irreconcilable with what we know from biology that our human species should be descended from a pair,"[540] a problematic assertion given Jesus' explicit teaching on that first pair (Matthew 19:5). Still yet, Chardin is famous for his synthesis of mystical religion, evolution, and ET belief. In *The Jesuits*, Martin wrote, "This man's influence on Jesuit thinking and on Catholic theologians as well as on the thought processes of Christians in general has been and still is colossal."[541] This suggests that Chardin's mystical evolutionary synthesis could be the demonic spirituality driving the VORG and the recent Roman Catholic embrace of extraterrestrials, a prospect we will take up in the final chapter.

SECTION THREE

WHEN CHARIOTS OF THE GODS APPEAR

12 | First Incursion of the Chariots of the (Fallen Star) Gods

Birds skipped among groves of date palms along the marshy banks of the Euphrates in the year 3500 BC. As the sun arose above Sumer, the alluvial desert of the Middle East came alive with agricultural activity. In a valley forged between the twin rivers of the Tigris and the Euphrates, magnificent walled cities awoke to the chatter of busy streets and marketplaces. In what the Greeks would later call "Mesopotamia" (between the rivers), the world's first great trade center and civilization had developed. The opulent Sumerian cities of Ur (the home of Abram), Uruk, and Lagash had become the economic machines of the ancient Middle East, and industries from as far away as Jericho, near the Mediterranean Sea, and Catal Huyuk, in Asia Minor, competed for the trade opportunities they provided. Laborers from the biblical city of Jericho exported salt into Sumer, and miners from Catal Huyuk prepared obsidian, used in making mirrors, for shipment into the ancient metropolis. But while the prehistoric people of the East looked to the Sumerians for their supply of daily bread, the Sumerians themselves gazed heavenward, as they had from time immemorial, to the early rising of Utu (Shamash), the all-providing sun god, as he prepared once again to ride across the sky in his *flying chariot*. And, in 3500 BC, Utu was not alone among the gods. By now, the Sumerian pantheon provided the earliest known description of organized mythology, consisting of a complex system of more than three thousand deities covering nearly every detail of nature and human enterprise. There were gods of sunshine and of rain. There were vegetation gods, fertility gods, river gods, animal gods, and gods of the afterlife. There were the great gods—Enlil (prince of the air), Anu (ruler of the heavens), Enki (the god of water), and so on. Under these existed a second level of deities, including Nannar the moon god; Utu the sun god; and Inanna, the "Queen of Heaven," a mother goddess who much later would be called by some, "Mary, the Queen of Heaven and the Mother of Jesus Christ."

Sumerian deity with reptilian features

Having so noted—and this is the big question—where did the gods of Sumeria come from? Since the religion of Sumeria was the first known organized mythology and would greatly influence the foundational beliefs of the forthcoming nations of Babylon, Assyria, Egypt, Greece, Rome, the ancient Hebrews, and others, this question has interested scholars and historians for more than a millennium. Specifically, where does one find the historical beginning of the ancient gods of Sumeria? Were the Sumerian deities the product of human imagination or the distortion of some earlier prehistoric revelation? Were they the "mythologizing" of certain ancient heroes or, as some believe today, the result of an extraterrestrial "alien" visitation whose appearance gave birth to the legends and mythological gods? Equally important, did the sudden appearance of these deities reflect a literal intrusion into man's reality by *supernatural power*, or were they purely the creation of primitive imaginations?

These questions are both fascinating and difficult, since the gods and goddesses of ancient Sumeria/Mesopotamia continue to be shrouded in a history of unknown origins. It was as though from out of nowhere the Sumerians sprang onto the scene over fifty-five hundred years ago, bringing with them (what seemed like overnight) the first written language and a corpus of progressive knowledge—from complicated religious concepts to an advanced understanding of astrology, chemistry, and mathematics. The questionable origin of the Sumerian culture thus caused some theorists to conclude that the gods of Sumeria, and the subsequent mythologies that grew out of them, were the diabolical scheme of an ancient "presence" that arrived on Earth, something we would call a *Fallen Star*. If this is true, does this power persist within parallel dimensions of our world? Do primordial and living *things*, once worshipped as gods, continue observing man? And do they scheme at present to repeat on a grander scale something they did once before? Will man soon experience something unexpected on a universal level, causing humans to focus intently on the skies, at manifested "flying wonders," and at winged geniuses inside them?

They Said They Came from Orion, Pleides, and Zeta Reticuli

Among scholars, there are three competing theories regarding the origin of the early mythological gods: 1) The Euhemerus View; 2) The Ancient Astronaut Theory; and 3) The Biblical View. The Euhemerus View was based on the historical theories of the Greek scholar Euhemerus, who claimed that the pagan gods originated with certain ancient and famous kings who were later deified. The more widely adopted theories—the Ancient Astronauts Theory and, alternatively, the Biblical View of the origin of alternative deities—have succeeded to become the popular authorities regarding original paganism and are therefore the beginning of our investigation into a larger, potentially imminent phenomenon, one that took the authors of this work from moldy corridors in forgotten libraries to the Vatican's Advanced Technology Telescope and the Large Binocular Telescope with its new LUCIFER instrument.

Infernal infrared notwithstanding, a growing doctrine within modern ufology claims that the true origin of the gods, and the human race as we know it today, is the direct result of extraterrestrial UFO activity. In the introduction to his bestselling book, *Chariots of the Gods?*, Erich von Däniken, who, it might be argued, is one of the fathers of modern ufology, said:

> I claim that our forefathers received visits from the universe in the remote past, even though I do not yet know who these extraterrestrial intelligences were or from which planet they came. I nevertheless proclaim that these "strangers" annihilated part of mankind existing at the time and produced a new, perhaps the first, *Homo sapiens*.[542]

As was illustrated in the Hollywood films *Contact* and *Close Encounters of the Third Kind*, von Däniken's hypothesis took America by storm starting in the 1960s with the proposition that mankind was possibly the offspring of an ancient, perhaps ongoing, extraterrestrial experiment. Ufologists like von Däniken assert that the gods of mythology themselves may have been evidence of, and a reaction to, an encounter with other-world beings. He means by this that ancient men would have considered space travelers as gods and would have recorded their arrival, their experiments, and their departure in hieroglyphs, megaliths, and stone tablets as a "supernatural" encounter between gods and men.

Erich von Däniken continues:

While [the] spaceship disappears again into the mists of the universe our friends will talk about the miracle—"The gods were here!"…they will make a record of what happened: uncanny, weird, miraculous. Then their texts will relate—and drawings will show—that gods in golden clothes were there in a flying boat that landed with a tremendous din. They will write about chariots which the gods drove over land and sea, and of terrifying weapons that were like lightning, and they will recount that the gods promised to return. They will hammer and chisel in the rock pictures of what they had seen: shapeless giants with helmets and rods on their heads, carrying boxes in front of their chests; balls on which indefinable beings sit and ride through the air; staves from which rays are shot out as if from a sun…"[543]

Around the world, ancient records repeat such stories of flying craft, which bore the gods throughout the galaxies. For example, the Metternich Stela (a magical stela from the thirtieth dynasty of Egypt currently housed as part of the Egyptian Collection of the Metropolitan Museum of Art in New York City) tells the story of a heavenly "Boat of Millions of Years," which it describes as a "Celestial Disc" that transported the Egyptian gods like Isis and Thoth. In ancient Chinese folklore, we find a distant land where "flying carts" originate, while a Sanskrit text—the *Drona Parva*—actually documents "dogfights" by gods in flying machines. In Hindu mythology, these gods traversed the cosmos in flying vehicles called *Vimanas*, which are mentioned many times in the Ramayana, dating to approximately the fourth century BC. From *Book 6, Canto CXXIII: The Magic Car*, we find:

> Is not the wondrous chariot mine,
> Named Pushpak, wrought by hands divine…
> This chariot, kept with utmost care,
> Will waft thee through the fields of air,
> And thou shalt light unwearied down
> In fair Ayodhyá's royal town.[544]

Then from *Book 6, Canto CXXIV: The Departure:*

> Swift through the air, as Ráma chose,
> The wondrous car from earth arose.
> And decked with swans and silver wings
> Bore through the clouds its freight of kings.[545]

Numerous other ancient sources describe flying machines associated with gods, and we will discuss some of these later in this work. But men like von Däniken go further, claiming the Holy Bible itself is the best record and "greatest UFO book of all time!" The "wheel" in Ezekiel 1:15, the "pillar of cloud" in Exodus 13:21–22, and Elijah's "chariot of fire" in 2 Kings 2:11 are all viewed as examples of UFO sightings by such researchers. Additionally, von Däniken believes the odd appearance of some of the gods as depicted in various hieroglyphs (human-like creatures with falcon heads, lions with heads of bulls, etc.) can be viewed as evidence the "aliens" who visited Earth in celestial transport devices also conducted genetic experiments on ancient people and animals, cross-mutating or transgenically altering them. Some see this aspect of Däniken's hypothetical Ancient Astronaut Theory as an alternative to the "fallen angel" theory that is based in part on Genesis chapter 6 (the "angel theory"), which postulates mutant "mighty men" were born to rebel angels known as *Watchers*. These powerful beings—according to early Christians, church fathers, and a growing list of modern writers—mingled their matter with humans, giving birth to part-celestial, part-terrestrial hybrids called *Nephilim*. This happened when men began to increase on Earth and daughters were born to them. When the sons of God saw the women's beauty, they took wives from among them to sire their unusual offspring. In Genesis 6:4 we read the following account: "There were giants in the earth in those days; and also after that, when the sons of God came in unto the daughters of men, and they bare children to them, the same became mighty men which were of old, men of renown."

When this Scripture is compared with similar ancient texts, including Enoch, Jubilees, Baruch, Genesis Apocryphon, Philo, Josephus, Jasher, and others, it unfolds to some that the giants of the Old Testament, such as Goliath, were the part-human, part-animal, part-angelic offspring of a supernatural interruption into the divine order and natural propagation of the species.

Earth History Immediately Following the Fallen Star Incursion

Regardless of one's interpretation of these and other ancient records, one thing seems clear. Thousands of years ago, heavenly beings visited the Earth. They engaged in genetic experiments resulting in a race of mutant creatures. This, in turn, led God to order Israel to destroy the Nephilim and their descendants. Thousands of years later, Jesus spoke of the events that occurred during these days (of Noah) as being comparable to the time leading up to His return (Matthew 24:36). This prophecy is remarkable when one realizes that after God judged the celestial beings that cohabited with the Noahtic women, all such comparable activity diminished until about the year 1947. Then, following the infamous Roswell incident that occurred in New Mexico in that year, people from around the world once again began encountering strange creatures conducting genetic experiments.

As we shall see in a different chapter, our dear old friend, former college professor, and BBC correspondent, Dr. I. D. E. Thomas, in his highly recommended book, *The Omega Conspiracy*, chronicled the burgeoning of this so-called alien abduction activity and tied it to the end-time predictions in Matthew 24 concerning a return of the Nephilim. Documentation by "abductees" worldwide and the stories of DNA harvesting by "aliens" reminded him of the history of biological misuse by the Watchers and led Thomas to conclude that the identity of the Watchers and whoever the alien entities are were somehow connected. Dr. Thomas told us personally that the special desire by these unknown agents for human and animal molecular matter explained "why animals have been killed, mutilated, and stolen by the aliens in UFO flap areas." Respected UFO researcher, Dr. Jacques F. Vallée, raised similar questions.

> In order to materialize and take definite form, these entities seem to require a source of energy…a living thing…a human medium.… Our sciences have not reached a point where they can offer us any kind of working hypothesis for this process. But we can speculate that these beings need living energy which they can reconstruct into physical form. Perhaps that is why dogs and animals tend to vanish in flap areas. Perhaps the living cells of those animals are somehow used by the ultraterrestrials to create forms which we can see and sense with our limited perceptions.[546]

Whether or not there is a connection between the ancient power behind the Watcher narrative and the modern "alien abduction" activity documented by Vallée and others involving biological harvesting from humans and animals, records from antiquity speak of yet another mysterious possibility regarding these Watchers and their offspring—*that they can return to "physical form" at particular moments in time, something some believe they are planning to repeat very soon.*

Did Ancient Records Document the Arrival of Advanced Alien Life Forms...Or Something Else?

The biblical (and we believe correct) interpretation of what happened following the first incursion of the Chariots of the Fallen Star begins with *Original Revelation*. This means there was a perfect revelation from God to man at the time of Creation. The first man, Adam, was at one with God and perceived divine knowledge from the mind of God. The human was "in tune" with the mental processes of God and understood, therefore, what God knew about science, astronomy, cosmogony, geology, eschatology, and so on.

After the Fall, Adam was "detached" from the mind of God, but retained an imperfect memory of the divine revelation, including knowledge of God's plan of redemption. Two things began to occur in the decades after the Fall: 1) Information from the Original Revelation became distant and distorted as it was dispersed among the nations and passed from generation to generation; and 2) The realm of Fallen Star (Satan) seized upon this opportunity to receive worship and to turn people away from Yahweh by distorting and counterfeiting the Original Revelation with pagan ideas and "gods." This point of view seems reasonable when one considers that the earliest historical and archaeological records from civilizations around the world have consistently pointed back to, and repeated portions of, an *original story*. In their startling book, *The Discovery of Genesis*, the Rev. C. H. Kang and Dr. Ethel R. Nelson confirm that prehistoric Chinese ideographic pictures (used in very ancient Chinese writing) report the story of Genesis, including the creation of the man and woman, the garden, the temptation and Fall, the Flood, and the tower of Babel. In his book, *The Real Meaning of the Zodiac*, Dr. James Kennedy (another friend who has since gone to be with the Lord) claimed that the ancient signs of the zodiac also indicate a singular and Original Revelation—a kind of Gospel in the stars—and that the message of the stars, though demonized and converted into *astrology* after the Fall of man, originally recorded the Gospel of God. He wrote:

There exists in the writings of virtually all civilized nations a description of the major stars in the heavens—something which might be called their "Constellations of the Zodiac" or the "Signs of the Zodiac," of which there are twelve. If you go back in time to Rome, or beyond that to Greece, or before that to Egypt, Persia, Assyria, or Babylonia—regardless of how far back you go, there is a remarkable phenomenon: Nearly all nations had the same twelve signs, representing the same twelve things, placed in the same order.... The book of Job, which is thought by many to be the oldest book of the Bible, goes back to approximately 2150 B.C., which is 650 years before Moses came upon the scene to write the Pentateuch; over 1,100 years before Homer wrote the *Odyssey* and the *Iliad*; and 1,500 years before Thales, the first of the philosophers, was born. In chapter 38, God finally breaks in and speaks to Job and to his false comforters. As He is questioning Job, showing him and his companions their ignorance, God says to them: "Canst thou bind the sweet influences of Pleiades, or loose the bands of Orion? Canst thou bring forth Mazzaroth in his season? or canst thou guide Arcturus with his sons?" (Job 38:31, 32). We see here reference to the constellations of Orion and Pleiades, and the star Arcturus. Also in the book of Job there is reference to *Cetus, the Sea Monster*, and to *Draco, the Great Dragon*. I would call your attention to Job 38:32a: "Canst thou bring forth Mazzaroth in his season?" *Mazzaroth* is a Hebrew word which means "The Constellations of the Zodiac." In what may be the oldest book in all of human history, we find that the constellations of the zodiac were already clearly known and understood.... Having made it clear that the Bible expressly, explicitly, and repeatedly condemns what is now known as astrology, the fact remains that there was a God-given Gospel [universally acknowledged Original Revelation] in the stars which lays beyond and behind that which has now been corrupted.[547]

In Dr. Kennedy's book and sermons on this issue, he strongly condemned the practice of astrology while asserting his view that the constellations of the zodiac were likely given by God to the first man as "record-keepers" of the Original Revelation of God. If the primary assumption of the Biblical View is correct—that an Original Revelation was corrupted after the Fall of man and subsequently degenerated into the mythologies of the pagan gods—one should be able to find numerous examples of such corruption from as far back as the beginning of history and within various civilizations around the world. Since the myths behind the gods would thus be "borrowed" ideas, the corrupted texts would be similar to the original truth, and, in that sense, evidence of a singular and Original Revelation. Furthermore, if the distortions of the Original Revelation were in fact energized by an *evil supernaturalism*, the goal of the alterations would be to draw people away from the worship of Yahweh and into deception. In certain ancient legends—such as the *Enuma elish*, the *Adapa Epic*, and the *Epic of Gilgamesh*—we discover just such early traces of an *Original Revelation* plagiarized for the purpose of constructing the mythologies of the pagan gods.

This is intriguing on several levels. First of all, while the meaning of the Mazzaroth is uncertain, the majority understanding of the word is "constellations," a variant of a similar term *mazzālôt*, also seen in 2 Kings 23:5. This seems to be the correct reading as we see its use in rabbinical Hebrew where it refers generally to the signs of the zodiac, planets, or constellations. The Hebrew Bible reveals that stars were used by sorcerers to predict the future (Isaiah 47:13) and the worship of astral deities was widespread in ancient Near Eastern culture (cf. Deuteronomy 4:19; 2 Kings 17:16). While stars were worshiped as deities by wayward Israelites (Jeremiah 8:2), this is rejected as idolatry in the Old Testament (Amos 5:26) because God created them (Genesis 1:16). In the writings of the prophet, Daniel, astrologers are conspicuously featured in the court of Babylonian King Nebuchadnezzar (Daniel 2:27; 4:7; 5:7, 11). Let's now examine the passage in Job which many believe speaks to the Original Revelation.

The book of Job records three cycles of debate between Job and his friends (first: 3–14; second: 15–21; third: 22–26) that rise in passionate intensity as his three friends claim that Job is suffering because of his sins, while Job defends his innocence with mounting vigor. The Lord, Himself, ends the debate by speaking to Job of His power and wisdom in creating and sustaining the world, all its creatures, and even the stars in the heavens (38–39). As to the latter, in Job 38:31–33 the Lord speaks specifically, even naming names:

> Canst thou bind the sweet influences of Pleiades,
> Or loose the bands of Orion?
> Canst thou bring forth Mazzaroth in his season?
> Or canst thou guide Arcturus with his sons?
> Knowest thou the ordinances of heaven?
> Canst thou set the dominion thereof in the earth?

The Bible also tells us that God, "telleth the number of the stars; he calleth them all by their names" (Psalms 147:4) and the book of Enoch attests that an angel revealed the figures of the constellations to Enoch. Although those constellations were later perverted by pagans, there is evidence that the Original Revelation was not entirely lost. While the evidence is scant, a medieval Persian astrologer, Albumasar (787–886 AD), wrote in the eighth century, "In the sphere of Persia, saith Aben Ezra, there ariseth upon the face of the sign Virgo a beautiful maiden, she holding two ears of corn in her hand, and a child in her arm: she feedeth him, and giveth him suck... She bringeth up a child in a place which is called Abrie [the Hebrew land], and the child's name is called Eisi [Jesus]."[548]

This theory states that God encoded the Original Revelation in the twelve constellations and decans. Each constellation has three decans for a total of thirty-six decans. As an example of how this works, Virgo and its three decans are explained like this:

1. Virgo: a virgin holding a branch and sheaves of wheat and corn
   a. Coma, the desired: a virgin holding a boy

    b.   Centaurus, the centaur: the desire son has two natures and kills the "Victim"

    c.   Bootes, the coming one: a man holding a spear and a sickle

The Original Revelation reveals Mary who bears a Son, the righteous branch of Judah (Jeremiah 23:5). In Coma, that child is "the desire of all nations" (Haggai 2:7), and is on the virgin's lap. The Son is pictured full-grown in Centaurus; a centaur symbolizes His dual nature as God and man. In Bootes, the "coming one" with a sickle has become a judge and conqueror (Mark 4:29; Revelation 19:11). In this way, each of the twelve constellations records salvation history in the sky. This idea was virtually lost to history.

In the early nineteenth century, Frances Rolleston, a scholar of ancient languages, discovered the basic outline of how the constellations testify of Christ. Her work *Mazzaroth, or the Constellations* (1802*)* was almost ignored until it was popularized by two biblical scholars: an American, Joseph Seiss with his book, *The Gospel in the Stars or Primeval Astronomy* (1910); and a Britain, E. W. Bullinger with his book, *The Witness of the Stars* (1893). While it is beyond the scope of our book to provide a detailed account we commend the reader to these works. (All three are included on the data DVD accompanying this book when purchased from SurvivorMall.com.)

It is important to consider the magnitude of what is being stated here. Physicists understand the laws of celestial mechanics to work with such precision that the universe runs like a finely designed clock. Consequently, we can know with great precision where the stars will be in the future as well as where they were in the past. This reveals much about God considering the evidence He recorded the *precise date* of Jesus' birth in the stars, and then inspired John to record it in the book of Revelation. Many scholars understand this as astral prophecy, "And there appeared a great wonder in heaven; a woman clothed with the sun, and the moon under her feet, and upon her head a crown of twelve stars" (Revelation 12:1). Dr. Ernest L. Martin explains Revelation 12:1–5 matches the alignment constellations to a matter of minutes.

The birth of this child in Revelation 12 (whom John identified with Jesus) should have occurred while the Sun was "clothing" the woman, when the Sun was mid-bodied to Virgo. This period of time in 3 B.C.E. covered 20 days (August 27 to September 15). If Jesus were born within that 20-day period, it would fit most remarkably with the testimony of Luke (relative to the birth of John the Baptist and the eighth course of Abijah). Indeed, the chronological indications associated with the priestly course of Abijah place Jesus' birth exactly within this period. But there is a way to arrive at a much closer time for Jesus' birth than a simple 20-day period. The position of the Moon in John's vision actually pinpoints the nativity to within a day—even to within a period of an hour and a half (within 90 minutes) on that day. This may appear an absurd assessment on the surface, but it is quite possible.[549]

Dr. Martin's book, *The Star that Astonished the World*, is available to read for free on the internet so you can follow the endnote above to read more. Also, Dr. Michael Heiser made a short video demonstrating all these details addressed above about Christs' birth using astronomy software. We commend you to watch it here: http://youtu.be/RED3iE3JLQc. The implications are profound. Since God encoded the precise time of Jesus' birth within a ninety-minute window and the laws of physics are deterministic and predictable, this implies from the very first second of Creation all of this was planned. We have an awesome God!

But naturally, God's enemies would want to suppress such astounding information. Keeping in mind that the constellation Bootes is a decan of Virgo and would symbolize Christ in the Original Revelation, let's examine what happened to it after the Great Flood of Noah.

Arcturus

The Hebrew term that the King James translators understood to be the brilliant star Arcturus, the fourth brightest star in sky, is עיש ‹ayiš. In Mesopotamia, it was linked to the god Enlil, the leader of the Babylonian pantheon, and was also known as Shudun in Sumerian (Akkadian *niru*), "the Yoke" that is in the constellation Boötes.[550] This derives from one of the earliest known sources for the zodiac constellations known as MUL.APIN, an ancient Babylonian compendium dealing with many diverse aspects of astronomy and astrology. Written in cuneiform on a collection of clay tablets, the MUL.APIN includes more than two hundred astronomical observations. By accounting for the observed positions in the sky, this ancient work has been dated to 1,370 BC, give or take a century, by Brad Schaefer, an astronomer at Louisiana State University.

In classical Greek mythology, the constellation Boötes is identified with Arcas, the son of Zeus and Callisto, a virgin nymph raped by Zeus.[551] Due to Zeus' infidelity, Arcas was brought up in secret by his maternal grandfather, Lycaon. One day Zeus paid a visit to Lycaon and his son to have a meal. In order to verify that his guest was truly the king of the gods, Lycaon murdered his grandson and served him for dinner. Zeus became enraged at the cannibalistic ruse, resurrected his son Arcas, and transformed Lycaon into a wolf. In the meantime, the violated nymph, Callisto, had been transformed into a she-bear by Zeus' jealous wife, Hera. This is corroborated by the Greek name for the constellation, Boötes, which is Arctophylax, meaning "Bear Watcher."

Later, Callisto, in form of a bear, was almost killed by her son, Arcas, who was out hunting. Zeus rescued her and took her into the sky where she became the constellation Ursa Major, "the Great Bear." Accordingly, the name Arcturus (the constellation's brightest star) comes from the Greek word meaning "guardian of the bear." This is an interesting correlation because modern English Bible translations render the Hebrew

ʿayiš as "the Bear" which is Ursa Major or the Great Bear associated with Callisto. Adjacent to Boötes, this constellation is widely observed as part of the Big Dipper.

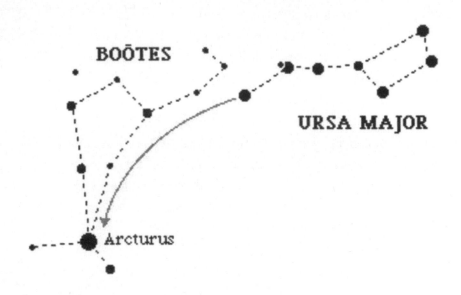

The Latin Vulgate and the Original Revelation

Eusebius Hieronymus Sophronius, better known as Saint Jerome (347–420), is the patron Saint of translators in the Roman Catholic religion. Living in the fourth century, his Vulgate translation is responsible for many theological errors. One particularly egregious translation error endowed Moses with horns based on Exodus 34:29: "And when Moses came down from the mount Sinai, he held the two tables of the testimony, and he knew not that his face was horned from the conversation of the Lord." This is because Jerome mistook the Hebrew קָרַן which means "radiant" in the Qal stem as the Hiphal stem indicating horns. This translation error led to various depictions of a rather demonic looking horned Moses within Roman Catholicism.

Michelangelo's horned Moses at the Basilica San
Pietro in Vincoli, Rome, Italy

Let's return to the text, "Canst thou bring forth Mazzaroth in his season? Or canst thou guide Arcturus with his sons?"(Job 38:32). Quite astonishingly, Jerome rendered the term "Mazzaroth" as **Lucifer**: The Vulgate reads,"*Numquid producis Luciferum in tempore suo et vesperum super filios terrae consurgere facis.*"[552] Of course, because Lucifer also means "morning star," an alternate name for Venus, Jerome likely had in mind a contrast between the morning and evening star. But Jerome's misunderstanding of the Hebrew yields an unexpected coincidence in light of recent astronomical developments. Indeed, a viable English translation of the Vulgate reads:

Can you bring forth Lucifer in its time?
And make the evening star rise upon the children of the earth?

While LUCIFER is the acronym for the infrared instrument in use at the Mt. Graham Observatory complex, the evening star would either be Arcturus, the guardian of the bear in the Boötes constellation, or the Great Bear herself, the constellation Ursla Major. While both host a plurality of alien worlds, it is intriguing that amongst the many uninhabitable gas giants and frozen spherical wastelands, astronomers have recently discovered potentially life-encouraging worlds.

One of the closest exoplanets known also happens to be in the Boötes constellation. The planet, Tau Boötis b, was one of the first exoplanets to be discovered back in 1996. Boasting a mass six times that of Jupiter, it is called a "hot Jupiter" because its temperature is a hellish 2,420 Fahrenheit! Of course, the planet would be unsuitable for life as we know it, and like other gaseous planets, would have no solid surface to contain seas for a watery, life-supporting medium. The gargantuan planet was dubbed the "Millennium Planet" because it was thought to be the first visually discovered exoplanet.[553]

A much more promising candidate in the constellation Boötes is exoplanet "HD 136418 b." This extrasolar planet orbits the G-type star, "HD 136418," which is remarkably similar in temperature to our sun. Additionally, it has a most promising orbit, staying within the known habitable (or "Goldilocks") zone within a comparable range between Earth and Mars in our solar system. Its orbit is 464.3 days, making for a longer year than Earth, but this is extraordinarily analogous to our own by exoplanet standards. Listed as potentially habitable, this planet is a leading candidate in astrobiological research.[554] While HD 136418 b represents the best that the home constellation of the Bear's Guardian has to offer, the Great Bear herself offers otherworldly promise.

The Great Bear constellation hosts a plurality of extraterrestrial worlds. The star 47 Ursae Majoris is a sun-like star with a three-planet system. The exoplanet, 47 Ursae Majoris B, was discovered in 1996, orbits every 1078 days and is 2.53 times the mass of Jupiter.[555] It is considered somewhat promising by astrobiologists because it orbits its parent star at a distance where liquid water may still exist. Even more interesting is that being twice as massive as Jupiter, it may have Earth-sized moons holding liquid water.

This adds intrigue to the current use by astronomers at Mt. Graham International Observatory to employ the LUCIFER device in hopes of finding ancient "aliens" and perhaps even the original home of the Fallen Star. Is there a time when he is to be brought forth and introduced to the world as a savior in the form of an intergalactic wise man? Evidence suggests the original legends of mythology were preceded by a belief in "the God" (*Yahweh* to the Hebrews) as the Creator of all things and the "ruler of heaven." Yet, later, *Satan* was described as "the god of this world" (2 Corinthians 4:4), and the prince of the "air" (Ephesians 2:2). A fascinating struggle between the "ruler of the heavens" versus the "power of the air" occurred in early Sumerian mythology after Enki, the god of wisdom and water, created the human race out of clay. It appears that Anu, who was at first the most powerful of the Sumerian gods and the "ruler of the heavens," was superseded in power and popularity by Enlil, the "god of the air." To the Christian mind, this is perceived as nothing less than Satan, the god of the air, continuing his pretense to the throne of God and his usurpation of Yahweh—"the Lord of the heavens." It also indicates a corruption of the Original Revelation and perhaps an effort on the part of Satan to trick pagan Sumerians into perceiving him as the "supreme" god (above the God of heaven) and therefore worthy of adoration. Correspondingly, in the *Enuma elish* (a Babylonian epic), Marduk, the great god of the city of Babylon, was exalted above the benevolent gods and extolled as the creator of the world. Marduk was depicted as a human but symbolized as a dragon (as is Satan in Revelation 12:9) called the *Muscrussu*, and his legend appears to contain several distortions of the important elements of the biblical account of Creation. The *Adapa Epic* tells of another Babylonian legend that is also roughly equivalent to the Genesis account of Creation. In it, Adapa, like Adam, underwent a test on food consumption, failed the test, and forfeited his opportunity for immortality. As a result of the failure, suffering and death were passed along to humanity. Finally, the *Epic of Gilgamesh* is a Sumerian poem, which, like the *Adapa Epic*, is also connected to ancient Assyrian and Babylonian mythology. In 1872, George Smith discovered the Gilgamesh tablets while doing research on the Assyrian library of Ashurbanipal at the British Museum. Because of the strong similarity to the biblical account of Noah and the Great Flood, Bible scholars have viewed the Gilgamesh epic with interest (and suspicion) since discovery. As the legend goes, Gilgamesh, the king of the city of Uruk, was told about the Flood from his immortal friend, Utnapishtim (the Sumerian equivalent of Noah). Utnapishtim described for Gilgamesh how the great god Enlil decided to destroy all of mankind because of its "noisy" sins. A plague was sent, but failed to persuade mankind of better behavior, and, consequently, the gods determined a complete extermination of the human race. Enki, the lord of the waters, was not happy with the other gods for this decision and warned Utnapishtim of the coming deluge, instructing him to tear down his house and build a great boat. Utnapishtim obeyed Enki, built a great vessel, and sealed it with pitch and bitumen. The family of Utnapishtim loaded onto the boat together with various beasts and fowl. When the rains came, the doors were closed and the vessel rose above the waters. Like Noah, Utnapishtim sent out a dove, and later a swallow, to search for dry land. They both returned. Later, a raven was released and it never came back. After several more days, the boat came to rest on the top of a mountain, where Utnapishtim built an altar and offered a sacrifice of thanksgiving to the gods. As the gods smelled the sweet offering, all but Enlil repented for sending the flood.

The Web of Deception Gets Deeper

But isn't it true that the Sumerian tablets predate the Hebrew Bible? Yes, they are older, but the veracity of *both* traditions presupposes the Sumerian anteceding the Mosaic. Plainly, they both speak to the same Flood, but the Babylonian traditions hold that their pre-Flood stories were buried at Sippar and later recovered.[556] In contrast, the Hebrews believed their accounting went back to Noah, who preserved the antediluvian material. Thus, we should expect the Sumerian tablets to be older. Because the Flood was an actual historic event, it follows that both cultures share a common memory. Even so, the Hebrew Bible presents a more realistic account with a seaworthy ark design, one that has proven to be immensely stable. In contrast, the four-sided tub described by the Sumerians is hardly seaworthy. While the existence of similarities is beyond dispute, the charge of plagiarism is no longer accepted by modern scholarship. The peoples of the ancient Near East shared a common history and worldview. One would expect similarities, given the patriarch Abraham was from Ur and the Israelites were held captive in Babylon just prior to the Hebrew Bible's completion. Even so, ancient astronaut theorists, relying on the discredited Sumerian translations by Zecharia Sitchin, lead many people astray.

Sitchin promotes the canard that the Hebrew Bible was derived from the Sumerian tablets, which are records of human origins involving the Anunnaki, a race of extraterrestrials from a planet beyond Neptune called Nibiru. In truth, his theory concerning the origin of the Hebrew Scripture is traceable to a 1902 lecture, "Babel and Bible," by a German scholar Friedrich Delitzsch. He was an early proponent of the idea that the Genesis Creation account and Flood history were borrowed from the ancient Babylonians. Like Sitchin, Delitzsch concluded that not only was the Sumerian religion and culture older than that of the Israelites, it was superior.[557] In a later book, he wrote:

> The so-called "Old Testament" is entirely dispensable for the Christian church, and thereby also for the Christian family. It would be a great deal better for us to immerse ourselves from time to time in the deep thoughts, which our German intellectual heroes have thought concerning God, eternity, and immortality.[558]

One detects a diabolic intelligence attacking the Original Revelation as this unholy union of German nationalism and anti-Semitism fueled the rise of the Third Reich. Conveniently, the Sumerian tales were retrofitted to the Aryan mythology of the Nazis based on dubious connections to Sanskrit writings in the Vedas. In fact, although he is Jewish, most of Sitchin's ideas about the Hebrew Bible are demonstrably based on this sort of anti-Semitic German higher criticism. Interestingly, much of this German higher criticism is accepted by the Vatican.

Sitchin & Balducci: A Meeting of Like Minds

The Vatican theologian Monsignor Corrado Balducci, famous for his assertion that UFOs are extraterrestrials visiting the Earth, met with Zecharia Sitchin in April 2000 at a conference themed "The Mystery of Human Existence" held in Bellaria, Italy. According to Sitchin, they agreed on three principal points: 1) Extraterrestrials can and do exist on other planets; 2) They are more advanced than us; 3) Man could have been fashioned by them from a preexisting sentient being.[559] This agreement is especially problematic, given Sitchin's belief that humanity was created as a slave race for advanced extraterrestrials whom the Sumerians called the Anunnaki and the Hebrews called the Nephilim. As Sitchin spins it, these ETs visited our planet around three hundred thousand years ago to genetically engineer Earth's hominids, "the Adam," into the first Homo sapiens, modern man.[560] There are numerous problems with Sitchin's theories.

Paramount, the biblical text does not support the notion that the Nephilim had anything to do with the creation of Adam. In fact, it is the Nephilim who are the *products*—not the instigators—of hybridization. Scholarly sources affirm the Nephilim were "a group of antediluvians who were the product of the union of the sons of God (*hā᾿ĕlōhîm*) with the daughters of humans (*hā᾿ādām*)."[561] Even so, Sitchin has written that *Nephilim* means "those who came down from above" or "those who descended to Earth" and, even more incredible, "people of the fiery rockets."[562] Of course, these translations support his ET mythology, but no credentialed scholar approves. He begins with a common assumption that *Nephilim* derives from the Hebrew root *naphal*, meaning "to fall." This commonly held theory leads to the meaning "fallen ones." Even so, he goes further, pounding a square peg into a round hole, imposing the meaning "to come down" rather than "fall," manufacturing his "to come down from above" translation. It's also notable that Sitchin holds no pertinent academic credentials, neither as a linguist nor in Semitic languages. However, his arch nemesis Michael Heiser holds a PhD in Hebrew and Semitic studies as well as an MA in ancient history.

Following Heiser's lead, morphology is the study of word forms and, as it turns out, even the starting point, *naphal* ("to fall"), is a poor choice, given Hebrew morphology. According to Heiser, "In the form we find it in the Hebrew Bible, if the word *Nephilim* came from Hebrew *naphal*, it would not be spelled as we find it. The form *Nephilim* cannot mean 'fallen ones' (the spelling would then be *nephulim*). Likewise Nephilim does not mean 'those who fall' or 'those who fall away' (that would be *nophelim*)."[563] However, as suggested by Heiser and renowned German scholar Hermann Gunkel, there is an Aramaic term *npyl*, meaning "giant," which works with the morphology and is also suggested by the context of the passages (Genesis 6:4; Num. 13:33).[564] For instance, "And there we saw the giants, the sons of Anak, which come of the giants: and we were in our own sight as grasshoppers, and so we were in their sight" (Numbers 13:33). The grasshopper comparison makes sense in light of them being unusually large. The Authorized King James Version gets this correct. This understanding is further supported by translation into Greek *gigantes* ("giant") in the Septuagint and by several passages in the Dead Sea Scrolls.[565] It seems that Sitchin's translation is a product of his own imagination and circular reasoning. Finally, the Anunnaki are represented as divine beings in the Sumerian texts, roughly equivalent to the "sons of God" in the Hebrew Bible. There is simply no justification from either the Sumerian or Hebrew texts to support Sitchin's notion that, "It is modern Man as we know him that the Nefilim created."[566] Nearly all of his fanciful notions are debunked at Heiser's website: www. SitchinIsWrong.com. It seems beyond dispute that Sitchin laid a minefield of false ideas sowing the seeds of strong delusion.

Back to the Future…and the Second Coming of the Gods!

Time does not allow for full disclosure of the many other examples of corruption that occurred with regard to the *Original Revelation*. These include distortions or "knock-offs" of the virgin birth, heaven and hell, the resurrection and final judgment, water baptism, communion, and many more. In addition to such corruptions of the *Original Revelation* that predates the gods of mythology, the Biblical View of the origin of the gods makes the following important assumptions: 1) that there exist within our universe real and supernatural powers; 2) that these powers are divided by their nature into two separate camps or "kingdoms"— one evil, the other good; 3) that these kingdoms are presided over by rulers—the biblical Satan over the evil and Yahweh over the good; and 4) that the kingdom of Satan provided the historical energy or "life" within and behind the first appearance of the gods of mythology as Satan's kingdom solicited human worship through deception and idolatry.

This happened on this order—in the beginning, Yahweh created the heavens (celestial beings, planets, etc.) and the Earth. Lucifer, "the light bearer," was a crowning achievement of God's heavenly Creation and a chief servant of the creative Yahweh. When this powerful angel became jealous of the worship Yahweh was receiving from His many creations, he proudly proclaimed, "I will exalt my throne above the stars of God.... I will be like the most high" (Isaiah14:13–14). Somehow, Lucifer convinced one-third of the celestial creatures to join him in rebellion, ultimately resulting in the mighty angel and his followers being cast out of heaven, becoming *Fallen Star* (Isaiah 14:12; Luke 10:18). While this event coincides with historical traits of an ancient "invasion" into man's reality—which men like Erich von Däniken, Zecharia Sitchin, Robert Temple, and others view as the first visit to Earth by extraterrestrial intelligence—in the biblical worldview, the same antediluvian records attest to a different set of facts altogether. They are a record of the fall from heaven to Earth by Lucifer (now Satan) who, driven by a quest for worship and thirsty for revenge with Yahweh, not only tempted Eve in the garden, but as a result of man's subsequent and heritable separation with God, moved to corrupt the divine truths contained within the *Original Revelation* by proclaiming himself (the god of the air) more worthy of worship than was the God of heaven.

If such an assumption of the Biblical View is correct—that a real and diabolical presence entered man's materiality, harvested and manipulated the genetics of Creation, and set in motion a cosmic conspiracy concerning the true origins of life on Earth (the Ancient Astronaut Theory)—the following questions arise: 1) Do the living *entities* of such ancient "gods" continue to manipulate human and animal DNA as part of an eons-old plan?; and 2) Are they currently at work preparing a final act, something similar in appearance to the first incursion of Earth, but so astonishing and of such inexplicable technological and intimidating contrivance that the very appearance of it will, if possible, deceive the very elect? Readers will be stunned to learn in the following chapters that institutional forces—both governmental and religious—have already started preparing for just such a scenario. The investigation you are reading uncovers this clandestine blueprint...and, along the way, an astonishing exotheological plan by the Vatican itself for the arrival of an *alien Savior intelligence...and its connection with Petrus Romanus, the Final Pope. Pope Benedict resigned as this book headed to the printer. By now, the world knows who Petrus Romanus is. But do you know his role for the alien savior?*

Be aware. Scripture did not leave those with ears to hear and eyes to see in the dark concerning this eventuality. This day was foretold, and it will be accompanied by "fearful sights and great signs…from heaven" (Luke 21:11). For "then shall that Wicked [one] be revealed…whose coming is after the working of Satan with all power and signs and *lying wonders*… And for this cause God shall send them *strong delusion*, that they should believe a lie: That they all might be damned who believed not the truth, but had pleasure in unrighteousness" (2 Thessalonians 2:8–12; emphasis added).

13 | The Extradimensional Hypothesis

"And Elisha prayed, and said, LORD, I pray thee,
open his eyes, that he may see.
And the LORD opened the eyes of the young man;
and he saw: and, behold,
the mountain was full of horses and chariots of fire
round about Elisha."—2 Kings 6:17

The king of Syria was in a rage. This was no trivial fit; it had been a long time coming. Over the last few months, his frustration had mounted following defeat after devastating defeat at the hands of inferior rivals…those impudent Israelites. Their repeated anticipation of his every stratagem suggested something beyond a gifted general's battle-honed acumen. Thinking back, it now seemed painfully obvious that a mole was afoot; all along, a pernicious traitor had leaked his battle plans. Now the time had arrived for decisive action! Pondering his best options, he resolves to offer a magnificent bounty for the head of the rat. If no one claimed the reward, then fearsome consequences must fall upon all until the spy is routed from their ranks. Before issuing this decree, he summons his wisest advisor and asks for the enemy agent's identity. The royal counselor explains that there is no rat; rather, "Elisha, the prophet that is in Israel, telleth the king of Israel the words that thou speakest in thy bedchamber" (2 Kings 6:12). Enraged by his apparent exposure, the king sends an entire division to capture Elisha.

Early the next morning, Elisha's compatriot is dismayed by Syrian troops surrounding the normally sleepy city of Dothan. In a panic, he cries to his overly calm mentor, "What should we do?" Showing no fear, Elisha beckons the Lord, "Open his eyes, that he may see" and as if from nowhere, the mountains are suddenly "full of horses and chariots of fire," a vastly superior divine force to that of the Syrian raiders. There is an otherworldly army protecting Elisha that cannot be seen by regular folks. Even so, no battle is necessary as Elisha prays and the Syrian soldiers are led off in a blind trance right into the clutches of the king of Israel and his army. The Israelite king is merciful and sends them home bewildered with sheepish promises to stop their raids.

What are we to make of this astonishing text? Over the years, preachers have made great use of the story as a way of encouragement in the face of overwhelming odds. Of course, such encouragement depends on the belief in this unseen dimension and the reality of the Lord's superintendence. Interestingly, the chariots of fire actually appeared prior, in 2 Kings 2:11, when Elisha's predecessor, Elijah, was carried up to heaven in a whirlwind. It seems quite fair to infer that the otherwise unseen army was in a parallel dimension, one that transcends normal human perception. We suggest that other glimpses of this unseen world include the army of angels encamped around Jacob (Genesis 32:1–2) and the heavenly visions of the prophets (Ezekiel 1; Is. 6). In the New Testament, Ephesians 6:12 reinforces the idea that unseen spiritual warfare is an ongoing reality.

Since Scripture supports the notion of an unseen dimension, it should not be too much of a leap for Christians to accept that this notion might find modern analogs. A helpful illustration comes by way of a nineteenth-century Victorian satire called *Flatland* by Edwin Abbot. The fantasy is set in an absolutely flat world of two physical dimensions where all the residents are geometric shapes like squares, circles, and triangles who believe that all of reality is completely explained by length and width.

However, the protagonist, just your average square, is visited by a peculiar circle that appears out of nowhere, expands to a typical size, diminishes to a dot, and then disappears. It turns out that the circle is no ordinary circle but a three-dimensional sphere! In an especially poignant scene, the sphere attempts to describe to the incredulous two-dimensional square, with great difficulty, how he passed into Flatland from the third dimension: "See now, I will rise; and the effect upon your eye will be that my Circle will become smaller and smaller till it dwindles to a point and finally vanishes."[567] While this confuses the square very much, it amazes him even more when he experiences the extra dimension firsthand.

Of course, the square is skeptical at first, but his life is forever altered once he becomes aware of this hitherto unknown dimensionality. Indeed, the sphere takes the square on a mystical voyage to the third dimension, transforming him to a cube. Upon arrival, this passage captures the square's astonished naiveté and the sphere's rebuke:

> Awestruck at the sight of the mysteries of the earth, thus unveiled before my unworthy eye, I said to my Companion, "Behold, I am become as a God. For the wise men in our country say that to see all things, or as they express it, *omnividence*, is the attribute of God alone." There was something of scorn in the voice of my Teacher as he made answer: "Is it so indeed? Then the very pickpockets and cut-throats of my country are to be worshipped by your wise men as being Gods: for there is not one of them that does not see as much as you see now. But trust me, your wise men are wrong."[568]

Much like Elijah's servant marveling at the angelic chariots of fire, this new three-dimensional perspective reveals what the Flatlanders never saw. Even more, the attributes our naïve square friend had assumed were exclusively divine are, in fact, everyday trivialities for three-dimensional beings, *even evil cutthroats*. Perhaps the moral implications of this analogy apply to the fiery chariot-riders as well?

The Flatland illustration is useful on many other levels (pun intended). For instance, imagine the perceived supernatural abilities a three-dimensional being has over a two-dimensional being. It would be possible to literally run circles around the two-dimensional entity while only appearing for a couple brief moments, alternately in front and behind, as the three-dimensional being briefly intersected the two-dimensional plane. If we press this analogy forward to our four-dimensional spacetime and imagine entities with access to spatial dimensions unseen to us, then the impossible abilities of RUFOs (residual UFOs) start to make more sense. These sorts of RUFO sightings are ubiquitous in the literature.

RUFOs are frequently seen making ninety-degree turns at speeds that would destroy conventional craft. For instance, veteran investigator John Keel once marveled, "They execute impossible maneuvers, such as sudden right angle turns, and disappear as mysteriously as they had come."[569] While ufologists universally acknowledge a snowballing caseload of craft exhibiting such impossible physics, the scientific mainstream is largely uniformed. The evidence is certainly available, but the UFO taboo as discussed elsewhere in this book discourages objective inquiry. Because ignorance rules the day, a brief survey of a few representative cases is in order.

The Nash-Fortenberry sighting is a compelling classic example of RUFO behavior that seems to defy known physical laws. On the clear night of July 14, 1952, a PanAmerican passenger plane, piloted by Captain William B. Nash and copiloted by William Fortenberry, encountered a RUFO over the skies of Virginia. The pilots described the craft:

We judged the objects' diameter to be a little larger than a DC-3 wingspread would appear to be—about 100 feet—at their altitude which we estimated at slightly more than a mile below us, or about 2,000 feet above ground level. When the procession was almost directly under and slightly in front of us—the pilot had to rise hurriedly from the left-hand seat and lean to see them—the objects performed a change of direction which was completely amazing. All together, they flipped on edge, the sides to the left of us going up and the glowing surface facing right. Though the bottom surfaces did not become clearly visible, we had the impression that they were unlighted. The exposed edges, also unlighted, appeared to be about 15 feet thick, and the top surface, at least, seemed flat. In shape and proportion, they were much like coins. While all were in the edgewise position, the last five slid over and past the leader so that the echelon was now tail-foremost, so to speak, the top or last craft now being nearest to our position. Then, without any arc or swerve at all, they all flipped back together to the flat altitude and darted off in a direction that formed a sharp angle with their first course, holding their new formation.

The change of direction was acute and abrupt. The only descriptive comparison we can offer is a ball ricocheting off a wall.[570]

This classic law-defying behavior suggests extradimensionality, but what makes this sighting particularly striking is that not only was it reported by expert witnesses, but the RUFOs were also observed between the airliner and the ground, allowing for accurate measurements of altitude, size, speed, and motion as compared to landmarks below that provide perspective. Furthermore, they were seen and reported by several groups of independent ground witnesses within an hour of the pilot's observation, long before the event was reported by the mass media. This case was classified as "unknown" by the US Air Force's Project Blue Book.

Another representative but lesser-known example comes from Robert Laing, an accomplished electrical engineer who describes a RUFO witnessed by his University of Michigan astronomy professor along with the entire class of thirty-five students:

My belief in flying saucers is based on a sighting of a UFO twice from the roof of the astronomy building at University of Michigan by an entire astronomy class of about thirty-five students and their professor, Dr. Lawler in the fall of 1957 while charting the stars. Dr. Lawler told the class the next day that she received about a hundred phone calls from local residents that night. I was in that astronomy class. What we saw was a disk travel at least three thousand miles an hour with no sonic boom, stop above us instantaneously without slowing down for about ten or twenty minutes with a pulsating red light all the way around it, and then instantaneously move from a dead stop to about three thousand miles per hour again, make a sharp ninety-degree turn at the same speed without slowing down, and race off to the horizon. About twenty minutes later it returned at the same speed from the place it left, made another sharp ninety-degree turn and left. No human could be in a vessel that goes from 3000 mile[s] per hour to a dead stop without being crushed and vaporized. No human being could go from a dead stop to an instantaneous velocity of 3000 miles per hour without disintegrating. No human could stand a right angle turn at 3000 miles per hour and live. This event was reported about eleven years later in the NICAP Journal, the National Investigation Committee on Arial Phenomena.[571]

This life-changing sighting, coupled with his Christian faith, eventually inspired Laing to publish the *Intelligent Design Theory* website, where he competently muses over various theological and scientific topics.

A more recent and well known case is the RUFO that appeared over Brussels, Belgium, on the night of March 30, 1990. After a policeman reported strange lights in the sky, which were confirmed by ground radar as a large unknown craft, two Belgian Air Force F-16s were scrambled to intercept. The pilots established radar lock three times, but within seconds, the strange craft executed incredible evasive maneuvers, later estimated to have gravitational forces of 40gs (g-force is force due to acceleration felt as weight). From the perspective of the fighter pilots, the craft seemed to be aware of their targeting. The elusive escapes were fantastic because even thrill rides like roller coasters are designed not to exceed 3g. This is because sustained g-forces above 10g can be fatal or lead to permanent injury. Even for unmanned drones, a turn eliciting 40g defies conventional aeronautics. This incident remains unexplained, and the Belgian defense minister has publicly admitted being mystified by it.[572] These sorts of sightings are by no means unusual, as RUFO reports go, and we could cite many more examples. We will discuss two ongoing 2012 cases at the close of this chapter, but the point we wish to press is the parallel between these RUFO reports and the experience of the square in Flatland. It seems likely that the RUFOs are taking advantage of a similar extradimensionality.

While both the interdimensional hypothesis (IDH) and extradimensional hypothesis (EDH) posit that RUFOs are craft navigating between different realities, there is a distinction. The prefix "inter" means "between" or "among." The IDH proponents think of flying saucers as concentrated blobs of energy that manifest based on wavelength. A useful analogy can be drawn with radio signals. We are all being bombarded by encoded, information-rich signals completely unawares. However, a receiver dialed to the right frequency can decode these signals. Did something like that occur when Elijah's servant was suddenly able to perceive the army and fiery chariots? Keel, an early advocate of the IDH, explains in paranormal terms:

> Your eyes are also receivers tuned to very specific wavelengths of the spectrum, and they turn the signals from those wavelengths into pulses, which are fed to your brain. Your brain, in turn, is also a very sophisticated, little-understood receiver, and it is tuned to wavelengths far beyond the receiving capabilities of manufactured electronic instruments. Most people are running

around with crude biological "crystal sets" in their heads and are not consciously receiving any of the sophisticated signals. However, about one-third of the world's population possesses a more finely tuned instrument. These people experience telepathy, prophetic dreams and other bizarre signals from some central source. If you are one of that 30 percent, you know precisely what I mean. If you belong to the larger, ungifted two-thirds, you probably regard all this as nonsense, and we may never be able to convince you otherwise.[573]

Following this line, Keel linked UFOs to ghosts and demons. While this idea has merit, it is extremely hard to prove. The extradimensional theory is similar, but has more scientific support. Perhaps there is room for both?

In her recent bestseller, Leslie Kean argued that "the hypothesis that UFOs are of extraterrestrial or interdimensional origin is a rational one and must be taken into account, given the data we have."[574] Though many of the top minds in ufology have adopted extradimensional theory, the greatest champion is Jacques Vallée. Long before it was popular or had much scientific support, he wrote, "I believe that the UFO phenomenon *represents evidence for other dimensions beyond spacetime;* the UFOs may not come from ordinary space, but from a *multiverse* which is all around us."[575] Vallée famously collaborated with the "father of ufology," J. Allen Hynek, on several books, and it seems their thinking runs parallel. At the 1977 International UFO Congress in Chicago, Hynek advocated what he called the "extradimensional intelligence hypothesis" and argued that the UFO phenomenon is neither entirely material nor mental. He stated, "I hypothesize a 'M&M' technology encompassing the mental and material realms."[576] This seemingly bridges the gap between extradimensional and interdimensional.

In other words, extradimensional entities may be interacting with our world interdimensionally (e.g., psychically and spiritually). Philosopher Michael Grosso notes that the phenomenon is able to, "affect radar, cause burns, leave traces in the ground and at the same time pass through walls, appear and disappear like ghosts, defy gravity, assume variable and symbolic shapes, and strike deep chords of psychic, mystic, or prophetic sentiment."[577] After years of investigation, Lieutenant Colonel Nelson Pacheco of the United States Air Force determined, "The five-or-so percent of UFO reports that are not misrepresentations, delusions, or hoaxes are real in the sense of being *intelligent* but *peripheral* psycho-physical intrusions into our experiential universe by *metaphysical intelligent entities* that exist outside our spacetime continuum (what some would call a parallel universe)."[578] A similar hypothesis was offered by the prolific paranormal author, Brad Steiger: "We are dealing with a multidimensional paraphysical phenomenon that is largely indigenous to planet Earth."[579] Indeed, many competent researchers believe that these beings have always been nearby, an idea congruent with a biblical worldview. Even though the extraterrestrial hypothesis (ETH) gets preference in popular parlance, intellectually honest secular researchers at least allow for extradimensional ideas. But what about the scientific community? Do hard-nosed, skeptical scientists entertain such fantastic notions? Indeed, they do.

Braneworld: Science Meets the Heavenly Places

We are all familiar with the three dimensions of length, width, and depth, but how can we begin to think about higher dimensions? The illustration from *Flatland* is helpful. Just like a square living on a sheet of paper would have no concept of depth, we may be similarly unaware of unseen dimensions. Extrapolate the *Flatworld* epiphany forward, and you have the basic concept behind braneworld theory. Braneworld cosmology posits that our four-dimensional spacetime is like the sheet of paper, a membrane or "brane" that is simply a subspace of a larger, multidimensional space. The big idea is that our visible, four-dimensional spacetime universe is restricted to its own brane inside a higher-dimensional space called "the bulk." The bulk could contain other branes that are, for intents and purposes, parallel universes. While it is hard to conceive, a parallel universe might be present only a micron away from this universe. We cannot see it because its photons of light are stuck to its brane just like our photons are stuck to our brane, but, even so, scientists theorize that gravitational forces can reach from one membrane-universe to another. If so, we should detect the existence of other braneworlds.

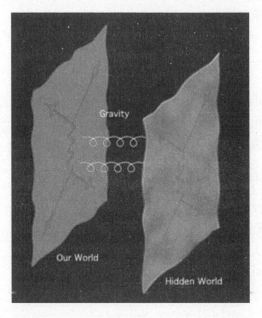

Dark Matter: Could gravity from a parallel world
influence our own?

This might sound like science fiction, but concepts of higher dimensionality, once considered on the fringes of cosmology, have entered the mainstream. Paul J. Steinhardt is the Albert Einstein Professor in Science at Princeton University, where he serves on the faculty of both the physics and astrophysics departments. Best known for his work in theoretical brane cosmology, he explains, "Our three-dimensional world can be viewed as a membrane-like surface embedded into space with an extra, fourth spatial dimension."[580] Thus, our universe is one "brane world" and there exists another brane world, a parallel universe, less than an atom's width away. This is likely a strange domain where the laws of physics might be entirely different. Does this seem too much like a science fiction novel? Not so fast; Steinhardt believes we have already quantifiable evidence for it.

Scientists have come to the troubling realization that they can only account for a small percentage of the observed gravitational effects in space. In the last decade, astronomers have discovered that every galaxy is surrounded by super massive, yet unseen, sources of gravity. They know this because galaxies rotate far too quickly given the amount of matter we see. Something huge and invisible is exerting a powerful gravitational force on these star clusters. Because we cannot see it, it is called *dark* matter. David Spergel, a leader of the Wilkinson Microwave Anisotropy Probe space mission, divulges:

> "From our experiments, the periodic table which comprises the atoms or normal matter that are said to make up the entire universe actually covers only 4.5 percent of the whole," lead theorist Spergel said. "Students are learning just a tiny part of the universe from their textbooks. It would be dark matter and dark energy that comprise the next 22 percent and 73.5 percent of the universe."[581]

This is an astonishing admission of ignorance. It seems the recent, high-handed pronouncement by Stephen Hawking in *The Grand Design* concerning the Creator was based on an incomplete data set.

Accordingly, dark matter suggests greater humility is in order because scientists now admit they only have a working knowledge of a very small percentage of reality. How does dark matter provide evidence for braneworld cosmology? Steinhardt argues, "Although we can't touch feel or see any matter on the other brane, we can, nevertheless, sense its existence because we can feel its gravity."[582] He is arguing that there is no dark matter within our universe after all; rather, it is matter existing in a parallel universe. A nearby parallel reality, immune from our light, is producing gravitational effects. This readily explains dark matter, an otherwise cosmological conundrum. More interestingly, Steinhardt proposes that these two membranes might even touch at points, transferring matter and radiation from one to the other. This suggests that black holes may, in fact, be points of connection between parallel braneworlds. If an excess of matter collects at one point on either brane, its gravitational field becomes so strong that it draws the other brane towards it, and what is a black hole on one side is a white hole on the other. In this way, black holes might be gateways to a parallel universe. This idea from mainstream science seems remarkably similar to the IDH and offers a solution as to the perplexing origin of RUFOs.

Another astrophysicist, Bernard Haisch, a principal investigator on several NASA research projects who served as the scientific editor for *Astrophysical Journal* for ten years, has suggested that RUFOs could indeed represent visitations from a parallel brane world. On his website, www.UFOSkeptic.org, he accounts for the seemingly impossible maneuvers exhibited by RUFOs in terms of braneworlds cosmology:

> Perhaps it is possible to lift off the membrane-universe constituting our four-dimensional spacetime, move in one of the additional dimensions where speed-of-light limits may not apply, and reenter our membrane-universe very far away. All of this is speculation of course, but it is worth noting that disappearing in place, changing shape or sometimes jumping discontinuously from location to location is frequently reported in UFO observations. Such behavior could conceivably be associated with motion into and out of a perpendicular dimension.[583]

Haisch's theory makes sense of otherwise baffling behavior. It seems that most open-minded scientists who study the RUFO evidence come to similar conclusions.

Of course, this begs the question: If otherwise skeptical scientists can so readily embrace such otherworldly concepts, then why are they so opposed to belief in God, miracles, and supernatural phenomena? Christian apologist Dinesh D'Souza made this point in his 2008 best-seller, *What's so Great about Christianity?*:

> It seems worth pointing out here what Harvard astronomer Owen Gingerich seems to be the first to have noticed: anyone who can believe in multiple universes should have no problem believing in heaven and hell. Just think of them as alternate universes, operating outside space and time according to laws that are inoperative in our universe. Even the atheist should now be able to envision a realm in which there is no evil or suffering and where the inhabitants never grow old.[584]

Indeed, the New Testament testified that our observed reality is merely a subset of a larger unseen one: "For we wrestle not against flesh and blood, but against principalities, against powers, against the rulers of the darkness of this world, against spiritual wickedness in high places" (Ephesians 6:12). We suppose it is refreshing that twenty-first century astrophysics is finally catching up to the Apostle Paul.

Dr. Hugh Ross is somewhat unique in that he is an astrophysicist with a biblical worldview. Thus, he is more qualified than most to assess ideas on the fringe of science and theology. Although they often are conflated, Ross draws a distinction between interdimensional and extradimensional:

> In the end, it seems best to abandon the ETH and consider the second option: the interdimensional hypothesis, or IDH. While in its more popular versions the IDH departs from verified and verifiable reality, the extradimensional hypothesis holds promise. And here the investigator stands on firmer ground, scientifically speaking. The space-time theorems show that supernature

must exist, because nature was plainly originated by something beyond itself. Therefore, a scientifically credible possibility exists that RUFOs come from beyond the four familiar dimensions of the universe.[585]

Ross is drawing a distinction between the paranormal approach and the extra dimensions posited by String theory. Even so, braneworld cosmology seems to have room for elements of both. Quite interestingly, two ongoing cases from 2012 display the sort of preposterous performance that has led so many scientists to embrace some variant of the IDH.

The Chilean Air Force Gets Buzzed: Berserkers or Bumble Bees?

The first case was broken worldwide by Leslie Kean in a March 13, 2012, piece in the *Huffington Post*: "UFO Caught On Tape Over Santiago Air Base."[586] On the sunny afternoon of November 5, 2010, the Chilean Air Force put on an air show celebrating a change of command at El Bosque Air Base in Santiago. The show offered the typical fare of acrobatics and screaming flybys. Naturally, many in the exuberant crowd had their cell phones and video cameras trained on the aviator acts of daring. All seemed to go as planned, and no one noticed anything peculiar. That is, not until later when an engineer from the nearby Pillán aircraft facility examined his digital camera footage. When viewing the video in slow motion (the low-altitude, overhead flyby made by F16, F5, and Halcone jets), the engineer was shocked to see the high-speed jets being shadowed by a peculiar, erratically moving UFO!

The silvery looking saucer, which seemed to reflect sunlight in a few frames, flew past the jets so fast that no one on the ground was able to see it. It literally seemed to be running circles around the high-tech military fighter planes, perhaps toying with them. The aviation enthusiast turned his footage over to the *Comité de Estudios de Fenómenos Aéreos Anómalos* ("Committee for the Study of Anomalous Aerial

Phenomena," [CEFAA]), the Chilean government's official investigating unit, for analysis. According to Kean, the CEFAA collected seven videos of the UFO taken from different vantage points. In examining videos from multiple angles of the same event, the initial panel of experts came to a consensus:

> Each video included three different, mainly horizontal loops flown by the UFO within seconds of each other. The object made elliptical passes either near or around each of three sets of performing jets. It flew past the Halcones, F5s and F16s at speeds so fast it was not noticed by the pilots or anyone on the ground below.[587]

The skipping-stone-like flight pattern of the craft is really too peculiar to describe in words, so we suggest you journey to the *Huffington Post* online article, where you can watch the footage in slow motion. One digital-imaging expert, Alberto Vergara, observed, "When we examine the whole scene frame by frame, we have been able to realize that [the object] has, apparently, moved at a speed far superior to any flying object of known manufacture."[588] Truly, this seems to be yet another example of the law-defying aerial acrobatics associated with RUFOs that continually confound investigators and suggests exploitation of extra dimensions.

Of course, a case like this involving Air Force personnel and footage from multiple angles deeply challenges the worldview of the skeptic. Accordingly, Internet debunkers were quick to argue that the inexplicable anomaly was simply an insect flying close to the lens. Yet, these skeptics were only viewing one of the clips in isolation. The CEFAA is taking the case seriously, because the UFO appeared on multiple videos taken too far apart to capture the same insect. Kean went so far as to enlist the expert opinions of a few entomologists. Brett C. Ratcliffe, professor at University of Nebraska Department of Entomology, concluded, "No idea what it is but it does not seem to be an insect."[589] The

CEFAA enlisted two expert studies in order to reach a more scientific conclusion as to what this might be.

Bruce Maccabee, retired Navy physicist, and Richard Haines, chief scientist for the National Aviation Reporting Center on Anomalous Phenomena (NARCAP), painstakingly analyzed the tapes. The fact that the anomaly was caught on more than one camera is the operative factor in verifying that it is not insects flying close to camera lenses giving the false impression of distant object flying at super high speed. Both experts sought to find instances in the video sources that showed the same Unidentified Aerial Phenomenon (UAP) from distinct, far-removed, observational perspectives (i.e., Camera 1, Camera 2). While Maccabee was unable to decisively determine, Haines documented an instance of multiple camera corroboration. He explains, "It has been shown that the UAP recorded by both cameras…was at least 42 feet from Camera 1 and probably much further. This would effectively eliminate all flying insects since they don't fly at 90 mph."[590] In his conclusion, he drives the point home:

> Could all of the UAP here be flying insects? On balance, the answer is very likely no because of the linearity of their flight, their high angular velocity, their occasional spontaneous and unexpected appearance within a video frame, their apparent trajectories relative to the different airplane formations, their almost consistent oval shape and nearly horizontal orientation, their lack of any color other than gray and white and perhaps most importantly, for one UAP…its relatively large distance from the two cameras.[591]

The CEFAA issued this statement: "After hearing from the ento-mologists who have looked at the images, we at the CEFAA agree that these photos do not show anything which allows for the conclusion that they are bugs."[592] As of November 2012, the case is still categorized as officially *unsolved*.

Pleiadean Berserkers Buzz the Mile High City?

On November 8, 2012, a local *Fox31* affiliate *KDVR* in Denver, CO aired a news story, "Mile High Mystery: UFO Sightings in Sky Over Denver" by investigative reporter Heidi Hemmat, and subsequently published it to their website.[593] Because we were then closely following the above Chilean case, this one caught our eye. The UFO spotted in this video is remarkably similar with its agitated, lightning quick, almost violent manner of flight. Exactly as in the Chilean case, the entity is not visible to the naked eye but appears only when the video is slowed down. Even more astonishingly, this case also has multiple videos of the same phenomenon.

As a reputable journalist, she was necessarily dubious when first approached by a local man (who remains anonymous) promising footage of a genuine UFO. To her amazement, she watched a bullet-like entity takeoff from within the city and dart about the Denver sky with impunity. The witness froze the frame to point out an apparent burst of fire as it executed a hairpin turn. The acrobatics continued, weaving in and out of frame, until it surreptitiously returned to the apparent point of origin within the Denver metro area. The video was shot atop a hill in Federal Heights, celebrated for its scenic overlook of Denver to the sSouth. During the news story, the unnamed, blacked-out videographer is heard marveling that before going public, he caught the same mysterious airborne performance between noon and 1:00 p.m. regularly for the preceding several months! In analyzing the brief clips in the news feature, pause the video at the 1:43 mark as the object ascends. Notice it appears to turn and reflect sunlight. Pause again at 1:47, this time on a downward trajectory, and observe another reflective flash. This reflectiveness supports a substantive, external object rather than an internal camera anomaly or digital artifact. Better still, this case boasts an unprecedented corroborating video independently shot by *KDVR* photojournalist Noah Skinner.

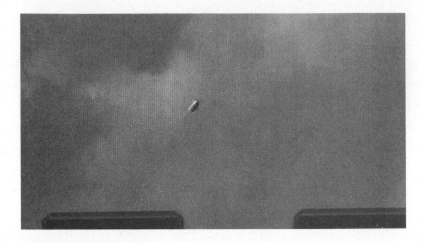

Denver UFO reflects light

The professional video journalist set up at the exact same spot and shot during the designated time slot. He did not notice anything unusual. To his surprise, while reviewing the footage in slow motion, he saw the same UFO! His footage is also available on the *KDVR* website below the original story. At the very least, independent corroboration demonstrates the original footage is legitimate. Of course, the identity of the entity buzzing Denver remains unresolved. To that end, *KDVR* consulted Steve Cowell, a former commercial pilot, flight instructor, and FAA accident prevention counselor. After scrutinizing the video evidence, Cowell seemed bewildered that a conventional explanation was not forthcoming. He laments, "It's very strange; that is not an airplane; that is not a helicopter; those are not birds...hmmm, I can't identify it."[594] Appearing perplexed, he surmises that its incredible velocity allows it to evade naked eye detection and public scrutiny. Speaking directly, the expert clarifies, "As it fits the definition, it is an *Unidentified Flying Object.*"[595] According to the reporter, he also said it was definitely *not* an insect. Since it flies so frequently during a specific time slot, perhaps it has been captured on radar?

The station checked with the Federal Aviation Administration (FAA), who denied having any information whatsoever, as well as consulting the North American Aerospace Defense Command (NORAD), located eighty miles away in Colorado Springs, who responded, "Our command center reviewed their records and they did not have any noted air activity in the Denver area during the times you indicated."[596] After the initial story went viral on the Internet, the station was inundated with inquiries, and hundreds of folks offering various explanations, including windblown debris, remote-controlled aircraft, a government surveillance drone, and top-secret military aircraft. While the station didn't say, surely someone proffered extraterrestrials? A plethora of possibilities aside, the most popular conventional explanation was, as with the Chilean case, insects flying close to the lens that appear to be distant, fast-moving objects. Despite aviation expert Steve Cowell's denial, the prevalence of the bug hypothesis warranted analysis by an entomologist and other experts.

After the aviation expert, a retired military drone expert, and other investigators unanimously dismissed drones and radio-controlled aircraft, the journalists took the video to Mary Ann Hartman, a professional entomologist employed as the vice president of science and conservation at nearby Denver Butterfly Pavilion. After viewing the video many times, she offered her professional opinion: "After watching the various shots, I would have to say, 'no.' I do not believe it's an insect. The shape is inconsistent with an insect."[597] Even so, this has not satisfied the skeptics, and, as this book goes to press, controversy still rages. In closing, a few observations are in order.

1: The original cameraman, who has spent months studying the phenomenon, believes the UFOs are launching and landing near 56th Avenue and Clay Street in Denver. The fact that the phenomenon is somewhat predictable and originates and returns to the same location belies the insect hypothesis.

2: He went to the area and watched for anyone operating a remote-control aircraft and interviewed the neighbors as well—to no avail.

3: The craft appears to rotate and reflect sunlight as it crosses the frame in several of the shots. This is not consistent with a bug near the lens.

4: At 1:06 in the original newscast, something akin to a jet thruster burst concurrent with an acute change of direction. Surely, skeptics must admit that insects do not emit visible energy bursts as they execute mid-air, right-angle turns.

5: The news reported that the "T" intersection of 56th Avenue and Clay Street (shown below) was a residential area, but they neglected to mention the nearby Kingdom Hall of Jehovah's Witnesses compound at 2675 West 56th Avenue with additional facilities located directly across the street.

Point A is 56th Avenue and Clay Street in close proximity to the Kingdom Hall; image from Google maps street view

While adequate evidence is lacking, the investigator is convinced that the UFO regularly originates and returns to this location. The founders of Jehovah's Witnesses held beliefs remarkably similar to nineteenth-century occult groups and modern UFO cults. The proximity of the UFO's observed trajectory to the Kingdom Hall compound is at least suggestive that this is a paraphysical spiritual entity.

Berserkers and Eschatological Judgment of God

At this point, you have probably followed the links to watch the footage. Consequently, you likely agree that the frantic flight patterns exhibited by these UFOs merit the title "Berserker." Originally, Berserkers were legendary Norse warriors who fought with a notorious, trance-like fury, a distinction that subsequently inspired the English word "berserk."[598] While employed with creative license in the headings above, the Berserker name was recently enlisted by writer Fred Saberhagen for a series of science-fiction short stories and novels. In his apocalyptic tales, the Berserkers are self-replicating flying machines sent to destroy all life on Earth. We think it not by chance that these biomechanical entities find functional parallels with the demonic locust hordes predicted in biblical prophecy (Joel 2 c.f. Revelation 9). We are not the first to suggest a connection between these insectoid instruments of divine judgment and the UFO phenomenon.

In a posthumously released textbook, *The Kingdom of the Occult*, by Dr. Walter Martin, a portion of his 1970s UFO presentation is transcribed. Although not widely known, he not only took the UFO phenomenon seriously, but he was also an eyewitness to a flying saucer.[599] In fact, he blew up a photograph of the craft he witnessed as a display supporting his lecture. Like ourselves, Martin was inclined toward the extradimensional hypothesis rather than space aliens. He likewise ventured that UFOs might be instrumental in Jesus' description of the events prior to His return: "Men's hearts failing them for fear, and for looking after those things which are coming on the earth: for the powers of heaven shall be shaken" (Luke 21:26, underline added). "Things which are coming on the earth" implies that they themselves are not of the Earth; rather, they are, by definition, *extraterrestrial*. In reference to this text and parallels in the book of Revelation, Martin offered this prophetic hypothesis:

> In addition to what is coming upon the earth, the book of Revelation speaks of the bottomless pit being opened (9:2). A

bottomless pit does not have to be one that is down—it could very well be one that is *up*, since in space there is neither up nor down, but *out* from the earth. This could reveal that what comes upon earth is from space, and not from under the earth. The symbolic language may easily refer to the manifestations of the powers of darkness near the consummation of the age. It is biblically predicted that Antichrist will reveal himself with signs and lying wonders so that if it were possible, he would deceive the elect (2 Thessalonians 2:9; Matthew 24:24).[600]

This is a fascinating, if not frightening, concept in light of the early Greek writer Hesiod, who is credited with Homer as a major source on early Greek mythology, particularly the "origins" of the gods of Greek religion. In his *Theogony*, Hesiod describes the "place" of imprisoned Titans—the old and powerful gods that ruled the world during the legendary Golden Age:

> And there, all in their order, are the sources and ends of gloomy earth and misty Tartarus and the unfruitful sea and starry heaven, loathsome and dank, which even the gods abhor.
>
> It is a great gulf, and if once a man were within the gates.... There stands the awful home of murky Night wrapped in dark clouds. In front of it the son of Iapetus stands immovably upholding the wide heaven upon his head and unwearying hands, where Night and Day draw near and greet one another as they pass the great threshold of bronze.... And there the children of dark Night have their dwellings, Sleep and Death, awful gods. The glowing Sun never looks upon them with his beams, neither as he goes up into heaven, nor as he comes down from heaven. (Lines 736–744)

Hesiod's *Theogony* takes on a fascinating mystery when one considers that the Bible characterizes the place of imprisoned rebel angels using the same words Hesiod employs to describe the place of Titan gods—"Tartarus" and the "Bottomless Pit" (see 2 Peter 2:4; Revelation 9:1–11; 11:7; 17:8; 20:1–3). Couple this with eerily similar discoveries on the actual moon Iapetus, the third-largest natural satellite of Saturn, and you understand why a growing number of researchers are open to the possibility that synthetic-looking planetoids like Iapetus may be, as it appears to be, artificial. Could it be the bottomless pit?

In Greek mythology, Iapetus was the son of Uranus and Gaia, and father of Atlas, Prometheus, Epimetheus, and Menoetius. Because Atlas was a "father of mankind," Iapetus was understood in myth to be a progenitor, a creator god, of Homo sapiens. Italian astronomer and engineer Giovanni Domenico Cassini discovered Saturn's moon Iapetus in 1672 using his small refracting telescope. Cassini correctly deciphered the disappearing and reappearing act of Iapetus as due to the moon synchronously rotating with one hemisphere continuously facing Saturn. Iapetus is also divided by a great gulf formed by a giant, walled threshold at its equator as seen in the picture of Iapetus below. This feature was discovered during a New Year's Eve flyby in 2005, when NASA's Cassina spacecraft photographed the 1300-by-20-kilo-meter-high rim (the equivalent of 808 by 12 miles) stretching over one-third of the moon's equator. No other moon in the solar system has been found with such a stunning feature: literally a 60,000-foot-high wall. Compare this fact again with Hesiod's description of a great threshold of bronze:

> It is a great gulf….murky Night wrapped in dark clouds. In front of it the son of Iapetus…where Night and Day draw near and greet one another as they pass the great threshold of bronze…. And there the children of dark Night have their dwellings, Sleep and Death, awful gods. The glowing Sun never looks upon them with his beams, neither as he goes up into heaven, nor as he comes down from heaven. (Lines 736–744)

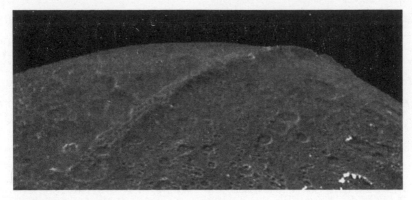

808 mile-long, 60,000-foot-high wall stretching over one-third of Iapetus equator

In *The Search for Life in the Universe,* Tobias Owen, the man at NASA who discovered the face on Mars, and Donald Goldsmith wrote, "This unusual moon [Iapetus] is the only object in the Solar System which we might seriously regard as an alien signpost—a natural object deliberately modified by an advanced civilization to attract our attention."[601]

In an email to Tom Horn a few years ago, the late David Flynn made an interesting point about this, including the possibility of the "bottomless pit" (mentioned previously) actually being a "star" (or an extraterrestrial object) in heaven:

Tom, you are intrepid enough to address an issue many are afraid to investigate.… And you are right about gates [and that various beings have come through them].…

[Flynn then quotes from Revelation 9.] "And he opened the bottomless pit.… And there came out of the smoke locusts upon the earth.…and the shapes of the locusts [were] like unto horses prepared unto battle; and…their faces [were] as the faces of men. And they had hair of women, and their teeth were as of lions…" (Revelation 9.1–8).

[Flynn continues.] Here is described an army of beings with mixed genetics [transgenics], but all species of terrestrial origin. The similarities between the "locusts with faces of men" and the modern reports of "insectoid" aliens [descending through dimensional gates] stand out in John's prophecy.… It is assumed that the locusts of Revelation 9 "ascend" from a bottomless pit somewhere on earth because the story of the locust invasion begins with a "star" falling from heaven to earth and an angel with a key. The Greek word translated "fall" is Pipto, which means to "descend from a higher place to a lower." If the star itself IS the bottomless pit, Revelation 9 could be describing an extraterrestrial object—a mother ship—moving into orbit around earth with myriad beings. From this same place in Scripture the word "bottomless" is bathos, often translated as "height" and the word "pit" is Phrear. A phrear in Greek mythology is an orcus, a deep chasm bound by a gulf where fallen beings are imprisoned.… Revelation 12 explains the surety of Satan and his angels coming down from heaven to the earth in the future. For now, they wait…somewhere out in space. (Flynn, 2005)[602]

David Flynn's complete study on this was published in his groundbreaking book *Cydonia: The Secret Chronicles of Mars* (available again in *The David Flynn Collection*), and one can easily imagine, if Flynn is correct, how Official Disclosure of aliens could be forced on hysterical Earth societies by sudden, inexplicable movement of an extrasolar planetoid like Iapetus or a similar "moon" unexpectedly turning and heading toward Earth as the bottomless pit!

It is probably no accident that this sounds remarkably similar to braneworld cosmology's dimensional bridges. Indeed, our intention with this book is to reiterate and amplify Dr. Walter Martin's early warning. One dark day, perhaps sooner than you think, the prophecy Jesus Christ delivered to His Apostle John on the island of Patmos will surely come to pass. John foresaw this impending event:

I saw a star fall from heaven unto the earth: and to him was given the key of the bottomless pit. And he opened the bottomless pit; and there arose a smoke out of the pit, as the smoke of a great furnace; and the sun and the air were darkened by reason of the smoke of the pit. And there came out of the smoke locusts upon the earth: and unto them was given power, as the scorpions of the earth have power. And it was commanded them that they should not hurt the grass of the earth, neither any green thing, neither any tree; but only those men which have not the seal of God in their foreheads. (Revelation 9:1–4)

While it is of the greatest peril imaginable to be an unbeliever when these sure trials come to pass, in light of the apocalyptic locusts, perhaps the flying insect solution to the aforementioned UFO cases is at least partially correct? Of course, those in Christ need not fear. But perhaps you think our imaginative correlations are too fanciful? The prophecies predict the locusts' release following specific unprecedented judgments. Thus, we warily concede that the recent sightings are probably not berserkers on reconnaissance. Even so, if they *do* turn out to be end-time portents, at least we suggested a connection. Nevertheless, these recent captures of objects flying too fast to see do fit the paraphysical profile associated with extradimensional entities. If the UFO phenomenon is legitimately connected to end-time prophecy, then it will increase in frequency and intensity. Yet, quantifying something so elusive is extremely problematic. So, like Elijah, pray for supernatural eyes to see.

Recalling Elijah's prayer for his servant's supernatural perception, it seems noteworthy that a whirlwind replete with fire and divine chariots appears yet again in prophetic Scripture. However, in this case, they are explicitly associated with the eschatological judgment of God, essentially the Great Tribulation climaxing in the battle of Armageddon. The prophet Isaiah foretold:

For, behold, the LORD will come with fire,
and with his chariots like a whirlwind,
to render his anger with fury,
and his rebuke with flames of fire.
For by fire and by his sword will the LORD plead with all flesh:
and the slain of the LORD shall be many. (Isaiah 66:15–16)

14 | Fátima: Harbinger of the Great Deception?

"UFOs are real, burgeoning and not going away."
—L. A. Marzulli

"The opaque sphere moved outward slightly, either spinning, or moving from left to right and vice versa. But within the sphere, you could see marked movements with total clarity and without interruption."—Pope Pius XII, after the sighting on October 30–31, 1950[603]

The Miracle of the Sun was an Unidentified Aerial Phenomenon (UAP)witnessed on October 13, 1917, by up to one hundred thousand people gathered near Fátima, Portugal. Several newspaper reporters in attendance recorded testimony from people who claimed to have witnessed an extraordinary aerial phenomenon in which a silvery disc flew about the sky. Of course, this was long before the term "flying saucer" was coined, and many thought the disc was the sun. Also, because it had been raining and the clouds broke just as the phenomenon occurred, many believed it was a solar miracle. However, if the sun had actually moved in the described manner, the gravitational effects would have devastated the Earth. Even so, the sighting was officially declared a miracle by the Roman Catholic Church in 1930. During a commemorative celebration on October 13, 1951, the papal legate, Cardinal Tedeschini, told the million people gathered at Fátima that Pope Pius XII had witnessed the same miracle of the sun from the Vatican gardens thirty-three years later, in 1950.[604]

Note the dark ball or disc that looks nothing like the sun

Mass UFO sighting, Fátima, Portugal, October 13, 1917

While the bulk of this chapter will discuss the Fátima sighting in 1917, a lesser-known fact is that thirty-three years later, the pope claimed to have seen the same thing above the Vatican gardens in Rome. A note signed by Pope Pius XII states that on October 31, 1950, "The sun, which was still quite high, looked like a pale, opaque sphere, entirely surrounded by a luminous circle."[605] The disc-shaped object "moved outward slightly, either spinning, or moving from left to right and vice versa. But within the sphere, you could see marked movements with total clarity and without interruption."[606] That this sort of Unidentified Aerial Phenomenon (UAP) is associated with Mary is astonishing; however, what makes this especially interesting is that this pope approved the Fátima apparitions in 1940 and then consecrated the entire world to the Immaculate Heart of Mary two years later. More provocative is that he saw the spinning spherical anomaly on the day he defined the dogma of the Assumption of Mary—the Catholic belief that Mary ascended bodily into heaven—which he, himself, made official dogma shortly thereafter. In other words, this UFO sighting inspired the pope to promulgate the dogma of the Assumption! Considering Constantine's fourth-century sighting got it started, the event in Fátima, and all the sightings over the Vatican, Roman Catholicism arguably qualifies as a UFO religion.

What this suggests is that the entities behind the aerial phenomenon are influencing Catholic dogmas. Other officially recognized apparitions are similarly suspicious. Every year, nearly 6 million pilgrims visit Lourdes, France, because Mary was said to appear there. People report being healed from diseases and seeing apparitions of her. However, few Catholics are aware of the origin of "Our Lady of Lourdes." The apparition first appeared to an impressionable teenager, Bernadette Soubirous, under very questionable circumstances. But what is astounding is that Bernadette originally never believed it to be Mary—that is, until she was pressured by a local priest. According to Lynn Picknett's excellent book on the paranormal, *Flights of Fancy*:

> In February 1858, fourteen-year-old Bernadette Soubirous had discovered a strange creature, apparently suspended between the branches of a tree. It glowed, smiled and beckoned. The future Catholic Saint did not, as in the Hollywood version, fall enraptured to her knees, but ran home to grab a bottle of holy water to throw at "that thing", as she called the vision. She believed it to be a demon, sent by the devil to lure her to doom, and perhaps she was right....
>
> She took her extraordinary secret to the parish priest, the only man of letters she knew. History might have taken a different turn, had he not been a fierce defender of Mariolatry at a time when the status of the Virgin was being challenged within the Catholic Church.[607]

The priest spun this phantasm into evidence for Marian dogma, and the rest is history. Astonishingly, Bernadette was heralded as a mystic, canonized as a saint in 1933, and even given her own feast day on the sixteenth of April. See a pattern emerging? Like at Fátima, it always speaks through naïve children (see Marzulli's material in the following pages). While a few credulous Portuguese children could be easily deceived by a supernatural entity, the events at Fátima had nothing to do with the biblical Mary.

Many scholars are now categorizing Fátima as a mass UFO sighting. A Portuguese scholar, Joaquim Fernandes, professor of history at the Universidade Fernando Pessoa, assembled an international panel to subject the Fátima apparitions to the scrutiny of modern scientific analysis. In *Fátima Revisited* (2008), Jacques Vallée and Eric Davis discuss the psycho-spiritual nature of the UFO phenomenon and assert Fátima as a representative case:

> As one example among many, it will be recalled that the events at Fátima involved luminous phenomena, atmospheric and thermal effects, and descriptions of an apparently metallic disk in the sky, while many of the 70,000 witnesses also experienced spiritual and psychological effects. The main percipients reported psychic states conducive to a form of extrasensory communication with a non-human Being assumed to be the Virgin Mary.[608]

While Fernandes has several books discussing Fátima in ufological terms, we want to offer the rest of this chapter to our friend and colleague, L. A. Marzulli, the author of the best-selling Nephilim Trilogy novels: *The Nephilim* (2000); *The Unholy Deception: The Nephilim Return* (2003); and *The Revealing: The Time Is Now* (2004). In the nonfiction genre, he has published *Politics, Prophecy & the Supernatural* (2007); *The Alien Interviews* (2010); and *The Cosmic Chess Match* (2011). As of late, Marzulli has teamed up with film producer Richard Shaw to create *The Watchers* video series available on DVD. We are excited and honored to include this excerpt from *Politics, Prophecy & the Supernatural*, which discusses the miracle at Fátima as a harbinger of the great deception predicted in end-time prophecy.

L. A. Marzulli writes:

> Before entering the strange and enigmatic world of Marian apparitions, I want to set something straight (for the record). In no way do I intend to demean those who believe in, or have faith in, these apparitions. There are many sincere people who

believe that these manifestations are what they appear to be: that of Mary.

I, however, have a completely different take on the subject and, like others who have delved into the events (including some Catholic priests), believe that these apparitions might be a deception by Luciferian/Satanic elements. Keeping this in mind, we will focus on one particular event that happened in Fátima, Portugal, in 1917. This event has been "approved" by the church and has been a source of inspiration and faith for millions of Christians. (By church approval I mean that the event of Fátima has been examined by the Catholic church and deemed to conform to the true teachings of Jesus Christ and is in harmony with church teachings.) Again, the purpose of the following discussion is not to denigrate but rather to express my utmost concern that the events in question may, in fact, be a harbinger of deception.

The Event

In my research for the Nephilim Trilogy, I found myself in some pretty strange areas of study. One area that piqued my interest in particular was the Fátima apparitions that took place in the early part of the twentieth century. For those of you who are unfamiliar with these events, I will provide a thumbnail sketch. This accounting comes from having read multiple sources regarding the event.

In 1917 three children (who would later become known as seers), Lucia Santos and her two cousins Francesco and Jacinta Marto, were tending sheep when they beheld an apparition of, what it would later refer to itself as, "a lady from heaven." The apparition told them to come to the same place—Cova da Iria (Irene's Cove, a place located near the town of Fátima, Portugal)—on the thirteenth day of the following month. The children told their parents about what they had seen and this set off an uproar in the town. The apparitions continued for months, finally culminating in the local priest instructing the children to ask the apparition for a sign. They did as they were asked, and the apparition told them that the following month, which was October, there would be a sign, for all to see. The next month upwards of seventy thousand people gathered in the field at Cova da Iria. It had been raining all day, and there was a thick layer of clouds overshadowing the crowd. A cross section of humanity gathered that day: bankers, peasants, clergy, bakers, young, old, reporters, believers, and skeptics alike all waited for the sign that the apparition had promised would appear. The appointed time for the "sign" to manifest, which was noon, came and went, and nothing happened. The crowd grew restless. An hour passed and one of the "seers" called out, "It's the Lady." The crowd could not see her, but the children apparently did, and everyone waited to see what would happen next. The dark sky suddenly parted to reveal what many onlookers described as "the sun." It spun around throwing off an array of colors and then, to the terror of everyone, began to fall in a pendulum like motion to earth. What followed was mass hysteria, as people thought the end of world was upon them. Some dropped to their knees, while others ran about screaming hysterically. (This event is now called, "the Miracle of the Sun.")

The "sun" then began to ascend to its rightful place in the heavens, and when it had departed, the crowd realized that their clothes, which had been soaked by the constant rain, were dry. Most everyone in the crowd that day had his or her worldview altered for all time—many choosing to believe in the apparition that called herself the Lady from Heaven. Imagine yourself standing in that field and experiencing what would later be hailed as, "The Miracle of the Sun." Would you examine your belief system? If you were from another faith, perhaps Judaism, would this event cause you to wonder as to what you were seeing? If you were an atheist, would not seeing the "miracle of the sun" make you pause and consider that there may be an unseen world? And finally, if you were a Catholic, how would it affect you? Would you start going to church everyday or maybe join the priesthood or a convent?

Before I continue, I must once again issue a caveat: the following critique of this event is not meant in any way to demean the Catholic Church or those who have a different opinion—specifically the belief that this apparition was the Mother of God or the biblical figure of Mary—than I do regarding the apparitions at Fátima. The purpose is rather to point out what I believe was a cosmic deception that fooled most everyone.

Following is a section from my third book in the Nephilim Trilogy, *The Revealing*. It has a scene where an aged Nazi (called "the Hag") tells a defrocked priest (Fitzpatrick, or his nickname, "Fitz") what really happened that day in Fátima. Afterward I will expound on why I wrote this fictional account and why I believe that what transpired at the Cova da Iria, in Fátima, is in fact a harbinger of deception—a precursor to events that will come upon the earth.

Excerpt from *The Revealing* by Lynn Marzulli

"I have much to show you, Fitzpatrick, and I can't be concerned with what you might do. Bruno will see that you behave. Let's begin, shall we? You are asking yourself why?" Without waiting for a reply the Hag continued.

"It is because I want to show you deeper things, the hidden mysteries, what has been kept in the secret places for millennia, but now, in our day, will be revealed."

Fitz glanced at Bruno then at the Hag realizing that there was no choice but to listen.

"Look at the screen Fitzpatrick," the Hag said, as he dimmed the lights very low, but not completely dark as before. Fitzpatrick stared at the screen, a feeling of dread coursing through his body, like a poison. The screen flickered a few times, and then he saw a black and white movie. The quality was poor, grainy.

"This was taken in 1917," the Hag began, "In Fátima, Portugal."

Fitz wondered, as he stared at the screen.

"There is no sound, Fitzpatrick, so if you don't mind I will narrate for us," the Hag informed. "You see the crowd? Over seventy thousand people were gathered in Fátima. And do you know why? Because three children claimed to see an apparition of the Blessed Virgin Mary. They had been told that she would appear and perform a miracle. So on that day people gathered, peasants, workers, farmers, the intelligencia of the day, newspaper reporters. It had been raining all morning, Fitzpatrick. But the 'pilgrims' remained vigilant. The miracle was supposed to happen at twelve noon. But the Virgin was late. Can you imagine, late?"

And he burst out laughing again.

"She finally showed up an hour later. One of the children pointed to where she was. Of course no one else saw anything but the children. But watch here Fitzpatrick. You see the film—how jerky it becomes? It is because the cameraman is pointing the camera in a new direction, toward the sky. Look. The sky is parting, and what do you see now? The sun spinning? Watch …see it fall to the earth. Now the people fall to their knees. Everyone is terrified. The world is coming to an end. The 'sun' is dancing and falling down to earth. Like your Chicken Little story."

The Hag laughed again.

"Stupid peasants. What do you see Fitzpatrick? It's

not the sun, is it? It's a disk. Look at it reflect the sun off its shiny exterior. See the way it comes close to the crowd. Everyone who had been standing in the rain experienced his or her clothes becoming dry. Some even reported miracles. And here's something that you should know. This is the only film remaining of that day. Every other photograph was confiscated. Are you aware that a Catholic priest devoted his entire life to discovering what really happened? He is dead now, and his work remains unpublished, confiscated by the Vatican."

Of course the above scene is completely fictional, but it is based on several books, most notably, *Celestial Secrets* by Joaquim Fernandes and Fina d'Armada, *Heavenly Lights* by Fernandes and d'Armada, and *Messages from Heaven* by Jim Tetlow, about the events at Fátima. Remember in 1917 the word "UFO" or "flying saucer" was not in the lexicon of the local inhabitants. Those terms would come later in the twentieth century. The people who saw the "Miracle of the Sun" had no reference point, nothing in their realm of experience to compare with what they were looking at. I realize that the Catholic Church has embraced the apparitions, and the previous Pope, Pope John Paul II, credited the failure of his assassination attempt to "Our Lady of Fátima." He also entrusted the third millennium to the apparition as well as entrusted the world to the "Lady of Fátima."

However, one must remember that the Pope is a man and that the priests, bishops, and clergy who witnessed the event were also men and that all of us are, in fact, not infallible. In their two coauthored books *Heavenly Lights: The Apparitions and the UFO Phenomenon* and *Celestial Secrets: The Hidden History of the Fátima Cover-Up*, Portuguese historians Dr. Joaquim Fernandes and Fina d'Armada cite eyewitness accounts of the Fátima event. I have included these eyewitness accounts from

Heavenly Lights because they add an important perspective that was not addressed in my previously provided thumbnail sketch and fictional accounts of the event.

Eyewitness Testimonies of the Event as Taken from *Heavenly Lights*

JOSE' PROENCE DE ALMEIDA GARRET, A LAWYER:
Moments before, the sun had broken overhead through a dense layer of clouds that would have otherwise hidden it, allowing it to shine clearly and intensely. I turned toward that magnet that attracted every gaze, and I could see that it was similar to a disk with a distinct and lively border, luminous and lucent, but harmless.

NEWSPAPER, BEIRA BAIZA:
The sun uncovered itself, and had a diverse gradation, appearing sometimes like a solar globe…enclosed by an aureole of flames, other times a metallic disk as if of silver.

MARIO GOHINO, AN ENGINEER:
In a radiant sky, the Sun could be looked at straight-on and with eyes wide open, without blinking, as if we were looking at a disk of polished glass illuminated from behind, with a rainbow of iridescence on its periphery, seeming to have a rotating movement.… And the Sun did not have the brilliance that hurt our eyes on normal days, as it was a majestic disk, magnetic, which attracted us and sort of revolved in the immense sky.…

RAIO DE LUZ, A RELIGIOUS PERIODICAL OF THE TIME:
Suddenly a luminous disk, the size of a great host, but one which could be gazed upon as one gazes at the moon,

appeared, as if it stood out from the Sun, descending visibly…

GILBERTO DOS SANTOS:
I saw the Sun, seeming a dull, silver disk, but more luminous than the moon.

MARIA ROMANA:
The Sun gave the appearance of a globe of dull silver fire, surrounded by a very dark purplish disk.

ANA MARIA CAMARA:
I saw a very clear, silvery blue disk, without rays…

More eyewitness accounts could be cited, but I think the point has been made. The official version of the story was packaged in the religious terminology, specifically Catholic dogma, of the day. What I mean by Catholic dogma is that the apparition was declared to be Mary, the mother of Jesus. Authors Fernandes and d'Armada have researched this aspect and, according to them, they believe that there was a rush to judgment in this regard. They have interviewed a fourth witness to the events that until recently had been overlooked. However, based on the multiple descriptions of a "silver disk" and a "sun" that did not have the blinding qualities of the sun, it appears from the eyewitness accounts above that what people were looking at was a craft of some sort. I believe that if you or I could somehow transport ourselves back to 1917 in Fátima, Portugal, we would point overhead and say, "I can't believe it, a flying saucer!" Or maybe, "Look at that, a UFO.…"

One extremely interesting aspect of the Fátima apparitions was the secrets that were told to the seers. There were three secrets in total, and the first two were revealed to the public. One of which was a vision of hell and the other a request to "consecrate" Russia, or there would be turmoil in the world, and Russia would spread her errors (Communism?) throughout the world.

The third and final secret was recorded in a letter and was supposed to be revealed publicly after 1960. It was not and caused speculation both inside and outside of the Catholic church as to the letter's contents. Pope John Paul II finally revealed it on June 6, 2000, and, in doing so, created controversy regarding the authenticity of the secret. The Pope declared that the secret had to do with an assassination attempt on his life and the persecution of the Catholic Church. There are those within the church that believed that what the Pope read was not the third secret, hence the controversy.

The lone surviving visionary, Lucia, had been in a Carmelite convent for most of her life, which prevented her from talking to anyone because of her vows. She remained silent until her death.

So why am I bringing all of this to your attention? In my opinion the "secrets" of Fátima drew people away from biblical truth. They usurped the authority of scripture with extrabiblical revelations. Why else would Pope John Paul II dedicate the world to "Our Lady of Fátima"? This one supernatural event, that of the Fátima apparition, which is controversial at best, shifted millions of peoples' belief from the solidity of biblical scripture to the "visions" of the three seers who may have been part of a great deception.

Here are some interesting questions that I raise regarding the event.

1. Since there are photographs of the various details of the event, just not the object that appeared, we know that there were photographers at Cova da Iria on October 13, 1917. So where are the photographs of the "miracle of the sun"?

2. Why was the surviving seer, Lucia, whisked off to a convent and essentially silenced?

3. Why have the revelations or "secrets" of Fátima seemed to have overshadowed the relevancy of biblical scripture?

4. Why has the testimony of many eyewitnesses who claimed to have seen a disk been ignored?

Since 1917 the events that transpired at Fátima changed the worldview of millions of people. The "Miracle of the Sun" lasted less than half an hour; yet, the event continues to affect millions of people around the world.

What I take umbrage with is that the revelations of Fátima— the secrets that I mentioned earlier, especially the third secret— have usurped the Bible as the source for truth, and in its place provided "secrets" that play upon the superstitions and gullibility of the masses. What is interesting is that some of the clergy of the Catholic Church state that the third secret has never been revealed. Although the Pope John Paul II claimed to have read the third secret in 2001, there are those within the church that believe it was not the secret written down by the seer, Lucia. What is more, if this secret is so important to the church, then why was not it read when it was supposed to be in 1960?[609]

In our book *Petrus Romanus*, we, too, investigated the secrets of Fátima and found an intriguing connection between the Vatileaks scandal of 2011–2012 and a possible Vatican cover-up of the complete vision of Fátima (and related prophecies). Our discovery began with a work by famous Italian media personality, journalist, and author, Antonio Socci, whose manuscript *The Fourth Secret of Fátima* claims the Holy See has repressed information concerning the true secrets delivered in Marian apparitions to three shepherd children in the rural Portuguese village of Fátima in 1917. At the center of his investigation, Socci focuses on a powerful papal contender for the role of Petrus Romanus or "Peter the Roman" (the Final Pope)—Cardinal Tarcisio Pietro (Peter) Bertone, who was born in Romano Canavese (the Roman). Among other things, Cardinal Bertone is, at the time this book heads to the printer, second in command at the Vatican. As the Secretary of State and the pope's Camerlengo (Italian for "Chamberlain"), he is responsible during a papal vacancy to serve as acting Head of State of the Vatican City until "the time of agreement" and the election of a new pope. Within uncharacteristically explosive accusations against Cardinal Bertone published online ("Dear Cardinal Bertone: Who—Between You and Me—Is Deliberately Lying?"[610]) we first discover how, after significant time and investigation, Mr. Socci concluded the Vatican had withheld an important part of the Fátima revelation during its celebrated press conference and release of "The Message of Fátima," June 26, 2000. On pages 456–465 of *Petrus Romanus*, we wrote:

> Socci describes in the introduction to his book how at first he truly believed the Vatican's official version of the Fátima message, prepared at that time by Cardinal Ratzinger (current Pope Benedict XVI) and Monsignor Tarcisio Bertone (possible next and final pope), which with its release to the public claimed to be the final secret. Then Socci came across an article by Italian journalist Vittorio Messori, entitled "The Fátima Secret, the Cell of Sister Lucy Has Been Sealed," and a series of questions for which Socci had no answers cast suspicions on the Vatican's authorized publication. Why would Messori, whom Socci describes as "a great journalist, extremely precise...the most translated Catholic columnist in the world,"[611] want to challenge the Church's official version of the third secret without good cause, he reasoned. Not long after, Socci came across a second similar thesis published in Italy by a young and careful writer named Solideo Paolini. The thesis convinced Socci to begin a probe of his own focusing on the biggest question of them all: Was a portion of Lucy's handwritten document, which contained the principal words "of the Blessed Virgin Mother" concerning end-times conditions at Rome, being withheld from public view by the Vatican due to its potentially explosive content?

Socci's suspicions only deepened after he requested an interview (well ahead of his work, *The Fourth Secret of Fátima*, which later cast doubts on Rome's official story) with Cardinal Bertone, who, together with Joseph Ratzinger, had coauthored the June 26, 2000, Vatican document that purportedly released the final segment of the "The Message of Fátima."[612]

"I've searched many influential authorities inside the Curia, like Cardinal Bertone, today Secretary of State in the Vatican, who was central to the publication of the Secret in 2000," Socci says. "The Cardinal, who actually favored me with his personal consideration, having asked me to conduct conferences in his former diocese of Genoa, [now] didn't deem it necessary to [even] answer my request for an interview. He was within his rights to make this choice, of course, but this only increased the fear of the existence of embarrassing questions, and most of all, that there is something (extremely important) which needs to be kept hidden."[613]

Though not expecting to uncover such a colossal enigma, in the end Socci was left convinced that two sets of the Fátima secret actually exist: one that the public has seen, and another, which for reasons yet unknown, the Vatican is keeping buried.

At the beginning of this possible plot was a description of the third secret given by Cardinal Angelo Sodano a full five weeks before the June 26, 2000, "Message of Fátima" was delivered by Rome. Sodano's comments came during Pope John Paul II's beautification of Jacinta and Francisco at Fátima, when he surprised many in a speech, saying the vision of a "bishop clothed in white" who makes his way with great effort past the corpses of bishops, priests, and many laypersons, is only "apparently dead" when he falls to the ground under a burst of gunfire.[614]

Using the added language "apparently dead," Cardinal Sodano went on to suggest the Fátima vision had been fulfilled in the 1981 assassination attempt against John Paul II. "It appeared evident to His Holiness that it was 'a motherly hand which guided the bullet's path,' enabling the 'dying Pope' to halt 'at the threshold of death.'"[615]

Though some applauded Sodano's presentation that day, others saw in it, and him, a concerted cover-up, as the Fátima prophecy and the alleged fulfillment in 1981 bore significant differences. The *Washington Post* was happy to point out these glaring contradictions on July 1, 2000, when under the stinging headline, "Third Secret Spurs More Questions: Fátima Interpretation Departs from Vision," the newspaper opined:

On May 13, Cardinal Angelo Sodano, a top Vatican official, announced the imminent release of the carefully guarded text. He said the Third Secret of Fátima foretold not the end of the world, as some had speculated, but the May 13, 1981, shooting of Pope John Paul II in St. Peter's Square.

Sodano said the manuscript...tells of a "bishop clothed in white" who, while making his way amid corpses of martyrs, "falls to the ground, apparently dead, under a burst of gunfire."

But the text released Monday (June 26) leaves no doubt about the bishop's fate, saying that he "was killed by a group of soldiers who fired bullets and arrows at him." Everyone with the pontiff also dies: bishops, priests, monks, nuns and lay people. John Paul survived his shooting at the hands of a single gunman, Mehmet Ali Agca, and no one in the crowd was harmed in the attack.[616]

Other facts the *Washington Post* did not point out is how, according to the prophecy, the pope is killed in "a big city half in ruins" while walking to the top of a mountain and kneeling at the foot of a cross. John Paul was riding in the pope's car through St. Peter's Square, not walking; there was no big mountain or kneeling at a cross; and the city was not half destroyed. And then there is the contradictory testimony by Cardinal Ratzinger (current Pope Benedict XVI) himself from 1984, which he gave in an interview with the Pauline Sisters' newsletter (*Jesus Magazine*) and which was republished a year later in *The Ratzinger Report*, in an article titled "Here Is Why the Faith Is in Crisis." In this discussion, Ratzinger, who had read the actual Fátima secret, said the vision involved "dangers threatening the faith and the life of the Christian and therefore [the life] of the world" as well as marking the beginning of the end times.[617] Additionally, he said, "the things contained in [the] third secret correspond to what has been announced in Scripture and has been said again and again in many other Marian apparitions" and that, "If it is not made public, at least for the time being, it is in order to prevent religious prophecy from being mistaken for a quest for the sensational."[618]

Concerned Catholics have since contrasted this 1984 testimony with the more recent report by Ratzinger, and have wondered when, where, and under what circumstance his account changed. The 1981 assassination attempt against John Paul II certainly did not fulfill the published parts of the Fátima vision or correspond to the "last times" as depicted in the Bible. And then there is the affirmation by the Vatican's most respected scholars who had deduced from years of studying the Fátima prophecy that it concerned an end-time global crisis of faith emanating from the highest echelons at Rome. Celebrated Cardinal Mario Luigi Ciappi (1909–1996) served as the personal theologian to five popes including John Paul II and unreservedly held that in "the third secret it is foretold, among other things, that the great apostasy in the Church *begins at the top*" (emphasis added).[619] Cardinal Silvio Oddi added in a March 1990 interview with

Il Sabato magazine in Rome, Italy: "The Third Secret alluded to dark times for the Church: grave confusions and troubling apostasies within Catholicism itself.… If we consider the grave crisis we have lived through since the [Vatican II] Council, the signs that this prophecy has been fulfilled do not seem to be lacking."[620] Even more impressive in his testimony was the late Father Joaquin Alonso, who knew Sister Lucy personally, had conversations with her, was for sixteen years the archivist at Fátima, and,before his death in 1981, stated the following concerning the third secret:

The text makes concrete references to the crisis of faith within the Church and to the negligence of the pastors themselves [and the] internal struggles in the very bosom of the Church and of grave pastoral negligence *by the upper hierarchy*… terrible things are to happen. These form the content of the third part of the Secret… [and] like the secret of La Salette, for example, there are more concrete references to the internal struggles of Catholics or to the fall of priests and religious. Perhaps it even refers to the *failures of the upper hierarchy* of the Church. For that matter, nonc of this is foreign to other communications Sister Lucy has had on this subject.[621]

Perhaps most unvarying among those who actually had access to and read the Fátima message was Jesuit Malachi Martin, a close personal friend of Pope Paul VI who worked within the Holy See doing research on the Dead Sea Scrolls, publishing articles in journals on Semitic paleography, and teaching Aramaic, Hebrew, and sacred Scripture. As a member of the Vatican Advisory Council and personal secretary to renowned Jesuit Cardinal Augustin Bea, Martin had privileged information pertaining to secretive church and world issues, including the third secret of Fátima, *which Martin hinted spelled out parts of the plan to formerly install the dreaded False Prophet (Petrus Romanus?) during a "Final Conclave."* Comparing the conflicting statements between Cardinal Ratzinger and Malachi Martin, Father Charles Fiore, a good friend of the murdered priest Alfred J. Kunz (discussed elsewhere in this book) and the late eminent theologian Fr. John Hardon, said in a taped interview: "We have two different Cardinal Ratzingers; we have two different messages. But Malachi Martin was consistent all the way through."[622]

Wikipedia's entry on the "Three Secrets of Fátima" adds:

On a syndicated radio broadcast, Father Malachi Martin was asked the following question by a caller: "I had a Jesuit priest tell me more of the Third Secret of Fátima years ago, in Perth. He said, among other things, the last pope would be under control of Satan…. Any comment on that?" Fr. Martin responded, "Yes, it sounds as if they were reading, or being told, the text of the Third Secret." In a taped interview with Bernard Janzen, Fr. Martin was asked the following question: "Who are the people who are working so hard to suppress Fátima?" Fr. Martin responded, "A bunch, a whole bunch, of Catholic prelates in Rome, who belong to Satan. They're servants of Satan. And the servants of Satan outside the Church, in various organizations; they want to destroy the Catholicism of the Church, and keep it as a stabilizing factor in human affairs. It's an alliance. A dirty alliance, a filthy alliance…." In the same interview, Fr. Martin also said with respect to Lucia [Lucy of Fátima] that, "They've (The Vatican) published forged letters in her name; they've made her say things she didn't want to say. They put statements on her lips she never made."[623]

One thing is certain: Something unnerving did seem to be happening around and with Sister Lucy in the lead-up to the release of the so-called final secret. After all, the first two parts of the message of Fátima had been publically issued by her bishop in 1941, and the third secret had been sent to the Holy See with instructions that it be made public in 1960. That year was chosen, according to Lucy, because the "Holy Mother" had revealed to her that it would then be when "the Message will appear more clear." And, lo and behold, it was immediately following 1960 that Vatican II set in motion what many conservative Catholics today believe is a crisis of faith in the form of Roman heresies. And though there could have been much more to the revelation than just a Vatican II warning, and the secret was not released in 1960 as it was supposed to be anyway (so we may never know), when Pope John XXIII read the contents of the secret, he refused to publish it, and it remained under lock and key until it was supposedly disclosed in the year 2000. If the first two secrets were any indication of the scope and accuracy of the third one, they had been amazingly insightful, including the "miracle of the sun" that was witnessed "by over 70,000 persons (including nonbelievers hoping to dispel the apparitions), whereby the sun itself [seemed to be] dislodged from its setting and performed miraculous maneuvers while emitting astonishing light displays; the end of World War I; the name of the pope who would be reigning at the beginning of World War II; the extraordinary heavenly phenomenon that would be witnessed worldwide foretelling of the beginning of World War II; the ascendance of Russia (a weak and insignificant nation in 1917) to an evil monolithic power that would afflict the world with suffering and death."[624]

But something about the third and final secret was different, a phenomenon evidently to be avoided and obfuscated at all costs by the hierarchy of Rome. At a minimum, it spoke of the apostatizing of the clergy and dogma that followed Vatican II. And yet perhaps these were simply devices to lead to something more sinister, elements so dark that it was keeping Lucy awake at night. When she finally had written down the secret in 1944 under obedience to Rome, she had a hard time doing so because of its terrifying contents. It had taken a fresh visit from the "Holy Mother" herself to convince Lucy it was okay. Then in the years following, she had been ordered by the Vatican to remain silent concerning its disclosure.

Under orders from the pope, visits to her for hours at a time were made by Cardinal Bertone. During the visits, the two of them would go over the diminutive aspects of the vision in private. This happened in 2000, again in 2001, and again in 2003. When, at age ninety-seven, the Carmelite nun finally passed away (2005), taking whatever secrets remained with her to the grave, her behavior at the last seemed odd to Catholics who understood Roman doctrinal "salvation" implications. Antonio Socci comments on this, pointing out that the long visits with the aged seer were not videotaped or recorded for posterity because viewers would have seen for themselves the psychological pressure that was being exerted on the cloistered sister. "These thoughts came back to my mind while I was reading a passage of Bertone's book, in which the Cardinal remembers that at one point the seer was 'irritated', and she told him 'I'm not going to confession!'" About this, Socci wonders, "What kind of question could Sister Lucy answer to so strongly? Maybe someone was reminding the old Sister of the ecclesiastical power, and hinting that she would 'not get absolution'? We don't know, because the prelate [Bertone]—who knows and remembers the Sister's (quite tough) answer very well—says he literally 'forgot' what his question was."[625]

It appears in truth that poor Lucy was trapped inside a sinister ring of *Romanita Omertà Siciliani* or "Mafia Code of Silence" imposed by Rome. Yet Socci believes the full truth of Fátima may have gotten out anyway, and based on his investigation, he offers a brave theory in his book *The Fourth Secret of Fátima* about what actually transpired in 2000 behind the Vatican's walls. John Vennari summarizes Socci's shocking hypothesis this way:

> Socci believes that when John Paul II decided to release the Secret, a power-struggle of sorts erupted in the Vatican. He postulates that John Paul II and Cardinal Ratzinger wanted to release the Secret in its entirety, but Cardinal Sodano, then Vatican Secretary of State, opposed the idea. And opposition from a Vatican Secretary of State is formidable.

A compromise was reached that sadly reveals heroic virtue from none of the main players.

The "Bishop dressed in white" vision, which is the four pages written by Sister Lucy would be initially revealed by Cardinal Sodano, along with his ludicrous interpretation that the Secret is nothing more than the predicted 1981 assassination attempt on Pope John Paul II.

At the same time, at the May 13 2000 beatification cere- mony of Jacinta and Francisco, Pope John Paul II would "reveal" the other part—the most "terrifying part"—of the Secret obliquely in his sermon. It was here that John Paul II spoke on the Apocaplyse: "Another portent appeared in Heaven; behold, a great red dragon" (Apoc. 12:3). These words from the first reading of the Mass make us think of the great struggle between good and evil, showing how, when man puts God aside, he can- not achieve happiness, but ends up destroying himself... The Message of Fátima is a call to conversion, alerting humanity to have nothing to do with the "dragon" whose "tail swept down a third of the stars of Heaven, and dragged them to the earth" (Apoc. 12:4).

The Fathers of the Church have always interpreted the stars as the clergy, and the stars swept up in the dragon's tail indicates a great number of churchmen who would be under the influ- ence of the devil. This was Pope John Paul II's way of explaining that the Third Secret also predicts a great apostasy.[626] (brackets and emphasis in original)

If Socci is correct in this analysis, Bishop Richard Nelson Williamson, an English traditionalist Catholic and member of the Society of Saint Pius X who opposes changes in the Catholic Church brought on by Vatican II, may have verified his hypothesis in 2005 when he related how a priest acquaintance of his from Austria shared privately that Cardinal Ratzinger had confessed: "I have two problems on my conscience: Archbishop Lefebvre and Fátima. As to the latter, my hand was forced." Who could have "forced" Ratzinger's hand to go along with a false or partial statement on the final Fátima secret? Was it pressure from the papal office, or, as Williamson questions, "Some hidden power behind both Pope and Cardinal?"[627] If Pope John Paul II's sermon at Fátima did in fact speak to the "terrifying part" of the final secret—*as in the dragon's tail sweeping down a third of the clergy to do his bidding*—we are left with the unsettling impression that at least 33 percent (Masonic marker) of the Vatican's hierarchy *are committed to a satanic plan.* Will this involve a return of that "disc" that first appeared in Fátima as a harbinger of deception?

15 | When Chariots of the Fallen Star Gods Appear

"It was the darndest thing I've ever seen. It was big, it was very bright, it changed colors and it was about the size of the moon. We watched it for ten minutes, but none of us could figure out what it was. One thing's for sure, I'll never make fun of people who say they've seen unidentified objects in the sky." —Former US President Jimmy Carter to reporters during the 1976 presidential election campaign

In 2006, Dr. Michael S. Heiser, Hebrew scholar and expert in ancient Semitic languages, was invited to speak at the formative meeting of a new think tank for evangelical Christian scholars, pastors, and lay researchers concerned with the spread of neo-pagan/occult worldviews in society and the Church. His lecture was entitled, "Ancient Mysteries and Alien Gods: Why People Reject Christ for a Paranormal Worldview." According to Dr. Heiser, there were perhaps only a half dozen people in the room who had ever heard about ufology in any academic sense, and even those aware of it had never been confronted with the physical evidence and peer-reviewed research with respect to UFOs and alleged alien abductions. They, like so many leaders in Christendom, had simply dismissed the subject altogether. "My task," he later wrote, "was to convince them in one hour that the subject was real, merited academic study, and was of special concern to Christians, primarily because these phenomena are a critical means of advancing an occult, worldview agenda. This is true even if those behind UFOs and abductions are not demonic manifestations, though that approach is a coherent one."[628]

Heiser went on to explain that the majority of Americans believe that Earth has been visited by aliens, that they have seen a UFO (and believe it to have been extraterrestrial in origin), and that the US government is deliberately hiding proof of alien life and contact. Thus, if Christian leaders substantially ignore the subject of UFOs, alien visitations, and evidence of a government cover-up, they forfeit their ability to answer a number of sincere and compelling questions from people within the Church and in secular communities and, thus, become worldview irrelevant to a large percentage of the culture.

Over the near decade since Heiser's presentation to the evangelical think tank, the need for Christian leaders to remain relevant on the issue of UFO-related phenomena has increased significantly. This is partly due to a new global wave of unidentified objects observed around the world; increasing openness by public observers with readily available technology (such as cell phones with cameras) who are progressively more comfortable sharing what they have captured on film; and, finally, what can only be described as a watershed moment in history in which former high-ranking members of the military, airline pilots, aviation experts, and government officials are coming forward now to admit compelling accounts of UFO and alien-contact events and top-secret government investigations, which, disconcertingly, appear designed to move mankind toward an imminent tipping point of acceptance of the larger extraterrestrial implications.

Among those who have stepped forward recently are former Air Force Colonol Charles Halt, retired Army Colonel John Alexander, retired Air Force Colonel Bill Coleman (chief spokesman for Project Blue Book 1961–1963), and Nick Pope, who served for twenty-one years at the British Government's Ministry of Defence, specifically heading up their department responsible for investigating UFOs. The occasion that most recently brought these men and others together was a September 22, 2012, symposium hosted by the Smithsonian-affiliated National Atomic Testing Museum (NATM).

Moderator Allan Palmer, CEO and executive director of the National Atomic Testing Museum; retired Air Force Colonol Robert Friend; retired Air Force Colonol William Coleman; retired Air Force Colonol Charles Halt; former UK Ministry of Defense UFO investigator Nick Pope; and retired Army Colonel John Alexander

During the NATM event, which presented experts who had worked directly and indirectly in official government capacities investigating UFOs in the past, Charles Halt accused the federal government of having a "secret agency" that is concealing from the public UFO activity directly related to extraterrestrial visitations. Halt was the deputy base commander at Brentwaters Air Base during the famous Rendlesham Forest UFO incident, and it was his official "Unexplained Lights" memo (below, dated January 13, 1981) to the British Ministry of Defence detailing the event that was later released under the Freedom of Information Act and published in British Press that cast light on the unusualness of what happened there.

DEPARTMENT OF THE AIR FORCE
HEADQUARTERS 81ST COMBAT SUPPORT GROUP (USAFE)
APO NEW YORK 09755

REPLY TO
ATTN OF. CD   13 Jan 81

SUBJECT: Unexplained Lights

TO: RAF/CC

1. Early in the morning of 27 Dec 80 (approximately 0300L), two USAF security police patrolmen saw unusual lights outside the back gate at RAF Woodbridge. Thinking an aircraft might have crashed or been forced down, they called for permission to go outside the gate to investigate. The on-duty flight chief responded and allowed three patrolmen to proceed on foot. The individuals reported seeing a strange glowing object in the forest. The object was described as being metalic in appearance and triangular in shape, approximately two to three meters across the base and approximately two meters high. It illuminated the entire forest with a white light. The object itself had a pulsing red light on top and a bank(s) of blue lights underneath. The object was hovering or on legs. As the patrolmen approached the object, it maneuvered through the trees and disappeared. At this time the animals on a nearby farm went into a frenzy. The object was briefly sighted approximately an hour later near the back gate.

2. The next day, three depressions 1 1/2" deep and 7" in diameter were found where the object had been sighted on the ground. The following night (29 Dec 80) the area was checked for radiation. Beta/gamma readings of 0.1 milliroentgens were recorded with peak readings in the three depressions and near the center of the triangle formed by the depressions. A nearby tree had moderate (.05-.07) readings on the side of the tree toward the depressions.

3. Later in the night a red sun-like light was seen through the trees. It moved about and pulsed. At one point it appeared to throw off glowing particles and then broke into five separate white objects and then disappeared. Immediately thereafter, three star-like objects were noticed in the sky, two objects to the north and one to the south, all of which were about 10° off the horizon. The objects moved rapidly in sharp angular movements and displayed red, green and blue lights. The objects to the north appeared to be elliptical through an 8-12 power lens. They then turned to full circles. The objects to the north remained in the sky for an hour or more. The object to the south was visible for two or three hours and beamed down a stream of light from time to time. Numerous individuals, including the undersigned, witnessed the activities in paragraphs 2 and 3.

CHARLES I. HALT, Lt Col, USAF
Deputy Base Commander

The January 13, 1981, Halt Memo (declassified)

Three weeks following the September 22, 2012, NATM presentations mentioned above, Nick Pope was back in the news under the fantastic headline: "Britain Has Alien-War Weapons, Says Former

Government Advisor [Nick Pope]." The story unveiled how, behind the scenes, the United Kingdom's Ministry of Defence (MoD) evidently takes the idea of aliens and even potential conflict with malevolent extraterrestrials very seriously. Hinting at what Britain is doing to anticipate intergalactic war, Pope admitted: "We do have several prototype aircraft and drones and other weapons you won't see on the news for another 10–15 years so if we did face a threat from the unknown then even if there is no Torchwood around now [Torchwood is the alien-hunting team from the BBC science-fiction series of the same name], there would be something like it by then and they certainly would have some great kit to help in the fight."[629] Pope then explained how such a threat from a source beyond Earth could lead to a global world front, saying, "One possibility would be trying to unite all the nations of the world. For those who think that far-fetched, Ronald Reagan once hinted at it in a speech to the UN. He said, 'I occasionally think how quickly we would set aside our difference[s] if we faced some alien threat from the other side.'"[630] John Dewey, professor of philosophy at Columbia University, reflected the same as far back as 1917 when he remarked, "The best way to unite all the nations on this globe would be an attack from some other planet,"[631] an idea confirmed by political scientists Alexander Wendt and Raymond Duvall in their landmark essay, "Sovereignty and the UFO," which argued, "The ontological threat is that even if the ETs were benign, their confirmed presence would create tremendous pressure for a unified human response, or world government."[632]

We wanted to know more about the potential alien threat; the Rendlesham Forest event (what Nick Pope now calls "Britain's Roswell"); the actual 1947 Roswell, New Mexico, incident; and UFO investigations in general, so we contacted experts in these specific fields, including Nick Pope, Dr. Bruce Maccabee, nuclear physicist Stanton Friedman, and Colonol Jesse Marcel Jr. (the only man the US government admits handled the Roswell debris). What follows are excerpts from the larger transcripts of those discussions.

Interview with Nick Pope:[633]

HORN: Nick. Thanks for joining me today. Earlier this year, I emailed you when Britain declared it was going to open its MoD UFO files to the public. Because you had run this department for the British government, I wanted to know if we should expect anything unusual in these materials. You emailed me back to say that I should not expect a smoking gun, but that there were some devils in the details. What has been the result of the MoD files going public?

POPE: Although a good deal of material is already available at the National Archives and on the MoD website, the rest of the UFO files have yet to be made public. Two separate things are happening right now. Firstly, 24 Defence Intelligence Staff UFO files are going to be considered for release. These were part of a much larger batch of files (on various subjects) that had been contaminated with asbestos. Originally it was feared they'd have to be destroyed, sparking outrage from historians and leading to various conspiracy theories. At huge cost, the files have now been decontaminated and can be considered for release in the normal way. Numerous ufologists have made Freedom of Information Act requests in relation to these files. The second thing that's happening is that the MoD has decided to release its entire archive of UFO files, not least because of the increasing burden of responding to FOI requests (the MoD get more FOI requests in relation to UFOs than on any other subject, including the war in Iraq). This is a massive job and may take months, if not years, as personal details of witnesses have to be removed, along with any information that would genuinely compromise national security—e.g. information on the capability of military radar systems.

HORN: When and why was the MoD's UFO project set up?

POPE: The MoD's UFO project has its roots in a 1950 initiative by the then Chief Scientific Adviser, Sir Henry Tizard. He said that UFO sightings shouldn't be dismissed out of hand without some form of proper scientific study. The MoD then set up a body called the Flying Saucer Working Party, to look into the phenomenon. It reported its sceptical conclusions (that UFO sightings were attributable to misidentifications, hoaxes or delusions) in 1951 and recommended that no further action be taken. But there was a series of high-profile UFO sightings in 1952 when UFOs were tracked on radar and seen by military pilots. This forced the RAF and the MoD to think again, and the Department has been investigating UFO sightings pretty much continuously since then. To date, there have been over 10,000 sightings reported to the MoD.

HORN: What is the MoD's policy on UFOs?

POPE: The policy is to investigate UFO sightings to see whether there's evidence of anything of any defence significance, i.e. evidence of any threat to the defence of the UK, or information that may be of use to us, scientifically or militarily. Having a UFO project in no way implies a corporate belief in extraterrestrial visitation. It simply reflects the fact that we keep a watchful eye on our airspace and want to know about anything operating in the United Kingdom's Air Defence Region. Although the British effort was on a much smaller scale, the terms of reference and methodology were virtually identical to that of the United States Air Force study, Project Blue Book.

HORN: MoD also acknowledged that a government UFO unit, known as S4(Air) and DI55, existed. Tells us about this unit and what it did (or does).

POPE: S4(Air) no longer exists. It was a division that had responsibility for UFO investigations some years ago. Like any bureaucracy, the MoD undergoes frequent reorganisations where divisions are opened, closed, merged, split or restructured. It's a nightmare! So, over the years, all sorts of different areas have had responsibility for UFOs, leading some researchers to wrongly conclude there are many different areas of the MoD all working on the subject. In fact, at any one time, there'll be a division that has the lead for policy and investigations (i.e. where I worked) and a number of other areas on whose specialist skills and expertise the lead division can call. DI55 is part of the Defence Intelligence Staff. They were one of the specialist branches that I could bring in to assist me with certain aspects of my UFO investigations. Up until a few years ago I couldn't talk about this aspect of my work at all, or even acknowledge the existence of DI55. Recently, however, details have emerged under FOI, including some documents relating to my own dealings with them. But as I'm sure you'll understand, this is still an area of my work that I can't discuss in any great detail.

HORN: How were you recruited into the UFO Project?

POPE: I joined the Ministry of Defence in 1985. At the time, the policy was to move people every 2 or 3 years—either on level transfer or promotion—so that everybody gained experience in a wide range of different jobs: policy, operations, personnel, finance, etc. I'd done 2 or 3 different jobs and prior to taking up my post on the UFO project I was working in a division called Secretariat(Air Staff), where I'd been seconded into the Air Force Operations Room in the Joint Operations Centre. I worked there in the run-up to the first Gulf War, during the war itself, and in the aftermath of the conflict. It was while working there that I was approached and asked whether, after I was released from duties in the Joint Operations Centre, I would like to run the UFO project, which was embedded in another part of Secretariat(Air Staff). I accepted the invitation. So, in a sense, I was headhunted.

HORN: Did your views change from the time you started working with MoD until you left the department?

POPE: I knew little about the subject before I joined and I certainly had no belief in extraterrestrials. So while I was open-minded in all my investigations, my start point was broadly sceptical. As I began to read into the archive of previous files, and as I began to undertake my own official research and investigation, my views began to change and I became more open to the possibility that some UFOs had more exotic explanations. What impressed me most were cases where UFOs were seen by trained observers such as police officers, where they were tracked on radar, where they were seen by pilots, and where there was evidence to suggest that UFOs were performing speeds and manoeuvres way ahead of the capabilities of even our most advanced aircraft. My position now is that while I can't say what these UFOs are, the phenomenon raises important defence, national security and flight safety issues. I've seen no proof that these things are extraterrestrial, but I don't rule out this possibility.

HORN: What were your procedures / protocols for investigating UFO sightings?

POPE: We used to receive 200–300 reports each year and the methodology of an investigation is fairly standard. Firstly, you interview the witness to obtain as much information as possible about the sighting: date, time and location of the sighting, description of the object, its speed, its height, etc. Then you attempt to correlate the sighting with known aerial activity such as civil flights, military exercises or weather balloon launches. We could check with the Royal Greenwich Observatory to see if astronomical phenomena such as meteors or fireballs might explain what was seen. We could check to see whether any UFOs seen visually had been tracked on radar. If we had a photograph or video, we could get various MoD specialists to enhance and analyse the imagery. We could also liaise with staff at the Ballistic Missile Early Warning System at RAF Fylingdales, where they have space-tracking radar. Finally, on various scientific and technical issues, we could liaise with the Defence

Intelligence Staff, although as I've said previously, this is an area of my work that I can't discuss in any detail.

HORN: What did you conclude about the majority of your investigations?

POPE: I concluded that sightings could be categorised as follows. Around 80% could be explained as misidentifications of something mundane, such as aircraft lights, weather balloons, satellites, meteors, etc. In approximately 15% of cases there was insufficient information to make a firm assessment. That left around 5% of sightings that seemed to defy any conventional explanation. But while we could say with reasonable certainty what these 5% weren't, we couldn't say what they were. They were by definition unknown, unexplained, or whatever word you care to use.

HORN: The Flying Saucer Working Party was set up in October 1950 by Ministry of Defence Chief Scientific Adviser Sir Henry Tizard. Was this a reaction to the 1947 Roswell incident or something else?

POPE: It wasn't a reaction to the Roswell incident, but to increasing numbers of UFO sightings in the UK and elsewhere, and to the associated media coverage. As a scientist, Tizard knew that any assessment of UFOs not based on investigation was assumption and guesswork, and therefore meaningless. He didn't have any firm view on the phenomenon but he knew UFOs were being reported in considerable numbers and he wanted to know what they were.

HORN: Britain's most sensational UFO case occurred in December 1980 in Rendlesham Forest, between RAF Bentwaters and RAF Woodbridge. Tell us about that.

POPE: This is the UK's most famous UFO incident and it's sometimes referred to as "Britain's Roswell". Over a series of nights in December

1980 UFOs were seen by dozens of United States Air Force personnel at Bentwaters and Woodbridge, two RAF bases operated by the Americans. On the first night the UFO landed in Rendlesham Forest (which lies between the two bases) and one of the witnesses got close enough to touch it. Sketches from the USAF witness statements clearly show a craft with strange markings on its hull, which have been likened to Egyptian hieroglyphs. The UFO returned on another night and was seen by more witnesses, including the Deputy Base Commander, Lieutenant Colonel Charles Halt. At one point the UFO illuminated the spot where Halt and his team were standing and at another time the UFO was directly over Woodbridge, firing beams of light down at the base. Subsequently, radiation readings were taken at the location where the UFO had been seen on the first night. They peaked in three indentations found where the craft had apparently landed. The MoD's Defence Intelligence Staff assessed that the radiation levels were significantly higher than background levels. Subsequently it emerged that a radar operator at RAF Watton had tracked an object briefly, over the base. I re-opened the investigation into this case but was unable to determine what happened. It remains unexplained.

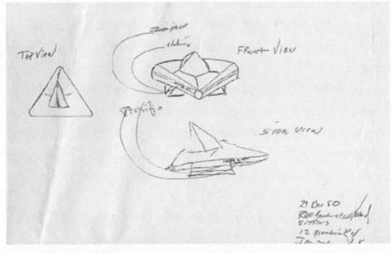

Sketch of the Rendlesham Forest UFO by USAF SSgt Jim Penniston from his official witness statement in 1980 (declassified in 1998 under the Freedom of Information Act [FOIA])

HORN: On 1 November 2006, you were involved with a Channel Five documentary, *The British UFO Mystery*. The programme focused on a wave of UFO sightings that occurred on 30 and 31 March 1993—The Cosford Incident—where many of the witnesses were police officers and military personnel. What did you conclude about this case?

POPE: We had a wave of UFO sightings over the UK for a period of about six hours. Many of the witnesses included police officers and military personnel. At one point the UFO flew over RAF Cosford and RAF Shawbury. Witnesses described a vast triangular-shaped craft capable of moving from a virtual hover to speeds of well over a thousand miles an hour in seconds. I led the investigation at the time and even my Head of Division, who was extremely sceptical about UFOs, was intrigued by this case. We even briefed the Assistant Chief of the Air Staff, one of the UK's most senior RAF officers. Channel Five's recent investigative documentary exposed the case to over a million viewers on primetime terrestrial TV and led to over 30 new witnesses coming forward. The production company had obtained the MoD case file on the incident (which ran to over 100 pages of documentation) under the Freedom of Information Act and asked me to front the programme, talking viewers through the case and the MoD investigation. As a result of the interest generated by the programme, the MoD made the file available on its website. The file includes my sceptical Head of Division's briefing to the Assistant Chief of the Air Staff, which states "In summary, there would seem to be some evidence on this occasion that an unidentified object (or objects) of unknown origin was operating over the UK". This is as close as the MoD will ever get to saying that there's more to UFOs than misidentifications or hoaxes.

HORN: What were some of the other interesting UFO cases you investigated?

POPE: It's difficult to single out interesting cases unless they're on the scale of something like Rendlesham Forest or the Cosford Incident. Also, it's difficult for me to talk about cases the MoD hasn't yet released.

I can't anticipate what the Department will release and what they may withhold, so you'll have to await the release of the files. But in general terms I can say that other interesting cases included some radar/visual cases, cases where UFOs were seen close to military bases, and some interesting sightings by civil and military pilots—including a few near-misses, where collisions were only narrowly avoided. Both the MoD and our Civil Aviation Authority has information on several such cases, and whatever one's beliefs about UFOs, the flight safety implications should be of concern to everyone. When the MoD released Project Condign (a highly classified study that had its roots in discussions I had with the Defence Intelligence Staff in 1993) some of the most interesting recommendations related to this point. One read "No attempt should be made to out-manoeuvre a UAP during interception". Another recommendation states "At higher altitudes, although UAP appear to be benign to civil air-traffic, pilots should be advised not to manoeuvre, other than to place the object astern, if possible". UAP was the abbreviated form of Unidentified Aerial Phenomena, a term we decided to use instead of UFO, as it sounded more scientific.

HORN: Why did you leave the MoD's UFO department?

POPE: After having done the job for 3 years I was promoted and moved to another post at a higher grade. There's certainly no truth to the rumour that I was moved because I was getting too close to the truth, as some conspiracy theorists allege. After I left, I took up a financial policy post, before moving to a security-related job.

HORN: I once asked Stanton Friedman a similar question I'd like to ask you. How do you respond to allegations that you're involved in a cover-up or that you're a disinformation agent?

POPE: How can I respond? You can't prove a negative. The rumour isn't true, but if people believe this sort of thing they won't believe my denial, or the MoD's confirmation of my departure. I can't win. It does amaze me though, how many people genuinely seem to believe this. I get asked it a lot and see the theory discussed frequently on various websites and discussion lists. The bottom line is that I worked for the Government for 21 years, for the very people who many conspiracy theorists believe are covering up the truth about UFOs. To them, the government are the bad guys, so I'm the bad guy, who's part of the conspiracy.

HORN: Your investigations ultimately led to other unexplained phenomena. What do you make of so-called alien abductions?

POPE: While none of these other subjects were in the UFO project's terms of reference, they inevitably ended up on my desk, because there was nowhere else to send them. I've probably looked into around 100 cases of alien abduction. Some of these cases were reported to me at the MoD, but most people contacted me after I'd written a book on the subject, called *The Uninvited*. Some sceptics say these people are attention seekers after their 15 minutes of fame, but this clearly isn't true. Out of the hundred or so abductees I've been involved with, maybe half a dozen are interested in engaging with the media or the UFO community. Most aren't interested. Other people suggest these people are delusional, but again, this theory doesn't stand up to scrutiny. The few scientists who have looked at this phenomenon have found no signs of psychopathology in the abductees, and [have seen] evidence (in terms of increased heartrate and perspiration) that they genuinely believe they've had these experiences. The use of regression hypnosis in some of these cases clouds the issue. The scientific community generally doesn't accept the validity of the technique in recovering suppressed memories, and indeed many believe it can distort memories or even create false ones. But regression hypnosis isn't used in all abduction cases, so we can't say False Memory Syndrome is the answer. Something's going on with these people, but the truthful answer is that we don't know what's happening.

HORN: Could it be something we call "ghosts"?

POPE: People associate ghosts with old houses, churches or pubs, but in my experience there are just as many reports of ghosts on military bases as anywhere else. I've received numerous such reports, often from the MoD Police officers or guards who have to patrol these areas at night. Now, these are pretty tough guys, as you can imagine, but some of them have been really spooked by what they've seen. All the classic signs are present in many of these cases: unexplained cold spots [and] guard dogs growling, with their hackles rising, at certain locations. And actual ghosts [have been] seen at sites where people have been killed. Ghosts have even been seen in MoD Main Building itself, where the modern headquarters is built on the site of the much older Whitehall Palace. The remains of Henry VIII's wine cellar are perfectly preserved in the basement, and there are some areas of the building where guards don't like to patrol alone at night. Perhaps the oddest report I received was an animal ghost story. During the Second World War, Wing Commander Guy Gibson (who led the famous Damn Busters raid) had a dog that was knocked down by a car and killed, shortly before the raid. The ghost of this dog has been seen several times at RAF Scampton.

HORN: You've written extensively about your work with MoD. Is this not a problem since you signed the Official Secrets Act?

POPE: I signed the Official Secrets Act on my first day in the MoD and even though I've left, it binds me for life. But it doesn't preclude writing or speaking about my work. Politicians invariably keep diaries and write memoirs, and military officers often write accounts of their careers. There's no bar on this sort of activity, provided you follow various rules and procedures, the most obvious one being the absolute prohibition on revealing any classified information.

After the initial interview with Nick above, he was in the news again with the latest batch of MoD UFO files released, and so we contacted him with follow-up questions:

HORN: Nick, a few days ago, you called the latest batch of MoD UFO files "absolutely fascinating." Why did you choose to describe them in this way?

POPE: I worked on these files and have been involved in the ongoing program to declassify them and release them to the National Archives, so the media inevitably come to me for a quote when each new batch of files is released. Sometimes they'll want an in-depth interview and on other occasions, just a soundbite. The "absolutely fascinating" quote was a quick soundbite.... That said, I think it's a fair comment—who wouldn't be fascinated by having the chance to peek into what I have called the real-life X-Files....including sightings from police officers, pilots and military personnel, and cases where visual sightings were backed up by radar evidence, or by photos and videos that MoD's imagery experts assessed as genuine.

HORN: File DEFE 24/1987/1 is a MoD 1998 briefing for Tony Blair after you wrote to the prime minister and urged him to make all UK UFO reports available to the public. What can you tell us about this?

POPE: I can't remember the exact sequence of events here, but I'd been warning MoD for some time that UFOs would be a major issue once the UK's Freedom of Information Act came fully into force. With that in mind, I'd certainly proposed that proactively releasing the files would be a way of defusing the situation and avoiding the inevitable workload that dealing with hundreds of UFO-related FOI requests on a case by case basis would generate. I didn't discuss this with Tony Blair personally, but with one of the Defence Ministers at MoD and with a Member of Parliament. Clearly this was relayed to Blair. The decision to release the files was made in 2007 and I was briefed on this by MoD (I'd left in 2006, but spoke to them regularly in my capacity as a broadcaster and journalist) and I broke the story in the media (in *The Daily Telegraph*). The interesting postscript to this is that Tony Blair now says that the

Freedom of Information Act was the biggest mistake of his political career!

HORN: File DEFE 24/2090/1 discusses how some UFOs may be the result of atmospheric plasmas and that "Russia was interested in harnessing these plasmas for potential military use." Is there anything you can add to this intriguing possibility?

POPE: This isn't an area I can discuss in detail, but clearly we were (and still are) concerned about any Russian research that might result in their acquiring novel military capabilities and technologies. So we were interested in the Russian work on this, and in the phenomenon more generally. This isn't going to be a popular statement with the New Age community (who would regard this mind-set as a militaristic and negative response to looking at UFOs and anomalous phenomena), but the question "can we weaponize that?" is a logical and obvious one when it comes to looking at things like exotic atmospheric plasmas.

HORN: In more recent years, you have also investigated so-called alien abduction cases including psychological orders, folklore, and demonology ascribed by some to the reported phenomenon. Have you considered that other-dimensional, spiritual, or occult forces could be at play in some of these cases?

POPE: I've considered these possibilities and certainly can't rule them out [but I'm really] not sure what to make of alien abductions. It's interesting that the few scientific experiments undertaken with abductees show no evidence of psychopathology or falsehood and suggest that in recalling their experiences they exhibit physiological reactions (e.g. increased heart rate and perspiration) not seen in control groups of non-abductees. Just as the UFO phenomenon has no single explanation, I believe there are various different explanations for the alien abduction phenomenon. Some cases will be hoaxes and some may be attributable to some form of hallucination or delusion. To this we can probably add vivid dreams, sleep paralysis, false memory syndrome and various other factors. However, this doesn't explain all the cases and I suspect there's some other factor at work here. But what that factor is, I don't know.

HORN: Are you familiar with Nick Redfern's book *Final Events* and the "Collins Elite"? If so, what do you make of it, if anything, and are you aware of any British government groups that reached similar conclusions, i.e., that "aliens" might be angels and/or demons?

POPE: I think the way I'd characterize it is this: elements in the British Establishment have always been interested in—and dabbled with—the occult. Such people are sometimes in government. Other times, their views can influence government policy. When such people or groups look at something like the UFO phenomenon, they often gravitate towards angelic/demonic theories, as a consequence of their pre-existing beliefs. None of this should be taken as implying this represents an official position, but I guess you could say that it's semi-official, given the power and influence of the sorts of people involved.

(NOTE FROM TOM HORN: When I pressed Pope to explain just who among the "British establishment" might be involved in alien occultism, he answered, "Tom, I'm not going to go into specifics, as there are considerable sensitivities here, but for whatever reason, one finds such beliefs most strongly held in certain parts of the aristocracy and the intelligence community." We follow the trail on this later in the book.)

Interview with Dr. Bruce Maccabee:[634]

HORN: Dr. Maccabee, thank you for taking time to do this interview. I understand you received your BS in physics at Worcester Polytechnic Institute in Worcester, Massachusetts, and then your MS in 1967 and PhD in physics in 1970 at the American University in Washington, DC. Please correct me if I have these facts wrong.

MACCABEE: That is correct.

HORN: You had a long career at the Naval Surface Warfare Center. You've worked on optical data processing, underwater sound, lasers, and the Strategic Defense Initiative and Ballistic Missile Defense using high-power lasers and most recently on technologies related to homeland security and defeating IEDs [improvised explosive devices]. With this background, I'm curious how you became interested in the study of UFOs.

MACCABEE: Like most kids of the '50s I was intrigued by the early space movies like *The Day the Earth Stood Still*, *War of the Worlds*, *It Came from Outer Space*, etc., but I never assumed they had any basis in reality. I probably paid little or no attention to the very few sightings reported in the local (Rutland, Vermont) newspaper until perhaps 1958 or so when I read Capt. Edward Ruppelt's book, *Report on Unidentified Flying Objects* (published in 1955). I presume I was intrigued by what he wrote, but there was nothing I could do about it so I promptly "forgot" it.

About nine or ten years later, when I was more interested in the subject, I recalled that I had read it years before. I found the book and reread it and realized that he was close to saying they were real and from outer space. In 1966 or 67, while studying for my physics degree at The

American University in Washington, DC, I read *UFOs Serious Business* by Frank Edwards and later went to a lecture by NICAP [National Investigations Committee on Aerial Phenomena] representatives at the university (Hall and Berliner?). Of course, I was aware of the newspaper stories of sightings (1965, 1966 UFO flap). So, when the NICAP guys said help was needed at headquarters, and I knew that headquarters was only a few miles away in DC, I decided to visit and see what they had.

I well remember the first case. It was a report of green lights passing over Tuckerman Lane, a road just west of what is now the beltway around Washington, DC. I have been told by other people who became interested in the subject that they carried out investigations and found nothing but trivial explanations for the sighting reports they investigated. This turned them off to the subject and they lost interest. It was different for me. This first case was a simple but strange sighting, a basic "night light" type, by a lady who had good credibility (teacher). We rode with her in her car along the road where this happened (Tuckerman Lane) and could see no normal reason for why green lights would have been seen passing over the road as she drove. She didn't want any publicity. We ended up classifying it as an unknown. (In the years since there have been reports of green lights traveling through the sky in the DC area and other places around the world.) The next case, which occurred in the early 1970s, was even more strange: a multiple witness sighting in the Shenandoah Valley of a rocket shaped object hovering stationary over a mountain. Another early 1970s case consisted of two incidents that involved several teenagers in Passapatanzy, Virginia, oddly enough, not far from where I have worked for the last ten years. That case was published in the NICAP Bulletin as the "Case of the Virginia Giant." The two events involved a UFO landing, a creature which came out of the craft holding a glowing ball in its hand (this preceded by several years a better-known sighting report from Pennsylvania of a creature holding a glowing ball), an animal reaction (dog ran away and didn't return for more than a day), a car that stopped when a UFO was hovering over it, that car's radio that stopped working and needed repair, TV interference and multiple witnesses. There may also have been an abduction, although at the time abduction was the furthest thing from the minds of the several investigators of that case. So, anyway, my initial foray into the subject, which included reading books, reading the Condon Report and investigating cases got me thoroughly interested in the subject.

After the publication of the Condon study in early 1969 there was a general feeling in the press that everything had been explained and UFOs had "gone away." At NICAP headquarters we knew that wasn't true, but there wasn't much we could do about it. Then in August 1973 it was "We're BaaaaaacK!" as police officers and others began reporting sightings in the southeast and moving over the succeeding weeks into the Midwest. (This flap included humanoid sightings and includes two well publicized incidents, the Hickson/Parker abduction in Pascagoula, Mississippi and the Coyne/helicopter case in Mansfield, Ohio.) Because the fall, 1973 flap regenerated interest in the UFO subject I wrote up a report on the Shenandoah Valley sighting that I had thoroughly investigated and sent it to Science Magazine. It was returned in about 2 weeks with the comment by Editor Philip Abelson that I should consider publication elsewhere because they already had lots of articles to publish. Of course, I would have been willing to wait, but I got the point: get lost! (A shortened version was eventually published by NICAP.) More importantly, at about this time Stanton Friedman alerted me to the importance of the statistical study known as Project Blue Book Special Report #14 (SR14). I managed to obtain NICAP's original copy of that document and I began a re-evaluation of the statistics (see below). I then decided to study the one case that William Hartmann, the Condon Study photo-analyst, claimed was probably real (McMinnville; see discussion below). I initially assumed that he had made a mistake somewhere, but at least there was real physics (optics) involved in analyzing the photos. So, I learned how to do the type of analysis that Hartmann had done, studied the arguments of the skeptics (Klass, Sheaffer) managed to get the original negatives (because of a suggestion by Philip Klass!) and it was uphill from then on!

I should point out that while investigating I was also reading and doing historical research during the years following 1973. I was one of the first to study the Blue Book files released to the Archives in 1975 and was the first to obtain the FBI file on flying discs. I guess you could say that by the middle of 1970's I was off and running and never looked back.

HORN: Among your published papers was a reanalysis of the statistics and results of the famed Battelle Memorial Institute Project Blue Book Special Report No. 14, which included thirty-two hundred Air Force cases through the mid 1950s. What was your conclusion?

MACCABEE: This document proved to me that there was strong statistical evidence that at least some UFOs were not explainable as mundane phenomena or, in the vernacular, it showed that "UFOs are real," even though the official Air Force press release (in 1955) had tried to convince everyone that the study showed nothing of significance.

The scientists and Air Force personnel who compiled this report studied each sighting carefully and assigned it to one of three groups: Known (K) if it could be identified with at least reasonable certainty, Unknown (U) if it definitely could not be identified, and Insufficient Information (II) if there was not enough information for a decision of K or U. The study used chi-squared tests to compare the statistical distributions of several sighting characteristics of the K and U sightings under the assumption that if the U sightings were merely unrecognized K sightings, the distributions should match. The characteristics tested included various "values" of color, number, duration, shape, speed and light brightness. The chi-squared tests showed less than 1% probability of a match for all characteristics except brightness, for which the probability was less than 5%. Combining the characteristics the probability of a match is much less than 1%. I revised the statistical calculations and came up with a similar result. The most unique and interesting statistical result involved the comparison between the percentages of K, U and II sightings and the credibility of the observer and the quality (self-consistency, completeness) of his report. When the sightings were placed into quality groups Poor, Doubtful, Good and Excellent (a large fraction of Excellent were military reports), the report showed higher percentages of Unknowns in the Excellent and Good groups than in the Doubtful and Poor groups. This is not what one would expect if UFO sightings were all mundane phenomena because, if that were true, the analysts would be more likely to make correct identifications from the better quality sighting reports than from the low quality reports and so the percentages of U and II cases would be lower in the group of high quality reports.

Of course, the Air Force did not even mention this important statistical result that the better the quality of the sighting the more likely it was to be unexplainable. Another important contribution to the study of UFOs is the brief discussion of the Rogue River Sighting (Case 10 of SR14). I had never heard of that before, but its presence in SR14 alerted me to its existence and so I searched for it in the Blue Book microfilm file. Eventually I found it and after analyzing it I concluded that it is one of the most convincing reports of the early years. I have an in-depth discussion of this case at my web site: http://brumac.8k.com/Rogue /RogueRiver.html. The published analysis of SR14 is at http://brumac.8k.com/SSUFOs. This is a downloadable Power Point presentation.

HORN: The McMinnville Annual UFO Festival finished up a couple weeks ago, which has grown to be second only to the Roswell festival in the United States as I understand it. The festival started in 2000, the 50th anniversary of the Trent UFO sighting near McMinnville, Oregon, when McMenamins began hosting a UFO fest in memory of the Trents and their experience. The story goes that Evelyn Trent was feeding rabbits on the farm when suddenly an object appeared overhead. She yelled for her husband Paul, who "came-a-runnin'" with his Kodak Roamer camera in hand. Paul was able to get two photographs of the large, metallic-disc hovering silently northeast of the farm just before sunset.

Photoanalyst William Hartmann (for the Condon Report) felt the pictures were consistent with the assertion that an "extraordinary flying object" flew within sight of two witnesses. The National Investigations Committee on Aerial Phenomena went on to study the photos, eventually listing them as "…one of the top cases demonstrating very strong evidence for the existence for unknown structured objects in our atmosphere." The Air Force couldn't find a better explanation. Neither could the University of Colorado, and researchers afterward concluded that the Trent sighting and its physical evidence was one of the best records ever made for a true UFO event. The story was placed on the Top Ten Best Evidence List and I believe it has remained there for the last forty years. Tell me about your research analysis and what you believe about the Trent UFO pictures.

The Trent UFO

MACCABEE: Although the history of the sighting itself is simple to describe the history of the investigation and analysis requires pages and pages. My extensive report on the McMinnville investigation, which includes analysis and discussions that took place over a period of about 25 years, is at http://brumac.8k.com/trent1.html, http://brumac.8k.

com/trent1b.html and http://brumac.8k.com/trent2.html. The "bottom line" is that there is no information that clearly points to a hoax. This is important because it was either a hoax or the real thing, there is no half-way point or "insufficient information" to arrive at a conclusion.

Years ago I realized that "a photo a UFO does not make." The best that a photo can do is act as an aide to the witness' recollection. It cannot by itself prove the sighting was real because virtually any photo could be faked, given the necessary desire, photographic skill, knowledge, economic resources and ability to create a reasonable sighting story and stick to it. The worst it can do is contain clear evidence of a hoax (e.g., strings, supports, etc.) In the Trent case the photos clearly show an unidentifiable object which has been variously "identified" as a garbage can lid, a Frisbee, a pie pan, a hand-made model or a truck mirror (at least pelicans play no role in this sighting [inside joke—see below]). However, there has been no particular mundane object that has been positively identified as explaining the image. The photos themselves provide no clear evidence of a hoax. (shadow arguments notwithstanding; see my web site). That means the investigation must center on the witnesses. The witnesses have been "tracked" from the time [of] the sighting in 1950 until they died in the middle 1990s. Over this whole period of time, despite the repeated "harassment" by investigator types (such as me) they maintained their simple story that they saw the object passing by and photographed it. So far as I and other investigators could tell, they were basic farmers who had no time or any good reason for creating any flying saucer hoax. Perhaps the newspaper photographer, Bill Powell, who first published the photos put it best when he said that he examined the photos every which way (after retrieving them from behind the sofa at the Trent's house) and couldn't figure out how they had faked them. So he published them because, in his opinion, the Trents were (paraphrase) incapable of thinking of such a thing as a flying saucer hoax. And that has been the opinion of numerous investigators, including myself, in the years since.

HORN: Another paper you authored was a reanalysis of the results of the Condon Committee UFO study from 1969, which I referred to in my last question. Do you think Edward Condon lied about the results?

MACCABEE: I don't recall writing an analysis of the Condon Report (Dr. Peter Sturrock of Stanford University did publish an analysis). However, I think Condon made an effort to cover up any significance of the work done by "his" investigators. In particular, Condon tried to confuse the reader in his discussion of the McMinnville case. According to Condon, an experienced photoanalyst (Everett Merritt) claimed that the Trent photos were worthless for photogrammetric analysis. This type of analysis involves angles between images, sighting lines and directions. (Actually, he was wrong, but that's beside this point.) Condon knew that Hartmann's conclusion that the Trent photos could be real was based on photometric analysis, which involves the relative brightnesses of images, not the directions or angles. Thus anyone reading only Condon's summary and conclusions at the beginning of the report would not know the photogrammetric criticism by Merritt had nothing to do with Hartmann's conclusion.

HORN: Of course before the Trent sighting, American businessman Kenneth Arnold claimed to have witnessed nine elliptical-shaped objects moving over Mt. Rainier in Washington, June 24, 1947. Have you studied his case, and if so, what were your findings?

MACCABEE: I have what may be the largest and most complete analysis to be found anywhere at my web site see http://brumac.8k.com/ KARNOLD /KARNOLD.html. It is the first publicized sighting and deserves extensive critical analysis because Arnold had no reason to hoax such a sighting and he made "measurements" during the sighting which indicate that the objects were not mirages, or fast moving clouds or motes in his eye or nearby jet aircraft or reflections from his airplane window or low-flying meteors or high-flying geese or pelicans (yes, pelicans). The bottom line is that the Arnold case remains unexplained.

HORN: What about some of the other old case files, such as the Gemini 11 [http://en.wikipedia.org/wiki /Gemini_11] astronaut photos? What do you make of these, and are there other astronaut and military photos you have found to be substantial?

MACCABEE: Again, there is a discussion of this case at my web site: http://www.brumac.8k.com/Gemini_11/GEMINI_11.html. There is no doubt that they saw and photographed something that has not been identified. There is a suggestion that it might have been an object ejected earlier by the spacecraft, but this is only a guess. Owen K Garriot photographed a red object seen by the Skylab 3 astronauts in 1973. Of course, there have been many allegations by people who study videos and photos taken during other spaceflights. Very often the claims made are based on faulty analysis. There may have been some UFOs seen and photographed or videotaped by astronauts, but it would be hard to prove.

HORN: You were the first to obtain the secret "flying disc file" of the FBI, what I believe you have called "the REAL X-Files." For those not familiar, tell us how you did that and why it is significant.

MACCABEE: I was told by Mrs. Trent in 1975 that "FBI men" came to her house and investigated her sighting soon after the photos were published. In 1976 I wrote to the FBI to ask if they had a file on Paul Trent. As an aside I asked them to also send any UFO documents they might have. I didn't expect to get anything because Capt. Edward Ruppelt wrote in The Report on Unidentified Flying Objects that (so far as he knew!) the FBI never took an interest in flying saucer sightings. I was, therefore, surprised to receive a phone call from an FBI agent about 6 months later who told me that there were 1,600 pages (approximately) of material in a file on flying saucers. He subsequently sent me a selection of the best of the documents and I wrote articles about them that appeared in the journals of all three major UFO groups (NICAP, CUFOS—Center for UFO Studies, and APRO—Aerial Phenomena Research Organization).

The documents showed that, starting in early July, 1947, the FBI acted as a "black hole" with information from the Air Force going in and nothing coming out (until my FOIPA [Freedom of Information and Privacy Act] request was answered). J. Edgar Hoover's director of the FBI, stated in letters to people requesting information in the 1960s that the FBI had never investigated UFOs. He lied. The FBI interviewed witnesses in 1947 at the request of the Air Force. In later years the FBI (and the CIA) collected documents from the AF but did no further investigations. By order of Congress, the Headquarters of the FBI could destroy no records, so all these documents were available when I made my FOIPA request. The FBI had the only documents that provide us with the high level secret opinion of Air Force intelligence officials in late 1952. The opinion was that several percent of the sightings could not be explained and that at least some sightings might be of "interplanetary vehicles." This opinion was never stated publicly. The whole story is in my book *THE UFO FBI CONNECTION*. Used copies are available at Amazon and other places. Some of the most important documents are from 1952. They are discussed in my history of 1952 at http://brumac.8k.com/1952YEARO FUFO/1952YEAROFUFO.html. As for my original request for information on the Trents it was officially denied, but unofficially the agent who handled my request said that he had made a search and found no FBI record on the Trents. He then pointed out that any Trent investigation would have been carried out by a local office. The local office may have found nothing of official interest to the FBI since the FBI had stopped investigating sightings several years before 1950. If that was the case the local office would not have sent a report to headquarters. Then the agent pointed out that the local offices generally destroyed unneeded records every five years. So I never did find out whether or not the FBI visited the Trents.

HORN: You've collected other documents from government agencies including the CIA, the US Air Force, the US Army, and so on. What are the most important of these documents, in your opinion?

MACCABEE: To some extent I guess they are all important because they show a tendency of the government to assign at least some importance to sightings of strange things in the sky. The *UFO FBI CONNECTION* combines files from the FBI, Air Force Intelligence and the CIA to show that the government has had, for 50 years or more, essentially conclusive evidence (even without Roswell or other supposed crashes) that "UFOs are real" and some may well be "interplanetary craft."

HORN: On the heels of the 1947 Roswell UFO incident, green balls of light and saucer-shaped objects began appearing in the sky near areas where top-secret nuclear weapon research was being carried out. This was happening repeatedly, and the US military was increasingly concerned. Eventually, something called "Project Twinkle" was set up in hopes of figuring out what was going on. Did you look into this case?

MACCABEE: I did indeed study the "green fireball" sightings and the Project Twinkle report. Again, there is a discussion of this at my web site. The first green fireball sightings were in December, 1948, in the southwestern areas near government laboratories where nuclear research was being carried out (Los Alamos, Sandia, Albuquerque area, etc.). A famous meteoricist (person who studies meteors), Dr. Lincoln La Paz analyzed many sightings and even had his own sighting. These fireballs were characterized by their green color and by the fact that they appeared to travel in flat trajectories, mostly in a southerly direction. So many of these events occurred in 1949 and 1950 that eventually, in the spring of 1950, the Air Force set up Project Twinkle to get photographic evidence of these objects. For more information and to see how Project Twinkle proved UFOs were real and covered up the proof, see http://www.brumac.8k.com/WhiteSandsProof/WhiteSandsProof.html.

HORN: I've talked with Jesse Marcel Jr. and Stanton Friedman on numerous occasions. They both believe something extraordinary actually happened outside Roswell, New Mexico, in 1947. What do you believe?

MACCABEE: I have never thought that Maj. Jesse Marcel, the intelligence officer at the base who retrieved the material found on the Foster Ranch by rancher Brazel, could not identify plastic or rubber or balsa wood sticks which were used in the construction of balloons, Mogul [top-secret project; see online report at link below] or otherwise. When Sheridan Cavitt, the counter-intelligence officer who accompanied Marcel, finally "talked" he claimed that he immediately recognized the debris as balloon material. If so, why didn't he tell Marcel and Brazel? For this and other reasons Cavitt's testimony is valid evidence against the balloon/Mogul explanations. I have an analysis of his testimony at my web site: http://www.brumac.8k.com/Roswell/CavittEmptor.html.

HORN: You've been on the who's who of television shows on this subject—*Unsolved Mysteries, A Current Affair, Encounters, Sightings, CNN News, Fox News, Nightline,* and the rest. Have you found serious investigative journalism into the subject of UFOs?

MACCABEE: These and other shows I have been on generally treat the subject as entertainment. Very often the shows try to present a "balanced" viewpoint which means that for every UFO-positive statement there has to be a UFO-negative statement. This is consistent with Maccabee's First Rule for Debunkers: any explanation is better than none. The result is that explanations which are illogical, make no sense, or are simply stupid get "equal play." The 2006 O'Hare Airport sighting is an example of this. It was suggested that the people saw airport lights reflected from clouds. The object was described as a greyish circular thing, darker than the clouds above it, completely inconsistent with being lights on clouds which would appear brighter than clouds (and there still was skylight at 4:30 PM in November, 2006, so how could one see ground lights reflected from the clouds anyway?).

HORN: What did you personally make of the O'Hare Airport sightings?

MACCABEE: Certainly seems like a good solid report. Fortunately the press did not pick up on it immediately. This gave the UFO investigators time to obtain testimony without the pressure from publicity. Then reporter [Jon] Hilkevitch did a very credible job of reporting. The story in the Chicago paper garnered more world-wide response, we are told, than any other newspaper story at the time. The sighting occurred in November, 2006, almost exactly 20 years after the famous Japan Airlines sighting over Alaska. This sighting is reported in detail at my web site: http://brumac.8k.com/JAL1628 /JL1628.html.

HORN: If you had to list the top five best UFO cases in terms of analytical evidence, which ones would they be?

MACCABEE: It is always difficult to pick the best of something like UFO sightings because there are so many. Therefore I concentrate on cases I have studied. Certainly at or near the top would be the New Zealand (December 31, 1978) sightings from a freighter aircraft is way up there. It is the only civilian UFO sighting, as far as I know, that includes multiple witnesses, radar, both ground and air, tape recordings made on the airplane and at the ground radar, and a professional 16 mm color movie that shows most of the strange lights/objects they saw. The White Sands movie case would be another if we had the film. Of course there is McMinnville. One can also consider the August 1980 police car damage case in Warren, Minnesota, reported by Officer Val Johnson (a case that Philip J. Klass couldn't explain). Then there is the Iranian Jet case (see http://brumac.8k.com/IranJetCase and download the Microsoft WORD document).

Interview with Stanton T. Friedman:[635]

HORN: Stanton, Roswell is the preeminent story of ufology. Some say whatever occurred near Roswell, New Mexico, in July 1947 will never be known. Others like you disagree on some levels. You and Bill Moore brought this story to light many years ago. This is the most appropriate place to start this interview, so please tell us how that happened.

STAN: I first heard of Roswell in the early 1970s from a woman named Lydia Sleppy whose son was a forest ranger in California. He had had a good sighting. My associate (Bobbi Ann Slate Gironda, long deceased) and I spoke with him and he suggested we talk to his mother who had had a good sighting near Albuquerque. We did speak to her and after she told us about the sighting, she mentioned that when she had been working at an Albuquerque Radio Station in the late 1940s, she was asked to type the story coming in from a broadcaster at their Roswell affiliate station for a newswire. He dictated how a flying saucer had been recovered and was being sent to Wright Field. Part way through the story the bell went off on the machine she was using to put the story on the news wire. The FBI instructed her not to continue the transmission. She remembered the names of some of the people and I located several, but came to a dead end. I should stress that New Mexico was a hotbed of classified Research and Development activities and certainly it was expected that there would be spies and counter intelligence concerns.

In 1978 I was in Baton Rouge, Louisiana, at a TV station to do three interviews before my lecture "Flying Saucers ARE Real!" that evening at Louisiana State University. I had done two, but the third reporter was nowhere to be found. The station manager was giving me coffee, looking at his watch, and was embarrassed as he knew the person who had brought me to the station and I had other things to do. Out of the blue he told me that the person I ought to talk to was Jesse Marcel over in Houma, Louisiana. I asked, "Who is he?" He answered, "Oh, he handled wreckage of a flying saucer when he was in the military. We are old Ham radio buddies." The reporter finally showed up and I was busy the rest of the day. Next day from the Airport I called information and then spoke with Jesse who told me his story. This is described in detail in *Crash at Corona: The Definitive Story of the Roswell Incident* by Don Berliner and myself. Jesse didn't have a precise date. I shared the story with Bill Moore (we had known each other in Pittsburgh, years before). I also saw him months later in Minnesota the day after meeting with Vern and Jean Maltaise of Bemidji, MN, who told me a story of their friend Barney Barnett who had come across a crashed saucer and strange bodies in New Mexico. Bill had a 3rd story (From the Flying Saucer Review) about an English actor named Hughie Green who heard a story on the radio about a New Mexico crashed saucer when driving from Los Angeles to Philadelphia. He could pin down a date (early July, 1947). Bill went to the U. of Minnesota Library and found the stories in newspapers in the periodicals department. These gave us an independent check on Jesse's story and the names of many more people. By 1980 we had located 62 people. That is when the first Roswell book *The Roswell Incident* by Bill Moore and Charles Berlitz was published. Bill and I did 90% of the research. By 1986 we had published several more articles and the total was up to 92. This was all before the internet made searching a lot easier and cheaper. I instigated, and was in, the *Unsolved Mysteries* NBC TV program about Roswell in 1989. It was well done and was seen by 28 million people.

Many others have joined in, some of the noisy negativists from their armchairs, and, of course, the government has issued two large reports full of misrepresentation and anti-UFO propaganda. I am still checking on some leads…and correcting the false information put out by the noisy negativists.

HORN: In 1984, a Hollywood movie producer named James Shandera was investigating the UFO phenomena and received an anonymously mailed package of 35-mm film. It supposedly contained images of a top-secret government report, later named the "Majestic Twelve" (or "MJ-12") documents. You wound up with these documents. Tell us about that, and do you still believe some of the Majestic 12 documents are genuine?

STAN: I had introduced Jaime to Bill Moore while I was living in California and worked with Jaime and Bill briefly on a fictional movie that didn't get very far in 1980 before I moved from California to New Brunswick, Canada. Jaime and Bill worked closely together, saw each other often and worked with several insiders. We kept in touch by phone and during my travels. The film had two identical sets of 8 negatives each. The document was classified TOP SECRET/MAJIC. The title on the first page is "Briefing Document: Operation Majestic 12" Prepared for President Elect Dwight D. Eisenhower, 18 November, 1952. I was notified about its receipt and we cooperated on trying to determine whether the original two documents, the briefing and p.8, a memo from President Truman to Secretary of Defense Forrestal (Sept. 24, 1947) authorizing Operation Majestic 12, were genuine. Another brief Top Secret Restricted document, a memo, July 14, 1954, from Robert Cutler to General Nathan Twining, one of the MJ-12 members, was discovered at the National Archives. A very important part of my research dealt with my very surprising finding that Dr. Donald Menzel, who was an astronomy Professor at Harvard and had written 3 anti-UFO books, and who was listed as an MJ-12 member, actually led a double life doing highly classified work for decades for the NSA [National Security Association], the CIA, and 30 companies.

My book *TOP SECRET/MAJIC* gives the whole story and demonstrates that none of the myriad of anti-MJ-12 arguments stand up to careful scrutiny based on my visits to 20 archives and my 14 years of work on classified programs. It also demonstrates that there are a number of phony MJ-12 documents out there as well.

HORN: I talked with Jesse Marcel Jr. again not long ago. He does not buy the Mogul/balloon explanation about Roswell. What's your take on this?

STAN: The ridiculous MOGUL explanation put forth by Colonel Richard Weaver simply doesn't stand up to careful review as is noted in *Crash at Corona* and in several other of my papers. That his specialty is disinformation becomes quite clear. Mogul doesn't cut it. The materials don't match witness descriptions in terms of the characteristics and the quantity. Dr. David Rudiak at his website shows that no Mogul balloon could have landed on the Brazel ranch. Engineer Robert Galganski shows the amount of material is a total mismatch. If it doesn't fit, one must acquit.

HORN: Could the crash-test dummies explain reports of alien bodies?

STAN: This attempt to explain the bodies observed by witnesses to the Roswell crashes is certainly one of the silliest of many totally false explanations put forth by government propagandists in a long history of such nonsense. There are 3 major problems with it:

1. All were dropped in 1953 or later; a minimum of 6 years after the Roswell crash. Last I heard, nobody had invented time travel, even for crash test dummies.

2. I met with Colonel Madson, who had been in charge of that program. For the tests to be meaningful, he noted that the dummies were 6' tall and weighed 175 pounds to match pilots. There was no way to morph them down to 4 foot tall skinny little guys with four fingers and big heads.

3. The Air Force report uses the same map of test drop locations three times. There were no dummy drops near either of the 2 crash sites (Brazel Ranch and Plains of San Agustin).

HORN: So you believe the government is covering up the truth about flying saucers?

STAN: It isn't a question of belief. One needs only to look at the multitude of lies over 60 year period of time, as well as the blacked out UFO documents from the CIA [and] the whited out UFO documents from the NSA (156 pages) on which one can only read one or two sentences.

HORN: Now let's turn to some technical questions. Doesn't relativity prevent interstellar travel?

STAN: Of course not. Time slows down as things approach the speed of light. This has been demonstrated. At 99.99% of the speed of light it only takes 6 months pilot time to go 37 light years. I worked on nuclear fusion propulsion systems in 1961. Using the right isotopes of hydrogen and helium one can eject charged particles having 10 million times as much energy per particle as in a chemical rocket.

HORN: Wouldn't it take too much energy to get to another galaxy?

STAN: Who cares? Andromeda is over 2 million light years away. But within just 55 light years of Earth there are about 2000 stars of which roughly 50 are very similar to the sun. If I need a loaf of bread for dinner I don't worry about going to that great bakery in Sydney, Australia, or even one in Sydney, Nova Scotia. I go to the supermarket 2 miles away. The amount of energy required depends on the details of the trip. One astronomer calculating the required initial launch weight of a rocket able to get a man to the moon and back was too high by a factor of 300 Million. One thing he neglected was cosmic freeloading, letting mother nature do much of the work as we do on all our deep space flights. Astronomers have very little knowledge of space travel.

HORN: What technique might be used to move around in the atmosphere the way saucers are reported to?

STAN: One of Friedman's laws is that technological progress comes from doing things differently in an unpredictable way. Lasers aren't just better light bulbs. The nuclear fission rockets I helped test almost 40 years ago are not just better chemical rockets. Entirely different physics in both cases. As I noted in my 1968 Congressional testimony, an attractive approach is magnetoaerodynamics similar to the electromagnetic submarine successfully tested in the mid 1960s by Dr. Stewart Way, but replacing seawater, an electrically conducting fluid, with ionized air another one. One technical-report literature search I had done noted 900 references; more than 90% were classified. Gets around all the problems of highspeed flight in the atmosphere.

HORN: Here's a big question I'm personally interested in. Where do you think these visitors originate?

STAN: The only UFO case that I know of that provides an answer is the fascinating abduction of Betty and Barney Hill in New Hampshire in September, 1961. Betty described a star map (model) under hypnosis. She drew it as a post hypnotic suggestion by the skilled psychiatrist hypnotist Dr. Benjamin Simon. It is in the first book *The Interrupted Journey*. A brilliant woman named Marjorie Fish built 25 models of the local galactic neighborhood and was able to determine that the base stars in the map were Zeta 1 and Zeta 2 Reticuli in the Southern sky constellation of Reticulum. They are unique being the closest to each other pair of sun-like stars in our neighborhood. They are only 39.2 light years from here and only 1/8th of a light year apart from each other, and a billion years older than the sun. The work is described in detail in the book: *Captured! The Betty and Barney Hill UFO Experience* by Kathleen Marden (Betty's niece) and myself. We deal with the objections to both the case and the star map work. Not surprisingly none of the critics accurately described either.

Interview with Colonel Jesse Marcel Jr.:[636]

HORN: Jesse, it's good to talk to you again. As the only man alive whom the government admits handled material from the debris field in 1947, material your dad let you and your mother see as he stopped off at home on his way back to the base, how did that night affect you? It changed the course of ufology and put Roswell and your family on the map.

MARCEL: It was then that I came to believe that our civilization was not alone certainly in the galaxy and that we were in fact being visited by others more advanced because they could get here from wherever they come from. I took it to mean that we were being studied from a scientifically curious race just as we would be curious about other life forms on our planet.

HORN: During the 1947 Roswell event, Colonel [William "Butch"] Blanchard authorized a press release saying the military had recovered a flying disc. I assume he had some facts about what was recovered before he allowed the press release.

MARCEL: Certainly he had been briefed by my dad as to the true nature of the debris and that it represented an artifact from elsewhere which went along with all of the unusual sightings seen in the skies at that time.

HORN: Your father was ordered to load the debris onto a B-29, which was then flown to Wright Field, where Gen. Roger Ramey took over. Correct?

MARCEL: He took a small representative portion of the debris for

General Ramey's inspection and I am convinced that he realized that this was too big of a story to be unleashed on the public at that time.

HORN: What happened then?

MARCEL: My dad was told to participate in the cover story. And when he came home he sat my mother and myself down and said in no uncertain terms that we were never to discuss what we had seen. I later recalled him stating that he was part of the cover up.

HORN: Let me ask something more personal. What were your dad's qualifications to evaluate a crash site?

MARCEL: He was the intelligence officer for the 509th and had training in aircraft accident investigation and in addition he had gone to radar school so he was familiar with the types of radar targets used on weather balloons etc. He was a natural to have been sent out on the initial investigation of the debris.

HORN: The material your dad brought home—tell us what you saw.

MARCEL: He had pre-positioned the debris on the kitchen floor so my mother and I could realize the unusual nature of the debris. What we saw was something certainly different from mundane material. I have described the debris itself many times so I don't know if you want that repeated here.

(NOTE: Jesse Marcel Jr.'s first-published recollection of the debris was that they were composed of "foil-like stuff, very thin, metallic-like but not metal, and very tough. There was also some structural-like material too—beams and so on. Also a quantity of black plastic material which looked organic in nature.... Imprinted along the edge of some of the beam remnants there were hieroglyphic-type characters. I recently questioned my father about this, and he recalled seeing these characters also and even described them as being a pink or purplish-pink color. Egyptian hieroglyphics would be a close visual description of the characters seen, except I don't think there were any animal figures present as there are in true Egyptian hieroglyphics."[637])

HORN: You are a military man, too. Have you ever seen anything that matches those materials?

MARCEL: As a flight surgeon, I was trained myself in aircraft accident investigations and have never seen anything that would match the debris.

HORN: What about the theory that this was a Mogul balloon?

MARCEL: A balloon is a balloon and the Mogul balloon had a classified mission, but it used off the shelf materials that were not unique.

HORN: Did you ever see the movie *Roswell*? Were you and the other events portrayed accurately in it?

MARCEL: For the most part it reflected what happened, there was of course some poetic license in depicting the event.

HORN: Last year in McMinnville, you told me an interesting story about a trip to Washington, DC, where you wound up in the dungeons of the Capitol building talking to somebody I believe was later identified as Dick D'Amato, an aide to Sen. Robert Byrd, who wanted to know where the Roswell UFO debris was. Tell us that story.

MARCEL: It was there that I was told that the event was not fiction. I am sorry that Mr. D'Amato's name came out because hopefully this would not cause any difficulties for him. [NOTE: To this day, Jesse Marcel doesn't know how the participants in Washington, DC, knew where he would be at that particular time. When he arrived at his motel, there was a message waiting for him on the phone in his room. It was from Dick D'Amato. He wanted to meet with Jesse the following day at 1:00 p.m. in a certain room at the Capitol building. Jesse felt uneasy, but agreed to go to the meeting. On arrival, he was ushered into D'Amato's office, who got right down to business. He wanted to talk to Jesse about Roswell, and he asked if he would be more comfortable "in a secure room." When Jesse explained that he wouldn't be saying anything he hadn't said before, D'Amato pressed the idea of the alternate meeting area, explaining, "Well, maybe I want to tell you something you don't already know." Leaving the office, they proceeded to the secure room where no listening devices existed, in an area Jesse described as "the dungeons of the Capitol building." They sat at a table where Jesse noticed a book about alien abductions, UFO technology, and Roswell. D'Amato tapped on the book with his finger and said outright, "This is not fiction." He continued talking for a while and then asked him if he knew where the material recovered from the Roswell ranch was being kept. Jesse found the question curious and said, "No. Don't you?" D'Amato's answer was as enigmatic as the question, so Jesse responded with an inquiry of his own: "If extraterrestrial activity is real, and you guys know it, when is the government planning official disclosure of what really happened at Roswell?" D'Amato said, "If it was up to me, we'd be doing it now" (as told to Tom Horn by Jesse Marcel Jr. in a personal 2006 interview; at that time, Jesse did not use Mr. D'Amato's name).]

HORN: A lot of people are saying we are getting close to an official disclosure event from either the US government or maybe the United Nations concerning some evidence of extraterrestrial intelligence. Other people point to the discovery of extra solar planets like Gliese 581 that was found recently that might be able to sustain life. What can you tell us, or what do you suspect, with regard to official disclosure?

MARCEL: It just confirms what I already knew. It is only a question of time before a radio signal will be picked up by the SETI team, and that will probably be the catalyst for our government *to make the big announcement.* (emphasis added)

FINAL NOTE ON THE FIRST FOUR INTERVIEW EXCERPTS: Jesse Marcel Jr. is a Catholic and his excitement about the forthcoming "big announcement" concerning extraterrestrial intelligence conveys a different worldview than most evangelicals may have. Nonetheless, it is one that will be on the lips of the world soon, as the Vatican has a plan for "their" arrival, and, as the reader will learn, Rome is busy now hypothecating the astonishing doctrines that will facilitate **the coming of a Galactic Savior.**

16 | Christians, UFOs, and Alien Abduction

"What I found was compelling evidence to claim that most of these aerial objects far exceeded the terrestrial technology of the era in which they were seen. I was forced to conclude that there is a great likelihood that Earth is being visited by highly advanced aerospace vehicles under highly 'intelligent' control indeed."—Dr. Richard F. Haines, retired NASA senior research scientist, Ames Research Center

"For many years I have lived with a secret, in a secrecy imposed on all specialists in astronautics. I can now reveal that every day, in the USA, our radar instruments capture objects of form and composition unknown to us. And there are thousands of witness reports and a quantity of documents to prove this, but nobody wants to make them public."—Colonel L. Gordon Cooper, Mercury and Gemini Astronaut

In the mid 1970s, Tom Horn and his wife, Nita, were crossing the Scholes Mountain on their way to Aloha, Oregon, to visit with Nita's mother, when suddenly, a brightly colored object moved erratically across the sky and caught their attention. At first, Tom thought it was a reflection on the windshield, the sun, or something creating light echoes on the glass. Then, as he watched, he realized he was seeing a solid, three-dimensional form. The thing was silvery, very bright, and circular, as best he could tell. It must have been at an altitude over fifteen thousand feet, and it was doing things known aircraft cannot do—shooting around at a phenomenal rate of speed, abruptly stopping, rocketing this way, then that, with hard-angle turns. He looked at Nita and pointed.

"Do you see that? What is that?"

It was the middle of the day, and she had seen it, too. Whatever they were watching, it was bright enough that they had no problem keeping it in view until they could stop the car. They got out and observed the phenomenon for another thirty seconds to a minute before it shot miles across the sky and stopped on a dime, then abruptly zoomed upward out of sight at an incredible rate of speed.

"What in the world did we just see?" Tom asked. Like him, Nita didn't have a clue. Spooky space effect in broad daylight? Top secret experiment? Angel? Demon? No idea.

As they got back in the car and continued on their way, they decided not to say anything to anybody.

"They'd think we were hallucinating," they decided.

But the next morning, they were amazed to see Salem, Oregon's top newspaper, *The Statesman Journal*, featuring a front-page article about how hundreds of people from across Washington and Oregon had seen a "UFO" the day before.

As it turns out, Tom and Nita are not the only Christians to have seen an Unidentified Flying Object. What follows are the testimonies of three other well-known and respected Bible teachers. We begin with the executive director of the popular Christian television program *Prophecy in the News*. Gary Stearman's story is additionally important due to his family's background in aircraft, plus Gary's personal experience as an experienced pilot of many air hours. (The Stearman family's Model 75 "Kaydet" was so popular during World War II that it was made the primary trainer aircraft for the US military. In 1934, Boeing purchased Stearman Aircraft and turned it into a subsidiary, and in 1989,

Lloyd Stearman, the family member who started the Stearman Aircraft Corporation in 1927, was inducted into the National Aviation Hall of Fame in Dayton, Ohio.)

Gary gave us permission to publish his story just as he told it in 2011.

Gary Stearman: The Story I Never Told...Until Now[638]

The following is a story that I've never publicly related. Except for a handful of people I've told over the last four decades, it has been my secret. Nevertheless, it is a true story that played a large role in the development of my thinking. Ultimately, it caused me to come to a deep belief in the absolute veracity of Scripture. As I relate the experience, I'm delivering a personal testimony, accompanied by a deep desire to sound a warning and to issue a challenge to Christians everywhere.

As a Bible-believing Christian, I hold to the conviction that the Tribulation period lies in our near future. According to prophecy, this time will be heralded by the release of dark spiritual forces, posing as saviors of planet Earth. Soon, the restraining effect of God's Spirit will be lifted from this planet and hell, itself, will be released to torment mankind.

When the Age of the Church comes to an end, these forces will convince many that they are presenting the super-scientific solution to man's problems. Instead, they will enthrall a gullible mankind into bondage and spiritual deceit. "Aliens from outer space," is their camouflage in our present age.

Their current message to mankind is, "Let us help you overcome your warlike, polluting ways, and build a bridge to future peace." That message is the oldest lie on earth, spawned by their chief scientist/sociologist, Satan.

As long as we remain here, Christians must endeavor to expose these dark spirits for what they really are.

Now to the Story.

As part of an aviation-oriented family, I was literally raised around airplanes from my earliest childhood. I was an airport brat when my father managed an airport. I determined to get my pilot's license at the earliest possible date…which I did as a teenager. I'm telling you this just to illustrate that flying has always been a big part of my life.

Stearman Aviation was known for having produced aircraft from the late 1920s through the 1940s, ending with the famous Model 75 Kaydet, which was the basic trainer for most of the pilots in World War Two. Over 8,500 of them were built, of which about 3,500 remain to this day. My father, uncles and cousins all felt the push toward flying and aeronautical engineering. So did I, until in the midst of my college years, I discovered that I was more interested in writing than engineering.

After graduation, with degrees in English and Psychology, as well as minors in descriptive linguistics, radio and television writing and literary analysis, I went to work, first for Beech Aircraft Corporation in commercial publications, then for Cessna Aircraft Corporation in the Merchandising and Marketing division. At both enterprises, my job was to write corporate publications and sales materials.

One of my tasks was to supply Cessna dealers across the United States with point-of-sale materials, such as brochures, product information, banners, posters, and films. This would include everything the local aircraft dealer would need to make a sale. After producing these products, we would personally deliver them by air in time for company representatives to put on sales meetings that introduced the new models.

It was midsummer in the late 1960s in Wichita, Kansas, and I prepared to take off from the delivery center airfield at Cessna Aircraft to make such a routine trip. On a Saturday afternoon, several of us in the Merchandising Division had spent time loading about a thousand pounds of displays into a brand-new Cessna 207 (rigged for cargo) preparatory to delivering it to a Texas dealer.

The next day—Sunday morning—I departed for my first stop, Love Field in Dallas, Texas, about 330 miles south. The trip took a normal and uneventful two hours. I arrived at the Cessna dealership late in the morning, where the dealer and I unloaded about half the materials I had brought for the meetings. We discussed his upcoming meeting over lunch. Then, a little after noon, I departed Love Field and headed west toward Lubbock, Texas, where I was to meet another Cessna dealer and unload the other half of the supplies for him. This leg of my flight, I thought, would be as ordinary as the first.

Climbing to a cruise altitude of 6,500 feet, and leveling off, I relaxed, expecting a 300-mile trip of about an hour and forty-five minutes. Routinely monitoring my nav-com and right on schedule, I was (as always) enjoying my flight. The air was smooth and cool. Then, without warning, a low-voltage warning flashed on my instrument panel!

My first reaction was simple annoyance: This had started as a perfect flight, but now I had to manage a failure. I was somewhat disgusted; this was after all, a brand-new airplane. I noted that the electrical system voltage was steadily dropping and after trying every alternative and discovering that there was no cure, I took one last reading on my heading and position, then shut down the entire electrical system. On an airplane, you can do that, because the engine has its own separate ignition system.

I believed that by doing this, I could save battery power till I got to Lubbock, then turn it back on in time to call the tower and make my landing. Again, I settled down, expecting the remaining hour to be uneventful. How wrong I was!

At this point, I would remind you that all electrical power was shut down, including of course, the radios. Yet, at that moment, I heard a crisp, clear voice that sounded just like a tour guide. It said, "If you look to your left, you'll see a UFO." My instant reaction was: "Now, that's the stupidest thing I've ever heard. I'm not gonna look to my left!"

And I didn't. Facing forward, I set my jaw and determined to continue as before.

But then it hit me: Although the radios were off, I had heard a clear voice. It was then that I decided for sure I was not going to look to my left!

Then, for the second time, loudly and clearly, the voice said (and I really couldn't tell where it was coming from), "If you look to your left, you'll see a UFO." Its intonation sounded just like a tour guide, and I laughed out loud. Then, curiosity finally got the best of me and I couldn't stop myself from looking to my left.

And there, slightly below my altitude, and a mile or two away, was a bright light. I watched it for a good while. It was matching my speed and direction. As we continued for a few minutes, it appeared to be slowly drawing closer to me. It occurred to me that if we were both homing in on Lubbock radio, we would be on converging courses. I then decided that this thing that I thought was a "UFO" was really an Air Force airplane (a Cessna T-41), which I knew they were using for basic training at Lubbock. This was no UFO after all…it was a silver-winged T-41, gleaming in the sunlight. Mystery solved!

We flew on together for a few minutes more, still on merging courses, drawing ever closer to each other. It looked like we'd get to Lubbock at about the same time. Then, something startling happened. We both flew under a high, solid cloud deck that was a few thousand feet above us. Now, at virtually the same moment, we had both flown into shadow. But amazingly, the light that came from this mystery aircraft was as bright as it had been in the sun. It was generating its own light! It was brilliant! Suddenly, I believed the voice I'd heard fifteen minutes ago. It was a UFO!

Now, the moment I had this thought, the bright ship reacted by flying quickly sideways toward me, covering about a mile in less than two seconds! What had earlier registered in my mind as a T-41 was now a circular aluminum craft…at least it looked like polished aluminum! It was about a hundred feet in diameter and maybe fifteen feet thick. It was shaped like an upside-down Reese's Peanut Butter Cup…even to the detail of being corrugated around the outside, though its corrugations weren't as deep as those on the traditional peanut butter cup. As it approached, I had seen its top because it was a little below me. It had a gleaming center spot and bright radial lines that went like pie slices to its edge.

Its corrugations were spaced about three feet apart. And here it was, flying with me in close formation about seventy-five feet off my left wing. Then, as unbelievable as it may sound, I felt something like waves of energy coming off this thing. I felt like I was being "probed" or "scanned"...that it literally knew what I was thinking! And I wasn't at all bothered by this. Quite the opposite, I felt an elation I've never experienced, either before or since.

I felt as though something terrifically good and beneficial was happening to me, something on the order of a rescue. Remember, I had entered into this situation with an electrical emergency.

I was magnetically drawn to this beautiful machine...if one can call it a machine. For several minutes, we flew along together. But as I looked, I wanted to get closer to it, to see how it was built. So I nudged the controls, causing my plane to slip stealthily closer to this thing... seventy feet...sixty-five feet...sixty feet...and I felt a magnificent connection with the giant ship...as though it was concerned about my condition. I perceived it as a gracious benefactor, though at the moment, I didn't connect its actions with my electrical failure.

Fifty-five feet...fifty feet... As I slowly drew closer and closer, I was looking for clues as to how it was built. Did it have rivets or seams? I could see none. It looked like one solid piece of material. Forty-five feet...and then I felt this thing alarmed by my intentions. It didn't want me to get too close.

In an instant, and with blinding speed, it zoomed back to its original position, about a mile off my left wingtip. It astonished me by banking to the right in order to turn left...exactly the opposite of the way an airplane flies. Now, in the distance, it still gleamed with a luminous silver light, and once again, flew along with me as we both headed for Lubbock, which was now less than twenty miles away! It seemed that we had covered what should have been an hour's flight in about ten minutes!

And here, the time had arrived to see whether my earlier strategy had worked. I reactivated the electrical system, and yes, there was enough battery power left to call Lubbock tower, and to deploy the flaps for a landing, all of which turned out to be routine. Rolling southward, I slowed and departed the runway in a left turn and taxied up to the Cessna dealership.

And through my windshield, looking back toward the east, about ten miles away, was the ship, still hovering in the distance, absolutely still. After shutdown, I walked into the dealership in something of a daze, where I met the dealer and mumbled something about having seen a UFO on my way.

There was nothing subtle about his reply: "I don't believe in those things!" I quietly resolved that I would never mention this to anyone else. Furthermore, he was angry: "You were supposed to be here earlier! What happened?" I told him about the electrical failure and it somewhat calmed him down. It didn't occur to me until years later that I had left Dallas just after noon on a trip that should have taken less than two hours. Now, it was after six o'clock…perhaps closer to seven. This man had waited on me all afternoon…on a Sunday! But he was sympathetic after he heard about my emergency.

Another thing didn't register with me until years later: I had refueled in Dallas, giving me enough fuel for four or five hours of flying time at the very most. I had landed over six hours later, and still had half my fuel left! But I just didn't think about it; it didn't cross my mind that there was anything strange about this.

I had intended to fly back to Wichita that evening after dropping off the rest of the load. But now, the airplane was in the shop with electrical problems, and I was forced to stay overnight.

The next morning…bright and early…the dealer picked me up and we headed for the airport to see what they had found wrong with my aircraft. Needless to say, I was quite anxious to fix the problem and head back home to Wichita and the factory. The shop foreman approached us as we entered. He was in an excited state as he almost shouted, "You ain't gonna believe what we found!"

And he proceeded to show us the brand new V-belt that had fallen off the alternator drive and ended up in the bottom of the cowling.

There was not a mark on it. It was factory new. And the pulleys from which it had escaped were still tensioned and safety wired. It was impossible for the belt to have fallen off in this way. Five men, including an FAA inspector, stood around marveling at the sight. At the very least, the belt should have been scarred. Most likely it would have broken. But it was pristine, and what's more, they had to loosen the fittings to replace it. It couldn't have fallen off the engine.

Of course, my mind was racing in a different direction: What had really happened? Why had the flying disc come alongside me at a critical moment? Had "they" actually caused that critical moment? Of course, I didn't utter a word about a UFO to any of those present on that Monday morning. I would have been laughed out of the hangar!

And so, after re-installing the drive belt, test-running the engine and discovering a healthy system voltage, it was pronounced airworthy. I took off and headed for Wichita.

A little over two hours later, I landed, went back to the office and essentially kept my mouth closed...to this day. Over the last 42 years, I've told maybe four or five people about the incident...more or less swearing them to secrecy in the process.

I have many questions. Was the UFO good or evil? Was it from outer space or inner space; perhaps another dimension? Was it angelic or demonic? Did it cause the failure of my electrical system, or did something else cause the calamity, and the UFO came to my aid? One thing is certain: I felt that the UFO had good intentions; contact with it had been both exhilarating and positive. I was disappointed when it stayed behind as I went on to land.

I must tell you that at that time, I had not yet given my life to Christ. And I was more aware than most people of the entire UFO phenomenon. This encounter, of course, had brought me to an entirely new level of perception. It opened my mind to the absolute reality of beings who have what appears to be a technology that's eons ahead of ours.

Here, it is important to mention that from my early childhood years, I had heard adults—family and close relatives—discuss the reality of UFOs. They were all totally convinced of their reality. In fact, two of my closest relatives were affiliated with the development of military aircraft, and later, with the establishment of our Intercontinental Ballistic Missile system. One of them, charged with developing protective systems that prevented false alarms, once casually mentioned that his major problem had been alarms tripped by passing UFOs. Another had seen a government-issued 16-millimeter film of a crashed UFO, which had been presented to them as a craft from outer space.

I, myself, had been employed in the building of test equipment for a wind tunnel, where I worked with two military officers who both had close encounters with UFOs.

From many sources, I had learned of the military's intense preoccupation with what they termed "extraterrestrial technology." It was rumored that from the 1948 Roswell crash and the years immediately following it, much technical knowledge was obtained by "trade agreements" with the little aliens and their overlords. Since that time, a veritable flood of books and articles have documented exactly that.

As the narrative goes, government leaders agreed to let these "spacemen" operate within our atmosphere, in return for scientific and industrial advances. Many researchers have related that the transistor, developed by Bell Labs in the 1950s, was said to have come from such a deal, that it began as "UFO technology." I hardly need remind you how radically our society has been changed by the introduction of solid-state electronics.

Not long after the personal encounter described above, I married the woman to whom I remain married to this day. She had been raised a Christian; I was not to become one until about a couple of years later. I began to read the Bible voraciously. It was the first book I'd ever found that explained the mysterious things that happen on this planet, as having to do with God, Creation and Redemption.

Because of my own encounter, I sought biblical answers that could explain what I had seen. I learned of God's angels in their chariots of fire that flew in the realms just beyond the reach of man's vision.

And I learned of the, "…principalities and powers in heavenly places…" mentioned by Paul in Ephesians 3:10. They are good as well as evil: The dark forces answer to their master, Satan, called in Ephesians 2:2, "…the prince of the power of the air."

Like Job, I can say, "For I know that my redeemer liveth, and that he shall stand at the latter day upon the earth" (Job 19:25). Without a shadow of a doubt, Jesus is my Lord and Savior.

In my own personal case, however, many questions remain. I continue to believe that I was rescued; I would like to believe that the beautiful ship that came alongside me was on a mission to save me from a possible crash.

But I don't exclude the possibility that the ship was demonic, representing a mission far beyond my ability to understand. I just can't say. I do know, however, that the Spirit of the Lord spoke clearly to me in the period that followed.

Afterward, I came, not only to saving faith in Christ, but to a consciousness that we are living in the last days, said by our Lord to resemble the days when fallen angels began to traffic among men. For eons, there has been a heavenly battle raging. Good and evil angels defend territories and causes that are far beyond our perception. Occasionally, they penetrate the dimensional barriers and for a moment, we see them.

The reality of these beings is beyond question to me. And since I am safe in Christ, I never worry that they might harm me. In the Spirit of the Lord, we are on the winning side of the battle.

Legendary Broadcaster Noah Hutchings' UFO Encounter[639]

Dr. Noah Hutchings, president of Southwest Radio Ministries in Oklahoma City, has been in Christian broadcasting for more than sixty years. He has written over a hundred books and booklets covering Bible commentary and prophetic topics and has led mission tours to the continents of Asia, Europe, South America, and Africa, as well as the Middle East. What many may not know is, like Tom Horn and

Gary Stearman, he, too, is a Christian who witnessed firsthand what some today call UFOs. We asked him to send us a short report of what he saw and when, and he happily replied:

In 1939 I lived with my family on a farm in SE Oklahoma, five miles south of Hugo, the county seat. At the time I was 15 years old. I daily rode the school bus at a pick up point about one half mile east of my home. I would usually cut across a short cut to and from the bus stop through a semi-wooded pasture.

One evening in, what I remember was October, as I was walking through the pasture toward my home, the sun was just setting. As I glanced northward past a grove of trees, an intense bright and glowing object suddenly ascended over the woods into the sky. About three seconds later as I watched, another object rose up and followed the same trajectory, followed by a third object a few seconds later doing the same. Then all three objects, radiating orange, white, and blue, lined up to form a triangle in the sky.

I sat down until it was dark and watched waiting to see if they would move. Later I walked the short distance to my home where my mother had saved supper for me. After eating, I rushed back to see if the three objects were still up in the sky, but they were gone.

At the time I was 15 years old, but there are some events in life so dramatic or beyond the ordinary that you never forget them. This was one of those incidents.

Years later, in 1942, I was called for Army duty in World War II. After basic training in Field Artillery Fire Direction I was sent overseas to New Caledonia for assignment. I was checking out a new radar to detect and identify all aircraft within fifty miles of our port. Attached to the radar unit were cables leading to sixteen anti-aircraft guns that could land a 90 mm shell in the lap of a Japanese fighter pilot at 12,000 feet. About half way through World War II, the Japanese converted all their military aircraft into Kamikaze planes, and the land based 90s were not effective in anti-Kamikaze attacks. I was thrown a set of firing tables for the 90s and spent the rest of the war supervising field artillery operations for the First Calvary Armored Division.

In the 18 months I operated a radar system I kept in mind the three objects I had seen on a late afternoon in 1939. However, I never picked up another thing in the sky that I could not identify, including a pelican that had swallowed a piece of gum from one of the ships that had been thrown overboard with the garbage. But no UFOs.

I remain convinced that the three objects I saw suddenly rising swiftly into the sky in 1939 [were] something beyond the identification and scientific knowledge of that time, or even today.... I think we have to consider seriously many of the seemingly reliable reports of UFO activity today, especially that of five retired Air force officers [640] who testified of the problems with UFOs during their service years.

Whether UFOs are something out of another dimension or angelic visitors from heavenly places is something that someday will be determined.

Dr. Walter Martin Had Time to Snap a Picture of the UFO[641]

Broadcaster, debater, and lecturer Dr. Walter Martin was a recognized Christian apologist who passed away in 1989. He pioneered organizations in the Christian counterculture movement including the Christian Research Institute in 1960 for Christian apologetics. Martin's colleagues included well-known radio Bible teacher Donald Grey Barnhouse; noted lawyer, professor, and Lutheran theologian John Warwick Montgomery; and founder of the Koinonia House ministry based in Coeur d'Alene, Idaho, Dr. Chuck Missler. But, as with Tom Horn, Gary Stearman, and Noah Hutchings, most people probably do not know that the cult-buster also had a UFO encounter. In fact, he and his partner even had time to take a clear picture of it as it hung suspended above a seminary. From a portion of his 1970s UFO presentation, we transcribed the following short excerpt:

> I possess, and it has been printed, the only color picture of a UFO, taken at an altitude of eight hundred feet, on a clear day in New Jersey, hovering near a seminary. And this particular one [the UFO picture], generally, I blow up on a wall about ten by fifteen feet so people can see it…and we have blown up large pictures of it…is of a circular ship with opaque windows circling it. Its dimensions, as far as we were able to determine, figure about fifty to seventy-five feet across and at least fifty feet thick. It made no noise whatsoever; it was bluish-grey in color. It hovered and then lazily took off, straight up over the mountains. My assistant took the picture with a 35-millimeter camera on a clear day. And that picture was used on the front cover of a national publication as the first "bonafide UFO sighting, verified by unimpeachable sources." After all, seminary professors would hardly be lying about Unidentified Flying Objects [sounds of audience laughing]. Particularly since my assistant who took the picture didn't believe they existed until he took the picture. Now, he is a firm believer in the existence of Unidentified Flying Objects…
>
> The question in my mind is not "what," but "who." I know what they are. Hynek knows what they are [Dr. Josef Allen Hynek was a United States astronomer, professor, and lead scientific adviser for UFO studies undertaken by the US Air Force under Project Sign, Project Grudge, and Project Blue Book]. The United States government knows what they are. The Soviet government knows what they are.… They are some form of extremely sophisticated aircraft, not made by any government occupying territory on our Earth that we know of… [Dr. Martin went on to explain his belief about the "who" that is piloting UFOs. He concluded they are demonic agents of deception].

The Difference between UFO Sightings and Alien Abduction

Because efforts have been made in some circles to renounce all unexplainable UFO activity as demonic and/or lump this phenomenon together with so-called alien abduction, we have listed below the current evolution of UFO encounter "types" as first developed by J. Allen Hynek and then revised in succeeding years:

1) Close Encounters of the First Kind (CEI) involve "visual" sightings of an Unidentified Flying Object.

2) Close Encounters of the Second Kind (CEII) include visual plus physical traces such as burned spots on the ground, radiation, strange markings, or wreckage debris appropriate for investigation.

3) Close Encounters of the Third Kind (CEIII) involve sightings of the UFO "occupants" near the UFO.

4) Close Encounters of the Fourth Kind (CEIV) include a human abducted by a UFO or its occupants (this was not included in Hynek's original scale).

5) Close Encounters of the Fifth Kind (CEV), developed by Steven M. Greer's Center for the Study of Extraterrestrial Intelligence (CSETI) group, are described as "joint, bilateral contact events produced through the conscious, voluntary, and proactive human-initiated or cooperative communication with extraterrestrial intelligence."[642]

6) Close Encounters of the Sixth Kind (CEVI) are described as "UFO incidents that cause direct injury or death."[643]

7) Close Encounters of the Seventh Kind (CEVII) involve abduction for the purpose of mingling human and extraterrestrial "DNA" to produce a hybrid.

"Close Encounters of the First Kind" is how we would describe the testimonies of Tom and Nita Horn, Gary Stearman, Noah Hutchings, and Walter Martin. They saw something that appeared to be solid, operated under what appeared to be intelligent control, yet defied identification and behaved in ways inconsistent with physical laws of the universe as we understand them. The UFOs could have been good, evil, or neither, but they were extraordinary, whatever they were.

For Tom Horn, the question over "what" and "who" UFOs and aliens are began a long time ago.

In fact, it dates back to his childhood. He was not yet a teenager when his father, Clarence, a Korean War veteran and territory officer in the state of Arizona, came home one day very excited. He'd been deer hunting not too far from Snowflake, Arizona. This was an area that Clarence loved to travel to, if for no other reason than that the man *loved to drive* (as anybody who knew him would testify, especially his kids), including along the Salt River Canyon up into the Apache-Sitgreaves National Forest. He'd stop at every little town along the way, including Show Low, an early settlement town named after a famous poker player. On this particular trip, Clarence had parked in the woods and was on foot, following an animal trail near Snowflake that he was very familiar with. He headed toward a waterhole that antelope, elk, and mule deer (his target) were known to habit, and that's when he came across something that had not been there before: several large, near-perfect, spherical craters, perhaps twenty feet across and eight feet deep. The mysterious cavities were so precise that it looked as if an enormous, white-hot ball had pushed them into the rock, and the finish on the walls was sealed so perfectly that rainwater filled the orbs. The sides of the holes were slick, not like they would have been if explosives had been used to create them (or somehow if gigantic drilling equipment had been lowered by a military transport helicopter into the remote location without disturbing the natural habitat or leaving behind signs of commercial or military activity), and each "pool" contained deer that had fallen in and drowned while attempting to drink the water.

Clarence took pictures of the obscure holes, had them developed, and showed them to the family. Tom remembers being especially impressed. Clarence also reported the finding to the police department where he worked and led a representative of the Army Corps of Engineers to the location. The origin of the puzzling craters was never determined, including by locals who frequented the area and thought they had appeared overnight. The Corps of Engineers also could not determine how the holes were made or what they could have been for. *The Phoenix Gazette* ran an article called "Mysterious Mountain Holes" about the discovery, reprinting photographs of Clarence kneeling beside the orbs with his 30-06 hunting rifle, and not long afterward, the Corps dynamited the pools so they would fill with rocks and protect the wildlife. About the same time, Tom's "crazy" aunt who lived next door to his family and whom nobody paid attention to was petrified by what she claimed was a dish-shaped object hovering above their home. But as they all knew, she was "nuts," so that, for a while, seemed to be the end of the story.

One of the holes Clarence Horn found. Bend in old picture distorts perfect circular pattern at top.

Officer Clarence Horn in the late '50s–early '60s

However, years later, something else happened near the site. On November 5, 1975, along the northeastern ridge of the same mountain range, Travis Walton stepped out of his pick-up to look at a mysterious, glowing object. While a crew of loggers waited nearby, Travis approached the UFO and was jolted by a blast of inexplicable energy. As his companions fled in terror, Travis was taken aboard the alien spacecraft and subjected to a variety of physical examinations. His story, *Fire in the Sky*, became a motion picture. It reports what's considered to be the best documented account of a UFO abduction ever recorded. Is Travis Walton's story true? Was there a connection between the Walton UFO and the mysterious mountain holes? Travis wanted to know, and once gave Horn his business card in Roswell, New Mexico, and asked him to call. Horn never did, but now, for the first time ever, we will disclose part (though not all of the complete story until the time is right) of what legendary American radio broadcaster, Paul Harvey, used to call "the rest of the story."

The Mysterious Case of Vida Bell

Throughout the first two decades of his public ministry, and to a large extent since, Tom Horn has held a secret. It involved a mystery concerning his family that he could neither understand nor talk about. If he had, too many in the Christian community would not have known how to advise him, or worse, would have thought he was nuts.

Across Arizona, Horn's father, Clarence, had been a well-known and liked individual. He had grown up riding fence lines for the old Bard Ranch, the largest open-territory cattle farm in the state, and later served in the Korean War. After his tour of duty, Clarence took a job as a police officer, married, and made a name for himself as a powerful but friendly man who literally would give you the shirt off his back. During his service in law enforcement, he would earn at least one commendation from the FBI as well as influential friends on both sides of the law…but that is another story. After he retired from the El Mirage Police Department, he would go on to work for over twenty-five years in the Del E. Webb Construction Company, building parts of Las Vegas and then Youngtown and Sun City near Phoenix. Webb, an associate of Howard Hughes, Bing Crosby, Bob Hope, and Robert and Barry Goldwater, was a good man to work for, and the company offered Clarence numerous opportunities to move up in the organization. But Clarence preferred keeping it simple, living in a modest home in El Mirage, Arizona, right where the Horns would be when the first of "the events" took place.

It was about 2:00 a.m. in 1964, just a few weeks after Clarence first discovered those mountain holes, when the screaming began. Tom may have been the first to hear it, as he recalls jumping from bed, terrified by the awful sound of his sister calling frantically for help. As he stood there, frozen in the darkness, his dad and mom suddenly pushed passed him in the shadows, and then his older brother Amil followed them, as they hurriedly made their way toward Vida's bedroom. Tom must have fallen in behind Amil, because the next thing he recalled was standing in his sister's chamber. She was on the mattress, clutching her blanket with both hands, holding the cover near her neck and wearing an emotionally harrowed expression. Tom would not understand her haunting gaze until years later, following his substantial experience as both a pastoral and hospital trauma counselor, when he would learn to recognize that expression as psychological shock. Vida was around thirteen years of age at the time, which means she had probably just started menstruating. That, too, was key, though Tom would not understand why or what had begun with his sister that night, until more than twenty years later, when finally one day she opened up to him while he was pastoring a church near Roseburg, Oregon. That's when she told him about something that had not even been defined in the early 1960s (the Betty and Barney Hill abduction story was the first widely publicized claim of alien abduction and wasn't made public until the best-selling 1966 book, *The Interrupted Journey*, and the 1975 television movie, *The UFO Incident*)—a story about her first visit by small, bulbous-headed grey men in her bedroom so many years before, facts Tom would confirm with his mother soon thereafter. What Tom could not have known, of course, was what would follow his sister's first admission: a series of disturbing events in her life—and then in her daughter's—that would crystallize something so preternatural and improbable that it nearly defied incredulity. In fact, it would have been easy for Tom to dismiss it all as the product of disturbed or fantastic imaginations if it had not been for the detectives, federal employees and attorneys, a vanished nuclear physicist from Los Alamos, Stephen Spielberg, and even what was possibly a recording of *their* voice and a picture of one of *them* that would follow. After that initial confession from his sister, Tom took a pen and wrote:

> Vida had "awakened" as if from a deep sleep and thought she saw something. Her eyes slowly examined the darkness, straining to identify the vague images filling the space around her. What little light she had was coming from moonlight through the window and the imperfect seal around the entry door. She could just make out a presence of some kind and the outline of

the closet and bathroom a short distance away. A small statue, or something like it, stood beyond the footboard of her bed near several "suspended" attachments.

Unaccountably, the smell of sulfur began wafting through the room.

No, not sulfur, more like gas: cadaverous, decomposing, a rotting stench of some kind lacing the air.

As she considered the odor, the "statue" by the footboard inexplicably bobbed. It appeared as if a cluster of balloons had been jerked sideways by a hidden, invisible clown.

Her eyes jumped to it, trying desperately to make out the image in the darkness.

Her stomach filled with nausea.

She forced herself to think, *Your mind is playing tricks on you, your mind is playing tricks on you…*

Then the form twitched…and she defined it; *them*…vacuous, horrible creatures, studying her.

The floating monstrosities acknowledged her glare, made a clicking sound, and slunk along the bedside, their bodies turning but not their heads, until spider-fast they formed a semi-circle near her feet. The vague light cast golden sheens on their bulbous-headed bodies, chalky and decrepit, as if their elliptical, horrifying eyes were windows into hell. The light vanished into them like into black holes: dead ocular cavities probably not unlike those of the minions of Dante's *Inferno*.

She wanted to scream, but couldn't at first. Beyond eye movement she was somehow paralyzed in the company of this malevolence. She could feel herself sweating profusely, her heart beating rapidly, and the inner urge to call out growing slowly toward a boiling point…until finally, one of the beings jumped forward and touched her forehead and that is when she shook herself and shrieked at their dreadful presence.

A moment later, she could hear scuffling elsewhere in the

house, the sound of people running toward her as the *things* seemed to dematerialize like ectoplasm through a fantastic, spinning void.

And then, a trace glow of the vanishing phantoms—like psychic shadows searching for ways to rush through spectral dimensions—lingered before her. The pungent smell of decaying flesh wafted away as her distant and unfamiliar expression fell upon her parents and brothers. Even now, malevolent beings could be watching them through shadows, angles in the walls, the very thought of which caused gooseflesh to crawl over her skin. She'd felt superstitious terror before, but this had been different—a nervous dread crouching deep inside her like an evil portent; this was but a shadow of things to come.[644]

Hidden Secrets, Private Investigations

Most of the details of the events following the first visit to Vida by unknown intelligence (improperly referred to in modern times as "alien abduction") will remain sealed for the time being due to a binding agreement and settlement between her, state authorities, and federal investigators. Perhaps the day will come when the complete "Mysterious Case of Vida Bell" will be told. What can be disclosed at this juncture is how the initial revelation to Tom Horn concerning what started that night in 1964 with his sister (and later his niece, a federal employee) pushed him to begin investigating what was truly behind the activity, and whether it was the same phenomenon that later would be reported by tens of thousands of people from around the world. Eventually, one thing became clear to Horn: The activity seemed demonic, but it was not possession; this was something else. He had worked for years in exorcism with a team of specialists, and so-called alien abduction was a malevolence of an entirely different kind. He wanted to understand and combat it.

At first, Horn was flying blind for many reasons: 1) The model for so-called alien abduction had not even been defined or circulated in the early '60s, and it wasn't much better in the '70s; 2) Christian leaders in particular were not formerly educated or trained to deal with the related psychosis often associated with those who experience the phenomenon (they were treated superficially as mentally unstable or demon possessed); 3) the social stigma connected to UFOs and abduction had created an atmosphere in which the phenomenon could not be openly discussed or studied, especially by clergy; and 4) as a result of the points above, there had been no serious effort by Christian academia that believers could turn to, to thoroughly investigate these circumstances or to determine the origin or causes of "abduction."

For Horn, these implications were deeply disturbing, and his investigation into the ramifications had to be done inconspicuously. After all, he was a respected pastor of a large and growing church and held ministerial association positions in the wider community, not including his responsibility to the denomination he was a part of. So, on Sundays, he would don his three-piece suit, step to the pulpit, and preach on subject matters of importance to victorious Christian living, while on his own time, he would be on the phone and in libraries (there was no Internet back then) looking for crime scenes and abduction reports that included "mysterious" facts or things that seemed to be out of place. In particular, he noted cases involving details such as traces of radiation; strange, "glassy" particles in the home; unexplained markings on the ground; and especially reports of sudden changes to the personality of the abductee, such as severe dissociation marked by unusual mood swings, manic depression, hallucinations, memory blocks, and so on, some of which he had seen in his own sister. He also wondered more conspiratorially if his father had unwittingly opened a metaphysical doorway that somehow invited an entry into his sister's life. Had she also somehow agreed with the activity? None of the family had been practicing Christians in the '60s, though they knew about God and had gone to church for a while. This would be an important fact as he reached back into his past, contacting people he could trust with this information who might be qualified to explain whether something truly was happening, and if so, weighing the possibilities of whether it was related to supernaturalism.

In the beginning, this private search for answers failed to produce any substantial results. Then in the late 1970s, a message arrived by mail. He should "read two books," he was told. One was called *The Cosmic Conspiracy*, which had just been written by a man named Stan Deyo, and a second was titled *The Omega Conspiracy*, by Dr. I. D. E. Thomas (Tom came to know both authors years later, and even republished the book by Dr. Thomas in 2007).

He ordered the books, read them, and for the first time, a window into the unknown cracked open. Here were other Christians—one a scientist and the other a seminary professor—who believed a factual phenomenon was occurring in which nondescript persons were being visited and in some cases reportedly carried away to laboratories or ships, where some kind of medical procedure was being performed on them. In the 1970s, Dr. Thomas encouraged Horn to take a closer look at deliberate cases of outright abductions, which sometimes included larger beings than the ones his sister had come face to face with. Dr. Thomas wrote:

> Mark Albrecht and Brooks Alexander in their excellent article in the *SCP Journal* (August 1977) refer to what can be considered a prototype of abduction encounter. It happened in 1971 near the Superstition Mountains of Arizona to a man called Brian Scott. He was on a camping trip when he found himself levitated into a large UFO. In the report of the doctor who directed Scott's hypnotic regression, he states that Scott had an authentic and detailed memory of what happened.
>
> The subject finds himself.... In a small room, paralyzed and unable to resist. Suddenly several 7-foot-tall beings enter and undress [him]... The beings are ugly, with sloping shoulders, crocodile-scaled skin, elephant-like feet, and hands with three fingers and a recessed thumb... Heavy fog or mist is everywhere... Two of the 7-foot-beings station themselves at consoles

of some kind, and a third stands beside a pole on which there is a moveable box with many tiny colored blinking lights… The subject experiences a series of uncomfortable if painless sensations from his feet upward; he senses he is bleeding; he urinates; he feels water run from his stomach; he feels his chest opened and he thinks his heart has left his body briefly; finally his head feels "pulled" violently… The subject detects a distinct unpleasant odor. Then from across the room out of the fog comes a 9-footer…[and] apparently communicates telepathically with the subject without moving his mouth. A message is communicated to the subject. Then the subject experiences an out-of-body trip. The message is a combination of vague philosophical statements, general information about the alien's origin and purpose, and a promise that they will return.[645]

The Superstition Mountains where Brian Scott claimed to have been abducted is part of the same Tonto National Forest boundary that includes the Apache-Sitgreaves National Forests, where Horn's father stumbled upon the mysterious mountain holes and where Travis Walton years later said he was taken aboard an alien spacecraft and subjected to medical procedures. This range also runs through the Agua Fria River valley, a dry riverbed bordering the town of El Mirage, where Vida was first visited by shadowy beings. It makes one wonder if this has any relationship with the ancient Pima and Maricopa Indians, who avoided these mountains as being the home of "bad medicine." Traditional Indian medicine included anything sacred, mysterious, or of "supernatural power" often connected to their shaman or medicine man who communicated with the spirit world for the benefit of the community. Bad medicine was evil supernaturalism that had to be avoided; thus, they called these the "Superstition Mountains," because they were historically connected with the presence of evil spirits who frequented the territory. Interestingly, this location is also where the giants known as the Jian-du-pids mentioned in chapter 2 ("The Sky Island's Assimilation for

Extraterrestrial Evangelism") were said to be destroyed by the Apache sun god.

For Vida Bell, something evil had definitely come this way. She had been well liked among boys and girls in the Dysart School District through junior high, where she was voted most popular student and often held leadership positions within cabinets and various groups. She maintained a cheery outlook on life both in and out of class, until that fateful night in 1964. Following her first "visit" by the strange unknowns, her life seemed to quickly fall apart, the details of which will not be included in this book out of respect for her privacy. Instead, we fast-forward now to the 1990s, when Vida was married to a man we will call Joey Luciano (not his real name). Luciano reportedly knew nothing of Vida's strange background and was a nuclear physicist with the uppermost security clearance doing research into nuclear and biological warfare at General Atomics in San Diego, California. For reasons Vida never knew or cannot remember, Luciano was transferred after some time from General Atomics to Los Alamos National Laboratory in northern New Mexico, where he was involved with a top-secret project, the details of which Vida was oblivious to. Of course, this is the same facility that was founded during World War II as a covert laboratory to coordinate the Manhattan Project—the Allied undertaking to develop the first nuclear weapons. More sinisterly, the site has also been connected to an alleged secret alien underground facility beneath Archuleta Mesa on the New Mexico border near Dulce, and to genetic experiments on humans, UFOs, and even five alien bodies or "Extraterrestrial Biological Entities" recovered from the 1947 Roswell crash site that were purportedly sent to a safe house at the Los Alamos National Laboratory north of Albuquerque.[646]

It was during this time while Luciano was conducting top-secret research for the US government at Los Alamos that one night after he returned home, Vida, under the influence of alcohol, opened up and revealed her secretive, inexplicable life, including past (and more recent) visitations by "little grey men with large heads and black, elliptical eyes."

She was utterly shocked by his response. He didn't bat an eyelid as he revealed his knowledge of the phenomenon and acknowledged that it is real. And, under the influence of alcohol himself, he admitted that the laboratory where he was working was involved with these things. He bragged of things we cannot publish herein, but what happened next speaks for itself. Soon after that discussion, he disappeared, never to be heard from again. (Was the house bugged, or did "they" report his conversation?)

Los Alamos National Laboratory where Luciano "disappeared" during top-secret research

When her husband did not return home, Vida started calling everybody she could think of. Nobody had heard from him, not family or friends. She finally called the police department to report him as missing. Soon afterward, she received a return call from somebody at Los Alamos who told her that Luciano had been killed "in a job-related accident." It took a few minutes to get past the initial shock before she thought to request the body for burial. That's when she was told the remains were unavailable and information surrounding her husband's death was a security issue. Vida was devastated and didn't know what to do. For the first time in years, she was entirely alone…and afraid. The person on the phone had been so matter of fact and had offered no sympathy or advice. Adding insult to injury, within weeks, her bills began stacking up as she no longer had an income. Her daughter Lavida, a federal employee with the Social Security Division, told her to apply for Luciano's pension and survivor's benefits. She made the application and quickly learned that in order for the application to be approved, she would need proof of her husband's death—either documentation from the funeral home (there was none because there was no body) or the death certificate, and that, too, was not to be provided through Los Alamos. If the classified research center arranged for information pertaining to Luciano's death for the certificate, the accident could be investigated, and this was not something they were going to allow. How they could refuse this information was beyond Vida, who thought it had to be illegal and turned to Lavida again, who subsequently started "rattling chains" up the halls in the Social Security Department. That action had an immediate effect, triggering something unprecedented. Vida was suddenly informed she would receive Luciano's pension and survivor Social Security benefits without need of any proof of death. To this day, nobody knows who intervened on her behalf or why, but Vida's application was simply "approved by decree," ostensibly in order to stop further inquests into her husband's disappearance. Somebody somewhere was powerful enough to simply say, "Make this go away," and that was that.

Yet, this would not be the last enigmatic suggestion that earthly government was somehow participating with "them" or covering up their presence. This show was just getting started.

Like Mother, Like Daughter

Approximately one month later, Vida and Lavida were driving to Vida and Tom's mother's home near Wickenburg, Arizona, after dropping off Vida's grandkids in Phoenix. Lavida was at the wheel, and they were following the back roads through the country, the way they always went because it was faster. As they approached a familiar intersection, somebody had placed a construction barrier in the lane. They decided to bypass the roadblock and continue forward, because they didn't want to turn around and go the long way.

Lavida noticed an amber glow in a field off the road ahead.

"What is that?" she asked.

Vida thought maybe the highway department or somebody was burning a field and said as much, following her inclination with, "They'll probably make you turn around."

Suddenly, a blinding flash dazed them. What seemed like a moment later, they were inexplicably parked in the middle of the road. Lavida looked at her mother and saw that her mouth and eyes were wide open, and she was staring straight ahead, as if frozen.

"Mom!" she yelled. "Mom!"

Vida appeared to be confused and responded with a slur, "Huh?"

Lavida surveyed their surroundings. They were sitting at a stop sign, many miles ahead of where they should have been.

"How did we get to the end of the road already, Mom?" She glanced at the rearview mirror. The amber-glowing fire was gone. There was nothing but blackness. Nightfall was deeper now.

"Where is the fire?!" Vida suddenly yelled. "Lavida, where is the fire?!"

Confused, Lavida started to pull the car over onto the curb, but Vida slammed her door lock down and screamed, "Just drive! Don't dare park this car!"

All the way to the house, Vida kept repeating that she needed to get there in order to call her brother (Tom) so he could pray for them.

He recalls their terror that night when he spoke with them on the phone, wanting to pass it off as two women afraid of the dark, but accepting that it may have been something more.

Soon afterward, Lavida developed a pseudotumor and started losing her eyesight. She began sleepwalking and finding herself standing in places she couldn't remember going. At one point, she awoke standing by the back door. Her ex-boyfriend had come to see her and found her there. He was yelling, "Lavida! What did you do!"

She remembers saying, "What?" then unexpectedly adding, "Look at that." She was pointing to a shadow in the backyard where she thought a tall, grayish-green figure that looked like a praying mantas stood. It had thin, large eyes, with just a line for a mouth.

The ex-boyfriend said, "What? Look at your head!" Blood was running down her back from a two-inch gash in the back of her head that later required stitches.

"Look," she repeated, pointing. The man glanced out the door and saw what he thought was somebody in a zoot suit, ducking away. Believing that somebody had mugged her, he rushed her to the emergency room, where her blood registered with high toxicity.

Tom's brother Amil, an Assemblies of God pastor, came by the hospital and prayed for her. She told him that a "teacher" and a "flight attendant" had come to her room, and when she had asked them what they wanted, the flight attendant had said, "It's not what you are now, but what they are going to make of you."

Spielberg and the Entity

Not long after this incident, the now-married Lavida went to Seattle, Washington, to see a football game with her friends. Before the event started, she was at the Space Needle when she and her husband became separated from the rest of the group. Right at that moment, as though from out of nowhere, a well-dressed man and woman approached them and said, "Come with us, you have been chosen." The man looked military—tall, with crew-cut hair and a firm disposition—and the woman was equally disposed. Both wore "passes" imprinted with barcodes around their necks. After a brief conversation, it was revealed that they were working with Stephen Spielberg. A promotional facility had been set up across the street to promote his new television miniseries, titled *Taken*, which was to air on the Sci-Fi Channel in 2002. The show would follow the lives of three families—the Crawfords, "who were seeking to cover-up the Roswell crash and the existence of Aliens, the Keys who are subject to frequent experimentations by the Aliens, and the Clarkes who sheltered one of the surviving Aliens from the crash."[647] Lavida and her husband agreed to be "interviewed" and crossed the road with Spielberg's representatives. Once inside the structure (which was guarded; only those chosen by Spielberg could get in, and this is where Lavida and her husband temporarily parted ways), Lavida was asked a series of bizarre questions about her health and dreams, and was given a set of headphones with which she listened to "abductees" rehearsing their stories. She was then led to a black object that she put her head into. She saw a suspended Earth surrounded by planets and heard a voice saying, "My life changed the day I was abducted." The select group of people she was with was taken into a room and told to form a circle and hold hands. The lights went out, and it felt to her like the building was spinning as fog filled the area and bright lights flooded in, followed by a voice saying, "You have just been abducted."

A girl's voice rang out from one side, saying, "You never know when they will come and take you."

Another voice, from a different part of the room, said, "You never thought it would happen to you," followed by another asking, "Why are they keeping the truth from you?"

Following this, Lavida's answers and reactions to the questions were evaluated and she was singled out by Spielberg as having most likely been abducted by aliens (the odds that Lavida of all people would have been picked out of a huge crowd and evaluated this way is highly improbable). She was shown alien replicas in glass boxes and Spielberg's private collection of authentic "implants," metallic objects taken from the bodies of abductees, and then she was given a copy of the book *Taken*, a high-tech amulet to wear, and a private pass to online information about aliens and the upcoming television series. She learned from reading the book on the ride home that abductees commonly develop a tumor that cannot be removed. She developed such a pseudotumor right after the night she and her mother witnessed the amber glow in the field and their journey was interrupted by missing time.

The high-tech amulet and security pass was a computer CD she mailed to Tom, together with other items. When he plugged it into his computer, it auto-launched to a hidden web page where various information on abduction, as well as facts involving "The Taken Experience" and "UFO Classification Systems," were archived by Spielberg. None of this was a surprise to Tom. He had known for some time of Spielberg's fascination with UFOs and abduction. In his 1977 sci-fi spectacular, *Close Encounters of the Third Kind*, Spielberg had, in fact, based his script on real-life witness testimonies and a government conspiracy to hide the facts from the public. These included multiple UFO sightings over southeastern Michigan in March of 1966 when Washtenaw County sheriffs and police in neighboring jurisdictions observed and reported disc-shaped objects flying at incredible speeds and diving, climbing, making sharp turns, then hovering. At the same time, officials at Selfridge Air Force Base confirmed that they were tracking the UFOs over Lake Erie. Another aspect of *Close Encounters* included an abduction event, portions of which were caught on audiotape. The Smithsonian produced a documentary titled *The Real Story: Close Encounters of the Third Kind* about these facts behind Spielberg's film. The documentary can be viewed online for free at the Smithsonian's YouTube channel.[648]

In any case, what happened next to Lavida may or may not have been connected to the Spielberg/Washington event, but as she arrived home, she found several messages on her telephone answering machine. The third message was very strange. Somebody named "Sharon" had started leaving a message when a signal from somewhere else bled over onto the recording. It is electrical and spooky-sounding, and it is difficult to make out exactly what is being said, but the recording sounds like, "This is Seir…I'm going to have to call her and see if I'm making her menstruate…Now, colly."

In demonology, Seir (also known as Seire, Seere, or Sear) is a Prince of Hell with twenty-six legions of demons under his command. He can go to any place on Earth in a matter of seconds to accomplish the will of the conjurer, while "colly" is a verb meaning "to make soiled, filthy, or dirty."

This audio file was professionally analyzed, resulting in the production of the original, plus three enhanced versions, that can be listened to at this book's website: ExoVaticana.com.

Additional digital phenomena happened again a few nights following this discovery. It took place as Lavida was using a webcam to send images in real time during a videoconference, when suddenly she felt very strange. Just then, the camera caught a glimpse of what looked like a "being" at her side and behind her. The picture "freaked her out," as it seemed to show a creature standing half inside the frame. Its slender, thin arm extended downward, while a reddish, praying mantis-like eye was observing her. When she spun around, nothing was there.

She sent the image to Tom, who had it evaluated by an image expert who concluded that whatever is in the frame was real and that it had not been doctored or photoshopped (later, the same picture was submitted to a police crime lab that concluded the same). Though we make no claim as to what is actually in the image, it is possible that this is the first legitimate capture of an "alien" entity on film.

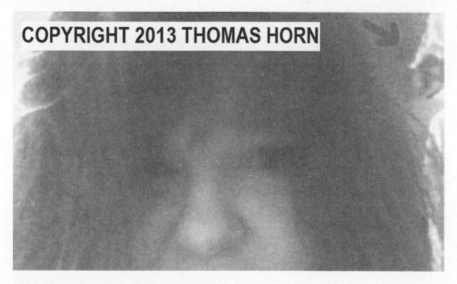

Image appears to show entity half in frame

As a federal employee and trained analyst for a particular state government Social Security Division, Lavida sought internal agency help over what was happening to her. She spoke privately with both the chief medical examiner and the head psych doctor about her sanity and, incredibly, they assured her that she is sane, that aliens exist, *and that the phenomenon is real!* One of the consultants even alleged that, at his last medical conference, the point was made how part of human DNA encodes something unknown, something "alien."

There is substantially more to this story that cannot yet be told, including information about other government "counselors" and what can only be thought of as highly placed "covens" within national agencies that direct abductees according to certain protocols—the most explosive of which was uncovered by a federal investigator working with Vida and over which a particular state had to monetarily settle with her and a dozen other *experiencers* (as alien abductees are called) in which an agreement was reached for their silence. Tom Horn attended two of these meetings at the behest of his sister. The investigator and the attorneys for both sides attended the meeting, and it was held inside the state building where the agreement was reached. Following that, Horn provided strong advice to both Vida and Lavida about the need to remain vigilant in their walk with Christ, to keep themselves covered in prayer and, at this time, this appears to have resulted in the final cessation of their "events." Besides Vida and her daughter Lavida, no other members of the extended Horn family have ever been troubled by the phenomenon, but related facts as reported above, and especially those withheld from this report, led Horn to conclude: 1) at least some UFO activity is supernatural deception; 2) true "alien abduction" is demonic in nature; and 3) both are ultimately subject to the authority of Jesus Christ.

SECTION FOUR

THE COMING GREAT DECEPTION

GARY SINISE and TIM ROBBINS

"THRILLING!"
— Paul Wunder, WBAI Radio

"EXHILARATING!"
— Bill Wine, FOX-TV

A BRIAN DE PALMA FILM

MISSION TO MARS

DVD

17 | If Artificial Structures Are Found on Another Planet (Xenoarchaeology), Will You Lose Your Religion?

"Many of the impressive [earliest civilization] buildings are made up of huge stones, with very little evidence testifying to how the ancient people fitted them into place. Such megalithic stones can be found all over, from the pyramids of Egypt to the stone circles of Britain to the Moai of Easter Island in the middle of the Pacific Ocean. Many unexplainable examples found in Peru have odd polygon shapes fitted precisely together like puzzle pieces with no mortar in between. Still more interestingly, many underwater cities have been discovered with the same megalithic construction."—Don Landis, *The Genius of Ancient Man*

In 2000, a movie directed by Brian De Palma titled *Mission to Mars* was released to theaters. It was based on an original screenplay by Jim Thomas, John Thomas, and Graham Yost, which depicted a NASA commander (Luke Graham, played by actor Don Cheadle) who, together with a crew of four astronauts, lands on the red planet. While exploring parts of the infamous "Cydonia" region, the "truth" about the Face on Mars as a genuine artificial structure is discovered together with remnants of advanced alien technology.

At the time the movie was in theaters, De Palma said he had set the narrative in the year 2020, "because that's the date the experts predict we should have a manned landing on Mars."[649]

The film inferred that when we do set foot on Mars, the remains of pyramids, city structures, and past alien presence could be made near the sphinx-like "face" and anomalous shapes photographed by the Viking Mars probe. A staple doctrine among many ufologists is that such a discovery on any exoplanet would confirm that the hero myths of ante-diluvian history, as well as the sudden appearance of man, himself, were the direct result of ancient, intelligent, extraterrestrial activity. The Great Sphinx in Giza, pyramidal structures around the world, and legends of early cultures would be seen as but trace evidence of this encounter, they believe, when ET astronauts arrived in our galaxy and on our planet a long time ago and genetically upgraded Homo sapiens from primates like apes. Such theorists also claim primitive men would have considered these spacefarers gods and would have recorded their arrival, experiments, and departure in steles and stone tablets as a supernatural encounter between gods and men. Having engineering help from the flying geniuses, the same men likely would have modeled the temples and holy sites they built on Earth in dedication to those "deities" based on designs they had been led to believe reflected similar configurations on the home planets of their creators; thus, pyramids, monuments, mounds, and sphinx-like formations not only dot the ancient Earth, but similar buildings could be (or have been) found on Mars or elsewhere and would be "the loaded gun" that New Age ufologists have been waiting for.

Admittedly, all around the world there are very old and mysterious constructions that do seem to defy explanation. These include gigantic edifices built from the largest stones ever cut and put into place and that seem to indicate manufacturing skills well beyond what we know of primeval man. One example of such a herculean slab weighs nearly four hundred tons, which was transported to Tiahuanaco, twelve miles south of Lake Titicaca in Bolivia, South America, from a quarry over two hundred miles away. A second example of an even larger stone, weighing a record-setting 2 million pounds, can be found at the southern entrance of Baalbeck, a city in eastern Lebanon famous for its magnificent temple ruins.

Some Christians agree that these colossal materials and structures do, indeed, attest to a time when superhuman intelligence was upon Earth and that, in fact, the builders of some magnificent arrangements really did originate from the heavens. It occurred while biblical Adam was still alive when powerful angels known as Watchers "descended [in the days] of Jared on the summit of Mount Hermon"[650] (brackets in original). *The Encyclopedia Britannica* says this port of entry at "Hermon" means a "Forbidden Place."[651] It is named as such ostensibly because the extraterrestrial beings that landed there are those that used women to birth the original giants called Anakim and Nephilim (and other abnormal creations) in the Days of Noah. God destroyed the first wave of these monstrosities in the Flood, but Moses records that the same type of beings reappeared again after the waters seceded (Genesis 6:4). These formidable, gigantic beings were attributed in ancient records as the builders of some of the most famous megalithic monuments, including the Great Pyramid and the Tower of Babel. J. R. Church once wrote that the structures these builders erected may also have been for metaphysical purposes, serving as a "gate" or doorway through which powerful beings could come. In the January 2007 *Prophecy in the News* magazine, he stated: "Perhaps the original group of Nephilim were scouts for a much larger force of demonic angels who, under the leadership of Satan, came to earth after the Flood. It seems to me that the Tower of Babel (meaning 'Gate to God') may have been built in an effort to contact these dark forces and forge a defense against the threat of another judgment."[652] Also connected to these sites are the ashes of both human and animal sacrifices that were made to the old gods or "Baals" of antiquity. Reginald C. Haupt Jr. participated in an archaeological expedition to Mt. Hermon and describes the ashes of sacrifices his group found there. In his book, *The Gods of the Lodge*, he wrote:

In the excavations of Baalbek, renamed Heliopolis by the Greeks, temples were uncovered honoring Baal and Bachus. The same is true of the site at Sidon. The Temple there is named the Temple of Baal of Sidon. But by far, of greater importance was the temple of Baal found on Mt. Hermon. Perhaps it would be more meaningful to you if I [Reginald Haupt] quote direct from my source. In the 1982 edition of the Thompson Chain Reference Bible (Fourth Improved Edition), the archaeological supplement was provided by G. Fredrick Owen, D.D., Ed.D. Dr. Owen wrote on page 376 of his supplement the following: "Mount Hermon, the 'chief' of the mountains of Palestine is five miles wide and twenty miles long. It has three peaks, the tallest of which is 9,166 feet above the Mediterranean Sea. For centuries before Abraham's time, the mountain had been venerated in connection with Baal.

"Baal worship was the leading religion of Canaan. On most of the high peaks of the country were shrines known as 'high places,' the higher the holier. Here groves were planted and shrines erected for worship. Since Mount Hermon towered above all the other mountains in the region, it was the chief high place, the shrine of shrines. Canaanites looked to Mount Hermon much as the Moslems face Mecca when they pray.

"During the summer of 1934, Dr. Stewart Crawford and this writer [Reginald Haupt] led a small expedition, in which we studied the ancient Baal shrines surrounding Mount Hermon. We located many ruins and in each case the shrine was so oriented that when the priests and the devotees were at the altar, they faced the chief Baal sanctuary, or Quibla, located on the highest of the three peaks of Hermon.

"We then ascended the mountain and found the ruined temple of Baal, constructed of Herodian masonry, which dated it to just previous to and during the early Christian era. In a low place near the northwest corner of the temple, we excavated and found loads of ash and burnt bone, which had been dumped there as a refuse from sacrifices."[653]

Mythology involving Watchers, fallen angels, and giants as builders of some of these mysterious sites is repeated in legends around the world. These stories are consistent with Sumerian and Hebrew accounts of the Great Flood and of the subsequent destruction of giant Nephilim whose history of human sacrifices parallel those found on Mt. Hermon.

A most dynamic question then arises concerning whether those megalithic builders known as Watchers would have also built similar structures on other planets, which perhaps were under their jurisdiction before the great war between God and Lucifer. This could be echoed in places like Ezekiel chapter 28, where the proud angel is called "the anointed cherub that covereth [Lucifer]" who was upon the holy mountain of God and who "walked up and down in the midst of the *stones of fire*" (v. 14, emphasis added). Because of the fallen angel's sins, God declared, "I will cast thee as profane out of the mountain of God: and I will destroy thee, O covering cherub, from the midst of the *stones of fire*" (v. 16, emphasis added). These "stones of fire" are believed by some scholars to represent the planetary belt, and it is not unreasonable to imagine that Lucifer and his angels once held command over certain of the planetoids. These worlds may have had artificial structures built on them—maybe even pyramidal or sphinx-like in shape—somehow related to the presence of those mighty angels, the ruins of which could be rediscovered someday. In the book of Job, where the prophet details how God destroyed the literal dwelling places of the angels who made insurrection against Him (Job 26:11–13), it specifically mentions the destruction of Rahab, a planetary body also known as "Pride," from which God drove "the fugitive snake."

This also brings up a second hypothetical question: If edifices on Earth were built to mirror those on these angel planets, what was their purpose? Could it have been to somehow create a binding or "unholy symmetry" between the fallen angels and man's sphere? We find indications of such a scheme all over the ancient world, where structures, circular mazes, altars, and mounds related to the Watchers and their giant offspring served the purpose of making contact with and homage to those beings. For instance, in the Golan Heights, there is a huge, Stonehenge-like monument that archaeologists believe to be as many as five thousand years old. It is called *Gilgal Rephaim* or "The Circle of the Rephaim" (the Rephaim are studied elsewhere in this book as offspring of the Watchers who were associated throughout the ancient world with deceased Nephilim, demons, ghosts, hauntings, the "shades of the dead," and spirits in Sheol). One feature of the Gilgal Rephaim circle is "the meaning of two large openings, somewhat like doorways, one facing northeast, the other southeast," notes Israeli journalist Barry Chamish.[654] "In 1968 Professor Yonathan Mizrahi of the Department of Anthropology at Harvard University and Professor Anthony Aveni of Colgate University discovered that in 3000 BCE, the first rays of the summer solstice would have appeared directly through the northeast opening as seen from the central tumulus. At the same time, the southeast opening provided a direct view of Sirius."[655] Thus, one function of the Gilgal Rephaim circles, as with similar sites, appears to have been the desire to create a connection between Earth with certain astronomical locations (in this case, the star Sirius). This particular cosmological site (Sirius) was considered by ancient Egyptians as the heavenly whereabouts of the goddess Isis and by Freemasons *as the home of Lucifer.* Such a nexus between this planet and the mythological home of Lucifer is suggestive, including the idea that discovery of artificial structures on a planet in that region bearing eerie similarity to buildings on Earth could be made someday. If they were, could this play a role in the great deception spoken of in 2 Thessalonians, chapter 2? Wouldn't people be quick to point to the other world and then to the Egyptian desert and say, "See! Here's proof! We came from aliens! The Bible is a hoax!" Such an extraordinary finding would undoubtedly challenge a great deal of our Earth-centric theology and contribute strongly to the delusion of the masses.

Gilgal Rephaim on the Golan Heights

Even science communities in recent years have speculated that artificial structures may just be waiting to be discovered on other planets. In fact, teams of astronomers have of late argued that the best way to find extraterrestrial intelligence—either dead and gone or still alive— would be to search for their "signposts" in the form of megastructures that may stand out as unnatural on other worlds or artificial satellites in orbit around ET planets called "Dyson Spheres."[656] (A Dyson Sphere is a hypothetical structure originally described by theoretical physicist and mathematician, Freeman Dyson, who speculated that extraterrestrial societies that survived long enough would eventually build massive starlight or solar collectors to harness their energy. Searching for such artificial structures might lead to the detection of advanced alien life, he believed.) Still others think discovery of artificiality has already been made on at least one other planet and massively covered up by a league of nations, being held back until a specific time of "Official Disclosure." This find was made right where *Mission to Mars* director Brian De Palma suggested it would be—Cydonia.

Before he died of cancer in 2009, we were privileged to interview Dr. Tom Van Flandern, who held a PhD in astronomy, specializing in celestial mechanics (the theory of orbits), from Yale University. He had spent twenty-one years (1963–1983) at the US Naval Observatory in Washington, DC, where he became the chief of the Celestial Mechanics Branch of the Nautical Almanac Office. For the last decade of his life, Professor Flandern was a research associate at the University of Maryland Physics Department in College Park, MD, and a consultant to the Army Research Laboratory in Adelphi, MD, working on improving the accuracy of the Global Positioning System (GPS). *The American Spectator, Salon* magazine, and others often quoted him regarding his challenges to Einstein's theory of relativity, but it was his outspoken belief that artificial structures dotted the Martian landscape and were being obfuscated by NASA and other national powers that caught our attention. In an excerpt from our 2007 interview, we asked:

HORN: On your website, there is a page where high-resolution spacecraft photos of Mars appear to show artificial structures. Tell us about these.

VAN FLANDERN: The biggest surprise of the space program to date has been the finding of several categories of anomalies on the surface of Mars that, if seen on Earth, would certainly be attributed to human activity. These include an abundance of special shapes not normally found in nature, such as closed triangles and pyramids; vehicle-like tracks and trails across otherwise featureless desert terrain; mostly underground networks of huge "glassy tubes" apparently extending for hundreds of miles, visible in places where the surface is cracked, and seeming to connect interesting surface places; odd patterns and symbols; and an abundance of large-scale "artistic" imagery such as the five known faces on Mars and some geoglyphs reminiscent of those on the plains of Nazca in Peru.

HORN: What stands out to you the most as special shapes on Mars that do not normally arise in nature?

VAN FLANDERN: Closed triangles with sharp vertices and straight sides are not normally seen in nature. 3, 4, and 5-sided pyramids are also rare. Yet many of these are found on Mars, but not on any other planet or moon yet examined in similar detail. On the Elysium plains of Mars there may be an entire field of pyramid-shaped objects laid out in linear arrays.

HORN: Describe the objects on Mars you called "glassy tubes."

VAN FLANDERN: From an examination of hundreds of these objects, we know that they are tube-like shapes typically 50–100 meters in diameter. White bands wrap around the tube about every ten meters along its entire length. The material between bands is translucent, and we can faintly see the white bands on the underside through the tube. When direct sunlight is available, it reflects from the tube in a mirror-like way instead of just scattering the light. Where a boulder has damaged a tube, we often see a collapsed tube section, where broken white bands lie flat on the surface, and sharp, spine-like portions of broken bands jut out from an intact-but-torn tube section. Tubes are visible mainly in fissures or where a flood has eroded away the topsoil. In some places, they can be traced underground in infrared images that can detect such things if they are not too far below the surface. Some tubes cross one another (one above, one below) in perpendicular intersections, while others have junctions where one tube becomes two or vice versa. In a few places, many tubes come together in patterns suggestive of "terminals" for train stations.

HORN: What else is seen that might be of special interest?

VAN FLANDERN: In certain places on Mars, especially near the location of the former equator of the planet, we see "artistic imagery", sometimes in abundance, although not always with distinct clarity. Moreover, the shapes seen are not random, but depict familiar terrestrial images in organized groupings. For example, in one region of Mars named

"Cydonia", we see an apparent mosaic scene showing impressions of sky, land, and water, with animal shapes organized in appropriate sections of the mosaic. Amphibious creatures are in the water area, animals on the land area, and aviary creatures in the air area. However, millions of years of dust storms and erosion have left many of the images more impressionistic than life-like. Had the images been as distinct as the words I must use to describe them, the shock waves from this discovery would have already traveled around the world.

HORN: What distinguishes the many artistic faces and other familiar shapes on Mars from faces and shapes seen in clouds and natural landscapes here on Earth?

VAN FLANDERN: It is possible to see even very detailed shapes in random, noisy backgrounds. But some of the Martian shapes appear against flat, featureless backgrounds. The context and relationship appropriateness is additional evidence these are not products of geology or random processes. But the most compelling proof, to a scientist at least, is the fulfillment of what we call a priori predictions. For example, if you are dealt a 13-card hand and get all 13 spades, you might wonder if that was an accident or the result of a fixed deck because the odds against that happening by chance are 635-billion-to-one. Yet every specific randomized deal of 13 unique cards had the same odds against happening by chance. So unlikely events, like unlikely card hands, can and do happen by chance. Yet if I predicted that on the next deal, your hand would contain 13 spades, and it did, you could be sure at odds of 635-billion-to-one that was not a lucky guess but the result of a controlled process. That's how the a priori principle works—through the power of predictions.

When the Viking spacecraft saw an apparent face on Mars in the Cydonia region, that was interesting but could easily have been a "trick of light and shadow". So scientists formulated tests to tell whether the object was natural (a product of geology and illusion) or artificial (a product of intelligences). The first eight such tests initially gave a split decision, 5 to 3 in favor of artificiality. Two of those tests were based on the fact that the Cydonia face-object cannot be seen from the ground but must be viewed from above, for example from an orbiting space station. So if artificial, it would logically be built on the equator of Mars and built upright. But the Cydonia face was far from the equator (latitude 41 degrees north) and was tilted from upright by an angle of about 35 degrees. Those statistics favored a natural origin. Then in 1996 we took a look at the pole shift of Mars to see where the face-like object was before the pole shift. The answer was exactly on the old equator and upright to within two degrees! The odds against that happening by chance were roughly 1000-to-one. So if the builders were active before the cataclysm that tipped the pole of Mars (the explosion of the other moon 3.2 million years ago), then both these tests indicated an artificial origin. By the end of that year, all eight tests favored an artificial origin over a natural one.

As compelling as this conclusion was to any mind open to either possibility, it still needed confirmation. So in 1997, the Society for Planetary SETI Research (SPSR), an association of about 30 independent scientists, sent a few representatives to NASA to request priority imaging of the Cydonia face-like object by the high-resolution camera on the newly-arrived Mars Global Surveyor spacecraft. SPSR then set down criteria for distinguishing artificial from natural well before any results were known. In brief, if and only if the object was artificial, the impression of a humanoid eye, nose, and mouth in the original images should be supplemented by secondary facial features in any detailed new image. These specifically included an eyebrow over the eye socket, an iris inside the eye socket, nostrils at the large end of a tapered nose, and evidence of lips in the mouth feature. Specifics were set down for the qualifying size, shape, location, and orientation of these features on the mesa. Moreover, the test required that no qualifying features appear in the background so that our minds could form apparent facial features from randomness, as our minds are prone to do.

When the spacecraft images were returned to Earth in April 1998, every prediction was fulfilled. This was like predicting a deal of 13 spades in advance, except that the combined odds against this happening by chance at Cydonia were 1000-billion-billion-to-one. That left no doubt in the minds of scientists familiar with the a priori principle that the Cydonia Face had to be an artificial structure.

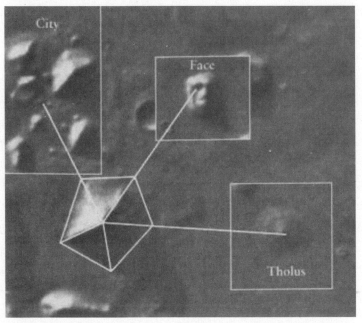

Cydonia region showing face, five-sided pyramid, and other artificial configurations

HORN: Can you give another example of ruling out a natural origin for some of these artistic features?

VAN FLANDERN: Yes. One of the animal shapes elsewhere on Mars resembled a puma, but it wasn't detailed enough to be persuasive and the edge of the spacecraft photograph left the hindquarters cut off and unseen. So the scientist who found the image, J. P. Levasseur, predicted that the image was artificial if and only if the missing hindquarters completed an animal hind-section and legs and contained a puma-like tail extending from the right place on the hindquarters. Anything else from an unlimited number of possibilities would indicate a natural origin. A few years later, the spacecraft (by request) took another image that included the hindquarters area, and showed the completion of an animal hindquarters and hind legs and a marvelous tail of the right proportions extending from just the right place.

HORN: So what is the connection between possible artifacts on Mars and the exploded planet hypothesis you discuss on your website?

VAN FLANDERN: The explosion of the "water-world" body Mars was orbiting until 3.2 million years ago produced the most recent pole shift on Mars that moved the Cydonia Face from the equator to its present location, tilting it by 35 degrees. This tells us that the builders of these amazing surface features predated the explosion, and that their civilization was probably terminated by that explosion.

Moreover, we see no evidence of a primary civilization on Mars, making the exploded water world the most likely location for that civilization. Indeed, that speculation makes sense on several levels. For example, if we project our own civilization ahead a few thousand years, trips to our Moon will by then be routine for tourists. The first thing such tourists will wish to do is board an orbiting space station to get a close-up overview of the entire Moon. It will then be a natural step for the many activities on the lunar surface—telescopes, mining operations, laboratories, communication centers, and all manner of commercial operations—to attract tourists and tourist dollars by building surface exhibits that can be seen from the orbiting space station. So we can reasonably project that the future of our Moon will be not unlike what we are seeing today on Mars—surface exhibits that can be best viewed from an orbiting space station. However, if that was the function of the artistic Mars images, that would imply Mars was the civilization's moon, not its home world. And the latter was lost by explosion 3.2 million years ago—a date that is reliably determined from the orbital period of new comet orbits [one cannot help wonder if this "exploded" planet "3.2 million years ago" in close proximity to Mars was not the "Rahab" (also known as "Pride") of Job 26 from which God drove "the fugitive snake"].[657]

Did Disney Almost Let the Cat Out of the Bag?

In the lead-up to the release of *Mission to Mars*, Disney had worked with an army of NASA scientists, astronauts, and technicians to produce the script for the film. Soon after, a row reportedly took place between NASA and Disney, as it seemed the space agency didn't like what the film was set to insinuate: that a discovery had been made of past alien presence on Mars, that an artificial, sphinx-like "face" and pyramidal shapes near it (photographed by the Viking Mars probe) had actually been discovered, and that a twenty-five-year cover-up was being perpetrated by NASA and the US government in collusion with other world powers who were waiting for a mysterious "right time" to disclose the findings. Even former consultant to President Bill Clinton, Dick Morris, once told his call girl that documented evidence of past intelligent life existed on Mars and was concealed by the US military.[658]

One thing is certain: A cover-up of global proportions involving an alien presence—past and present—that includes supranatural sites, machines, devices, and entities has become abundantly convincing in recent years as expert testimony from astronauts and military personnel (including generals, pilots, aviation experts, and government officials), as well as documents on official government letterheads released through the Freedom of Information Act, have piled sky high. No reasonable person can any longer survey the *known* evidence and doubt that *someone* or *something* is operating outside the average man's purview in league with at least some of the world's elite. Smack dab in the middle of this conspiracy is not only NASA and other aeronautics and space administrations like the European Space Agency, but the Vatican. In some ways, this makes perfect sense. Official Disclosure of so-called extraterrestrial intelligence and habitable alien worlds, which is likely to be announced in 2013, according to scientists like Abel Mendez, who runs the Planetary Habitability Laboratory at the University of Puerto Rico at Arecibo, "will have a profound effect on humanity."[659] This will be true both psychologically and spiritually, and, due to the nature of man, most of the world's peoples will be looking for traditional religious leaders to put the revelation of exo-worlds and "aliens" (whom we believe to be deceptive fallen angels) into context. As the most powerful Church on Earth with its own diplomatic corps of ambassadors posted throughout the industrialized nations of the world, the Vatican is uniquely positioned and has been actively preparing for this moment. According to Monsignor Corrado Balducci, who, during his life, was an exorcist, theologian, member of the Vatican Curia (governing body at Rome) and official mouthpiece of the Church *concerning the reality of aliens here now*, the Vatican has not only been closely following the phenomenon, but has also been using its embassies (Nunciatures) around the world to quietly compile material evidence on the extraterrestrials and their mission. The Vatican has never refuted this revelation from Balducci, and in further evidence of the covert research, in 1976, a high-profile attorney named Daniel Sheehan (with degrees from Harvard in government law and divinity and who had served as legal counsel on numerous famous cases, including the Karen Silkwood case, Iran-Contra, Three Mile Island, Watergate, and—with funds from Laurance Rockefeller—even as counsel for famous abduction researcher Dr. John Mack) sought to crack open the secret UFO files held in the vaults of the Vatican library. If anybody should have been given access to them, it would have been Sheehan, as in addition to his legal profession, he was general counsel to the United States Jesuit Headquarters in Washington DC. Furthermore, his request was made at the behest of the US government and then president of the United States, Jimmy Carter. During a 2001 radio interview, Sheehan explained what happened when he requested access to the Vatican's highly guarded alien files:

It turned out that President Carter, then in 1977…had actually asked to have the information regarding the existence of extraterrestrial intelligence and the UFO phenomena sent to him. This procedure of asking the United States Congress—the Science and Technology Committee of the House of Representatives to have the Science and Technology Division of the Library of Congress Congressional Research Service— [to] gather all this information together, and make a determination about what information was going to be released to the public, and how much was going to be made available to Congress, could be made in that context. So, it was in that context that I was talking to Marcia Smith, and Marcia asked me whether, as General Counsel to the United States Jesuit Headquarters, there at their National Office in Washington DC, whether or not I could get access to the section of the Vatican library in Rome that would contain this information…on extraterrestrial intelligence and the UFO phenomenon. I was very pleased to try to do that. So I asked Father Bill Davis, who was the Director of the National Office at that time [1977], if I could follow that process of trying to get that information from the Vatican. He gave me his official approval, so I undertook that process, but much to my surprise in fact, and much to the surprise of Father Davis I might add, we were refused access to that particular portion of the Vatican Library. So, I sent back a second letter to the Jesuit who was the head of the Vatican library, and explained to him that this was an official request that had come from the Congressional Research Service of the Library of Congress—that it had come from the Congress of the United States, and that the President, himself, had wanted to get this information. So, I thought that would get us the information, but I received a second response from the Vatican Library saying no—the Jesuit National Headquarters would not be provided with this information. So, I had to regretfully report that back to Marcia Smith letting her know that I was not able to get it.[660]

While the Vatican is certainly the biggest duck in the puddle with responsibility for controlling the flow of disclosure information for the world's religious communities, it is not alone among consulting academia. For instance, the astronomers we mentioned earlier who are working to pinpoint the alien home bases by searching for their "Dyson Spheres" are funded in large part by the Templeton Foundation, a philanthropic organization interested in genetics and alien-sounding transhumanist aspirations as the path toward hybridizing humanity to posthuman. As mentioned in chapter 1 ("Mount Graham and the L.U.C.I.F.E.R. Project: The Investigation Begins"), the Templeton Foundation has been funding a series of lectures titled, "Facing the Challenges of Transhumanism: Religion, Science, Technology," at Arizona State University, which led to another undertaking launched in 2009 called the SOPHIA project (after the Greek goddess who helps man make contact with "them"), the express purpose of which is to verify communication with and to contact "Other-Worldly Entities/Extraterrestrials, and/or a Universal Intelligence/God."[661]

Another university that we suspect could be involved in the cover-up of the alien presence, artifacts, and/or mysterious technology is Pennsylvania State—or at least one of its well-known lecturers. This story goes back to 2005, when Tom Horn and Steve Quayle were doing a series of *Q-File* radio shows, and suddenly a story shot across the World Wide Web of a giant, Leviathan-type creature that had been discovered in the polar ice of Franz Josef Land.[662] The colossal being was described as having horns "immense in dimension" that protruded from its head "with incredible length. The body is covered with a combination of coarse fur and what can best be described as 'body armor' (like an American armadillo) that protects its enormous joints and head."[663]

Both Horn and Quayle started investigating the story at the time—including analyzing the audio and video files—and within days, Quayle had tracked down the helicopter pilot who had flown over and filmed the Leviathan video. According to the pilot, Sony had created a docu-drama hoax to virally promote the release of a new Playstation 2 game called, *Shadow of the Colossus*. Quayle reported his discussion with the pilot to George Noory on *Coast to Coast AM* that same week, but before the whole thing could be put to rest, new evidence unearthed by Horn suggested that both he and Quayle might have only scratched the surface of a much deeper mystery or "bait-and-switch" designed to throw people off the trail of legitimate recovery efforts at or near the Franz Josef Land site. Among the most interesting and potentially telling pieces of the puzzle was a senior lecturer in anthropology and American studies at Pennsylvania State University, Abington College in Abington, by the name of P. J. Capelotti. Just before the so-called hoax was perpetuated, the professor had been conducting archaeological studies of Franz Josef Land and followed his research of the site by immediately advocating the need to establish international laws and/or treaties to *preserve alien artifacts*.

Photo of Leviathan-type creature on Franz Josef Land

Among other things, Capelotti pointed out that:

The late biochemist and science fiction writer Isaac Asimov once speculated that the galaxy may contain 325 million planets with traces of civilizations in ruins. Perhaps our astronomers and their SETI stations are hearing only static through their radio telescopes because they are, in effect, listening for a message from the extraterrestrial equivalent of the ancient Maya or the Sumerians—dead civilizations that can speak to us now only through archaeology. Constructing a catalog of visual signatures of advanced civilizations will someday be within the province of aerospace archaeology. And with a potential cultural resource database of 325 million planets with civilizations in ruins, there sure is a lot of fieldwork to do "out there."[664]

Did Capelotti's team discover something in Franz Josef Land and/or nearby expedition sites needing international protection…something that corresponds to artificial remains elsewhere in the galaxy that also need international protection…something big enough to, let's say, employ Sony to concoct a cover-up? Was the helicopter pilot paid off or threatened against admitting the truth about what he had actually filmed? As extraordinary as that sounds, history has shown repeatedly how governments have participated in similar scenarios on more than one occasion. (Just look at the ridiculous Roswell weather balloon cover-up story.)

Another intriguing aspect of the 2005 case is how, like the pro-transhumanist Templeton Foundation's funding to locate Dyson Spheres and "Other-Worldly Entities/Extraterrestrials" in order to promote the alien-hybridizing of man, Capelotti seems to have come away from his Franz Josef Land findings with a similar belief that "aerospace archaeology" is somehow connected with the next step in human evolution (something the film *Mission to Mars* also strongly suggested). In a now-removed Pennsylvania State Personal Webserver entry preserved on the "Aerospace Archaeology Wiki," Capelotti wrote:

I prefer the term "aerospace archaeology" if for no other reason than it includes the study of sites from the space age, which I believe will become increasingly important to the study of modern man as *technological possibilities* continue their course of *altering the possibilities of human evolution.*[665] (emphasis added)

What type of "technology" could Capelotti's team have recovered in Franz Josef Land that convinced him that: 1) man's evolution will be altered via "aerospace archaeology"; and 2) international laws and/or treaties must be established now to preserve alien artifacts?

Amazingly, a few years after Horn and Quayle's investigation, Capelotti followed his 2005 expedition with a book published by McFarland Publishing titled, *The Human Archaeology of Space: Lunar, Planetary and Interstellar Relics of Exploration*, in which he discusses the *Shadow of the Colossus* Leviathan conspiracy and admits to making two voyages to the North Pole on board the Russian icebreaker Yamal at the time. "During the second voyage," he writes, "as we returned from the pole, we landed by helicopter on Rudolf Island in the Franz [Josef] Land archipelago."[666] Capelotti describes his team's excursion to the site to examine the remains of "an enormous aircraft," which he then claims was a Soviet TB-3 bomber whose destruction the former Soviet Union had also "buried as deeply" as the government could. Again, how and why surveying a crashed airplane could be described as needing international laws and/or treaties to preserve "alien artifacts" as well as having the power to alter humanity via "aerospace archaeology" simply does not add up. Capelotti then takes several pages of his book to focus on Tom Horn as he seeks to downplay the *Raiders News Update* original inquiry:

> This fairly benign aerospace archaeology—albeit in very extreme environment—was taken up as a central element of an argument for the presence of artifacts of extra-terrestrial intelligence here on earth. In a series of articles called "Stargates, Ancient Rituals, and Those Invited Through the Portal" and posted on the internet news site Raiders News Update, author Thomas Horn speculated that it was the disbelievers that were being conned, in this case by a specially created hoax that was in fact part of a larger cosmic conspiracy involving, you guessed it, me.[667]

After republishing a large part of Horn's 2005 investigation in his *Human Archaeology of Space* work, Capelotti repeats his claim that nothing otherworldly was discovered at Franz Josef Land, but he does so, once again, without explaining how neither a crashed Soviet airplane could lead to the next step in human evolution nor why—following *whatever* was discovered in the Arctic Ocean north of Russia—this had provoked his immediate advocacy of international treaties to preserve alien artifacts.

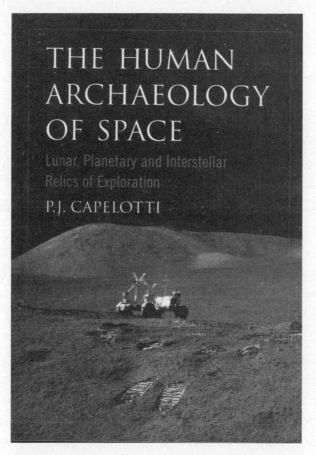

Capelotti takes on Tom Horn in *The Human Archaeology of Space: Lunar, Planetary and Interstellar Relics of Exploration* book

It's also interesting that, according to Capelotti, the former Soviet government wanted to "bury as deeply as possible" the massive craft they had discovered near where "Sony" had filmed the Leviathan. This attempt to capture, suppress, and control "alien artifacts" is the modus operandi of earthly governments and is a reminder of what happened in 2003 when archaeologists discovered a magnetic anomaly in the ground where the Euphrates River once flowed. It turned out to be (according to the archaeologists) the lost tomb of King Gilgamesh, the legendary ruler of ancient Sumeria known in the Bible as Nimrod and in the New Testament as the spirit of Antichrist that rises again during the end times. This is interesting, given that the same location is mentioned in the book of Revelation (chapter 9) where John describes the "bottomless pit" opening up. Does this imply the gate to the underworld is located near the Euphrates where ancient Babylon stood? Whatever the case may be, within hours of the Gilgamesh find, the United States military set up a barrier around the site and removed the materials, secreting them away to places unknown. Members of the media, who had been set to cover the Gilgamesh findings, suddenly found themselves without a story and in the dark. This included journalists from the *Assyrian International News Agency*,[668] *ABC News*,[669] and *BBC News*.[670] According to Graham Hancock and Robert Bauval, in *Message of the Sphinx*,[671] the US and Egyptian governments also blocked independent investigations around the Great Sphinx at Giza, where it is believed a "Hall of Records" or mythical library exists containing the lost knowledge of the Egyptians on papyrus scrolls and the history of the lost continent of Atlantis, which psychic Edgar Cayce claimed is buried beneath the Sphinx.

All this should catch the reader's attention given how the Brookings Institution, considered the number-one policy think tank in the world with contributors from every field of science and industry, philosophy, and religion, published a secret report in the 1960s for the Committee on Long-Range Studies of the National Aeronautics and Space Administration in which they argued in favor of NASA and other national agencies withholding from the public knowledge or evidence of alien artifacts. Brookings speculated that advances in technology and space frontierism would soon allow extraterrestrial exploration and even armchair astronomers to locate artifacts on other planets, and this was of great social concern to them. The report, titled "Proposed Studies on the Implications of Peaceful Space Activities for Human Affairs" (provided with the purchase of this book from the publisher), describes how "artifacts left at some point in time by these life forms [intelligent aliens] might possibly be discovered through our space activities on the Moon, Mars, or Venus."[672] The policy setters then suggested such a discovery could lead to the acquisition of "unknown knowledge" or even "contact" with entities, and this was an uncalculated danger. They wrote:

Anthropological files contain many examples of societies, sure of their place in the universe, which have disintegrated when they have had to associate with previously unfamiliar societies espousing different ideas and different life ways; others that survived such an experience usually did so by paying the price of changes in values and attitudes and behavior. Since intelligent life might be discovered at any time via the radio telescope research presently under way, and since the consequences of such a discovery are presently unpredictable because of our limited knowledge of behavior under even an approximation of such dramatic circumstances, two research areas can be recommended:

- Continuing studies to determine emotional and intellectual understanding and attitudes—and successive alterations of them if any—regarding the possibility and consequences of discovering intelligent extraterrestrial life.
- Historical and empirical studies of the behavior of peoples and their leaders when confronted with dramatic and unfamiliar events or social pressures. Such studies might help to provide programs for meeting and adjusting to the implications of such a discovery. Questions one might wish to answer by such studies would include: How might such information, under what circumstances, be presented to—*or withheld*—from the public for what ends? What might be the role of the discovering scientists and other decision makers regarding release of the fact of discovery? (emphasis added)[673]

Of particular concern to the Brookings Institute was how fundamentalist Christians might react to—and even define—the issue through broadcast and print media. As such, they should be infiltrated and gradually steered toward a particular mindset, which the government could favor. "Consider the following," they wrote:

> The Fundamentalist (and anti-science) sects are growing apace around the world and, as missionary enterprises, may have schools and a good deal of literature attached to them. One of the important things is that, where they are active, they appeal to the illiterate and semiliterate (including, as missions, the preachers as well as the congregation) and can pile up a very influential following in terms of numbers. For them, the discovery of other life—rather than any other space product—would be electrifying. Since the main ones among these sects are broadly international in their scope and are, in some places, a news source, the principal distributors of mass media materials, an important source of value interpretation, a central social institution, an educational institution, and so on, some scattered studies need to be made both in their home centers and churches and their missions, in relation to attitudes about space activities and extraterrestrial life.[674]

The wide-ranging Brookings Institute report thus determined: 1) Aliens and/or their artifacts are likely to be confirmed this century on other planets, including Mars and the moon; 2) The impact on society and religion is unpredictable and potentially dangerous; and 3) Confirmation of alien intelligence should thus be withheld until the appropriate time, when the world's masses have been properly "climatized" to the idea.

One is therefore left to conclude that, whether it is the tomb of Gilgamesh, the Hall of Records, the Franz Josef Land findings, or more recent alleged discoveries such as the underground Dark Pyramid fifty miles from Mount McKinley in Alaska, the idea that artifacts that may be connected to otherworldly knowledge and extrasolar locations exist on or beneath Earth's soil is possible and even perhaps should be thought of as waiting instruments of end-times deception, something established long ago in anticipation of a final conflict when the armies of darkness shall gather in contest for the souls of humankind.

On this, the question for the reader is, if artificial structures are revealed on another planet similar to or linked with structures on Earth, will you lose your religion? Not if you understand where they originated and how *they* plan to use them.

18 | The Power and Principality's Planetary Control System

The UFO Mythos

"Any sufficiently advanced technology is indistinguishable from magic."[675]—Arthur C. Clarke

"Any sufficiently advanced magic is indistinguishable from technology."—Anonymous

The UFO phenomenon is nuanced, complex, multidimensional, and, above all, uncooperative to analyze. No matter what one believes, it cannot be denied that a UFO mythos permeates modern culture. It subtly animates and steers cultural consciousness. A myth is a tale believed as true. It's usually sacred, and is set in the distant past, otherworlds, or other parts of the world featuring heroic, superhuman, or nonhuman characters.[676] In this sense, the alien invasion has already occurred. Psychoanalyst Bruno Bettelheim explains: "Myths and fairy stories both answer the eternal questions: What is the world really like? How am I to live my life in it? How can I truly be myself?"[677] Myths answer fundamental worldview questions. Thus, rather than trying to explain flying saucer propulsion technology, perhaps we are better served by asking what sort of worldview it promotes. Jacques Vallée has pointed out, "If UFOs are acting at the mythic and spiritual level it will be almost impossible to detect it by conventional methods."[678] It is important to analyze how myths function in order to assess how the UFO phenomenon shapes public opinion.

Myths are not necessarily fictional; rather, they are transcendent, dreamlike, and psycho-social. We can see this in the way Hollywood affects culture. For this reason, professional screenwriters make use of classical mythic devices in movies and television drama. A student of the famous mythologist Joseph Campbell who teaches storytelling to screenwriters explains:

> What is a myth? For our purposes a myth is not the untruth or fanciful exaggeration of popular expression. A myth, as Joseph Campbell was fond of saying, is a metaphor for a mystery beyond human comprehension. It is a comparison that helps us understand, by analogy, some aspect of our mysterious selves. A myth, in this way of thinking, is not an untruth but a way of reaching a profound truth.[679]

While this is an excellent working definition, it is important to recognize that this is how the secular world explains Christianity. Campbell and his disciples have little room for Christian truth claims, seeing things like Jesus' resurrection as a metaphor to be reinterpreted through a mythical hermeneutic. Campbell writes, "We are all manifestations of Buddha consciousness, or Christ consciousness, only we don't know it."[680] Of course, this begs the question of how he knows *that*. In the end, Campbell's sort of spirituality, which is increasingly popular, amounts to Gnostic, pantheistic monism—through knowledge, mankind awakens to realize that all is one. Interestingly, this is the dominant UFO spirituality as well.

Thus, we are not endorsing Campbell's spirituality but rather his insight into how beliefs and stories mold culture. At a fundamental level, God providentially allows the world to be so molded. C. S. Lewis pointed out that the world's mythologies consistently hint at the redemption realized through Christ. Lewis wrote, "The heart of Christianity is a myth which is also a fact. The old myth of the dying God, without ceasing to be myth, comes down from the heaven of legend and imagination to the earth of history. It happens—at a particular date, in a particular place, followed by debatable historical consequences. We pass from a Balder or an Osiris, dying nobody knows when or where, to an historical Person crucified (it is all in order) under Pontius Pilate."[681] Accordingly, Christianity has all the features of myth, but uniquely stands on a documented historical basis that all other such myths lack—it is the *actualized* hope behind man's mythic yearnings. The UFO phenomenon is promoted as an alternative.

UFO accounts influence society in subtle yet important ways. The mythos has a factual basis—photographs and video, physical effects, radar data, radiation signatures, ground impressions, abductees with physical trauma—that cannot be dismissed. Yet, the mythic elements forecast a future evolution, communion with our space brothers, and the savior from above. By examining its mythological impact, perhaps we can discern something about its true intent. From a literary and psychological perspective, the UFO myth evokes psychic symbols deep in our unconscious minds, influencing our thinking and worldview. A range of experts—Carl Jung, Jacques Vallée, and Ted Peters, among others—recognizes that a UFO savior myth is molding modern man, irrespective of contact. Many people who have never seen a UFO still *believe* in them. In this way, the phenomenon exerts broad influence with minimal exposure. After a brief examination of myth, we will suggest a connection between Jacques Vallée's control-system hypothesis and biblical theology in order to draw some conclusions.

The UFO Mythos Synchronicity and Archetype

In the 1950s, the famous Swiss psychiatrist and founder of analytical psychology, Carl Gustav Jung, spoke of the UFO phenomenon as a modern myth in the making. Jung famously created some of the best-known modern psychological concepts, including synchronicity, archetype, and the collective unconscious. Researching the first has yielded some surprising results. Synchronicity refers to "a non-causal connection between two or more various phenomena (psychic and/or physical)."[682] Additionally, Jung offered, "We could also use the concept of a *meaningful coincidence* if two or more events, where something other than probability of chance is involved."[683] Synchronicities give one the impression that circumstances have been arranged for a purpose. Christians speak of these sorts of occurrences in terms of "God opening doors." When circumstances favorably align in accordance with God's will, believers interpret synchronicity as God encouraging a particular course of action. Often these involve impossible circumstances that defy coincidence. Synchronicities suggest that reality is a lot stranger than commonly accepted.

Jung's ideas were inspired by experiences that the naturalistic worldview fails to explain. The mechanistic determinism common to atheism leads to a hopeless existence. Rather than accepting humans as biological robots, he believed in a deeper reality beyond the physical world and tried to parse it in scientific terms. Roderick Main, a Jungian scholar from the Centre for Psychoanalytic Studies, wrote:

> The culmination of Jung's lifelong involvement with the paranormal is his theory of synchronicity, the view that the structure of reality includes a principle of acausal connection which manifests itself most conspicuously in the form of meaningful coincidences. Difficult, flawed, prone to misrepresentation, this theory nonetheless remains one of the most suggestive attempts yet made to bring the paranormal within the bounds of intelligibility.
>
> It has been found relevant by psychotherapists, parapsychologists, researchers of spiritual experience, and a growing number of non-specialists. Indeed, Jung's writings in this area form an excellent general introduction to the whole field of the paranormal.[684]

An example of a common synchronicity is when you are thinking about a friend you have not seen for a long while, and at that precise moment he or she calls on phone. Is it a mere coincidence? Perhaps…but what about a few minutes later, when a relative stops by unexpectedly—bearing an old photograph of that same friend? How many coincidences are necessary before we take note? Most people have experienced events like this and may believe this is the way God gets our attention. If so, it seems fair to suggest that UFOs are a portent of His imminent intervention into the world.

Once one sifts out the nonsense, even the residual UFOs are notoriously difficult to classify. Jung concluded, "*Something is seen, but one doesn't know what.* It is difficult, if not impossible, to form any correct idea of these objects, because they behave not like bodies but like weightless thoughts."[685] To Jung, it looked as if "this obviously complicated phenomenon had an extremely important psychic component as well as a possible physical basis."[686] In this way, a minimal amount of material manifestation provides the more influential psychic layer with philosophical legs to stand on. They peel the curtain of spacetime back just enough to exert an influence and then they vanish. Jung also considered that, in some cases, they could be manifestations of consciousness—synchronistic phantasms. Interestingly, indicative of the high strangeness involved, UFO abductees have said things like, "Synchronicity is like a language to *them*" and "synchronicity is the language that *they* use to communicate."[687] Actually, in writing this chapter, an interesting synchronicity occurred while acquiring sources for those quotes.

In researching this project, I (Putnam) listened to a number of UFO-related podcasts. One episode was *Truth Out Radio with Richard Dolan*, who had Mike Clelland, an abductee and writer of Hiddenexperience. blogspot.com, as a guest.[688] During the course of their conversation, the two men talked about how abductees experience a remarkable amount of synchronic high strangeness, ostensibly more than most folks. This is when I first heard Clelland mention, "Synchronicity is the language that *they* use to communicate." As the conversation progressed, Dolan and

Clelland discussed how the number "333" seems to manifest in strange synchronicity to the phenomenon. Clelland talked about how many abductees report waking up to see their clocks at exactly 3:33 a.m., and his research indicated that this is the time when the body, in its deepest sleep, is at its weakest and consequently nearest to death. He inferred a connection between abduction and near-death experiences, a parallel NDE researcher Dr. Kenneth Ring observed as well. In response, Dolan agreed that the number "333" was ubiquitous and said that all he had come up with was a possible Christian connection in that it is exactly half of "666," seemingly implying a connection to the biblical number of the beast (Revelation 13:8). Being that neither man is a professing Christian, I found their discussion provocative, to say the least.

After listening to their fascinating conversation, I decided to contact Mike Clelland to get a reference for that quote about synchronicity as a language. He was kind enough to send me a link to download his essay, "Synchronicity and the UFO Abductee," but I discovered it was part of a published collection called *The Sync Book 2*. Being drilled by my seminary course work to always provide accurate documentation, I asked him what page that quote appeared on in the published version. It turns out (and this is the sort of stuff you just cannot make up) the citation is on *page 333*. Coincidence? Now, to me, that seems like a significant synchronicity, albeit to anyone else it likely seems fanciful. However, if it is, I believe it's the sort of thing only God can providentially produce and, since this occurrence, I have been praying for Mike Clelland, specifically that he might consider his hidden experience through a Christian lens. Perhaps you might pray for him as well.

In lieu of being misunderstood, we are not endorsing Jungian psychology but rather examining how one of the twentieth century's great minds connected the UFO phenomenon to religious and mythological motifs. Given our hypothesis that all of this heralds the strong delusion of biblical prophecy, Jung's insights are valuable. We do not necessarily have to buy into all of psychoanalytic theory to acknowledge that stories and symbols affect the mind in subtle yet profound ways. In order to understand Jung's thought, a brief discussion of Jungian psychology is necessary.

The two big ideas are the archetype and collective unconscious. An archetype is defined as a "primary structural element of human psyche" or a universal symbol that is theoretically shared by all humans and "the collective unconscious is made of archetypes or primordial images."[689] While an adequate treatment is beyond the scope of this work, Jung described it in this way:

> My thesis then, is as follows: in addition to our immediate consciousness, which is of a thoroughly personal nature and which we believe to be the only empirical psyche (even if we tack on the personal unconscious as an appendix), there exists a second psychic system of a collective, universal, and impersonal nature which is identical in all individuals. This collective unconscious does not develop individually but is inherited. It consists of pre-existent forms, the archetypes, which can only become conscious secondarily and which give definite form to certain psychic contents.[690]

In this sense, archetypes are symbols that serve as models or images in the subconscious mind. Myths are a powerful means of communicating at this level.

One of the last books Jung published, *Flying Saucers: A Modern Myth of Things Seen in the Skies* (1959), analyzed the archetypal meaning and psychological significance of UFO encounters. Describing the phenomenon as a living myth, he wrote, "Since the second World War they have appeared in masses, obviously because an imminent landing is planned."[691] Though he acknowledged that they are tracked on radar as well as reported anecdotally, his treatment of the subject of flying saucers demonstrates that, historically, circular symbols have invoked totality and divinity. He concluded that "the UFOs could easily be conceived as 'gods.'"[692] Accordingly, he noted that they often take on messianic qualities, among other ideas: "These space-guests are sometimes idealized figures along the lines of technological angels who are concerned for our welfare, sometimes dwarfs with enormous heads bursting with intelligence, sometimes lemur-like creatures covered with hair and equipped with claws, or dwarfish monsters clad in armor and looking like insects."[693] Professor of philosophy at Denver Seminary, Dr. Douglas Groothuis, writes: "Christians should reinterpret [extraterrestrials] as very possibly the malevolent masquerading of some very low demonic beings and monsters."[694] One needn't look long at the literature to confirm all of this and more.

Jung saw this mythos as filling the gap left by the waning Christian consensus. Speaking to secularization, he wrote: "The dominating idea of a mediator and god who became man, after having thrust the old polytheistic beliefs into the background, is now in its turn on the point of evaporating. Untold millions of so called Christians have lost their belief in a real and living mediator."[695] He argued that secularized man projects his deep psychological need for a savior and that the UFO mythos "has a highly suggestive effect and grows into a savior myth whose basic features have been repeated countless times."[696] He saw them as a replacement for Christ. No matter what the underlying reality is behind UFOs, the myth is molding culture and forming a worldview. We think this is by design.

Building on Jung's analysis, Lutheran theologian Ted Peters writes, "I suggest that the study of UFOs has the appearance of being scientific—hence, it offers the opportunity to discuss religious feelings in seemingly scientific terms. Whether we say it in public or not, many of us believe science is good and religion is bad. Science is for modern educated people; religion is for old-fashioned superstitious people."[697] He suggests that some people see aliens as diplomats or scientific explorers, but his third explanatory model, the "celestial savior," resonates best with our hypothesis.[698] This savior model, common in channeled messages and contactee literature, was thought to be a projection of Cold War angst. Peters writes: "He or she is the messiah from a 'heavenly' civilization where there is peace and no more war. In this religious model, we believe that the reason for the alien mission to earth is to help us achieve the same utopian level of existence that the aliens have."[699] Similarly, astrobiology and SETI serves this religious need as much as, if not more than, a scientific one. Although Peters has criticized our position, we find many points of agreement even though he offers a different Christian perspective from our own.

Peters has characterized the Christian fundamentalist argument in three steps: 1) an argument from biblical authority that ETs do not exist; 2) a subversive connection to naturalistic evolution; and 3) a declaration that UFOs are demonic. We addressed the first point in our chapter entitled "Astro-Apologetics" by arguing that while Scripture is silent on the existence of ETs, biblical prophecy predicts a great deception rather than a cosmic awakening. Furthermore, Peters' own celestial savior model connects the predicted end-time false messiahs to UFOs. The second point is addressed in our critique of astrobiology, but Peters has also noted how the UFO mythos connects to Darwinism:

> The UFO phenomenon and the concept of evolution converge in our culture to form a mythic view of reality. Since the 1950s and perhaps even before, a myth has been under construction in our society that pictures Ufonauts as coming from a civilization in outer space that is further advanced than ours—further advanced in science, technology and morality. This means they have evolved further than we on earth. According to this emerging myth, the Ufonauts are traveling to earth to teach us how to evolve faster, to save ourselves from disaster as we cross the nuclear threshold. The space beings constitute our own future coming back in time as well as they see in this emerging UFO myth is the human imagination gone wild. By presuming validity to the theory of evolution, earthling imagination has projected evolutionary advance to the point of development salvation onto imaginary civilizations in outer space. What we

find here, complain the fundamentalists, is a subversive plot to convince our people to believe in evolution and, of course, then to deny the authority of the biblical account of creation in the book of Genesis.[700]

While we would qualify that we do not see it as merely an imaginative phenomenon, the subversive promotion of the naturalistic worldview is a premise in our argument. The third step, according to Peters, is to simply declare all of it demonic. Rather than providing a simple declaration, we have offered biblical exegesis establishing the atmosphere as the demonic realm. Even so, we acknowledge, the UFO/ET phenomenon is a murky subject full of misidentifications and hoaxes. Additionally, they aren't all necessarily evil. Certainly, broad-sweeping generalizations are bound to miss the mark somewhere. Even so, the widely acknowledged association between the occult, paranormal, and UFOs makes such an inference not only viable, but wise. A synthesis of Jacques Vallée's hypothesis and biblical theology offers much promise.

Jacques Vallée's Control System Hypothesis

Jacques Vallée came of age in postwar 1950s, France, just as the modern UFO wave was hitting its peak. It was also the dawn of the space age with the launch of the famous *Sputnik* satellite. All of this captured his imagination and motivated him to study physics and astronomy; he earned his master's degree in astrophysics. One of his early jobs for the Paris observatory where he witnessed data recordings and films of UFOs being destroyed had a profound influence on his career.[701] Later, when he moved to America to earn a PhD in computer science from Northwestern, he sought out astronomer and UFO expert, J. Allen Hynek, and the rest is the stuff of legend.

Although early on, Hynek was explaining away UFOs as swamp gas and other such absurdities, Vallée began assisting him on Project Blue Book in 1963 and the two became friends. Twenty-two years of government employment studying the phenomenon (1947–1969) convinced Hynek that, after the wheat was sifted from the chaff, a genuine phenomenon remained unexplained—the residual UFO (RUFO). The collaboration inspired Vallée's first two books: *Anatomy of a Phenomenon* (1965) and *Challenge to Science* (1966). Then, Vallée and Hynek wrote one together: *The Edge of Reality* (1975). While the *UFO Encyclopedia* calls Vallée's first two books the most scientifically sophisticated defenses of the extraterrestrial hypothesis (ETH) ever mounted,[702] as more evidence was analyzed and his thinking matured, he came to view the phenomenon as interdimensional rather than extraterrestrial. In 1990, Vallée published a paper, "Five Arguments against the Extraterrestrial Origin of Unidentified Flying Objects," in the *Journal of Scientific Exploration* arguing against the space alien explanation (included free on the data disc provided with the first release of *Exo-Vaticana*).[703] His opposition is discounted by many prominent ufologists, prompting Vallée to refer to himself as a "heretic among heretics."[704] He adds humorously, "I will be disappointed if UFOs turn out to be nothing more than spaceships."[705] But this begs the question of what he thinks UFOs really are…

It was *Passport to Magonia* (1969) that marked the major turning point in Vallée's thought. Within, he argued that modern reports of UFOs and aliens parallel appearances of occult entities like demons, ghosts, faeries, sylphs, and cryptids from religion, folklore, witchcraft, and magic. However, it was his subsequent book, *The Invisible College* (1975), that introduced the hypothesis that UFOs are a component working in a "control system" meant to influence and steer human culture.[706] Vallée reasoned the control system is analogous to a thermostat that controls room temperature. When a room gets too hot, the air conditioning is triggered, and when it gets too cold, the heat activates. In this way, he asserts that UFOs are a component in a control system influencing human consciousness and beliefs. This not only explains why they seem evasive and deceptive, it clarifies why the phenomenon appears to deliberately promote a level of absurdity that evades rational scrutiny, because most people dismiss the subject as nonsense—something Vallée calls "metalogic."

A helpful analog is the word "paradox," meaning a statement, proposition, or situation that seems to be absurd or contradictory, but in fact may speak to a deeper truth inexpressible in common language. For example, if someone says to you, "I'm a compulsive liar," do you believe them or not? Another humorous example is, "Nobody goes to that restaurant because it is too crowded." Vallée made an analogy to Buddhism:

> For example, in Zen Buddhism the seeker must deal with such concepts as "the sound of one hand clapping"—an apparently preposterous notion which is designed to break down ordinary ways of thinking. The occurrences of similar "absurd" messages in UFO cases brought me to the idea that maybe we're dealing with a sort of control system that is subtly manipulating human consciousness.[707]

In this way, seemingly nonsensical information has a deconstructive purpose. Recalling the full citation in chapter 3 ("Days of Noah"), Vallée provides a rationale for this behavior: "It would have to disturb and reassure at the same time, exploiting both the gullibility of the zealots and the narrow-mindedness of the debunkers."[708] This has a lot of explanatory scope. The saucer enthusiasts accept almost any Unidentified Aerial Phenomenon as space aliens, and the debunkers will argue that it all has a natural explanation, be it hallucinations, insects, or swamp gas. This enforces the UFO taboo in academia as summarized in chapter 3 and prevents much serious investigation. However, in the grey area in between, there is a remarkable result in terms of shaping worldviews.

It only takes a few to influence the many. Witnesses, contactees, and abductees experience a staged spectacle they cannot deny, and eventually, they, in turn, influence society by suggesting alien intervention from outer space. The paradoxical metalogic is visible in that despite the widespread snickers and scholarly dismissals, polls indicate that 56 percent of Americans believe it is "very likely" or "somewhat likely" that intelligent life exists on other planets, and up to 48 percent think they have already visited Earth.[709] Commenting on the UFO mythos, author Keith Thompson concluded:

> Without our notice, the human mythological structure has been undergoing a fundamental shift. Public opinion surveys and other measures of collective pulse reveal that more people than ever now take for granted that we are not alone in the universe— "inner" as well as "outer" universes, if such a division is finally possible.[710]

Without ever landing on the White House lawn, the phenomenon is profoundly altering culture. Roughly, half the American population believes ETs are already here! For such a fringe phenomenon, it has a disproportionally prevalent influence.

Vallée's recent essay written with Dr. Eric W. Davis, "Incommensurability, Orthodoxy, and the Physics of High Strangeness—A 6-Layer Model for Anomalous Phenomena," for a collection called *Fátima Revisited* examining the Fátima apparition, updates the control system hypothesis. The essay serves to elucidate "the issues surrounding 'high strangeness' observations by distinguishing six layers of information that can be derived from anomalous events, namely, (1) physical manifestations, (2) anti-physical effects, (3) psychological factors, (4) physiological factors, (5) psychic effects, and (6) cultural effects."[711] The essay chides the skeptics who say the phenomenon is too absurd to be real and the believers who assume it is necessarily space aliens. Remarkably, they also critique the SETI scientists' extrapolation from the mediocrity principle as short-sighted anthropocentrism. They argue that the ufology researchers and SETI scientists could bridge their studies if both would acknowledge this fact: "No experiment can distinguish between phenomena manifested by visiting interstellar (arbitrarily advanced) ETI and intelligent beings that may exist near Earth within a parallel universe or in different dimensions, or who are (terrestrial) time travelers."[712]

Naturally, this applies to the supernatural entities that world religions have been acknowledging from time immemorial as well.

Of the six-layered approach for analyzing Unidentified Aerial Phenomenon, three are of special interest. The second, antiphysical effects, describes observations that contradict our normal understanding of physics. These include objects: becoming fuzzy or invisible, dividing into two or more objects, merging with several other objects into one, disappearing and instantaneously reappearing elsewhere, being visually observable while not detected by radar, and producing missing time or time dilatation. Anyone familiar with the literature has read about these sorts of behaviors often witnessed by pilots and highly trained military personnel. Yet, these sorts of descriptions lead most academic scientists to reject such accounts as hallucinations or hoaxes. While some are, the pervasiveness of such cases suggests this might be an intentional ploy to avoid scrutiny.

The next item of special significance is the fifth category, labeled "psychic" because it involves parapsychological effects. These include telepathy or psychic communication, prophetic dreams, poltergeist phenomenon, levitations, UAP maneuvering in anticipation of the witness' thoughts, witnesses developing unusual abilities, and healings. The sixth category is cultural, which is concerned with public reactions and how the phenomenon is perceived. Vallée explained in an interview:

> But perhaps we're facing something which is basically a social technology. Perhaps the most important effects from the UFO technology are the social ones and not the physical ones. In other words the physical reality may serve only as a kind of triggering device to provide images for the witness to report. These perceptions are manipulated to create certain kinds of social effects.[713]

In the modern era, UFOs have fostered a general acceptance of life in space and nonhuman intelligence, whereas in the past, such phenomena tended to confirm religious beliefs like with Constantine's fourth-century UAP or the silver disc witnessed by thousands at Fátima. The conclusions are extraordinary:

> Everything works as if UAPs were the products of a technology that integrates physical and psychic phenomena and primarily affects cultural variables in our society through manipulation of physiological and psychological parameters in the witnesses....
>
> The purpose of the technology may be cultural manipulation—possibly but not necessarily under control of a form of non-human intelligence—in which case the physiological and psychological effects are a means to that end.[714]

Remarkably, their proposal that this control system is maintained by a form of nonhuman consciousness that manipulates our world supports our central thesis. Masquerading in various guises to various cultures, these entities have been active throughout human history. They may manifest in a silver disc associated with the Virgin Mary in Fátima; as colored lights connected to *Konohanasakuya-hime* on Mount Fuji in Japan; or as a huge, delta-shaped craft over Phoenix, Arizona, linked to space aliens. In Vallée's opinion, the intelligence behind the phenomenon manipulates human culture by using deception based on the beliefs of the particular audience. More intriguing is that, although he realizes this confirms a biblical worldview, he qualifies his position accordingly:

> When I speak of a control system for planet earth I do not want my words to be misunderstood: I do not mean that some higher order of beings has locked us inside the constraints of a space-bound jail, closely monitored by psychic entities we might call angels or demons. I do not propose to redefine God. What I do mean is that mythology rules at a level of our social reality over which normal political and intellectual action has no real power.... Myths define the set of things scholars, politicians, and scientists can think about. They are operated upon by symbols,

and the language these symbols form constitutes a complete system. This system is metalogical, but not metaphysical. It violates no laws because it is the substance of which laws are made.[715]

We find it intriguing that he recognizes the intersection enough to feel the need to specifically distance himself from redefining God and from saying that angels and demons are the perpetrators. He suggests an underlying plan for the deception of mankind and documents myriad examples within *Messengers of Deception* (1979). We believe the ultimate motivation for this is the breaking down of the biblical worldview while simultaneously implementing a new one based on Darwinism and pantheistic monism. This is a form of idolatrous spirituality, which places the creature above the Creator (Romans 1:23) and is widely promoted by the powers that be.

Behind the Curtain of the Control System

The Bible confirms something remarkably analogous to Vallée's hypothesis. It seems that he has correctly surmised that the world is being manipulated and controlled. The control system was explained two thousand years ago in a letter Paul wrote to the Ephesians: "For we wrestle not against flesh and blood, but against principalities, against powers, against the rulers of the darkness of this world, against spiritual wickedness in high places" (Ephesians 6:12). With all the political rhetoric and culture war posturing coming from evangelicals, we often wonder if they ever consider that our battle is *not* against flesh and blood. You would never know it, given the tenor of the last presidential election. Regrettably, many Christians think like naturalists, but, even so, they are at least familiar with the supernatural powers about whom Paul wrote. However, fewer still are familiar with the Old Testament background undergirding Paul's thought.

As a Jew educated in the Pharisaic tradition, Paul was certainly familiar with the concept of the divine council, a concept that has been lost in most contemporary evangelical Bible scholarship. It actually explains a lot of mysteries surrounding Old Testament Israel and the Gentile nations. Semitics expert Dr. Michael Heiser calls this the "Deuteronomy 32 Worldview," a theological construct based on the oldest manuscript's reading of verse 8. Where we read in the King James Bible, "according to the number of the children of Israel," in the Dead Sea Scrolls as well as the Greek Septuagint, this verse is translated, "according to the number of the sons of God," which is a clear reference to angels (Deuteronomy 32:8, ESV [the ESV translation used the DSS reading]).

The passage is teaching that the number of the nations is proportional to the number of the *bene ha elohim*, the "sons of God" mentioned in Genesis 6:2 and Job 1:6, among other passages. This is a more logical reading, because at no time in history was mankind divided in reference to the number of Israelites, an idea that doesn't add up. Of the seventy nations in the Genesis 10 table, certain "sons of God" or "powers and principalities" are associated with specific geographic areas and people groups. In ancient Judaism, it was understood that the dispersal at the Tower of Babel entailed not only the confusion of the languages but Yahweh's disinheriting of the other nations. In order to display distinction, Deuteronomy 32:9 indicates that He chose Israel as His own. This explains why God was so concerned that His people stood out as pure and holy. It explains the exacting rules and God's frustration with them. Israel was an example. However, revealed in the New Testament as a "mystery," God's plan was always to reconcile the nations through the Messiah (Ephesians 3:6). However, the foreign gods still exact a rebellious influence. The territorial nature of these powers is supported by Scripture.

In the book of Daniel, the angel Gabriel reports to Daniel that he was delayed twenty-one days due to a battle with the "prince of the kingdom of Persia," and was only able to escape when Israel's champion, the archangel Michael, came to assist (Daniel 10:13–14). Even more, he reports that once he is done battling the Persian spirit, he must then fight the "prince of Greece." What immediately comes to mind is that at the time of Daniel's writing, the Persian Empire was in control of most of the world, but it was soon to be conquered by Alexander the Great of Greece. What we have in Daniel is a peek behind the curtain of an extradimensional battle, which finds its analog in our material world. It seems the purveyors of the control system have their own rivalries. The prophet Isaiah foretells the future judgment of these so-called gods: "On that day the LORD will punish the host of heaven, in heaven, and the kings of the earth, on the earth" (Isaiah 24:21). This is also seen in the Psalms.

With this background in mind, we suggest reading Psalm 82, where you will read that Yahweh was not pleased with the way these spirits— referred to as "gods" with a little "g"—misgoverned and abused their people. The same passage supporting the division according to the number of the sons of God also identifies them as devils (Deuteronomy 32:17). In fact, God says that because of their manipulation and deceitfulness, they are doomed to "die like men" (Psalms 82:7). Thus interpreting Psalm 82 to argue the "gods" are human men violates the context. After all, men sentenced to "die like men" is hardly a meaningful punishment. Furthermore, Psalm 89:5–7 locates this assembly "in the heaven" (v. 6) and clarifies the deeper meaning behind the "sons of the mighty" as *bene ha elohim*, "sons of God," which always refers to heavenly beings. Other passages that mention the divine council include the following: 1 Kings 22:10–23; Isaiah 6:1–8; 40:1–11; Psalms 29:1–2; 58:1; 89:5–8; 103:20–21; 148:2; Job 1:6–12; 2:1–7; 15:8; Jeremiah 23:18; Daniel 7:9–10; 10:13–14, 20–21. If you would like to learn more concerning the Old Testament background, we suggest visiting Dr. Heiser's website: http://www.thedivinecouncil.com/.

The New Testament makes it clear that Jesus has already defeated these demon-gods who deceive the nations. Paul writes that Jesus "spoiled principalities and powers, he made a shew of them openly, triumphing over them in it" (Colossians 2:15). This was done through Jesus' work on the cross when God enticed the devil into checkmate. When a supremely overconfident Satan thought he could secure his position by having Jesus crucified, he ensured his own defeat. Yet there remains a tension, because the New Testament acknowledges that still, "the whole world lieth in wickedness" (1 John 5:19), or in the Greek original, "ὁ κόσμος ὅλος ἐν τῷ πονηρῷ κεῖται," which best reads, "the whole world lies in the power of the evil one." Thus, the New Testament confirms that the world is in the grip of a deceptive control system, but that spiritual rebirth leads to clarity and freedom.

Scholars refer to this as the "already/not yet" paradigm. Basically, it means God chose to inaugurate the kingdom at Christ's first coming, but has postponed fully realizing it until the second. The kingdom is here now in the Church—the "already"—but we eagerly await Jesus' return to rule—the "not yet." This "already/not yet" eschatology can be seen in the epistle to the Hebrews (with the "not yet" underlined): "Thou hast put all things in subjection under his feet. For in that he put all in subjection under him, he left nothing that is not put under him. But now we see not yet all things put under him" (Hebrews 2:8, underline added). This explains our current situation: the powers and principalities were defeated, but they still mislead many. Their deceptive control system helps evil, false religion, and blasphemy flourish. The fearsome judgments in the book of Revelation describe the final battle that will realize the Kingdom of God on Earth. This final victory is described in 1 Corinthians 15:24–25: "Then cometh the end, when He (Christ) shall have delivered up the kingdom to God, even the Father; when He shall have put down all rule and all authority and power. For He must reign, till He hath put all enemies under His feet." Those enemies are not humans. This is where we see a remarkable parallel to what Jacques Vallée calls the control grid.

In our chapter titled "Astro-Apologetics and the End Times," (chapter 8) we make a biblical case that the realm of Satan ("the prince of the power of the air") and his demons is essentially the Earth's atmosphere. We believe that exegesis is decisive, and we need not repeat it here. With scriptural basis established, we note that occultists also recognize the sky as their dominion. For example, Francis Barret's compendium *The*

Magus, in accord with Aristotelian physics, classifies principalities as airy entities: "Also, according to the different orders of spirits or angels, some are fiery, as seraphims, authorities, and powers—earthy, as cherubim—watery, as thrones and archangels—airy, as dominions and principalities."[716] We need not accept the four-element cosmology to acknowledge they were believed to inhabit the sky. Kabbalistic occultism yields similar conclusions. According to the *Encyclopaedia Judaica*, there is a distinction between demons of the Earth and sky-devils:

> Apparently, the author of the Zohar distinguishes between spirits that have emanated from the "left-side" and were assigned definite functions in the "palaces of impurity" and devils in the exact sense who hover in the air. According to later sources, the latter fill with their hosts the space of the sky between the earth and sphere of the moon.[717]

Given that the biblical and occult sources agree, we have ample grounds to posit that the atmosphere—where the majority of strange sightings occur—is the realm of these rebel spirits.

It seems inescapable that fallen angels are the source of some UAP or UFOs. There are several New-Testament terms for entities that correlate to the control-system hypothesis, specifically the "principalities" (*archons*), "powers" (*exousia*), and "rulers of the darkness of this world" (*kosmokrators*), of whom Paul warned (Ephesians 6:12). It seems almost self-evident in translation, but the original language is utterly convincing, as these entities are described in a Greek lexicon as "a supernatural power having some particular role in controlling the destiny and activities of human beings—'power, authority, lordship, ruler, wicked force.'"[718] If one accepts biblical authority, it's tempting to say, "Case closed, Jacques," but there is more supporting data to be mined from the New Testament.

A prime example is "στοιχεῖον" (*stoicheon*), which is used by Paul three times in the expression "στοιχεῖα τοῦ κόσμου," meaning "elemental spirits of the world" (Galatians 4:3; Colossians 2:8, 20). Unfortunately, sometimes the author's intentions are masked in translation. Where the KJV reads, "Beware lest any man spoil you through philosophy and vain deceit, after the tradition of men, after the rudiments of the world, and not after Christ" (Colossians 2:8), other translations render "according to the elemental spirits of the world," (ESV) reflecting the ancient understanding that spiritual entities, known as elementals, are promoting deceitful philosophies—*like the mediocrity principle*. A scholarly lexicon supports this translation:

> στοιχεῖα, ων *n* (always occurring in the plural): the supernatural powers or forces regarded as having control over the events of this world—"the supernatural powers over this world." εἰ ἀπεθάνετε σὺν Χριστῷ ἀπὸ τῶν στοιχείων τοῦ κόσμου "now that you have died with Christ and are free from the supernatural powers ruling over this world" Colossians 2:20.[719]

Other aerial entities can be lost in translation as well; Paul mentions "ὕψωμα" (*hupsoma*) rendered "height" in Romans 8:38–39. In the ancient context, this often meant "supernatural powers in the region above the earth—'powers of the world above'" and, on the opposite end, the word "βάθος" (bathos), rendered "depth" in the same verse, meant "powers of the world below."[720] The verse in question assures born-again believers freedom from subjection to these entities: "For I am sure that neither death nor life, nor angels nor rulers, nor things present nor things to come, nor powers, nor height (*hupsoma*) nor depth (*bathos*), nor anything else in all creation, will be able to separate us from the love of God in Christ Jesus our Lord" (Romans 8:38–39). Thus, even though the world at large is under their influence, believers are free notwithstanding their sinful natures.

While we believe we have a viable explanation for the control system, there is no room for arrogance. The first few verses of Ephesians 2 remind us that at one time we all were all so deceived. Unfortunately, very smart and nice people are often unable to find freedom because of the sin nature. Indeed, the Scriptures affirm that fallen humanity's thinking is so infected by sin that reality is "darkened" (Ephesians 4:17–22). Even more: "The god of this world hath blinded the minds of them which believe not" (2 Corinthians 4:4). It's more than blind confusion; we are born as slaves (Romans 5:12; John 8:34), unable to see reality unless reborn (John 3:3). Probably the most difficult factor is the devil's masquerade: "Satan himself is transformed into an angel of light" (2 Corinthians 11:14). For this reason, many are sincere but deceived. This seemingly impossible state of supernatural deception is why true conversions are celebrated as God's merciful grace. While many in the UFO research community have ostensibly analyzed the phenomenon correctly, rebirth in Jesus Christ is the only way to escape the deluding influence. But the powers have initiated counter measures.

The Control System's Social Deconstruction

While the UFO phenomenon exerts a broad influence with minimal exposure, the control system is much more elaborate and reaches into every area of culture, *especially politics*. Professor Carl Raschke of the Religious Studies Department at the University of Denver, suggests that UFOs are agents of cultural deconstruction, meaning they are slowly and subtly tearing down foundational beliefs. He states, "So far as UFOs are concerned, the deconstructive movement works upon human culture as a whole, although it may also have devastating effects at times on individual lives."[721] Dr. Leo Sprinkle, a professional counselor formerly at the University of Wyoming, also believes that UFO activity could be a conditioning process: "It is possible that we are being slowly introduced to ETs through movies and science fiction, until the evidence of ET visitation becomes more acceptable to the 'morality' of physical scientists."[722] Vallée has said, "We are seeing the emerging UFO phenomenon is not gradual contact but rather gradual control."[723] When one surveys the moral decay of the last few decades, there is no need to argue where that control is leading.

In *Project: Mindshift* (1998), Michael Mannion asserts a hypothesis: "Our world has been, and now is being visited by advanced intelligent entities from elsewhere, and this reality has been known to a limited number of people in the US government since at least 1947."[724] The *Collins Elite* meets the description, albeit they are not promoting belief in extraterrestrial life. Even so, Mannion makes a good case for a covert government reeducation campaign to prepare the public for disclosure. He argues that, since 1947, propaganda designed to desensitize the public to an ET reality has been systematically promoted. But he also writes that people who report even trivial UFO contact begin to experience poltergeist activity and out-of-body experiences. Although we do not discount government involvement, the social engineering isn't necessarily being perpetrated by humans. Perhaps the elite echelons of above top-secret are unwitting shills for spiritual wickedness in high places.

The Materialist and the Magician

The Apostle Paul wrote that the elemental spirits promote deceptive philosophies. It goes without saying that they play on both sides, too. Author C. S. Lewis famously wrote in *The Screwtape Letters*, "There are two equal and opposite errors into which our race can fall about the devils. One is to disbelieve in their existence. The other is to believe, and to feel an excessive and unhealthy interest in them. They themselves are equally pleased by both errors and hail a materialist or a magician with the same delight."[725] The UFO world has plenty of both. We see plenty of magicians in the New Agers and contactees and an abundance of materialists in the scientists. The general population is indoctrinated by both. First, let's look at the materialist.

On a worldview level, UFO/ET belief serves as a subtle confirmation of the mediocrity principle. Recalling this tenet entails that there is nothing very unusual about our solar system, the Earth, and humans. As an extrapolation from naturalism, it undergirds the astrobiological project. It is antithetical to God's truth. In advocating the many worlds interpretation of quantum mechanics, cosmologist Alexander Vilenkin, the materialist, seems poignantly pleased, pronouncing:

> In the worldview that has emerged from eternal inflation, our Earth and our civilization are anything but unique. Instead, countless identical civilizations are scattered in the infinite expanse of the cosmos. With humankind reduced to absolute cosmic insignificance, our descent from the center of the universe is now complete.[726]

He reasons that since the universe is teeming with life, humans are trivial skin-bags of bones, blood, and water. Even though the mediocrity principle is taught as an amoral scientific tenet, Vilenkin implies that the significance of humankind is a function of its abundance or rarity in the cosmos, a horrid devaluation of life that has subtly infected public consciousness. The depreciation of humankind and Christian values has chilling moral and spiritual repercussions; ultimately, it amounts to a deconstruction of the spiritual armor that can protect people from the influence of the powers (Ephesians 6:13–18). This is where we find C. S. Lewis' magician.

Because the powers and principalities offer so much explanatory power, some in the UFO community have adopted a neo-Gnostic interpretation promoted by John Lash. Whereas Lash mixes Gnosticism with occultism and Eastern religion, the ancient Gnostics also created their own mythology by twisting and perverting ideas from the Bible with Zoroastrianism. There were two types of Gnostics ascetics who denied physical pleasures and antimonians who indulged the flesh. Lash, who also practices tantric Buddhism, is of the latter variety. He describes himself as "self-educated free-lance scholar who combines studies and experimental mysticism to teach *directive* mythology: that is, the application of myth to life, rather than its mere interpretation."[727] Lash writes, "I do accept the reality of reincarnation based on my own memories and a great deal of testimonial evidence."[728] While he identifies UFOs with the rulers (archons), his Gnostic spirituality plays right into the hands of the entities he proclaims to oppose. Gnosticism was the enemy of primitive Christianity long before Roman Catholicism came into existence.

The Gnostics were followers of a variety of spiritual movements that emphasized salvation through *gnōsis*, or "knowledge." Cosmological dualism was an essential feature of Gnosticism—an opposition between the spiritual world and the evil, material world, created by the demiurge associated with the God of the Old Testament. The principal aspects that unify Gnostic creation myths are that an original divine being produced other, lesser-divine entities in the spiritual realm—associated with the archons in Ephesians 6. However, something went dreadfully wrong, and a defect occurred in the spiritual realm that brought physical matter into existence. Some of the original spiritual matter, a divine spark, was implanted into material persons as a soul. Unfortunately, people are now trapped in the evil, defective, material realm. However, a savior came to impart knowledge that will emancipate the divine spark. Through this gnosis, a soul can free itself and battle through a series of levels controlled by the archons until one is back home in the pure spiritual realm.[729]

As an archon shill, John Lash argues that Christianity is the control system. He wrote: "Working through telepathy and suggestion, the Archons attempt to deviate us from our proper course of evolution. Their most successful technique is to use religious ideology to insinuate their way of thinking and, in effect, substitute their mind-set for ours. According to the Gnostics, Judeo-Christian Salvationism is the primary ploy of the Archons, an alien implant."[730] Astonishingly, in opposing the sacramental legalism of Roman Catholicism, he labels Christian salvation an *alien implant.* However, Lash's work reveals that he advocates the same evolutionary pantheistic spirituality promoted by the aliens and contactees. He is an ardent advocate of occultism, teaching "interactive magic with Gaia" and tantric Buddhist practices with the goal "to guide the species and align one person at a time to Gaia, the living planet."[731]

Whereas Lash wants to unify with the Earth goddess, Gaia, Catholic mystics believe they become one with God in a process called *theosis*. The Jesuit priest Pierre Teilhard Chardin also imagines an eschatological process in which all consciousness evolves to the Omega Point, a remarkably similar idea to New Age religions and saucer spirituality.

They all share the central premise or goal of monism, that "all is one" or evolving to become one. But this line of thinking is fatally flawed. All is not one, nor will it ever become one. In surveying Eastern thought, pantheistic philosophers simply assume that "being" (existing) is univocal (has a single definition) and then offer arguments for monism. However, if the word "being" is defined in such a way that it always means exactly the same thing, then anything that "is" is necessarily the same. This does not prove that "all is one"; rather, it betrays circular reasoning and equivocation of the worst kind. Being or existing is *not* always the same sort of thing. A rock does not exist in the same way as a person. A thought does not exist in the same way as a car. Even more, we must account for *qualia*, a term for ideas like "the redness of red" or "wetness of water." It does not exist anywhere other than in a mind. They are mental realities wholly other than matter. But it gets worse… If everything is one, are monism and dualism then the same? While this is obviously absurd, it shows that monism is fundamentally incoherent.

Of course, the biblical worldview makes a Creator/Creation distinction (Genesis 1:1; John 1:1; Romans 1:18–32). It also speaks of an *eternal* separation between two groups based on one's response to Jesus Christ (John 3:36). The most troublesome aspect of monism is the denial of sin's significance and the trivialization of evil. Evil is real, but monism makes everything relative. While his spiritual system has serious problems, Lash correctly identified the archons as perpetrators of the UFO phenomenon and works-based salvation as an alien implant. Unfortunately, his internally contradictory spirituality inverts reality and also leads to spiritual slavery. This is one of the enemy's most clever counter measures.

Confronting the Matrix

Theologian Neil Andersen contends, "Freedom from spiritual conflicts and bondage is not a power encounter; it's a truth encounter."[732] The truth we stand on is: "That if thou shalt confess with thy mouth the Lord Jesus, and shalt believe in thine heart that God hath raised him from the dead, thou shalt be saved" (Romans 10:9). We should place no confidence in our own authority or we risk ending up like the sons of Sceva in Acts 19. Still yet, we need not fear because Colossians 2:15 and Luke 11:21–22 tell us that Satan is a defeated foe. Thus, he only gains the power that one gives to him through fear and ignorance. While he can hinder, he has no authority over a Christian. Andersen argues from Ephesians 2:5–6 that we are seated with Christ at the right hand of God and through Him we have authority over the demons. He lists four qualifications for believers who confront these powers: 1) Belief is essential; 2) Humility is confidence properly placed because we can do nothing without Christ; 3) Boldness is having courage (2 Timothy 1:7); 4) Dependence, in that our authority is in God's calling to kingdom ministry. We put *first things first*.[733] These entities have no authority over those in Christ.

The spiritual armor described by Paul in Ephesians 6 is especially noteworthy in that we do not find special rituals or prayers for casting out demons; rather, we see the helmet of salvation, which the Christian always has on; the sword of the spirit, which is God's Word one can study and memorize; and the belt of truth, which one should always have on by walking with integrity. In other words, the more you know and live by the truth, the more impenetrable your spiritual armor. This supports the assertion that spiritual warfare is largely in the realm of ideas—on the mythological level as discussed at the beginning of the chapter. The UFO mythos has profoundly permeated the public psyche, promoting the advent of the alien savior.

19	## Petrus Romanus and Project LUCIFER

The Vatican's Astonishing Plan for the Arrival of an Alien Savior

"Currently, the group of beings referred to as 'aliens' are…preparing the earth for a massive…paradigm shift, while also continuing the education that they maintain is crucial if the human race is to be spared destruction. The nonhuman intelligences are feigning good intentions by warning humans of their potential fate, and the offer to assist humans is all but altruistic in that it is <u>designed to unite mankind under a global authority, with their candidate on the Throne of the World</u>."—David Flynn, 2005 (underline added)

"One thing is apparent: We are witnessing a masterful satanic subterfuge that appears to involve the appearance of 'angels' and 'aliens.' Many are asking whether the coming of Antichrist can be far removed. From the Bible we learn that such an evil day surely lies ahead. The question for our consideration, then, is this: Are we in the throes of that final otherworldly deception now?"
—Timothy J. Dailey, PhD, Senior Fellow Family Research Council

From the very beginning of this arduous investigation, we knew we were facing a daunting task. To breach that labyrinthine monument to religion, the Roman Catholic Church, and to ascertain subterranean secrets concealed beneath its layers of classified documentation had been tried and failed by thousands before us. The Vatican is impenetrable, we were warned, the very inventor of the term "above top secret." As the world's oldest-running bureaucracy, it is an amalgamation of secrets, vaults, and esoteric traditions dating back to the Dark Ages. Steeped in complexity and guarded by a procession of popes, cardinals, and multileveled priests, it is obsessed with maintaining "the need to know." When spokesmen for the Church do tantalize the outside world with commentary, it often turns out to be duplicity designed to keep researchers running in circles and in the wrong direction. And yet, of late, we have heard enough consistency from Jesuit astronomers to wonder now if, for some reason, Rome was actually slowly moving the religious world toward a definite revelation, a period in time coupled with a momentous disclosure that somehow required specific public comments and the development of theological arguments concerning extraterrestrial intelligence that ultimately will, they believe, impact the religion of Christianity.

On this, we have provided: 1) first-person testimonies by qualified authorities that agree with the assessment above; 2) public statements, interviews, and scholarly papers issued by the Vatican and its academics in recent years that substantiate our conclusions; and 3) the threshold of what is called in the court system "a presumption of fact." This is a legal term that offers an argument of proof through inference to the existence of a fact not certainly known but about which the existence of other facts known and proved point, and that is grounded on probable evidence that entitles the presumed fact to be believed based on other sufficient, corroborative information. This is an established legal methodology for ascertaining judicious conclusions "beyond reasonable doubt," which is the standard of evidence required to validate verdicts in most legally recognized systems. Criminal convictions are routinely held up in courts of law that include such presumptions of fact. This is also true in war colleges and battlefield decisions where the amount of indirect data suggests a preponderance of evidence beyond reasonable doubt leading to a conclusion and subsequent actions or reactions. Likewise, every day around the world, tribunals, judges, and grand juries reach agreements to indict or convict persons or institutions using arguments based on this precedent. In the same way, when reading *Exo-Vaticana*, the number of documents and the amount of commentary evidence on the part of Rome's astronomers and the Vatican's emerging theology as conveyed herein would be enough in a legal proceeding to convince the majority of a grand jury to determine "probable cause"—that is, to conclude beyond reasonable doubt that the Vatican has intentionally positioned itself to be the religious authority on, and ecclesiastical benefactor of, Official Disclosure: the imminent and authorized public admission by world governments of advanced extraterrestrial intelligence.

Why the Vatican has taken this carefully designed and deliberate course over the last few years is the greater mystery, but implies knowledge on their part of facts yet hidden to most of the world that may hold far-reaching and historic implications. It also illustrates how Rome has wittingly or unwittingly set itself up to become the agent of mass end-times deception regarding "salvation from above." That's because, historically, there exists a clear pattern wherein man's psychological need of a savior is displayed during times of distress—a time like today—when people look skyward for divine intervention. As Ted Peters, professor of systematic theology at Pacific Lutheran Theological Seminary, wrote, "With the constant threat of thermonuclear destruction in the post-World War II era leaving our planet in a state of insecurity and anxiety, it is no wonder many have begun to hope for a messiah to save us. The holiness of the sky and the need for a salvation converge and blend when the bright clean powerful UFO zooms up onto the horizon. Could it be our celestial savior?"[734] Jesuit Brother Guy Consolmagno must think so, as he assured us that if highly advanced ET saviors from outer space touch down on planet Earth soon, it will not mean what Catholics believe is wrong, but rather, "We're going to find out that everything is truer in ways we couldn't even yet have imagined."[735]

In truth, Consolmagno's advice for the religious faithful could be leading mankind into a gigantic setup, as many religions have at least one apocalyptic myth describing the end of the world accompanied by a redeemer who appears in the sky at the last minute to rescue the chosen from annihilation or wrath. Mayans, Assyrians, Egyptians, and Greeks held similar beliefs, while the Hopi Indians foresee times of great hardship when they will be preserved by the "power" of a blue star, far off and invisible, that suddenly makes its appearance in the heavens. Today, even factions of the New Age look for a techno-savior to arrive in the atmosphere in the nick of time to save mankind. Although Jesus, Himself, is prophesied to appear in the clouds during an era of great earthly trials (1 Thessalonians 4:16–18), predominant among prophecy scholars is the idea that coupled with any heavenly appearing and concurrent salvation of believers from chaos will first be the materialization of a false Christ or "man of sin." Where Hopi see a blue star and Vatican astronomers see their "space brothers" en route to guide us into the light, evangelical Christians understand the Antichrist will initially assume the role of a fabricated end-times messiah who mimics the return of Christ with a false second coming *that also happens to be attended by heavenly "signs and lying wonders"* (2 Thessalonians 2:8–9). Could these deceptive "wonders" be: 1) the discovery of artificial structures on another world; 2) a "contact" scenario, or; 3) maybe even something more dramatic, like a flying saucer armada piloted by creatures who appear to be advanced humanoids but who are in fact evil supernaturalism on a quest to mislead and destroy the human race? Even secular ufologists suspect demonic activity in the interaction between humans and "aliens." Whitley Streiber, author of *Communion* and other books on the subject, once wrote: "There are worse things than death, I suspected. And I was beginning to get the distinct impression that one of them had taken an interest in me. So far the word *demon* had never been spoken among the scientists and doctors who were working with me. And why should it have been? We were beyond such things. We were a group of atheists and agnostics, far too sophisticated to be concerned with such archaic ideas as demons and angels" (emphasis added).[736]

Alien Saviors, Demonic Plots

In 1958, a peculiar novel was published under the title, *A Case of Conscience*, by James Blish. In the story, a Jesuit priest named Father

Ruiz-Sanchez and a team of scientists travel to a newly discovered planet dubbed "Lithia" to study the Lithians who live there. Unknown to the science team, the Vatican secretly advises the Catholic father to investigate whether the aliens have redeemable souls. What he finds in the Lithians are intelligent creatures whose morality fits perfectly with Christianity but who are devoid of any concept of religion or God. This dilemma grows, and soon the priest is invited to visit with a Lithian family. He writes:

> Here was the first chance, at long last, to see something of the private life of Lithia, and through that, perhaps, to gain some inkling of the moral life, the role in which God had cast the Lithians in the ancient drama of good and evil, in the past and in the times to come. Until that was known, the Lithians in their Eden might be only spuriously good: all reason, all organic thinking machines, ULTIMACs with tails and without souls.[737]

Original cover of *A Case of Conscience* by James Blish

Because the publisher of *Exo-Vaticana* is giving away the pdf version of *A Case of Conscience* in the data-dvd provided with the first release of this book, we will not spoil the ending—which includes the Jesuits (described as "the cerebral cortex of the Church") dealing with the knotty moral, theological, and organizational issues surrounding a papal proclamation and the seed of Satan—for those who want to read the novel. However, it is important to note that the fictional Father Ruiz-Sanchez warns the Vatican to classify Lithia as X-1—a planet to be forever quarantined from Earth and humans due to its potential *for great deception*.

> "What we have here on Lithia is very clear indeed. We have—and now I'm prepared to be blunt—a planet and a people propped up by the Ultimate Enemy. It is a gigantic trap prepared for all of us—for every man on Earth and off it. We can do nothing with it but reject it, nothing but say to it, Retro me, Sathanas. If we compromise with it in any way, we are damned."[738]

When Ruiz-Sanchez uses the phrase, "Retro me, Sathanas," he is annunciating the medieval Catholic formula for exorcism, "Vade retro Sathanas" ("Go back, Satan"), a clear reckoning that the aliens on Lithia are part of a satanic plot to be avoided at all costs, an astro-theological conspiracy designed to mislead mankind. He eventually convinces the pope (Pope Hadrian in the story) of the satanic stratagem, but, ironically, he is unable to convince all of the Church's theologians. Did the author of *A Case of Conscience* foresee how such great deception would eventually be embraced by the Vatican as a result of some of Rome's celebrated scholars and astronomers? When science-fiction writer Jo Walton asked real-life Jesuit Brother Guy Consolmagno—whom we also interviewed from Rome—what he made of these issues posed by Blish in his novel, Consolmagno admitted that the Jesuits are: 1) the strongest advocates of "inculturation" (allowing alien cultures to maintain their paganism while modifying expressions of Christian ideas within those beliefs); 2) accepting of "alien cultures for who they are"; and 3) willing to adapt alien "religious practices into a form and a language that can be accepted."[739] So, if Brother Consolmagno had been on Lithia, Walton concluded, we'd already be in contact with aliens "and finding out as much as we could about them."[740]

From what we have seen, Walton may not have to wait much longer for contact, which raises a *hidden* aspect of *A Case of Conscience* involving wordplay around the term "Lithia." While Blish makes an obvious connection to the name of the planet and its inhabitants as reflecting the abundance of "Lithium" ore on the alien world (ore that could be mined and exploited for use in making nuclear weapons), mention of the goddess I-Lithia or "Ilithyia" is strangely missing from the work. This stands out as possibly a secret code in the book that specifically relates to the deductions of Father Ruiz-Sanchez and the "seed of Satan" being debated by the Church back on Earth. If the similarity between Lithia and the goddess Ilithyia is coincidental, it is extraordinary, as it was the job of this goddess in antiquity to protect the very "seed of the serpent" that in turn generates the birth of the "serpent child" and future "serpent-savior." So important was the goddess Ilithyia's role in ancient days as the preserver of this serpent seed toward the birth of the serpent-savior that shrines were erected to her by cult followers across Greece (including at Athens, Megara, Korinthos, Argos, Mycenae, Sparta, etc.) in which terra-cotta figures of immortal nurses were depicted watching over the divine children in whom the bloodline would survive. For example, on the mainland at Olympia, a shrine dedicated to Ilithyia (called Eileithyia by the Greeks) was witnessed by traveler and second-century geographer, Pausanias, in which a small inner chamber (cella) sacred to the serpent-savior hosted a virgin-priestess who "cared for a serpent that was fed on honeyed barley-cakes and water."[741] The shrine memorialized *the appearance of a Marian-like woman with a babe in her arms* who, "at a crucial moment when Elians were threatened by forces from Arcadia," was placed on the ground between the contending forces and changed into a terrifying serpent, "driving the Arcadians away in flight, before it disappeared into the hill."[742]

Interestingly, the myth of Ilithyia is also connected in ancient history with the birth of Apollo, whose coming as "the promised seed" formed the *novus ordo seclorum* prophecy of the Great Seal of the United States. This "messiah" who returns to rule the Earth in the latter days is also described (by the same name) in the book of 2 Thessalonians as the Antichrist who becomes the progeny or incarnation of the ancient seed (or spirit) of Apollo. The warning in 2 Thessalonians 2:3 reads: "Let no man deceive you by any means: for that day shall not come, except there come a falling away first, and that man of sin be revealed, the son of *perdition* [*Apoleia*; Apollyon, Apollo]" (emphasis added). Revelation 17:8 also directly ties the coming of Antichrist with the seed of Apollo, revealing that the Beast shall ascend from the bottomless pit and enter him: "The Beast that thou sawest was, and is not; and shall ascend out of the Bottomless Pit, and go into *perdition* [*Apoleia*, Apollo]: and they that dwell on the Earth shall wonder, whose names were not written in the Book of Life from the foundation of the world, when they behold the Beast that was, and is not, and yet is" (emphasis added).

The verses above elucidate a very important and central eschato-logical issue concerning how all of the Bible is really a story about the ancient and future struggle between the "seed" of the woman (Jesus) and that of the serpent. Genesis 3:15 says, "And I will put enmity between thee and the woman, and between thy seed [*zera*, meaning "offspring," "descendents," or "children"] and her seed." Besides the pre-preaching of the Gospel of Christ in this verse (known in theology as the *protoevan-gelium*), another incredible tenet emerges here that was first pointed out by Dr. Chuck Missler in his superior book *Alien Encounters: The Secret Behind The UFO Phenomenon*—that Satan has "seed" and it is at enmity (hostility, hatred, antagonism) with Christ.

We believe an example of Satan's hostile seed can be found in Genesis chapter 6, where fallen angels mingled with humans and produced Nephilim. More importantly, elsewhere in this book we have discussed how Church leaders including Roman Catholics from the Middle Ages forward believed the Antichrist would be spawned of this demonic seed.

Saint Augustine wrote about this in the *City of God*,[743] and in the *De Daemonialitate, et Incubis, et Succubi*, Father Ludovicus Maria Sinistrari de Ameno (1622–1701) argued how the coming of Antichrist represented the biological hybridization of demons with humans. "To theologians and philosophers," he wrote, "it is a fact, that from the copulation of humans with the demon…Antichrist must be born."[744] Thus, as Jesus Christ was the "seed of the woman," the "Man of Sin" will be the "seed of the serpent." And if the serpent seed represents the second coming of Apollo as prophesied by the Apostle Paul, not only will he be the exact opposite of Jesus (Son of God), but the forerunner of the return of these Nephilim.

Preparing Religious People to Accept the Alien Serpent-Savior

Initially, when reading *A Case of Conscience*, one is tempted to puzzle why a novel written in 1958 furtively touched on (or was guided by a warning or mocking spirit to forecast) how some of Rome's then-quiet Jesuit astronomers and theologians might later become the ones to argue in favor of what could become end-times deception involving the "fertility" of Satan or an alien serpent-savior from the prophesied seed of the Evil One. Upon further contemplation, however, this is really not that astonishing. It was, after all, the Roman Catholic theologians who provided the "liveliest speculation" on the existence and nature of extraterrestrials four years after Blish's book was printed, when the executive secretary of the American Rocket Society published conjectures on the subject.[745] Since then, other Vatican authorities have further contended the extraterrestrials might actually express the glory of God better than we humans do, even leading mankind to venerate them as gods, a recurrent theme articulated among numerous Jesuit astronomers. Father Daniel C. Raible thought the acceptance of aliens as objects of worship might naturally occur as a result of them having godlike qualities and preternatural gifts ascribed by humans to divinity:

For example, they might enjoy infused knowledge (they would literally be born with extensive knowledge and would find the acquisition of further knowledge easy and enjoyable); they might be blessed with harmony and concord in the working of their bodily and spiritual faculties; they might be spared the ultimate dissolution of death, passing to their reward at the end of their time of trial as peacefully as the sun sinks below the horizon at the end of the day. They might possess all these preternatural gifts or only some of them in any of various combinations that are limited only by the omnipotence and providence of God.[746]

Father Domenico Grasso not only thought such beings would be "far ahead of us in science and related fields,"[747] but that their version of salvation might be based on a savior *other than Jesus...even a messianic member of their own race.* These beings, closer to God than man (perhaps even unfallen), would possess superior theology that could "expand markedly" our terrestrial understanding of redemption and knowledge of God, something current Vatican theologians such as professor of fundamental theology at the Pontificia Università della Santa Croce in Rome [connected with Opus Dei], Giuseppe Tanzella-Nitti, agree with. Another Church scholar, Father Thomas F. O'Meara, a theologian at the University of Notre Dame, imagined these godlike beings spread out across universes "on untold planets called to a special relationship with God" and that "it is a mistake to think that our understanding of 'covenant,' the 'reign of God,' 'redemption,' or 'shared life' exhausts the modes by which divine power shares something of its infinite life."[748] Such Catholic leaders believe these spiritually superior aliens may even have been created by God with the future redemption of humanity in mind—beings who know their place in the eternal scheme of things to evangelize humans when the time is right. This disturbing and potentially prophetic belief is partially based on theological arguments made during the 1800s by such men as Monsignor Januaris De Concilio, professor of theology at Immaculate Seminary in New Jersey, who believed "that the immense distance in intellect between human beings and the angels suggest that God would create intermediate species to fill in the gap, and these species would be ETI [Extraterrestrial Intelligence]."[749] Monsignor Corrado Balducci (who during his life was the official mouthpiece of the Roman Catholic Church concerning the reality of aliens) agreed with De Concilio, saying, "It is entirely credible that in the enormous distance between Angels and humans, there could be found some middle stage—that is, beings with a body like ours but more elevated spiritually."[750] When imagining how this issue could finally be settled, Paul Thigpen for *The Catholic Answer* section of *Our Sunday Visitor* resolved that "nothing short of a public, thoroughly documented encounter between earthlings and aliens (or their relics) will be conclusive."[751] According to the Quran, the primary religious text of Islam, this encounter may happen sooner than most suspect and at a specific and hidden time that God Himself has already chosen. In *Revelation, Rationality, Knowledge & Truth*, Muslim scholar Mirza Tahir Ahmad quotes verse 42:30 of the Quran, which says, "And among His Signs is the Creation of the heavens and the earth, and of *whatever living creatures [da'bbah] He has spread forth in both....* And He has the power to *gather them together [jam-'i-him]* when He will so please" (emphasis added).[752] Ahmad says of this:

> Jam-'i-him is the Arabic expression in this verse which specifically speaks of bringing together of life on earth and the life elsewhere. When this meeting of the two will take place is not specified, nor is it mentioned whether it will happen here on earth or elsewhere. One thing however, is definitely stated: this event will most certainly come to pass whenever God so desires. It should be kept in mind that the word jama' can imply either a physical contact or a contact through communication. Only the future will tell how and when this contact will take place, but the very fact that more than fourteen hundred years ago such a possibility was even predicted is miraculous in itself.[753]

Furthermore, the expectation that aliens are headed our way extends to the nonreligious worldview as well. Lewis White Black, a philosopher at the University of Rochester, writes, "I believe even responsible scientific speculation and expensive technology of space exploration in search of other life are the peculiarly modern equivalent of angelology and Utopia or demonology and apocalypse."[754] Black then adds, "Exobiology recapitulates eschatology. The eschatological hope of help from heaven revives when the heavens of modern astronomy replace the Heaven of religion. That we can learn from more advanced societies in the skies the secret of survival is the eschatological hope which motivates, or at least is used to justify, the work of exobiologists."[755] This applies broadly to other spiritualities as well. For instance, the founder of analytical psychology, Carl Jung, wrote concerning ET belief: "In addition to their obviously superior technology they are credited with the superior wisdom and moral goodness which would, on the other hand, enable them to save humanity."[756] Speaking of the UFO as an archetype, Jung describes its messianic qualities as creating "the image of the divine-human personality, the Primordial Man or Anthropos, a *chen-yen* (true or whole man), and Elijah who calls down fire from heaven, rises up to heaven in a fiery chariot, and is a forerunner of the Messiah, the dogmatized figure of Christ, as well as of Khidir, the Verdant one, who is a parallel to Elijah: like him, he wanders over the earth as a human personification of Allah."[757]

Thus a belief in "godly" aliens that will ultimately come in contact with man has wide interfaith acceptance among secularists, spiritualists, and the world's largest religions, who seem ready and even excited about embracing their Official Disclosure moment—something these authors believe holds dangerous and deceptive end-times ramifications.

The Role of Petrus Romanus for the Alien Savior

In our previous work, *Petrus Romanus*, we carefully detailed a prophecy by Malachy O'Morgair, or "Saint Malachy" as he is known to Catholics, having to do with "the last pope." This prophecy was hidden for hundreds of years inside the highly guarded vaults of the Vatican library. It contains a list of Latin verses predicting each of the Roman Catholic popes from Pope Celestine II to the final pope, *Petrus Romanus* or "Peter the Roman," whose reign assists the rise of Antichrist and ends in the destruction of Rome. According to this nine-hundred-year-old prophecy, the pope following Benedict XVI is this final pontiff. The last segment of the prophecy reads:

> In the extreme persecution of the Holy Roman Church, there will sit Peter the Roman, who will nourish the sheep in many tribulations; when they are finished, the City of Seven Hills will be destroyed, and the dreadful judge will judge his people. The End.[758]

While investigating this mysterious prophecy, we learned of the long line of other Roman Catholic leaders who, down through time, also foresaw Rome being destroyed after becoming an engine of the Antichrist. A remarkable example of this was Dr. Henry Edward Cardinal Manning, who delivered a series of lectures in 1861 under the title, "The Present Crises of the Holy See Tested by Prophecy," in which he predicted a future crisis in the Roman Catholic Church resulting in apostasy and the rise of the False Prophet and Antichrist. Of the prophecy in the book of Revelation (chapter 18) concerning the end-time destruction of Mystery Babylon, Manning wrote:

> We read in the Book Apocalypse, of the city of Rome, that she said in the pride of her heart, "I sit as a queen, and am no widow, and sorrow I shall not see. Therefore shall her plagues come in one day: death, and mourning, and famine; and she shall be burned with fire, because God is strong who shall judge her." Some of the greatest writers of the Church tell us that…the great City of Seven Hills…the city of Rome will probably become

apostate…and that Rome will again be punished, for he will depart from it; and the judgment of God will fall.[759]

Manning continued, explaining how Catholicism's greatest theologians agreed with this point of view:

The apostasy of the city of Rome…and its destruction by Antichrist may be thoughts so new to many Catholics, that I think it well to recite the text of theologians, of greatest repute. First, Malvenda, who writes expressly on the subject, states as the opinion of Ribera, Gaspar Melus, Viegas, Suarez, Bellarmine, and Bosius, that Rome shall apostatize from the faith, drive away the Vicar of Christ, and return to its ancient paganism. Malvenda's words are:

But Rome itself in the last times of the world will return to its ancient idolatry, power, and imperial greatness. It will cast out its Pontiff, altogether apostatize from the Christian faith, terribly persecute the Church, shed the blood of martyrs more cruelly than ever, and will recover its former state of abundant wealth, or even greater than it had under its first rulers.

Lessius says: "In the time of Antichrist, Rome shall be destroyed, as we see openly from the thirteenth chapter of the Apocalypse;" and again: "The woman whom thou sawest is the great city, which hath kingdom over the kings of the earth, in which is signified Rome in its impiety, such as it was in the time of St. John, and shall be again at the end of the world." And Bellarmine: "In the time of Antichrist, Rome shall be desolated and burnt, as we learn from the sixteenth verse of the seventeenth chapter of the Apocalypse." On which words the Jesuit Erbermann comments as follows: "We all confess with

Bellarmine that the Roman people, a little before the end of the world, will return to paganism, and drive out the Roman Pontiff."

Viegas, on the eighteenth chapter of the Apocalypse says: "Rome, in the last age of the world, after it has apostatized from the faith, will attain great power and splendor of wealth, and its sway will be widely spread throughout the world, and flourish greatly. Living in luxury and the abundance of all things, it will worship idols, and be steeped in all kinds of superstition, and will pay honor to false gods. And because of the vast effusion of the blood of martyrs which was shed under the emperors, God will most severely and justly avenge them, and it shall be utterly destroyed, and burned by a most terrible and afflicting conflagration."[760]

Recent Catholic priests have confirmed this vision of apostate Rome, some going farther than Cardinal Manning did regarding the inevitable danger of the False Prophet rising from within the ranks of Catholicism. As discussed in *Petrus Romanus*, this includes:

Father E. Sylvester Berry, whose book *The Apocalypse of Saint John* foretold the usurpation of the papacy by a false prophet; Father Herman Bernard Kramer, whose work *The Book of Destiny* painted a terrifying scenario in which Satan enters the church and assassinates the true pope (possibly during conclave) in order that his false pope can rise to rule the world; as well as similar beliefs by priests like Father John F. O'Connor, Father Alfred Kunz, and Father Malachi Martin.... In a two-hour presentation (available on DVD), Father O'Connor gave a homily titled "The Reign of the Antichrist," in which he described how changes within [the Roman Catholic] institution were already at work before his death to provide for the coming of Antichrist. (brackets in original)[761]

O'Connor's worst fears have certainly been realized. An associate of Popes John Paul II and Benedict XVI who is considered one of the most important Catholic theologians of the twentieth century, Hans Urs von Balthasar, wrote a provocative essay, "Casta Meretrix," ("Chaste Harlot") that not only identified the Roman Catholic Church as the Great Harlot, but embraced it:

> The figure of the prostitute [*forma meretricis*] is so appropriate for the Church...that it...defines the Church of the New Covenant in her most splendid mystery of salvation. The fact that the Synagogue left the Holy Land to go and be among the pagans was an infidelity of Jerusalem, the fact that "she opened her legs in every road in the world."
>
> But this same movement, which brings her to all the peoples, is the mission of the Church. She must unite and merge herself with every people, and this new apostolic form of union cannot be avoided.[762]

While the embrace of whoredom is astonishing, the convicting words of prophecy, "Come out of her, my people, That ye be not partakers of her sins, And that ye receive not of her plagues" (Revelation 18:4), seem to forecast such apostasy. In sharp relief, Paul's letter to the Ephesians implies that Christ's "Bride" is the body of believers who comprise the universal Christian Church (ἐκκλησία "called-out ones"). The one's called out in order, "That he might present it to himself a glorious church, not having spot, or wrinkle, or any such thing; but that it should be holy and without blemish" (Ephesians 5:27). The stage is set for the judgment of the harlot as predicted in Revelation and the prophecy of Saint Malachy.

Speaking of *Petrus Romanus*, some have found the most tantalizing aspects of that investigation to be our preemptive work on the so-called Vatileaks scandal of 2011–2012 before news services had even broke most of the details across the wire. The world understands today that it involved the trial of Pope Benedict XVI's butler, Paolo Gabriele, who was arrested by magistrates as the source behind leaked documents that plagued the Vatican starting in 2011. A Vatican computer expert named Claudio Sciarpelletti was also convicted of aiding and abetting the butler in the crime, and at least one cardinal was suspected of operating behind the scenes as well, with the butler likely just a pawn in a deeper internal power struggle. "This is not just a leak of documents that can be defined as a betrayal," Church historian Alberto Melloni wrote at the time of the trial, concluding that it was part of a power struggle among cardinals in the Curia, the Vatican's central administration.[763] "This is a strategy of tension, an orgy of vendettas and pre-emptive vendettas that has now spun out of the control of those who thought they could orchestrate it."[764] Other Vatican insiders were equally blunt in their assessment of Vatileaks, believing it was a smoke screen covering a larger hidden agenda involving Machiavellian maneuverings—what Phillip Pullella for *Reuters* called "a sort of 'mutiny of the monsignors'"[765]—playing out behind the scenes among cardinals jockeying for the role of the final pope. After thoroughly investigating the matter over a period of several months, we concluded:

> The unpleasant reality is that a conflict over who will become Petrus Romanus is boiling beneath the surface, largely unknown to the public but nevertheless foreseen by Catholic mystics such as Father Herman Bernard Kramer in his work, "The Book of Destiny." Let us remind the reader of his frightening prophecy and strange interpretation of the twelfth chapter of the book of Revelation concerning "the great wonder" mentioned in verse one. Father Kramer prophesied:
>
> > The "sign" in heaven is that of a woman with child crying out in her travail and anguish of delivery. In that travail, she gives birth to some definite "person" who is to RULE the Church with a rod of iron (verse 5). It then

points to a conflict waged within the Church to elect one who was to "rule all nations" in the manner clearly stated. In accord with the text this is unmistakably a PAPAL ELECTION, for only Christ and his Vicar have the divine right to rule ALL NATIONS.… But at this time the great powers may take a menacing attitude to hinder the election of the logical and expected candidate by threats of a general apostasy, assassination or imprisonment of this candidate if elected.

While we disagree with Kramer's interpretation of the book of Revelation, the idea that a specific "person" was born and is now of the appropriate age to fulfill the incarnation of St. Malachy's Prophecy of the Popes and to produce the Man of Sin, is without question. Kramer's fear that "great powers may take a menacing attitude to hinder the election of the logical and expected candidate" also reverberates the sentiment of other priests, past and present, including Cardinal Archbishop Paolo Romeo, the leader of Sicily's Catholics, who made headlines February 10, 2012, when the Italian newspaper *Il Fatto Quotidiano* (which is famous for breaking exclusives) published parts of a secret *communique* involving the cardinal and a criminal conspiracy to assassinate Pope Benedict.… Evidently at the center of the *Mordkomplott* (or contract to kill the pope) are political machinations in Rome involving Vatican Secretary of State Cardinal Tarcisio Bertone, whose growing thirst for power Benedict has come to hate, according to the leaked document, and another Italian now favored as successor by Benedict, Cardinal Angelo Scola, currently the Archbishop of Milan. The contract against the pope and the prediction by Cardinal Paola that was allegedly made in secret to his Italian and Chinese business partners in Beijing…were apparently believed serious enough that somebody among Paola's listeners "suspected that he himself was involved in a specific plot to assassinate Pope Benedict XVI. At least one of those present therefore reported the Cardinal's words to Rome, and a special report on the incident—complied by Cardinal Darío Castrillón Hoyos and written in German in an attempt to stop it from being leaked—was presented to the Pope on 30 December last year."[766]

Whether or not the threat whispered by Paola was actually formulated, it illustrated that efforts were being made while Benedict XVI was still pope by at least some members of the College of Cardinals to align themselves as candidates for Petrus Romanus. Besides Francis Arinze, Tarcisio Bertone, Peter Turkson, and Angelo Scola, we rounded out our top candidates for this final pontiff with Cardinals Gianfranco Ravasi, Leonardo Sandri, Ennio Antonelli, Jean-Louis Tauran, Christoph Schönborn, and Marc Quellet.

As this book headed to the printer we still did not know whether the last pope would turn out to be a person on our short list, but, whoever he is, intrigue surrounds how he may accommodate the newly celebrated astro-theology of Rome's top astronomers and theologians and whether this will somehow fulfill the Catholic prophecies of the coming Man of Sin—the seed of Satan—either *as* an alien serpent-savior, or as a deceiver that points mankind to a god of another world.

In point of fact, the Bible describes both the False Prophet (Petrus Romanus?) and the Antichrist as having allegiances and endowments not of this Earth. Not only can both of them call "fire" down from out of those heavens suspected to be the host-location of aliens (see Revelation 13:12–14 as a clear alliance with the "powers" of the celestial realm), but the prophet Daniel tells us their belief system will actually honor a "strange, alien god." In Daniel 11:38–39 we read:

But in his estate shall he honour *the God of forces*: and a god whom his fathers knew not shall he honour with gold, and silver, and with precious stones, and pleasant things. Thus shall he do in the most strong holds [Hebrew *Mauzzim*] with a ***strange god***, whom he shall acknowledge and increase with glory: and he shall cause them to rule over many, and shall divide the land for gain. (emphasis added)

Several parts of Daniel's prophecy stand out as very unusual. First, the "God of forces" or alternately "god of fortresses" (מעזם אלה) has been connected to Baal-Shamem, literally "Lord of the Heavens," a deity whom the Manichaean Gnostics later worshipped as "the greatest angel of light."[767] His second reference to the deity as "a strange god" is also intriguing. The Hebrew text "עִם־אֱלוֹהַּ נֵכָר" can be literally rendered "with an alien god." Add to this how the turn-of-the-century Protestant scholars translated this text as directly related to the Vatican and Roman Catholicism, and things get really interesting. The British Methodist theologian and biblical scholar Adam Clarke (1762–1832) took forty years to write his voluminous *Clarke's Commentary on the Bible*, which has remained a primary theological resource for centuries. In it, he says of Daniel's statement rendered in the authorized version as "in the most strong holds with a strange god" that it directly refers to the institution—not necessarily the laypeople of—the Roman Catholic Church:

Bishop Newton proposed the following translation [of this text as]: "Thus shall he do to the defenders of Mauzzim, together with the strange god whom he shall acknowledge: he shall multiply honor, and he shall cause him to rule over many; and the earth he shall divide for a reward." The defenders of Mauzzim, these saint and angel gods protectors, were the monks, priests, and bishops; of whom it may be truly said, "They were increased with honor, ruled over many, and divided the land for gain." They have been honored and reverenced almost to adoration; their jurisdiction was extended over the purses and consciences of men; they have been enriched with the noblest buildings and largest endowments, and the choicest lands have been appropriated for Church lands. These are points of such public notoriety, that they require no proof.[768]

English Baptist pastor, biblical scholar, and theologian, John Gill (1697–1771), likewise wrote and published expositions on the entire Bible. He interpreted the same text as: "Thus shall he do in the most strong holds with a strange god…. Or, 'in the strong holds of Mahuzzim,' that is, in the temples, churches, and chapels, dedicated to angels and departed saints; deck and adorn their images with gold, silver, precious stones, and with desirable things, which is notorious."[769]

With this in mind and based on other information from the previous few pages, it's evident that for hundreds of years, both Catholic prophets and Protestant reformers believed the Antichrist would ultimately champion a strange, alien deity through an apostate priesthood seated in Rome (and this fits perfectly with what we have documented and have even been assured of in person by today's Vatican authorities, astronomers, and theologians). They also saw how this union would ultimately lead to war and destruction from the heavens. And these visionaries were not alone in their assessment concerning a powerful alien-christ and his coming war as the result of otherworldly alliances. Government leaders around the globe have believed this for some time, and as far back as 1955, General Douglas MacArthur warned:

> You now face a new world, a world of change. We speak in strange terms, of harnessing the cosmic energy, of ultimate conflict between a united human race and the sinister forces of some other planetary galaxy. The nations of the world will have to unite, for the next war will be an interplanetary war. The nations of the earth must someday make a common front against attack by people from other planets.[770]

Over thirty years later, one of America's most beloved presidents, Ronald Reagan, echoed the same before the United Nations when he said:

In our obsession with antagonisms of the moment, we often forget how much unites all the members of humanity. Perhaps we need some outside, universal threat to make us recognize this common bond. I occasionally think how quickly our differences worldwide would vanish if we were facing an alien threat from outside this world.[771]

In Britain, the five-star admiral and former head of the British Ministry of Defence, Lord Hill-Norton, expressed his opinion that "some UFO encounters are definitely antithetical to orthodox Christian belief" and helped to form an international group called UFO Concern to assess the phenomenon as it pertains to religion and national security.[772] More recently, the former UFO adviser for the UK Ministry of Defence, Nick Pope, acknowledged that Britain has even prepared (and is preparing) top-secret sophisticated aparati in anticipation of this future military engagement against space invaders.[773] Global leaders outside the United Kingdom who have hinted similar knowledge of a potential external threat include former presidents Jimmy Carter and Gerald Ford, former US Senator Barry Goldwater, J. Edgar Hoover when he was director of the FBI,[774] and the former president of the old Soviet Union, Mikhail Gorbachev, who believed "it must be treated seriously."[775] It makes one wonder if something of this knowledge was behind recent Vatican comments when it criticized the Ridley Scott film *Prometheus*, saying that it is "a bad idea to defy the gods."[776]

The Gospel According to ET—Ready or Not, Here it Comes

Over the last decade especially, the Vatican has ramped up its production of science and theology studies aimed at developing an ecclesiastical position for disclosure of extraterrestrial intelligence. This includes November 2009, when it convened a five-day study week on astrobiology at the summer residence of the pope on the grounds of the Pontifical Academy of Sciences, during which astronomers and scientists from countries around the world joined prominent churchmen to evaluate "the origin of life and its precursor materials, the evolution of life on Earth, its future prospects on and off the Earth, and the occurrence of life elsewhere."[777] Whether any discussion was held at that time concerning the LUCIFER device and what it might be monitoring in deep space from atop Mt. Graham is unknown (the meetings were private), but just three months later, in January 2010, the Royal Society, the National Academy of Science of the UK, and the Commonwealth hosted representatives from NASA, the European Space Agency, and the UN Office for Outer Space Affairs to discuss "The Detection of Extraterrestrial Life and the Consequences for Science and Society."[778] Lord Martin Rees, president of the Royal Society and Astronomer Royal, announced at that time that aliens may be "staring us in the face"[779] in a form humans are unable to recognize, while other speakers referred to "overwhelming evidence" and "unprecedented proof" to signify how close we are to making irrefutable discovery and/or disclosure of alien life. This had Vatican spokesmen in the news again with increasingly candid statements regarding the future of the Church and Jesuit preparations to accommodate a dynamic ET reality.

In the lead-up to the Vatican-sponsored conference on astrobiology, the official Church newspaper, *L'Osservatore Romano*, interviewed Father José Gabriel Funes, an astronomer and director of the Vatican Observatory who made it clear that accepting the reality of intelligent aliens does not contradict the Catholic faith and that, in fact, *to believe otherwise* is the real heresy, as it puts "limits on God's creative freedom." Attorney Daniel Sheehan, who served for ten years as general counsel to the United States Jesuit Headquarters in Washington, DC, said Funes' explicit statement that disbelief in extraterrestrial intelligence "puts limits on God's creative freedom" was code-talk for those in the know. He wrote:

> On the face of it, this statement may not seem like an important event…. However, unbeknownst to the non-Catholic world,

Father Funes' specific choice of words tracks precisely the exact wording of the key aspect of the official Catholic Church Edict that was issued in 1277 by Bishop Etienne Tempier, the Bishop of Paris, in which the Catholic Church officially condemned St. Thomas Aquinas' Theological Proposition #34 in which Aquinas had publically asserted that "the first cause [meaning God] cannot possibly have created other worlds." Proposition #34 was officially condemned by the Catholic Church on the specific grounds that "it seems to set limits on God's creative freedom," the precise words that were deliberately used by Father Funes in 2008.[780]

Sheehan went on to explain why the reassertion of this theological position by Roman Catholic leaders is very important:

The fact that these precise words were chosen by the official Jesuit director of the Vatican Observatory to announce the new official policy of the Roman Catholic Church acknowledging the likelihood of the existence of extraterrestrial life elsewhere in the universe is understood by those of us who are familiar with such matters to be no mere coincidence. It may, indeed, prove to be of extraordinary importance. For this specific 1277 Catholic Edict that condemned Proposition #34 of Thomas Aquinas is deemed, by Church authorities and by secular historians alike, to have been the action which opened "the plurality of worlds debate" in Western civilization, which led directly to the removal of earth from the center of the universe four-hundred years ago. *And these words may point the way, here in the twenty-first century, to our removal from our position on the pinnacle of the pyramid of life."* (emphasis added)[781]

What Sheehan here identified is the belief by most Catholic theologians that Christianity as we know it is based on a pre-Copernican cosmology. Once cosmology changes as a result of new discovery or disclosure of alien life, so, too, will theology, whether explicitly or implicitly. To believe otherwise is "cosmic hubris," thought Andrew Burgess, who wrote:

> As long as someone is thinking in terms of a geocentric universe and an earth-deity, the story has a certain plausibility.... As soon as astronomy changes theories, however, the whole Christian story loses the only setting within which it would make sense. With the solar system no longer the center of anything, imagining that what happens here forms the center of a universal drama becomes simply silly.[782]

While the Catholic apologists will object that there is no official church teaching on Extraterrestrial Intelligence (ETI), it is possible to derive their trajectory from officially sanctioned literature. Kenneth J. Delano's *Many Worlds, One God* (1977) is described on its dust jacket as "an intelligent discussion of the existence of extraterrestrial life and its impact upon mankind." The thing that makes this book important is that it advocates belief in ETs and boasts a *nihil obstat* and an *imprimatur*. A *nihil obstat* is an official approval granted by a designated censor in the Roman Catholic Church. Its presence certifies that a work does not contradict Catholic teachings on matters of faith and morals. An *imprimatur* is the final approval and official declaration by the bishop in the diocese where the work is to be published, indicating the content is free from errors concerning Catholic doctrine.

In this hard-to-find work, Delano states, "Extraterrestrial visitors to our planet might display an astonishing knowledge and understanding of the universal laws of nature as well as psychic abilities that enable them to exercise powers of mind over matter to an equally amazing degree. To our bewildered human race, their wondrous deeds would be indistinguishable from the miraculous. An experience of this sort would shake the foundations of many a person's religion."[783] He continues, "In our dealings with ETI, we will have to adopt a way of thinking called 'cultural relativism' by anthropologists. Like cultural relativists who do not assume that their way of life is better than the 'weird' or 'evil' practices of other peoples, we must not assume that our species, Homo sapiens, is morally superior to any other species of intelligence in space."[784] This sort of relativism leaves mankind wide open for a great deception scenario. Furthermore, the idea that "moral truth is relative" is dangerously false. An extreme example makes this self-evident. For example, we ask, "Is there ever a circumstance in which 'killing babies for fun' is morally virtuous?" Of course, no one in his or her right mind will answer affirmatively. Thus, moral truths are not relative. If something is evil, it is evil for all. The sanctioned Roman Catholic position treating ETI in terms of cultural relativism demonstrates just how susceptible the Vatican is to evil supernaturalism cloaked in an alien guise.

Philosopher J. Edgar Burns held similar views and saw space exploration as the cosmic center for the birth of a new "space-faith" (what he also called "cosmolatry") that ultimately would give birth to a new religion. "By 'new religion' it is not entirely clear whether Burns meant an annihilation of the past or a breakthrough in religious consciousness that renders our 'truth claims' obsolete," wrote Ilia Delio in *Christ in Evolution*. "What the term does connote, however, echoes an insight of Pierre Teilhard de Chardin, namely, that Christianity is reaching the end of one of the natural cycles of its existence. 'Christ must be born again,' he said, 'he must be reincarnated in a world that has become too different from that in which he lived.' It is in light of this insight that 'exoChristology,' a term Burgess used to discuss Christological issues 'raised by discoveries in outer space,' takes on new import for Christian faith."[785] This also casts significant light on the new official position of the Vatican that *not believing* in aliens and being willing to accept their superior morality and coming new religion is not only paramount to heresy, but is based on a dying and antiquated belief system. Given that the Vatican holds sway to over 1 billion followers as well as influencing an even greater number of peoples, governments, and policies worldwide, any puny obstacles to their revised Christianity will thus hardly keep most of the world's "spiritual" people from wholeheartedly embracing the alien serpent-saviors on their arrival. In fact, acquiescence to ET gods will be widely and positively received by the masses of the world, according to Vatican astronomer and professor of fundamental theology, Father Giuseppe Tanzella-Nitti, exactly because:

> Extraterrestrial life contexts re-propose the intervention of mediators from faraway worlds, the delivery of moral messages that awaken in human beings the existential questions that ordinary terrestrial life has made dormant. Moreover… contact with civilizations different from our own is…a powerful conceptual place in which the human family *returns to wisdom and self-understanding*.
>
> As Paul Davies has intelligently pointed out… "The powerful theme of alien beings acting as a conduit to the Ultimate— whether it appears in fiction or as a seriously intended cosmological theory—touches a deep chord in the human psyche. The attraction seems to be that by contacting superior beings in the sky, humans will be given access to *privileged knowledge, and that the resulting broadening of our horizons will in some sense bring us a step closer to God."* (emphasis added)[786]

Professor Tanzella-Nitti further elaborated on this alien-derived "privileged knowledge" in his doctrinal paper for the Vatican in which he expressed theologically how, upon contact with highly advanced aliens, the Church will "have to conclude that our understanding of Revelation until that moment had been largely imprecise and even ambiguous [or, nowhere near the truth]."[787]

But all is not lost, as a new and improved religious "revelation" based on information acquired from another world *is coming*. It will involve a "strange, alien God" according to prophecy and (according to both ancient and modern authorities) be advocated for by a priesthood seated in Rome. Just be aware that there is a considerable downside. To reject the mysterious new gospel or even to neglect bowing down before the image that the deity sets up in its place (Daniel 11:38–38; Revelation 13:15) will result in "as many as [will] not worship the image of the beast [to] be killed." There will be no place for those heretics Father Funes referred to who reject the (papal?) decree and refuse to accept the alien dogma. Any such denial will definitely not go unpunished.

Alien Evangelists with Leathery Wings, Little Horns, and Barbed Tails

During his life, Sir Arthur C. Clarke (1917–2008) was a famous science-fiction author, inventor, futurist, and television commentator who, together with Robert A. Heinlein and Isaac Asimov, was considered to be one of the "Big Three" of science fiction. Clarke in particular had an uncanny knack at foreseeing the future. As an example, modern video games were unheard of in 1956 and virtual reality games had not even been imagined. That is, until Clarke wrote about them in *The City and the Stars*:

> Of all the thousands of forms of recreation in the city, these were the most popular. When you entered a saga, you were not merely a passive observer.... You were an active participant and pos-sessed—or seemed to possess—free will. The events and scenes which were the raw material of your adventures might have been prepared beforehand by forgotten artists, but there was enough flexibility to allow for wide variation. You could go into these phantom worlds with your friends, seeking the excitement that did not exist in Diaspar—and as long as the dream lasted there was no way in which it could be distinguished from reality.[788]

Or who could have believed in 1968 that the "newspad" technol-ogy set in 2001 would be realized nine years late as the iPad in 2010? Yet Clarke in his novel, *2001: A Space Odyssey*, clearly described the technology:

When he tired of official reports and memoranda and minutes, he would plug his foolscap-sized Newspad into the ship's information circuit and scan the latest reports from Earth. One by one he would conjure up the world's major electronic papers; he knew the codes of the more important ones by heart, and had no need to consult the list on the back of his pad. Switching to the display unit's short-term memory, he would hold the front page while he quickly searched the headlines and noted the items that interested him.[789]

Unfortunately, that Clarke showed such remarkable prescience may hold important (and frightening) realities for our investigation, too. This is because in the sci-fi seer's classic, *Childhood's End* (1953), giant silver spaceships appear in the future over every major city on Earth. After the dust settles, the peaceful yet mysterious "Overlords" inside them help form a world government, which ends all war and turns the planet into a utopia. Oddly, only a select few people get to see the Overlords, and their purpose for coming to Earth remains shrouded as they dodge questions for years, preferring to remain in their spacecraft, governing by proxy. Overlord Karellen, the "Supervisor for Earth," (an alien god) speaks directly only to the UN Secretary-General. Karellen tells him that the Overlords will reveal themselves in fifty years, when humanity will have become used to (and dependent on) their presence. When the revealing finally takes place, at Karellen's request, two children run into the ship as the crowd below finally gets a glimpse of what the aliens look like. Clarke writes:

There was no mistake. The leathery wings, the little horns, the barbed tail—all were there. The most terrible of all legends had come to life, out of the unknown past. Yet now it stood smiling, in ebon majesty, with the sunlight gleaming upon its tremendous body, and with a human child resting trustfully on either arm.[790]

According to the narrative, the revelation that these beings—historically known as the devil and his angels—were in fact always our benefactors does not lead to chaos but rather to technological and spiritual utopia, quickly resulting in the dissolution of all previously existing religions. The world celebrates as people are described as having overcome their prejudices against the devilish sight of Karellen, or, as he had been known in the Bible, Satan.

> Here was a revelation which no-one could doubt or deny: here, seen by some unknown magic of Overlord science, were the true beginnings of all the world's great faiths. Most of them were noble and inspiring—but that was not enough. Within a few days, all mankind's multitudinous messiahs had lost their divinity. Beneath the fierce and passionless light of truth, faiths that had sustained millions for twice a thousand years vanished like morning dew.[791]

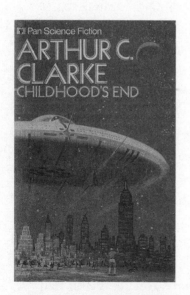

As the story continues, the children on Earth—set free from outdated Abrahamic religions such as Christianity—begin displaying powerful psychic abilities, foreshadowing their evolution into a cosmic consciousness, a transcendent form of life. Indeed, this is the *end* of the human species as it was known as everyone merges into a cosmic intelligence called the Overmind.

Those familiar with eastern religions will recognize Clarke's narrative as a clever ET version of pantheistic *monism* (the view that there is only one kind of ultimate substance). Overmind is quite similar to the Hindu concept of Brahman, and given that Atman is, simply stated, the concept of self, the Hindu doctrine "Atman is Brahman" is roughly equivalent to absorption into the Overmind. Similarly, Buddhism advocates the dissolution of the self

into Nirvana. In fact, nearly all New Age, spiritualist, and occult traditions have comparable monistic dogma. Some shroud this doctrine of
deceit in terms like "Christ Consciousness," giving it a more appealing
veneer, but Jacques Vallée recorded interesting examples of such twisted
ET theology, replacing biblical prophecy with the Overmind. One contactee told Vallée:

> I was told that I was to come out at this time with this informa-
> tion because mankind was going to go through the collective
> Christ experience of worshipping UFOs and receiving informa-
> tion. It would help mankind balance its political focus. You see
> the interesting thing, Jacques, is that we must emphasize the fact
> that we are receiving a new program! *We do not have to go through
> the old programming of Armageddon.* (emphasis added)[792]

That such New-Age babble as described above has been the
doctrine of non-Christians this century is one thing, but in recent
homilies, Pope Benedict XVI's end-times views have taken on a
troubling and similar tome. This may not come as a surprise to those
Catholics familiar with Father Malachi Martin's warnings in his
book, *The Jesuits*, which documented how priests like Pierre Teilhard
de Chardin were deeply influencing the Church and its academia
toward occultism this century. In our historical survey we established
Chardin's belief in extraterrestrials and offered a brief discussion on his
sorcerous Darwinian mysticism. But it was his connection with monistic
occultism and what is called the "Omega Point" that takes us through
the alien-deity rabbit hole. According to Chardin, in his *The Future of
Man* (1950), the universe is currently evolving towards higher levels of
material complexity and consciousness and ultimately will reach its goal,
the *Omega Point.* Chardin postulated that this is the supreme aspiration
of complexity and consciousness, an idea also roughly equivalent to the
"Technological Singularity" as expressed in the writings of transhumanists
like Ray Kurzweil. Indeed, one finds a remarkable coalescence of all

non-Christian systems under the banner of Singularity, Monism, Omega Point, and Overmind. Yet, like the nebulous "Christ consciousness" advocated by occultists, Chardin's writings are easily misunderstood because he not only created new vocabulary for his Darwinian religion, he also redefined biblical terminology to mean something alien to its original intent. For instance, when Chardin writes about "Christ," he usually does not mean Jesus of Nazareth. Instead, he is describing the Ultra-Man, the all-encompassing end of evolution at the Omega Point. As an example, consider when Jesus said, "Think not that I am come to destroy the law, or the prophets: I am not come to destroy, but to fulfill" (Matthew 5:17). Chardin exegetes this as, "I have not come to destroy, but to fulfill Evolution."[793] To most Christians, this probably seems overtly heretical, but its infiltration into Roman Catholic thought and the dangerous alien-christ implications it brings with it has infiltrated the highest levels at Rome—*including the papacy.*

Unbeknownst to most Roman Catholics, Pope Benedict XVI is a Chardinian mystic of the highest order. The pope's book, *Credo for Today: What Christians Believe* (2009), follows the lead of the Jesuit and states unequivocally that a belief in Creationism (the idea that life, the Earth, and the universe as we know it today did not "evolve" but rather were created by the God of the Bible) "contradicts the idea of evolution and [is] untenable today."[794] Following his rejection of Creationism and support of evolution, Pope Benedict XVI uses the doctrine of the Second Coming of Christ to advance Chardin's "Omega Point," *in which a "new kind" of God, man, and mind will emerge.* From page 113 we read:

> From this perspective the belief in the second coming of Jesus Christ and in the consummation of the world in that event could be explained as the conviction that our history is advancing to an "omega" point, at which it will become finally and unmistakably clear that the element of stability that seems to us to be the supporting ground of reality, so to speak, is not mere unconscious matter; that, on the contrary, the real, firm ground

is mind. Mind holds being together, gives it reality, indeed is reality: it is not from below but from above that being receives its capacity to subsist. That there is such a thing as this process of 'complexification' of material being through spirit, and from the latter its concentration into a new kind of unity can already be seen in the remodeling of the world through technology.[795]

The term "complexification" was coined by Chardin (and the technological allusions it suggests is akin to transhumanism and Ray Kurzweil's Singularity) and the pope's complete devotion to this theology is again laid bare in his book, *Principles of Catholic Theology* (1987), which states:

The impetus given by Teilhard de Chardin exerted a wide influence. With daring vision it incorporated the historical movement of Christianity into the great cosmic process of evolution from Alpha to Omega: since the noogenesis, since the formation of consciousness in the event by which man became man, this process of evolution has continued to unfold as the building of the noosphere above the biosphere.[796]

This "noosphere" is taken very seriously today in modernist Catholic theology, academia, and even science. It is explained in the *Encyclopedia of Paleontology*, this way:

Teilhard coined the concept of the "noosphere," the new "thinking layer" or membrane on the Earth's surface, superposed on the living layer (biosphere) and the lifeless layer of inorganic matter (lithosphere). Obeying the "law of complexification/conscience," the entire universe undergoes a process of "convergent integration" and tends to a final state of concentration, the "point Omega" where the noosphere will be intensely unified and will have achieved a "hyperpersonal" organization. Teilhard equates this future hyperpersonal psychological organization with *an emergent divinity* [a future new form of God]. (emphasis added)[797]

The newly sanctioned doctrine of an approaching "emergent divinity" in place of the literal return of Jesus Christ isn't even that much of a secret any longer among Catholic priests (though the cryptic Charindian lingo masks it from the uninitiated). For instance, in his July 24, 2009, homily in the Cathedral of Aosta while commenting on Romans 12:1–2, the pope said:

The role of the priesthood is to consecrate the world so that it may become a living host, a liturgy: so that the liturgy may not be something alongside the reality of the world, but that the world itself shall become a living host, a liturgy. *This is also the great vision of Teilhard de Chardin: in the end we shall achieve a true cosmic liturgy, where the cosmos becomes a living host.* (emphasis added)[798]

This is overtly pantheistic and, of course, the text he was discussing (Romans 12) teaches the exact opposite: "Be not conformed to this world" (Romans 12:2a). While the pope thus aggressively promotes Chardin's process of "noogenesis" in which the cosmos comes alive and everyone unifies as a "living host," one can readily see that Brahman, Nirvana, Overmind, and Singularity are roughly equivalent to this monistic concept. Interestingly, noogenesis (Greek: νοῦς=mind; γένεσις=becoming) actually has two uses: one in Chardin's Darwinian pantheism—and another, more *telling* rendering—within modern astrobiology.

In Cardin's system, noogenesis is the fourth of five stages of evolution, representing the emergence and evolution of mind. This is the stage we are said to be in currently, and as noogenesis progresses, so does the formation of the noosphere, which is the collective sphere of human thought. In fact, many Chardinians believe that the World Wide Web is an infrastructure of noosphere, an idea intersecting well with trans-humanist thought. Chardin wrote, "*We have as yet no idea* of the possible magnitude of 'noospheric' effects. We are confronted with human vibrations resounding by the million—a whole layer of consciousness exerting simultaneous pressure upon the future and the collected and hoarded produce of a million years of thought."[799]

However, this concept gets more translucent in astrobiology, where scientists have adopted noogenesis as the scientific term denoting *the origin of technological civilizations capable of communicating with humans and traveling to Earth*—in other words, the basis for extraterrestrial contact.[800] Consequently, among many if not most of Rome's astronomers and theologians, there is the widespread belief that the arrival of "alien deities" will promote our long-sought spiritual noogenesis, and according to a leading social psychologist, the world's masses are ready for such a visitation and will receive them (or *him*) as a messiah.[801] This is further reflected in a 2012 United Kingdom poll, which indicated that more people nowadays believe in extraterrestrials than in God.[802] Consequently, whether or not it is the ultimate expression, the noogenic "strong delusion" is already here.

While we aren't suggesting a direct equivocation per se, the conceptual intersection between the two uses of noogenesis (the occultic and astrobiological) is thought provoking, especially in light of Clarke's scenario in *Childhood's End*, where noogenesis in the astrobiological application (the arrival of the alien Overlords) was the impetus for evolution toward the Overmind and dissolution of humanity. It seems Rome has connected these dots for us. In his sanctioned treatise, Kenneth J. Delano linked the concept of maximum consciousness and alien contact, truly noogenesis in both senses of the word:

> For man to take his proper place as a citizen of the universe, he must transcend the narrow-mindedness of his earthly provincialism and be prepared to graciously accept the inhabitants of other worlds as equals or even superiors. At this point in human

history, our expansion into space is the necessary means by which we are to develop our intellectual faculties to the utmost and, perhaps in cooperation with ETI, achieve the maximum consciousness of which St. Thomas Aquinas wrote in *Summa Theologica*:

> This is the earthly goal of man: to evolve his intellectual powers to their fullest, to arrive at the maximum of consciousness, to open the eyes of his understanding upon all things so that upon the tablet of his soul the order of the whole universe and all its parts may be enrolled.[803]

Viewed through this lens, the Vatican's promotion of Darwinism and astrobiology intrigues. Following Chardin and Delano, perhaps Pope Benedict, the VORG astronomers, and theologians like Tanzella-Nitti, O'Mera, and Balducci pursued astrobiological noogenesis so that when Petrus Romanus assumed his reign as the final pope, they might usher in the Fifth Element of the Omega Point known as "Christogenesis." (Authors note: one cannot help recall the movie *The Fifth Element* that involved a priesthood who protects a mysterious Fifth Element that turns out to be a messianic human who ultimately combines the power of the other four elements [noogenesis] to form a "divine light" that saves mankind.) In Chardin's book, *The Phenomenon of Man*, the five elements of evolution are: 1) "geogenesis" (beginning of Earth); 2) "biogenesis" (beginning of life); 3) "anthropogenesis" (beginning of humanity); 4) noogenesis (evolutionary consolidation to maximum consciousness); leading to finally 5) "Christogenesis," the creation of a "total Christ" at the Omega Point. With that in mind, be aware that astrobiology and transhumanist philosophy suggest this noogenesis is being driven by *an external intelligence*, whether it be respectively artificial or extraterrestrial, which leads these authors to conclude we are on the cusp of a noogenesis unlike the one Rome's theologians may have anticipated. We would redefine the terms and instead suggest aggressive preparation for an *Antichristogenesis*—an Alien Serpent-Savior—the ultimate Darwinian Übermensch who may even bare leathery wings, little horns, and a barbed tail. But regardless how he appears, it is obvious to all now that the Vatican has cleverly prepared for his coming, perhaps even monitored his approach from atop Mt. Graham, using the LUCIFER device.

Also NEW From These Authors!

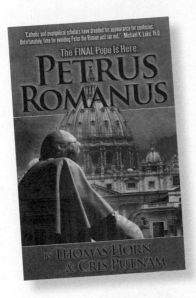

In *Petrus Romanus: The Final Pope Is Here*, internationally acclaimed author Thomas Horn and respected theologian and apologist Cris Putnam predicted the resignation of Pope Benedict XVI and tell readers what to expect to unfold in the coming days, and, more importantly, what they can do to be prepared for the arrival of Petrus Romanus and the kingdom of Antichrist.

Pandemonium's Engine is the vehicle through which Tom Horn, Cris Putnam, and an elite team of commentators inform a still-sleeping public about radical changes coming to our culture… very soon. In particular, the technological advances in genetics, robotics, artificial intelligence, nanotechnology, and synthetics biology (G.R.I.N.S.) that will bring us all to the doorstep of life-altering realities almost too incredible to believe.

Available at www.SurvivorMall.com

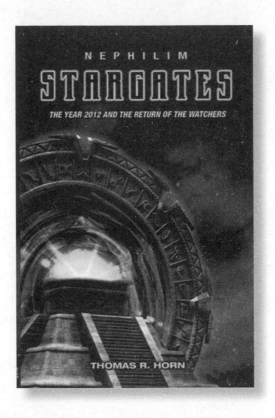

One myth from the history of every great civilization spoke of beings descending from heaven and using human and animal DNA to create giant offspring. Rabbinical authorities, Septuagint translators, and early church fathers understood this as a factual record of history. The phenomenon began with the "Watchers" who spawned "Nephilim" resulting in judgment from God. *Nephilim Stargates and the Return of the Watchers* is a glimpse into this past, present, and future phenomena, with an eye on what sages and scientists believe and what futurists and prophets may fear.

Available at www.SurvivorMall.com

When English theologian George Hawkins Pember, in his 1876 masterpiece, *Earth's Earliest Ages*, analyzed the prophecy of Jesus Christ in Matthew 24 that says the end times would be a repeat of "the days of Noah," he concluded the final and most fearful sign heralding the Lord's Second Coming would be the return of the "Nephilim, the appearance upon earth of beings from the Principality of the Air, and their unlawful intercourse with the human race." It is time for a new generation to discover his warning, as it now appears set to unfold.

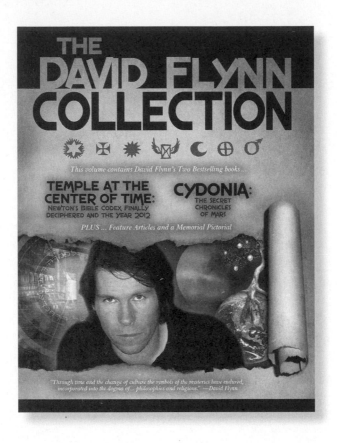

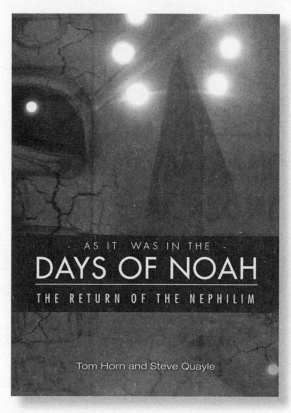

As it Was in the Days of Noah: The Return of the Nephilim has been called "the best ever series" by popular radio personalities Tom Horn and Steve Quayle. This is a fascinating and sometimes frightening exposé on little-known passages from the Bible and apocryphal texts, which speak of an alien agenda, great deception giving rise to the Antichrist, and in the last two parts of this series, the most incredible information ever revealed over the airwaves about the return of the giants in the last days. Tom's newest revelation from the Book of Enoch left Steve Quayle speechless for several seconds and led to newshounds seeking additional information and a feature editorial at WorldNetDaily, the world's #1 online news site.

Available at www.SurvivorMall.com

Notes

1. Malachi Martin, *Keys of This Blood: Pope John Paul II Versus Russia and the West For Control of the New World Order*, 1 ed. (New York: Simon & Schuster, 1991), 632.

2. Bob Pratt, "More than 30 Years of Triangle Sightings," *MUFON*, last accessed January 24, 2013, http://www.mufon.com/bob_pratt/triangles.html.

3. Richard H. Hall, *The Ufo Evidence—Volume 2: A Thirty Year Report* (Lanham, Maryland: Scarecrow Press, 2001), 349. Also see: http://www.ufoinfo.com/onthisday/September14.html.

4. The following website cites *Raiders News Update* as its source: "UFO Filmed Over Vatican," *HotSpots*, last accessed February 5, 2013, http://www.hotspotsz.com/UFO_Filmed_Over_Vatican_%28Article-13991%29.html.

5. "Unusual Light Appears over Vatican," *Unknown Country*, April 9, 2005, last accessed January 24, 2013 http://www.unknowncountry.com/news/unusual-light-appears-over-vatican#ixzz2Ios0QqGe.

6. Piotr Cielebiaś, Robert Morningstar, and Dirk Vander Ploeg, "UFO Over the Vatican," *UFO Digest*, last accessed January 27, 2013, http://www.ufodigest.com/news/0407/omegasecret7.html.

7. John Allen, "Bertone Named Secretary of State," *National Catholic Reporter*, June 23, 2006, last accessed 01/23/2013, http://www.nationalcatholicreporter.org/word/word062306.htm.

8. Italian specialist Giuseppe Stilo explained that this alleged photo case was first known when the Italian weekly *L'Europeo* released it on February 3, 1957. For more information, see: http://www.ikaros.org.es/fotocat1954.pdf.

9. Martin Shough, "Oct/Nov. 1957, United Kingdom," *NICAP*, addendum at bottom of report, last accessed January 26, 2013, http://www.nicap.org/reports/5410XXUnitedKingdom_report.htm.

10. Gordon Creighton, "'Great Crosses' Over Rome and Washington, D.C., in November 1954," *Flying Saucer Review*, vol. 30, no. 4 (1985), as viewable here: http://www.ignaciodarnaude.com/avistamientos_ovnis/Creighton-Perego,Crosses%201954,Rome-Washington%20D.C.,FSR85V30N4.pdf.

11. Ibid.

12. Ibid.

13. Ruth Gledhill, "Defense Chief Warns of 'Satanic UFOs'" *The Times of London*, as cited in *AUFORA News Update* March 1, 1997, last accessed January 25, 2013, http://www.mufon.com/MUFONNews/arch011.html

14. Karin Laub, "Scroll Said Resembles Sea Scrolls," *Washington Post* (September 27, 1999), last accessed January 28, 2013, http://www.washingtonpost.com/wp-srv/aponline/19990927/aponline195514_000.htm.

15. The Mysterious Angel Scroll, *Science Ministries*, last accessed February 5, 2013, http://www.starwire.com/partner/Article_Display_Page/0,,PTID4859_CHID5_CIID131000,00.html.

16. Barry Chamish, "New 'Angel' Dead Sea Scroll Contains Astral Implications," *Rense*, October 5, 1999, last accessed January 28, 2013, http://rense.com/politics5/astral.htm.

17. Michael S. Heiser, *The Façade* (SuperiorBooks.com Inc., 2001), 211. Also verified in personal email to Cris Putnam.

18. Rachel Donadio and Nicholas Kulish, "A Statement Rocks Rome, Then Sends Shockwaves Around the World," *New York Times*, February 11, 2013, last accessed February 13, 2013, http://www.usatoday.com/story/weather/2013/02/12/lightning-bolt-strikes-vatican-pope-benedict-resignation/1913095/.

19. "A Possible Naked-eye Comet in March," *NASA Science*, February 6, 2013, last accessed February 13, 2013, http://science.nasa.gov/science-news/science-at-nasa/2013/06feb_panstarrs/.

20. Michael D. Lemonick, "Coming in 2013: The Comet of the Century?," *Space.com*, December 20, 2012, last accessed February, 13, 2103, http://science.time.com/2012/12/20/coming-in-2013-the-comet-of-the-century/#ixzz2KoIzilud.

21. Hildergard Von Bingen, cited at Irene Hahn, "The Incredible Life and Prophesies of St. Hildegard," last accessed February 13, 2013, http://www.unitypublishing.com/prophecy/HildigardSaint.htm.

22. Thomas F. O'Mera, "The Salvation of Extraterrestrials," *Huffington Post*, July 16, 2012, last accessed January 28, 2013, http://www.huffingtonpost.com/thomas-f-omeara-op/salvation-of-extraterrestrials_b_1671783.html.

23. "The Constancy of Constants," *Scientific American*, June 2005, 57–63.

24. So dubbed by Henry Luce in 1941.

25. Allan Bloom saw it all coming in his *Closing of the American Mind: How Higher Education Has Failed Democracy and Impoverished the Souls of Today's Students*, 1987. Also, David Breese's *The Seven Men Who Rule the World from the Grave*.

26. NDAA, signed December 31, 2012, abrogated the Bill of Rights. Even the legality of the current president is under question: Cf. several books by Jerry Corsi, and WorldNetDaily, et al.

27. Cf. *Petrus Romanus* for a detailed review of the related legends and prophecies.

28. "Safford, Arizona," *Wikipedia, The Free Encyclopedia*, last modified November 24, 2012, http://en.wikipedia.org/wiki/Safford,_Arizona.

29. Taken from the "Abstract": Dumke, Michael, "Sub-Millimeter Science with the Heinrich-Hertz-Telescope," *Harvard-Smithsonian Center for Astrophysics*, last accessed December 3, 2012, http://adsabs.harvard.edu/abs/2000yera. confE..64D.

30. "Welcome to the Vatican Advanced Technology Telescope," *VaticanObservatory. org*, last accessed December 3, 2012, http://vaticanobservatory.org/VATT/ index.php.

31. Guy Consolmagno, *Intelligent Life in the Universe: Catholic Belief and the Search for Extraterrestrial Intelligent Life* (London: Catholic Truth Society, 2005), 5.

32. Ibid., 33–34.

33. Ibid., 37.

34. Roger Highfield and Tom Leonard, "American Association: Martian Life Will Change God's Image, Says Vatican," *Watcher's Website*, February 17, 1997, http://www.mt.net/~watcher/ufovatican.html. (Article originally appeared on *The Electronic Telegraph*: http://www.telegraph.co.uk.)

35. "Vatican Astronomer Says it's OK to Think Aliens Exist," *USA Today*, May 14, 2008, http://www.usatoday.com/news/religion/2008-05-14-vatican-aliens_N. htm.

36. Father José Gabriel Funes, S.J., "Believing in Aliens Not Opposed to Christianity, Vatican's Top Astronomer Says," *Catholic News Agency*, May 13, 2008, http://www.catholicnewsagency.com/news/believing_in_aliens_not_ opposed_to_christianity_vaticans_top_astronomer_says/.

37. Richard Boylan, PhD, "Vatican Official Declares Extraterrestrial Contact is Real" *UFO Digest*, last accessed December 4, 2012, http://www.ufodigest.com/ balducci.html.

38. Paola Leopizzi Harris, "Monsignor Corrado Balducci Says Mexico Blessed with UFO Sightings," *MUFON [Mutual UFO Network] Journal*, March 28, 2006, http://www.mufon.com (site requires membership; alternatively, see full article online on the following page: David Ben Yakov, "Catholicism and the UFO Reality," *DelusionResistance.org*, last accessed December 4, 2012, http://www. delusionresistance.org/ufo/catholicism-ufos.html).

39. "Comet and Father Malachi Martin" (ART BELL INTERVIEWS FATHER MALACHI MARTIN: Transcript of the April 5th, 1997 interview with late Father Malachi Martin by Art Bell), *Godlike Productions*, January 7, 2007, http://www.godlikeproductions.com/forum1/message326615/pg1.

40. This quote came from a personal interview in an email correspondence between Thomas Horn and Guy Consolmagno on November 7, 2012.

41. Sharon Begley, "The Vatican and Little Green Men," *Newsweek*, May 15, 2008, http://www.newsweek.com/blogs/lab-notes/2008/05/15/the-vatican-and-little- green-men.html.

42. Neil Mackay, "And On the Eighth Day—Did God Create Aliens?" *Sunday Herald—Scotland*, November 28, 2005, http://www.sundayherald.com/53020

(site discontinued; see alternatively, from *Signs of the Times*: http://www.sott.
net/articles/show/106410-And-on-the-eighth-day-did-God-create-aliens-).

43. Father Josè Funes, "The Extraterrestrial is My Brother," *L'Osservatore Romano*,
May 14, 2008 (English translation of article viewable here: http://padrefunes.
blogspot.com/).

44. As quoted by article: Brother Guy Consolmagno, "Would You Baptize an
Extraterrestrial?: A Jesuit Priest Says the Discovery of Life Elsewhere in the
Universe Would Pose No Problem for Religion," *Beliefnet*, last accessed
December 4, 2012, http://www.beliefnet.com/News/Science-Religion/2000/08/
Would-You-Baptize-An-Extraterrestrial.aspx?p=2.

45. Giuseppe Tanzella-Nitti, "EXTRATERRESTRIAL LIFE," *Interdisciplinary
Encyclopedia of Religion and Science*, last accessed December 4, 2012, http://
www.disf.org/en/Voci/65.asp.

46. Ibid.

47. Ibid.

48. J. Antonio Huneeus, "The Vatican Extraterrestrial Question," *Open Minds
Magazine*, June/July 2010, Issue 2, 59.

49. See: http://www.vaticanobservatory.org/VO-NEWS/index.php/videos/item/79-
lucifer.html.

50. Paul Ogilvie, "How Does an Infrared Telescope Work?" *eHow*, last accessed
December 4, 2012, http://www.ehow.com/how-does_4926827_infrared-
telescope-work.html.

51. Thomas and Nita Horn, *The Ahriman Gate* (Sisters, Oregon: Musterion Press,
2005), 205.

52. Ibid., 218.

53. Nick Bostrom, "Transhumanist Values," last accessed December 4, 2012,
http://www.nickbostrom.com/ethics/values.html.

54. For more information on these lectures, see: "Facing the Challenges of
Transhumanism: Religion, Science, Technology," *Arizona State University*, last
accessed December 4, 2012, http://transhumanism.asu.edu/.

55. "The SOPHIA Project, *Arizona State University*, http://lach.web.arizona.edu/
Sophia/ (site discontinued; see alternatively, from Arizona State University:
http://lach.web.arizona.edu/veritas_research_program and http://www.lach.
web.arizona.edu/sophia_project).

56. Ludovico Sinistrari, *De Daemonialitate et Incubis et Succubis* (Demoniality; or,
Incubi and succubi), from the original 1680 Latin manuscript translated into
English (Paris, I. Liseux, 1872) 53. (The 1879 English translation of the book is
available in full and for free online in scanned format by the *California Digital
Library* here [last accessed December 4, 2012]: http://archive.org/details/
demonialityorinc00sinirich.)

57. Annette Yoshiko Reed, *Fallen Angels and the History of Judaism and Christianity:
The Reception of Enochic Literature* (Cambridge, 2005), 214.

58. Father Malachi Martin and Art Bell, "Father Malachi Martin on Exorcisms,"
The Art Bell Show, April 5th, 1997, last accessed January 16, 2013, http://
en.gloria.tv/?media=22060.

59. Timothy B. Benford, "UFO, Aliens and the Vatican: And Why Astronaut Gordon Cooper Lied to Me," *Yahoo Voices*, June 11, 2008, http://voices.yahoo.com/ufo-aliens-vatican-why-astronaut-gordon-1521705.html.

60. John Wetenhall, "Arizona Spends $1.25M to Save 250 Squirrels," *ABC News*, June 17, 2010, http://abcnews.go.com/US/Broadcast/arizona-spends-125-million-endangered-squirrels/story?id=10934895#.UMyK73fNmSo.

61. To learn more, see: "Richard Dawkins Interviews Father George Coyne," *Catholic Truth*, January 27, 2009, http://www.catholictruthscotland.com/blog/2009/01/richard-dawkins-interviews-father-george-coyne/.

62. To learn more about these programs, see: "Center for Astrobiology," *The University of Arizona*, last accessed January 16, 2013, http://www.astrobiology.arizona.edu/.

63. *Science and Theology: Ruminations on the Cosmos* (ND From Vatican Observatory Foundation) by Chris Impey and Catherine Petry (Jan 13, 2004); also *International Symposium on Astrophysics Research and on the Dialogue between Science and Religion* (ND From Vatican Observatory Foundation) by Chris Impey and Catherine Petry (Feb. 26, 2004).

64. Compiled with data from Ohio State University; see more here: "The Large Binocular Telescope," *Ohio State University*, last accessed January 16, 2013, http://www.astronomy.ohio-state.edu/LBT/.

65. Elizabeth Brandt, "The Fight for Dzil Nchaa Si An, Mt. Graham: Apaches and Astrophysical Development in Arizona," *Cultural Survival*, March 24, 2010, http://www.culturalsurvival.org/ourpublications/csq/article/the-fight-dzil-nchaa-si-an-mt-graham-apaches-and-astrophysical-developme.

66. Information viewable here: "Arizona," *The Nature Conservancy*, last accessed January 16, 2013, http://www.nature.org/ourinitiatives/regions/northamerica/unitedstates/arizona/index.htm.

67. David Chidester and Edward Tabor Linenthal, *American Sacred Space (Religion in North America)* (Bloomington, IN: Indiana University Press, 1995), 120; viewable here: http://books.google.com/books?id=-C9pugPeqhMC&lpg=PA149&ots=9LCZK7sSRb&dq=Steve%20Yozwiak%2C%20%E2%80%9CPriest%20calls%20telescope%20foes%20part%20of%20%E2%80%98Jewish%20conspiracy%E2%80%99%E2%80%9D&pg=PA120#v=onepage&q=Graham&f=false.

68. To learn more about this, see: Thomas Horn and Cris Putnam, *Petrus Romanus: The Final Pope Is Here* (Crane, MO: Defender), 226.

69. Associated Press, "Ex-Fish and Wildlife Director Dies from Heart Complications: Embattled Boss Resigned in '89," *The Spokesman Review*, October 26, 1993, http://news.google.com/newspapers?id=KzsqAAAAIBAJ&sjid=hAkEAAAAIBAJ&pg=4313%2C4134214.

70. Peter Warshall, "The Heart of Genuine Sadness—Astronomers, Politicians, and Federal Employees Desecrate the Holiest Mountain of the San Carlos Apache," *Whole Earth* No. 91, (Winter 1997). http://www.mountgraham.org/content/heart-genuine-sadness-astronomers-politicians-and-federal-employees-desecrate-holiest

71. "Locutus of Borg," *Memory Alpha*, last accessed January 16, 2013, http://en.memory-alpha.org/wiki/Locutus_of_Borg.

72. Steve Yozwiak, "Priest Calls Telescope Foes Part of 'Jewish Conspiracy,'" *Arizona Republic* (August 14, 1992), B1; as quoted in: Jeffrey St. Clair, "Star Whores, Astronomers vs. Apaches on Mount Graham," February 1–3, 2003, http://www.counterpunch.org/2003/02/01 star-whores-astronomers-vs-apaches-on-mount-graham/.

73. "Personal Biography of Randy Maddalena, Ph.D.," *Environmental Protection Agency*, last accessed January 16, 2013, http://www.epa.gov/scipoly/sap/pubs/biographies/maddalena.htm.

74. Randy Maddalena, "The Price We Pay to See the Stars: Mt. Graham Red Squirrel v. Madigan," *Environs: Envtl. L. & Pol'y J.* 16 (1992), 26; viewable here: http://environs.law.ucdavis.edu/issues/16/1/articles/maddalena.pdf.

75. Steve Yozwiat, "Priest Calls Telescope Foes Part of 'Jewish Conspiracy'"; as quoted in: Jeffrey St. Clair, "Star Whores, Astronomers vs. Apaches on Mount Graham," http://www.counterpunch.org/2003/02/01/star-whores-astronomers-vs-apaches-on-mount-graham/.

76. Sandra Rambler, "Mount Graham Coalition Included in Notice of Intent to Sue U.S. Forest Service," *Arizona Silver Belt*, January 12, 2011, http://www.silverbelt.com/v2_news_articles.php?heading=0&story_id=2264&page=77.

77. Jeffrey St. Clair, "Star Whores: Astronomers vs. Apaches on Mount Graham," *Counter Punch*, weekend ed., February 1–3, 2003, http://www.counterpunch.org/2003/02/01/star-whores-astronomers-vs-apaches-on-mount-graham/.

78. Bruce Johnston, "Vatican Sets Evangelical Sights on Outer Space," *Daily Telegraph* (London, October 28, 1992), http://www.skeptictank.org/treasure/UFO2/VATICAN.SPA.

79. Correspondence, Freedom of Information Act Officer Patricia Riep, *NASA*, January 8, 1993, as cited in *The Southwest Center for Biological Diversity News Advisory*, December 2, 1997.

80. Michael S. Heiser, "The Mythological Provenance of Is. XVIV 12–15: A Reconsideration of the Ugaritic Material," *Vestus Testamentum* LI, 3, (2001): 356–357.

81. Ibid., 356–357.

82. Kaufmann Kohler, "Lucifer," last accessed March 5, 2011, http://www.jewishencyclopedia.com/view.jsp?artid=612&letter=L.

83. C. S. Lewis, *Mere Christianity* (NY: Harper Collins. 2001), 122.

84. Origen, "Origen de Principiis" book 1, chapter 5, as quoted in: Alexander Roberts, James Donaldson and A. Cleveland Coxe, *The Ante-Nicene Fathers Vol. IV : Translations of the Writings of the Fathers Down to A.D. 325* (Oak Harbor: Logos Research Systems, 1997), 259.

85. Alison Abbott, "Max Planck Society admits to its predecessor's Nazi links" *Nature* 411, 726 (14 June 2001) http://www.nature.com/nature/journal/v411/n6839/full/411726b0.html

86. Chelsea Schilling, "What the devil? Scientists Tap Power of 'Lucifer'" *World Net Daily*, January 20, 2013, http://www.wnd.com/2013/01/what-the-devil-scientists-tap-power-of-lucifer/#dpSowKyTDCvgbzM6.99.

87. Ibid.

88. "Teufel," *Reverso*, last accessed January 29, 2013, http://dictionary.reverso.net/german-english/Teufel.

89. "Large Binocular Telescope Interferometer," *LBTI*, last accessed January 17, 2013, http://lbti.as.arizona.edu/LBTI/index.html.

90. Daniel Stolte "Scientists Prepare to Take First-Ever Picture of a Black Hole," *UANews*, September, 23, 2012, http://uanews.org/node/44218.

91. David Chidester and Edward Tabor Linenthal, *American Sacred Space (Religion in North America)* (Bloomington, IN: Indiana University Press, 1995), 126; viewable here: http://books.google.com/books?id=-C9pugPeqhMC&lpg=PA149&ots=9LCZK7sSRb&dq=Steve%20Yozwiak%2C%20%E2%80%9CPriest%20calls%20telescope%20foes%20part%20of%20%E2%80%98Jewish%20conspiracy%E2%80%99%E2%80%9D&pg=PA120#v=onepage&q=Graham&f=false.

92. Jacques Vallée, *Dimensions: a Casebook of Alien Contact* (New York, NY: Contemporary Books, 1988) 200.

93. Dr. Alexander Roman, "Lourdes, Fátima and Medjugorje," *Orthodox Christianity*, last accessed January 17, 2013, http://www.orthodoxchristianity.net/forum/index.php?topic=2186.0;wap2.

94. To learn more, see: "Theotokos," *Orthodox Wiki*, last modified October 22, 2012, http://orthodoxwiki.org/Theotokos#Ever-Virginity.

95. Leslie Kean, *UFOs: Generals, Pilots and Government Officials Go On the Record* Kindle ed. (Random House, Inc., 2010) 262.

96. To learn more, see: Clair Millet, "The Legend of the Tuar-Tums," last accessed January 17, 2013, http://www.connieleemarie.com/library/papago.html.

97. "Creation Myths," *Mercer*, last accessed January 17, 2013, http://physics.mercer.edu/balduz/sci105/creationMyths/creationMythsF07.htm.

98. G.H. Pember, *Earth's Earliest Ages and Their Connection with Modern Spiritualism and Theosophy* (Crane, MO: Defender Publishing, 2012), Kindle locations 48–51.

99. Ibid., Kindle location 3528.

100. Ibid., Kindle locations 3271–3273.

101. Al Mohler, as reported by Cathy Lynn Grossman, "Many Beliefs, Many Paths to Heaven?" *USA TODAY*, December 18, 2008, http://www.usatoday.com/news/religion/2008-12-18-saved-heaven_N.htm.

102. "History of Marriage and Divorce," *eDivorce Papers*, last accessed December 7, 2012, http://www.edivorcepapers.com/marriage-and-divorce/history-of-marriage-and-divorce.html.

103. "Divorce Statistics in America," last accessed December 7, 2012, http://www.divorcestatistics.org/.

104. "Study: 'Living Together' Before Marriage a Statistical Risk," *Christian Telegraph*, last accessed December 7, 2012, http://www.christiantelegraph.com/issue1349.html.

105. Ibid.

106. A.W. Tozer, "Knowledge of the Holy," 1961 (See: http://www.heavendwellers.com/hdt_knowledge_of_the_holy.htm, last accessed December 7, 2012), 14–15.

107. David Roachon, "Pastors Say Porn Impacts Their Churches, Many Unsure to What Degree," *LifeWay*, November 10, 2011, http://www.lifeway.com/ArticleView?storeId=10054&catalogId=10001&langId=-1&article=Lifeway-Research-Pastors-say-porn-impacts-their-churches.

108. Stephen Hawking, *The Grand Design* (New York, NY: Bantam Books, 2010),14.

109. Mireya Navarro, "Openly Gay Priest Ordained in Jersey," *The New York Times*, December, 17, 1989.

110. ELCA News Service, "ELCA Assembly Opens Ministry to Partnered Gay and Lesbian Lutherans," *ELCA.org*, August 21, 2009, http://www.elca.org/Who-We-Are/Our-Three-Expressions/Churchwide-Organization/Communication-Services/News/Releases.aspx?a=4253.

111. Eric Marrapodi, "First Openly Gay Pastor Ordained in the PCUSA Speaks," *CNN.com*, October 10, 2011, http://religion.blogs.cnn.com/2011/10/10/first-openly-gay-pastor-ordained-in-the-pcusa-speaks/.

112. Steve Baldwin, "Child Molestation and the Homosexual Movement" *Regent University Law Review*, last accessed December 7, 2012, http://www.mega.nu/ampp/baldwin_pedophilia_homosexuality.pdf.

113. NAE Member Academies, "IAP Statement on Population Growth" last accessed December 7, 2012, http://www.interacademies.net/10878/13940.aspx.

114. "Crime in the United States," *FBI.gov*, last accessed December 7, 2012, http://www.fbi.gov/about-us/cjis/ucr/crime-in-the-u.s/2010/crime-in-the-u.s.-2010/tables/10tbl01.xls.

115. For a list of 2012 zombie events, see the following article: Neva Happel, "Zombie Apocalypse List of Attacks in 2012, Real or Just Covered More?" *Z6Mag*, July, 30, 2012, http://z6mag.com/featured/zombie-apocalypse-list-of-attacks-in-2012-real-or-just-covered-more-1612871.html.

116. G.H. Pember, *Earth's Earliest Ages* (Kindle locations 3433–3434).

117. Hugh Ross, Kenneth Samples, and Mark Clark, *Lights in the Sky & Little Green Men: A Rational Christian Look at UFOs and Extraterrestrials* (Colorado Springs, CO: NavPress, 2002), 29.

118. Edward J. Ruppelt, *The Report on Unidentified Flying Objects* (Cherry Hill Publishing; eBook; 2012). (Ruppelt writes,"UFO is the official term that I created to replace the words 'flying saucers.'" See: http://books.google.com/books?id=Fjdg1CtLNUQC&lpg=PP1&pg=PT6#v=onepage&q&f=false.)

119. Ibid.

120. "The Twining Memo" *The Roswell Files*, last accessed December 7, 2012, http://www.roswellfiles.com/FOIA/twining.htm.

121. Edward J. Ruppelt, *The Report on Unidentified Flying Objects*.

122. "Neil deGrasse Tyson: UFO Sightings," YouTube video, 5:27, a short excerpt from his Keynote presentation at the Amazing Meeting 6 in Las Vegas, NV, posted by AmazingMeetingVideos, last updated February 24, 2009, last accessed December 7, 2012, http://www.youtube.com/watch?v=xag3oOzvU68. (accessed 09/25/2012). Time 00:14 -00:35.

123. Jacques Vallée, *Dimensions: a Casebook of Alien Contact* (Chicago, IL: Contemporary Books, 1988), 249.

124. "Good Chance UFOs Exist in Some Form," *Industrial Research/Development 21* (July, 1979): 139–40.

125. Bernard Haisch, "An Information Site on the UFO Phenomenon By and For Professional Scientists," last accessed December 7, 2012, http://www.ufoskeptic.org/.

126. Stanton T. Friedman, "The UFO 'Why?' Questions," *StantonFriedman.com*, last accessed December 7, 2012, http://www.stantonfriedman.com/index.php?ptp=articles&fdt=2006.11.10&prt=1.

127. Richard M. Dolan, *UFOs and the National Security State: Chronology of a Cover-Up: 1941–1973* (Hampton Roads Publishing Company, Inc.), Kindle location 9325.

128. Ibid., Kindle location 9307–9327.

129. Ibid., Kindle location 691.

130. Ibid., Kindle location 304.

131. Leslie Kean, *UFOs: Generals, Pilots and Government Officials Go On the Record* (New York, NY: Random House, Inc., 2012), chapter title heading, 153.

132. For more information on this movie, see the *I Know What I Saw* website here: http://www.iknowwhatisawthemovie.com/.

133. J. Allen Hynek, "The Roots of Complacency," *The J Allen Hynek Center for UFO Studies*, last accessed December 7, 2012, http://www.cufos.org/hynek_prefix.html.

134. Natalie DiBlasio, "A Third of Earthlings Believe in UFOs, Would Befriend Aliens," *USA TODAY*, June 26, 2012, http://www.usatoday.com/news/nation/story/2012-06-26/ufo-survey/55843742/1.

135. Stanton T. Friedman, "The UFO 'Why?' Questions."

136. Hugh Ross, Kenneth Samples, and Mark Clark, *Lights in the Sky & Little Green Men*, 32.

137. Jacques Vallée, *Dimensions: A Casebook of Alien Contact* (Chicago: Contemporary Books, 1988), x.

138. John A. Keel, *Operation Trojan Horse* (Lilburn, GA: Illuminet Pr, 1996), 126–127.

139. "Alien species, 57 catalogued varieties," YouTube video, 3:56, part of *The Disclosure Project*, posted by "Tommy Tajeda," updated November 2, 2008, http://www.youtube.com/watch?v=K6uC0CKBWaM.

140. Jacques Vallée, *Dimensions*, 178.

141. Jacques Vallée, *Dimensions*, 226.

142. Alexander Wendt and Raymond Duvall, "Sovereignty and the UFO," *Political Theory*, last accessed (member access or registration required to view article) December 7, 2012, http://ptx.sagepub.com/content/36/4/610.

143. Ibid., http://ptx.sagepub.com/content/36/4/607.

144. Ibid., http://ptx.sagepub.com/content/36/4/621.

145. Ibid., http://ptx.sagepub.com/content/36/4/609.

146. "*They Live*," *Wikipedia, The Free Encyclopedia*, last modified January 7, 2013, http://en.wikipedia.org/wiki/They_Live.

147. Ibid., http://en.wikipedia.org/wiki/They_Live#Cast.

148. E. A. Speiser, Semitic language specialist at Yale University, remarks, "A pertinent noun is otherwise unattested in this language, but is well known in Akkadian as rābiṣum, a term for 'demon.'" E. A. Speiser, Genesis: Introduction, Translation, and Notes (New Haven; London: Yale University Press, 2008), 33.

149. John H Walton, *Zondervan Illustrated Bible Backgrounds Commentary (Old Testament) Volume 1: Genesis, Exodus, Leviticus, Numbers, Deuteronomy* (Grand Rapids, MI: Zondervan, 2009), 38.

150. M. L. Barre, "RĀBIṢU," *Dictionary of Deities and Demons in the Bible*, 2nd ed., editors K. van der Toorn, Bob Becking, and Pieter Willem van der Horst (Leiden; Boston; Grand Rapids, MI: Brill; Eerdmans, 1999), 682.

151. M. L. Barre, "RABIṢU," Dictionary of Deities, 682.

152. Francis A. Schaeffer, *Genesis in Space & Time: The Flow of Biblical History* (Glendale, CA: IVP Books, 1997), 125.

153. William W. Hallo and K. Lawson Younger, The Context of Scripture (Leiden; New York: Brill, 1997), 392.

154. Personal email correspondence between author, Tom Horn, and Guy Consolmagno, 2012. Also see: "Intelligent Life in the Universe: Catholic belief and the search for exraterrestrial intelligent life," Catholic Truth Society, London, 2005, 4.

155. Flavius Josephus, *Antiquities of the Jews - Book I*, chapter 3:1.

156. "The Demonstration of the Apostolic Preaching," *Book of Iranaeus*, chapter 18, *Christian Bookshelf*, last accessed January 10, 2013, http://christianbookshelf. org/irenaeus/the_demonstration_of_the_apostolic_preaching/chapter_18_and_ for_a.htm.

157. David Flynn, "Seraphim, Cherubim & Ezekiel's Wheels: Aliens, Nephilim & the Days of Noah" *Watcher Website*, last accessed January 10, 2013, http://www. mt.net/~watcher/nephelim.html.

158. James H. Charlesworth, *The Old Testament Pseudepigrapha and the New Testament, Volume 2: Expansions of the "Old Testament" and Legends, Wisdom, and Philosophical Literature, Prayers, Psalms and Odes, Fragments of Lost Judeo-Hellenistic Works*, Includes Indexes (New Haven; London: Yale University Press, 1985), 2:64.

159. Josef Karst, Eusebius Werke, 5. Band: die Chronik (Leipzig 1911).

160. J. R. Church, "Mt Hermon: Gate of the Fallen Angels," *Prophecy in the News*, February 2009.

161. "4Q Amram[b] (4Q544)," Geza Vermes, *The Dead Sea Scrolls in English*, revised and extended 4th ed. (Sheffield: Sheffield Academic Press, 1995), 312. (Previous ed.: London: Penguin, 1987.)

162. John E. Mack, *Abduction* (NY: Charles Scribner and Sons, 1994), 212.

163. Jacques Vallée, *The Invisible College: What a Group of Scientists Has Discovered About UFO Influences on the Human Race* (New York, NY: Dutton, 1975), 233.

164. "Giants in the Earth, Part I: Giants of the Ancient Near East," *Mysterious World*, Spring 2003, http://www.mysteriousworld.com/Journal/2003/Spring/Giants/.

165. Brian Vastag, "Sex with Early Mystery Species of Humans Seen in DNA, US Researcher Says," *The Washington Post*, July 26, 2012, http://seattletimes.com/html/nationworld/2018783144_humans27.html.

166. James Montgomery Boice, "Notes on the Nephilim: The Giants of Old," *Lambert Dolphin's Library*, last accessed January 10, 2013, http://www.ldolphin.org/nephilim.html.

167. T. Shinn and Richard P. Whitley, *Expository Science: Forms and Functions of Popularisation* (Springer, NY: D. Reidel, 1985), 148.

168. Neil T. Anderson, *The Bondage Breaker* (Eugene, OR: Harvest House Publishers, 2006), 33.

169. "Notes (W. B. Yeats)," *Sacred-Texts.com*, last accessed January 10, 2013, http://www.sacred-texts.com/neu/celt/vbwi/vbwi19.htm. (Material in public domain.)

170. Father Sinistrari of Ameno, *Demoniality* (Paris: Isidore Liseux, 1879), this quote is from the book's extended title.

171. Sinistrari, *Demoniality*, 165. Viewable here: *Internet Archive*, last accessed January 10, 2013, http://archive.org/details/demonialityorinc00sinirich.

172. Geoffrey W. Bromiley, *The International Standard Bible Encyclopedia, Revised* (Wm. B. Eerdmans, 1988; 2002), 4:440.

173. "(KTU 1.161:2–1.161:10)," as quoted in William W. Hallo and K. Lawson Younger, *The Context of Scripture* (Leiden; New York: Brill, 1997), 356.

174. *The Septuagint*, Translation by Sir Lancelot C. L. Brenton, 1851.

175. *Pseudepigrapha of the Old Testament*, ed. Robert Henry Charles (Bellingham, WA: Logos Research Systems, Inc., 2004), 2:198.

176. George W. E. Nickelsburg and Klaus Baltzer, *1 Enoch : A Commentary on the Book of 1 Enoch, Includes the Text of the Ethiopic Book of Enoch in English Translation* (Minneapolis, MN: Fortress, 2001), 274.

177. James H. Charlesworth, *The Old Testament Pseudepigrapha and the New Testament, Volume 2*, 2:76.

178. John MacArthur, *Revelation 1–11* (Chicago: Moody Press, 1999), 259.

179. Arnold G. Fruchtenbaum, *The Footsteps of the Messiah : A Study of the Sequence of Prophetic Events*, Rev. ed. (Tustin, CA: Ariel Ministries, 2003), 226.

180. "*Conspiracy Theory with Jesse Ventura*," *Wikipedia, The Free Encyclopedia*, last modified January 11, 2013, http://en.wikipedia.org/wiki/Conspiracy_Theory_with_Jesse_Ventura.

181. Jesse Ventura, "Conspiracy Theory—Season 3, Episode 4: 'Manimal,'" *JesseVentura.net*, at the time of this writing, article is on front of official website, last accessed January 11, 2013: http://www.jesseventura.net.

182. Kate Kelland, "Scientists Want Debate on Animals with Human Genes," *Reuters*, November 9, 2009, http://www.reuters.com/article/2009/11/10/us-science-animal-human-idUSTRE5A900R20091110.

183. "Animals Containing Human Material," *The Academy of Medical Sciences*, last accessed January 11, 2013, http://www.acmedsci.ac.uk/p47prid77.html.

184. Ibid., in full report.

185. Ibid., in full report.

186. Daniel Martin and Simon Caldwell, "150 Human Animal Hybrids Grown in UK Labs: Embryos Have Been Produced Secretively for the Past Three Years," *UK Mail Online*, July 22, 2011, http://www.dailymail.co.uk/sciencetech/article-2017818/Embryos-involving-genes-animals-mixed-humans-produced-secretively-past-years.html.

187. Kate Kelland, "Scientists Want Debate on Animals with Human Genes," *Reuters*, November 9, 2009, http://www.reuters.com/article/2009/11/10/us-science-animal-human-idUSTRE5A900R20091110.

188. Ibid.

189. "What is the Chuman?" *Opentopia*, last accessed January 11, 2013, http://encycl.opentopia.com/term/Chuman.

190. Mary Loftus, "Jewish Law Supports Emerging Reproductive Technology, Broyde Says," *Emory*, October 7, 2011, http://www.law.emory.edu/faculty/faculty-news-article/article/jewish-law-supports-emerging-reproductive-technology-broyde-says.html.

191. Michael Hanlon, "World's First GM Babies Born," *UK Mail Online*, last accessed January 11, 2013, http://www.dailymail.co.uk/news/article-43767/Worlds-GM-babies-born.html#ixzz2Cg03IwTl.

192. Dr. Joseph Mercola, "Dozens of Genetically Modified Babies Already Born—How Will They Alter Human Species?" *Mercola Health*, July 17, 2012, http://articles.mercola.com/sites/articles/archive/2012/07/17/first-genetically-modified-babies-born.aspx#_edn1.

193. Ethan A. Huff, "GMO Babies Now Being Engineered in Labs Under Guise of Preventing Incurable Disease," *Natural News*, November 16, 2012, http://www.naturalnews.com/037993_GMO_babies_incurable_disease.html.

194. Alex Newman, "Genetically Engineered Babies are Moral Duty, 'Ethics' Guru Claims," *The New American*, August 22, 2012, http://www.thenewamerican.com/culture/faith-and-morals/item/12564-genetically-engineered-babies-are-moral-duty-%E2%80%9Cethics%E2%80%9D-guru-claims.

195. "Richard Seed," *Wikipedia, The Free Encyclopedia*, last modified March 26, 2009, http://en.wikiquote.org/wiki/Richard_Seed.

196. Gregory Stock, *Redesigning Humans: Choosing Our Genes, Changing Our Future* (Boston, MA: Houghton Mifflin Harcourt, 2003), 13.

197. Joe Garreau, *Radical Evolution: The Promise and Peril of Enhancing Our Minds,*

Our Bodies—and What it Means to Be Human (New York: Broadway, 2005) 116.

198. "Ilya Ivanovich Ivanov," *Wikipedia, The Free Encyclopedia,* last modified December 12, 2012, http://en.wikipedia.org/wiki/Ilya_Ivanovich_Ivanov#Human-ape_hybridization_experiments.

199. Jerome C. Glenn, "The State of the Future," *Kurzweil Accelerating Intelligence,* July 14, 2012, http://www.kurzweilai.net/the-state-of-the-future.

200. John Naish, "Genetically Modified Athletes: Forget Drugs. There Are Even Suggestions Some Chinese Athletes' Genes Are Altered to Make Them Stronger," *UK Mail Online,* July 31, 2012, http://www.dailymail.co.uk/news/article-2181873/Genetically-modified-athletes-Forget-drugs-There-suggestions-Chinese-athletes-genes-altered-make-stronger.html.

201. Ibid.

202. "Human enhancement and the future of work," science report by the Academy of Medical Sciences, British Academy, the Royal Academy of Engineering and the Royal Society (October, 2012), 26.

203. "Animals Containing Human Material," *The Academy of Medical Sciences,* last accessed January 11, 2013, http://www.acmedsci.ac.uk/p47prid77.html.

204. Case Western Reserve University, "Case Law School Receives $773,000 NIH Grant to Develop Guidelines for Genetic Enhancement Research: Professor Max Mehlman to Lead Team of Law Professors, Physicians, and Bioethicists in Two-Year Project" (press release, April 28, 2006).

205. George W. Bush, in his January 31, 2006, State of the Union address.

206. Joseph Infranco, "President Barack Obama Warped and Twisted Science with Embryonic Stem Cell Order," *LifeNews* April 13, 2009, http://www.lifenews.com/bio2823.html.

207. Leon R. Kass, *Life, Liberty, and the Defense of Dignity: The Challenge for Bioethics* (New York, NY: Encounter, 2002), introduction.

208. Jacques Vallée, *Confrontations—A Scientist's Search for Alien Contact* (New York, NY: Ballantine Books, 1990), 159.

209. Jacques Vallée, *Dimensions: A Casebook of Alien Contact* (New York, NY: Ballantine Books, 1988), 143–144.

210. John A. Keel, *UFOs: Operation Trojan Horse* (Atlanta, GA: Illuminet Press, 1996), 192.

211. Elizabeth L. Hillstrom, *Testing the Spirits* (Downers Grove, IL: InterVarsity Press, 1995), 207–207.

212. John A. Keel, *UFOs: Operation Trojan Horse,* 299.

213. John E. Mack, *Passport to the Cosmos: Human Transformation and Alien Encounters* (New York: Crown, 1999), 209.

214. John E. Mack, *Passport to the Cosmos,* 209.

215. Jacques Vallée, *Confrontations,* Reprint ed. (New York, NY: Ballantine Books, 1991), 13.

216. Ibid., 86.

217. "St. Cecilia," *Catholic Culture,* last accessed January 14, 2013, http://www.catholicculture.org/culture/liturgicalyear/calendar/day.cfm?date=2012-11-22.

218. Ludovico Maria Sinistrari, *Demoniality: Or Incubi and Succubi* (Isidore Liseux, 1879), 235–241.

219. Philip Schaff, *The Nicene and Post-Nicene Fathers Vol. II – St. Augustin's City of God and Christian Doctrine* (Oak Harbor: Logos Research Systems, 1997), 303.

220. Ludovico Maria Sinistrari, (Whitefish, MT: Kessinger, 2003), 27.

221. "Notes (W. B. Yeats)," *Sacred-Texts.com*, last accessed January 14, 2013, http://www.sacred-texts.com/neu/celt/vbwi/vbwi19.htm.

222. "Paracelsus," *Wikipedia, The Free Encyclopedia*, last modified December 20, 2012, http://en.wikipedia.org/wiki/Paracelsus.

223. Jacques Vallée, *Dimensions*, 15.

224. Abbé N. de Montfaucon de Villars, *Comte de Gabalis, ou entretiens sur les sciences secrete* (London: The Brothers/Old Bourne Press, 1913), 29.

225. Robert Pearson Flaherty, "These Are They," *ET-Human Hybridization and the New Daemonology, Nova Religio: The Journal of Alternative & Emergenct Religion* (Nov 2012, Vol. 14 Issue 2), 86.

226. Ibid., 87.

227. Ibid.

228. Thomas G. Aylesworth, *Science Looks at Mysterious Monsters* (New York, NY: Julian Messner, 1982), 30.

229. Noah Hutchings, *Marginal Mysteries* (Crane, MO: Defender Publishing, 2011), 141.

230. Thomas G. Aylesworth, *Science Looks at Mysterious Monsters*, 32–33.

231. Joseph Jacobs, "The Truth Behind The Exorcist," *TAT Journal* 12 (1981), last accessed January 14, 2013, http://www.searchwithin.org/journal/tat_journal-12.html#1.

232. Viewable here: "Demons: The Answer Book," *Anchor Distributors*, last accessed January 14, 2013, http://www.anchordistributors.com/ProductInfo1.aspx?item=13214.

233. Ibid.

234. Will Stewart, "Sasquatch in Siberia? Hair Found in Russian Cave 'Belonged to Unknown Mammal Closely Related to Man,'" *UK Mail Online*, October 30, 2012, http://www.dailymail.co.uk/news/article-2225276/Yeti-latest-Russian-scientists-say-DNA-tests-hair-samples-existence-man-like-mammal.html.

235. "'Bigfoot' DNA Sequenced in Upcoming Genetics Study," *PRWeb*, last accessed January 14, 2013, http://www.prweb.com/releases/2012/11/prweb10166775.htm.

236. Ibid.

237. Linda S. Godfrey, *Real Wolfmen: True Encounters in Modern America* (New York, NY: Tarcher/Penguin, 2012). See quote and learn more about the book here: "Summary of *Real Wolfmen*," *Penguin*, last accessed January 14, 2013, http://www.us.penguingroup.com/nf/Book/BookDisplay/0,,9781585429080,00.html?Real_Wolfmen_Linda_S._Godfrey.

238. "The Book of Were-Wolves," *Sacred-Texts.com*, last accessed January 14, 2013, http://www.sacred-texts.com/goth/bow/bow09.htm.

239. "Werewolf," *Wikipedia, The Free Encyclopedia*, last modified January 12, 2013, http://en.wikipedia.org/wiki/Werewolf.

240. Frank Joseph, *The Lost Worlds of Ancient America* (Pompton Plains, NJ: New Page Books, 2012), 252.

241. "Skinwalker Ranch," *Wikipedia, The Free Encyclopedia*, last modified January 4, 2013, http://en.wikipedia.org/wiki/Skinwalker_Ranch.

242. George Knapp, "Is a Utah Ranch the Strangest Place on Earth? (Part 2)," *Las Vegas Mercury*, November, 29, 2002.

243. Natalie Patton, "UNLV Unplugs Program on Human Consciousness: Donor Behind its '97 Birth Decides to Fund Scholarships Instead," *Review Journal*, November 8, 2002, http://www.reviewjournal.com/lvrj_home/2002/Nov-08-Fri-2002/news/20024414.html.

244. Ibid.

245. George Knapp, "Is a Utah Ranch the Strangest Place on Earth?"

246. Ibid.

247. Ibid.

248. "Fairy stroke," *Oxford Dictionary of Celtic Mythology*, as quoted in: "Fairy stroke," *Answers.com*, last accessed February 8, 2013, http://www.answers.com/topic/fairy-stroke-1.

249. "The Fairy-Faith in Celtic Countries," *Sacred-Texts.com*, last accessed February 8, 2013 http://www.sacred-texts.com/neu/celt/ffcc/index.htm.

250. Dr. Jacques Vallée, *Passport to Magonia: From Folklore to Flying Saucers* (Chicago, IL: Henry Regnery Company, 1969), 100–101.

251. "17th Century Disclosure Martyr—Rev Kirk," You Tube video, 2:11, posted by Andrew Hennessey, last updated July 14, 2012, last accessed February 8, 2013, http://www.youtube.com/watch?v=F8SGgXtiNMs.

252. Dr. Jacques Vallée, *Passport to Magonia*, 102.

253. Ibid., 104.

254. Ibid., 105.

255. *JARMAG*, last accessed February 8, 2013, http://www.jarmag.com/2007/vol001_hopkins.htm.

256. "Watchers, Aliens, UFOs, Angels, Demons: Tom Horn on PITN (pt 5)," YouTube video, 9:57, posted by Thomas Horn, last updated February 21, 2008, last accessed February 9, 2013, http://www.youtube.com/watch?v=pE7qT3IK8lc.

257. Thomas Horn, *Nephilim Stargates: The Year 2012 and the Return of the Watchers* (Crane, MO: Anomalos Publishing House, 2007), 94; first set of brackets in original; second set of brackets added by authors.

258. Nick Redfern (works full-time as an author and lecturer; is well-known in UFO circles as a hardworking investigative journalist) in discussion over personal email communication with the author, Thomas R. Horn, January–February 2013.

259. Talk notes of Gregory Richford (Ball Aerospace contact who works with advanced systems and technologies for Space Control and Special Missions),

in documents provided over personal email communication with the author, Thomas R. Horn, during 2012.

260. Dr. Jacques Vallée, *The Invisible College: What a Group of Scientists Has Discovered about UFO Influences on the Human Race* (New York, NY: Dutton; 1st edition, 1975), 233.

261. Philip J. Corso, *Dawn of a New Age, Part II*, 28, as retrieved November 23, 2012 from: "Full Text of 'Philip J. Corso—Dawn of a New Age,'" *Internet Archive*, last accessed February 8, 2013, http://archive.org/stream/PhilipJ.Corso-DawnOfANewAge/PhilipJ.Corso-DawnOfANewAge_djvu.txt.

262. Dr. Jacques Vallée, *Revelations: Alien Contact and Human Deception* (San Antonio, TX: Anomalist Books, 2008), 236.

263. David M. Jacobs, *The Threat: Revealing the Secret Alien Agenda*, 1st Fireside ed. (NY: Simon & Schuster, 1999), 121.

264. David M. Jacobs, *Secret Life: Firsthand, Documented Accounts of UFO Abductions*, (New York, NY: Touchstone, 1999), 309.

265. John E. Mack, *Abduction: Human Encounters with Aliens* (New York, NY: Ballantine Books, 1995) 404–405.

266. Gary Stearman, "The Ghastly Truth About the Days of Noah," *Prophecy in the News Magazine*, November 1999, 15.

267. David Flynn, "Seraphim, Cherubim & Ezekiel's Wheels: Aliens, Nephilim & the Days of Noah," *Watcher Website*, last accessed February 8, 2013, http://www.mt.net/~watcher/noah.html.

268. Vladimir Moss, "Genetics, UFOs, and the Birth of the Antichrist," last accessed February 8, 2013, http://www.orthodoxchristianbooks.com/articles/205/genetics,-ufos-birth-antichrist/.

269. Ibid.

270. "G. H. Pember: A Short Biography," *Raiders News Network*, last accessed February 8, 2013, http://www.raidersnewsupdate.com/pember.pdf.

271. Quote by Arthur Charles Clarke, *Quote World*, last accessed January 18, 2013, http://www.quoteworld.org/quotes/2909.

272. T. S. Eliot, from the poem "Little Gidding," viewable here: *Allspirit*, last accessed January 18, 2013, http://allspirit.co.uk/gidding.html.

273. Jonathan L. Lunine and José G. Funes, "Vita e Cosmo a Rapport" *'Osservatore Romano*, November 7, 2009, http://www.vatican.va/news_services/or/or_quo/cultura/2009/258q04a1.html (translation Putnam).

274. Program for "The Pontifical Academy of Sciences Study Week on Astrobiology November 9–11, 2009," 4.

275. Ibid., 11.

276. "Chris Impey," as quoted on "Western Educators," *Science for Monks*, last accessed January 20, 2013, http://scienceformonks.org/About/WesternEducators.

277. "Pontifical Academy Studies Possibility of Extraterrestrial Life," *Catholic World News*, November 11,2009, http://www.catholicculture.org/news/headlines/index.cfm?storyid=4568.

278. George Gaylord Simpson, "The Nonprevalence of Humanoids," *Science* 143 (1964): 769–775.

279. "About Astrobiology," *NASA Astrobiology*, August 15, 2012, https://astrobiology.nasa.gov/about-astrobiology/.

280. Jeffrey Bennett and Seth Shostak, *Life in the Universe*, 3rd ed. (San Francisco: Addison-Wesley, 2012), Glossary G1.

281. Carl Sagan, *Pale Blue Dot: A Vision of the Human Future in Space*, Reprint ed. (New York, NY: Ballantine Books, 1997), 5–7.

282. "100 Billion Alien Planets Fill Our Milky Way Galaxy: Study," *Space.com*, January 2, 2013, http://www.space.com/19103-milky-way-100-billion-planets.html.

283. "17 Billion Earth-Size Alien Planets Inhabit Milky Way," *Space.com*, January 7, 2013, http://www.space.com/19157-billions-earth-size-alien-planets-aas221.html.

284. Guy J. Consolmagno, S.J. (astronomer and coordinator of public relations for the Vatican Observatory Research Group; received a PhD in Planetary Science from the University of Arizona in 1978; later studied philosophy and theology at Loyola University, Chicago; and took vows as a Jesuit brother in 1991), in discussion over personal email communication with the authors, Tom Horn and Cris Putnam, dated November 5, 2012.

285. "The Habitable Exoplanets Catalog" *The Planetary Habitability Laboratory*, January 11, 2013 http://phl.upr.edu/projects/habitable-exoplanets-catalog.

286. Ibid.

287. José Funes in an interview with Francis M. Valiante, "The Extraterrestrial is My Brother," viewable here: http://www.vatican.va/news_services/or/or_quo/interviste/2008/112q08a1.html, (translation Putnam) last accessed January 6, 2013.

288. "Kepler: A Search for Habitable Planets," *NASA*, last accessed January 20, 2013, http://www.nasa.gov/mission_pages/kepler/main/index.html.

289. Sara Seager, "Exoplanets and the Search for Habitable Worlds," lecture 3 in "Are We Alone? The Scientific Search for Extraterrestrial Life— Linda Hall Library 2010 Lectures," https://itunes.apple.com/ne/podcast/are-we-alone-the-scientific/id385112506.

290. "'Habitable' Planet Discovered Circling Tau Ceti Star," *The Guardian*, December 19, 2012, http://www.guardian.co.uk/science/2012/dec/19/habitable-planet-discovered-tau-ceti.

291. Peter D. Ward and Donald Brownlee, *Rare Earth: Why Complex Life Is Uncommon in the Universe* (New York, NY: Springer, 2003), xxix.

292. Ibid., 222.

293. Ibid., 220.

294. Casey Luskin, "Darwin's Dilemma: Evolutionary Elite Choose Censorship over Scientific Debate," *CNSNews.com*, October 14, 2009, http://www.discovery.org/a/12871.

295. Guillermo Gonzalez and Jay W. Richards, *The Privileged Planet: How Our Place*

in the Cosmos Is Designed for Discovery (Lanham, MD: Regnery Publishing, Inc., 2004), 334.

296. Transcribed from the documentary film: *The Privileged Planet*, written by W. Peter Allen, Wayne P. Allen, and Jonathan Witt, directed by Ladd Allen, Wayne P. Allen, *Illustra Media*, 2004, quote at 11:16–11:32; viewable here: http://www.imdb.com/title/tt0495399/.

297. Hugh Ross, Kenneth Samples, and Mark Clark, *Lights in the Sky & Little Green Men: A Rational Christian Look at UFOs and Extraterrestrials* (Colorado Springs, CO: NavPress, 2002), 39.

298. Hugh Ross, "Planet Habitability Requires a Lifetime of Fine-Tuning," *Reasons to Believe*, November 1, 2012, http://www.reasons.org/articles/planet-habitability-requires-a-lifetime-of-fine-tuning.

299. Hugh Ross "Part 1. Fine-Tuning for Life in the Universe" *Reasons to Believe*, last accessed January 19, 2013, http://www.reasons.org/files/compendium/compendium_part1.pdf.

300. Ibid.

301. Hugh Ross, *The Creator and the Cosmos: How the Greatest Scientific Discoveries of the Century Reveal God* (Colorado Springs, CO: NavPress, 2001), 147.

302. Antony Flew and Roy Abraham Varghese, *There Is a God: How the World's Most Notorious Atheist Changed His Mind* (New York, NY: HarperOne, 2008), 114. Flew's second piece of evidence is built around the anthropic principle. Given how our universe seems finely tuned to support life, Flew considers two possible reasons. One reason postulates divine design; the other assumes a multiverse. Flew argues that the multiverse theory is vacuous, because by suggesting infinite universes, it explains everything and nothing (118).

303. Hugo de Garis "From Cosmism to Deism," *Kurzweil Accelerating Intelligence*, Jaunary 18, 2011, http://www.kurzweilai.net/from-cosmism-to-deism.

304. Ibid.

305. David Allen Lewis and Robert Shreckhise, *UFO: End-Time Delusion* (Green Forest, AR: New Leaf Press, 1991), 120.

306. Hugh Ross, *Creation as Science: A Testable Model Approach to End the Creation/Evolution Wars* (Colorado Springs, CO: NavPress, 2006), 192.

307. Fazale Rana and Hugh Ross, *Origins of Life: Biblical and Evolutionary Models Face Off* (Colorado Springs, CO: NavPress, 2004), 133.

308. Richard Dawkins, *The Blind Watchmaker: Why the Evidence of Evolution Reveals a Universe Without Design* (New York, NY: W. W. Norton & Company, 1996), 5.

309. David Derbyshire, "I'd Love to Baptise ET, Says Vatican's Stargazer," *UK Mail Online*, September 17, 2010, http://www.dailymail.co.uk/sciencetech/article-1312922/Pope-astronomer-Guy-Consolmagno-Aliens-souls-living-stars.html#ixzz2GyHmVqio.

310. Francis Crick, *Life Itself* (New York, NY: Simon and Schuster, 1981), 88.

311. Roger White, "Does Origins of Life Research Rest on a Mistake?" *Noûs* 41, no. 3 (2007), 453–577.

312. Lauren Aguirre, "The Drake Equation,"*PBS*, July 1, 2008, http://www.pbs.org/wgbh/nova/space/drake-equation.html.

313. Fraser Cain, "Galaxy Has 1,000 Times Our Rate of Star Formation," *Universe Today* December 19, 2007, http://www.universetoday.com/2007/12/19/galaxy-has-1000-times-our-rate-of-star-formation/.

314. Stuart Burgess, *He Made the Stars Also : What the Bible Says About the Stars* (Epsom: Day One Publications, 2001), 134.

315. Michael Shermer, "Why ET Hasn't Called," *Scientific American* (August 2002).

316. Michael Crichton, "Aliens Cause Global Warming" Caltech Michelin Lecture, January 17, 2003, available online at http://online.wsj.com/article/SB122603134258207975.html (accessed 01/04/2013).

317. Hugh Ross,"Summary of Reasons To Believe's Testable Creation Model," *Reasons.org*, last accessed January 5, 2013, http://www.reasons.org/articles/summary-of-reasons-to-believe-s-testable-creation-model.

318. Eric Jones, "Where is Everybody?" An Account of Fermi's Question," *Los Alamos* Technical report LA-10311-MS, March, 1985, http://www.fas.org/sgp/othergov/doe/lanl/la-10311-ms.pdf.

319. Hugh Ross, Kenneth Samples, and Mark Clark, *Lights in the Sky & Little Green Men*, 56.

320. Helmholtz, *Populare Wissenschaftliche Vortrage*. vol. iii., (Braunschweig, 1876), 101; as quoted in Svante Arrhenius, *Worlds in the Making: the Evolution of the Universe* (New York, NY: Harper Brothers, 1908), xiv.

321. Svante Arrhenius, *Worlds in the Making: the Evolution of the Universe* (New York, NY: Harper Brothers, 1908), 229.

322. Margaret Wertheim "Looking for GOD and ALIENS," *Science & Spirit* magazine (2002), last accessed January 19, 2013, http://vaticanobservatory.org/News/GOD_ALIENS.html.

323. Gerda Horneck, "Surviving the Final Frontier" *Astrobiology* magazine, November 25, 2002, http://www.astrobio.net/exclusive/318/surviving-the-final-frontier.

324. "No one at the Vatican Observatory is currently directly involved in astrobiology research; there are some of us who have worked in the field of exoplanets." Email correspondence between Guy Consolmagno and Tom Horn/Cris Putnam dated November 5, 2012.

325. Henry Bortman, "Interview with Brother Guy Consolmagno" *Astrobiology* magazine, May 12, 2004, http://www.astrobio.net/interview/966/interview-with-brother-guy-consolmagno.

326. F. H. Crick and L. E. Orgel, "Directed Panspermia," *Icarus* 19 (1973), 341–348.

327. F. H. Crick and L. E. Orgel, "Directed Panspermia," 343.

328. Dialog from *Expelled: No Intelligence Allowed*, written by Ben Stein and Kevin Miller, directed by Nathan Frankowski, performed by Richard Dawkins and Ben Stein, *Premise Media*, 2008.

329. Dr. Michael Heiser, "Panspermia," in *How to Overcome the Most Frightening*

Issues You Will Face This Century (Crane: Defender, 2009), Kindle location 3750.

330. Dr. Michael Heiser, "Panspermia," in *How to Overcome*, Kindle locations 4078–4080.

331. Dr. Michael Heiser, "Panspermia," in *How to Overcome,* Kindle locations 4114–4115.

332. An interesting video is available here: "The Centrality of Earth in the Universe—Cosmic Microwave Background Radiation," MetaCafe video, posted by TheWordisalive, 7:21, last updated on March 1, 2010, http://www.metacafe.com/watch/4240304/the_centrality_of_earth_in_the_universe_cosmic_microwave_background_radiation/.

333. "The Energy of Empty Space That Isn't Zero: A Talk with Lawrence Krauss," *Edge*, July 6, 2006, http://www.edge.org/3rd_culture/krauss06/krauss06.2_index.html.

334. "About Astrobiology," *NASA Astrobiology*, August 15, 2012, https://astrobiology.nasa.gov/about-astrobiology/.

335. Stephen J. Dick, *Life on Other Worlds* (Cambridge University Press, 1998), 238.

336. Carl Sagan, "Cosmos," *IMDB*, last accessed January 19, 2013, http://www.imdb.com/title/tt0081846/quotes.

337. Paola Leopizzi Harris, "Monsignor Corrado Balducci says Mexico is Blessed with UFO Sightings," www.paolaharris.it March 28, 2006, http://www.delusionresistance.org/ufo/catholicism-ufos.html.

338. Timothy J. Dailey, *The Millennial Deception: Angels, Aliens, and the Antichrist* (Grand Rapids, MI: Chosen Books Pub Co, 1995), 11.

339. Benedict XVI, *"Caritas In Veritate" Vatican*, last accessed January 14, 2013, http://www.vatican.va/holy_father/benedict_xvi/encyclicals/documents/hf_ben-xvi_enc_20090629_caritas-in-veritate_en.html.

340. The World Economic Forum, last accessed January 19, 2013, http://www.weforum.org/.

341. World Economic Forum Global Risks 2013, *World Economic Forum*, last accessed January 17, 2013, http://reports.weforum.org/global-risks-2013/section-one/executive-summary/, 12.

342. Ibid., 59.

343. Charles Caldwell Ryrie, *Dispensationalism*, revised ed. (Chicago, IL: Moody Publishers, 1995), 20.

344. John Sailhamer, *Genesis Unbound* (Sisters, OR: Multnomah Books, 1996), 38.

345. For a discussion of the debate, see: R. Laird Harris, Robert Laird Harris, Gleason Leonard Archer, and Bruce K. Waltke, *Theological Wordbook of the Old Testament* (Chicago, IL: Moody Press, 1999, c1980), 826.

346. Johannes P. Louw and Eugene Albert Nida, *Greek-English Lexicon of the New Testament: Based on Semantic Domains*, electronic ed. of the 2nd ed. (New York, NY: United Bible Societies, 1996), 1.4 κτίσις.

347. Ibid.

348. C.S. Lewis, "Religion and Rocketry," as quoted in *The World's Last Night: And Other Essays* (Orlando, FL: Houghton Mifflin Harcourt, 2002), 92.

349. "20th Century Democide," last accessed January 18, 2013, http://www.hawaii.
edu/powerkills/20TH.HTM.

350. Ted Peters, "Exo-Theology" essay (article or chapter in a collection) in James
R. Lewis, ed., *The Gods Have Landed: New Religions from Other Worlds* (Albany,
NY: State University of New York Press, 1995), 199–200.

351. Donald N. Michael, Jack Baranson, et al. (December 1960), "Footnotes for
Proposed Studies on the Implications of Peaceful Space Activities for Human
Affairs" (PDF), Washington, DC: Brookings Institution. NASA Document ID:
19640053194; NASA Report/Patent Number: NASA-CR-55640, http://ntrs.
nasa.gov/archive/nasa/casi.ntrs.nasa.gov/19640053194_1964053194.pdf. page
102, n.34.

352. John B. Alexander, *UFOs: Myths, Conspiracies, and Realities* (New York, NY:
Thomas Dunne Books, 2011), 242.

353. Jeff Levin, "Revisiting the Alexander UFO Religious Crisis Survey
(AUFORCS): Is There Really a Crisis?" *Journal of Scientific Exploration*, vol. 26,
no. 2 (2012), 278.

354. Ted Peters, "The Peters ETI Religious Crisis Survey," last accessed January 19,
2013, http://www.counterbalance.org/etsurv/index-frame.html.

355. Donald N. Michael, Jack Baranson, et al.,"Footnotes for Proposed
Studies," http://ntrs.nasa.gov/archive/nasa/casi.ntrs.nasa.
gov/19640053194_1964053194.pdf, page 103, n. 34.

356. "Hawking: Aliens May Pose Risks to Earth," *NBC News*, last accessed January
19, 2013, http://www.msnbc.msn.com/id/36769422/ns/technology_and_
science-space/t/hawking-aliens-may-pose-risks-earth/#.UPRyvGdyGSo.

357. Jim Marrs, Richard M. Dolan, and Bryce Zabel, *A. D. After Disclosure: When
the Government Finally Reveals the Truth About Alien Contact* (Pompton Plains,
NJ: Career Press, 2012), Kindle locations 3631–3636.

358. Ibid., Kindle locations 3634–3637.

359. David Fetcho, "A Sum of Shipwrecked Stars UFOs and the Logic of
Discernment," *Spiritual Counterfeits Project Journal*, vol. 1, no. 2 (August 1977),
30.

360. C. Fred Dickason, *Angels: Elect & Evil* (Chicago, IL: Moody Press, 1995), 128.

361. Clinton E. Arnold, *Powers of Darkness: Principalities & Powers in Paul's Letters*
(Downers Grove, IL: IVP Academic, 1992), 125.

362. William Hendriksen and Simon J. Kistemaker, *New Testament Commentary :
Exposition of Ephesians*, vol. 7 (Grand Rapids, MI: Baker Book House, 1953–
2001), 113.

363. Gary Stearman, "What Does the Bible Say About UFOs?" *Prophecy in the News*,
vol. 38, no. 11 (August 2011), 15.

364. Ted Peters, *Ufos—God's Chariots? Flying Saucers in Politics, Science, and Religion*
(Atlanta, GA: John Knox Press, 1977), 9.

365. Jacques Vallée, *Dimensions: A Casebook of Alien Contact* (New York:
Contemporary Books, 1988), xiii.

366. Jacques Vallée, *Messengers of Deception: UFO Contacts and Cults* (Daily Grail
Publishing, 2008), vi.

367. "John A Keel UFO Researcher Has Died at Age 79" *National UFO Center,* July 8, 2009, http://www.nationalufocenter.com/artman/publish/article_287.php.

368. John A. Keel, *Operation Trojan Horse* (Lilburn, GA: Illuminet Press, 1996), 193.

369. Daniel R. Jennings "Similarities Between UFO Encounters And Demonic Encounters," last accessed January 18, 2013, http://www.danielrjennings.org/SimilaritiesBetweenUFOActivityAndDemonicActivity.html.

370. Guy Malone, *Come Sail Away,* last accessed January 18, 2013, http://www.alienstranger.com/seekye1/CSA-UFO-Bible.htm.

371. David Ruffino and Joseph Jordan, *Unholy Communion* (Crane, MO: Official Disclosure, 2010), Kindle locations 720–724.

372. To learn more, see: "Testimonies," *CE4 Research Group,* last accessed January 18, 2013, http://www.alienresistance.org/ce4testimonies.htm.

373. Richard Boylan, "Vatican Official Declares Extraterrestrial Contact Is Real" *UFO Digest,* last accessed January 18, 2013, http://www.ufodigest.com/balducci.html.

374. Michael Heiser, "UFOs, ETs, and Religion, Part 2 (Balducci's Conundrum Continued)" *UFO Religions,* last accessed January 19, 2013, http://michaelsheiser.com/UFOReligions/2008/05/ufos-ets-and-religion-part-2-balduccis-conundrum-continued/#fn-12-5.

375. Corrado Balducci, "Ufology and Theological Clarifications,"*Pescara,* (June 8th, 2001), viewable here: http://www.spiritofmaat.com/archive/mar3/balducci.htm.

376. "4Q Amram[b] (4Q544)," in Geza Vermes, *The Dead Sea Scrolls in English,* 312.

377. Philip Elmer-De Witt, "No Sympathy for the Devil," *Time,* March 19, 1990, 55–56.

378. Chuck Missler and Mark Eastman, *Alien Encounters* (Coeur d'Alene, ID: Koinonia House Inc, 1997), 108.

379. Linda Lyons, "Paranormal Beliefs Come (Super)Naturally to Some" *Gallup,* November 1, 2005, http://www.gallup.com/poll/19558/Paranormal-Beliefs-Come-SuperNaturally-Some.aspx.

380. "UFO Evidence," last accessed January 18, 2013, http://www.ufoevidence.org/topics/publicopinionpolls.htm.

381. "Recent Polls—Belief in Aliens & UFOs," last accessed January 18, 2013, http://www.alienresistance.org/ufo-alien-deception/recent-polls-trends-belief-aliens-ufos/.

382. Richard M. Dolan, January 6, 2002, *UFOs and the National Security State: Chronology of a Cover-Up*: 1941–1973, 17.

383. Merrill F. Unger, *Biblical Demonology: A Study of Spiritual Forces at Work Today* (Wheaton, IL: Scripture Press Publications, 1952), 201.

384. Robert James Utley, *Paul Bound, the Gospel Unbound: Letters from Prison (Colossians, Ephesians and Philemon, Then Later, Philippians),*vol. 8, Study Guide Commentary Series (Marshall, TX: Bible Lessons International, 1997), 85.

385. David Allen Lewis and Robert Shreckhise, *UFO: End-Time Delusion* (Green Forest, AR: New Leaf Press, 1991), 216.

386. In this film, select people are saved from a global cataclysm by alien space ships; see: http://www.knowing-themovie.com/.

387. Giuseppe Tanzella-Nitti, "Extraterrestrial Life" *Interdisciplinary Encyclopedia of Religion and Science*, last accessed August 21, 2012, http://www.disf.org/en/Voci/65.asp.

388. Catechism of the Catholic Church, 846, viewable here: last accessed January 18, 2013, http://www.scborromeo.org/ccc/p123a9p3.htm.

389. Karl Rahner, "Christianity and Non-Christian Religions" in *Theological Investigations* (Baltimore: Helicn, 1969). 5:115-34 and "Anonymous Christian" in Theological Investigations, 6:390-98.

390. Thomas F. O'Meara, "The Salvation of Extraterrestrials" *Huffington Post*, July 21, 2012,http://www.huffingtonpost.com/thomas-f-omeara-op/salvation-of-extraterrestrials_b_1671783.html.

391. Giuseppe Tanzella-Nitti, "Extraterrestrial Life," http://www.disf.org/en/Voci/65.asp.

392. Guy Consolmagno, *Brother Astronomer: Adventures of a Vatican Scientist* (New York, NY: McGraw-Hill, 2000), 152.

393. Dr. Michael Heiser, "Panspermia," in *How to Overcome*, Kindle locations 4078–4080.

394. Kenneth J. Delano, *Many Worlds, One God* (Hicksville, NY: Exposition Press, 1977), 105.

395. Ibid., 106.

396. Bruce Johnston , "Vatican Sets Evangelical Sights on Outer Space," *Daily Telegraph* (London, England, Oct. 28, 1992), 15.

397. Jack Hitt, "Would You Baptize an Extraterrestrial?" *New York Times* magazine, last accessed January 19, 2013, http://www.nytimes.com/1994/05/29/magazine/would-you-baptize-an-extraterrestrial.html?pagewanted=all&src=pm.

398. Richard Alleyne, "Pope Benedict XVI's Astronomer: The Catholic Church Welcomes Aliens," *The Telegraph*, last accessed January 19, 2013, http://www.telegraph.co.uk/news/religion/the-pope/8009299/Pope-Benedict-XVIs-astronomer-the-Catholic-Church-welcomes-aliens.html.

399. Millard J. Erickson, *Christian Theology.*, 2nd ed. (Grand Rapids, MI: Baker Book House, 1998), 1100.

400. "It (The Roman Church) teaches…that the souls…of those who die in mortal sin, or with only original sin descend immediately into hell; however, to be punished with different penalties and in different places." Henry Denzinger, Roy J. Deferrari, and Karl Rahner, *The Sources of Catholic Dogma* (St. Louis, MO: B. Herder Book Co., 1954), 193. The Council of Trent declared: "If anyone denies that by the grace of our Lord Jesus Christ which is conferred in Baptism, the guilt of original sin is remitted; or even assert that the whole of that which has the true and proper nature of sin is not taken way…let him be anathema." Henry Denzinger, *Sources of Catholic Dogma*, 247). Thus, without baptism, original sin is not remitted and according to the above infants would descend immediately into hell. Older Catholic theologians speculated about a place called "limbo," which was less severe than hell.

401. Henry Denzinger, Roy J. Deferrari, and Karl Rahner, *The Sources of Catholic Dogma* (St. Louis, MO: B. Herder Book Co., 1954), 247.

402. Jim Marrs, Richard M. Dolan, and Bryce Zabel, *A. D. After Disclosure*, Kindle locations 3559–3561.

403. Jim Marrs, Richard M. Dolan, Bryce Zabel, *A.D. After Disclosure*: Kindle locations 3559–3561.

404. Bruno Mobrici interviews Father Corrado Balducci, *RAI 1*, "Speciale TG1," October 8, 1995; audio transcript viewable here: "Father Balducci Assertions about Extraterrestrials," last accessed January 18, 2013, http://www.edicolaweb. net/nonsoloufo/baldu01e.htm; also see video here: "Vatican man says Aliens exist & describes them," YouTube video, 3:02, posted by commonagenet, last updated February 12, 2010, http://www.youtube.com/watch?v=5MYCfq4uA7k &feature=share&list=PLDE6EC924F348F0C9.

405. Ibid.

406. Paola Leopizzi Harris, "Monsignor Corrado Balducci says Mexico Is Blessed with UFO Sightings," http://www.delusionresistance.org/ufo/catholicism-ufos. html.

407. Gregory L. Reece, *UFO Religion: Inside Flying Saucer Cults and Culture* (New York, NY: I. B. Tauris, 2007), 104–105.

408. To learn more, see: "Lucifer," *The Blavatsky Archives*, last accessed January 18, 2013, http://www.blavatskyarchives.com/luciferreprints.htm .

409. Helena Petovna Blavatsky, *The Secret Doctrine: The Synthesis of Science, Religion, and Philosophy*, vol. 2 (London: The Theosophical Publishing House, 1883), 569.

410. Ibid., 405.

411. George Adamski, "The Kingdom of Heaven on Earth" *Adamski Foundation*, last accessed January 18, 2013, http://www.adamskifoundation.com/html/heaven. htm.

412. Professor Solomon, *How to Make the Most of a Flying Saucer Experience* (Baltimore: Top Hat Press, 1998), 75.

413. "Pacem in Terris, Encyclical of Pope John XXIII, on Establishing Universal Peace in Truth, Justice, Charity, and Liberty," *Vatican*, April 11, 1963, para 137, http://www.vatican.va/holy_father/john_xxiii/encyclicals/documents/ hf_j-xxiii_enc_11041963_pacem_en.html.

414. John Masson, The Atomic Theory of Lucretius Contrasted with Modern Doctrines of Atoms and Evolution, (London: George Bell and Sons, 1884),70.

415. For more information, see: "Ancient Aliens Debunked," last accessed January 9, 2013, http://ancientaliensdebunked.com/; "Sitchin Is Wrong," last accessed January 9, 2013, http://www.sitchiniswrong.com/.

416. We are indebted to the work of scholars Michael Crowe and Stephen J. Dick for their surveys of the ET debate.

417. Kurt Seligmann, *The History of Magic and the Occult* (New York, NY: Gramercy, 1997), 48.

418. Andrew G. M. van Melsen, "Atomism," in *Encyclopedia of Philosophy*, volume 1,

2nd ed. Edited by Donald M. Borchert (Detroit, MI: Gale/Cengage Learning, 2006), 384.

419. Hippolytus, *Refutation of the Heresies Book 1*, chapter 11, viewable here: "Refutation of All Heresies," *New Advent*, last accessed January 9, 2013, http://www.newadvent.org/fathers/050101.htm.

420. Jerry Coffey, "Democritus Model," *Universe Today*, March 19, 2010, http://www.universetoday.com/60137/democritus-model/.

421. Epicurus, "Letter to Pythocles," in *Cyril Bailey, Epicurus, the Extant Remains* (Westport, CT: Hyperion Press, 1980), 59.

422. Epicurus, "Letter to Herodotus," translated by C. Bailey in *The Stoic and Epicurean Philosophers*, ed. Whitney J. Oates (New York, NY: Random House), 5.

423. Epicurus, "Letter to Herodotus," 13.

424. Titus Lucretius Carus, "On the Nature of the Universe," translated by R.E. Latham (Middlesex: Penguin Books, 1975), 91.

425. Lucretius, "On the Nature of the Universe," as cited in Kurt Seligmann, *The History of Magic*, 81.

426. Daniel Devereux, "Plato: Metaphysics" in *The Blackwell Guide to Ancient Philosophy*, ed. Christopher Shields (Malden, MA: Wiley-Blackwell, 2003), 78.

427. Aristotle, *Aristotle's Metaphysics*, ed. W. D. Ross (Oxford: Clarendon Press, 1924), Perseus Collection, last accessed January 9, 2013, http://www.perseus.tufts.edu/hopper/text?doc=Perseus:text:1999.01.0051:book=12:section=1072a. Translation Putnam.

428. *Theological Dictionary of the New Testament*, vols. 5–9, edited by Gerhard Friedrich. Vol. 10 compiled by Ronald Pitkin., ed. Gerhard Kittel, Geoffrey William Bromiley and Gerhard Friedrich, electronic ed., 3:871 (Grand Rapids, MI: Eerdmans, 1976).

429. Aristotle, *On the Heavens*, book 1, chapter 8, lines 11–13; as quoted in Steven J. Dick, *Plurality of Worlds: The Extraterrestrial Life Debate from Democritus to Kant* (Cambridge University Press, 1984), 6.

430. Lactantius, "On the Anger of God, 13.19," under U374, last accessed January 9, 2013, http://www.epicurus.info/etexts/epicurea.html.

431. Philastrius, *Diversarum Hereseon Liber*, 86; as cited in Marie George, *Christianity and Extraterrestrials?: A Catholic Perspective*, Kindle ed (iUniverse: 2005) Kindle locations 1337–1339.

432. Origen, *De Principis*, 3.5.3; as cited in Marie George, *Christianity and Extraterrestrials?: A Catholic Perspective*, Kindle ed (iUniverse: 2005) Kindle locations 1295–1296.

433. Philip Schaff, *The Nicene and Post-Nicene Fathers Vol. II, St. Augustin's City of God and Christian Doctrine*, (Oak Harbor: Logos Research Systems, 1997), 207.

434. Ibid., 208.

435. "Contact (film)," *Wikiquote*, last modified May 21, 2012, http://en.wikiquote.org/wiki/Contact_(film).

436. Thomas Horn and Cris D. Putnam, *Petrus Romanus: The Final Pope Is Here* (Crane MO: Defender, 2012), 208.

437. Agobard, *Liber De Grandine Et Tonitruis*, chapter II cited in *Abbé de Montfaucon de Villars, Comte de Gabalis, ou Entretiens sur Us Sciences Secretes*, English ed (Paterson, NJ: The News Printing Company, 1914), 194.

438. Ibid.

439. "Nevertheless, as they escaped with their lives they were free to recount what they had seen, which was not altogether fruitless for, as you will recall, the age of Charlemagne was prolific of heroic men. This would indicate that the woman who had been in the home of the Sylphs found credence among the ladies of the period and that, by the grace of God, many Sylphs were immortalized. Many Sylphids also became immortal through the account of their beauty which these three men gave; which compelled the people of those times to apply themselves somewhat to Philosophy; and thence are derived all the stories of the fairies which you find in the love legends of the age of Charlemagne and of those which followed." Villars, *Comte de Gabalis*, 193.

440. Albertus Magnus, as quoted in Steven J. Dick, *Plurality of Worlds: The Extraterrestrial Life Debate from Democritus to Kant* (Cambridge University Press, 1984), 23.

441. Albertus Magnus, *De Mineralibus*, translation by Dorothy Wyckhoff; from *The Book of Minerals*, (Oxford, 1967); viewable here: "Albertus Magnus on Talismans," *Renaissance Astrology*, last accessed January 9, 2013, http://www.renaissanceastrology.com/albertusmagnustalisman.html.

442. Julian Franklyn, *A Survey of the Occult* (London: Electric Book Company, 2005), 29.

443. Thomas Horn and Cris D. Putnam, *Petrus Romanus*, 307.

444. Saint Thomas Aquinas and Fathers of the English Dominican Province, *Summa Theologica*, Translation of: *Summa Theologica*, I q.47 a.3 obj. 1; ad 1 (Bellingham, WA: Logos Research Systems, Inc., 2009).

445. Etienne Tempier, as quoted in Everett Ferguson, *Church History Volume One: From Christ to Pre-Reformation: The Rise and Growth of the Church in Its Cultural, Intellectual, and Political Context*, Kindle ed (Grand Rapids, MI: Zondervan, 2009), Kindle locations 9554–9555.

446. Etienne Tempier, as quoted in Michael J. Crowe, *The Extraterrestrial Life Debate, Antiquity to 1915: A Source Book*, edited with commentary (Notre Dame, IN: University of Notre Dame Press, 2008), 21.

447. "Letter to Cardinal Guliano Cesarini," as quoted in Christopher M. Bellitto, Thomas M. Izbicki, and Gerald Christianson, *Introducing Nicholas of Cusa: A Guide to a Renaissance Man* (New York, NY: Paulist Press, 2004), 206.

448. Peter M. J. Hess and Paul L. Allen, *Catholicism and Science* (Westport, CT: Greenwood, 2008), 22.

449. Nicolas of Cusa, *Of Learned Ignorance*, translated by Germain Heron (London: Routledge and Kegan Paul, 1954), 111–118; as cited in Michael J. Crowe, *The Extraterrestrial Life Debate, Antiquity to 1915: A Source Book* (Notre Dame, IN: University of Notre Dame Press, 2008), 31.

450. N. R. Hanson, "The Copernican Disturbance and the Keplerian Revolution," *Journal of the History of Ideas 22* (1961): 161–184; as cited in Michael J. Crowe, *The Extraterrestrial Life Debate*, 37.

451. *The Complete Works of Montaigne*, translated by Donald F. Frame (Stanford, 1958), p. 390.

452. Giordano Bruno, *The Heroic Frenzies* (Parigi, Appresso Antonio Baio, 1585), translated by Paulo Eugene Memmo, Jr., 1964. Viewable here: *Esoteric Archives*, last accessed January 9, 2013, http://www.esotericarchives.com/bruno/furori. htm.

453. William Turner (1908), "Giordano Bruno," *The Catholic Encyclopedia*, (New York, NY: Robert Appleton Company). Viewable here: "Giordano Bruno, *New Advent*, last accessed January 9, 2013, http://www.newadvent.org/ cathen/03016a.htm.

454. Karen Silvia De León-Jones, *Giordano Bruno and the Kabbalah: Prophets, Magicians, and Rabbis* (New Haven: Yale University Press, 1997), 9.

455. Frances A. Yates, *Giordano Bruno and the Hermetic Tradition* (New York, NY: Routledge, 1999), 155. See the book here: http://books.google.co.uk/ books?id=V5DMa7eWOlkC&lpg.

456. Frances A. Yates, *Giordano Bruno and the Hermetic Tradition*, 248. See the book here: http://books.google.co.uk/books?id=V5DMa7eWOlkC&lpg.

457. Frances A. Yates, *Giordano Bruno and the Hermetic Tradition*, 422.See the book here: http://books.google.co.uk/books?id=V5DMa7eWOlkC&lpg.

458. Karen Silvia de León-Jones, *Giordano Bruno and the Kabbalah*, 21.

459. Karen Silvia de León-Jones, *Giordano Bruno and the Kabbalah*, 67.

460. Giordano Bruno, *The Cabala of Pegaus*, translated and annotated by Sidney L. Sondergard and Madison U. Sowell (New Haven: Yale University Press, 2002), xxxii. Viewable here: http://www.yale.edu/yup/pdf/092172_front_1.pdf

461. Adam Kadmon depicted as Cosmic Christ on the schematic Tree of Life. The Kabalistic Trinity—Atika Kadisha ("Holy One of Old"), Meleka Kadisha ("Holy King"), and the Shekhinah ("Feminine presence of God") are above Christ's head. Picture viewable here: "KABBALAH," *A. G. DEI*, last accessed January 9, 2013, http://agdei.com/Davincicode2.html.

462. Giordano Bruno, *Essays on Magic, in Cause, Principle, and Unity & Essays on Magic* translated and edited by Richard J. Blackwell and Robert de Lucca (Cambridge, UK: Cambridge University Press, 1998), 128. See the book here: http://books.google.com/books?id=0E565t7WozQC&lpg=PA186&ots=SeZpc5 VNvH&dq=Cause%2C%20Principle%20and%20Unity.%20Ed.%20R.J.%20 Blackwell%20and%20Robert%20de%20Lucca%2C%20with%20an%20 Introduction%20by%20Alfonso%20Ingegno.&pg=PA106#v=onepage&q&f=f alse.

463. Giordano Bruno, *Essays on Magic*, 139. See the book here: http://books.google. com/books?id=0E565t7WozQC&lpg=PA186&ots=SeZpc5VNvH&dq=Cau se%2C%20Principle%20and%20Unity.%20Ed.%20R.J.%20Blackwell%20 and%20Robert%20de%20Lucca%2C%20with%20an%20Introduction%20 by%20Alfonso%20Ingegno.&pg=PA106#v=onepage&q&f=false.

464. Giordano Bruno, *Essays on Magic*, 131. See the book here: http://books.google. com/books?id=0E565t7WozQC&lpg=PA186&ots=SeZpc5VNvH&dq=Cau se%2C%20Principle%20and%20Unity.%20Ed.%20R.J.%20Blackwell%20 and%20Robert%20de%20Lucca%2C%20with%20an%20Introduction%20 by%20Alfonso%20Ingegno.&pg=PA106#v=onepage&q&f=false.

465. For number values see: "Gematria Chart," *Inner.org*, last accessed January 9, 2013, http://www.inner.org/gematria/gemchart.php.

466. "AGLA," *Wikipedia, The Free Encyclopedia*, last modified August 14, 2012, http://en.wikipedia.org/wiki/AGLA.

467. Rav Shimon Bar. Commentary by Yehuda Ashlag, Edited & compiled by Rabbi Michael Berg. Yochai, The Zohar: the First Ever Unabridged English Translation with Commentary (23 Volume Set) Vol. 3: Lech lecha Vayera (Los Angeles: Kabbalah Centre Intl, 2003), 486. Google Books link Quoted here.

468. Giordano Bruno, *Cause, Principle and Unity*, with introduction by Alfonso Ingegno. ed. R.J. Blackwell and Robert de Lucca (Cambridge, UK: Cambridge University Press, 1998), xxvii.

469. Giordano Bruno, *On the Infinite Universe and Worlds*, *Positive Atheism*, last accessed January 9, 2013, http://www.positiveatheism.org/hist/brunoiuw0.htm.

470. Edward Howard Griggs, *Great Leaders in Human Progress* (Freeport, NY: Books for Libraries Press, 1969), 121.

471. Dorothea Waley Singer, *Giordano Bruno, His Life and Thought* (New York, NY: Henry Schuman, 1950). Viewable here: *Positive Atheism*, last accessed January 9, 2013, http://www.positiveatheism.org/hist/bruno07.htm.

472. William Turner, "Giordano Bruno," *The Catholic Encyclopedia*, vol. 3 (New York, NY: Robert Appleton Company, 1908). Viewable here: *New Advent*, last accessed November 15, 2012, http://www.newadvent.org/cathen/03016a.htm.

473. Charles Seife, "Vatican Regrets Burning Cosmologist" *Science*, last accessed November 15, 2012, http://news.sciencemag.org/sciencenow/2000/03/01-04. html.

474. Steven J. Dick, *Plurality of Worlds: The Extraterrestrial Life Debate from Democritus to Kant* (Cambridge: Cambridge University Press, 1982), 176.

475. Ibid., 47.

476. Giancarlo Genta, *Lonely Minds in the Universe* (London: Springer, 2007), xi.

477. Ibid.

478. Translated with a commentary by Edward Rosen, *Kepler's Somnium: The Dream, or Posthumous Work on Lunar Astronomy* (Mineola, NY: Dover Publications, 2003), 63.

479. ChiaLynn, "This Week in Odd History: Kepler's Mother Arrested for Witchcraft (August 7, 1620)," August 2, 2010, last accessed February 12, 2013 http://www.popbunker.net/2010/08/ week-odd-history-keplers-mother-arrested-witchcraft-august-7-1620/.

480. For more information, see http://www.theflatearthsociety.org/forum/index. php?topic=7026.35;wap2.

481. Charles Singer, *A Short History of Science to the Nineteenth Century* (London: Clarendon Press, 1941), 217.

482. Robert Bellarmine, "Letter to Foscarini" from Giorgio de Santillana, *The Crime of Galileo*, (New York: Time, Inc 1962), pp. 104-106 as cited by Carl J. Wenning, "The Life and Times Of Galileo" last accessed February 10, 2013 http://www.phy.ilstu.edu/~wenning/galileo/galileo.html.

483. Galileo Galilei, "Letter on Sunspots," as quoted in: Michael J. Crowe, *The Extraterrestrial Life Debate, Antiquity to 1915: A Source Book* (Notre Dame, IN: University of Notre Dame Press, 2008), 52.

484. As recorded in J.J. Fahie, *Galileo: His Life and Work* (London: J. Murray, 1903), 135-36 as cited in Michael J. Crowe, *The Extraterrestrial Life Debate, Antiquity to 1915: A Source Book* (Notre Dame, IN: University of Notre Dame Press, 2008), 52.

485. Steven J. Dick, *Plurality of Worlds*, 37.

486. Daniel N. Robinson citing John Paul II in: Daniel N. Robinson, Gladys M. Sweeney, and Richard Gill, eds., *Human Nature in Its Wholeness: A Roman Catholic Perspective* (Washington, DC: Catholic Univ of Amer Pr, 2006), 169.

487. Kenneth J. Delano, *Many Worlds, One God* (Hicksville, NY: Exposition Press, 1977), 37.

488. Sabino Maffeo, S.J. *The Vatican Observatory: In the Service of None Popes* (Città del Vaticano: Vatican Observatory Publications, 2002), 10.

489. Donald K. McKim and David F. Wright, *Encyclopedia of the Reformed Faith* (Westminster: John Knox Press, 1992), 61; viewable here: http://books.google.com/books?id=MJPsgwN789gC&pg=PA61#v=onepage&q&f=false.

490. Thomas Chalmers, *Discourse VI: On the Contest for an Ascendancy Over Man, Amongst the Higher Orders of Intelligence*, last accessed February 12, 2013, http://www.newble.co.uk/chalmers/astronom6.html.

491. Michael J. Crowe, *The Extraterrestrial Life Debate, 1750–1900* (Mineola, NY: Dover Publications, 2011), 249.

492. Joseph Pohle, *Die Sternenwelten und ihre Bewohner* ("Steller Worlds and Their Inhabitants"), (Kolne, 1906), 457; viewable here: http://books.google.com/books?id=uyIyAQAAMAAJ&dq=Joseph+Pohle%2C+Die+Sternenwelten+und+ihre+Bewohner&jtp=0.

493. Richard Harter, "Piltdown Man: The Bogus Bones Caper," *Talk Origins* (1996), last accessed February 12, 2013, http://www.talkorigins.org/faqs/piltdown.html.

494. Pierre Teilhard de Chardin, *Christianity and Evolution* (New York, NY: A Harvest Book, 1971), 232.

495. Ibid., 234.

496. Mission statement of *100 Year Starship* program, viewable on its website here: last accessed January 17, 2013, http://100yss.org/mission.html.

497. Clara Moskowitz, "Are Aliens Part of God's Plan, Too? Finding E.T. Could Change Religion Forever," *Space.com*, October 2, 2011, http://www.space.com/13152-aliens-religion-impacts-extraterrestrial-christianity.html#.

498. Merrill F. Unger, *Biblical Demonology: A Study of Spiritual Forces at Work Today* (Wheaton, IL: Scripture Press Publications, 1952), 203.

499. Millard J. Erickson, *Christian Theology.*, 2nd ed. (Grand Rapids, MI: Baker Book House, 1998), 532.

500. C. S. Lewis, "Religion and Rocketry," as quoted in *The World's Last Night: and Other Essays* (Orlando, FL: Houghton Mifflin Harcourt, 2002), 92.

501. Millard J. Erickson, *The Concise Dictionary of Christian Theology*, rev. ed., 1st Crossway ed. (Wheaton, IL: Crossway Books, 2001), 97.

502. Michael S. Heiser, *The Facade* (Bowling Green, KY: Superiorbooks.Com Inc., 2001), 168.

503. Peter Kreeft, *Yes or No?: Straight Answers to Tough Questions About Christianity* (San Francisco: Ignatius Press, 1991), 150.

504. Michael S. Heiser, "Panspermia" as quoted in *How to Overcome the Most Frightening Issues You Will Face This Century* (Crane: Defender, 2009), Kindle locations 4047–4050.

505. Wayne A. Grudem, *Systematic Theology: An Introduction to Biblical Doctrine* (Leicester, England; Grand Rapids, MI: Inter-Varsity Press; Zondervan, 1994), 442.

506. Wayne A. Grudem, *Systematic Theology,* 443.

507. Paul Davies, *God and the New Physics* (New York, NY: Simon & Schuster, 1983), 71.

508. Peter Kreeft, *Yes or No?*, 150.

509. Christopher Corbally, "What if There Were Other Inhabited Worlds?" as quoted in: Niels Henrik Gregersen, Ulf Görman, and Christoph Wassermann, *The Interplay between Scientific and Theological Worldviews, Volume 1* (Paris, *Labor et Fides*, 1997); viewable here: http://books. google.com/books?id=ylKZFty_OdsC&lpg=PA77&ots=K9TMN-q2wP&dq=Christopher%20Corbally%2C%20%E2%80%9CWhat%20 if%20There%20Were%20Other%20Inhabited%20 Worlds%E2%80%9D&pg=PA77#v=onepage&q&f=false.

510. Karl Rahner, "Natural Science and Reasonable Faith," in *Theological Investigations*, vol. XXI, trans. Hugh M. Riley (New York, NY: Crossroad, 1988), 51.

511. Thomas Paine, *The Age of Reason* (New York, NY: The Truth Seeker Company, 1898), 283.

512. Lewis, "Religion and Rocketry," as quoted in *The World's Last Night*, 91.

513. Pierre Teilhard de Chardin, *Christianity and Evolution*, (New York, NY: A Harvest Book, 1971), 233.

514. Thomas F. O'Meara, *Vast Universe: Extraterrestrials and Christian Revelation.* Kindle ed. (Collegeville, MN: Liturgical Press, 2012), Kindle location 560.

515. C. Stephen Evans, *Pocket Dictionary of Apologetics & Philosophy of Religion* (Downers Grove, IL: InterVarsity Press, 2002), 124.

516. Francis A. Schaeffer, *The Francis A. Schaeffer Trilogy: the Three Essential Books in One Volume.* (Westchester, Ill.: Crossway, 1990), 211.

517. Ibid., 209.

518. George Coyne, as quoted in: Margaret Wertheim, "The Pope's Astrophysicist,"

Catholic Education Resource Center, last accessed January 17, 2013, http://catholiceducation.org/articles/science/sc0047.html.

519. "Pope Leads World Prayer Day," *BBC News*, January 24, 2002, http://news.bbc.co.uk/2/hi/europe/1779135.stm.

520. Phillip E. Johnson, *The Wedge of Truth: Splitting the Foundations of Naturalism* (Downers Grove, IL: InterVarsity Press, 2000), 148,

521. "Previous Prize Winners: Michael Heller," *Templeton Foundation*, last accessed January 17, 2013, http://www.templetonprize.org/previouswinners/heller.html.

522. "About the Prize: Purpose," *Templeton Foundation*, last accessed January 17, 2013, http://www.templetonprize.org/abouttheprize.html.

523. Statement by Professor Michael Heller at the Templeton Prize News Conference, March 12, 2008; viewable here: http://www.templetonprize.org/pdfs/heller_statement.pdf.

524. R. C. Sproul, *Not a Chance: The Myth of Chance in Modern Science and Cosmology*, electronic ed. (Grand Rapids, MI: Baker Books, 2000, c1994), 3.

525. Giuseppe Tanzella-Nitti, "Extraterrestrial Life" *Interdisciplinary Encyclopedia of Religion and Science*, last accessed August 21, 2012, http://www.disf.org/en/Voci/65.asp.

526. Ibid.

527. "Pell says Adam and Eve Didn't Exist," *The West Australian*, April 10, 2012, http://au.news.yahoo.com/thewest/a/-/newshome/13381016/pell-says-ad/.

528. Jack Hitt, "Would You Baptize an Extraterresrial?" *New York Times* magazine, May 29, 1994, http://www.nytimes.com/1994/05/29/magazine/would-you-baptize-an-extraterrestrial.html?pagewanted=all&src=pm.

529. Ibid.

530. Richard Dawkins, "Is Science a Religion?" *The Humanist*, January/February 1997, viewable here: http://www.thehumanist.org/humanist/articles/dawkins.html.

531. Stanley Grenz, David Guretzki, and Cherith Fee Nordling, *Pocket Dictionary of Theological Terms* (Downers Grove, IL: InterVarsity Press, 1999), 50.

532. Henry Bortman, "Interview with Brother Guy Consolmagno," *Astrobiology Magazine*, last accessed January 17, 2013, http://www.astrobio.net/interview/966/interview-with-brother-guy-consolmagno.

533. Nancy Pearcey, *Saving Leonardo: A Call to Resist the Secular Assault on Mind, Morals, and Meaning,* Kindle ed. (Nashville, TN: B&H Publishing), 25.

534. Chris Corbally, "Faith Matters God's Stargazers," *In Focus* on DW-TV 2009; viewable here:"NASA And The Vatican's Infrared Telescope Called (LUCIFER) PT 2," You Tube video, 8:00, posted by migfoxbat, last updated April 13, 2010, last accessed January 17, 2013, http://www.youtube.com/watch?v=_GCEl1-9LCw&feature=plcp, 2:33–3:34.

535. Malachi Martin, *The Jesuits* (New York, NY: Simon & Schuster, 1988), 86.

536. Ibid., 287.

537. Ibid., 287.

538. Pius IX, Letter, 1877, as quoted in Maureen Fiedler and Linda Rabben, eds.,

Rome Has Spoken: a Guide to Forgotten Papal Statements and How They Have Changed through the Centuries (New York, NY: The Crossroad Publishing Company, 1998), 178.

539. "On the Historical Character of the First Three Chapters of Genesis," as quoted in Maureen Fiedler and Linda Rabben, eds., *Rome Has Spoken,* 179.

540. Malachi Martin, *The Jesuits,* 287.

541. Malachi Martin, *The Jesuits,* 293.

542. Erich von Däniken, *Chariots of the Gods* (NewYork: G.P. Putnam's Sons, 1970), 10.

543. Ibid., 26.

544. "Ancient astronauts," *Wikipedia, The Free Encyclopedia,* last modified December 2, 2012, http://en.wikipedia.org/wiki/Ancient_astronauts.

545. Ibid.

546. Jacques Vallée, *The Invisible College: What a Group of Scientists Has Discovered About UFO Influences on the Human Race* (New York: Dutton, 1975), 233.

547. Dr. James Kennedy, PhD, *The Real Meaning of the Zodiac* (Ft. Lauderdale, FL: TCRM, 1993), 6–8.

548. *Ancient Universal History, vol. 5, pp. 415 to 419.* Viewable here:*Sacred-Texts.com,* last accessed January 11, 2013, http://www.sacred-texts.com/astro/ptb/ptb03. htm.

549. Ernest L. Martin, *The Star that Astonished the World* (1996), as quoted here: "The Time of Jesus' Birth," *Associates for Scriptural Knowledge,* last accessed January 11, 2013, http://askelm.com/star/star006.htm.

550. "SHUDUN," *Star Catalog* , last accessed January 9, 2013, http://www. astronomy.pomona.edu/archeo/outside/starlog.html.

551. "Arcus," *Encyclopedia Mythica,* last accessed January 9, 2013, http://www. pantheon.org/articles/a/arcas.html.

552. Holy Bible, Latin Vulgate Translation (Joseph Kreifels), 510.

553. Steve Connor, "Scientists Catch the 'Millennium Planet's Glow," *The Independent,* December 16, 1999, http://www.independent.co.uk/news/ scientists-catch-the-millennium-planets-glow-1132737.html. Also see: "Tau Boötis b," *Wikipedia, The Free Encyclopedia,* last modified January 2, 2013, http://en.wikipedia.org/wiki/Tau_Bo%C3%B6tis_b.
List of stars in Boötes http://en.wikipedia.org/wiki/List_of_stars_in_Bo%C3%B6tes

554. For more information on planet profile, see: "HD 136418 b," *NASA,* last accessed January 11, 2013, http://exep.jpl.nasa.gov/atlas/atlas_profile. cfm?Planet=593. *The TutorGig Encyclopedia* lists this planet as potentially habitable here: "Habitable Zone," *The TutorGig Encyclopedia,* last accessed January 11, 2013, http://www.tutorgigpedia.com/ed/Habitable_zone.

555. "Planet 47 Uma b," *Exoplanet,* last accessed January 11, 2013, http://exoplanet. eu/catalog/47_uma_b/.

556. John Walton, *Ancient Israelite Literature in Its Cultural Context* (Grand Rapids, MI: Zondervan, 1994), 40.

557. Bill T. Arnold and David B. Weisberg, "Babel und Bibel und Bias: How Anti-

Semitism Distorted Friedrich Delitzsch's Scholarship," *Bible Review*, 18:01 (Biblical Archaeology Society, 2004; 2004).

558. Friedrich Delitzsch, *Die Grosse Täuschung* (*The Great Deception*) as quoted in Arnold and Weisberg, "Babel und Bibel und Bias" *Bible Review* 18:01.

559. Zecharia Sitchin, "Dialogue in Bellaria" *The Official Website of Zecharia Sitchin*, last accessed August, 11, 2012, http://www.sitchin.com/vatican.htm.

560. Zecharia Sitchin, *The 12th Planet (the Earth Chronicles, Book 1)* (New York: Harper Collins, 1999), 341.

561. David Noel Freedman, *The Anchor Bible Dictionary*, 4:1072 (New York: Doubleday, 1996, c1992).

562. Zecharia Sitchin, *The 12th Planet*, vii, 128ff.

563. Michael S. Heiser, "The Nephilim," *Sitchin is Wrong*, last accessed December 5, 2012, http://www.sitchiniswrong.com/nephilim/nephilim.htm.

564. Heiser, "The Nephilim," and H. Gunkel, *Genesis* (Göttingen 1910) 58–59. (See: http://books.google.com/books?id=-ZtH3hbGITkC&lpg=PP1&ots=QvC iOAVLUP&dq=inauthor%3A%22Hermann%20Gunkel%22&pg= PA58#v=onepage&q&f=false.)

565. P. W. Coxon, "Nephilim" in *Dictionary of Deities and Demons in the Bible*, 2nd ed. Edited by K. van der Toorn, Bob Becking, and Pieter Willem van der Horst (Leiden; Boston; Grand Rapids, MI: Brill; Eerdmans, 1999), 619.

566. Zecharia Sitchin, *The 12th Planet*, 341.

567. Edwin Abbott, *Flatland: A Romance of Many Dimensions* (Boston, MA: Roberts Brothers, 1885), 112. Viewable here: http://books.google.com/books?id=R6E0A AAAMAAJ&ots=BaLaIlYilo&dq=Flatland&pg=PA112#v=onepage&q&f=false

568. Ibid., 125-126. http://books.google.com/books?id=R6E0AAAAMAAJ&ots=BaLaIlYilo&dq=Flatland &pg=PA125#v=onepage&q&f=false

569. John A. Keel, *Our Haunted Planet* (Lakeville, MN: Galde Press, Inc., 2002), 89.

570. William B. Nash and William H. Fortenberry, "TRUE Report On Flying Saucers," originally printed in *TRUE* magazine, 1967; viewable here: "We Flew Above Flying Saucers," *UFO Evidence*, last accessed January 16, 2013, http:// www.ufoevidence.org/Cases/CaseSubarticle.asp?ID=94.

571. Robert L. Laing, "UFO Sightings; Reports and the Government Response – Aliens, the Pyramids, Obelisks and Extraterrestrial Life," *Intelligent Design Theory*, last accessed January 16, 2013, http://www.intelligentdesigntheory.info/ ufo_sightings_reports_evidence_aliens_government_response_flying_saucers_ egyptian_pyramids_obelisk_extraterrestrial_life.htm

572. This case is detailed in Leslie Kean, *UFOs: Generals, Pilots and Government Officials Go On the Record* (New York, NY: Three Rivers, 2010), 37.

573. John A. Keel, *Operation Trojan Horse* (Lilburn, GA: Illuminet Press, 1996),44.

574. Leslie Kean, *UFOs: Generals, Pilots and Government Officials Go On the Record*, Kindle ed. (New York, NY: Harmony Books, 2010), 13–14.

575. Jacques Vallée, *Dimensions: A Casebook of Alien Contact* (New York, NY: Contemporary Books, 1988), 284.

576. Curtis Fuller, *Proceedings of the First International UFO Congress* (New York, NY: Warner Books, 1980), 164–165.

577. Michael Grosso, "Transcending the 'ET Hypothesis,'" *California UFO 3*, no. 3 (1988), 10.

578. Nelson S. Pacheco and Tommy R. Blann, *Unmasking the Enemy: Visions and Deception in the End Times*, rev. ed. (Arlington, VA: Bendan Press, 1994), 30.

579. Brad Steiger, *Blue Book Files Released*, as quoted in *Canadian UFO Report*, volume 4, number 4, 1977, 20; also as cited at http://www.mt.net/~watcher/quotes.html.

580. Paul Steinhardt transcribed from: *Through the Wormhole*, season 2, episode 10. "Are There Parallel Universes?" (Original air date: August 3, 2011), Discovery Channel.

581. "WMAP Space-Mission Survey of the Universe After the Big Bang Completed—Its Results Hint at a Far Stranger Cosmos," *The Daily Galaxy*, October 8, 2010, http://www.dailygalaxy.com/my_weblog/2010/10/-wmap-space-mission-survey-of-the-universe-after-the-big-bang-completed-but-its-results-may-hint-at-.html.

582. Paul Steinhardt transcribed from: *Through the Wormhole*, season 2, episode 10. "Are There Parallel Universes?"

583. Bernard Haisch, "Extraterrestrial Visitation: The Speed-of-Light-Limit Argument," *UFO Skeptic*, last accessed January 16, 2013, http://www.ufoskeptic.org/.

584. Dinesh D'Souza, *What's so Great about Christianity* (Washington, DC: Tyndale House Publishers, Inc., 2008), 85.

585. Hugh Ross, Kenneth Samples, and Mark Clark, *Lights in the Sky & Little Green Men: A Rational Christian Look at UFOs and Extraterrestrials* (Colorado Springs, CO: NavPress, 2002), 168.

586. Leslie Kean and Ralph Blumenthal, "UFO Caught On Tape Over Santiago Air Base," *Huffington Post* March, 13, 2012, http://www.huffingtonpost.com/leslie-kean/the-extraordinary-ufo-sig_b_1342585.html.

587. Ibid.

588. Leslie Kean, "Update on Chilean UFO Videos: Getting the Bugs Out," *Huffington Post*, April 13, 2012, http://www.huffingtonpost.com/leslie-kean/update-on-chilean-ufo-vid_b_1424008.html.

589. Brett C. Ratcliffe, as quoted in Leslie Kean, "Update on Chilean UFO," http://www.huffingtonpost.com/leslie-kean/update-on-chilean-ufo-vid_b_1424008.html.

590. Richard F. Haines, "The El Bosque Video Case: A Preliminary Study of Anomalous Objects in Active Airspace," *International Air Safety Case Report IR-5*, 2012, 94, http://www.cefaa.gob.cl/web/videosfinal/halcones/NARCAP%20IR%2015a.pdf

591. Ibid.

592. Leslie Kean, "Two New Reports on the Chilean 'UFO' Videos Produce Conflicting Result," *Huffington Post*, November 15, 2012, http://www.huffingtonpost.com/leslie-kean/ufo-chile_b_2123947.html.

593. Heidi Hemmat, "Mile High Mystery: UFO Sightings in Sky Over Denver," *KDVR*, November 8, 2012, http://kdvr.com/2012/11/08/ mile-high-city-mystery-ufo-sightings-in-sky-over-denver/.

594. Steve Cowell, statements during *KDVR* video interview, "Mile High Mystery," 2:17–2:30, http://kdvr.com/2012/11/08/ mile-high-city-mystery-ufo-sightings-in-sky-over-denver/.

595. Ibid., 2:50.

596. NORAD statement in response to *KDVR* station inquiry, "Mile High Mystery," 3:25, http://kdvr.com/2012/11/08/ mile-high-city-mystery-ufo-sightings-in-sky-over-denver/.

597. Heidi Hemmat, "Insect Expert: UFOs Over Denver Not Bugs; Images On Video Remain a Mystery," *KDVR*, November 20, 2012, http://kdvr.com/2012/11/20/ insect-expert-ufos-over-denver-not-bugs-images-on-video-remain-a-mystery/.

598. "Berserk," *Online Etymology Dictionary*, last accessed January 16, 2013, http:// www.etymonline.com/index.php?search=berserk.

599. Dr. Walter Martin, "A Christian View: UFO Encounters," audio recording, *Sermon Audio*, last accessed January 15, 2013, http://www.sermonaudio.com/ sermoninfo.asp?SID=2190615720. This audio sermon was also included as a transcript in the following book: Dr. Walter Martin, Jill Martin Rische, and Kurt van Gorden, *The Kingdom of the Occult* (Nashville, TN: Thomas Nelson Inc., 2008), viewable here: http://books.google.com/books?id=n1qaOUDfCeE C&printsec=frontcover&dq=The+Kingdom+of+the+Occult&hl=en&sa=X&ei =vKL2ULH6B4Os8QS_pYHwCQ&ved=0CC0Q6AEwAA#v=onepage&q&f= false.

600. Dr. Walter Martin, Jill Martin Rische, and Kurt Van Gorden, *The Kingdom of the Occult* (Nashville, TN: Thomas Nelson Inc, 2008), 372–373.

601. Thomas Horn, *Nephilim Stargates*, 53.

602. Thomas Horn, *Nephilim Stargates: The Year 2012 and the Return of the Watchers* (Crane, MO: Anomalos Publishing, 2007), 60–61.

603. Antonio Gaspari, "Pope Pius XII Saw the 'Miracle of the Sun,'" as quoted in: *Catholic.org*, November 5, 2008, http://www.catholic.org/international/ international_story.php?id=30396.

604. Antonio Gaspari, "Pius XII Saw 'Miracle of the Sun,'" *Zenit*, November, 04, 2008, last accessed February 2, 2013, http://www.zenit.org/ article-24149?l=english.

605. Ibid.

606. Ibid.

607. Lynn Picknett, *Flights of Fancy* (London: Ward Lock, 1987), 82–83.

608. Jacques F. Vallée and Eric W. Davis, "Incommensurability, Orthodoxy, and the Physics of High Strangeness — A 6-Layer Model For Anomalous Phenomena" in *Fátima Revisited: The Apparition Phenomenon in Ufology, Psychology, and Science* Kindle Edition ed. Fernando Fernandes (Anomalist Books 2010), Kindle locations 5568-5571.

609. L. A. Marzulli, *Politics, Prophecy & the Supernatural* (Crane, MO: Anomalos Publishing, 2007), 110–120.

610. Antonio Socci, "Dear Cardinal Bertone: Who—Between You and Me—Is Deliberately Lying?" *The Fátima Network: Our Lady of Fátima Online*, May 12, 2007, last accessed February 6, 2013, http://www.fatima.org/news/newsviews/052907socci.asp.

611. John Vennari, "The Fourth Secret of Fátima," *Catholic Family News*, last accessed February 13, 2012, http://www.cfnews.org/Socci-FourthSecret.htm.

612. See: http://www.vatican.va/roman_curia/congregations/cfaith/documents/rc_con_cfaith_doc_20000626_message-fatima_en.html.

613. John Vennari, "The Fourth Secret of Fátima," *Fátima.org*, last accessed February 13, 2012, http://www.fatima.org/news/newsviews/010207fourthsecret.asp.

614. "Cardinal Sodano Reads a Text on the 'Third Secret,'" *The Fátima Network: Our Lady of Fátima Online* , May 13, 2000, http://www.fatima.org/news/newsviews/thirdsecret01.asp?printer.

615. Ibid.

616. John Vennari, "The Fourth Secret of Fátima," *Catholic Family News*.

617. "Joseph Ratzinger as Prefect of the Congregation for the Doctrine of the Faith," *Wikipedia*, last modified November 14, 2011, http://en.wikipedia.org/wiki/Joseph_Ratzinger_as_Prefect_of_the_Congregation_for_the_Doctrine_of_the_Faith.

618. "Published Testimony: Cardinal Ratzinger (November 1984)," *The Fátima Network: Our Lady of Fátima Online* , last accessed February 13, 2012, http://www.fatima.org/thirdsecret/ratzinger.asp?printer.

619. John Vennari, "The Fourth Secret of Fátima," *Catholic Family News*.

620. Cardinal Oddi on the REAL Third Secret of Fátima: "The Blessed Virgin was Alerting Us Against the Apostasy in the Church," last accessed February 13, 2012, http://www.tldm.org/news7/thirdsecretcardinaloddi.htm.

621. Published Testimony: Cardinal Alonso (1975–1981)," *The Fátima Network: Our Lady of Fátima Online* , last accessed February 13, 2012, http://www.fatima.org/thirdsecret/fralonso.asp.

622. "Three Secrets of Fátima," *Wikipedia*, last modified February 6, 2012, http://en.wikipedia.org/wiki/Three_Secrets_of_F%C3%A1tima.

623. Ibid.

624. Erven Park, "'Diabolic Disorientation' in the Church," *New Oxford Review*, October 2006, http://www.newoxfordreview.org/article.jsp?did=1006-park.

625. Antonio Socci, "Dear Cardinal Bertone: Who—Between You and Me—Is Deliberately Lying? And Please Don't Mention Freemasonry," last accessed February 13, 2012, http://www.fatimacrusader.com/cr86/cr86pg35.asp.

626. Thomas R. Horn and Cris Putnam, *Petrus Romanus: The Final Pope Is Here* (Crane, MO: Defender Publishing, 2012), 456–465.

627. Bishop Richard Williamson, "Bishop Fellay of the Society of St. Pius X to Meet Pope August 29," August 15, 2005, http://www.freerepublic.com/focus/f-religion/1464382/posts.

628. Dr. Michael S. Heiser, "Why Should Christians Care About Ufology?"*ANOMALOS MAGAZINE*, Premier Edition, June–July 2006 (Portland, OR: Thomas R. Horn), 30.

629. Zoe Catchpole, "Britain Has Alien War-Weapons, Says Former Government Advisor," *MSN News*, October 12, 2012, http://news.uk.msn.com/exclusives/britain-has-alien-war-weapons-says-former-government-adviser.

630. Ibid.

631. Carnegie Endowment for International Peace. Division of Intercourse and Education; Ishii, Kikujiro, Viscount, 1866–1945; Iyenaga, Toyokichi, 1862–1936; Clarke, Joseph Ignatius Constantine, 1846–1925, *The Imperial Japanese mission, 1917* (Press of B.S. Adams), 1918, 105.

632. Alexander Wendt and Raymond Duvall, "Sovereignty and the UFO," *Political Theory* (June 11, 2008), 620–621, http://ptx.sagepub.com/content/36/4/607.

633. Nick Pope (headed the UFO department for twenty-one years at the British government's Ministry of Defence), in discussion over personal email communication with the author, Thomas R. Horn, between 2011–2012.

634. Bruce Maccabee (American optical physicist formerly employed by the US Navy, and a leading ufologist), in discussion over personal email communication with the author, Thomas R. Horn, between 2011–2012.

635. Stanton Friedman (nuclear physicist and the original civilian investigator of the Roswell incident), in discussion over personal email communication with the author, Thomas R. Horn, between 2011–2012.

636. Jesse Marcel Jr. (colonel and the only man whom the US government admits handled material from the Roswell debris field in 1947, when his father let him and his mother to see fragments of the crash material as he stopped off at home on his way back to the base), in discussion over personal email communication with the author, Thomas R. Horn, between 2011–2012.

637. Charles Berlitz and William Moore, *The Roswell Incident* (New York, NY: Berkley, 1988), 78–80.

638. Gary Stearman (executive director of programming at Prophecy in the News), in discussion over personal email communication with the author, Thomas R. Horn, between 2011–2012.

639. Noah Hutchings (author of over one hundred Christian books and president of Southwest Radio Ministries in Oklahoma City since April 1951), in discussion over personal email communication with the author, Thomas R. Horn, between 2011–2012.

640. Clay Dillow, "Former Air Force Officers Claim UFOs Visited Bases, Tampered with Nukes," *Popular Science*, September, 28, 2012, http://www.popsci.com/technology/article/2010-09/former-air-force-officers-claim-ufos-tampered-our-nukes.

641. Dr. Walter Martin, "A Christian View: UFO Encounters," audio recording, *Sermon Audio*, last accessed January 15, 2013, http://www.sermonaudio.com/sermoninfo.asp?SID=2190615720. This audio sermon was also included as a transcript in the following book: Dr. Walter Martin, Jill Martin Rische, and Kurt

van Gorden, *The Kingdom of the Occult* (Nashville, TN: Thomas Nelson Inc., 2008), viewable here: http://books.google.com/books?id=n1qaOUDfCeEC&pr intsec=frontcover&dq=The+Kingdom+of+the+Occult&hl=en&sa=X&ei=vKL2 ULH6B4Os8QS_pYHwCQ&ved=0CC0Q6AEwAA#v=onepage&q&f=false.

642. "Close encounter," *Wikipedia, The Free Encyclopedia*, last modified January 4, 2013, http://en.wikipedia.org/wiki/Close_encounter.

643. Ibid.

644. Tom Horn's private notes following a visit with Vida.

645. Dr. I. D. E. Thomas, *The Omega Conspiracy* (Crane, MO: Anomalos, 2008), 142–143.

646. Jerome Clark, *UFOs in the 1980s* (Canada: Apogee Books, 1990), 85.

647. "*Taken* (TV miniseries)," *Wikipedia, The Free Encyclopedia*, last modified January 14, 2013, http://en.wikipedia.org/wiki/Taken_(TV_miniseries).

648. "The Real Story: Close Encounters of the Third Kind," YouTube video, 46:41, posted by smithsonianchannel, last updated August 19, 2012, last accessed January 15, 2013, http://www.youtube.com/watch?v=m8Hjb98-j5I.

649. Thomas Horn, *Nephilim Stargates: The Year 2012 and the Return of the Watchers* (Crane, MO: Anomalos), 154.

650. *The Researchers Library of Ancient Texts, Volume 1, The Apocrypha* (Crane, MO: Defender, 2011), *Book of Enoch*, chapter 6, verse 6, page 3.

651. J. R. Church, "Mount Hermon: Gate of the Fallen Angels," May 1, 2011, http://www.prophecyinthenews.com/mount-hermon-gate-of-the-fallen-angels/.

652. Ibid.

653. Reginald C. Haupt, Jr., *The Gods of the Lodge* (Austin, TX: Victory, 1990), 126.

654. Barry Chamish, "Did Biblical Giants Build the Circle of the Refaim?" *Christian Churches of God/Bible Prophecy Research*, May 30, 1998, http://www.ccg.org/_ domain/ccg.org/Creation%20Articles/Circle%20of%20the%20Refaim.htm.

655. Ibid.

656. Ross Andersen, "The Best Way to Find Aliens: Look for Their Solar Power Plants," *The Atlantic*, October 4, 2012, http://www.theatlantic.com/technology/archive/2012/10/ the-best-way-to-find-aliens-look-for-their-solar-power-plants/263217/.

657. Dr. Tom Van Flandern (PhD in astronomy, specializing in celestial mechanics from Yale University; twenty-one years at the US Naval Observatory in Washington, DC, where he became the chief of the Celestial Mechanics Branch of the Nautical Almanac Office), in discussion over personal email communication with the author, Thomas R. Horn, in 2007.

658. Pickett and Prince, *The Stargate Conspiracy* (New York, NY: Berkley Trade, 2001), 153.

659. Mike Wall, "First 'Alien Earth' Will Be Found in 2013, Experts Say," *Space. com*, December 27, 2012, http://www.space.com/19044-alien-earth-exoplanets-2013.html.

660. Interview with Daniel Sheehan, July 14, 2001, *Strange Days…Indeed*, with Errol Bruce-Knapp and Scott Robins. http://www.ufoevidence.org/documents/ doc836.htm.

661. "The SOPHIA Project," *Arizona State University*, http://lach.web.arizona.edu/
Sophia/ (site discontinued; see alternatively, from Arizona State University:
http://lach.web.arizona.edu/veritas_research_program and http://www.lach.
web.arizona.edu/sophia_project).

662. "Forgotten UFO and alien retrieval footage from Siberia," YouTube video, 1:13,
posted by cohenparanormal, last updated April 3, 2011, last accessed January
15, 2013, http://www.youtube.com/watch?v=tRQZIqElcfE. Also viewable
here: http://teamico.wikia.com/wiki/Polarneft_conspiracy and here: http://web.
archive.org/web/20060211043125/http://giantology.net/videos/Siberian_Ice_
Giant.mov.

663. "Siberian Ice Giant Video: Cryptozoological Cover-Up," online discussion
board, quote excerpt from post by Libertus Invictus, November 3, 2005, last
accessed January 15, 2013, http://www.unexplained-mysteries.com/forum/
index.php?showtopic=54391.

664. P. J. Capelotti, "Space: The Final (Archeological) Frontier," *Archeology Archive*
(volume 57, number 6 November/December 2004), last accessed January 15,
2013, http://archive.archaeology.org/0411/etc/space.html.

665. P. J. Capelotti, "Aerospace archaeology," *Space Archaeology Wiki*, last
modified November 3, 2007, last accessed January 15, 2013, http://www.
spacearchaeology.org/wiki/index.php?title=Aerospace_archaeology.

666. P. J. Capelotti, *The Human Archaeology of Space: Lunar, Planetary and Interstellar
Relics of Exploration* (Jefferson, NC: McFarland, 2010), 86–87.

667. Ibid., 87.

668. "Gilgamesh Tomb Believed Found," *Assyrian International News Agency*,
January 25, 2005, last accessed January 15, 2013, http://www.aina.org/
news/20050125100240.htm.

669. "Experts Search for Grave of Legendary Gilgamesh," *ABC News*, May 6, 2003,
last accessed January 15, 2013, http://www.abc.net.au/news/2003-05-06/
experts-search-for-grave-of-legendary-gilgamesh/1849534.

670. "Gilgamesh Tomb Believed Found," *BBC News*, last modified April 29,
2003, last accessed January 15, 2013, http://news.bbc.co.uk/2/hi/science/
nature/2982891.stm.

671. Graham Hancock and Robert Bauval, *The Message of the Sphinx*, first ed. (Three
Rivers Press, 1997), 59; 71.

672. The Brookings Institution—Final Report: "Proposed Studies on the
Implications of Peaceful Space Activities for Human Affairs" (July 1993),
182–183.

673. Ibid., 182–184.

674. Ibid., footnotes.

675. Arthur C. Clarke, *Profiles of the Future: An Inquiry into the Limits of the Possible*,
1st American ed. (New York: Henry Holt & Co, 1984), 36.

676. William Bascom, "The Forms of Folklore: Prose Narrative," *Journal of American
Folklore* 78, (1965): 3.

677. Bruno Bettelheim, *The Uses of Enchantment: The Meaning and Importance of
Fairy Tales*, (New York: Random House, 1989), p. 45.

678. Jacques Vallée, *Dimensions: A Casebook of Alien Contact* (New York, NY: Contemporary Books, 1988), 274.

679. Christopher Vogler, *The Writer's Journey* (Studio City, CA: Michael Wiese Productions, 1992), vii.

680. Joseph Campbell, *The Power of Myth* (New York: Anchor, 1991), 69.

681. C. S. Lewis, *God in the Dock: Essays on Theology and Ethics* (Grand Rapids, MI: Wm. B. Eerdmans Publishing Co., 1972), 66.

682. "Glossary of Jungian Terms," *Carl-Jung.net*, last accessed January, 22, 2013, http://carl-jung.net/glossary.htm.

683. Roderick Main, C. G. Jung, *Jung on Synchronicity and the Paranormal* (London: Routledge, 1997), 90.

684. Roderick Main, C. G. Jung, *Jung on Synchronicity and the Paranormal* (London: Routledge, 1997), 1.

685. C. G. Jung, *Flying Saucers* (New York: MJF Books, 1997), 6.

686. C. G. Jung, *Flying Saucers,* 7.

687. Mike Clelland, "Synchronicity and the UFO Abductee," essay within Alan Abbadessa et al., *The Sync Book 2: Outer + Inner Space, Shadow + Light: 26 Essays On Synchronicity (volume 2)* (New York: Sync Book Press, 2012), 333. Essay available from Mike Clelland here: http://hiddenexperience.blogspot.com/2012/10/sychronicity-and-ufo-abductee.html.

688. Podcast I listened to is available here: Richard Dolan and Mike Clelland, "Richard Dolan in Conversation about Abductions," recorded July 28, 2012, posted by Mike Clelland July 30, 2012, http://hiddenexperience.blogspot.com/2012/07/richard-dolan-in-conversation-about.html

689. Ibid.

690. C. G. Jung, *The Archetypes and the Collective Unconscious*, 2nd ed., vol. 9, of *The Collected Works of C. G. Jung* (Princeton, NJ: Princeton University Press, 1969), 43.

691. C. G. Jung, *Flying Saucers*, 15–16.

692. Ibid., 21.

693. Ibid., 16.

694. Douglas Groothuis, *Confronting the New Age* (Downers Grove, IL: InterVarsity Press, 1988), 31.

695. C. G. Jung, *Flying Saucers,* 108.

696. Ibid., 109.

697. Ted Peters, *UFOs—God's Chariots? Flying Saucers in Politics, Science, and Religion* (Atlanta, GA: John Knox Press, 1977), 9.

698. Ibid., 25.

699. Ibid., 25.

700. Ted Peters, "Exo-Theology" essay (article or chapter in a collection) in James R. Lewis, ed., *The Gods Have Landed: New Religions from Other Worlds* (Albany, NY: State University of New York Press, 1995), 199.

701. Jacques Vallée, *The Invisible College* (New York: E. P. Dutton, 1976), 4, 46.

702. Jerome Clark, *The UFO Encyclopedia* (Detroit, MI: Omnigraphics Inc, 1990), 66.

703. Jacques Vallée, "Five Arguments against the Extraterrestrial Origin of Unidentified Flying Objects," *Journal of Scientific Exploration*, vol. 4, no. 1, 1990, 105—117.

704. "Heretic Among Heretics: Jacques Vallée Interview," *UFO Evidence*, last accessed January 17, 2013, http://www.ufoevidence.org/documents/doc839.htm.

705. Ibid.

706. Jacques Vallée, *The Invisible College*, 1.

707. Jerome Clark, "Jacques Vallée Discusses UFO Control System," *UFO Evidence*, original in FATE Magazine, 1978, online article last accessed February 5, 2013 http://www.ufoevidence.org/documents/doc608.htm.

708. Jacques Vallée, *Dimensions*, 178.

709. A 2008 poll in America revealed that 56 percent of the respondents said it is either "very likely" or "somewhat likely" that intelligent life exists on other planets but a decisive 74 percent of the eighteen- to twenty-four-year-olds believe alien life is likely, 33–48 percent of the population believes they have already visited Earth, and around 10 percent have personally seen a UFO. Scripps Survey, Research Center, "UFO Poll," *The Grand Rapids Press*, July 20, 2008, last accessed January 22, 2013, http://search.proquest.com/docview/2936 60669?accountid=12085.

710. Keith Thompson, *Angels and Aliens: UFOs and the Mythic Imagination* (Reading, MA: Addison-Wesley, 1991), 182.

711. Jacques F. Vallée and Eric W. Davis, "Incommensurability, Orthodoxy, and the Physics of High Strangeness—A 6-Layer Model for Anomalous Phenomena," as quoted in: Jacques Vallée and Eric Davis, *Fatima Revisited: The Apparition Phenomenon in Ufology, Psychology, and Science*, Kindle ed. Fernando Fernandes (Anomalist Books 2010), Kindle locations 5486–5488).

712. Jacques Vallée and Eric Davis, *Fátima Revisited*, Kindle locations 5547–5549.

713. Jerome Clark, "Jacques Vallée Discusses UFO Control System," http://www.ufoevidence.org/documents/doc608.htm.

714. Jacques Vallée and Eric Davis, *Fátima Revisited*, Kindle locations 5651–5661.

715. Jacques Vallée, *The Invisible College*, 201–202.

716. Francis Barrett, *The Magus or Celestial Intelligencer Containing the Constellatory Practice, or Talismanic Magic* (1801), 84. Viewable here: http://www.sacred-texts.com/grim/magus/ma127.htm.

717. Gershom Scholem, "DEMONS, DEMONOLOGY" in *Encyclopaedia Judaica*, last accessed January 9, 2013, http://www.jewishvirtuallibrary.org/jsource/judaica/ejud_0002_0005_0_05094.html.

718. Johannes P. Louw and Eugene Albert Nida, vol. 1, *Greek-English Lexicon of the New Testament: Based on Semantic Domains*, electronic ed. of the 2nd ed. (New York: United Bible Societies, 1996), 146–47.

719. Ibid., 146.

720. Ibid., 148.

721. Carl Raschke, "UFOs: Ultraterrestrial Agents of Cultural Deconstruction," *Archaeus Cyberbiological Studies of the Imaginal Component in UFO Contact Experience 5* (1989), 24.

722. Keith Thompson, *Angels and Aliens*, 193.

723. Keith Thompson, *Angels and Aliens*, 195.

724. Michael Mannion, *Project Mindshift: The Re-Education of the American Public Concerning Extraterrestrial Life, 1947-Present* (New York: M. Evans & Company, 1998), 82.

725. C. S. Lewis, *The Screwtape Letters* (New York, NY: HarperCollins, 2009), ix.

726. Alex Vilenkin, *Many Worlds in One: The Search for Other Universes* (New York, NY: Hill and Wang, 2007), 117. Viewable here: http://books.google.com/boo ks?id=9nRGwQnvGx0C&lpg=PA117&ots=XecbUQcTUs&dq=Vilenkin%20 %22A%20Farewell%20to%20Uniqueness%2C%22&pg=PA117#v=onepage& q=Vilenkin%20%22A%20Farewell%20to%20Uniqueness,%22&f=false.

727. John Lash, "Contact," *Metahistory.org*, last accessed February 5, 2013, http:// www.metahistory.org/siteauthor.php.

728. John Lash, "The Ambivalent Power of Compassion," *Metahistory.org*, last accessed February 5,2013, http://www.metahistory.org/RiteAction/ RiteActionintro.php.

729. Kurt Rudolph, "Gnosticism," as quoted in: *The Anchor Bible Dictionary* ed. David Noel Freedman (New York: Doubleday, 1996), 2:1039.

730. "Archon," in Index, *Metahistory.org*, last accessed February 5, 2013, http://www. metahistory.org/LEX/lexicon_A.php.

731. Description in green box at *Metahistory.org*, last accessed February 5, 2013, http://www.metahistory.org/.

732. Neil T. Anderson, *The Bondage Breaker* (Harvest House Publishers, Kindle ed.), 23.

733. Ibid., 87.

734. Ted Peters, *UFOs—God's Chariots?: Flying Saucers in Politics, Science, and Religion* (Atlanta: John Knox Press, 1977), 147.

735. Carol Glatz, "Do Space Aliens Have Souls? Inquiring Minds Can Check Jesuit's Book," *Catholic News Service*, November 4, 2005, http://www.catholicnews. com/data/stories/cns/0506301.htm.

736. Whitley Strieber, *Transformation: The Breakthrough* (Sag Harbor, NY: Beech Tree Books, 1988), 44–45.

737. James Blish, *A Case of Conscience* (New York, NY: Ballantine Books, 1958), 26.

738. Ibid., 92.

739. Jo Walton, "Aliens and Jesuits: James Blish's *A Case of Conscience*," *TOR*, November 29, 2010, http://www.tor.com/blogs/2010/11/ aliens-and-jesuits-james-blishs-a-case-of-conscience.

740. Ibid.

741. "Eileithyia," *Wikipedia, The Free Encyclopedia*, last modified January 24, 2013, http://en.wikipedia.org/wiki/Eileithyia.

742. Ibid.

743. Augustine, *City of God*, 23:15.

744. Father Ludovicus Maria Sinistrari de Ameno, *De Daemonialitate, et Incubis, et Succubi* (1622–1701), English translation of this portion provided by Jacques Vallée in *Passport to Magonia* (Contemporary Books, 1993), 127–129.

745. James Harford, "Rational Beings in Other Worlds," *Jubilee: A Magazine of the Church and Her People*, vol. 10, 1962, 19.

746. Daniel C. Raible, "Rational Life in Outer Space?" *America: A Catholic Review of the Week*, vol. 103, 1960, 533.

747. "Missionaries to Space," *Newsweek Magazine*, February 1960, 90.

748. Thomas F. O'Meara, "Christian Theology and Extraterrestrial Intelligent Life," *Theological Studies 60* (1999): 23–24.

749. Paul Thigpen, "Life on Other Planets: Are Catholics Free to Debate the Issue?" *Our Sunday Visitor*, November 1, 2010, http://www.osv.com/tabid/7631/itemid/7002/Life-on-Other-Planets.aspx.

750. Zecharia Sitchin, "Sitchin and Vatican Theologian Discuss UFO's, Extraterrestrials, Angels, Creation of Man," last accessed February 6, 2013, http://www.sitchin.com/vatican.htm.

751. Paul Thigpen, "Life on Other Planets," http://www.osv.com/tabid/7631/itemid/7002/Life-on-Other-Planets.aspx.

752. http://www.alislam.org/library/books/revelation/part_4_section_7.html.

753. Ibid.

754. Lewis White Black, "Extraterrestrial Intelligent Life," as quoted in: E. Regis, *Extraterrestrials* (London: Cambridge University Press, 1987), 13.

755. Ibid., 13–14.

756. C. G. Jung, *Flying Saucers* (New York, NY: MJF Books, 1997), 11.

757. Ibid., 21–22.

758. "Prophecy of the Popes," *Wikipedia, The Free Encyclopedia*, last modified, February 6, 2013, http://en.wikipedia.org/wiki/Prophecy_of_the_popes.

759. Thomas Horn and Cris Putnam, *Petrus Romanus: The Final Pope Is Here* (Crane, MO: Defender Publishing, 2012), 79–80.

760. Ibid., 81–82.

761. Thomas Horn and Cris Putnam, *Petrus Romanus*, 442–443.

762. Hans Urs von Balthasar, *Casta Meretrix, in Sponsa Verbi*, (Brescia: Morceliana, 1969), 267. Translated here: http://www.traditioninaction.org/ProgressivistDoc/A_043_BalthasarMeretrix.htm.

763. Ibid.

764. Ibid.

765. "Monsignors' Mutiny" revealed by Vatican leaks, Philip Pullella, *Reuters*, February 13, 2012.

766. Thomas Horn and Cris Putnam, *Petrus Romanus*, 479–480.

767. "GOD OF FORTRESSES מעזים אלה Θεὸς μαωζιν" as quoted in: K. van der Toorn, Bob Becking, and Pieter Willem van der Horst, *Dictionary of Deities and Demons in the Bible DDD*, 2nd extensively rev. ed. (Leiden; Boston; Grand Rapids, MI: Brill; Eerdmans, 1999), 369. Source states "E. Nestle (ZAW 4 [1884] 248) saw a satirical pun on the name → Baal Šamêm, a high god of Semitic origin." Thus, see: "BAAL-SHAMEM ממש־לעב, וימש־לעב" in *Dictionary of Deities and Demons in the Bible DDD*, 151.

768. "Daniel 11:39," *Biblos*, last accessed February 7, 2013, http://bible.cc/daniel/11-39.htm.

769. Ibid.

770. General Douglas MacArthur, *New York Times*, Oct 9, 1955, as quoted in: Michael S. Heiser, *The Facade* (Superior, Colorado: Superior Books, 2001), 14.

771. Ibid., 152.

772. Ruth Gledhill, "Defense Chief Warns of 'Satanic UFOs'" *The Times of London*, as quoted in: *AUFORA News Update*, March 1, 1997, last accessed January 25, 2013, http://www.mufon.com/MUFONNews/arch011.html.

773. JohnThomas Didymus, "Nick Pope: Britain Is Armed and Ready for UFO Alien War," *Digital Journal*, October 14, 2012, http://www.digitaljournal.com/article/334805.

774. "UFO Quotes by Government Sources," *UFO Evidence*, last accessed February 7, 2013, http://www.ufoevidence.org/documents/doc1737.htm.

775. Mikhail Gorbachev, Soviet Youth, May 4, 1990, as quoted in: Michael S. Heiser, *The Facade*, (Superior, Colorado: Superior Books, 2001), 162.

776. Ben Arnold, "Vatican Newspaper Criticises Prometheus," September 25, 2012, http://uk.movies.yahoo.com/vatican-newspaper-criticises-prometheus.html.

777. J. Antonio Hunecus, "The Vatican: Extraterrestrial Connection," *Open Minds Magazine*, June–July 2010, 59.

778. To see more information on this event, see: "The Detection of Extraterrestrial Life and the Consequences for Science and Society," *The Royal Society*, last accessed February 7, 2013, http://royalsociety.org/Event.aspx?id=1887.

779. Heidi Blake, "Royal Astronomer: 'Aliens May Be Staring Us in the Face,'" *The Telegraph*, February 22, 2010, http://www.telegraph.co.uk/science/space/7289507/Royal-astronomer-Aliens-may-be-staring-us-in-the-face.html.

780. Daniel Sheehan, "Catholic Dogma Faces E.T.," *Open Minds Magazine*, June–July 2010, 68.

781. Ibid.

782. Ilia Delio, *Christ in Evolution* (New Delhi, India: Concept Publishing Company, 2010), 166.

783. Kenneth J. Delano, *Many Worlds, One God* (Hicksville, NY: Exposition Press, 1977), 99.

784. Ibid., 117.

785. Ibid., 251.

786. "EXTRATERRESTRIAL LIFE," *Interdisciplinary Encyclopedia of Religion and Science*, last accessed February 7, 2013, http://www.disf.org/en/Voci/65.asp.

787. Ibid.

788. Arthur C. Clarke, *The City and the Stars* (New York, NY: Harcourt, Brace, 1956), 10.

789. Arthur C. Clarke, *2001: A Space Odyssey*, as quoted in: Steven Sande, "Arthur C. Clarke's 2001 Newspad Finnally Arrives, Nine Years Late," *The Unofficial Apple Weblog*, January 28, 2010, http://www.tuaw.com/2010/01/28/arthur-c-clarkes-2001-newspad-finally-arrives-nine-years-late/.

790. Arthur C. Clarke, *Childhood's End* (New York, NY: Ballantine Books, 1953), 68.

791. Clarke, *Childhood's End*, 75.

792. Jacques Vallée, *Messengers of Deception: UFO Contacts and Cults* (Berkeley, CA: Ronin Pub, 1979), 136.

793. Malachi Martin, *The Jesuits* (New York, NY: Simon & Schuster, 1988), 290.

794. Pope Benedict XVI, *Credo for Today: What Christians Believe* (San Francisco: Ignatius Press, 2009), 34.

795. Ibid., 113.

796. Joseph Cardinal Ratzinger, *Principles of Catholic Theology: Building Stones for a Fundamental Theology*, translated by Sister Mary Frances McCarthy, S.n.d. (San Francisco: Ignatius Press, 1987), 334.

797. "TEILHARD DE CHARDIN, PIERRE," *Encyclopedia of Paleontology*, s.v, last accessed January 26, 2013, http://www.liberty.edu:2048/login?url=http://www.credoreference.com/entry/routpaleont/teilhard_de_chardin_pierre.

798. Pope Benedict XVI, "Homily of July 24, 2009," in the Cathedral of Aosta, last accessed January 26, 2013, http://www.vatican.va/holy_father/benedict_xvi/homilies/2009/documents/hf_ben-xvi_hom_20090724_vespri-aosta_en.html.

799. Pierre Teilhard de Chardin, *The Phenomenon of Man* (New York, NY: Harperperennial, 1955), 286.

800. M. M. Ćirković, "Fermi's Paradox: The Last Challenge for Copernicanism?" *Serbian Astronomical Journal 178* (2009), 1–20.

801. Robert Emenegger, *UFO's, Past, Present, and Future* (New York, NY: Ballantine Books, 1975), 130–147.

802. Lee Speigel, "More Believe in Space Aliens than in God According to U.K. Survey," *Huffington Post*, October 18, 2012, http://www.huffingtonpost.com/2012/10/15/alien-believers-outnumber-god_n_1968259.html (accessed 12/07/2012).

803. Kenneth J. Delano, *Many Worlds, One God*, 104.